Catching Lightning in a Bottle

CATCHING LIGHTNING IN A BOTTLE

How Merrill Lynch Revolutionized
the Financial World

WINTHROP H. SMITH JR.

This book is dedicated first to my father, a principled leader and a humble, generous man who lived his life with the highest integrity. It is also dedicated to my family, who by reading this will have an even greater appreciation for the Mother Merrill that my father and I knew and loved. And it is for the thousands of other Merrill Lynch families who contributed to our great company's success in its first hundred years.

Winthrop H. Smith Jr.
1840 Sugarbush Access Road
Warren, VT 05674

Orders and information: www.smith-merrillhistory.com
ISBN 978-0-9898543-0-6

First Printing 2013
© 2013 Winthrop H. Smith Jr.

Co-author: William Ecenbarger
Design: Barbara Justice, Barb Justice Designs

Printed in the United States of America

Contents

Part One

Part Two

Part Three

Author's Note

When my father graduated from Amherst College in the spring of 1916, he joined the two-year-old Merrill, Lynch & Co., thus beginning his life's work. It was an impressive career marked by significant achievements and lasted more than forty-five years. From the outset, he developed a personal friendship and business partnership with Charlie Merrill, a brilliant visionary and pioneer in the grocery and financial services industries. While Charlie was the better known of these two partners, I have come to understand the depth of the role my father played in shaping the Merrill Lynch of the future.

It was my father who convinced Charlie to reenter the brokerage business in 1940 after a decade of involvement with other enterprises. Together they brought Wall Street to Main Street, changing the paradigm of financial services in the modern age. But most important, they developed a uniquely powerful set of principles that became the North Star for future generations of Merrill leaders. The culture that this established was the primary reason for Merrill's success over the years. My father died in 1961.

Thirteen years later, I joined Merrill Lynch as an associate in the Investment Banking Division after receiving an MBA from Wharton. Since my dad passed away when I was only eleven, I never fully appreciated his leadership skills and the power of his humility. During nearly twenty-eight years at the company, however, I came to know him better and to appreciate the principles and the culture that he and Charlie Merrill had created. I was proud to be a member of the Mother Merrill family.

Being the son of Winthrop H. Smith had many benefits, but it also presented challenges. I had to work extremely hard every day to prove myself worthy of the name. Over the years I held line and staff positions in investment banking, wealth management, finance, human resources, and marketing prior to becoming Executive Vice President, Chairman of Merrill Lynch International and a member of the Merrill Lynch & Co. Executive Committee. I had a great career and feel so fortunate to have been at Merrill when I was.

In October 2001, the culture of Merrill Lynch was about to change as a result of a new management team with different ideas about how to maximize profits. I knew that I couldn't work within this new environment, so I decided to retire. And I resolved to write the story of Merrill Lynch.

Several years passed, and I had not begun writing. Then in 2007, the financial crisis hit and my former firm became a victim of greed and the lack of proper oversight by its Board of Directors. Two years later, two people motivated me to start a book. Bill Ecenbarger had been hired a decade earlier to write the corporate history of Merrill Lynch. Bill is a Pulitzer Prize winner, and he interviewed me in my Connecticut office in 2002. He was well along with the project when Stan O'Neal, Merrill's new CEO, decided there was no need for a history of the firm and his efforts ceased. In late 2009, Bill called me. "Win, I read the speech you gave at the final shareholders meeting," he said. "You need to write the history of Merrill Lynch. No one can tell it better than you, and I'd enjoy working on it with you." When I told Lili, my wife-to-be, about this conversation, she made me realize that this was not only something that I needed to do for my own therapeutic reasons, but also something that I was compelled to do so that future generations could know the truth about Merrill Lynch and appreciate its historical importance.

This book is about the history of Merrill Lynch and its leadership—the rise and fall of an American institution. The chapters are organized around the twelve leaders of Merrill Lynch, ending with John Thain—all of whom I had known. Each left his own mark on the company and, with one stark exception, respected and strengthened the firm's culture. It is a story about an idea that began with a man named Charlie Merrill, without a doubt one of the leading entrepreneurs in the history of American business. By bringing Wall Street to Main Street and democratizing investing, Merrill Lynch helped countless middle-class individuals save and invest and, in turn, helped thousands of companies, municipalities, and governments fund their growth. Merrill was at the center of the financial intermediation process that allowed the United States to grow into the economic powerhouse it became in the last half of the twentieth century. Like all companies, it made mistakes, but it was guided by principled leaders who always attempted to do the right thing and for the right reason.

Catching Lightning in a Bottle is based on three years of solid research but it is very personal, too. Besides being a history of one of America's great companies, it also reflects my personal memories of many of Merrill's leaders and of significant events over a twenty-eight-year career. During those years, I not only discovered more about the enormous impact my father had on Merrill Lynch, but I also learned to appreciate how important a corporate culture and a set of values can be in creating a successful company. Unfortunately, I also learned how quickly they can be destroyed. Because of this personal perspective, events are sometimes not presented in strict chronological sequence as they might be in a more traditional account.

For this book, hundreds of people shared their stories, documents, and memorabilia with me. They told me what working at Merrill Lynch meant to them and to their families. For so many, our firm was not only a place to work but an enormous source of pride. Although I have written mostly about the important leaders who shaped, influenced, and grew the firm, there are tens of thousands of others who contributed to its success as well. They embraced its culture, protected it, and passed it along to future generations. It was a remarkable family.

This has been an emotional book to write. I am grateful to my wife, Lili Ruane, for convincing me to begin in earnest. And I am indebted to so many friends and colleagues who helped me along the way. Special thanks are due to Bill Ecenbarger, my partner in writing this history. His research and co-authorship were invaluable.

Also special credit is due to Meg Drislane for her editorial skills, to Barb Justice for the design of the book, and to Susan Hemmeter, my executive assistant at Sugarbush. I also want to thank Bank of America for allowing us access to Merrill Lynch's archives, which are now located in Charlotte, North Carolina.

I hope that this book will enable every member of the Merrill Lynch extended family to remember and appreciate, even more, what we collectively accomplished and that it will help many others to know the real Mother Merrill. In particular, I hope that my own children and grandchildren will have a greater appreciation of what their grandfather and great-grandfather helped to create.

Prologue

I went into the meeting with every intention of saying yes. But the answer to my own seemingly simple question changed all that, and I knew in an instant that my life would never be the same. What I could not have imagined was how quickly Mother Merrill would metamorphose into something I would not even recognize.

It was October 2001, just a few weeks after the terrorist attacks on the World Trade Center. Merrill Lynch had been forced out of its offices in the neighboring World Financial Center. The new president and eventual CEO, E. Stanley O'Neal, was temporarily using our office at 717 Fifth Avenue in Midtown Manhattan. A few days before, as part of his broad reorganization, O'Neal had removed me from my twin positions as chairman of Merrill Lynch International and president of the International Private Client Group. He had asked me to stay on as vice chairman of Merrill Lynch & Co. to focus on our most important client relationships throughout the world. I was initially skeptical. I had become increasingly concerned about O'Neal's vision for Merrill Lynch, about how he was starting to shape his administration, and about his shabby treatment of some of my fellow executives. However, conversations with several ML colleagues whose judgment I respected convinced me to give the new role a try. We scheduled another meeting.

Stan was never big on small talk, so just as I was settling into my chair he said: "I hope that you're here to accept the job. I want you to be a core part of my team. We are going to have to change a lot of things about the way this place is being run. As soon as we get rid of Komansky, we can get started running this place the right way." Wow! I stared at him in disbelief. Here was the new president talking about discarding his nominal superior, David H. Komansky, the chairman and chief executive officer. O'Neal rambled on until I asked him where he stood on the Principles.

"The Principles" were our mantra at Merrill Lynch. Charlie Merrill and my father had built the firm on a core set of values, and through the years they had been carried forward by their successors. Every chairman and CEO up to O'Neal had always felt and acted as though they stood on the shoulders of the leaders who had preceded them. Dan Tully, Komansky's predecessor, capsulized these Principles and now they were displayed prominently in every Merrill Lynch office throughout the world. In our foreign offices, they were written in the local language. And they were etched in the concrete of our headquarters in New York:

CLIENT FOCUS
RESPECT FOR THE INDIVIDUAL
TEAMWORK
RESPONSIBLE CITIZENSHIP
INTEGRITY

Tully revered them and always referenced the Principles whenever we had to make difficult decisions. "Okay," he would ask in a weekly Executive Committee meeting, "is this really in the client's best interests?" But when I asked O'Neal about them, his face distorted with anger and I could see the arteries throbbing in his neck.

O'Neal launched into a scathing attack against "Mother Merrill"—he said the words the way a sick man names his disease—and he ridiculed the Principles and the culture that had made the company revered by both its customers and its employees. As he ranted on, I grew angrier and felt my cheeks quivering and the veins throbbing in my own neck. Clearly this man cared nothing about our heritage or our prestige in the business world. Finally, I interrupted him. I had heard enough. "Stan," I said, "thank you for your offer but I can't work for you." I stood up and walked out, to the silent amazement of O'Neal.

Back home in Connecticut that night, doubts began to fester as I tried to fall asleep. Had I acted impulsively rather than rationally? Was it the wrong decision—a huge mistake? Abruptly leaving a firm where my father had worked for forty-five years, finishing at the very top, and a place where I had been for twenty-eight years was not an easy decision. I knew that I would be disappointing many colleagues as well as my family. And I understood that I would be giving up many millions in future compensation.

But the next morning I awoke refreshed, with a sense of relief. I knew I had made the right decision. I looked out the window at a glorious autumn day. Every leaf looked like a flower. I got into my car and began driving north—first on Interstate 95, then on Interstate 91. As I passed the exit for Holyoke, Massachusetts, I thought about my father, who had been born and raised only a few miles from there in South Hadley Falls. Also nearby was Amherst College, where both Charlie Merrill and my father had studied and from which I graduated in 1971.

At that moment I was sure that my father would have been proud of my decision because it was based on principle—his Principles. The Merrill Lynch culture that I loved and respected was going to change dramatically, and I could not be a party to it. I could not be a member of this new management team.

While I was driving, I suddenly thought of the *matryoshka*, the Russian nesting dolls, in Dave Komansky's office. Dave had been presented with these as a gift when he succeeded Dan Tully as CEO in 1997. There were ten dolls, each with the face of a Merrill Lynch leader, beginning with Charlie Merrill. Next came my father. Then Mike McCarthy, George Leness, Jim Thompson, Don Regan, Roger Birk, Bill Schreyer, Dan Tully, and Dave Komansky. The dolls got progressively larger from Merrill up. The symbolism of the dolls was that each era of Merrill Lynch grew from what was inherited from the prior one and that each new leader built on the success of his predecessor rather than relied on what he could achieve alone. Each of us stood on the shoulders of those who came before us, those who built our successful firm and created a powerful and enduring culture. It was our responsibility to maintain the essence of what came before us while moving into the future. It was our obligation to adopt change without throwing out the Principles that were our solid foundation. It was our obligation to preserve the culture.

By the time I crossed the border into Vermont that day, I could really see that autumn had taken a firm grip on the landscape. The change is dramatic because Vermont has outlawed billboards and all you see is the vista. I drove past trees in gorgeous Van Gogh colors, past farmland that had been harvested to stubble. My destination was Sugarbush, a ski resort that I and a few other investors had purchased on September 10, the day before the terrorist attacks.

One nagging thought refused to go away, however, and it clung to my brain like a barnacle on a hull. Stanley O'Neal was dead wrong when he characterized my company—my former company—as inefficient, paternalistic, and bloated. On the contrary, Merrill had become one of the leading investment banking and private wealth firms in the world. We had a global footprint that was unmatched and envied by our competition. We were proud to wear "the Bull" on our sleeves and in our hearts, and we felt privileged to be a member of Mother Merrill's family. The "bloated" firm that O'Neal was about to disassemble had earned a record $3.8 billion the prior year, had a pre-tax margin of 21.3 percent, and had a return-on-equity of 24.2 percent. For the forty-eighth consecutive quarter we had led the Global Underwriting league tables with a 13.3 percent market share, and we ranked No. 3 in global mergers and acquisitions, with very little difference between us and No. 1. Our global research was ranked No. 1 in the world, and we were the dominant secondary equity trading firm in the world. Our private wealth business held $1.5 trillion in client assets and our global asset management business managed $557 billion. We had 72,000 employees, 21,200 financial advisers, and 975 offices in forty-four countries around the world. In the first quarter of 2001, our stock price hit a record high of $80.

However, O'Neal had no interest in continuing the culture that had allowed our firm to prosper. In my opinion he was enabled by a Board of Directors who valued their positions and compensation as directors more than they valued a culture that required integrity and respect. They allowed short-term profitability to blind their views of the highly leveraged and risky business Merrill would become, and they allowed a small group of greedy individuals to destroy an icon. What happened from 2001 through 2007 never should have been allowed to occur.

The real story of Merrill Lynch had to be written. There was a reason why Arthur Levitt, the former chairman of the Securities and Exchange Commission under President Clinton, called Merrill Lynch "the only firm on Wall Street with a soul." This is mostly a positive story about a firm that grew into greatness through principled leadership and a core set of values that shaped its culture and brought Wall Street to Main Street after World War II. Through innovation and principled leadership, it became one of the world's leading and most venerated financial firms. For the hundreds of thousands of us who knew the real Mother Merrill, our experience there was like catching lightning in a bottle. Unfortunately, the years after 2001 were not the same.

I sat down in the spring of 2010 to begin writing this book. Link by link, I retraced the glorious history of this company. It was a story I knew well. In considering where to begin, I finally settled on a scorching afternoon ninety-four years earlier in the dusty, sleepy town of Shaw, Mississippi.

Part One

A young and charismatic Charlie Merrill begins to charm Wall Street.

CHAPTER ONE

Little Doc

(1885–1907)

T he wooden sidewalks on either side of the single dirt street were perfectly still, without any moving thing. The town's commerce was conducted in false-fronted shacks, but all of the respectable enterprises—a drugstore, two hotels, and several cafés—were closed. On one side of town, there were nine churches—four white and five black. On the other side, on the banks of Porter's Bayou, there were at least that many brothels and saloons. But even they weren't open for business today.

It was August 1907, and all across small-town America, in each of the other forty-four states, it was the same as here in Mississippi. Everyone was just outside of town, at the ball park. Nearly every town in America had its own ball park and its own ball team, and both were sources of considerable civic pride. The smaller the community, the greater the pride. Challenges were issued to neighboring towns, and the games became festive occasions with bands and cookouts. Special trains brought in the out-of-town fans, though visiting teams were at a disadvantage because the home team supplied the umpires. Nevertheless, the betting was heavy.

Baseball really was the national pastime, and in Shaw, this really was the only game in town. No one missed it. It would be years before radio broadcasts of major-league games began eroding attendance. Typically, the games were played on rock-studded vacant lots and in cow pastures where sometimes dried fecal matter served as bases.

Shaw's ball park was an old cotton field that had been dragged more or less smooth with a huge steel rail. The backstop was fashioned from weathered, discarded lumber and chicken wire. The bases were burlap bags filled with sand. The field was surrounded by horse-drawn wagons and buggies, and fans watched attentively from chairs and spread-out quilts they had brought with them.

Shaw's center fielder that day was a short, wiry man just a few months away from his twenty-second birthday. While his teammates looked vaguely comic in their beanie caps and baggy uniforms, the man in center field was tailored to parade-ground neatness. The only shabby thing was his glove, which was nothing more than a flimsy lace-less pad, not unlike a hot pad, that required him to use his fingers when he caught the ball. He played a shallow center field—not because he had great range but because he had a weak arm, the legacy of a boyhood fight in which it was broken.

Like most town teams, Shaw's was semiprofessional, meaning the players, at least some of them, were paid, but not on a full-time basis. The Shaw nine played two games on Saturday, one on Sunday. The center fielder, along with the catcher, the pitcher, and the shortstop, were out-of-towners who were paid to play. Local, unpaid talent filled in the rest of the Shaw roster. In the middle of the game, a hat would be passed around and fans would be exhorted to "loosen their wallets." The center fielder was paid $25 a week, which is the equivalent of about $500 today.

From this we can conclude that the center fielder's baseball talent was above average, but just how far above is not known. At five foot four, he presented pitchers with a small strike zone and drew a lot of walks. What is certain is that he was one of the most popular players. He had a melon slice of a smile that crinkled the skin around intense, bleached-denim eyes. His teammates called him Merry Merrill, and he was the life of every party. One young lady of this day remembered in later years that "everyone loved it when Charlie Merrill came to town, especially the young women, because he was so much fun."

Charles Edward Merrill was born on October 19, 1885, in Green Cove Springs, Florida, to Dr. Charles Morton Merrill and Octavia Wilson Merrill. He was the eldest of their three children and their only son. He had ancestral roots in the North as well as the South; his grandfathers had fought on opposite sides in the Civil War.

As a boy and an adult, Merrill had an abiding respect for the values and traditions of the Old South, which he inherited from his mother, who had been born on a Mississippi cotton plantation in 1861. An intelligent young woman from a "good family," Octavia Wilson attended Maryville College, in Maryville, Tennessee. She was part of Maryville's secondary school program, which boarded its students. There, when she was fifteen years old, she met Ohio-born Charles Morton Merrill, who was studying medicine at the college. He was twenty years old. Octavia and Charles courted by letter for almost seven years while Charles pursued his studies. He received his medical degree in 1881 from New York's Bellevue College and Hospital, and on New Year's Day 1883, Charles and Octavia were married.

Dr. Merrill suffered from asthma and after their marriage the couple decided to settle in Florida for his health. They moved to Green Cove Springs, a trendy, prospering resort town with a reputation for the curative powers of its mineral springs. The nation's elite, including Astors and Vanderbilts, came there to drink and bathe. Charles Merrill became the town doctor and the owner of the village drugstore—a dual role that was common for the time.

At various times in his life, Charlie Merrill claimed to be a direct descendant, through his mother, of John Alden, the New England Puritan, signer of the Mayflower Compact and hero of a Longfellow poem. In successfully applying for membership in the Sons of the American Revolution, Merrill traced his father's roots back to Nathaniel Merrill, who came to America in 1633.

Octavia Wilson, CEM's mother, was the oldest of ten children of Edward and Emily Wilson, who owned Round Hill Plantation in Lexington, Mississippi. Her father, a private in the Confederate army, was captured during the siege of Vicksburg, and returned to fight again after being released in a prisoner exchange. The plantation survived the Civil War, but the family was impoverished during the Reconstruction years.

There is no question that the single most influential person in CEM's life was his mother. As the eldest child, she had learned about responsibility and duty at an early age. An avid, lifelong reader, particularly of poetry, she graduated from the Maryville boarding school in 1876 at the age of fifteen. Over and over, she told her only son of the value of education and the obligation he had to succeed at some worldly endeavor. CEM remembers her saying to him, "Charlie, you can get anything in the world you want, as long as you want it bad enough."

According to a story Octavia Merrill told her grandchildren, CEM had just learned to talk when she took him out on the porch one night to show him the moon. He pointed his arm straight up and began yelling, "I want it! I want it!" He threw a tantrum on her lap when he didn't get his wish.

CEM's entrepreneurial talents surfaced early in Green Cove Springs, which sat on the banks of the St. John's River, about thirty miles downstream from Jacksonville. Every winter the town hosted Northerners who came to drink its medicinal waters and bathe in its sulphur pools. White Sulphur Spring flowed at the rate of three thousand gallons per minute and was impounded into a pool that, according to the local Chamber of Commerce, offered the bather "long life and good health." At the age of eight, Charlie Merrill would bet visiting Yankees a dime that he could cross the pool underwater faster than the dupe could swim it above water. Diving down, Charlie would crawl across the bottom of the pool aided by a swift current unknown and unavailable to the swimmer above him.

Charlie worked all day on Saturdays and for four hours on Sunday in his father's drugstore, and he soon came to be called Little Doc. At the age of twelve, he decided to raise soda fountain revenues by adding grain alcohol, readily available in the pharmacy, to the standard soft drinks for selected customers. The new hard drinks cost more money, and for a few weeks in 1897 drugstore revenues soared to all-time highs as word spread that spiked drinks were available at the soda fountain. As soon as Dr. Merrill discovered his son's merchandising tactic, he ordered an end to it.

Forty-two years later in an interview for an unpublished biography, CEM said that his first retail experience convinced him there must be a better way to run a store: "Even as a boy, it was obvious to me that the best that could be expected from a retail store, under conditions that existed in those days, was a very poor return on the capital and risk in the business, and practically no return if the business had been charged the proper salaries for the efforts and time of my father and myself. The turnover was so slow, and the credit losses were so large, that notwithstanding a very high margin of profit, there was almost nothing left at the end of the year. Naturally, my father had to interview a steady stream of traveling salesmen, keep the books, and perform sundry duties in and about the store, all of which drew heavily on his time and resulted in the neglect of his practice. The hours of labor were long; the store opened at seven o'clock in the morning and closed, theoretically, at twelve o'clock at night; as a practical matter, it was open almost twenty-four hours a day. On the shelves of this store, there must have been twenty-four thousand items, and my best recollection is that more than half of these items didn't sell once a year, and incidentally, the soda fountain department and the store, generally, were quite unsanitary. Today in studying a modern drugstore, the mystery of how my father and I managed to eke out our living still remains unsolved."

In 1898 the Merrills attempted to improve their fortunes by moving to Knoxville, Tennessee, and when that didn't work out, they returned to Florida and set up residence in Jacksonville. However, this wasn't the answer to their cash-flow problems, either—and thirteen-year-old Charlie continued to be a young man of many enterprises. On his way to a Sunday-school picnic on May 8, 1898, he passed a railroad station where the latest copies of the Florida *Times-Union and Citizen* were being unloaded from a Tampa-bound train. The Spanish-American War was raging, and it was easy to read the headline: DEWEY TELLS STORY OF HIS VICTORY. Charlie spent all his money, $5, to buy a hundred copies, which he lugged out to the picnic grounds and hawked for twenty-five cents each. Patriotic, news-hungry buyers, eager to learn of the destruction of the Spanish fleet, gladly paid extra to read the good news. Merrill called this "my first financial coup."

Like Horatio Alger, Charlie became a newsboy. He peddled the *Times-Union* on Ward Street in the heart of Jacksonville's red-light district. Though family legend holds that the street's customers bought the papers to hide their faces, it was far more likely that the prostitutes bought most of them. And they tipped generously. He also repeated his Spanish-American War coup in 1901 when President

William McKinley was assassinated. So successful was the Ward Street adventure that when it came time to sell the concession, he asked for and received $75, the modern equivalent of about $1,500, from another boy.

Compared to the lure of his business activities, school held little interest for the young Merrill. This concerned his mother, who intended to prepare her son for success by sending him to one of the prestigious Northern colleges. In the fall of 1901, she took him out of Jacksonville's Duval High School and enrolled him in the John B. Stetson University, a preparatory school in Deland, Florida, about fifty miles south of Jacksonville. Stetson was considered the best prep school in the South—but by Northern standards that still wasn't very good.

During Charlie's final year at Stetson, his father was robbed and brutally beaten as he went for an after-dinner walk near his home in Jacksonville. Dr. Merrill was in a coma for several days, and his survival was in question. Charlie was called home from Stetson for what he later called "those dreadful weeks." The elder Merrill regained consciousness, but he was confined to a wheelchair for months and unable to practice. Word circulated among his professional peers and patients that his skills as a physician had been permanently impaired, and, in fact, Dr. Merrill, only forty-six years old, never recovered physically or economically.

Octavia Merrill responded to the financial crisis by opening two boardinghouses (one for whites, the other for blacks), but money was still scarce, and there was a steady stream of letters from Stetson financial officials, who were undergoing their own budget crisis, demanding payment for overdue bills. Charlie left Stetson before completing his final year—but apparently for disciplinary rather than financial reasons. According to CEM's son, Charlie was expelled from Stetson after he dropped a cracker box of water from a fourth-floor dormitory window on a professor, whom he had mistaken for a classmate.

Still, his mother was steadfast in her determination to send Charlie to one of the better colleges in the North. Toward that end, the family sold a small piece of land they owned in Miami, and with these profits, plus an athletic scholarship, Charlie went north to Massachusetts's Worcester Academy for another preparatory year.

CEM's time at Worcester, the 1903–04 academic year, was an unhappy one. As a Southern boy of modest means, he was shunned and ridiculed by the New England elitists of the all-male student body. Some of his Northern classmates complained that they could barely comprehend his drawling speech. And there was a definite stigma to receiving financial aid. CEM paid only $185 of the estimated $700 annual cost to attend Worcester and was obliged to live on the top floor of Davis Hall with the other athletes, who were scorned as "hired hands." Even with the scholarship, Charlie had to work by waiting on tables in a dining hall and selling suits for a local clothier on a commission basis to wealthier students on campus.

If the Worcester athletic program expected to get a superstar in Charlie Merrill in exchange for their scholarship, they were hugely disappointed. He was decent at baseball and became the team's center fielder. He also went out for football, but at 114 pounds or so he was relegated to the second and third strings, seldom actually played in a game, and suffered a broken nose in practice. There is a story—widespread, probably apocryphal and apparently originating with CEM himself—that lightweight Charlie Merrill would get into a game when the team needed a few yards because they could throw him over the line of scrimmage. This, like most of the stories passed on by CEM through his children, must be taken with not a few grains of salt. While there is a basic truth in them, this truth was often embroidered because they were usually intended as fatherly advice or cautionary tales.

With his work schedule and athletic obligations, Merrill had little time for academics at Worcester, and it is not surprising that at the end of the year he didn't have enough credits to qualify for a diploma. In the end, though, school officials agreed to an unusual arrangement whereby they would grant him his diploma if he could successfully complete his first year at Amherst College. Amherst officials allowed him to enroll through a backdoor provision of the admissions policy.

That summer CEM worked as a waiter in a hotel on an island off of Portland, Maine, where he received a salary of $5 a week plus lodging, meals, and tips. He was there for sixteen weeks, and at the end of each of them he walked to the post office, where he wrote a $5 money order to himself and mailed it to Amherst with a note on the envelope: "Hold Until Called For." When he arrived on campus in September, there was $80 waiting for him.

In the fall of 1904, Octavia Merrill fulfilled one of her dreams for her son by seeing him enroll in Amherst College as a freshman. Indeed, she was waiting for him when he arrived on campus from Maine. Merrill was initially flustered by this maternal presence, but his embarrassment dissipated when Octavia proved to be a popular figure with his new classmates. Still, later in life he told his own son that he "had every card in the deck stacked against him" at Amherst. He was short, poor, spoke with a Southern drawl—and arrived on campus with his mother. Charlie would remain at Amherst for two years, and though his time there had some shining moments, he was dogged by financial problems. Decades later, in a letter accompanying an academic gift, CEM said, "I want to help relieve the tensions which develop in young men from a lack of funds to carry out their education. During my high school and college years I felt a burden of pressure almost too heavy for me to bear."

He earned his meals by donning a white jacket every evening and waiting on his Chi Psi fraternity brothers at a boardinghouse (Amherst had no dining facilities). Again he sold men's suits, taking a portion of his 15 percent commission in clothes for his own wardrobe. This haberdashery operation netted him $1,300 in his sophomore year and allowed him to be fashionable and well-dressed. However, he was embarrassed by his modest finances, and he believed that wealthier students bought clothes from him "just to be nice to Charlie Merrill, who had no money." In the fall, Merrill supplemented his income by raking leaves for fifty cents an hour.

His athletic career at Amherst is encrusted with myth (the story about being tossed over the line of scrimmage in football games was often repeated). CEM tried out for the cross-country, football, track, and baseball teams—failing in each case to make the varsity squads. He played baseball on what today would be called intramural teams rather than at the intercollegiate level.

Work and athletics did not stand in the way of his social life. Although he always felt like an outsider at Amherst, Merrill's party spirit and Southern geniality made him popular among his peers. He joined Chi Psi immediately and lived his second year in the fraternity house, where he was assigned the smallest room. CEM was a typical and enthusiastic fraternity man. His good looks and sunny disposition won over both his Chi Psi brothers and the attractive women who flocked to fraternity parties. He achieved hero status early by managing to capture the class flag in the traditional freshman-sophomore rivalry. He also shone at the annual "Chapel Rush," a free-for-all in which freshmen tried to roll sophomores down a hill and vice versa. According to classmates, CEM jumped on the back of a huge football player, seized him around the neck, and managed to roll him down the hill—reminding one eyewitness of "a monkey riding an elephant."

There were about five hundred students and forty faculty members at Amherst at this time. Classes were small, and daily chapel attendance at 8:15 A.M. was compulsory. Academically, CEM was average. He showed some aptitude for mathematics, but none whatsoever for foreign language. At the end of his first year, his French professor offered to give him a passing grade on the condition that he not take French the following year. His best class was English, where he earned consecutive B's in his final three semesters. He was honing a talent for writing clear, direct, concise, and occasionally eloquent prose that would show up much later in hundreds of business letters and memoranda.

At least partially because of financial anemia (Amherst at this time cost about $300 a year, the equivalent of about $6,000 today), CEM left the school at the end of his sophomore year in 1906. He missed his fraternity buddies, but it was not until he had secured his fortune that he developed an affection for his ersatz alma mater. In 1927 he donated $100,000 (about $918,000 in current dollars) to the school—on the condition that it be used to help financially needy students. He funded several scholarships and received an honorary Doctor of Laws degree from the college in 1943. In a biographical form filled out in 1947, Merrill wrote, "For the past 20 years my main hobby has been to help promising boys through school and college—total now about 300—and have kept in close touch with educational problems in many schools and colleges."

Over the years, CEM took great pride and satisfaction in attending the annual Amherst reunions, though at first he got a cool reception. "It took me [many years] after leaving Amherst to be accepted by my former classmates as an equal, and as a friend," he wrote in a 1948 letter to his son. "In the first place, I went there only two years, and, in the second place, success came to me early. In the first ten years after leaving College, I could tell that the subject of the conversation would abruptly change when I entered the room. This I now know was perfectly understandable, and a characteristic trait of human nature. Most fellows, when they come back to a reunion simply cannot resist from bragging about their accomplishments. I know now it was difficult, if not impossible, for a Court Reporter, or Principal of a small High School, to continue his bragging when I came into the room. Please do not misunderstand me; I certainly was not shunned, but, on the other hand, I was not taken into the fold. However, as the years passed by, and my classmates found out that I didn't have horns or even antlers, they began to unbend, and ended up by according me the same welcome—no more and no less—that they gave to all their other old friends."

Charles Merrill, Amherst '08, enlivened many of the reunions. At one such affair during Prohibition, a breakfast meeting was moving at a painfully slow pace until CEM leapt to his feet and exclaimed, "Well, I used to do this in college—I guess I haven't forgotten how." He walked over to a serving table, pulled out a flask of forbidden bourbon, and filled each waiting grapefruit half with the amber liquid.

Near the end of his time at Amherst, CEM became embroiled in an issue that illustrates one of his strongest traits: loyalty. A fraternity brother was caught cheating on an exam and expelled from school. The fraternity hierarchy, spurred on by a powerful alumni segment, also sought to oust him for life from Chi Psi as an example to other brethren. Charlie opposed the move because it amounted to hitting a fraternity brother who was already down and it violated the principles of comradeship so important to fraternity life. The dispute ended in a hollow compromise that expelled the miscreant for only five years rather than life.

As he would later acknowledge, CEM was on the wrong side of this issue. Honesty was more important than blind loyalty, and as a Wall Street businessman, he would make that distinction many times. But as a twenty-year-old undergraduate, Merrill allowed his lifelong sense of personal loyalty to take precedence.

Two important non-academic events occurred in the life of Charlie Merrill during his final year at Amherst. In the first instance, he was spending Christmas break at a friend's house in Mount Vernon, New York, when he received the tragic news that his sister Mary had died from diphtheria at the age of three. Charlie had been away at school during her entire lifetime and he barely knew her. CEM remained convinced for the rest of his life that the financial straits of the Merrill family had prevented his sister from getting the proper medical care that would have saved her life. He told his son a half-century later in a letter: "The fact my father knew how to save his daughter's life, and yet, because of limited finances did not possess the equipment, crushed him. Money, of course, is not everything, but, my friend, emergency after emergency comes up in this world of ours, in which for a few brief moments, at least, and maybe longer, money is the equivalent of everything."

The other event was a happier one. He began dating Marie Sjostrom, a student at Smith College, which was a half-hour streetcar ride away in Northampton. They were seen together at college functions and fraternity parties, and by the spring of 1906, Charlie Merrill was in love for the first time—though certainly not the last.

Amherst also became an important bond between Charlie and my father. Eight years younger than CEM, my dad graduated from Amherst in 1916 and shared Charlie's love for baseball (he was the manager of the Amherst baseball team and a lifelong Yankee fan). Dad's baseball genes were passed down to my brother, Bardwell, who played varsity baseball at Yale with George Herbert Walker Bush. Years later Charlie donated the money that built three faculty houses and named one after my father. When I attended Amherst myself, I joined Chi Psi and the legacy of Charlie Merrill was manifested in the magnificent stained-glass window in our fraternity library that Charlie had donated. The new science building was also named in his honor.

By the time Charlie left Amherst, the Merrill family had moved to West Palm Beach, and at the end of Amherst's 1905–06 academic year, Charlie went home and spent the summer playing semipro baseball and helping to put out the local paper, the *Tropical Sun*. The editor of the paper had tuberculosis and Dr. Merrill had suggested he spend a few months in Arizona to improve his health, meanwhile recommending his son as a temporary replacement. Though CEM claimed later that he put out the paper single-handedly, there were at least two or three others who wrote and edited.

It was during this time that Palm Beach was beginning to emerge as a kind of American Riviera, attracting blue-blood families like the Vanderbilts, the Rockefellers, the Morgans, the Carnegies, the Mellons, and the Drexels. Within twenty-five years, they would be joined by the Merrills. The showpiece of West Palm Beach during the summer of 1906 was the Royal Poinciana Hotel, the largest hotel in the world, with facilities for two thousand guests. The six-story wooden structure, painted yellow and white, had a baseball diamond ringed with palm trees, and it was here that Charlie Merrill patrolled center field (and occasionally right field) for the town semipro team. Surviving box scores show that CEM batted low in the batting order (indicating he was not one of the better hitters) and seldom had more than one hit per game, often none at all.

Meanwhile, Charlie was a jack-of-all-trades at the semiweekly *Tropical Sun*—reporting, editing, selling ads. He came to work at seven-thirty every morning, took time off at noon to practice with the team, then went back to the newspaper until early evening. Weekends were for baseball. Charlie numbered these days among the happiest in his life.

Journalistic scruples were virtually nonexistent at this time, and CEM used every opportunity to promote the baseball team in print. The *Tropical Sun* for July 1, for example, promised readers that "those who want to witness what will doubtless be the very best game that will be played on the East Coast this season cannot afford to miss next Monday's game." On July 18, reporter Merrill wrote, "Decidedly the best baseball ever witnessed on the Poinciana diamond was the game played Monday afternoon, when West Palm Beach shut out St. Augustine by a score of 2 to 0." The August 1 edition described a road contest that was "the most exciting game ever played in Miami," and contained this item on the front page:

> West Palm Beach is soon to have another drug store.
> Dr. Chas. M. Merrill, a prominent local physician, having
> leased the store room in the Masonic Temple, Clematis

Avenue, formerly occupied by Miller & Co., in which he will, some time in the month of August, open an up-to-date retail drug store.

Dr. Merrill has had considerable experience in the drug business, having for a number of years successfully conducted a drug store in Green Cove Springs. He is now placing orders for his stock and fixtures, and will probably have his store open by the last of August.

There were no bylines on the articles, but Merrill's florid, cheerleader style is unmistakable.

CEM's brief journalistic career taught him the importance of public opinion and its role in shaping events. It was a happy summer for twenty-year-old Charlie Merrill, and he believed that he learned more than he had in his previous two years at Amherst. "On the *Sun*," he said later, "I learned to meet people and I learned human nature. It was the best training I ever had."

CEM earned $25 a week for his baseball skills and another $17 for his journalistic efforts, managing to save $75 during his three months in West Palm Beach. He needed every penny of it in September, when he enrolled in the University of Michigan Law School. With the continued decline of the family's finances and his father's practice, there was even more pressure on him to establish himself in a remunerative endeavor.

The idea of a law career was not CEM's but rather came from his maternal grandmother, Emily Wilson, who envisioned him entering politics and one day becoming governor of Mississippi, where many of his maternal relatives still lived. She raised the money for his tuition from family members, including his uncles, Augustus, Edward, and Bayard Wilson.

Charlie boarded the train for Ann Arbor on September 27, 1906, and almost immediately after his arrival he became a popular, sought-after figure on campus. Despite his Southern accent, the two years at Amherst had enabled him to affect an air of an Eastern sophisticate. Quickly he was inducted into the local Chi Psi chapter and installed as chapter steward, which paid for his room and board. The position involved buying supplies and planning meals, and he found this work far less menial and demeaning than waiting on tables.

Charlie continued his baseball career by playing for the law school's team under his own name and for the engineering school team under another name. When the two teams met on the field, he didn't show up for the game. As his campus social standing rose, his grades descended, and by the end of the year he failed to pass three of his six subjects—Contracts, Real Property, and English. His courtship of Marie Sjostrom continued with long letters, and he returned to Amherst in early 1907 to escort her to a Chi Psi dance. She came to Ann Arbor in June for the fraternity's commencement dance, and around this time, the couple became engaged.

After Marie returned East, it was clear that Charlie's law career was over and his days at Michigan were numbered. He took a job as a night clerk at a local hotel, and apparently caroused so extensively that he had to bribe the night watchman to keep him awake on duty. A few weeks later, he received with delight and relief a telegram from Uncle Augustus informing him that he had a summer job as Shaw's center fielder if he wanted it. So he went to Mississippi and spent the summer doing what he loved best.

At the end of the season, the people of Shaw gave their popular center fielder a going-away party. Earlier, they'd taken up a collection that paid for a one-way rail ticket to New York, and CEM wasted no time getting moving. The very next day found him heading north on the Yazoo and Mississippi Valley Railroad. The flat land seemed to blaze and buckle in the heat. It was a green sea of cotton plants that in a few weeks would be covered with fluffy white fiber.

If Charles Edward Merrill had had a résumé, it would not have been very impressive: prep school disciplinary problem, two-time college dropout, drinker, and all-around reveler. In these days semipro baseball players were on a level with sailors and carnival roustabouts in terms of public esteem. But now he had a job on Wall Street. He felt foolish because he only knew one person in New York: Marie Sjostrom's father, motivated at least partially by self-interest, had gotten him a job as a clerk at a salary of $15 a week.

In a few days, Charlie Merrill would be in New York, and in a few weeks he would be twenty-two years old. Not long after his thirtieth birthday, he would be among a few hundred Americans who would earn a million dollars in a single year.

Young Charlie Merrill (eighth from the left) at a church picnic in Green Cove Springs, Florida.

Charlie was an active member of Chi Psi at Amherst College. The stained-glass window he later donated to the fraternity was still there when I joined Chi Psi in 1968.

Charlie Merrill and Eddie Lynch met each other at the Twenty-third Street YMCA in New York City and within a couple of years they both became millionaires.

CHAPTER TWO

The Odd Couple

(1907–1915)

There were still more than two thousand working farms in New York City when Charlie Merrill arrived in the fall of 1907, but the city was well along the road toward becoming the nation's business colossus. Down at the southern tip of Manhattan, tall buildings climbed skyward like vines seeking sunlight. Henry James wrote of "the multitudinous skyscrapers standing up to the view, from the water, like extravagant pins in a cushion already overplanted." So concentrated was this accumulation of steel that the captains of ships approaching New York Harbor claimed their compasses strayed by as much as seven degrees. A third of America's exports and fully two-thirds of its imports were handled on the city's wharves. Meanwhile, new industries were being born almost daily. Indeed, the movie industry had just begun when CEM arrived. A few blocks from where Charlie rented a fourth-floor room for $6 a week, Scott Joplin had just set up an office to compose and arrange ragtime.

In Lower Manhattan, about half of America's two hundred largest corporations, including U.S. Steel, General Electric, Standard Oil, Western Union, and American Telephone & Telegraph, built towering "cathedrals of commerce" to house their growing armies of clerical workers. They overflowed from the real Wall Street, and the figurative Wall Street was ever-expanding to include Cedar, Pine, Broad, Nassau, William, Exchange Place, and Lower Broadway. Bells from the great Gothic tower of Trinity Church pealed the start of the

Wall Street day, and every New Year's Eve at midnight, masses of reveling people came down and listened to it chime in the calendric moment of change (though when *The New York Times* moved into its new Midtown quarters on January 1, 1908, it began a custom of dropping a ball to greet the new year in what everyone would soon be calling Times Square). The temple-like building housing the New York Stock Exchange had just been opened four years earlier, and sightseers still marveled at the seven white columns on the outside and the trading hall, which was one of the largest rooms, with one of the highest ceilings, in the world.

But just as there would be 101 years later, panic was in the air as CEM came on the scene. Wall Street's overextended financial markets were shredding; bankers were resigning under barrages of criticism, and when any bank was mentioned in the newspapers, lines began forming at its doors. The run on the banks began after a group of speculators headed by F. Augustus Heinze made an unsuccessful attempt to corner the stock of United Copper. J. P. Morgan engineered an end to the panic and averted further bank failures and the closing of the Stock Exchange itself. It was the last hurrah for the seventy-year-old Morgan, and it would be two decades before the emergence of Wall Street's next great figure: Charles Edward Merrill.

The Panic of 1907 was one of the worst in Wall Street history, and it crystallized growing concerns in Congress about stock market trading and its threat to the economic welfare of ordinary Americans. Investing in stocks was considered only slightly more respectable than gambling, and it was outlawed in several states. There was no Federal Reserve System to manage the flow of money, and there was no Securities and Exchange Commission to regulate the stock market. This was the Wall Street where Charlie Merrill began a kind of apprenticeship in finance that would last some six years.

T he Young Men's Christian Association had just opened a branch on Twenty-third Street, and in 1907 its ranks swelled to include Charles Edward Merrill, just arrived from Florida by way of Massachusetts, Michigan, and Mississippi, and Edmund Calvert Lynch, just arrived directly from Baltimore. Both young men were born on the nineteenth day of a month in 1885, both were the first of three children, and both came to the Y to swim in the yellow-tiled pool on the sixth floor.

Merrill had just started working as an office boy for a group of textile companies run by his prospective father-in-law, P. Robert Sjostrom, who had arrived in America with his parents from Sweden in 1868 when he was eight years old. Sjostrom was now a highly paid (about $800,000 a year in modern dollars) treasurer for the Einstein-Wolfe group, a holding company for six textile mills in the metropolitan New York area. Merrill was paid $15 a week, and his rent was $6.50 a week for a fourth-floor room that lacked, among other amenities, a closet. Lynch was earning $12 a week, plus commissions, as a salesman. He had a well-located, spacious apartment on West Thirty-sixth Street, but it cost $10 a week. Lynch was in a tight financial squeeze, but he had been told by his landlady that she would reduce his rent to $8 if he could find a roommate who would also pay $8.

Merrill and Lynch had been nodding acquaintances at the Y for a few weeks, until one day late in 1907 or early in 1908 (neither party ever recalled the exact date), Merrill had just descended the spiral staircase from the sixth-floor pool after his swim and was standing in line waiting to pay his fifty-cent monthly dues. The main lobby was finished in hardwood, mainly oak and walnut. An Oriental rug was centered on the floor, and marble columns rose to a high ceiling from which Victorian light fixtures, modern and electrified, were suspended.

An inscription over the main entrance read ENTER HERE TO BE AND FIND A FRIEND and beneath it strode Lynch—a stocky, square-jawed figure in a straw hat. Spying the waiting Merrill through his thick-lensed glasses, Lynch walked over. As Merrill remembered it, after a few minutes of chitchat Lynch asked him if he liked his present living quarters. When Merrill said no, Lynch invited him to inspect his place on Thirty-sixth Street. Merrill went there and was impressed, but he was put off when Lynch said he was paying $10 a week. Lynch did not mention the landlady's $2 reduction offer. Instead, he pressed his case, enumerating the advantages of his situation: The apartment was only three flights up instead of four; it was closer to work, so he could eat lunch at home and save money; there was a nice backyard, and it had a big closet. In addition, he had secured an agreement from the landlady to reduce CEM's cost to $8 a week. Surely, all this was worth another $1.50 a week.

The sales spiel droned on, and finally Merrill agreed to move in with Lynch "just to get him out of my hair." Only much later did he learn about Lynch's agreement with his landlady that reduced his own rent from $10 to $8. Thus Merrill had his costs raised by 25 percent while Lynch realized a 20 percent reduction. When he told this story decades later, Merrill said, "That son of a gun, in our very first deal he got the best of me."

It would be another seven years before they would become business partners, but the meeting at the YMCA marked the beginning of a bittersweet relationship that would span three decades until Lynch's untimely death in 1938. Moreover, their two names would be inseparably linked in the popular mind in the manner of Sears and Roebuck, Mason and Dixon, Barnum and Bailey, and by the time the century turned again, people would associate the name Merrill Lynch with financial services the way they associated Kleenex with tissues, Xerox with photocopies, and Scotch with tape.

The Merrill-Lynch living arrangement lasted only a few months, but the two young men became friends. Despite stark personality differences (Merrill was trusting, diplomatic, instinctive, imaginative, and an initiator; Lynch was suspicious, brusque, cautious, and a troubleshooter), they respected and complemented each other. They would spend hours together in public libraries boning up on business strategies.

"Those were the days when New York had more than its share of glamour for many people, and certainly for two poor boys from out of town," Merrill wrote in a memoir. "The very year that Eddie and I came to New York, we had to face a panic; dozens of banks failed; there were cues [he meant queues] of people sometimes two blocks long standing in line to draw money out of the banks that didn't fail. We, of course, were 'babes in the woods' and didn't know whether or not the companies we worked for would survive or fail."

Eddie Lynch, as he would become known on Wall Street, was born on May 19, 1885, in Baltimore to Richard Hinkle Lynch and his wife, the former Jennie Vernon Smith, who, like Octavia Wilson Merrill, would exert a powerful influence on her son well into his adult years.

When he met Charlie Merrill at the YMCA, Lynch had just come to New York to work as an office boy for Liquid Carbonic, a manufacturer of soda fountain equipment. He had studied economics, logic, and psychology at Johns Hopkins University in his hometown and graduated in three years rather than the usual four. As a sprinter on the college track team, Lynch sometimes used his wits to defeat speedier opponents. One story that would become a favorite of Merrill's (whether it was true or not) told how Lynch studied in minute detail the habits of starters just before they fired—thus enabling him to get off the mark a split-second before the rest of the field.

Charlie Merrill's strategy when he arrived in New York was to achieve financial security by marrying the boss's daughter; his choice of employer had nothing to do with career plans—but it was extraordinarily fortuitous. Sjostrom, though only forty years old, was a seasoned veteran of finance and a born teacher. Merrill, for the first time in his life, was an eager student. When Sjostrom died in 1937, Merrill wrote his widow: "I came to New York alone and friendless, except for the Sjostroms. Robert, from the start, took me to his heart, watched over me and trained me, as if I were his son. He was kind and gentle always to me, and so far as my career is concerned, he gave me, in two years, not only the rudiments of business, but a post-graduate course as well."

On Merrill's first day with Sjostrom, the company's Manhattan office was moved to a new location about a block away, and Merrill was conscripted to help carry books, files, and other items from the old place to the new. He feared greatly that he would come across some friend from Amherst who would witness his menial labors. Another early task was to deliver the payroll to a mill in Patchogue, New York, about fifty-five miles from the home office. During the Panic, employees insisted on being paid in silver dollars, and for a while Merrill had to lug two suitcases full of the coins to the train station, ride the Long Island Rail Road for two hours to Patchogue, and then trudge two miles to the mill.

As a twenty-two-year-old office boy, Merrill scored a financial coup by obtaining for his prospective father-in-law's company a badly needed $300,000 short-term loan from the new National Copper Bank—despite the tight money market of the Panic. CEM tells of being politely turned down by officer after officer but persisting until he was allowed into the office of Charles H. Sabin, the bank president, who—either because he was impressed by the young man's tenaciousness or wanted to get him out of his office—approved the loan. Sjostrom was very pleased and treated his precocious employee to a special lunch ("pig's knuckles, Rhine wine and coffee cakes," as Charlie remembered it) and gave him a blank check to buy "the best suit of clothes in New York City." CEM went to Sandford and Sandford, a popular and fashionable clothing store at the time, and spent $100, but he would have preferred to have gotten a salary increase. "The last thing I needed was another suit of clothes. I had a trunk full from college days. I did need a raise. Milk and crackers for lunch are not the proper prelude to a siesta."

Soon Merrill was promoted to credit manager and was making $100 a week (about $2,000 in today's dollars). He began saving money, and one of the first things he did was to pay off the $1,750 mortgage on his parents' home in West Palm Beach. He considered this to be his first investment, and throughout his life counseled that the very best investment anyone could make was to pay off one's debt. Merrill would work twelve hours at the Manhattan office and then often be summoned to Sjostrom's apartment in suburban New Rochelle to work long into the night. He also worked there on weekends—and rankled his fiancée for his lack of attention to her. The long hours went on for nearly two years, and in later life Merrill called the experience "the equivalent of a university course in business."

But Merrill didn't see this advantage for quite some time, and many years later he told an interviewer:

> I didn't realize at the time the training that I had under Mr. Sjostrom in accounting, cost accounting, elementary financing such as short-term notes, bank borrowings, and things of that routine character would come to help me or rather form the background of my thinking and activities in years to come. For instance, under Mr. Sjostrom I learned that a credit man, if too conservative, is a great handicap to the sales department. I remember distinctly going in to Mr. Sjostrom with a report on the losses of the credit

department of which I was manager. In my ignorance I was very much pleased and expected a pat on the back because of my phenomenal record. Under my regime the losses had been cut from a quarter of 1% on sales or more and I was very much taken aback when Mr. Sjostrom told me that was not my job—my job was to find growing concerns that had able management regardless of the capital, and if the moral risk was fine and the experience of the man running these companies or firms was good, then Patchogue Belsen and other companies for which I was credit manager should extend credit to these companies.

CEM's time at Sjostrom's company was important for another reason, for as credit manager he noticed that the best customers were the new chain stores. They were stable, they bought in large volume, and they paid promptly. Frank W. Woolworth's success in marketing low-cost consumer goods had sparked a revolution in retailing, and other merchants—S. J. Kresge, John G. McCrory, and S. H. Kress—had formed similar chains. Charles Walgreen had just launched a drugstore chain in Chicago. Their success intrigued him, and not only did Merrill invest his own money in chain-store equities, he studied these operations while he was with Sjostrom. "It was obvious to me that the chains offered standard merchandise to the public at substantially lower prices than were obtainable elsewhere. I became convinced that there was a wonderful opportunity for any business that would cut loose from obsolete methods on the one hand, and not attempt to profiteer on the public on the other."

But personal matters sidetracked Merrill from his interest in chain stores. For reasons that are unknown except to the immediate parties, the three-year engagement to Marie was broken. The romance was over and so was his career in the textile business ("[I] had to get the hell out of that situation," he recalled). The summer of 1909 found Charlie Merrill back at the University of Michigan Law School, where he told his friends he was enrolled as a student. However, Michigan Law had no summer session in 1909, and it is very likely that he spent most of his time enmeshed in the campus social life to soothe the wounds from his shattered romance. He had saved some money and didn't have to work. By autumn, apparently recovered, he was ready to go back to New York.

During his time with Sjostrom, Fred Bale, an old Amherst classmate, had introduced Merrill to George H. Burr & Co., a commercial paper dealer with offices at 43 Exchange Place. Burr's principal activity was the buying and selling of notes and accounts receivable. George Burr himself had taken a liking to the young Southerner and told him in general terms that he could always have a job. After his job with Sjostrom ended, Merrill wrote several letters to Burr in an attempt to take advantage of the offer, but he received no answer. When he arrived back in New York in early September, he called personally on Burr, who was cordial but said he did not have an opening. CEM moved into a room with Bob Underhill, an Amherst man, and launched a job search.

Initially, CEM was optimistic, for he believed he had much to offer—two years of college, on-the-job training in business practices, and a proven record of borrowing money for companies. But Wall Street did not erupt in a battle over the right to hire Charlie Merrill—in fact, no one wanted him on the payroll. For three weeks he made four or five personal calls a day. Then his spirits waned and he made only two calls a day. He turned down an offer to be assistant credit manager for a silk mill because he would have been working for a black man and he was unwilling to do so. "I had the suspicion he wasn't as much impressed by my record as the idea of having as an assistant a whipping boy, a Southerner." Thus, he passed up a respectable salary of $35 a week, and the rejections kept coming. He sold off stock and his savings dwindled to about $1,500. This experience—the long hours spent in reception areas, the rejections and, even worse, getting no response at all, the slow liquidation of his assets—was humiliating and discouraging, and Merrill would come to view this time as "the worst in my life."

While Merrill pounded the pavement, George Burr decided to expand his business into the growing and lucrative field of investment banking and established a bond department. He was motivated by what was happening with the McCrum-Howell Co., a plumbing supplier that had several overdue short-term loans with Burr. Burr feared the company was about to fail, and believed that the proceeds of a bond sale might rescue it. He hired a Chicago banker to head the new operation, but the banker caught pneumonia on his way to

New York and died soon after he arrived. Burr, committed to the new department and desperate for someone to run it, remembered the young Floridian and offered him $25 a week plus 10 percent of the new department's profits. Merrill jumped at the opportunity, and in doing so landed firmly on Wall Street at the age of twenty-four—albeit by default.

Down in West Palm Beach, Octavia Merrill must have sighed in relief. She had not seen her son in eighteen months, and she had read with growing anxiety his letters telling of the broken engagement, leaving the job with Sjostrom, and the long search for employment. As usual, she had some advice for the new job: Find out where George Burr buys his clothes and go there for some new suits without regard to cost. This was the beginning of CEM's long friendship with his tailor, E. R. Van Sickle, who kept him well-dressed for the rest of his life. Van Sickle liked to tell the story of a visit Merrill made to him in the dark days of 1914.

> The stock exchange was closed and business downtown at a standstill, and gloom was so thick you could mold it into balls. My business had prospered and I had accumulated a modest surplus in cash. Mr. Merrill had dropped into the shop to fit a couple of suits. It was snowing and we stood at the side window looking down the avenue in the growing dusk.
>
> I asked him how he happened to buy my expensive clothes when he was struggling along selling bonds. Mr. Merrill explained that his mother had encouraged him to, as it was her confirmed belief that a man starting out in business and contacting important businessmen should only wear the best obtainable in clothes, as a man was often judged by the clothes he wore, and a well-cut suit would surely impress his prospects.
>
> Standing there looking out at the falling snow, he told me he did not really know if I would ever be paid for the clothes I was making him. I told him I was not worried at all. He thought a few minutes and said, "Van, if I did not know how hard you worked for your dough, I would let you put a few thousand in our business and sometime it

might make you some real money, but I don't know, and you might lose it all."

If I had been real bright, I would have invested ten or fifteen thousand, which I had on hand. But I fumbled that pass, which was the opportunity of my lifetime, as later events proved.

When Merrill showed up for work the first day at 43 Exchange Place, he was given $25,000 in seed money to launch the new department. He also inherited the secretary hired for the recently deceased Chicago banker. Her name was Lilian Burton, and she would remain near Merrill's right hand for some forty years (longer than his three wives combined). She also would be an important force in his long efforts to use honesty and integrity to open the stock market to ordinary investors. It is therefore a powerful irony that Lilian Burton would influence Merrill by passing on information she had obtained while working in a bucket shop.

Bucket shops (the term apparently goes back to the practice of carrying beer by the bucket into brothels) were fly-by-night brokerage operations that catered to naïve small investors—and often fleeced them of their money. Bucket shops would take small investors' orders and place them, but not before they had put their own orders into the exchange first. Then they would sit back and allow their clients' orders to drive up the price, thereby benefiting themselves rather than their clients. If an investor made money, it was purely accidental. Bucket shops were one reason that Wall Street had an odious reputation that kept many hardworking Americans out of the stock market. Nevertheless, in the early part of the twentieth century, bucket shops were among the nation's largest brokerages.

One of the ways bucket shops hustled securities to the gullible was through direct-mail solicitation, and Lilian Burton showed Merrill some examples. Merrill was intrigued by the idea of using this technique for the legitimate marketing of securities. Despite respectable Wall Street's widespread taboo against any kind of direct solicitation, CEM saw nothing wrong with using direct mail so long as the information it contained was accurate and honestly presented. In one of his first direct-mail attempts, Burr prepared a letter comparing

McCrum-Howell favorably with a competitor, American Radiator, and mailed it together with a return postcard to a select list composed mostly of physicians. In less than a week he received a $2,500 check from one doctor, William Norris Hubbard, and one for $2,000 from another, Frederick E. D'Oench. He got fifty leads in all, twenty-five of which were strong.

Though CEM knew nothing about the securities business when he started his job with Burr, Burton, who had some experience in the field, was able to give him a crash course. It was an auspicious beginning for their relationship, and while Merrill wasn't always easy to work with, Burton usually stood her ground when she thought she was right. For example, in a joint memo to Merrill and his then-partner Lynch in 1930, she complained that a promised salary raise had not materialized: "I know that you have no conception of the burdens I have been carrying nor the share of responsibility which I have always taken.... It has been rather unfortunate for me, in so far as recognition from you two is concerned, that my work and efforts have been so varied and so far removed from under your very noses."

And when a suggestion of hers was rebuffed by Merrill with his trademark sarcasm, she fired off this note to him: "A person who thinks constructively and is trying to help certainly has a lonely job when the boss is given to continued sarcastic and disparaging remarks concerning any and all intelligent effort and honest thinking. Under such constant and apparently intentional discouragement, how can he expect the most prolific thinker to 'keep on thinking'?"

Still, the two worked well together, and during the Depression, Burton even insulated Merrrill from his own excessive generosity. After a long parade of once-proud, once-wealthy "friends" succeeded in wresting loans from Merrill, Burton instructed the office receptionist to tell such visitors—especially if they claimed to have gone to school with Merrill—that he was out of town and could not be reached.

CEM was fascinated by Wall Street, and he tackled his duties at Burr with vigor and enthusiasm. The timing was fortuitous because big businesses had come to realize that by selling bonds they could improve their factories, streamline distribution systems, and enhance efficiency—and ambitious, able young men like Charlie Merrill were successful in selling these investments to the public. Only six years earlier, the New York Stock Exchange had moved into its new building, a white marble and steel temple with a pediment supported by seven columns. In its shadow, CEM learned about the securities business in general, and his open, inquiring mind challenged some of its hidebound traditions. He noted, for example, that those longtime investor favorites, railroads and utilities, paid very little out of earnings, while better returns were available from less-known chain-store securities.

Soon after his twenty-sixth birthday, Merrill wrote an article on investing that was published in the November 1911 issue of *Leslie's Illustrated Weekly*, a popular magazine of its day. It summarized the philosophy that would guide him for the rest of his life. The piece was addressed to "Mr. Average Investor," and on the surface it was a radical plea for prudence and integrity in the buying and selling of securities to individual investors. But more than that, the article showed tremendous growth by CEM in just two years at Burr and revealed him to be a stunningly original thinker.

Merrill counseled investing in stocks and bonds that allow for a reasonable appreciation in market value from year to year. He urged the inexperienced investor to secure the advice of a reputable investment bank in searching out securities that would meet his particular needs: "The investment of money requires specific knowledge and experience. If it is impossible for you to get in touch with a representative of a banking house not only willing but competent to serve your every need, you should write to one or two bankers whom you know to be reliable, telling them frankly of the investment situation as it concerns you personally."

On the responsibility of broker to client: "To select intelligently the investment securities best suited to the needs of each individual requires of the investment banker long experience, special training and a thorough knowledge not only of the intrinsic merit of the securities he recommends, but also of the investment situation as it concerns that particular individual. For instance, your banker should know if you are dependent for livelihood on the return from your investments, your present holdings, if any, and size of income. To make effective this personal service, the cooperation of the prospective client is imperative."

A warning to his Wall Street colleagues: "While it is the business of the investment banker to buy good issues as cheaply as possible and to sell them at a profit, he that overlooks the fact that the best asset is a satisfied customer had better close shop today than await the inevitable. To have customers satisfied, it is necessary for the banker not only to sell good securities . . . . but also to offer them to his clients on a basis which allows for a reasonable appreciation in market value from year to year."

"And so it has come to pass," Merrill wrote, "that a new guild has sprung up in the banking profession, whose members despise not the modest sums of the thrifty, men who give the same thoughtful and careful attention to the wise investment of $100, $1,000 or $10,000 as to the funds of the opulent."

That sounds like boilerplate rhetoric from a brokerage today, but in 1911 it was on the outer edge barely, touching the fringe. However, despite Merrill's claim of a new day on Wall Street, the truth was that much of the financial establishment remained what it had always been—interested in the wealthy and unwilling to lower itself to serve "the penny public." Charlie Merrill was right on the money—he was just thirty years ahead of the times.

The *Leslie's* article prompted hundreds of calls to Burr & Co. and buttressed Merrill's growing conviction that advertising could be used legitimately to sell stocks and bonds to a wider range of investors. It was a radical idea because J. P. Morgan and the other established Wall Street investment houses used only "tombstone" ads—newspaper displays that simply listed interest rates, dates of maturity, the addresses of the underwriters, the nature of the issuing company's business, and some measure of its past performance. Such limited exposure discouraged the entrance of competing brokerages into the field and perpetuated the general public's ignorance of Wall Street.

In pursuing his belief in a wider role for advertising, Merrill found a kindred spirit and fellow maverick in Albert "Rudy" Guenther, the son of a Chicago newspaperman who came to New York in 1896 and was a familiar figure in brokerage houses. When he and Merrill met in 1909, Guenther was buying up newspaper space at a discount and then—while ignoring signs outside many offices that read NO DOGS, BOOK AGENTS, PEDDLERS OR ADVERTISING AGENTS ALLOWED—attempting to sell creative financial advertising.

Merrill greatly admired Guenther and told him in a letter in 1913: "One of the rarest things to find in an advertising agent is downright sincerity coupled with good judgment. You know that I have always felt that advertising would be more profitable to the advertiser if more banking houses put out good instructive copy, and I shall be very glad indeed to tell the actual results of our advertising to any responsible house that may inquire." Guenther would be both a significant influence on Merrill and a personal friend for a half-century, and they would prosper together. Indeed, Guenther would become known as "the dean of financial advertising."

By 1912, Merrill had turned the Bond Department's $25,000 in seed money into $750,000 in earnings for George H. Burr & Co., and his influence in the company swelled. Burr, who did not have the clout of the larger and more established names on the Street, began angling for larger investment banking mandates, bringing in his charming and brilliant young Southerner to negotiate. When CEM was authorized to begin dealing in equities, he looked around for help and immediately thought of his old roommate and current friend, Eddie Lynch. During Lynch's early tenure as an office boy at Liquid Carbonic, it became clear that one of his strongest traits was tenacity—and so he was promoted to the demanding job of collector of overdue accounts. He ran up an outstanding record tracking down deadbeats, and a grateful management promoted him to sales. He was earning $70 a week when he was contacted by Merrill, who offered him $25. After some soul-searching, Lynch took the pay cut in order to "learn the securities business."

To that end, Merrill instructed Lynch to sit at his desk for his first two weeks with Burr and study the basic principles of investment banking, but when he did, the Burr office manager upbraided the newcomer for loafing on the job. Merrill was furious at this misreading of his hardworking friend, and he sent Lynch out to seek an account from a promising client no one else had been able to secure, that of Diogenes Balsam, a Swiss-born missionary who, soon after his arrival in America, had switched from saving souls to making neckties. Wall Street folklore holds that Lynch showed up at Balsam's Brooklyn office at ten A.M. and was kept waiting all day. At five P.M. he spotted his target leaving for the day and cornered him. Balsam, impressed by the Lynch persistence that would become legendary, supposedly opened an account with Burr on the spot. Whatever the truth of the details of this event, the fact of Lynch's contact with Balsam was important to the future Merrill Lynch enterprise because about a year later Balsam would introduce the two young entrepreneurs to one of his best customers, John G. McCrory, who was seeking capital to expand his chain of five-and-ten-cent stores.

Charlie Merrill prospered at Burr, and at the beginning of 1912 he was earning $5,000 a year, plus 10 percent of the profits, and had built up a sizable nest egg in securities. Much of his savings centered on McCrum-Howell, which George Burr had assured him was a solid company. Merrill had even bought some of McCrum-Howell's common stock with a loan from the Mechanics and Metals Bank. But one day Burr summoned him to deliver shocking news: McCrum-Howell was failing and would be bankrupt in a few hours. Merrill dashed back to his office, called the loan officer at the Mechanics and Metals, whose name was Miller, and told him to sell all the company stock and apply the proceeds to his debt. Then he wrote a personal letter of apology and regret to every customer to whom he had sold McCrum-Howell and recommended other securities they could buy. Meanwhile, Miller for some reason failed to sell CEM's McCrum-Howell stock, resulting in a substantial loss to Merrill. Nevertheless, CEM did not report Miller's error, probably because he knew it would cost Miller his job.

Soon after he began working at Burr in 1909, Merrill had set up housekeeping with three former Amherst classmates—Sumner Cobb, Fred Bale, and Bob Powell—in a Brooklyn apartment, and he would look back on these years with great fondness. "We played as hard as we worked. This meant long hours at the office, and upon occasion longer hours investigating the mysteries of the city. Today that life seems like heaven—a room full of books, an open fire and oil lamps. From our windows, we had a fine view of the harbor and busy boats. Misty nights were grand; then the lights of the two cities, connected by a faintly gleaming necklace of the bridge, made an unforgettable picture. Equally unforgettable are the mornings, when homeward bound, we walked the bridge in that lovely green light that comes just before daybreak."

The "mysteries of the city" that CEM cherished most wore skirts, and he developed a reputation as a Lothario. But at a dinner party at

George Burr's house in 1912, he met Eliza Church, a twenty-year-old woman from Columbus, Ohio, who was a friend of Mrs. Burr's. Eliza had just graduated from Briarcliff College, an exclusive school north of New York City, and was a talented pianist. Like most women of her day, her lifetime goal was to marry a successful man or one with "prospects." Charlie Merrill fit that requirement nicely, and he was strongly attracted to her—at least partly because Eliza, cultured, refined, and shy, was a pleasant contrast to the women whose company he had been keeping. After a courtship of about one month, they were married in a Roman Catholic ceremony on April 8, 1912, then left for a ten-day honeymoon at a posh mountain retreat in Hot Springs, Virginia. But five days into the honeymoon George Burr summoned CEM back to New York to work on a possible underwriting for an important new client.

Sebastian Spering Kresge was born in 1867 in a small town not far from Scranton, Pennsylvania, in the heart of the anthracite coal region. He held various sales jobs as a young man, and by the time he was thirty he had amassed savings of $8,000 (about $156,000 today). He joined forces with John G. McCrory to open five-and-tens in Memphis and Detroit. Quickly he became manager and then sole owner of the Detroit store, and in 1900, with his brother-in-law, Charles J. Wilson, Kresge organized the Kresge & Wilson Company to operate five-and-tens in other cities. By 1907 he bought out Wilson's shares and changed the company name to S. S. Kresge.

Undoubtedly there were businessmen who were more different from each other than Charlie Merrill and Sebastian Kresge—but not very many. Once, Kresge explained his hobby of beekeeping: "My bees always remind me that hard work, thrift, sobriety, and an earnest struggle to live an upright Christian life are the first rungs of the ladder of success." His parsimony was already well established, and it was said that Sebastian Kresge had trained himself not to want anything. He kept wearing worn shoes by stuffing them with newspapers, bragged that he never spent more than thirty cents for lunch, took the upper berth on Pullmans because they were cheaper, and gave up golf because he couldn't stand losing balls. He was forty-four years old when he met Charlie Merrill, and he had about eighty-five stores at the time. He wanted to open many more.

Merrill went to Detroit to meet with Kresge in mid-April 1912 and returned with an agreement with him to issue $2 million in preferred stock and 10,000 shares in common stock—the latter to be reserved at below-market prices for the underwriters and their best customers. Burr did not have the resources to handle this undertaking by itself, and Hallgarten & Co., an investment banking house with better connections and more capital, was asked to join them in the deal. George Burr met with Hallgarten officials, who told him they were enthusiastic about joining in the underwriting, but were concerned about the unsavory reputation of George H. Burr & Co., which was just emerging from the McCrum-Howell fiasco of a few months earlier. Hallgarten agreed to participate in the Kresge underwriting and share the profits with Burr—only if the name of the Burr company did not appear anywhere in the offering.

Merrill recounts Burr's return from the meeting: "About six-thirty or seven, Burr returned to the office from a visit to Hallgarten. I was still working but most everyone else had gone for the day. He looked fifteen years older, gray, tired, depressed. He called me into his office, said, 'Close the door and sit down.' He told me the Hallgarten firm was upset at the failure of McCrum-Howell and worried about the standard of their own concern if Burr continued in the Kresge deal. They asked him to kindly refrain from using his name in the deal, said they would be glad for him to share the profits but none of the credit. I was twenty-six at the time. With all the patience I could muster I said, 'Mr. Burr, I would see them in hell first. Let Hallgarten have all the profit and you take all the credit. You need a success like the Kresge offering.' I was convinced the Kresge deal would be a great success. Burr listened intently, phoned Hallgarten and found a couple of the partners were still there. He went back as I advised him to do. Inside of twenty minutes he returned and looked like a new man. Said he: 'They recognized my point of view.'"

Early in 1913, Herbert Dillon, a senior partner in the underwriting firm of Eastman Dillon & Co., informed Rudy Guenther that he was looking for a sales manager. When Guenther passed the word on to his friend Charlie Merrill, he found a receptive ear partly because CEM thought he was undervalued and undercompensated at Burr. But in addition, Merrill believed that George Burr had been irresponsible in his handling of the 1909 McCrum-Howell financing that turned sour three years later. Specifically, he thought Burr had proceeded with the bond issue without regard to his customers, in turn forcing CEM to mislead his own clients. Dillon told Guenther the job paid $50 a week, but Guenther said he'd have to pay $100, and Merrill subsequently got it bumped up to $125. Meanwhile, Lynch stepped into Merrill's spot as head of the Burr Bond Department.

Almost from his first day on the job, Merrill knew he had made a mistake. He was put in charge of a mediocre sales force and found that Dillon undermined his authority. But more serious was that he questioned Dillon's business ethics. Because of Merrill's experience in Detroit with the Kresge deal, Dillon assigned him to market preferred stock in the Chalmers Motor Co., a new and untested auto manufacturer. After an investigation of the company that included discussions with Sebastian Kresge himself during a trip to Detroit, Merrill concluded that the company was unsound and told Dillon he could not recommend that investors buy its stock. Dillon was annoyed by his brash new employee and went ahead and sold the stock himself.

It was a different story when Dillon handed Merrill a file on McCrory Stores. CEM enthusiastically endorsed the department store chain and asked to take part in any underwriting and share in the profits, which he estimated to be between $200,000 and $250,000. "To my horror and amazement," CEM wrote, "he said I couldn't share because the contract had been made before I came to E-D." But like most Wall Street executives, Dillon viewed chain stores as a passing fad, and he did not follow up on the McCrory opportunity; Merrill put the file away in his desk drawer for future reference, but it wouldn't stay there for long.

Because things weren't working out for him at Dillon, with great reluctance CEM returned to George Burr and asked for a job. According to Merrill, "Burr with a big fat cigar and pleasant smile leaned back in the chair like the father of the boy who had seduced the housemaid [and] told me, 'It's bad policy to take back an employee.'" Then, a few days before Christmas 1913, Dillon called his upstart employee into his office and said he was cutting his salary from $125 to $75 a week because of grim business prospects for the coming year. On his way home to deliver the disastrous news to his wife, who was now pregnant, Merrill spotted a YWCA Christmas fund-raising sign. "I had $40 or $50 in my pocket. I'll be damned if I missed the train and instead got in the elevator and went to the YWCA headquarters. I spoke to the woman at the desk. 'Would you take a guy's last $40?' I asked. I had $5 left. It was stupid. You can't explain it."

After only a few days of contemplation, twenty-eight-year-old Charlie Merrill took a daring step: semi-independence. He went to Herb Dillon during the week between Christmas and New Year's and proposed that he set up his own company. He would continue to trade his accounts through Eastman Dillon, which in turn would grant him office space and the use of its telephones. The deal made sense for Dillon because business was slow and young Merrill had good accounts. Not only did Dillon agree, he moved out of his own office so CEM could set up shop there. And thus on January 6, 1914, in a thirteenth-floor sublet room at 71 Broadway, there occurred an event that would go totally unnoticed by Wall Street, but whose repercussions would one day shake it to its foundations and permanently alter it: The firm of Charles E. Merrill & Co. opened for business. The "& Co." in these first weeks consisted of Lilian Burton. Whimsically, to have his new firm appear a bit more substantial, CEM had "Operations Department" painted on the closet door.

"I have no fear of failure," CEM said around this time. "Provided I use my heart and head, hands and feet—and work like hell." The operation showed a profit of about $1,000 in January through the sale of unlisted securities. February brought in $5,000. On the evening of March 4, Eliza was rushed home by sleigh from a bridge party to the couple's home in Montclair, New Jersey, where she gave birth to a daughter, whom they named Doris. By April, Merrill was in a position to make a clean break from Dillon and move into his own quarters in an ancient building at 7 Wall Street, where a one-room office on the seventh and top floor was reached either by flights of iron steps or a creaking elevator that moved at glacial speed. Merrill wrote to his mother on May 26, informing her that the company had cleared about $900 in April and had already passed the $2,500 mark for May. "I have been sweating blood since the first of May—when we moved to Seven Wall Street," he added. "I have been working almost every night and twice on Sunday, and just now am almost petered out."

Soon after the move, CEM made another momentous decision: He asked Eddie Lynch, who was still working in the Bond Department at Burr, to become his partner. Lynch, characteristically, was skeptical about the new venture—especially because the only capital he had to put up was his mother's lifetime savings of $400. Lynch went to Baltimore for a family powwow, where he paced up and down the sitting room, going over pros and cons with various aunts and uncles. He left the final word to his mother, who counseled him to make the move. But when he got back to New York the doubts returned, and it was only after Rudy Guenther assured him that he could borrow the money that he would need to put up from the bank at 6 percent interest that Lynch agreed to become a partner. But for some reason, possibly an impatience with Lynch's vacillations, when the copartnership agreement was signed in July, it provided that Merrill would put up all of the firm's $4,000 capital and the profits would be split 62½ percent for Merrill, 37½ percent for Lynch. It was not a good time for a name change, and it was not until October 15, 1915, that the partnership became known as Merrill, Lynch & Co.

Superficially, it was an odd coupling. Merrill was small, trim, and extremely handsome, with clear blue eyes and an almost perpetual boyish grin; nearly everyone remembered his charm and relaxed, soft Florida accent that stretched his vowels and made his words seem farther apart. A friend once described him as "quite lovable." He was generous. Lynch was big-framed, square-faced, and plain-spoken. In his business dealings he was a table-pounder and a bully. He was parsimonious and would rage at a telephone booth that failed to give back his nickel after a failed call.

Merrill was the visionary, Lynch was the realist—and Merrill recognized that the business needed both. He leaned heavily at times on Lynch's detail-oriented, legalistic, skeptical mind—though he sometimes chafed at Lynch's caution in committing fully to many of his ideas until it was clear beyond all doubt that they were sound and would lead to success. He appreciated his partner's ability to remain impartial and to speak bluntly. One early Merrill Lyncher, H. H. (Pop) Melcher, an Amherst man who joined the firm in 1919, said Merrill used Lynch as a brake: "Charlie considered Lynch the best man he ever knew at spotting something wrong just by looking at a bunch of figures." For the next quarter-century, Merrill would depend so thoroughly on Lynch as a friend and as a business partner that at Lynch's death in 1938, a grieving Merrill would write to a friend: "I truly don't know how I am going to get along without him." Some two decades after Lynch's death, Merrill continued to credit him with much of the firm's success: "I think without Eddie's help, counsel, and his capacity to discover the weak points in a situation, this company wouldn't be here today."

Kenneth Martin, who started as an office boy in 1919 at the age of fourteen, said the two partners' roles were clear-cut: "Merrill was a very outgoing person. He'd come in and was always happy and gay, and if there was something wrong he'd raise hell—but that's all. Lynch stayed in his office most of the time and had a few people he talked with. He didn't have the rapport [with people] that Merrill had." Lynch's disdain for the opinions of others may well have been part of what made him so valuable to Charlie Merrill. Lynch willingly played "bad cop" to Charlie's "good cop," allowing Merrill to continue in the role of benign and loving "Chief," while Lynch handled the dirty work. "He was the finest troubleshooter, the most dependable, tough guy I ever knew in my life," Merrill said.

My father saved an early letter he'd gotten from Lynch in which the boss expressed his strong disapproval about the lateness of certain office employees, including Dad himself. "I understand that you were delayed on account of the railroad situation," Lynch wrote. "However, of this situation we all had ample notice and I suppose on occasions like this it is up to those depending upon the railroads to plan ahead." He demanded that Dad "please make this a rule that the telephone operator gets there at ten minutes to nine every morning, and the first morning she does not arrive at ten minutes to nine, pay her off and get another one." This was not a letter that Charlie Merrill ever could or would write. But no doubt he reaped its benefits.

Because of their different temperaments, the two partners had some raging, fundamental disagreements, and CEM sometimes found Lynch exasperating. "Of all the fine men I have known," he once said, "Eddie was the most difficult to handle." Looking back in 1955, some two decades after Lynch's death, Merrill would say: "My, what a terror he was. And yet I was devoted to him." In fact, when asked what he wanted on his tombstone, CEM wrote:

Here lies Charles Edward Merrill
October 19, 1885–April 1st, 1955
who for twenty-four years
was a partner of Edmund Calvert Lynch
AND
SURVIVED HIM

Along with all their other differences, what motivated the two men was also different. Lynch's goal was intensely personal: the accumulation of wealth. Merrill had a broader vision and loftier sense of purpose. Once angered by an insinuation that the business of securities investment was nothing but a game, CEM snapped back: "If the supplying of capital to the nation's industries and, for that matter, to the nation itself is a game, then the time has come to rewrite the dictionary."

At Merrill, Lynch & Co. the brokerage business was secondary to the investment banking business. In an early memo, Merrill said, "It is my ambition to build up a business that will endure, to create for M.L. & Co. a name that will stand for what is best in investment banking." And as early as 1914, he wrote to a colleague: "The business of investment banking is my life work." Merrill and Lynch saw themselves as venture capitalists and investment bankers who could envision the opportunities for expansion in the chain-store field, could convince the chains' owners that they could increase their sales by increasing the number of stores they owned, and could successfully market the securities of the expanding chains. Their payment for investment banking services, as was common at the time, would be in the form of stock in the companies they underwrote. And as major stockholders in those companies, they would exercise their management rights actively.

Cash flow was sluggish in these early days. Since the firm did not have an NYSE seat, it had to place its orders through brokers that did and then split the commission. Problems arose on large orders because payment was due at the end of each business day, and the firm could not cover the purchases with its own funds. Johnny Wark, the nimble eighteen-year-old office boy who was the company's first male employee, helped solve the problem in one of two ways: If the buyer handed CEM a check, Wark ran to the broker, bought the stock with the customer's money, then ran back to the office with the securities. If there was no check, Wark bought the stock on memorandum, delivered the securities to the customer, cashed the customer's check at the bank, took out the commission, then raced to the broker to pay for the stock. Wark would remain with Merrill for many years and become a partner when the modern Merrill Lynch was formed in 1940.

Back when Merrill and Lynch were working together for what was then Charles E. Merrill & Co., their first major underwriting had very nearly ended in calamity. Lynch parlayed his earlier contact with Diogenes Balsam, the necktie-maker, into a meeting between Merrill and John G. McCrory, Sebastian Kresge's onetime partner, who had opened a variety store in Scottsdale, New York, in 1881 and now ran his own chain of 113 five-and-tens in the East and South. CEM had to borrow $10 from a friend so he could pay for lunch, but he convinced McCrory, who was nearly twice his age, that an infusion of capital would permit faster growth while enabling him to obtain cash discounts through the wholesale purchase of goods. McCrory signed a handwritten contract authorizing the issuance of up to $2 million in preferred stock—for an underwriting fee of 20 percent of McCrory's common stock. The upstart Charles E. Merrill & Co. was able to land this lucrative piece of business because McCrory was relatively unknown and the older Wall Street firms had shied away from it. But CEM had studied the situation carefully, and he knew that McCrory had an uncanny knack for picking good store sites, and that the company was solid. For his part, Lynch visited five-and-dimes all over the metropolitan area and bombarded the managers with questions about location, profits, and inventory. McCrory would become the cornerstone of both their personal fortunes.

However, the Merrill firm could barely meet its payroll, let alone handle a deal of this magnitude, and thus CEM sought the help of one or more additional houses to participate in the venture. "I went to work," Merrill recalled. "Called on every important house in Wall St. . . . Blair & Co., Horn Blower [sic] & Weeks, Dominick, Kissell, Kinnecott, White Weld, F S Smithers, Laudenberg Thalmann, Hallgarten, Knauth,

Nacholds & Kuhne, Heidelbeck Ickeheimer, Speyer & Co. List covered about 30." To each one Merrill touted the up-and-coming McCrory company and preached his chain-store gospel (volume buying equals low prices), but no one was interested. Discouraged and desperate, Merrill went to Chicago, where he found a willing partner in S. W. Straus & Co., specialists in real-estate bonds. The package was set at $2.5 million—half in bonds, half in preferred stock. For successfully issuing the $1.25 million in stock, Merrill would receive 18 percent of McCrory's outstanding common stock. Merrill returned to New York and, along with Lynch and Sumner Cobb (his Amherst pal), went to work. It was a hard sell, much of it door-to-door canvassing. The investing public didn't know what a chain store was (some prospects asked if they sold chains, others asked what kind of chains they sold—logging, industrial, or watch?), but by July 1914 the entire $1.25 million had been subscribed. However, because the details of the contract had not been worked out, the certificates had not been printed, and the stock was sold on a "when issued" basis.

Late that month Merrill left for Chicago to close the deal with Straus, but as he was getting off the train in Union Station, the powder keg that was Europe exploded. Austria-Hungary declared war on Serbia. Three days later, on July 31, the New York Stock Exchange closed in an attempt to prevent panic selling by European investors that would be devastating for the American economy. American investors were uncertain what to do next, and the subscribers to the McCrory issue began backing out. Then the single-largest customer died, and his estate refused to honor his commitment to buy $100,000 in McCrory. Merrill and Lynch watched in mounting horror as their first big underwriting—the deal that would have made them wealthy, perhaps millionaires, and enabled them to buy a NYSE seat—unraveled.

Merrill gave up his house in New Jersey and moved to a small apartment in Manhattan and sold his car. Eliza, who had never known poverty and was greatly distressed by this sudden descent into it, went to live with her sister in Columbus, Ohio, taking with her Doris, who was less than a year old. She offered her husband the use of her personal inheritance of some $30,000, but it is not clear whether he used any of it. In the back of his mind, he had found some security from the knowledge that his mother had $2,000 in savings, but then he received the news that the Jacksonville bank where she kept it had failed. Merrill was glum, and in retrospect he would call these days in 1915 worse than the Crash of 1929. Initially, Lynch was paralyzed by the fact that his worst fears had come to pass, but he then rallied to action and got his old employer, Liquid Carbonic, to agree to take him back. After receiving Lynch's letter of resignation, Merrill made an emotional, weeping appeal for his partner to reconsider, and at the last minute Lynch agreed to stay on.

To keep the partnership afloat, Merrill went back to the Mechanics and Metals Bank, and after some lower-level rejections worked his way into the office of the bank president, Gates McGarrah. He told McGarrah how three years earlier he had paid off the loan to McGarrah's bank that he had taken out to buy McCrum-Howell stock even though the securities had become worthless and even though the bank had made an error in not selling them when he'd asked them to. He also told of protecting the loan officer's job. McGarrah was impressed and approved a $20,000 loan without collateral. Borrowing J.P. Morgan's phrase, he told Merrill, "Your character will be my collateral." Years later Merrill wrote: "If he had refused me that loan, I think I'd have simply given up and gone home to raise watermelons. I walked out of McGarrah's office with tears of gratitude in my eyes. Until I paid back that loan the one guiding principle in my life was to be found worthy of that man's trust. Is it any wonder that to this day we have maintained an active account in that bank?"

During the lull, while the stock market was shut down, Merrill honed his financial skills. "I would employ my spare time in making a thorough study of what information was available from annual reports and *Moody's Manual* and that sort of thing about General Electric. After getting all the data together that was available, I pretended I was a partner in J. P. Morgan & Co. and wrote a prospectus regarding a big issue, perhaps $50 million of convertible bonds for General Electric Company. Of course, this was all make-believe because we never had a chance to finance General Electric."

When the stock market reopened in December 1914, investors awakened to the fact that the war, far from being a financial calamity for America, was actually going to be a boon. The British and the French were issuing war bonds and placing orders with American munitions manufacturers. The surge bounced the market out of the skepticism that had smothered it since the Panic of 1907. Before long, commissions were rolling in to 7 Wall Street. Merrill paid off the bank loan and proceeded with the McCrory financing. This time he found a co-sponsor in Hornblower & Weeks, Boston, which he hoped would lend not only capital but respectability to the McCrory offering. Merrill put some twenty-five salesmen to work and supported them with a newspaper advertising campaign. The orders came in, and Johnny Wark raced from office to bank to broker. Even executives from McCrory's rivals, Kresge and Woolworth, bought some shares. The issue sold out by the end of the summer of 1915, and it became Wall Street's first major underwriting since the resumption of trading. As Merrill and McCrory were closing the deal in a lawyer's office, Merrill received a telephone call from his mother, who was in nearby Yonkers, New York, with his sister Edith, who was in labor with her first child and suffering terribly. Octavia Merrill told her son that if he wanted to see his sister alive again, he should get on a train immediately and come to her bedside. As Merrill recounted later: "She knew about the McCrory deal, and I told her that McCrory at that time was with me to sign the final papers, that I could not be of any help to my sister, and that if we didn't consummate the deal there would be no money available to pay the doctors' bills or funeral expenses. That was certainly one hell of a day for me, but she lived through that ordeal." With the return of income to the Merrill household, Eliza came back and they bought an even larger house in Montclair, but the separation had left bitterness on both sides.

As successful as the McCrory issue had been, a last-minute hitch forced Merrill and Lynch to make a rare descent into questionable practices. The trouble came when an external audit of McCrory showed that its 1914 profits had been considerably less than what Merrill and Lynch had been telling investors. According to CEM, Lynch reacted poorly: "I thought he was going to faint. He got pale and weak in the knees." But then Lynch rallied and dove into the books, where he discovered that three new stores—in Philadelphia, Louisville, and Lancaster, Pennsylvania—hadn't been included in the calculations. They confronted McCrory, who said it was his policy not to count such new stores because they distorted the true financial picture. The accountants disagreed. Rather than risk the loss of investors, Merrill and Lynch solved the problem by creating a separate corporation to house the three new companies—and then remained silent about their bookkeeping subterfuge. They didn't even tell Hornblower & Weeks about it. "We should have been ashamed of ourselves, pulling a trick like that," CEM said some three decades later. "And of course it was risky. Anybody, any clerk, any office boy, could have discovered the discrepancy simply by placing the two circulars, the original and the amended one, side by side and comparing." They turned in the revised paperwork and waited for someone to blow the whistle. "But the days went by and the deal wasn't called off. By some incredible oversight they never discovered the trick. . . . I don't believe to this day that Hornblower & Weeks learned of our little sleight of hand."

The McCrory financing set a pattern that Merrill and Lynch would use over the next few years to amass personal fortunes: By accepting options to buy common stock as part of their underwriting compensation, they became part owners in the firms whose expansion they were promoting. In doing so, they in effect sent a message to prospective investors that "what's good enough for our customers is good enough for us." And if the company used the stock proceeds well and prospered, Merrill and Lynch stood to realize sizable capital gains as the value of shares increased. Because the partnership needed cash in these early years, sometimes desperately, there was some risk in taking stock instead, but Merrill estimated that the partnership realized an immediate $200,000 profit from the McCrory deal; in addition, they received 12,500 shares of common stock that was then worth $30 a share. In little more than a decade, the value would zoom to $600 a share.

Other patterns were established that would repeat themselves again and again over the next half-century. One was challenging and breaking with tradition. The Wall Street establishment had set up seemingly impenetrable barriers to newcomers and business was conducted on a gentlemanly, man-to-man referral basis. Merrill was convinced that to break in he needed to shatter the old taboos against aggressive marketing strategies. One of his first steps after he went independent was to prepare a three-page circular contrasting Kresge and Woolworth. It was strictly informational, with graphs and statistics, but it showed Kresge in a favorable light. "I took that circular and carried it up and down Broadway and made literally hundreds of customers for an absolutely new and unknown firm," CEM said. Taking his cue from what Lilian Burton had taught him about the bucket shops, CEM compiled extensive lists of people who owned stock. In the loft of his makeshift office, he set up a "Multigraph and Mailing Department" and churned out thousands of letters seeking business. Rather than spend money for postage, he would hire between ten and fifteen runners who would fan out across the city and deliver the solicitations all night long. Meanwhile, Rudy Guenther did newspaper advertisements and told Merrill to pay him when he could. Guenther had an account with Postal Telegraph, and he let CEM run up the tab to send out telegrams to prospective clients.

The new Merrill, Lynch venture was strongly tied to the basic concept of chain stores—using mass purchasing power and low margins to offer customers low prices. The timing was just right. The early chains were now expanding exponentially as mass public transportation, a national commercial freight rail network, the electric motor, and the methods of mass production blossomed in America. In the coming years Merrill and Lynch would assist unknown, trailblazing entrepreneurs with names like Samuel H. Kress, James Cash Penney, George Romanta Kinney, Samuel Lerner, James Josiah Newberry, and Charles R. Walgreen. Most of them, like Merrill, were from rural, small-town America, and Charles E. Merrill would perform the vital service of bringing their companies to public ownership. Eventually he would come to see that the chain-store idea could be applied to services as well as goods. "It probably would not have occurred to anyone at the time that Charlie would someday carry that organizational strategy to its logical conclusion: a nationwide network with more than one hundred brokerage offices," writes Merrill's biographer, Edwin J. Perkins.

Merrill and Lynch quickly realized that honesty was not only the right thing, it could also be good for business. A major problem facing investors in these early days was how to find an honest broker, for stockbrokers had bad reputations—often with good reason. When they opened a Detroit office, CEM sent a handwritten note to its manager:

I want you to make all your customers and, for that matter, every investor in your territory realize that this firm has only one ambition—and that is to stand for all that is best in Investment Banking. The success of this house has been predicated upon the success of our customers—if we take care of them they will take care of us—Our business will continue to grow only as we serve the best interests of the investing public—Not much when it is put on a scrap of paper—but it spells success when put into effect. Stand for the best in our line of endeavor—every day—every year and the carpet at 1001 Penobscot Building will soon be worn threadbare.

In 1916 he sent this remarkable memo to his staff:

From conversations that I have overheard over the telephone between one or two of our salesmen and their clients, I notice a very unfortunate tendency to dwell upon the profits that a customer is likely to make on a certain transaction and not upon the merit of the issue as an investment. It is our business to buy and place for investment, issues of stocks and bonds that we think enough of in which to invest the money of our firm. It is not our idea to induce any client to buy today with the hope of immediate profit due to the popularity of the issue of the initial price.

A salesman deserves no credit for any sale made on the strength of exaggerated statements. The thing for you to bear in mind is that if you once get a customer's confidence in the integrity and honesty of the house, you have already paved the way for a long string of repeat orders; whereas, if you exaggerate or paint the picture too rosy on the security that you are selling at the time, you have to go through the same process when you come to sell him a second time. Please bear this in mind and remember that in every sale you are either increasing or destroying a good-will which up to this time has been our most valuable asset.

Partly to celebrate his McCrory success and partly to repair his marriage and get to know his young daughter, CEM took a cottage in

Ogunquit, Maine, in the summer of 1915 and stayed there for about a month. He had many visitors, including Lynch, Lilian Burton, his in-laws from Ohio—and Charles S. Mott, the second-largest stockholder in General Motors, who had invested in the Kresge offering. Mott tried to persuade CEM and Lynch to invest in the new automaker, and while the company had about $300,000 to invest at this point, they politely declined, thereby (assuming they had held on to the GM stock during the Depression) turning down a nine-figure fortune. But Merrill and Lynch already had plans to get into the burgeoning automobile industry—this time on the ground floor with a new company, Saxon Motors. Late in 1915, Merrill, Lynch & Co. underwrote a $6 million stock offering that enabled Saxon to build an assembly plant and develop plans for selling its high-powered, luxury product. But just as Saxon was gearing up to fill a backlog of orders, the new plant burned to the ground. Rather than wait and build another plant, the company put together makeshift production facilities at several locations—and came out with a lemon. When in 1916 the president of the firm died unexpectedly, the partners tried to lure Walter P. Chrysler, a forty-year-old GM vice president with a reputation as a comer, to take the job. Chrysler declined the offer, and Saxon Motors fell into a slow decline that ended in receivership in 1922. Chrysler, of course, would go on to organize a company that would bear his name and become one of the nation's Big Three automakers. Merrill speculated in later years that had he sweetened the offer to Chrysler with the kind of stock option he liked, Chrysler might have taken the job and rescued Saxon Motors.

Though Merrill was making attempts to improve his marriage, ironically it was a quarrel between him and Eliza that played a role in a second Kresge financing. Merrill had aggressively courted Kresge for several years, but in November 1915 he went to Detroit to see him because "I thought I'd better absent myself from Montclair to escape bombardments by Mrs. Merrill." In a previous meeting, Merrill had rashly promised Kresge that he would "come up with a financing idea to make us both rich." When Kresge reminded him of this boast, CEM proposed recapitalizing the company with a sale of $5 million in preferred stock and 500,000 shares of common. At the end of the meeting CEM dictated a letter authorizing the underwriting and

Kresge signed it. Merrill was pleased. Unlike McCrory, Kresge was already a prestige name. Although the deal eventually went to market at $2 million in preferred, CEM was still satisfied. "This was a piece of business any firm would have wanted to handle," he said. Out of a sense of loyalty and obligation for allying with him on the McCrory deal when no other firm was willing to take the chance, Merrill again turned to Hornblower & Weeks to be co-manager. This offended both Burr and Hallgarten & Co., who considered Kresge their client. Merrill was less concerned that "Mr. Burr's nose was out of joint," perhaps because he felt he had rescued Burr & Co. in the first Kresge issue. But Hallgarten & Co. was a different matter: "Hallgarten & Co. had always been kind to me, and I was embarrassed when they asked, 'Why didn't you invite us to join?'"

My father, Winthrop ("Win") Smith, joined Merrill Lynch right out of college in 1916 and went to work for fellow Amherst man Charlie Merrill as his office boy.

CHAPTER THREE

Mr. Smith
Goes to Wall Street

(1915–1929)

My father was born in South Hadley Falls, Massachusetts, on June 30, 1893, which was 259 years almost to the day after his ancestors first came to America. They arrived in Boston aboard the *Elizabeth* out of the English port city of Ipswich. He was the first of four children born to Frederick Merwin Smith and Evelyn Bardwell Smith. A daughter, Rachel, died in infancy, and my father had two younger brothers, Lincoln and Frederick.

My grandfather was a successful businessman who ran a printing plant in nearby Holyoke. He was, according to my father, "the hardest-working man I ever knew." He came from a long succession of distinguished Massachusetts men and women that stretched back to Samuel Smith, who was born in England in 1602 and sailed for America on April 30, 1634. He was accompanied by his wife, Elizabeth, and four children—Samuel, nine years old; Elizabeth, seven; Mary, four, and Philip, one. The parents were both thirty-two years old.

The family originally settled in Wethersfield, Connecticut, where Samuel Smith became a leading figure in the community. In 1661 the Smiths moved up the Connecticut River and helped to found the town of Hadley. Smith organized a militia to defend the new town against Indian attacks, and it was this role that earned him the title of "Lieutenant." He died in 1680 at the age of seventy-eight, and his wife passed away six years later at eighty-four. Those were incredible life spans in those days and perhaps explains why my father's mother lived to be 107.

My next noteworthy ancestor was Hiram Smith, who was born in 1793. Hiram might be an unusual name to many, but it dates back to Hiram Abbif, who was the architect of King Solomon's temple. In *The Book of Names*, one of the definitions of Hiram is "the exalted one." According to *The Annals of South Hadley*: "Hiram Smith. . . . early turned his attention to navigation on the Connecticut River, and by his energy and business ability probably did more than any other person to open up the commerce of the Upper Connecticut. This was before the days of railroads, when the river was the great highway of commerce in Western Massachusetts. Indeed, so great were his exploits as a boatman and so far reaching his ideas and plans, that he was universally known on the river as 'King Hiram.' He was a valuable and useful citizen, and served his town in various offices for many years. He represented South Hadley in the General Court of Massachusetts." Only a few years ago, I found a small ceramic cup that was given to Hiram Jr. by his father, King Hiram, on his third birthday.

In 1830 the Connecticut River Valley Steamboat Company issued stock for the construction of five steam ferries operating at different points between Hartford, Connecticut, and Wells River, Massachusetts. One of them, the *Ariel Cooley*, was commanded by Hiram Smith. But eventually the entire enterprise failed, and Hiram then opened a general store in the new community of South Hadley Falls. Like Charlie Merrill, Hiram seems to have inherited an entrepreneurial and retailing gene—one that would trace its way down to my father.

His son, Hiram Jr., born in 1848, was another solid citizen who ran the thriving store that, according to a contemporary newspaper advertisement, sold "dry goods, clothing, fine groceries, provisions, crockery, glass and wooden ware and hardware" plus "a full line of patent medicines." For more than thirty years, Hiram Jr. also was the South Hadley Falls postmaster, and as was common at the time, the post office was set up at the store. The mail came up by boat from Hartford. He died sorting the mail in 1890.

Hiram Jr. and his wife had four sons, the youngest of whom was Frederick Merwin Smith, my grandfather, who was born in 1862. Fred M. Smith received his early education first in the public schools of South Hadley and then at the Williston Seminary in Easthampton, where he finished in 1880. He went on to Amherst College and graduated with the class of 1884. He was very active in the Delta Upsilon fraternity and instrumental in the construction of the lodge, which was still present when both my father and I attended Amherst six decades apart. Several days after Fred graduated, he walked into the offices of the *Springfield Union* newspaper and asked the editor, Joseph S. Shipley, for a job. He was hired on the spot as a reporter. After two years in journalism, he took a middle-management job with the Valley Paper Company of Holyoke, Massachusetts. Three years later he moved over to the Holyoke firm of Griffith, Axtell & Cady and became company president in 1895. Griffith, Axtell & Cady was engaged in fine printing, engraving, and embossing; it had about thirty employees and an international clientele.

Fred married Evelyn Bardwell in 1892. My grandmother had been born on a farm in Shelburne Falls, Massachusetts, in 1861, and her homestead would be purchased nearly a hundred years later by the comedian Bill Cosby. Her ancestors had arrived in America about the same time as the Smiths. While I did not know her intimately, she was a very important influence in the life of my half brother, Bardwell, twenty-five years my elder, and she lived almost until the age of 108. For over thirty of those years Bardwell was very close to her. After school every year he spent two or three weeks with her in her home in South Hadley Falls, the same house where my father, who was born in 1893, grew up. Bardwell was her first grandson and so she lavished attention on him, and later she was very kind and solicitous of me. She was a devout, liberal-minded Congregationalist, and every Sunday went to church. Although I never went to church with her as Bardwell did, her faith made an indelible impression on me one day. I was sitting in a small antique child's chair in her living room when she walked by and said, "Winnie [as I was called then], do you like that chair?" "Yes, Nana," I remember saying, "I love this chair." "Winthrop," she firmly replied, "you love only God!" Nana enjoyed gardening and most days throughout the summer she could be found in her sizable garden on her knees, surrounded by her tulips and roses and pansies, a riot of beautiful colors. She was a bright and interesting person, and had a dear sister named Lucy who lived with her, who was much quieter, and who never married.

My grandfather, who died in 1928, was active in Republican politics, and succeeded his own father as town treasurer. Fred Smith was chairman of the Republican Town Committee from 1888 to 1902, and was elected to a two-year term in the Massachusetts Legislature in 1900.

When my father was a boy, South Hadley Falls was a bustling farming community and a rather typical New England small town. Mount Holyoke College was nearby, and across the river was Holyoke, which was a manufacturing center and the site of my grandfather's factory. Dad liked to skate and play hockey with his two younger brothers, Lincoln, who was born in 1895, and Fred, who was born in 1899. Fred went on to become Head of Orthopedics at Columbia Presbyterian in New York City and was someone I knew well when growing up in New York City. Lincoln stayed in nearby Holyoke, and was a tinkerer and ne'er-do-well who often returned to his parents' home to live for long periods. Linc loved archery, and I remember practicing archery in his backyard with his handmade arrows.

My father was imbued with an entrepreneurial bent very early in his life. "On the day I was born," he recalled, "my grandmother gave me one share of common stock in the Boston & Albany Railroad. If she had in mind instilling in me a proud sense of participating in American enterprise and its rewards in stock dividends, the gift failed of the mark. As a boy I was impressed only with the fact that as a stockholder I got a free trip to Boston each year, purportedly to attend the stockholders' meeting. Somehow I never managed to get around to any of the meetings, nor did it dawn on me that as one of the owners of the railroad I had some small part in giving myself the free ride."

After going to grammar school locally, my father attended Phillips Academy in Andover, graduating in 1912. He went on to Amherst College, his father's alma mater, where he was an average student, played football and hockey, and was manager of the baseball team. Everyone called him "Hi." One of my father's classmates was John J. McCloy, who became a dear friend. He was a lawyer and banker who served as Assistant Secretary of War during World War II, president of the World Bank, U.S. High Commissioner for Germany, and chairman of the Chase Manhattan bank. He would become a prominent presidential adviser, serve on the Warren Commission, and would become a member of the foreign policy establishment group of elders called "the Wise Men." Another of Dad's Amherst classmates and great friends was Seeley Bixley, who became the president of Colby College in Maine. Later, my father, John McCloy, and Seeley Bixley would be appointed trustees of Amherst. Coincidentally, years later when I began skiing at Sugarbush in Vermont (the resort I later purchased), I discovered that John McCloy's son was a longtime Sugarbush skier as well. He and his wife, Laura, have since become good friends of my wife Lili's and mine.

Although he was educated in a classic liberal arts curriculum and didn't take a single course in business or economics, Dad had a vague notion that he might like the securities field. Armed with a Bachelor of Arts degree in English literature and history, he went to Boston in June 1916 and applied for a job with an investment house. "But they treated me so coolly—didn't seem to care whether I came to work for them or not—that I felt just as cool toward them," he said. "I got on a train and headed for New York."

There, like so many future Wall Street executives of his generation, Dad began his career as a runner. His first employer was Bonbright & Co., and he was happy with his new job until his first payday. "They'd promised me a living wage, but hadn't said just what that would be. When I opened my paycheck that first week, I nearly fell over. It was for seven dollars." Two weeks later he happened upon an Amherst classmate, Brooks Johnson, who was working for a new firm, Merrill, Lynch & Co., and was making $10 a week, even though it was just a summer job. My father immediately walked a few blocks to the ML office at 7 Wall Street and was hired at $10 a week. Then, as he remembered it, "I went back that afternoon and told Mr. Wilcox at Bonbright that I wanted to resign. He said, 'Why?' I told him I could get a raise in salary at Merrill, Lynch. I never saw a man so disgusted in all my life. Mr. Wilcox did not think too much of the chances for the young, upstart firm of Merrill, Lynch. Bonbright & Co., on the other hand, was an old, established firm."

My father reported for work on September 1, 1916, and after just three weeks he was promoted to clerk in the cashier's department, ending his career on the runner's bench. "Early in November while working at some lowly job, I noticed someone standing behind me watching what I was doing. He finally asked, 'Are you Win Smith?' I replied, 'Yes,' looked around, and saw a pleasant, short, young man. He said, 'I'm Charlie Merrill.' I bounded to my feet and said, 'Yes, sir!' and shook hands with him. After a short conversation, he asked me if I would like to go see the Amherst–Williams game the next weekend. Naturally, I accepted, and on Friday afternoon we departed for Amherst." Thus began a personal friendship and business alliance that would last forty years and become one of the most successful examples of co-leadership in American business history. "My early relationship with him was a combination of boss and father," my father recalled. "Later it developed into an older brother relationship and then as a partner and a close friend." The Amherst connection would be of continuing importance in the history of Merrill Lynch as a number of its graduates joined the firm and played significant roles in its development.

From his job as clerk, Dad worked his way up to the position of statistician before entering the Army as an artillery officer. Immediately after graduation from Amherst, he'd spent three weeks at an Army training camp in Plattsburgh, New York. America's entry into World War I seemed imminent at the time, and by doing this, he was insuring himself of a place in the officers' school there. On April 6, 1917, the United States declared war on Germany, and a few days later my father reported to Plattsburgh again, trained there, and became a second lieutenant in the 4th Mountain Artillery. His Army service took him to Syracuse, New York, and posts in Mississippi, Texas, and South Carolina. Much to his regret, he was not sent overseas. However, his brother Lincoln served in the Army artillery in France.

Meanwhile, Charlie Merrill had been frustrated in his own attempts to get into the military, and Dad recalled CEM's reaction when he informed him of his military assignment: "Upon receipt of my orders, I asked permission to see Mr. Merrill, was ushered into his office, and told him that I wanted to resign to go to Plattsburgh. I remember vividly that instead of answering me, he put his head down on his desk and remained in that position for some two minutes, then looked up and said, 'Congratulations. How did you do it?'"

Shortly after the war broke out, Merrill and Lynch decided that in the interest of preserving the business through wartime, one of them should go into uniform, while the other should stay behind to mind the store. And, they reasoned further, since Merrill was a husband and father, bachelor Lynch should be the one to go. But Lynch failed the Army physical because of poor vision, and so Merrill applied for the officer training camp at Fort Myer, Virginia, and was promptly accepted. Ever eager to cut a handsome figure, CEM went to his tailor, Van Sickle, and put in a rush order for a complete set of uniforms—khakis, woolens, fatigues, an overcoat, and a dashing British officer's trench coat. Then he made the rounds of his friends and associates, bidding them all a soldier's farewell. But a backlog of officer candidates delayed his induction, and CEM fumed, embarrassed, at 7 Wall Street.

In an initial effort to break the stalemate, Merrill convinced an Army clerk to alter his application to include his ersatz military training as an adolescent at Stetson. Then he made a personal trip to Washington to promote his application with the War Department brass, who were impressed with his persistence. Finally, late that summer, thirty-one-year-old Charlie Merrill left civilian life. For his marriage, this unnecessary separation was another nail in the coffin. Eliza was so angry she didn't even kiss him good-bye. In its wisdom, the Army concluded that CEM's experience as a fraternity steward at Michigan Law School made him a perfect candidate for cooks and bakers school at Camp Lee in Petersburg, Virginia, where he seemed destined to become the Army's only millionaire mess steward. Merrill, chafing to get "over there" to fight, looked around for alternatives. Training films of the infantry in action persuaded him that trench warfare was not for him, and so he sought a transfer to a more glamorous branch—the Army Air Corps, which was the predecessor of the modern Air Force.

He was accepted, and in February 1918, "Pops" Merrill (as he was called by his younger comrades) began flight training at Kelly Field near San Antonio, Texas. It was dangerous, exhilarating duty. Merrill flew in Curtiss JN-4's—the notorious "Jenny"—little more than fabric stretched over a wooden skeleton. The planes looked like unwieldy mother hens, and it was a daily struggle to keep them aloft and out of spins. He communicated with his instructor through tin cans linked to a garden hose. But Merrill took to it with relish and he considered these days to be among the happiest in his life. A fellow trainee remembered him years later: "The cadet students were in their late teens or very early twenties, which made the student officers approaching thirty or more seem almost senile. Youthful reflexes and recklessness were what was needed in those days to be a good flier. Charlie was a natural-born flier. He had the moral and physical courage that enabled him to overcome the natural fear of flying and was as quick in his reflexes as men ten years his junior. He took flying seriously and was determined to excel." That he did, and in the summer of 1918 he was sent to Carlstrom Field, Florida, to be trained on pursuit planes called Gnomes, which Army specifications called "armored planes" but in fact were built of stiff canvas that was designed to look like armor plate. The Gnomes' engines often quit in mid-flight and pilots had to make emergency landings in the sandy bushes around the base. When he completed his training, CEM was informed that rather than going to Europe, he was going to remain stateside to train other pilots. Perhaps the highlight of his flying career was when he landed to a hero's welcome at Palm Beach and emerged from the cockpit in goggles, helmet, and spit-shined boots to greet the adoring crowd, which included his mother and father. It was a poignant moment, and he especially relished the look of pride and relief on his father's face.

While Merrill was engaged in his flying career, Lynch managed business on Wall Street—to the point where things appeared secure enough that he renewed his attempts to get into the Army himself. He finally succeeded by memorizing the eye examination wall chart and pulling strings in Washington.

On October 23, 1918, Edmund Calvert Lynch reported for duty as a private in the cavalry at Camp Leon Spring, Texas. *The Wall Street Journal* carried an announcement from Merrill, Lynch & Co:

> We desire to announce that because of entering the Military Service of the Government, CHARLES E. MERRILL and EDMUND C. LYNCH have withdrawn from the firm of MERRILL, LYNCH & COMPANY as general

partners and have become special partners therein; and
that the business will be continued under the firm name
of MERRILL, LYNCH & COMPANY by the undersigned as
general partners. Paul Bayne, Harold S. Matzinger, Herbert
D. Williams, Bernhard Benson.

Twenty-three days later the war ended. Though the Army did not
give Charlie Merrill the combat experience he wanted, it did provide
him with long-lasting lessons in leadership training and management
that would help him as a businessman. It is impossible to quantify
these values, but later he wrote about "a bit of knowledge that I
acquired in the Army":

> I had plenty of chances to learn it in business, but I didn't
> learn the lesson until I had charge of men. The prime quality
> that men like in a leader is sincerity. Chaps never did like
> company commanders that attempted to curry favor; they
> wanted fair, considerate and just treatment; commanders
> that babied the men one day, and ignored them the next,
> were cordially hated. It is not necessary—and, probably,
> not advisable—to set any great store on personal popular-
> ity. The thing a leader most desires in his men is respect;
> respect cannot be won by any other method than know-
> ing the job better than the men know it, and being quick
> to praise work well done, and slow to censure. Whatever
> censuring is necessary must be done in private, and not
> within earshot of the other men in the company; and what
> is equally important, you can't censure a fellow for mistake
> after mistake unless you are also willing and anxious to
> praise him for the things he does right. And last—but not
> least—most men, and all soldiers, at any rate, cordially hate
> a commander that has pets in the company, and, for that
> matter, hate and despise the pets, too.

Immediately after President Wilson's declaration of war, the U.S.
Treasury had launched a massive, unprecedented borrowing spree
to provide the huge sums of money needed to conduct a war. Over
the next two years, the total loans would come to a staggering $37

billion (about $500 billion today). To help pay off the loans, American citizens were asked to buy bonds, which came to be called Liberty Bonds. Slogans popped up across America to prime the patriotic pump: "LIBERTY BONDS OR GERMAN BONDAGE" . . . . "COME ACROSS OR THE KAISER WILL" . . . . "A BOND SLACKER IS A KAISER BACKER". . . . "LEND A HAND TO UNCLE SAM OR BEND A KNEE TO THE KAISER." Many Americans responded earnestly— and learned for the first time that their money could be used to make more money. Merrill, Lynch and Co. was one of the first firms on Wall Street—and perhaps the very first—to help Uncle Sam sell his bonds without commission. Charlie Merrill foresaw that the purchase of Liberty Bonds would kindle in many average Americans a habit of investing and an interest in other forms of securities that would last long after the end of hostilities. "Just consider the 3,000,000 who bought the last issue of Liberty bonds," CEM wrote in 1917. "It shows we must devote more and more of our time to the small investor. That is going to come to this country. It has been a long time coming, but I venture to predict that we will sell government bonds before the war is over to 8,000,000 to 20,000,000 people. People who start buying bonds from motives of patriotism will continue to do so because they are the most convenient form of safe investment." History would later agree with this on-the-spot assessment, and the World War I Liberty Bond drives are credited with bringing the American public into the stock market.

The company sent out 100,000 letters to investors urging them to support the government's campaign and ran newspaper ads announcing, "We are placing the facilities of our firm unreservedly at the disposal of both the Government and the Public and will handle subscriptions for the impending loan without profit or commission of any kind whatsoever." The ads got the company chastised by the NYSE establishment, which complained through its Committee on Business Conduct that Merrill, Lynch & Co. had failed to get its Liberty Bond advertising approved by the Exchange. Merrill apologized, but he and his successors would have many more clashes with the NYSE's rules and regulations through much of the twentieth century.

When the warriors returned to Wall Street, Merrill, Lynch & Co. was a success by any measure. The company had opened offices in Detroit and Chicago and it was a member of the New York Stock Exchange. On April 29, 1916, a Dow Jones news ticker had been installed in the firm's ground-floor offices at 7 Wall Street. The Dow opened that day at 117.16 and closed at 115.77. Merrill and Lynch were known as the "boy millionaires," at least in New York. They were wealthy men—though the federal income tax had just been enacted and they both fell into the top bracket of 15 percent. Some insight into just how wealthy they were can be gleaned from an incident in 1917 when CEM went out to Detroit to close a deal with A. H. Demory, president of the Timken-Detroit Axle Co., and there was a last-minute disagreement involving $75,000 ($1.2 million in current dollars), Merrill proposed breaking the impasse by flipping a coin. He called tails and won.

The closest that Merrill, Lynch ever came to going on strike was when the two principal partners were preparing to return to civilian life. They found that most of the sales force had quit because of slow business and the remaining clerical workers were putting forth a list of demands and organizing a work stoppage. Still in his Army uniform, Merrill appeared in the "cage"—slang for the operations center—and, as one witness recalled, said: "In case you don't realize it, a lot of guys will be back from the war looking for jobs in the next month. This firm will not be bullied. If you have any legitimate grievances, they will be arbitrated in proper, orderly fashion. If that doesn't suit you, clear out now. If you want to continue working here, get back to your desks and give me a chance to consider your requests."

Apparently, most of the clerks stayed on.

Shortly after the armistice in 1918, Dad returned to Wall Street and received a quick promotion. "I was made a bond sales-man, although I didn't get the title for a while. Actually, I was a mediocre salesman for a couple of years, until I began picking up the technique. It took four or five years and plenty of doorbell push-ing before I really caught on." Those were discouraging times for him. There had been an uptick of business activity in 1920 that was followed by the short but severe depression of 1921. There were days on end when he received only "no's" to his sales pitches. "One thing I learned then," he said, "was to try to work harder than anybody else. I started working early in the morning, and didn't finish until late at night. Even so, often it didn't seem like my efforts would pay off. Fortunately, there were a few boosts along the way. One man—a little guy named Mayer—did a lot for me. I'd been to see him a couple of times, and one day he gave me a large order. He said, 'You're just the man to handle my business—serious and honest.' That really set me up and made me feel that I hadn't been wasting my time. There was another prospect I would call on faithfully every month. Or, should I say, I called on his secretary, who inevitably reported that he was out or in a meeting or in a conference—or any place where I couldn't see him. One day I started to make the monthly call and then stopped. I was feeling very discouraged, and one more 'no' from this guy—sight unseen—would have been too much. Then I thought, *Just once more.* I went, and he saw me right away, gave me an order for fifty bonds. Those were the boosts that kept me going."

It was during these early days on Wall Street that Dad had a random brush with history—and danger. On September 16, 1922, he was walking down Wall Street to meet a friend for lunch when an anarchist's bomb went off in front of the offices of J. P. Morgan & Co. Dad was a block away and thanks to a last-minute phone call he made escaped injury, but thirty people died in the blast. This was the infamous "Wall Street Explosion," set off by a bomb in a horse-drawn cart.

In his history of the 1920s, *Only Yesterday*, Frederick Lewis Allen wrote: "That the Big Red Scare was already perceptibly abating by the end of the summer of 1920 was shown by the fact that the nation managed to keep its head surprisingly well when a real disaster, probably attributable to an anarchist gang, took place on the 16th of September." Allen described the scene: ". . . . just as the clerks of the neighborhood were getting ready to go out for luncheon, there was a sudden blinding flash of bluish-white light and a terrific crashing roar, followed by the clatter of falling glass from innumerable windows and by the screams of men and women." The bomb had gone off with such force that "it killed thirty people outright and injured hundreds, wrecked the interior of the Morgan offices, smashed windows for blocks around, and drove an iron slug through the window of the Bankers' Club on the thirty-fourth floor of the Equitable Building."

Allen also noted that "the victims of the explosion were not the financial powers of the country, but bank clerks, brokers' men, Wall

Street runners, stenographers." In the confusion Dad never found his friend, who, he learned later, was one of those killed in the blast. My mother later told me that Dad calculated that had it not been for the phone call, he would have been exactly at the spot of the explosion.

Dad's brush with fate notwithstanding, he continued to work hard selling bonds, and his efforts paid off in 1923 when he was sent to ML's uptown office at Madison Avenue and Forty-third Street as head of the Bond Department. A year or two later, he returned downtown as assistant sales manager of the main office. It was then that the rising young executive became close friends with the man whose future was to be so closely bound with his own: Charlie Merrill.

From his earliest days at Merrill Lynch, my father was aware that there were frequent battles between the two principal partners—a pattern that would persist for nearly a quarter of a century. Other managers as well remembered the two locked in sulfurous glares, faced off like the *Monitor* and the *Merrimac*, Lynch's forehead knotted in fury, Merrill's blue eyes turned into ice fields. The debates were bare-knuckled, and both were capable of extended, loud, and imaginative invective. At the root of these disagreements were fundamentally different approaches to life. Merrill was the visionary, Lynch the realist—but only Merrill recognized that a business needed both.

Because they were partners, though, there was a fundamental understanding between them that they both had to agree on any major action before it could be implemented. Usually it was a case of Merrill trying to convince Lynch of the need to take action. Lilian Burton recalled frequent instances of Lynch listening carefully to Merrill's entreaties over an entire day without uttering a word in reply. Then, often late in the evening, Lynch would simply say no, put on his hat, and go home. Merrill's daughter, Doris, vividly remembered her father engaged in loud arguments with Lynch over the telephone when she was growing up. "The language they used on each other was terrible," she said. Behind many of these clashes was Lynch's instinct to be a bully and Merrill's determination not to be bullied.

My father viewed Lynch as a critical brake on Merrill's impetuousness, and he told associates after CEM's death in 1956 that for every ten ideas that Merrill came up with, two were good ones. Michael McCarthy, who would head the firm after my father, called CEM "a dreamer," adding: "That's why he made. . . .such a good partner for Lynch. Lynch was a cold-blooded guy. And Charlie would have these ideas, and Lynch would take a look at the cold figures, and he said, 'Charlie, you can't do that, now. You can't, for this reason and that reason, and so forth.' And he'd put it on ice." At such times, Merrill found Lynch exasperating. Through it all, though, Octavia Wilson Merrill maintained a high regard for Lynch's abilities, and she would chide her son after the two men had a quarrel, saying, "You and Eddie make a good team. Never forget it."

Though Merrill could never fully explain the complicated chemistry between himself and his partner, he considered Lynch to be his best friend—an opinion that was not reciprocated. He asked Lynch to be best man at his second wedding in 1925—even though when Lynch was married for the first and only time a year earlier, Charlie had only been a spectator. Part of the friction between them resulted from Merrill's assumption that he, as the founder of the firm, was the senior partner (even though the two now shared profits equally).

There were fractious times when Lynch didn't measure up to Merrill's standards of business ethics. In April of 1929, for example, CEM wrote a strident letter to his partner chastising him for creating a conflict of interest for the firm by interfering in delicate negotiations with a grocery chain contrary to his express oral and written instructions. "You can imagine my chagrin and disgust to find that we had negotiated directly with the Joseloffs, for our own account, without being properly released by the First National Crowd," he told his partner.

Just as Charlie Merrill said it would, the Liberty Bond experience altered Americans' thinking on how they should handle their money. As the bonds matured and the holders saw how they had made money on their own money, expansion-minded capitalists found a waiting trove of new capital. Between them stood the investment bankers, eager to bring them together. There were profits to be made all around. The timing was fortuitous. Britain was staggering under the monetary burden of more than four years of war, and New

York had replaced London as the world's financial capital. All roads led to Wall Street.

Reliable statistics on stock ownership during this period are elusive, but it can be said with some certainty that before the war, between 500,000 and 2 million Americans owned stocks and bonds, and by 1929 the number of investors had reached between 5 million and 10 million. Million-share days on the New York Stock Exchange, once the reaction to a panic, became routine in the twenties.

After a postwar recession, the American economy picked up in 1922 and prosperity reigned for seven years, giving the entire decade of the twenties an almost permanent adjective: "roaring." The federal income tax enacted in 1913 did not, as many warned it would, deter consumer spending. The demand for goods, particularly cars, radios, and telephones, was strong, and eventually all three moved from being luxuries to necessities. In the case of cars, this made buying them on borrowed money acceptable. Credit, once the almost exclusive privilege of the wealthy, became democratized. Naturally, the idea spilled over into the stock market, and buying on margin became common for new accounts.

Although Merrill, Lynch & Co. set up several modest programs to educate the public about investing, they were nothing compared to what was to come in the 1940s and 1950s. Several other brokers did at least as much, or more, to encourage the small investor. At the same time ML grew its routine brokerage business, the firm continued its march off the beaten path as an underwriter for chain-store retailers. Between 1919 and 1929, it handled some seventy-five stock issues, about half of which were on behalf of chain stores. In nearly all these deals, Merrill and Lynch kept large blocks of the stock for themselves. Two of the underwritings were especially gratifying—Patchogue-Plymouth Mills (Merrill's would-be father-in-law's company) and Liquid Carbonic—the principal partners' first employers in New York.

Throughout the decade, Merrill, Lynch & Co. was easily Wall Street's most prolific advertiser, thereby offending much of the financial establishment, which believed advertising to be beneath its dignity, and solidifying its reputation as an outsider and a maverick. Merrill's near-obsession with truth in advertising was undiminished. Indeed, the firm stood out from the Wall Street pack by publishing detailed offering circulars on its underwritings, long before the days of SEC registrations and "full disclosure." If a security was intended as a long-term investment, the firm made that recommendation. If the venture held risks, those risks were spelled out. "Retail customers who bought and held the securities sponsored by the partners had every reason to be thankful for the dividends and capital gains over the long term," says Edwin J. Perkins in his Merrill biography, *Wall Street to Main Street*.

But not all Americans were so lucky. Millions of first-time investors got caught up in the investing binge, and for a while at least buying a stock was like betting on a horse race in which most of the horses had winning records. Between 1920 and 1928, the prices on the NYSE roughly doubled and about $50 billion in new securities were sold. By 1930 about half of them would be nearly or totally worthless.

L ess than a year after their return to civilian life, the partners fashioned a deal to underwrite $3 million in preferred stock for J. C. Penney Co., which operated several hundred department stores. James Cash Penney, the son of an unsalaried Baptist minister, had opened his first dry-goods store, called Golden Rule, in the frontier mining town of Kemmerer, Wyoming, in 1902, and from the very beginning he had a vision of a chain operation. The original store was a one-room, twenty-five-by-forty-foot shop sandwiched between a laundry and a boardinghouse off the main street with makeshift counters and shelves put together from packing crates. Penney and his wife lived above in the attic and water had to be hauled in from a nearby Chinese restaurant. The operation competed with stores owned by the mining companies, which offered easy and expensive credit, but Penney insisted that his customers, nearly all of them miners, pay cash. The company stores sat back and waited for him to fail. But the cash-only policy enabled Penney to keep prices low; moreover, as a convenience to his hardworking customers, he kept the store open from early morning to night, even on Sundays. He rang up sales of nearly $29,000 in his first year, and by 1910 he had twenty stores throughout the Western states. The company moved its corporate headquarters to New York during the war to prepare for national expansion, and it wasn't long before J. C. Penney Co.

and Merrill, Lynch & Co. found each other. Within four years of the initial financing, Penney opened its five-hundredth outlet by buying up a store where the founder himself had worked as a boy in his hometown of Hamilton, Missouri. By midcentury there would be some 1,700 stores, and Americans would petition the company to locate in their neighborhood.

For Charlie Merrill, there was an unexpected bonus in his dealings with Penney. For one thing, Penney's application of the Golden Rule to his business dealings reinforced CEM's own conviction that honesty was good business. In addition, the cash-only policy did indeed keep prices low, and what was lost in profit margins was gained back through high volume. Penney's most innovative policy was to allow store managers to become part owners of their respective outlets, and thereby participate in the success or failure of their own management. In time, Merrill would apply these lessons to his own ventures—first in the grocery business, then in the brokerage business.

My only personal memory of J. C. Penney was when my mother prepared to attend his hundredth birthday celebration. She had spent months finding a penny dated each year of his life and then put them together in a book. I remember how excited she was to present it to Mr. Penney.

But J. C. Penney wasn't Merrill Lynch's only success story. Along with Kresge, another early postwar underwriting was for G. R. Kinney, a chain of about one hundred stores selling shoes to average Americans that would one day grow to some 2,700 Foot Locker outlets. In order to handle its vastly increased flow of business, Merrill, Lynch & Co. expanded rapidly. In 1919 the firm moved its headquarters from 7 Wall Street to the thirty-first floor of the Equitable Building at 120 Broadway, and extended its brokerage business nationwide by opening branch offices in Los Angeles in 1919, Denver in 1920, and Milwaukee in 1921. In 1924, as part of its efforts to cater to "Mr. Average Investor," the firm kept its uptown New York office open every weekday evening from seven P.M. to nine P.M.

By the 1920s, the company had about fifty employees at its main office and six branches. They included CEM's old Amherst classmates like Herbert H. Melcher and Sumner W. Cobb; relatives like Harold S. Matzinger, Charlie's sister's first husband, and Douglas Findlay, her second husband; two men who would one day step up to lead the modern Merrill Lynch—my father and James E. Thomson—and others who would stay with Merrill and become major figures themselves, like Kenneth W. Martin, John F. Wark, George B. Hyslop, William H. Dunkak, Robert L. Rooke, and Milija Rubezanin. Lilian Burton headed the secretarial staff and was joined by Esther King and Marguerite Francis.

ML's Statistical Department began modestly. "Pop" Melcher, who would eventually become a partner, said that during his first interview with Merrill he was asked what he knew about the stock and bond business. "Not a damn thing," he replied. Merrill responded, "Well, we'll put you to work in the Statistical Department and you can learn." The grand-sounding department, however, consisted of only one other man and, as Melcher recalled: "Learning consisted of reading *Moody's* and *Standard & Poor's* for three months. That was followed by about six weeks of doorbell ringing to sell government bonds and then selling other investments on a 'Go out and sell these anywhere you can' basis."

There was even room on the sales staff for a woman. In 1919— still a year before American women could vote—Ann B. (Annie) Grimes was looking for a sales job on Wall Street. She was rebuffed at the first two firms she approached, but at the latter the personnel manager told her that Merrill, Lynch & Co. had just moved into 120 Broadway and was expanding. She went there and was greeted by Charlie Merrill himself, who told her that the decision on hiring her was up to Sumner Cobb, his sales manager. After Cobb interviewed her, he rose, pointed to a nearby desk, and said, "See that vacant place? Hang up your hat and get to work." With that she joined an expanding sales staff and rang doorbells with her male colleagues, including my father, and later, when CEM launched *Family Circle* magazine, she would be in charge of selling ad space.

Grimes's hiring was an aberration in the company's long-standing poor record in gender equality. Indeed, despite his mother's influence, CEM once told his son, "An educated woman makes me nervous." In the 1970s it took a suit by the federal Equal Employment Opportunity Commission to awaken Merrill Lynch and others on Wall Street to the fact that women, African-Americans, and Hispanics deserved the same opportunities as white males. To the credit of future leaders like Don Regan and his successors, talented women eventually gained a major role in the company and were important parts of the future legacy that would have made Annie Grimes proud, but it took far too long.

An informal, loosely defined division of work emerged after the war: Merrill handled chain stores, Lynch handled everything else. The latter included a foray into the petroleum business, which was growing right along with the automobile industry. Between 1919 and 1922, Merrill, Lynch & Co. underwrote nine security issues for six different oil companies, worth a total of more than $14 million. Each produced a nice profit for the partners. The firm's principal failure of the 1920s was its sponsorship of a $1 million preferred stock issue for Waring Hat Manufacturing, which occurred in 1920 and was decided on the basis of what most analysts saw as a rosy postwar future. In 1923, ML bought 24,000 shares of common stock and gave Waring Hat large loans on unsecured commercial paper, but soon thereafter it became clear that the prognosticators had erred, and then Waring Hat went into receivership. Both the company and its brokerage customers who had bought the stock on the firm's recommendation were hit by steep losses. The partners tried to ease the pain by offering these clients the opportunity to buy into a grocery chain at the underwriter's price—a practice that's illegal today but was widely accepted in the twenties. However, one of the more disgruntled investors sued the firm, and the New York Stock Exchange got involved. Worse yet, the ML official who was scheduled to show the Waring Hat books to Winthrop Burr, chairman of the NYSE Committee on Business Practices, failed to keep the appointment. An infuriated Burr summoned Charlie Merrill to explain this disrespect. "The session lasted about an hour," CEM remembered, "and throughout it Burr gave me plain and fancy hell. Burr pounded his desk and said his committee would show us once and for all its power and authority." Merrill apologized, but he believed that Burr's animosity went directly back to 1917 when the firm had upset the NYSE powers by advertising Liberty Bonds without prior approval.

One of the most important transactions in company history involved another industrial newcomer to the American scene: motion pictures. Merrill and Lynch had gotten personally involved in the movie business in 1915 when they were appointed board directors of Pathe Exchange, Inc., the new American subsidiary of Pathe Freres Cinema, which had headquarters in Paris and had been making films since 1896. The Pathe interests had heard of Merrill and Lynch through a legal connection, and made the appointments apparently to help safeguard the company's interests in the U.S. during the war. For their efforts, whatever they were, the partners each were paid $50,000—an astronomical salary (about $809,000 in current dollars) that is difficult to explain given their total lack of experience in the industry. Edwin J. Perkins, Merrill's biographer, speculates that "profits were perhaps so high in the U.S. market, and French executives were so accustomed to throwing money around, that few thought the remuneration for the partners' service on the board was excessive."

Before the war, most films shown in American theaters were made in Europe; this was still the silent, pre-talkies age, and language presented no barrier. But the war disrupted filmmaking on the Continent, and the American industry took up the slack. After the war, friction developed between Pathe's Paris headquarters and its American offshoot, and Merrill and Lynch were persuaded to purchase the subsidiary. As with some other Merrill, Lynch & Co. investment areas, motion pictures were still considered only semi-respectable ventures. In fact, the onstage theatrical world had even taken to applying the adjective "legitimate" to distinguish its own offerings from the movies. But by 1921, the American cinema had gone from nickelodeon peepholes to big screens and was emerging as a sophisticated narrative form. Lavish movie houses were being built, directors were experimenting with lighting and camera angles, film genres were being defined, and the star system was taking hold. All of these elements would soon be summed up in a single word: Hollywood. The big players were Fox, Loew, and Pathe. Box-office profits were handsome, but they were insufficient to handle industry expansion alone, and studio magnates sought the easiest road to quick capital, Wall Street.

Although Pathe turned out mostly run-of-the-mill fare, it was a steady and reliable moneymaker. It was famous for its *Perils of Pauline* serials. Pathe's brightest star was Harold Lloyd, the comedian who nimbly scaled the sides of tall buildings and jumped from roof to roof. Occasionally, the studio crossed paths with great actors like Douglas Fairbanks and Mary Pickford, but its best and most durable product was its newsreel serial, Pathe News, which eventually would be shown in some 13,000 American theaters week after week.

Merrill had resigned from the Pathe board when he entered the Army, but Lynch had stayed on, and so it was determined that he would go to Paris to work out the purchase. In line with his lifelong policy of careful preparation, Lynch decided that he would master the French language and use it exclusively for the negotiations. Toward that end, he retained a French-speaking butler named Hamel, who stayed by his side at home and at the office in the weeks leading up to his departure. Doggedly, daily and nightly, Lynch attacked vocabulary, grammar, and accent. The result was predictable. "When Mr. Lynch left for Paris," says Lilian Burton, "he spoke French horribly but with no qualms." After realizing that his hosts' English was better than their guest's French, though, Lynch dropped his linguistic adventure and over the next three months hammered out a deal that gave him and Merrill control of the company. Soon after he returned to New York, however, Lynch discovered that the company's books grossly overstated its inventory. When the partners revealed the mismanagement and possible fraud to the banks that had loaned Pathe money for production, the banks agreed to extend the repayment period only if Merrill, Lynch & Co. took over operation of the company. Thus the partners found themselves running a company they had bought only as an investment in a field they knew nothing about.

Starting from scratch, Lynch learned the movie business inside and out, and over the next five years Pathe would take up nearly all of his time and energy. Still a bachelor at thirty-six, he moved out of 120 Broadway to the Pathe offices in Midtown Manhattan and began a grueling work schedule. He ate lunch at his desk every day and barked out orders between bites. John Humm, the Pathe treasurer who would one day become a Merrill Lynch partner, described Lynch's approach: "The Lynch follow-ups were terrific. He had a slip of paper for everything, had his pockets stuffed full of them. If some piece of business had been going on for some time, he would jump into the middle of it without having a clear idea of all the detail that had preceded. But as time went on, his regular periodic checks brought him completely up to date. He never forgot a thing. He learned every angle of Pathe thoroughly; there wasn't an angle he didn't know. I never saw such a hardworking man. . . . Obstacles meant nothing to him. Nothing that he wanted to do was impossible." It all paid off, and Lynch turned Pathe into a profit machine. It was around this time that J. P. Morgan is reputed to have said that Lynch had the best business judgment in New York City—and told of the comment, Lynch is reputed to have replied, "If Mr. Morgan had considered the matter better, he would have realized that there are many men in New York City of sound judgment, and that no comparison of this sort is truly valid. I suppose that all he meant was that I take the trouble to get the facts."

Despite its ultimate success, still there were struggles early on in Lynch's management of Pathe. The recession of 1921–22 cut in to earnings, and Merrill and Lynch thought so little of their new Pathe common shares that they used them as stakes in their bridge games. But then the economy perked up. Lynch's draconian management made Pathe a model of efficiency for the entire film industry and put it back on a profitable course. Pathe joined with the DuPont Company and manufactured film to challenge the near-monopoly of Eastman Kodak. Then the nature of the industry changed as Pathe's competitors began building and acquiring their own theaters; if Merrill and Lynch wanted to continue in the film business, they would have to follow suit. Ultimately, neither wanted to commit their capital to such a venture, so they sold their Pathe interest in 1926 to a syndicate that included Joseph P. Kennedy, a Wall Street banker and future head of the Securities and Exchange Commission. Kennedy, whose nine-year-old son would become President of the United States, had already gained a reputation as a canny, shrewd manipulator of Hollywood stocks.

The selling price was $2.9 million, nearly all of which was profit. In addition, the partners had earned millions from dividends on their Pathe stock and from the liquidation of its bonds and stock. It was Lynch's finest hour. Merrill said throughout the rest of his life that none of what he achieved could have been possible without Eddie Lynch. More than anything else, it was Lynch's handling of Pathe that Merrill had in mind.

"The Pathe interlude was important, too, because it gave Lynch the opportunity to make his business relationship with Charlie something more akin to a two-way street," says biographer Perkins. "Charlie had created the firm in 1914, and he had taken the initiative in arranging most of the transactions involving chain stores. But Lynch made Pathe his personal bailiwick, and the success of the venture helped to cement the strong ties between the two partners. Through the film company, Lynch had the chance to return the favor by contributing significantly to Charlie's wealth and power."

I n all likelihood, Merrill and Lynch would have done well for themselves had they stayed in the movie business. The Depression, which sent so many industries spinning into bankruptcy, barely touched Hollywood. Indeed, box-office business boomed with the advent of sound. There was a rush to make more movies, and the motion picture industry, once considered inefficient and risky as an investment, became a Wall Street darling. But CEM wanted to focus his attention elsewhere, and saw great potential in applying the chain-store concept to America's largest retail business: food. He envisioned a system of joint buying in groceries, produce, and meats; joint warehousing, distribution, and transportation; and joint manufacturing operations for products such as bread, coffee, soft drinks, condiments, and extracts. A nationwide chain would mean good working capital and unheard-of economies of scale. Food would be purchased in bulk at low prices, housed in state-of-the-art warehouses, and delivered by modern delivery vans as speedily as possible to the retail stores, themselves clean and modern and carefully managed.

In other words, what we now call the supermarket. Charlie Merrill didn't invent the supermarket, but he certainly was an influential figure in its development, and today he deserves part of the credit for the fact that Americans use a smaller share of their income for food than any other people on earth. In fact, many years later he told his son, "If ever I get to heaven it will be because I helped lower the price of milk by a penny a quart in Los Angeles. Saint Peter would forgive many things for [my] having done that."

And thus the partners used their considerable profits from the sale of their Pathe interests in 1926 to purchase Safeway Stores, Inc., a West Coast grocery chain with 322 outlets in fast-growing Southern California. Safeway was started in 1914 by Sam Seelig, who built up a debt to one of his wholesalers, W. R. H. Weldon, and paid him off by giving him enough stock for a controlling interest. Around 1925, Weldon decided to sell his ownership as a means of attracting new capital and new management, both of which the chain badly needed. Merrill saw his opportunity and moved quickly. The purchase price was $3.5 million, and when the deal was completed, he asked Weldon for the name of "the best grocery man in America" to run the company. Weldon told him it was M. B. Skaggs, the head of Skaggs United Stores in Portland, Oregon.

Like James Cash Penney, Marion Barton Skaggs was the son of a Baptist minister; his father also owned a small grocery in American Falls, Idaho. At the age of twenty-seven, Skaggs bought the 576-square-foot store from his father for $1,088 and put to the test his theory that the key to success in the grocery business was volume buying and low profit margins. His store had efficient shelving that kept goods within easy reach, and all sales were cash-and-carry. In a few years his brothers joined him and the number of outlets grew. The company attracted first-rate store managers and kept them, in part, by offering them a profit-sharing plan. By 1926, Skaggs had more than four hundred stores, and the problem facing Charlie Merrill was not whether he had found the right man, but how to persuade him to join the new Safeway operation. CEM, perhaps remembering his failure to lure Walter P. Chrysler into the Merrill, Lynch & Co. fold in 1916, was determined to get Skaggs. However, his first move was a mistake. In June 1926 he dispatched Lynch and another partner, Joseph Merrill (no relation to CEM), to Portland, unaware that Skaggs harbored a withering prejudice against Eastern bankers—of which Lynch and Merrill, in their bowler hats and waistcoats, were the quintessence. The two emissaries returned empty-handed, and a few weeks later Merrill headed West to talk to Skaggs himself in his best Southern accent.

They met for eight days and seven nights in a suite at the Benson Hotel in Portland. When it was over, they'd reached a simple agreement: Charlie would provide the financing, Skaggs would run the company from a new headquarters in Oakland, California—and Charlie would come to the West Coast anytime Skaggs felt it was necessary. The purchase price for the Skaggs stores was $1.5 million and 30,000 shares of Safeway stock. The two new business associates found they were kindred spirits, and they would be trusted, close allies throughout the coming difficult years. CEM saw in Skaggs the work ethic and the rock-ribbed integrity he valued above all else. For his part, Skaggs never forgot the meeting.

"I think it is proper and I would like to say that the day I met Charles E. Merrill was one of the very best days in my life, both from a personal and business standpoint," he recalled later. "During the years we worked together, the mutual respect and confidence established in those first eight days in the hotel room were never marred. With me, Charlie Merrill—in addition to being smart, quick, honest—always did more than he promised all through the years of our association.

"His father was a doctor; my father was a preacher. We were both raised in the country. We had a lot in common. We each had a lot of self-confidence, and we were both quite independent. Nevertheless, we got along. Merrill could present his propositions in words and terms I could understand, and no doubt he could understand me because the two of us, each with a lawyer to advise [us], came to an agreement."

In relinquishing managerial control of Safeway to Skaggs, Merrill made a sharp departure from previous ventures in which the partners assumed an active management role. But CEM knew that if he wanted Skaggs, he would have to make this exception. My father later cited this concession as a good example of Merrill's brilliance as a negotiator: "Charlie was a genius in laying down the basic terms of agreement in a delicate, intricate transaction. The sincerity and logic of his proposals convinced the other side of his candor from the outset, always the first essential in any business deal. He could be awfully tough on a pleasant level in jockeying for a position favorable to him, but he immediately compromised if he saw the other fellow had a valid argument. The crux of the Safeway deal was a tremendous concession he made. Had he been bullheaded, the whole thing would have fallen through or, worse yet, resulted in heavy losses in the long run."

Skaggs wasted no time in getting down to business. He took a Los Angeles store and reorganized it to operate the way he thought a grocery should be run. Managers came in from other stores for a demonstration and were ordered to duplicate it. Safeway sales climbed steadily. For the next three years, Merrill worked out deal after deal, adding existing chains into the Safeway operation. Between trains in Phoenix, Arizona, he deposited his new wife at a hotel and opened negotiations with the management of the twenty-four Pay'n Takit stores. He impressed them with his knowledge of the grocery business, and a few hours later he put the sales contract into his pocket, met his wife at the station, and caught the next train out of town. In like manner, Safeway absorbed the twenty-four New Way Stores in the El Paso, Texas, area; the 429 stores of the Sanitary Grocery Company in Washington, D.C.; the 67 outlets of Eastern Stores, Incorporated, in Baltimore and vicinity; the 82-store Piggly Wiggly chain in California and Hawaii; the 224 Bird Grocery outlets in the Kansas City area, and on and on.

From 670 stores in 1926, Safeway grew to 2,660 outlets by the end of 1929. While desperately safeguarding Safeway during the Depression, CEM wrote to Lynch, "Safeway means more to me than money. I have poured my life into it." By the time Merrill had ceased active management of Safeway in the 1950s, the chain operated 2,000-plus stores across the country, with annual sales of more than $2 billion. And, even more significantly, it had been instrumental in the formation of Charlie Merrill's second great vision, which he would call Merrill Lynch, Pierce, Fenner & Smith.

By the late twenties, Safeway was the crown jewel in an empire of chain-store financings fashioned by CEM. It included other food retailers like National Tea, First National, Winn Dixie, and Jones Brothers Tea, as well as up-and-coming retailers like Western Auto, Peoples Drugs, Lerner Stores, J. J. Newberry, City Radio Stores, Sally Frocks, Oppenheim Collins, and Daniel Reeves. These underwritings brought Merrill into contact with people like Frank Melville, who wanted to sell a four-dollar shoe through outlets he would call Thom McAn, and Lena Bryant, a Lithuanian immigrant who created a special dress for pregnant women and was so flustered by her success that she opened her first bank account in the name of Lane Bryant. Fueled by Merrill financing, Kresge grew from 184 to 678 stores during the decade; J. C. Penney from 312 to 1,452; Melville from 19 to 480; Kinney Shoes from 366 to 756; Peoples Drug from 8 to 117, and Walgreen from 23 to 440. Most of these Merrill-financed companies survive today either under their original names or within new ones like Foot Locker, CVS, Grand Union, and K-Mart. Six years after Merrill died in 1956, Sam Walton opened his first Wal-Mart in Rogers, Arkansas, and with low prices and customer service made it into one of the most successful companies in the world. Charlie Merrill, son of a mom-and-pop retailer, had a role in all of it.

The investing public, prospering as never before, eagerly provided the capital, and Merrill, Lynch & Co. seemed invincible. The firm developed an excellent reputation and seldom offered an investment that was not sold out immediately. This led to a company policy whereby 10 percent of each issue was reserved for the salesmen for their individual clients. Still there was never enough to go around, and finally it was agreed that individual underwritings would go to the salesmen in turns, allowing at least one salesman, on any given issue, the chance to satisfy his customers fully.

As business grew, so did the number of offices, and by 1927, Merrill, Lynch & Co. maintained its main New York office at 120 Broadway; an uptown office at 11 East Forty-third Street; branch offices in Chicago, Detroit, Denver, and Los Angeles; representative offices in Cleveland, Cincinnati, Milwaukee, Minneapolis, and St. Louis; and correspondents in Youngstown, Ohio, and San Francisco. The firm was now a member of the New York, Chicago, Cleveland, and Detroit stock exchanges, as well as the New York Curb Exchange, which would become the American Stock Exchange in 1953. Merrill, Lynch & Co. underwrote sixteen chain-store companies for a total volume of $590 million in 1926 alone, and this gave it a market share in chain-store underwriting of more than 50 percent for that year. In addition to its Underwriting and Commercial Paper departments, which employed seventy-five sales representatives, the firm maintained an independent Research Department and a Publicity Department, which handled all advertising as well as supplied articles for newspaper publication. It was hard work, and Merrill complained to his mother in a letter, "I am so tired, even though I've been successful." Octavia Merrill replied, "Just be glad your tiredness comes with victories and you haven't known the tiredness of constant defeats."

During the 1920s, the firm founded by Charles Fenner and Alpheus Beane made bold steps that doubtlessly were observed by Charles Merrill and played a role in his decision to merge with the firm in 1941. Fenner & Beane was a leader in securities research, and in the twenties it began publishing *Fortnightly Comment*, a newsletter analyzing the securities and commodities markets that was widely followed in the financial world. Later it began its *Security and Industry Survey*, which would became a staple among the early customers of MLPF&B.

In 1928, Fenner & Beane began distributing to the public an annual statement of its financial condition. Though the practice was discontinued after three years, and the statements contained limited information, it did anticipate CEM's own decision in 1940 to begin publishing an annual report. When a market glut threatened to ruin many planters in 1926, Fenner & Beane launched a newspaper advertising campaign using the slogan "Disaster Threatens the South" and advocated low-interest bank loans that prevented disaster. The firm issued a basic financial statement in 1928 and gave it to all customers. It developed an internal training program and a professional research staff. And when the NYSE liberalized its advertising rules in 1938, it became the first firm to make use of them with a campaign to educate the public about stocks and commodities.

E ven as Merrill built his reputation and fortune, his marriage crumbled. The decline began soon after the birth of his son Charles in 1920. Eliza had had a particularly difficult pregnancy, spending the final trimester in bed with her feet elevated. After nearly a decade in Montclair, Merrill chafed at life in suburban New Jersey, and in order to escape its conventionality and be closer to his growing ranks of friends and business associates, he moved his family to Manhattan. Eliza resisted the move, but CEM was insistent. Immediately the pace of his social life quickened. The new Merrill residence at 471 Park Avenue became the scene of festive dinner parties several evenings during the workweek, and on weekends the family moved to an oceanfront retreat on the eastern end of Long Island for drinking, dining, and conviviality. In both places, the Merrill hospitality was reciprocated. Eliza, with two young children and a shy disposition, was acutely uncomfortable and the couple quarreled often. As Doris grew older, Eliza's Catholicism became an unavoidable issue. CEM was furious when he returned home from a business trip to learn that Doris, without his knowledge or consent, had had her First Communion. By this time, anger had become a household fixture. Merrill, ever the patient negotiator at the office, was intolerant and short-tempered at home. He engaged in several extramarital affairs. Merrill moved out of the house and into the Hotel Marguery in the summer 1924, and about this time he became involved with Hellen Ingram, the editor and publisher of *Silhouette*, a Jacksonville-based magazine for Florida socialites and a kind of local version of the nationally popular *Vanity Fair*. She was fourteen years younger than CEM, and possessed many qualities he found lacking in Eliza—sociability, liveliness, artistic energy. They had met in 1923 in Jacksonville, and the following year Hellen came north to attend journalism classes at Columbia University. Her arrival coincided with Merrill's marital separation.

At this time, the only grounds for divorce in New York State were adultery and extreme cruelty, and though Merrill clearly qualified on the former count, Eliza and the two children moved to Jacksonville to establish residency and pave the way for a less embarrassing legal proceeding under Florida law. The divorce was handled for both sides by Sam Marks, who had been CEM's roommate at Stetson. When the legalities dragged on, Merrill pressed Marks to speed things up because by this time he was deeply in love with Hellen and eager to marry her. On February 12, 1925, after nearly thirteen years of marriage, the decree was granted in Jacksonville. Five days later, also in Jacksonville, Charlie and Hellen were married in a big wedding and reception at the bride's home. Thirteen years and four days later they would be back in the same court seeking a divorce. Meanwhile, Eliza, along with Doris and Charles Jr., returned to New York, where she lived out her life in quiet solitude, barred from remarrying by her religion. Though there were occasionally disagreements over expenditures and child care, Merrill took care of his children and former wife financially—though he was not always there emotionally. "Although my mother and father were divorced and my father remarried, he remained on friendly terms with my mother," Doris wrote years later. "He had only words of praise about her to my brother and me."

Merrill began his second marriage by buying a house in Greenwich Village not far from where he and Eliza had started his first. He spent some $50,000 on remodeling, and he gave the project his personal attention, monitoring many of the details about floors, tiles, and furnishings, complaining to contractors about their bills and even deducting $55 from one invoice because it charged for a damaged table. Not long after he moved to the Village home, CEM proceeded to buy a white-shingled, tall-columned antebellum mansion in Southampton, a seaside playground for the wealthy on eastern Long Island. Charlie and Hellen had been driving around the town looking for a place, and he was dazzled by the property, which was called "the Orchard" because it had a grove of apple trees. It had been designed around the turn of the century by Stanford White and Charles McKim for James L. Breese, a New York financier, and originally had about thirty-five rooms, but through a series of additions it had grown to fifty-four rooms. With the usual impatience that always came to bear after he'd reached a decision, Charlie signed the papers closing the deal between acts at a Broadway theater.

With twenty-two bedrooms, the Orchard presented the Merrills with the possibility of Gatsby-like guest lists every weekend. Celebrities like Hoagy Carmichael, Helen Hayes, and Gloria Swanson stayed at the Orchard, and Hellen remembered sitting in the music room one night while George Gershwin and Gertrude Lawrence worked on a tune for a Broadway show. Robin Magowan, Merrill's grandson, recalled his childhood days at the Orchard: "To my begoggled eyes it had just about everything: an old-fashioned icehouse; extensive chicken and turkey coops; a pair of cows whose main function, it seemed, was to keep our two families supplied in homemade ice cream; four pigs; a great kennel of yelping flame-colored setters, the progeny of Mike, whose full-length portrait adorned the entrance hall. From behind the house, classic columns led the eye into a three-sectioned Italian garden, flanked with wisteria-hung pergolas and ornamented with Roman goddesses and copper fountains bubbling from within a labyrinth of formal boxwood. Until I came upon the Alhambra in my twenties, I had never seen a garden more paradisiacal." It is not clear how much Merrill paid for the Orchard, but he would put the home to good use for the rest of his life, and would use it as his base of operations to direct the new Merrill Lynch between 1944 and 1956.

Meanwhile, Lynch expanded his own personal life. In 1923 he gave up his rented quarters at a private Manhattan club and bought a spacious co-op apartment at 570 Park Avenue. That same year he was a weekend guest at a beach house in Westhampton on eastern Long Island and decided he needed a weekend retreat. In a single afternoon, he bought a twenty-two-bedroom mansion that he called "Lyndune" because it was his and it was near sand dunes. Merrill soon sent him a letter addressed to "Edmund, Duke of Lyndune." With his housing established, Lynch turned to finding a wife with the same care and precision he exercised in his business decisions. Several prospects were rejected, and then Lynch himself was rejected, but the disinclined woman introduced him to a friend—Signa Fornaris, an attractive, exotic New Orleans woman whose father was Spanish and her mother French.

Signa was in New York on her way to Paris when she met Eddie Lynch. The next day, as she embarked on her transatlantic journey, a huge basket of fruit was waiting for her at the pier with a note from Lynch. She was abroad for about six months, and during this time Lynch carefully considered this latest candidate. He was at Merrill's house when she returned to New Orleans, and he tried to telephone her. Eliza, who was nearby, recalled: "He got awfully mad at the operator because she couldn't locate a girl named Signa in New Orleans. He was at the telephone for an hour, hollering, 'But I tell you, I don't know her last name! Why can't you find her by her first name? It's unusual enough.' He even described her to the operator. By some miracle he finally reached her, learned her address, and decided to stop in New Orleans for a few days on his way to Los Angeles." Lynch proposed a few days later, and as he was leaving he told Signa he would telephone her from Los Angeles for her answer—and if it was affirmative, he would return immediately to New Orleans and they would marry. In later years, an invented story would make the rounds of financial and social circles that during this conversation Signa hesitated, and Lynch finally blurted out, "Hell, make up your mind, this is long distance!"

And so in 1924, Eddie Lynch, nearing his thirty-ninth birthday, finally ended his bachelorhood. Lynch made the transition to domesticity quickly, and by the end of the decade he was the father of three children who increasingly begrudged his time away from his family for business. Merrill bitterly reflected that by the critical year 1929, "I was in general charge, and the responsible and active partner, Mr. Lynch, was either south or abroad most of that year, and when he was in New York he was concerned almost entirely about taxes. [Sumner] Cobb was the managing partner; he did, generally speaking, what I told him to do, and yet had enough initiative and ability to run the business from day to day. His assistant was Win Smith, and after I mention these three, I have just about covered the entire subject. . . . Keep in mind this was a big firm, doing a lot of business, and yet it was run under my general supervision by only two people."

Meanwhile, in 1923, my father married Gertrude Ingram, a divorcée and Smith College graduate who had a five-year-old son by her first marriage. She was the daughter of a wealthy Minnesota farm equipment dealer who was very dominating and left her feeling inadequate as a child and young adult. Her first marriage was to an abusive alcoholic, whom she divorced in 1921. My father and Gertrude had a son, Bardwell Leith Smith, in 1925, and the family—father, mother, and two half brothers—lived in Englewood Cliffs, New Jersey. There was no George Washington Bridge in those days, and my father commuted to Wall Street on the ferry. By all accounts, it was a stable, perhaps even happy family throughout the 1920s, but the marriage would deteriorate rapidly during the Depression.

The stock market took on a life of its own in the late twenties, propelled by ordinary men's dreams of easy money. As with the state lotteries of modern times, success stories were widely publicized, thereby fueling the frenzy. The millions of tape-watchers included poets who swore by General Motors and chauffeurs who kept one ear cocked to the rear seat for the latest tips. People actually came to New York, rented rooms and apartments to be closer to the action, and vowed to stay until they struck it rich. Luxury cruise ships carrying wealthy clients to Europe provided on-board brokerage services so passengers could wheel and deal at sea.

As the Merrill, Lynch & Co. company prospered and grew, it became apparent that neither of the principal partners had any talent or interest in management. My father, on the other hand, had the special ability to make a web of offices hum with efficiency and generate teamwork. His managerial role at the firm expanded steadily, and on January 1, 1929, he became a full partner and worked closely with Sumner Cobb in learning his new role.

In the midst of it all, Charlie Merrill came to believe that stocks were overpriced and it was time for prudent investors to retrench. One evening at home in March 1928, he drafted a letter to all Merrill, Lynch & Co. customers, brought it into the office the next day, handed it to Robert L. Rooke, head of the Research Department, and told him to distribute it to all clients. Rooke stared at the title incredulously: "Now Is the Time to Get Out of Debt." Stunned, he showed it around the office, and the consensus was that "the boss must be out of his mind." Merrill had already gotten grudging approval from Lynch—but only because the two principal partners, concerned lest their growing differences paralyze the firm, had established a system of alternate vetoes to resolve disagreements. Recently Merrill, an aviation booster since his days in the Army Air Corps, had proposed support for a new plane being developed by Donald Douglas. Lynch had scuttled the idea. He wanted to do the same with the letter of warning, but now he owed one to Merrill, who cashed in the chip. Then CEM pushed aside the objections of the lesser partners and staff members and ordered Rooke to get the letter in the mail. Dated May 31, 1928, it read:

> We think you should know that with few exceptions all of the large companies financed by us today have no funded debt. This situation is not the result of luck, but of carefully considered plans on the part of the management and ourselves to place these companies in an impregnable position.
>
> The advice we have given important corporations can be followed to advantage by all classes of investors. We do not urge that you sell securities indiscriminately, but we do advise in no uncertain terms that you take advantage of the present high prices and put your own financial house in order. We recommend that you sell enough securities to lighten your obligations.

And thus, seventeen months before it happened, Charlie Merrill became the first major Wall Street figure to warn of a crash. Merrill also gave a copy of the letter to the press, and the next day *The New York Times* ran a piece calling it "the most outspoken advice given by a firm . . . . in the present phase of the market." There were a few other voices shouting from lonely rooftops, but they were dismissed as well-intentioned but naïve—and perhaps inspired by Bolshevists and other anticapitalistic forces. It is impossible to know how many Merrill, Lynch & Co. customers averted or mitigated disaster by following Merrill's counsel. According to my father: "A certain number of our customers followed his advice but, unfortunately, as the market advanced they regretted their action and blamed the firm for the loss of paper profits. On the whole, as I look back on the effects of this letter, I think the tide was altogether too strong for any one person to buck and furthermore, I think that the effects of this excellent advice were more or less inconsequential."

The lack of support from his colleagues in the financial community gave Merrill pause for thought—perhaps, as they were saying at the office, "the boss had gone out of his mind." When these self-doubts wouldn't go away, he consulted a psychiatrist—a truly radical step at the time—and after five or six visits went to hear his analyst's conclusion. CEM remembered: "The doctor asked me to sit down at his desk. He opened a drawer of the desk and pulled out some sheets of paper which I immediately recognized as brokerage statements with various firms I knew of. He said, 'Mr. Merrill, you are so crazy that I want to show you I have not a single share of stock in my accounts.'" The patient's advice had been heeded.

Thus reinforced, Merrill looked around for a nationally known figure to carry the message against the speculative fever, and he settled on President Calvin Coolidge, a fellow Amherst man, who had just announced he would not seek reelection. Playing the Amherst card, Merrill got an audience at the White House and made an offer: partnership in Merrill, Lynch & Co., at a salary of $100,000 a year or 10 percent of the profits; in return, Coolidge would serve in a public relations capacity, using weekly radio addresses and other means to preach common sense to American investors. It was a sweet offer (10 percent of the profits would have come to $400,000 that year), and besides, the President shared Merrill's pessimism about the economy. But Coolidge turned it down. He had gone into the White House with a substantial inheritance, and he used insider connections to amass a small fortune while in office. Upon his return to private life, he earned most of his money from various writing projects, including a dull and disingenuous autobiography. A few months after this meeting with Merrill, Coolidge offered his final State of the Union Address and gushed, "No Congress ever assembled has met with a more pleasing prospect than that which appears at the present time."

Merrill's activities during this period—the cautionary letter, the visit to the psychiatrist, the offer to Coolidge—were extraordinary and can be explained only as reflective of a genuine concern for his nation and its people. "He did not use his superior intuition merely to feather his own nest through secrecy, deceit or manipulation," notes Edwin Perkins in his Merrill biography. "While brokers with most other firms were encouraging customers to borrow more money to buy more securities, Charlie instructed his sales personnel to advise investors with regard to acquiring stocks on margin." What Charlie realized is that now, more than ever, his customers needed to understand the risk associated with buying on margin.

Throughout 1928 and into the new year, Merrill pressed Lynch and the rest of the partners to follow the advice he had given to customers. Dr. Charles Morton Merrill died on February 21, 1929, and after his father's funeral, CEM stayed in Palm Beach with his mother, brooding over his personal loss, his continued pessimism about the economy, and the failure of his colleagues to heed his warnings. The outcome was a strongly worded letter to Lynch, dated February 25; it listed $44.5 million in Merrill, Lynch & Co. investments and demanded a systematic plan for their speedy liquidation:

> Now, regardless of what these securities cost us, I think we have too many securities on hand. Furthermore, if we had twice the resources that we have got today, I would be in favor of liquidating all, or part, of our holdings. I have many reasons for this opinion; it is unnecessary to go into them again; it is simply prudent not to be "security poor." However, the financial skies are not clear. The

highest authority, and the strongest power in the land of finance, in the whole world—the Federal Reserve Banking System—has issued warning after warning that a storm is gathering. Anybody not "money drunk" can read these signs if he will. Regardless of the income tax problem it is good business for us to stand from under.

I do not like the situation at all; I do not like the outlook, and I do not like the amount of money we owe. Most of all I do not like the apathetic and indifferent attitude that seems to be prevalent in the New York office at this time. What has gotten into you, Cobby, and everybody else that you can close your eyes to the situation, and be absolutely nonchalant to a situation which is packed full of dynamite. If prices in general were not so high, if our holdings didn't show us such gigantic profits, and if the financial clouds were not gathering, I would still want to liquidate, and get our affairs in A-1 shape. Fortunately, for us, practically everything we own shows a great big profit; why there should be any resistance to turning a very substantial amount of this profit into cash is an absolute unending, insoluble mystery to me. What earthly difference does it make to you and to me whether we pay 12-1/2% tax, or 25% tax, so long as we can turn our holdings into cash, and have rest and comfort at night.

To me business ceases to be of any interest when I must carry an intolerable burden of worry and anxiety. I would prefer to have a great deal less money, if that is the price that must be paid for less anxiety. We went over all this last October, and it was definitely decided and agreed that we would adopt a careful and conservative policy; and would turn old investments into cash before we made any new investments. This policy has been followed only in part, and we now find ourselves approaching the point where we will have plenty of securities, but no money. I tell you I do not like it at all. . . . You do not come out flat-footed and say that you oppose liquidation, but I notice that you do not liquidate, and you do not let anybody else liquidate.

Many fine reputations have been built up in this era of extraordinary prosperity, which will not stand the acid test when troublesome times are here. I have noticed over and over again that when firms are poor, and times are hard, that the utmost cooperation prevails; that is perhaps due to the law of self-preservation, but money does make trouble and it just seems too bad to me that you and I should be pulling at cross-purposes and not together at a time when we are prosperous, and, at a time, when I, for one, think that the outlook is extremely questionable. . . .

I have only one more thing to say; if I am wrong in insisting upon liquidation, then that is a luxury which I can afford, and in which you, and all my partners, should indulge me. Turning securities into cash is my idea of running a business. I always intend to have the business run along those lines; all my partners know this, all know that it is my theory and my policy, and, that being the case, they should not go into business with me unless they are perfectly willing to follow this broad, basic policy. I prefer, as you know, to have harmony rather than friction; I would like to feel that my wishes are respected, and are carried out without the necessity of resorting to stronger and more objectionable methods. It seems to me, I am sorry to say, that nothing I can say or do, if my requests are couched in polite and reasonable terms has any effect. This, to me, is an intolerable situation. It is very distasteful to me, especially at this time, to write at length on this subject. This is not the first message, the second, or the third, but, I hope, it is the last. You and Cobby, the ones upon whom I rely the most, are on the job; it is not only your privilege, but it should be your duty to carry out a sane, reasonable plan for our mutual protection, and do it at once.

It was a remarkable letter. Here was Merrill accusing Lynch of being the principal culprit in a course of non-action that placed the firm in peril. But Lynch was moving away from mundane business concerns to a life of leisure, and he resented his partner's constant browbeating about the balance sheet and even suggested that CEM was mentally unbalanced because of his father's death. Instead of rolling up his sleeves along with Merrill, Lynch left for a long vacation in Paris (he had become a Francophile and devotee of French culture during his stay during the Pathe negotiations in 1921). The chasm between the two partners widened. Merrill began a course of unilateral action, using a power of attorney in Lynch's absence. After months of badgering, Lynch finally gave in and sent word from Paris: "I don't agree with your thinking, but I will not disagree with your actions. If you wish, sell all my holdings." Merrill continued the pruning process through the spring and summer of 1929. There is no evidence that Lynch ever thanked CEM for such prudent action with his personal portfolio, though two years later, Merrill reminded Lynch in a letter: "I have never found fault with you or any of the other fellows for not supporting me 100 per cent in my opinions. However, it is a matter of record that not once, but over and over again did I suggest and recommend liquidations, and, looking back on that situation, it is surprising that in view of the lack of encouragement so many securities were turned into actual cash." Lynch's lack of appreciation notwithstanding, many other business associates and customers who heeded CEM's counsel were openly and eternally grateful for his perspicacity in getting them and the firm out of a bear market that would drop 85 percent over the next three years.

One enduring image of the Crash, which has passed into American folklore, is that of ruined investors jumping out of windows and off bridges. The fact is that between Black Tuesday, October 29, and the end of 1929, about ten weeks later, there were eight such suicides recorded—only four of which were attributed to financial losses. Indeed, New York City's suicide rate that autumn was actually lower than it had been the previous summer.

The prevailing reaction on Wall Street and in brokerages all over America on October 29 was the frantic attempt to keep up with sell orders, contact customers with margin accounts, and take calls from customers demanding quotations, which were unavailable because the ticker was hours behind the action. Merrill was inspirational. "The physical strain upon us was terrific," my father said of that never-to-be-forgotten time. "At times many of us spent forty-eight hours in the office, catching a nap here and there on a sofa or in a chair. During all this period, Charlie was magnificent; he put in the same hours, he was calm and collected and displayed qualities of leadership that were inspiring. He gave us such confidence that we in Merrill Lynch never had the feeling that the world was coming to an end, as so many others in the financial district believed."

Lynch was there on Black Tuesday, but Esther King, CEM's secretary, says he was less than inspirational. "The margin clerks were working like mad, preparing lists of the customers whose accounts needed margin—more margin—and Mr. Lynch was in the cage with them driving them crazy—asking all the time, 'How much does Jones owe? How much does Smith et. al. owe?' So finally when they could not stand him any longer, one of the clerks came out and asked me if he could see Mr. Merrill. I took him into Mr. Merrill's office, and he told Mr. Merrill if he did not get Mr. Lynch out of that margin cage right away, all the margin clerks would quit. Mr. Merrill, in a very calm, cool way, told him to go back into the cage, and in a few minutes he would come to the rescue. Well, he did—he said to Mr. Lynch, 'Come out, Eddie, I want to talk to you,' and when he got him out, CEM told him to stay out."

At five P.M. all employees were asked to remain in the office to help prepare telegrams to customers who could not be reached by telephone. Esther King stayed until 2:30 A.M., and when she returned the next morning, CEM had just arrived. He said he had stayed until 7 A.M. and had just gone home to shower and change clothes. "He was still calm, smiling and cheerful," she said. Merrill told Lilian Burton that he was distressed by the events but relieved that they proved his sanity. For weeks, Merrill, Lynch & Co. partners and staffers continued to work around the clock. When on New Year's Day Herbert "Pop" Melcher walked in the office, he found Merrill at his desk. "Why are you so late?" Charlie asked in jest. "I've been here all night."

Early in 1930 it became clear that the firm had come through the market collapse in better shape than almost any other brokerage. The partnership still held substantial blocks of stock in some of the companies it had helped finance, like Safeway and McCrory, but Merrill, Lynch & Co. had trimmed its sails enough to survive. "We were far more fortunate than others," my father said, "for one very simple reason, and that was that both of our senior partners had cash credit balances with the firm totaling some twenty million dollars. Consequently, we were in an impregnable position and had the confidence of knowing during that panic that the firm could not be really hurt."

*During the Great Depression, Charlie Merrill was
focused on creating a chain of Safeway stores,
revolutionizing the grocery industry. He later applied
the chain-store technique to the securities business.*

CHAPTER FOUR

The Grocer

(1929–1940)

I t is often forgotten that the grave implications of the Crash were not immediately apparent to most people—not even the editors of *The New York Times*, who picked Admiral Richard Byrd's journey to the South Pole as the top news story of 1929. In the aftermath of the Crash, many brokerage houses sent out encouraging letters to their clients. While continuing to counsel its customers to maintain strong cash positions, Merrill, Lynch & Co. did note that there were some bargains on the market for those with available funds. Around Christmas there was a mild rally in stocks and bonds that extended into March, and Treasury Secretary Andrew Mellon declared that the depression—it had yet to earn a capital D—was over.

But the truth was clearer among ordinary Americans on Main Street, such as those who patronized chain stores, who saw their jobs being abolished, their goods repossessed, and their lifetime savings vanishing in bank failures. And Wall Street, that evangelist of the American Dream that so recently was preaching to full tents, was fast becoming a despised symbol of greed and swindling. How interesting that eighty years later we experienced such a similar environment. Charlie Merrill decided very soon after Black Tuesday that it was time to sell his seat on the stock exchange and get out of the brokerage business, which had always been second on the firm's priority list, anyway. Up to this point in his career, he essentially had been a deal man raising capital for companies.

Merrill casually mentioned his intention to withdraw from the retail security business at a chance meeting that fall with Latham Reed, a partner in E. A. Pierce & Co., which had recently built itself into the large "wirehouse"—Wall Street slang for a brokerage with a far-flung network of branch offices connected by telegraph wires. This led to talks about a merger that extended into the holidays, and an agreement was hammered out by January 18—just ninety-nine days after the Crash. It was a Saturday, and the pact was signed over lunch after the close of the market at noon. It was announced on February 3.

Under the agreement, Merrill, Lynch & Co. put up $5 million—about $1.9 million each from Merrill and Lynch and the rest from my father and other Merrill partners (including Sumner Cobb, Robert Rooke, and Wood Williams) who moved over to Pierce. Because the lawyers insisted on a strict separation of the two company operations, the two principal partners' money was listed in the names of their mothers—Octavia Merrill and Jennie Lynch. In addition, Merrill and Lynch never visited Pierce offices. Despite the legalistic distance, the two principal partners had access to Pierce balance sheets through their mothers' holdings, and a direct line into company operations through my father and the other former associates.

For both my father and Charlie Merrill, the 1930s were not only difficult financial years, but they both led troubled personal lives. In the first half of the decade, CEM would drift apart from his second wife, his sons, and his partner, and both his mother and his sister would die. He would engage in a series of extramarital affairs that would culminate in a messy divorce and a third marriage that would prove to be the least wise of them all. And in 1938, Lynch would die at the age of fifty-three before the two partners could reconcile their differences and resume their personal friendship.

However strained their personal affairs, though, both Merrill and my father did well in business during the 1930s. Merrill would thrive and prosper because once again his timing was judicious. After a division of assets with Lynch that gave him control of most of the Safeway holdings, Charlie turned his attention to the grocery chain, which was little affected by the Depression; most Americans continued to buy food and, indeed, now more than ever they were interested in finding the lowest possible prices. CEM consolidated

Safeway's financial position and streamlined its operations, and his management skills guided it into a period of expansion that would make it one of America's premier grocery chains. Safeway emerged from the Depression as a dynamic enterprise, and Charlie Merrill became known more as a food merchant than as an investment banker. Indeed, he seemed ready to let the old Merrill, Lynch & Co. operation drop out of existence.

Meanwhile, my father took on the challenges of making E. A. Pierce the nation's leading wirehouse investment firm. By 1930 he was thirty-seven years old and had grown into a brilliant business-man with a calm, even-handed management style. His genius was not in fashioning deals but in bringing together all elements of the company to form a unified, productive unit. Pierce took full advantage of his new partner by sending him first to the troubled Boston office, where the company had absorbed two competitive firms, and later to the big Chicago branch, where he stayed for the rest of the decade.

While working in Boston, Dad would take a train up there every Monday morning and return home to Englewood Cliffs, New Jersey, for the weekend on Friday night. The assignment was supposed to last a couple of weeks, but it dragged on as the principals of the two acquired firms wrangled over details. "As the months dragged by," my father recollected many years later, "it became obvious to me that the only way I could be relieved from my job was to find a suitable manager." He finally found one in Walter Trumball, a former Kidder Peabody partner, who was looking for work.

E ddie Allen Pierce (he apparently changed to "Edward" when he arrived on Wall Street) was born in 1875 in Orrington, Maine, a town of small farms and sawmills just south of Bangor on the Penobscot River. He was the great-great-grandson of Nathaniel Pierce, who helped found the town in 1788. Orrington prospered for its first hundred years, but the economy turned sour around the turn of the century, and the town's population dropped from 1,800 in 1870 to 1,200 in 1900. One of the émigrés was Eddie Pierce, who left town in 1901, taking a job as a junior clerk on Wall Street with the presti-gious firm of A. A. Housman & Co., where even J. P. Morgan kept an account, and in so doing got an immediate, firsthand lesson on the manipulative, devious and unregulated securities market that existed at the turn of the century. His first day on the job was Thursday, May 9, 1901—one of the darkest days in American financial history. It was the day of the Northern Pacific Panic, which was precipitated by a fight for control of the railroad by two powerful syndicates. When the stock started falling around noon, there was mayhem as traders punched and kicked one another while attempting to unload it. The entire market collapsed. Crowds surged down Wall Street, and the stock exchange was forced to close its gallery for the first time in history. Total financial catastrophe was averted only by a court order, but not before many ordinary investors had been wiped out in the power play. This was an "Occupy Wall Street" of a different era.

It was a difficult introduction to Wall Street for an idealistic, highly principled New Englander, and Pierce could only watch with wide eyes and distress. "At that time no holds were barred in the starting of false rumors for stock market effect," Pierce remembered forty-three years later, "and on the day of the panic a report was wired over to Boston to be relayed back to New York, to the effect that I. and S. Wormser and A. A. Housman & Co., both very prominent houses, had failed and that Arthur Housman had dropped dead at the Northern Pacific trading post. Such a report was well calculated to intensify a condition already bad enough. Upon its being brought to the attention of Mr. Housman, he rushed down to the money post on the Exchange and lent $3 million to the firm—which quite conclusively disputed the report that he was dead or that the firm was busted."

After a few years, Pierce saw that, for all its reputation, Housman's backstage operation was sloppy. He took his case to Clarence Housman, the managing partner, who told him to take over and do a better job. Pierce did just that, and in 1915 he was made a general partner. His business connections expanded exponentially and came to include J. P. Morgan and Bernard Baruch. After World War I, Pierce began building Housman into a wirehouse, and by 1923 he was managing partner and the network of branches and correspondent firms stretched all the way to the West Coast. He hired the fastest telegraph operators, including one who had only three fingers on his sending hand but was the fastest of them all and was paid $420 a month just to tap out market quotations five hours a day. While the prevailing pay for Morse operators in the twenties was $100 a month, nearly all the Pierce operators were earning substantially more.

Throughout the decade, Pierce engineered mergers with about twenty other brokerages, and in 1927 the company's name was changed to E. A. Pierce & Co. After the Crash, many of the Pierce partners were eager to cash in their interests, and the firm needed an infusion of new capital to keep operating. It was at this time that Charlie Merrill was looking to get out of the brokerage business. At first glance, Merrill and Pierce seemed an odd couple—Pierce, the Democratic New Dealer, Merrill, the Republican conservative. But both men had an unwavering belief in the ultimate dignity and value of business, and they shared the vision of a kind of democratic capitalism where ordinary Americans benefited from investing through a nationwide chain of brokerages.

Eddie Pierce would be a fixture at ML for nearly a half-century. A larger-than-life figure who came to work every day in striped pants and a frocked coat with a flower in its lapel, he was a slight man, with a gray pompadour, and was called "EAP" (rhymes with keep) by everyone. He was a workaholic, often showing up at the office at two A.M., sleeves rolled up, collar open, and hair tousled.

Pierce's most enduring trait was his good nature, and it is best illustrated by this anecdote. One day, as he leaned over to take a drink from the office water fountain, an employee, mistaking EAP for someone else, playfully dunked the boss's head in the water and held it there for a minute or more. When Pierce stood and was recognized, the joker was wide-eyed and petrified. But EAP simply buttoned his jacket, walked out trailing a stream of water on the floor—and never mentioned the incident.

Pierce chain-smoked cigarettes, ate wheat germ and other health foods, hobnobbed with Eddie Rickenbacker and Bernard Baruch, and worked at his desk standing up. He came to work at his office daily until he was ninety-eight, and died in 1974 at the age of one hundred. Dan Tully, a future Merrill CEO, recalled riding up in the elevator with EAP as he smoked a cigarette and joked afterward that smoking was going to kill the senior partner. At the time, EAP was ninety-eight years old.

During the Depression, using the money and expertise acquired from Merrill, Lynch & Co., Pierce & Co. made itself a Wall Street anomaly by continuing to expand, giving life to Pierce's steadfast belief that the brokerage business had to come back to sustain America's capitalistic economy. "The less the sun shone, the more it grew," *Fortune* magazine said of the firm in the 1930s. Its acquisition of ailing brokerages was so conspicuous that when Germany tottered on the brink of economic ruin, the joke on Wall Street was: "Nothing to worry about. E. A. Pierce will take them over." By 1938 the firm had absorbed the business of sixteen brokerages, and at the end of the decade it had offices in forty American and Canadian cities connected by twenty thousand miles of leased wire. Skeptics tried to guess the company's losses and took bets on how many days it would be until it folded. Among the doubters was Edmund Lynch, who did not trust the management skills of E. A. Pierce, and as long as he was around, the relations between the two companies would become no closer. But my father and the other former ML partners sent over to Pierce made many management improvements, especially in the areas of research and backstage operations. In their 1999 book, *Co-Leaders: The Power of Great Partnerships*, David A. Heenan and Warren Bennis wrote that after two years in the Pierce Chicago office, Dad had "revolutionized financial record keeping, introducing early IBM technology to the company's back-office operations."

The size of the Pierce firm and its appetite for smaller brokerages were not its only unusual features. One of its twenty-one partners was Miss Ethel E. Mercereau, who was the only female active partner on Wall Street at that time—and for decades to come. It was she, with Pierce's blessing, who made the New York office purr efficiently with her idiosyncratic rules that were issued from her office right next to the boss's. Mercereau believed that a healthy body was a prerequisite for a healthy mind, and her first rule was that all employees be physically fit. Applicants were examined by a physician, and there were periodic checkups to insure continued fitness. There was no smoking of any kind allowed in the office, an incredible hardship to nicotine addicts, as nearly all men were in those days (as a royal prerogative, Pierce was exempt from the smoking ban). Suit jackets were to be worn at all times, there were to be no personal telephone calls on company time, and personal use of company stationery was *verboten*. The guiding tenet of Mercereau's overall management philosophy was that anyone in the employ of E. A. Pierce & Co. was extremely fortunate to be there, and to insure the perpetuity of the system, she extracted from Pierce an agreement that neither of them would ever set foot on an airplane at the same time. Many of the Merrill, Lynch & Co. people sent over to Pierce in the thirties chafed under Mercereau's harsh regime, and when Charlie Merrill took command in 1940, one of the first steps he took to lift staff morale was to relieve her of her management responsibilities, though she was kept on for a time as a limited partner.

During the Depression, Pierce became a conscience of Wall Street. He was a staunch advocate of reform and believed that a certain degree of regulation of the financial industry was a necessity. It was not a widely popular position. Pierce strongly opposed the reelection of Richard Whitney as NYSE president, siding with government regulators who wanted to break up the clique of brokers who ruled the Exchange in their own interests. The battle lines were drawn in 1934 when President Franklin D. Roosevelt created the Securities and Exchange Commission and named Joseph P. Kennedy as its first chairman. Kennedy, who it was said bailed out of the market just before the Crash when he saw his shoeshine boy giving market tips, had become rich doing the kind of questionable manipulation he was about to stifle. "Send a thief to catch a thief," FDR later explained the seeming contradiction in his appointment of Kennedy.

Years later in the fall of 1960 when my father was near death, I visited him as he lay in his bed in Litchfield, Connecticut. One of my best friends, David Mortimer, was the grandson of Averill Harriman, and Harriman had recently visited our school to speak about his support for JFK, who was running for President against Richard Nixon. While he was there, Harriman gave out KENNEDY FOR PRESIDENT buttons, and I was wearing one as I walked over and gave my father a kiss on his forehead. Although he was weak and had difficulty even sitting up at that point, he reached up and grabbed the button, tearing it off my shirt. He was too weak to speak but his eyes said, *No Smith will ever vote for a Kennedy.* Joe Kennedy was the opposite of everything that Charlie Merrill, E. A. Pierce, and Win Smith stood for.

The stage had been set for reform in 1933 by a U.S. Senate subcommittee led by its chief counsel, Ferdinand Pecora, a relentless inquisitor who drew damaging testimony from a succession of witnesses from the Wall Street establishment. For two years the nation watched the Pecora Committee paint a picture of duplicity, fraud, and outright thievery that clearly showed an institution badly in need of reform. The most conspicuous villain was NYSE president Richard Whitney, a blue-blooded member of Wall Street's Old Guard. Whitney battled government regulation and called the NYSE "a perfect institution," but even as he spoke he was fraudulently manipulating funds of the Exchange to cover his personal losses. The forces for reform caught up with Whitney, and on a spring day in 1938 some six thousand people gathered in New York to watch this economic royalist, who had so recently ridden with the hounds on his New Jersey estate, be sent off to Sing Sing prison with two extortionists, a holdup man, and a rapist.

Meanwhile, Pierce and his allies established the NYSE presidency as a full-time, salaried job and elected William McChesney Martin to the new post. It signaled a new day—the NYSE would no longer be primarily responsible for protecting the interests of its members, but instead the investing public would be its main concern. It took many years for this message to filter down, and Charlie Merrill and my father would be the single most important figures in seeing that it did.

With its staff trimmed from a high of about 250 during the most euphoric years of the 1920s to about twenty-five or thirty, Merrill, Lynch & Co. moved from 120 Broadway to 40 Wall Street on June 2, 1930. Though the new office was far smaller, it still took up the entire fifty-fourth floor of the building's tower and was not bleak. The partners' suites were furnished in knotty pine taken from an old wooden bridge in Cambridge, Massachusetts, and the paneled walls held hidden, recessed cabinets. Each office had private bathroom facilities, including a shower-bath. Most of the furnishings were antique pieces purchased at auction in London. There were three secretaries—the redoubtable Lilian Burton, Esther King, and Marguerite Francis. There were no across-the-board salary cuts at the firm during the Depression.

In a reallocation of assets following the retrenchment, Merrill assumed ownership of most of the firm's grocery stocks, and he immediately turned his attention to the venture that would occupy most of his time in the thirties: Safeway. By the time of the Crash, CEM had quadrupled the number of Safeway stores to nearly 2,700, and in the early years of the Depression it continued to grow at a more modest pace. In 1933, Merrill boasted, "It is generally conceded that Safeway is in a class by itself in having fully 80 percent of its stores modern and up-to-date in every respect." The retail food market became more competitive during the thirties, though big supermarkets were often ridiculed as a temporary response to hard times.

Nevertheless, under Merrill's management, Safeway maintained its profit level and paid a dividend. The key to its growth was its merger with MacMarr Stores, Inc., a second grocery chain that CEM had fashioned just before the Crash and placed in the hands of Lingan A. Warren, who had come to Merrill, Lynch & Co. as a salesman in 1928. MacMarr had started out with 39 stores, and by 1931 it had grown to about 1,300 outlets in California, Washington, and Oregon. Many of the MacMarr stores operated in Safeway territory, but it was Merrill's intention from the very beginning to bring the two chains together.

Soon after the move to 40 Wall, CEM decided it was time for a firsthand look at "Safeway territory," and in 1931 he, Lynch, and Warren headed West by train. Merrill worked long days and stayed up late at night taking notes and making calculations, but Lynch was a reluctant participant. He had by this time decided more or less that he would lead a life of leisure and luxury, pausing only to protect his personal fortune from the ravages of taxation and depression, and his attitude toward business and the partnership was captured by Warren in his memories of the trip:

> We went to Winnipeg. I still have pictures of Lake Louise and Banff in the winter, snowing. Eddie Lynch falling through the ice. On this trip Mr. Lynch bet Merrill he could wear my belt (I'm not as big as he was, but fat in the wrong places) for an evening. Lynch won the bet. . . . We went down Bright Angel Trail on mules in the Grand Canyon. I was next to the end. Charlie was not very anxious

to go. His donkey shied and he started climbing off. Lynch
had an old mule named Missouri, and on the way back it
shied. It was funny because Lynch prided himself on being
a fine horseback rider, and Merrill and I were not. Charlie
jumped off to help Eddie. When we came to the Painted
Desert, Lynch got us up at 4 A.M. to take the trip through
it. We went along, reluctantly, with me driving. But Lynch,
though he was an inveterate sightseer, was always hungry.
After a big breakfast, he went to sleep and snored. So he
slept through the entire time.

Merrill returned from the trip believing that it was an appropriate
time to merge Safeway and MacMarr. M. B. Skaggs, who was in
bad health, was reluctant to take on the additional burdens, but he
agreed to go along after Merrill told him that Warren, as Skaggs's
heir apparent, would shoulder part of the management load. Thus,
at the very beginning of the Depression, CEM put together one of
the biggest deals of his career. The new Safeway, with nearly 4,000
stores, was the unchallenged food giant of the West and nationally
was outperformed only by A&P (with 15,000 stores) and Kroger
(5,600 stores). Merrill maintained a keen interest in Safeway for
the balance of the decade. Sometimes he would pay incognito visits
to groceries, both Safeway's and its competitors, wandering around
the aisles, checking prices, and chatting with clerks and customers.

CEM's many trips to Safeway headquarters in Oakland made him
one of the world's first frequent flyers. In fact, there were several years
when he logged more than 100,000 air miles. Commercial aviation
was just getting started, and for a workaholic like Merrill, it was an
incredible blessing. Flying in a plane was still something extraordinary to do, but unlike most of the American population, Merrill was
not afraid to fly. In the early 1930s, transcontinental flight involved
flying during the day and then transferring to a Pullman sleeper on a
train for the night. Regardless of the time of day, the meal was usually
the same—coffee, fruit cocktail, rolls, and fried chicken lifted out of
steam chests that were supposed to keep the food warm. A round-
trip coast-to-coast fare cost about $720 ($8,800 in current dollars).
CEM found air travel exhilarating, and he described a 1935 flight in

a note to Warren when he got back: "On the return trip I think I set a new record for air travel in 23 hours by a paid passenger. The total air mileage covered between 12:20 San Francisco standard time, and 2:20 Eastern Standard Time was 3544 miles. A heavy fog over Indianapolis accounts for the extra mileage. We were right smack over Indianapolis on scheduled time, but had to double back to St. Louis for safety sake."

M eanwhile, as the grocery business grew. Merrill began to consider the radical notion of giving away a women's magazine at checkouts in groceries. The idea appears to have originated with Harry Evans, a journalist who knew Hellen Ingram, CEM's second wife, when he worked as a sportswriter on his hometown newspaper in St. Augustine, Florida, in the 1920s. Eventually, Evans moved up to *Life* magazine and came to New York, where he developed a minor reputation as a journalist and a major reputation as a peerless raconteur, top-rated golfer, excellent tennis player, fair baseball player, all-around ladies' man, and a dancer so talented that even the reclusive Greta Garbo would get out on the floor with him. All of these qualities endeared him to Charlie Merrill, and after an introduction by Hellen, the two Floridians became friends. While he was at *Life*, Evans came to question the wisdom of using expensive subscription campaigns to obtain readers: Why not just give the magazine away and make the money from advertising?

CEM took the idea and refined it: Why not give away the magazine in a grocery and then advertise that grocery's products? In his trips to observe Safeway outlets firsthand, Merrill had noticed that consumers considered private labels to be inferior and tended to purchase national brands. Not only would the magazine be a good vehicle for grocery chains to advertise their own brands, but its direct, point-of-sale feature would appeal to national food advertisers, whose messages were now diluted in general-interest magazines. Merrill took a survey in the state of Washington that showed that belt-tightening families were canceling paid magazine subscriptions because of the Depression, and he foresaw that this trend would continue. Thus, in 1932, he took Evans's idea and gave it wings—and capital. CEM and Evans took their concept to Skaggs, who was unenthusiastic, and so

Merrill launched the magazine as his own venture, independent of both Safeway and Merrill, Lynch & Co.

In September 1932, a new weekly magazine called *Family Circle* debuted in chain groceries in the New York and Washington, D.C., metropolitan areas. Evans was managing editor and Annie Grimes sold ads. It was twenty-four pages, with about sixteen pages of editorial content and eight of advertising. The initial press run was for 250,000 copies. Skeptics pounced on it immediately, claiming that nothing given away is respected, but within a month circulation rose to 350,000, and by early 1934 it reached 1.3 million. Soon even Skaggs was rhapsodic, telling prospective advertisers that a dollar spent in *Family Circle* was worth five spent on radio. *Family Circle* went on to become a household staple, and a member of the so-called seven sisters of women's service magazines, joining *Ladies' Home Journal, McCall's, Woman's Day, Better Homes & Gardens, Redbook*, and *Good Housekeeping*. Merrill lost some $700,000 before the magazine turned a profit in 1937, but when he sold it for an unknown amount in 1954, circulation had reached 4 million. Once again, Charlie Merrill had successfully swum upstream against conventional wisdom and launched a visionary venture. In the context of Merrill's assets in 1932, the risk was not a great one, but it was taken in the darkest hours of the American economy.

Merrill, Lynch & Co. was an atypical firm on Wall Street because it had cash, but some of its attempts to put that money to work were not as successful as CEM's *Family Circle* enterprise. At one point, two Maine housewives persuaded the partners to invest in their invention, called Wet-Me-Wet, a window cleaner that came embedded in its own pad. It was a hot item in gas stations for a brief time, but competitors soon drove it out of business. Another endeavor was the Animated Illuminated Sign, a scheme for effecting the illusion of motion on signs, but the signs were dim and often didn't work. There was even a gold mine in Montana that the best engineering and geological minds concluded held substantial amounts of gold because the primitive method used in the first attempt to extract it had barely pierced the surface. Merrill, Lynch & Co. invested in the construction of a new mill, but the experts were wrong and the mill ended up closing. A proposal to merge several independent bus lines to compete with Greyhound was explored but ultimately abandoned, and there were exploratory talks about purchasing the Brooklyn Dodgers baseball team in 1935. Although most of these deals and near-deals were in the name of the firm, it is more than difficult to imagine Lynch having an active role in them—and the resulting losses may have contributed to the growing animosity between him and his partner.

Merrill's most embarrassing investment of the Depression involved Clarence Birdseye, an Amherst fraternity brother, who in 1924 had offered to sell him a one-quarter interest in a business that would freeze food for future use. The stake would have cost CEM about $10,000, but he turned it down. The Birdseye process ended up revolutionizing food retailing in stores and restaurants, including Safeway outlets, and with it what the world bought and ate. Just five years after Merrill spurned the proposition, Birdseye sold his process to the forerunner of the General Foods Corporation for about $22 million. Then, in 1934, multimillionaire Birdseye set up a small company to develop and manufacture a new type of incandescent lightbulb coated on the inside with silver that acted as a reflector to direct the beam. This time Merrill took him up on his offer to invest in the venture and sank about $700,000 of ML funds into it. In the end, General Electric beat them to the punch with a better product, and Birdseye filed for bankruptcy. Near the end of the decade, Merrill talked of "the futility of indulging in idle regrets," adding: "A businessman must either take his medicine with as much grace as possible, under the circumstance, or else grab hold of the problem with both hands and conquer it."

Though Merrill had known a mixture of failure and success, one of his most conspicuous successes in the 1930s occurred in politics, the only occasion during his career when he involved himself directly in the political sphere.

I n the early days of Colonial America, retail selling was done by peddlers, first on foot and later in wagons. As towns and villages sprang up, retailing shifted to tiny shops, whose owners put peddlers out of business either by charging them exorbitant license fees or banning them outright. For the next two centuries, America's retail business was conducted largely through small businesses that lined the Main Streets of its communities. They were owned by individuals and families, sometimes for several generations, but by 1935, about 23 percent of the nation's retail sales were being rung up in chain stores—due in no small part to the efforts of Charles Edward Merrill. The backlash was predictable—the nation's shopkeepers banded together to fight "the chain-store menace." It was the kind of classic, economic-based political struggle that still occurs today—lawyers versus insurance companies, doctors versus hospitals, truckers versus railroads.

Beginning in the thirties, there was a flurry of anti-chain activity that included attacks in the press, Congressional hearings, and anti-chain taxes in states and cities. The November 19, 1930, issue of *The Nation* described the manager of a chain store as "a transient, merely a representative of a non-resident group of stockholders who pay him according to his ability to line their pockets with silver. He can hardly be classed as a merchant. Since the chain manager must be a puppet, he is hardly capable of becoming a leading citizen of any town." One leading Congressional opponent was Rep. Emanuel Celler, a New York Democrat, who claimed the chains were making America a nation of clerks and robbing its citizens of opportunity. "Chain stores mean absentee control," he asserted. "Absentee control is the very antithesis of democracy." The chains were denounced as the creation of the now-hated Wall Street. Chain opponents also played on themes of the ingrained American sympathy for the underdog and nostalgia for the mom-and-pop grocery and the corner druggist. Many of the same arguments would be leveled sixty years later against Wal-Mart stores, which would be vilified as economic Godzillas sucking downtowns dry. Now, as then, the public continued to patronize the chains—often while paying lip service to their opponents' criticisms—because they offered lower prices. However, as the Depression deepened, the populist rhetoric resonated with politicians, and revenue-hungry states began enacting stiff taxes on chain stores. When the U.S. Supreme Court upheld the validity of an Indiana tax in 1931, the floodgates opened—more than five hundred special tax bills were introduced in state legislatures over the next two years.

With his usual prescience, Charlie Merrill saw the coming turmoil in 1930, and he tried to muster the defenses of chain stores by asking their executives to contribute funds toward a counter-propaganda campaign. The response was so meager that he eventually abandoned the idea, but in 1935 he took matters into his own hands when the California Legislature, by a huge majority, passed a chain-store tax that had a graduation feature—the more outlets in a chain, the higher the tax on each outlet. Such a progressive tax made huge chains particularly vulnerable, and it would have cost Safeway about $650,000 a year, or some 20 percent of its annual income. Merrill, who was steadfast in his belief that chain stores were good for Americans and that any public policy that supported higher consumer prices was wrong, convinced the doubters that it was time to stand and fight. He created the California Chain Store Association, which was funded almost entirely by Safeway, and set it to work securing petitions bearing enough signatures to place a referendum on the statewide ballot repealing the tax. This was accomplished in September 1935, and the question was certified for the November 1936 election. Merrill had thirteen months to convince a majority of voting Californians that the chain-store tax was unfair and not in the public interest.

At first, the deck seemed stacked against him. The tax repeal question was next to last on a list of twenty-three ballot measures going before the voters, whose attention was further diluted by the fact that 1936 was an important presidential election year. The state of California, whose treasury was drifting toward the fiscal shoals, could ill afford this loss in projected revenue, and state politicians, embarrassed by a huge budget deficit, looked askance on Proposition 22 because it would only enlarge the projected shortfall. But the repeal forces came up with a catchy slogan—"22 Is a Tax on You"— and a soft-sell, low-key voter education campaign was followed by a direct attack on the tax, one that used handbills, package inserts, print, radio, movies, billboards, and windshield stickers. A speakers bureau sent articulate repeal advocates to clubs and schools to discuss Proposition 22 with anyone who would listen. Voters were lured into large auditoriums by entertainment and door prizes to hear the gospel truth about chain stores. Other workers went door-to-door. This well-orchestrated campaign cost about $2 million, but it paid off. The chain-store tax was overwhelmingly rejected by the voters, and while anti-chain legislation would continue for another five years or so, it began to lose momentum.

Aside from the victory itself, CEM reaped a further bonus in the California referendum, for it introduced him to Theodore W. Braun, who masterminded the successful campaign and would become one of the most important figures in Merrill Lynch history. Ted Braun was born in Newark, New Jersey, in 1901, and he managed to enlist in the Army at the age of fifteen, emerging as an officer at the end of World War I. After the war, he returned to New Jersey and worked as a farmer in Parsippany until 1923, when he migrated to the West Coast. His first job there was driving a cab in Los Angeles, and he quickly developed a chart that helped him determine the next best place to go to pick up a fare after he dropped one off. The system impressed the cab company, and he was made foreman. In like manner, Braun helped to develop a better production system at his next employer, a milling firm, and his success came to the attention of a bank, which put him to work salvaging another milling company that threatened to default on a loan. Braun then put his management talents to work for a resort hotel, which he transformed from a loser to a profit-maker. As his reputation spread, referrals rolled in and he set up his own management consulting firm, Braun and Co., in 1928. Years after the California chain-tax referendum, Ling Warren, the Safeway president, would call Braun's work the best advertising campaign in the history of Safeway. Charlie Merrill spent the next five years dealing with pressing business matters and a dis-integrating personal life, but he never forgot about the management skills of Ted Braun, and in time would put them to good use for his firm.

Ted later became a close friend and adviser to my father, and when I was born in 1949, my father asked him to be my godfather. Ted also counseled Nelson Rockefeller in his various political campaigns and became the godfather to one of his children.

Charlie Merrill was known for his deep sense of loyalty and responsibility, and during the thirties he came to the aid of two of his oldest business friends, Sebastian Kresge and John G. McCrory, only to have his strenuous and largely effective efforts earn him the undying enmity of both men.

Early in the Depression, Kresge had pegged the price of his own company's stock at 26⅛—meaning that he was ready to buy from anyone at that price. It was an attempt to halt the steady erosion of the stock's value, but many shareholders, including Merrill, Lynch & Co., sold their Kresge shares, and by the end of 1931 the strategy had cost Kresge more than $8 million in personal funds. With his cash resources dangerously depleted and his company's financial condition perilous, Kresge asked Merrill for advice. CEM told him to set the stock loose and let it find its own market value. The price dropped to $6, and Merrill bought back in to the company. It was a risky move, but the stock started to rise—and Merrill sold at a nice profit. Kresge accused CEM of exploiting him in bad times, and thereby infuriated Merrill, who believed he had rescued his longtime business associate from financial ruin. The rift was never mended.

McCrory's company got into trouble because, contrary to advice from many quarters, including ML, it entered a series of long-term leases during the heady days of the twenties when its stock was selling at $65 a share. By 1932 the value of a McCrory share had tumbled to forty cents, and its unpaid landlords were threatening a takeover. The company went into bankruptcy and receivership, and both Merrill and Lynch put in long hours developing a restructuring plan. The principal recommendation was a renegotiation of the leases, and most of the landlords readily agreed because in the existing commercial real-estate market, their choice was a lower-paying tenant or no tenant at all. Merrill's strategy worked, and McCrory eventually came out of receivership in 1936 and resumed its profitable ways, but McCrory himself was bitter over CEM's handling of the bankruptcy. For his part, Merrill thought McCrory an ingrate. In a memo to Lynch at the conclusion of the McCrory affair, CEM bespoke a sense of frustration and fatigue:

> The main trouble with M L & Co. in general, and you and me, in particular, is that we are trying to do too much, in too many different lines of business. Just to keep M L & Co. alive, as an ordinary investment and promotion house, would be enough of a job for anybody in these times. . . . In times like these, men who have ability, courage and energy

are terribly driven and imposed upon; you are required
to work with and help McCrory along a hundred different
lines, and what is true of McCrory is true to a greater or
less degree with practically every account we are close to.
The demands upon our time, and, more important than
that, upon our thought, are simply incredible.

There was no letup in the demands Merrill referred to, and a few
months later, in February 1933, he wrote to his partner to complain
of "sheer physical fatigue" and warned that "when a fellow works too
hard at too many different things he ends up being incapable of doing
real good work at anything." Merrill went on to "analyze our blessings"
and to propose a more sensible regimen that included a limit on the
number of hours of work, regular meal times, a drive every morning
in Central Park, and the delegation of work to subordinates. Merrill
concluded: "So far I think we are incredibly lucky; we have been
through two small panics, and one international depression, and at
the outset of each of these three catastrophes we found ourselves free
and clear from debt. It is true that we have lost an incredible fortune,
but that disaster in itself is not as hideous as would be the disaster
of losing either our sanity or our self-respect."

Charlie Merrill understood the power of leverage and the folly of
too much debt. His views saved himself and his partners and were
ingrained in my father and his successors at Merrill Lynch until
Stan O'Neal levered the firm to unsustainable levels and ultimately
brought it down.

By the time Charlie was voicing his concerns about more balance,
though, Lynch already had lapsed into a de facto retirement and
was determined to lead a life of luxury broken only by his efforts to
protect his fortune. His daily mail was brought to his apartment at
570 Park Avenue by John Moritz, who would arrive just before nine
A.M. and wait in the foyer until Lynch awakened. "I had two folders,
one marked 'Desk' and one, 'Miss Francis,'" says Moritz, referring
to Marguerite Francis, Lynch's secretary. "Dressed in a robe, Mr.
Lynch went over every single piece of mail, advertisements and all,
as though they were all equally important. Everything that he read
he put a check mark on, surrounded by four dots. I thought at first

it was a secret code of some kind, but I found out later from Miss Francis that it was simply a mark to show he had read it, and that the four dots—never three or five—were just a habit he had picked up to round out the simple check sign, to individualize it so that it would be clear who had checked it. After he got through with the mail he'd come to the office, perhaps around ten-thirty or eleven o'clock."

In 1932, Lynch bought an eighty-foot yacht, the *Anahita*, and flew from it the ensign of a check mark encircled by four dots. He sailed around the Caribbean until he found a house he liked on Jamaica and had it duplicated on Hog Island in the Bahamas by Howard Major, the architect who had designed a home for Merrill in Palm Beach. Meanwhile, he bought other Long Island estates as hobbies and investments, including "Cherrywood" in Locust Valley (it had an indoor tennis court) and "Wooldon Manor" in Southampton (fifty-five rooms and a beach house). Through it all, Lynch never lost his innate frugality. Though he was driven by chauffeurs, all his cars were secondhand. If Signa and the children needed the car for the day, he used the subway. In his travels, he haggled with porters and cabdrivers over their prices. He examined every hotel and restaurant bill, and always counted his change. Unlike CEM, Lynch found marriage agreeable and enjoyed home life with his wife and three children. He took up tennis and quickly became a very serious player, hiring a member of the British Davis Cup team as a full-time professional coach (and putting him on the Merrill, Lynch & Co. payroll without informing his partner). Three months out of the year, Lynch was abroad, based in his beloved Paris and making trips to Spain, Italy, and England.

As early as 1932, Merrill was complaining directly to Lynch about his lack of participation in partnership affairs:

> I am feeling the burden, very keenly, of our investment in the Safeway Company, plus the enormous amount of extra work already descending upon me, on account of the FAMILY CIRCLE, with the promise of a great deal more to come; therefore, not only the fair thing to do, but the smart thing to do is for us to get together and work out ways and means whereby all, or almost all, of all the other work that passes over my desk will be attended to by somebody

else. I don't say that you are that somebody else, but I do say that you and I together must decide whether or not you are going to do it, or whether we must hire somebody else to do it, because I have simply come to the end of my rope as to these matters, and I cannot be held responsible any longer for attending to them.

It is unnecessary for me to mention the fact that Criscuolo, John Wark, Joe Merrill, and the Lord only knows who else, come to me over and over again for decisions, about minor matters on questions that arise during my absence, when you are in the office, that could very easily be decided right then and there by you.

We have been in business together a long time, and the time has now come when you must give me the benefit of your organizing ability, and devise not only ways and means by assuming the responsibility of employing sufficient additional human beings who some way, some how will take these burdens off my shoulders. How you manage to do this, and what the cost is I leave entirely to you. Anything that you decide to do, and how you do it, will be all right with me, but this you must keep in mind, that no longer can I be relied upon or expected to do all the thousand and one things that I have been called upon to do.

There is no indication how Lynch responded, or whether he responded at all, but in the ensuing years the bulk of his time was absorbed by his long trips to Europe, his cruises on the *Anahita*, his pursuit of tennis excellence, and the managing of his real-estate holdings and other personal matters.

The Merrill-Lynch relationship suffered a severe loss in 1933 when Octavia Merrill died at the age of seventy-one. She had continued to exert a strong influence on her son's life well into his adulthood, and more important, she was frequently a soothing agent in his relations with his business partner. Merrill's father had died four years earlier. When his sister Edith died in 1936 at the age of forty-three, Charlie Merrill became the sole survivor of his immediate family, and his loneliness was exacerbated by his increasing estrangement from Hellen. The couple had gotten along well for a few years, even had a son, and a heady social life in New York, Southampton and Palm Beach, but the marriage of two strong-willed individuals turned sour in the thirties. There were bitter arguments and second-guessing when they were bridge partners, and CEM would become infuriated by Hellen's habit of interrupting him and finishing his stories in company. But most of the damage was the result of a series of extramarital activities on his part that culminated in his beginning a long-term affair in 1935 with Kinta Des Mares, a New Orleans woman fifteen years his junior whom he had met through Signa Lynch and who would become his third wife.

Personal losses piled up for Charlie Merrill in the early years of the Depression. In addition to the family deaths, Sumner Cobb, one of CEM's earliest and most beloved business associates, died in 1934 at the age of forty-six. Merrill credited "Cobbie" with many things, the most important of which was introducing him to my father. Merrill met Cobb at Amherst, and both men ended up in New York, where they were roommates in Brooklyn from 1909 to 1911. Cobb was one of the first employees of the new Merrill, Lynch & Co., and he soon rose to sales manager. He earned his spurs in 1915 with a backbreaking, door-to-door campaign to sell the McCrory stock issue, the firm's first big deal. Cobb became a Merrill, Lynch & Co. partner in the 1920s, and after the Crash in 1929 he was among the group in the firm that went to work for E. A. Pierce, where he worked until his death.

By 1937, Merrill had attained a certain renown as a financier and socialite, and his and Hellen's protracted divorce proceedings provided fodder for New York City's tabloid newspapers. There were items like this: "The inevitable triangle took shape, according to Mrs. Merrill's separation suit, when her husband met Dorothy Stafford, Long Island beauty, in 1931. As time and Cupid marched on, the triangle quickly assumed proportions of a polyhedron as more and more affairs added more and more angles. She is suing on grounds of cruelty." And this: "Once he found his wife barricaded behind a chained and bolted door when he returned unexpectedly to their apartment at the swank Hotel Carlyle. 'I have since learned a man was in the apartment with my wife at the time and that he escaped down the service stairway,' he says." And this: "Both Merrill and his wife accuse each other of imbibing too much when champagne flowed. He locked her in a closet at the Hotel Carlyle for three hours one night in March 1937, because he was intoxicated, she stated. Merrill explained he did it because she was intoxicated."

The principal victim of this kind of publicity was the couple's son, Jimmy, a precocious adolescent who had to repeat a grade at boarding school and ballooned up to about two hundred pounds through compulsive overeating during the nasty divorce. The boy was the source of much friction between his mother, who defended and protected his frail, creative nature, and his father, who decried his lack of boyish energy. Jimmy became the object of a bitter custody battle that ended in an uneasy compromise. Charlie and Hellen were divorced in Jacksonville on February 19, 1939, in the same court that had granted his divorce from Eliza. Seventeen days later he married Kinta Des Mares. It would be the worst of his three marriages. Like the first two, it would last about thirteen years.

James Ingram Merrill would go on to become one of America's great poets and winner of the 1967 National Book Award. He died in 1996 with an artistic legacy of fifteen volumes of verse, two novels, two plays, and a memoir. In the 1940s, CEM became supportive of his son's early literary endeavors, but he never came to grips with his open homosexuality. Though he keenly felt the need to become closer to his two sons, Merrill's business and personal distractions kept him from developing a deeper relationship with either of them. Their rejection of business as a career extended this distance into adulthood. Charles Jr. disappointed his father by choosing to attend Harvard instead of Amherst and by his liberal political beliefs. When he married his college sweetheart in 1941, CEM was pointedly not invited to the wedding.

Far happier were Merrill's relations with his first child, Doris, whom throughout his life he called "My Number One Girl." He addressed her in numerous letters as "DDD" for "Dearest Darling Doris," and sometimes even drew smiling faces on his correspondence to her. Moreover, she in effect provided him with a son to enter the family business in 1935 by marrying Robert A. Magowan, who at the time was an executive with the advertising firm of N. W. Ayer & Son. The weekend after the wedding, the newlyweds visited Southampton, where another guest was Lingan Warren, who had just been installed as president of Safeway Stores. Before the weekend was over, Warren offered Magowan a job at $2,000 a year more than he was making with Ayer. He accepted, and the Magowans moved to Oakland, where Warren devised a training program designed to teach Magowan every aspect of the grocery business. Magowan started in the warehouse and then moved to checkout clerk in one of the Safeway stores. While his identity was supposed to be a secret, the secret didn't last long because he came to work every day in a Cadillac. When Ed Lynch died in 1938, Merrill invited his son-in-law to come into the firm as a vice president and director ("I think Mr. Merrill was lonesome for his daughter," Magowan once explained). Whenever anyone asked Bob Magowan for the secret of his success, he would reply, "Decisiveness. I decided to marry the boss's daughter." Despite his self-effacement, Magowan was a skilled executive in his own right and a major figure in Merrill Lynch history.

As a young boy, I remember both Bob and Doris fondly, and after my father's death they remained good friends of my mother's. After I started working for Merrill Lynch, I received a call from Bob one day in 1980. "The Merrill Trust is winding down," he said, "and because of Charlie's great affection for your father, I would like to have you direct a $50,000 gift to any charities that you like. You just can't give anything to either Amherst or Deerfield. They've received enough." After speaking with my then-wife, Maggie, I asked him to give $25,000 to the Winthrop H. Smith Memorial Foundation and $25,000 to Greenwich Academy, where my two daughters were enrolled. To both of those charities they were meaningful gifts and Greenwich Academy subsequently asked Maggie to join the Board of Trustees. Later I was chairman of the WHS Memorial Foundation for several years.

In both good marital times and bad, Merrill kept up an active social life in New York and at his two luxurious seaside retreats. Among his neighbors were Rockefellers, Mellons, Wanamakers, Kennedys, Vanderbilts, Drexels, Woolworths, and Morgans, but for the most part he eschewed contact with the socially prestigious, whom he scorned as the "striped pants crowd," and spent his nonworking hours with people he knew and liked from business. Recreation featured golf, tennis, bridge, good food, and, above all, good wine and spirits. During the Depression, the wealthy lived as they had always lived, very well. There were no bread lines in Southampton or Palm Beach, though many of its residents lost millions in investments, and from time to time "For Sale" signs were hammered into the palm-dotted, manicured lawns of great houses that lined the Atlantic beaches. Seventy years later Bernie Madoff had a greater impact on many residents of those affluent neighborhoods.

Nevertheless, CEM wanted his sons to realize what was happening to most of America, and so in 1936 he sent them to Wildwood, a cotton plantation he owned in the Mississippi Delta that was now struggling. Charles, who was sixteen years old at the time, was called "Young Master" by the workers and remembered that as he rode horseback through the fields, "old black women would stop by my horse and say that they had been my daddy's nurse." For Jimmy, a sensitive ten-year-old, it was an interesting and memorable experience: "We stayed with the manager and we worked a couple of hours in the little plantation store. . . . He [CEM] certainly wanted us to realize what was going on in that part of the country." Cotton prices plunged during the thirties, and Wildwood was a consistent loser. Merrill complained about indolent field workers and came to regret his decision to entrust management of the plantation with a maternal uncle, Jeff Wilson, whom he accused of mismanagement and collusion. The relationship ended badly in 1934 with a sarcastic letter from Wilson to his nephew and employer: "I trust your vacation in Florida has improved your health and morals. If 'wine, women and song' is your trouble, you must cut out one of the three. In your case, you will dispense with song."

Early in the Depression, Merrill was an easy mark for dozens of ruined men—business colleagues, college classmates, neighbors— seeking loans. In many cases, they were individuals he knew only slightly or not at all. In February 1937, he received a long letter from the wife of Robert Sjostrom, his first boss in New York and the father of his onetime fiancée. Mrs. Sjostrom said her husband had suffered a heart attack and required constant home care, which she was having trouble affording. She asked for a loan of $500. CEM wrote back the same day he received the letter, enclosing a check for $500 and offering it as a gift.

The friendship between Charlie Merrill and Eddie Lynch hit bottom in the summer of 1937 while both men were abroad. CEM was escorting Charles Jr., Ed Lynch Jr., and the son of M. B. Skaggs on a European grand tour while Lynch was traveling the Continent with Signa. CEM was undergoing mental anguish over his shattered personal life, and he sought advice and solace from his longtime partner and confidant. When Merrill learned that the Lynches were in London buying furniture for their new home in the Bahamas, he decided to fly over from Rome. When he arrived at the Lynches' hotel suite, it was in turmoil. The couple was about to sail for New York, and maids were packing trunks, Lynch was signing agreements with furniture dealers, and several other people were waiting for appointments. Through all the confusion, it was clear to everyone that Charlie Merrill had come all this way especially to see his friend Eddie Lynch in private. "I was in a desperate way," Merrill admitted later. "I just had to talk to Eddie, but it was like someone trying to have a chat with Napoleon during the Battle of Waterloo." Merrill waited patiently for several hours, but when Lynch finally agreed to have lunch, he insisted that a banker come along to make a threesome. "It was a miserable meal, for I saw my last chance to speak to him go glimmering. Eddie left right after lunch, and I went back to Italy without having unburdened myself to him."

Merrill had no communication from Lynch for the next eight months.

Milija Rubezanin, the head of research, who was taking on the role of Merrill's principal adviser in the absence of Lynch, urged both partners to pay more attention to their original business. "The name of Merrill, Lynch & Co. is too good to be lost," Rubezanin wrote in a memo to the two men, "and at the present time, it is steadily losing ground because the firm has not been active." But the fortunes of the partnership spiraled steadily downward, and in March 1938, CEM wrote a bitter letter to Lynch: "I realize, to my regret, that you have decided to do no more work. This is a very laudable decision provided you can afford to follow it out. But, in my opinion, Eddie, unless you and I do get down to brass tacks, and do put our respective abilities to work, the time will not be far distant when we will have nothing to work with, and nothing to worry about. . . . It is really too bad, in your own interest, that you pick out a year like 1938 to withdraw from the world." But Lynch attributed CEM's distress to his marital woes, and instead of heeding the call to action made plans for another trip to Europe. Just before his departure, he agreed to meet with CEM—despite the objections of Signa, who had taken Hellen's side in the divorce wrangle. Merrill insisted that the meeting take place in Lynch's apartment rather than his hotel "because the walls are so thin"—though the real reason appears to be that he did not want to encounter Signa Lynch. Neither party has left any account of what happened at the meeting on May 1, 1938, but it would be the last time the two men ever saw each other.

When Lynch left aboard the *Normandie* on May 4, he was ill with a bladder infection and throughout the voyage ran a fever and passed in and out of delirium. He was no better upon his arrival in France, and he was immediately transferred to a London nursing home. He appeared to rally after a few days, but on May 11 he died from a coronary embolism. It was eight days before his fifty-third birthday. After a funeral service in New York, which was attended by about a thousand people, Lynch's remains were placed on a private railroad car to be transported to Baltimore for burial in the family plot. Just as Merrill and a small party of Lynch's family and friends were about to board the train, a newsboy appeared hawking the latest tabloid, which carried an item about CEM's divorce proceedings that began, "A society marital hangover—attributed to too much champagne, a Latin-American Romeo, a couple of society playboys and two designing beauties—throbbed painfully in Supreme Court." Several copies made their way onto the funeral train, and Merrill's misery was compounded by embarrassment.

L ike Charlie Merrill, my father had devastating domestic problems in the 1930s. His wife, Gertrude, began drinking heavily soon after Dad left for the E. A. Pierce Boston office, leaving the family behind in New Jersey during the workweek for about a year. By the time the family moved to Chicago in 1932, she was a full-blown alcoholic. During this time, her teenaged son by her first marriage would also become an alcoholic, and he would not stop drinking until shortly before his death in 1966 at the age of forty-eight.

Gertrude wrote a fictionalized account of her life entitled *The Late Liz*, which would propel her into national prominence as a temperance speaker in the 1940s after she stopped drinking. My father was named Silas Adams in her narrative. In the book, she described those early days in Chicago:

> Along with alcoholism, within a year or so I began to take drugs. With all the servants in the house, all I had to do for breakfast about 11 in the morning was to push a button, and breakfast would come up. I would spend a few minutes doddling [*sic*] with that. Then I would take Benzedrine to get me up. Somewhat later, not much later, I would take liquor to keep me up. And then a sleeping pill to knock me out. Well, this makes a very short day. There were only about two hours that I was "compos mentis."

Bardwell, my father's son and my half brother, was seven when the Smiths moved to Chicago. In an autobiographical essay, he said this about his mother:

> I won't go into all the gory details about her drinking and the pain of those years. There was a Hollywood movie made out of *The Late Liz*. The movie was terrible, but the book was wonderful. The book sold a lot, so she was asked to speak in prisons, junior leagues, Lutheran churches, Episcopal churches, Jewish synagogues, black churches, colleges, universities, high schools as well, etc. She spoke all over the country for about 11 months each year. She was an excellent speaker: very funny, very bright, very honest about herself and in the process of these experiences her life came together in powerful ways. This book represents an extraordinary testimony of why there was a need for change. In the first half of the book she talks graphically about herself. The second half discusses at length the beginning and evolution of this change—as if it were a small blade of grass emerging from unlikely soil, with no guarantees, and then how this tiny growth became stronger and stronger.

My own mother, Vivian, whom my father married in 1947, hated the book and felt that Gertrude had ridiculed my father; she also had little affection for Bardwell and thought he only came to visit to get money from my father. As a result, unfortunately I grew up with a bad impression of both. I later read *The Late Liz* and now I agree with Bardwell's assessment. I got to know Bardwell much later in life and realized what a talented teacher and wonderful human being he is—and how proud my father must have been of him and would be now. I am fortunate to have a great older brother.

The family spent most of the 1930s in several rented homes in the posh Chicago suburb of Lake Forest, and from there my father commuted to work every day on the Chicago and Northwestern Railroad. When he and Gertrude were divorced in 1937, she stayed in Lake Shore and he moved to a hotel in Chicago. Gertrude sometimes complained that Dad was a workaholic and "boring," but her assessment of him in her book was that he was "a good and moral man." Bardwell was twelve when his parents divorced, and was sent to Brooks School in North Andover, Massachusetts, for the next three years. Before the divorce, my father would often take Bardwell to Wrigley Field to see the Chicago Cubs, and like his father, Bardwell became a lifelong baseball fan.

After serving in the U.S. Marines during World War II, Bard earned a bachelor of arts degree at Yale and remained there for a bachelor of divinity degree, a master's, and a doctorate. He taught East and South Asian religions and philosophies at Carleton College in Northfield, Minnesota, from 1960 to 1995, served as dean of Carleton from 1967 to 1972, and currently he's Carleton's John W. Nason Emeritus Professor of Religion and Asian Studies. Bard is widely published, and his special interests include religion and society in Sri Lanka and Buddhism in Japan. Over the years at Merrill Lynch I met numerous graduates of Carleton College who would seek me out to tell me what a great professor and person I had as a brother.

Dad managed Pierce's Chicago office for nearly a decade, and he considered this experience critical to his career. "I already knew the underwriting business," he recalled, "but it was my eight years in Chicago that gave me my best practical training in the commission business. And commodities—I never even had seen a grain of wheat before I went there."

Along with his full-time job, he served as chairman of the Business Conduct Committee of the Chicago Board of Trade, and as governor of the board. His top assistant was Homer P. Hargrave, who would go on to become resident partner for the new Merrill Lynch in Chicago, and a legendary figure on the Midwestern financial scene known as "Mr. Chicago." In 1935, Hargrave married Colleen Moore, the famous Hollywood star from the days of silent movies. Today Colleen Moore is best known for the Colleen Moore Dollhouse, an eight-foot-high miniature "fairy castle" that toured the United States in the 1930s. Since 1954 the dollhouse has been a featured exhibit at the Museum of Science and Industry in Chicago and attracts more than a million visitors annually. When I was born Colleen made me a needlepoint cushion with a scene of animals boarding Noah's Ark, and placed it in a small antique child's chair. It was my favorite place to sit in our living room in our New York apartment, and is now on display at Winivan, our former family home which is now a Relais & Chateaux Spa Resort in Litchfield, Connecticut.

After Lynch's death, Merrill, perhaps still in a precarious state from the sudden and untimely passing of his partner of nearly a quarter-century, insisted that both their names continue to appear on the letterhead even as the firm underwent some reorganization. Three months after Lynch died, the name of the firm was changed from Merrill, Lynch & Co. (with comma) to Merrill Lynch & Co. Inc. (no comma). The comma was dropped at the insistence of company lawyers, who said that using the name of a deceased individual could create legal problems under New York State law (under the legalism, the comma-less phrase "Merrill Lynch" represented the name of a company rather than the names of two individuals, one of whom was deceased). Soon the company began receiving letters addressed to "Mr. Merrill Lynch." The comma removal also sparked many false legends, some of which were impishly aided and abetted by Merrill himself. Merrill told some people that if he had finished his college education he might have known to insert the comma. Others were told that a printer erroneously struck the comma on a business letterhead in 1917, and he and Lynch couldn't afford to order more. A variation on the latter tale was that tightwad Lynch insisted on using up all of the erroneous stationery before correcting the error. In 1949, Merrill was interviewed by a cub reporter for the *New York Herald Tribune*, and he was asked about the comma. Merrill advised the young man not to ask silly questions about commas in a serious interview because "nitpicking never gets you anywhere in life." The reporter was William Safire, who went on to become a columnist for *The New York Times* and one of the world's leading (nitpicking) authorities on the English language. Personally, I've always liked the stories of the comma better than the facts and preferred to use the 1917 story when I would tell people the history of the firm.

Beyond the confusion over punctuation, the naming of the reorganized firm had a graver consequence in that it lent a measure of undeserved immortality to Edmund Lynch, who likely would have opposed the coming bold move that brought the modern Merrill Lynch into being. This injustice also took away that recognition for many years from the man who would come to be most deserving of it, Winthrop Hiram Smith. During the summer and fall of 1938, Merrill sometimes wondered aloud how he could manage to go on without Lynch. But in fact, as he must have come to realize, he was for the first time free to act on his own, with no one standing in the wings with a bucket of cold water. At fifty-four years of age, he was a seasoned, wise businessman, ready for a new challenge. Fortunately for him and the firm, he found another man ten years his junior who would become his best friend, partner, and co-leader for the next sixteen years.

Charlie Merrill worked hard and played hard. Here he is in the early days sailing on Long Island Sound. Standing in the background is Paul Shields, a onetime ML partner who would go on to head another prominent Wall Street firm, Shields & Co.

MERRILL, LYNCH & CO.

SEVEN WALL STREET

NEW YORK

We beg to announce that we have this day changed the name of our copartnership from

Charles E. Merrill & Co.

to

Merrill, Lynch & Co.

and shall continue to conduct a general investment business in Stocks and Bonds at our offices 7 Wall Street, New York 1004 Penobscot Building Detroit

Merrill, Lynch & Co.

October 15th 1915

Although Eddie Lynch only served in the Army for twenty-three days during World War I, he was a patriot. Here he is meeting with Admiral Richard Byrd.

Young Merrill was finally accepted into the Army and trained other pilots. Charlie was as dashing in his military gear as he was in civilian life.

Young Win Smith goes from Amherst to Wall Street to the army.

The underwriting of McCrorey stores was the first great success for Merrill and Lynch. The name was changed to "McCrory" a few years later.

Family Circle *magazine* was distributed free in Safeway Stores.

During the 1930s, Merrill set about to revolutionize the grocery industry, with special focus on growing Safeway Stores.

Charlie Merrill's home in Southampton, Long Island, was named "The Orchard."

During the early 1920s, Eddie Lynch focused on the Merrill, Lynch investment in Pathé. "Perils of Pauline" was one of its legendary films.

Part Two

*Charlie Merrill and Win Smith finalizing the deal that
brought Wall Street to Main Street. Together they
forged one of the greatest partnerships in American
business history.*

CHAPTER FIVE

Wall Street
to Main Street

(1940–1942)

O n the morning of April 3, 1940, the big golden revolving doors of the Waldorf-Astoria were spinning nonstop, slicing crowds into people. Most of them carried umbrellas as insurance against the rain that threatened to erupt from leaden skies at any moment. It was chilly and damp, raw as a skinned knee. When the eight-sided bronze clock in the lobby chimed the hour of ten, the doors of the famed Starlight Ballroom on the eighteenth floor were closed, and visitors were turned away for the rest of the day. Since it opened nine years earlier, the Waldorf had become a synonym for high society, wealth, and good breeding. It was, therefore, an unlikely setting for a revolution that would make Wall Street an ally of the thrifty as well as an agent of the privileged. Few that day appreciated that Wall Street would be coming to Main Street. Some three months earlier, men in tuxedos with boutonnieres in their lapels had guided bejeweled ladies in gowns across the dance floor as Guy Lombardo and his Royal Canadians ushered in the New Year. But now the images in the gilded mirrors were of men in white shirts and dark business suits with name badges pinned on their lapels. Seated at circular tables of eight were the sixty-eight branch managers in the latest permutation of Merrill Lynch: the newly formed firm of Merrill Lynch, E. A. Pierce & Cassatt. They were somber-faced, for the stock brokerage business had been moribund for a decade, and they could see no relief in sight. Action on the floor of the New York

Stock Exchange, just a few miles downtown, was so slow that traders regularly played baseball with crumpled pieces of ticker tape. The public had little faith in the stock market and even less understanding of what made Wall Street tick.

Here at the Waldorf, there was also bewilderment on many faces, for the managers had been abruptly summoned to New York with only the explanation that new and radically different policies were being established.

In deference to his longevity and reputation, E. A. Pierce opened the conference, but he soon gave way to the firm's new directing partner, and it was clear that he was the man in charge. Charles Edward Merrill was a trifle overweight as he walked to the podium, but at the age of fifty-four, he was at the top of his mental game. Characteristically blunt and irreverent, he told the assemblage, "I hope and believe that before this meeting is over, you will get it clearly through your heads that the reason why this firm has certain ideals, and certain methods, and certain aspirations is not because we hope to come into the kingdom of the Lord. Exclusive of all ethics, it simply pays to do business right."

The two-day 1940 Managers Conference may well have been the most important event in Merrill Lynch history. It was the blossoming of a seed Merrill had planted a quarter-century before as a twenty-five-year-old newcomer to the financial district when he called for "a new guild whose members despise not the modest sums of the thrifty." Merrill was firing the first shot in a revolution that would change Wall Street forever and propel him into the ranks of Jay Cooke and J. P. Morgan as one of its greatest figures. And the radical idea spawned that morning at the Waldorf had been set in motion just a few months earlier by my father.

Neither Charlie Merrill nor my father were superstitious by nature, and so when they met up on a crisp autumn day in the autumn of 1939, probably neither of them attached any significance to the fact that it was Friday the thirteenth. On that day, CEM was making a routine journey to the West Coast, which he had done by train or plane dozens of times in the 1930s, to confer with the top Safeway managers. But this time he stepped off the Pennsylvania

Railroad's crack Broadway Limited in Chicago's Union Station for a weekend stopover at the request of my father, his onetime office boy and former partner who was now a partner of E. A. Pierce & Company and running its big Chicago brokerage branch. Ever since my father left as a Merrill Lynch partner in 1930 to go to work for Pierce (after Merrill sold his brokerage business to Pierce), the two men had maintained regular communications by telephone and mail. In addition, Dad made annual visits to Merrill's homes on Long Island and in Florida, and they also often ran into each other at Amherst College reunions and football games. But now my father had a bold proposition for Merrill to return to the brokerage business; he knew it would be the biggest selling job of his life, for his timing seemed dreadful. Merrill would be fifty-four years old in less than a week, he had remarried just seven months earlier, and his fortune (estimated at $50 million) was secure. Moreover, World War II had begun six weeks earlier. But my father had made painstaking preparations before sitting down with Merrill in his comfortable home in suburban Lake Forest, for this was the most important meeting of his life. While my father was a modest and soft-spoken man, he was a superb salesman and like Charlie a born optimist. Years later, Merrill CEO Bill Schreyer used to say that he had never met a "rich pessimist," and I am sure my father felt the same way.

My father's motivation for seeking out Merrill now was simple enough: The days of E. A. Pierce & Co. were numbered. In fact, the agreement with Merrill Lynch that had kept the foundering Pierce organization afloat for a decade would expire in about ten weeks, and there was virtually no chance it would be renewed. The company was losing money at an ever-increasing rate as it continued to operate with an overhead geared to Wall Street's sunnier days. The average cost of executing a transaction exceeded the average commission. War was on the horizon in Europe. The nation had suffered through a decade of economic malaise. Dad hoped to convince Merrill to merge the two firms, arguing that fresh capital and an aggressive reduction of overhead could turn the combined firm into a moneymaker. Moreover, it would be the realization of Merrill's dream of a "department store of finance" operated in the chain-store mold—a high volume of transactions with a small return on each to maintain profitability.

"He became very much interested immediately, and for the rest of the weekend we went backwards and forwards over the figures and spent hours discussing the possibilities of a merger," my father recalled. "When he left he told me he would be back in three weeks and would spend another weekend with me and, in the meantime, asked me to get more information for him and gave me certain details that he was interested in."

When Merrill returned in early November, Dad had assembled a scenario that projected earnings of $1 million in the first year of the new firm, and considerably more if stock market activity increased. But CEM was unconvinced and asked my father to spend the period between Thanksgiving and Christmas in New York developing more definitive numbers. According to my father: "We worked late into the nights for the whole month and never seemed able to get the right combination of figures that satisfied Merrill. I went back to Chicago for Christmas and came to New York the first of the year and resumed work. We never seemed to be able to come up with the right answers, and it began to look very much as though Merrill was going to throw over the whole idea of a merger." But as the life of the partnership agreement ticked down to its final hours on December 31, CEM extended it for ninety days. He asked his longtime associates, "What would Eddie Lynch have done?"—though surely he knew that his old partner would have already killed the idea.

At the same time Merrill was questioning hard numbers, outside events were influencing his decision. For one thing, the public held a deep distrust of Wall Street. A poll by the Elmo Roper organization, commissioned by the New York Stock Exchange, found widespread public misunderstanding and distrust of the NYSE. Among its findings, Roper reported: About 35 percent of the respondents thought buying and selling stocks was "foolish," about half thought small investors were given short shrift by brokers, 24 percent thought grain could be bought and sold on the Exchange floor, and 8.7 percent believed the NYSE dealt in livestock. The general impression was that a major cause of the Depression was greed, duplicity, and fraud on the part of bankers and brokers. CEM was stunned by the findings, and he ordered Ted Braun, now a close adviser, to conduct a similar study of Pierce customers in California with the added goal of discovering what they wanted from their broker. Braun's findings mirrored those of the Roper poll and additionally found that brokers were so mistrusted that clients were reluctant to have them hold their securities in safekeeping. Most people preferred to keep their assets in banks, real estate, and insurance. Most of those who did buy stocks relied on advice from bankers; friends and relatives placed second as a source of advice, and brokers were in third place.

Again Merrill cringed. "The results of these two surveys are shocking," he wrote. "To us who have conducted our business along honorable and ethical lines, it is almost incomprehensible that so large a percentage of the public can have so poor an opinion of our character and honesty. No self-respecting broker can complacently sit by and ignore this criticism, some of which is unquestionably true." The Braun study was unprecedented on Wall Street. No insider had ever conducted such a rigorous self-examination. In later years, Dad would say, "This survey will be ever memorable in the annals of the firm; from it we based our policies and to it we are largely indebted for whatever success we may have achieved."

My father and Merrill agreed, and after Dad had completed his final research and number crunching, Merrill decided to go ahead with the merger. However, the methods of doing business would have to change. The new partnership would have to be guided by a set of core principles and the public would have to be convinced that Wall Street had the best interests of Main Street in mind. Main Streeters would also need to be educated before they could invest, and a new breed of broker would have to be developed. These were formidable challenges and risks for a man of wealth in his mid-fifties and a man of only modest means in his late forties.

Merrill invited my father to his office at 40 Wall Street on January 31, 1940, and told him that on April 1 the new firm's name would be changed to Merrill Lynch, E. A. Pierce & Cassatt, though that name would last only fifteen months. Cassatt & Co., an old-line Philadelphia investment house, had become a Merrill Lynch subsidiary in 1938, but the Cassatt name was probably more recognizable because of the financier's sister, Mary Cassatt, the great American Impressionist painter. Despite the long name and the partnership structure, it was clear that Charlie Merrill was in charge. Pierce, sixty-six years old, remained at the firm and lived to be one hundred years old. Among other skills, he was renowned for signing stock certificates at his stand-up desk with both hands simultaneously, a feat that my good friend and Manager of Employee Services at Merrill Lynch, Lee Roselle, also learned to do. Although Pierce became an elder statesman and a figurehead and surrendered a failing enterprise, his company had provided a ready-made structure for Merrill's return to Wall Street. CEM delegated the major tasks of implementing the new company to Dad, Ted Braun, and Robert Magowan, his son-in-law.

Meanwhile, my father moved into the No. 2 slot as managing partner and Charlie's unofficial chief of staff. Magowan, married to Charlie's daughter, Doris, and thirty-six years old, had returned to New York as a vice president and director of the newly organized Merrill, Lynch & Co. in 1938 after spending three years on the West Coast learning the chain-store business under Ling Warren at Safeway. Under the new operation, he was responsible for advertising and sales. By this time, Magowan had become a virtual third son to Merrill, who called him "Bobby" and signed his letters "Pop." Braun, thirty-eight years old, combined public relations expertise with a genius for organization, but perhaps his most important trait for the future of Merrill Lynch was that he was not a yes-man to anyone, including Charlie Merrill and my father, when he believed in something.

Braun's study of Pierce's operations in the Los Angeles area convinced him that it was critical that the new firm's brokers inspire trust in small investors. Not only should ML representatives avoid giving "hot tips," they should not give any advice at all unless it was asked for. Rather, they should provide their clients with the hard information they needed to make their own investment decisions. All clients, regardless of the size of their accounts, were to be treated equally. But the major complaint against brokers uncovered by Braun was the hallowed practice of "churning" accounts—buying and selling mainly for the purpose of generating commissions.

As a Wall Street outsider, Ted Braun could see better than other ML leaders, including CEM, that the churning problem was pivotal, and the gist of the issue was how brokers were compensated. Until now, they had always been paid commissions and therefore had always had an incentive to churn accounts. Braun proposed a drastic remedy for the churning problem: Pay Merrill Lynch brokers a straight salary, with annual bonuses to reward special contributions to the firm. Salaries would be based principally on success in providing services to customers. Any bonuses and their amounts would be judged by branch managers and based on the contribution to the overall profitability of the firm. This approach at Merrill Lynch lasted into the 1970s when competitive pressure forced the firm to change its method of compensation back to a commission-based one. Later, under Dan Tully and Launny Steffens, Merrill once again moved back closer to the model envisioned by Braun by charging clients a fee for "assets under management" and taking away the motivation of buying and selling specific financial instruments. In fact, the most successful financial advisers embraced this concept and apply it today. It is interesting that what Ted Braun saw and pushed for in 1940, more than seventy years ago, has once again become what the public is demanding in light of the recent financial crisis.

Despite the sound reasoning behind Braun's proposal, the older partners at Merrill Lynch, E. A. Pierce & Cassatt were appalled. Here was Ted Braun, a young California PR man and former cabdriver, suggesting a revolution on Wall Street, a place not known for embracing radical change. If part of each broker's commissions was siphoned off into the firm, how would this lost income be replaced? Charlie Merrill told Braun that he would never work in a firm that did not pay commissions, whereupon Braun (as CEM recalled it) "leaned back in his chair, relaxed, and said, 'This point is the keystone of all my suggestions. If you do not adopt it, it's no use talking about any of the rest.'" CEM slowly saw the wisdom of Braun's idea, which surely must have appealed to his chain-store ethic. In addition, he realized that the loss of income would be more than offset by increased business. By April 3, when all the branch managers were to meet in New York at the Waldorf for a kind of pep rally and indoctrination session, Merrill had totally accepted Braun's proposal. In later years Merrill conceded that "Ted was 100 percent right," and he called the change the single most important policy of the new Merrill Lynch. It became clear that if "the customer's interest was going to come first," the method of compensation would be paramount. Years later in 1994 Arthur Levitt, chairman of the SEC under President Clinton, established a blue-ribbon panel led by Dan Tully, the then-CEO of Merrill Lynch, "to recommend ways to reduce conflicts between investors and brokers by changing the broker compensation system." The panel of five, which included Warren Buffet, came up with a set of "best practices," but the industry basically rejected the recommendations even though, as Arthur Levitt said in his book *Take On the Street*, at least the "industry leaders acknowledged the existence of conflicts." Braun would have been appalled at their shortsightedness.

Merrill and the Pierce partners put about $5 million into the new venture, and about $2.5 million of that was from Merrill himself. CEM had placed another $1.9 million of his own money in the Pierce operation back in 1930, but nearly all of it had been lost in the lean years of the Depression.

Merrill never explained the rationale that led him to take on the financial risk and demanding workload that would inevitably accompany an attempt to save the Pierce operation. Why risk a substantial part of the fortune he had amassed and carefully sheltered through the Depression? Even my father, in the heat of his advocacy, admitted to CEM that "a man in your tax bracket would be a fool to come in." Why start a new, daring venture in a world darkened by war and with the very survival of democracy dangling uncertainly? And, until now, Merrill had shown little interest in the securities business. As Ling Warren put it, he was "a deal man" who had made his money by providing capital for new and expanding companies.

Three of those closest to Merrill during this period all offered different reasons for his decision. Robert Magowan, his son-in-law, put it irreverently: "Merrill was getting bored after sitting on his ass for ten years. It looked like an opportunity, the only one left, and he had all the money." Ted Braun says Merrill was trying to protect his investment in the dying Pierce operation. Doris Magowan, his daughter, puts a nobler spin on it: "He wanted to bring Wall Street to the people—the little people especially." All three were probably correct, but there was a fourth contributing factor: He knew he would not be going it alone, just as he had not when he and Eddie Lynch were partners. In my father, Ted Braun, and Bobby Magowan, he had three people whom he trusted and respected and who were able to work with his own brilliance and volatility.

Aside from whatever was at the heart of Merrill's decision, there were also structural reasons the merger made sense. Probably most important, Pierce provided a ready-made distribution network that could be coupled with Merrill's underwriting operation. Most of the major investment banking firms on Wall Street did not have their own distribution operations, but relied instead on close allies in the brokerage business. Pierce also had a commodities business that provided ties to big industrialists who might want Merrill's underwriting services. CEM's considerable ego probably responded irresistibly to the challenge, and his instincts were whetted by his new marriage, the return of Doris and his grandchildren to the East Coast, and the tensions of wartime. He was genuinely distressed by the low public esteem in which his chosen field was held. And the dream still burned of a chain store of finance, driven by high volume and low costs, that would bring Wall Street to Main Street.

A nd so Merrill reserved the Starlight Ballroom at the Waldorf-Astoria to hold the managers' meeting on April 3 and 4. To prepare for the conference, he worked day and night for the two months preceding it, and he demanded that my father, Magowan, and Braun do the same. In a series of crisp memoranda, Merrill attempted to instill his vision of the new venture into his managers. On March 18, he informed sales personnel:

> I want our customers' men trained to call up Mr. Jones, and say—"Mr. Jones, this is the news, and this is the dope; this is a guess, etc." And when Mr. Jones says in reply—"Well, Mr. _____ what do you advise me to do?" Our customers' man says in reply—"If I knew the answer to that question, I would have my share of the world's goods, and would not be calling you up. It is your money Mr. Jones; you make the bid. All I can do is keep you informed as to what we think, or hear, or guess, is going on. . . ." Today I doubt very much if anywhere in the U.S. you can find an expert investment man, with any sense of modesty, or humor, left who would be willing to claim that he was an investment expert. I don't believe there is any such animal, and I certainly am not going to let our organization in general hold itself out to the

world as experts in investment matters when at least one of the senior partners is positive that he himself is no expert. This investment counselor racket is sure to burn itself out.

On March 26, one week before the Waldorf meeting, a letter went out, signed by Merrill and Pierce:

> Essentially the job before us involves adapting our operations so that expenses will be in ratio to existing minimum standards of gross income; and then increasing the gross income by adapting our policies to meet the standards and requirements of our customers and public opinion. The sooner we recognize that the temper of living may never again be identical with what it was twelve or fifteen years ago, the sooner we shall gear ourselves for success under present and future conditions.
>
> E. A. Pierce & Co., which on Saturday becomes an integral part of our new firm, had approximately 50,000 accounts on its books January first last. About 13,000 of these had debit and credit balances. Really a small business, isn't it? It was handled by forty partners and 285 registered representatives. The figures are especially illuminating when we realize that they define the present scope of the biggest firm in our field.

The firm that would come to be known as the modern Merrill Lynch was born on April 3, 1940, and cumbersomely christened Merrill Lynch, E. A. Pierce & Cassatt. My father recalled that the sixty-eight managers came to New York "thoroughly bewildered by the merger and thoroughly downhearted because of the poor business they had been experiencing for years." Also weighing heavily on their minds was the fact that their calling was held in near-contempt by such a large portion of Americans. One of the conference attendees, J. Bryan Grubbs, Pierce's manager in Columbia, South Carolina, even claimed he'd had the windows of the brokerage painted over "because nobody wanted to be seen in a broker's office."

The meeting was opened by Pierce, who made very brief remarks and retired to polite applause after introducing Merrill, who now was firmly in control of the operation. The air was prickly with tension. "In the first place," Merrill began, "I will tell you something in advance which certainly all of you will find out before the next two days are over. I don't mind very much working hard, but God knows I would rather take a licking than make any kind of a talk or address." It was far from the truth, but it seemed to take the anxiety in the room down a few notches. He told them that he had learned in the grocery business that the one thing retailers were entitled to was "not a profit in accordance with our expenses, not a profit in accordance with our hopes, not a profit in proportion to our avarice, but what was left in our pockets after meeting the lowest competitive prices in town." These same guidelines, he said, would apply to the new Merrill Lynch.

Next came Ted Braun, who presented a sobering outline of the Roper survey and his own study of Los Angeles customers. "The conclusion that we were forced to arrive at," he told the managers, "is that the one thing that is vitally important to every customer, or potential customer, is the combination of honesty, integrity, and general reputation. This is on Page One. It must come first before they are interested in any other factor." When it came to what stock buyers wanted, he said, the hot tip was at the bottom of their lists. "No one wanted anything of that kind of monkey-shine."

After lunch, Merrill and my father alternated in describing what the new approach would be. My father said there would be a concerted public relations and advertising campaign to untangle the arcane world of investing and make it understandable to customers. There would be newspaper and national magazine advertising, a speakers' bureau would be established, and all branch managers would have public relations as one of their duties. Friendly relations with financial journalists would be seeded and nurtured. Merrill Lynch personnel would take an active role in the affairs of their local communities, including by joining service clubs like Rotary and Kiwanis. Merrill said research materials prepared for customers would disclose any interest Merrill Lynch partners might have in a security: "If we should prepare a circular or pamphlet on the Kresge Company, we will say that we have attempted to get figures together in the most scientific and impartial manner we know how, but we are only human beings. We will state that Mr. Merrill has been identified with this company since 1912. . . . He is not impartial about the Kresge Company. . . . He believes in it completely although he may be completely wrong."

All of this sounds like common sense today, but in 1940 it was radical. Wall Street did not advertise. It did not know the meaning of merchandising. Being part of a local community was beneath the "dignity" of Wall Street bankers, and icons like Joseph Kennedy earned their fortunes through inside information. One cannot overstate the importance of these core principles enunciated that April day in New York, and for years the transcript of those remarks would be read by future leaders of Merrill Lynch: Smith, McCarthy, Lenness, Thomson, Regan, Birk, Schreyer, Tully, and Komansky. Unfortunately, Merrill's second-to-last CEO, Stan O'Neal, had no interest in the history of the firm nor its core values, and this, in my opinion, was the root cause of the ultimate disaster that unwound in the fall of 2007 and ultimately led to the forced marriage with Bank of America. More on that later in this book.

On the second day of the meeting, CEM expanded on his vision for the new firm. For one thing, he told the assembled managers, it would provide detailed information to the public on its own finances: "I have seen very few balance sheets on any Wall Street house that I, personally, could understand. Now, that is probably because I am a dumb bunny, but, by George, if I can't understand reading an ordinary statement of an ordinary firm in thirty minutes, why should we assume that any customer can understand a statement glancing at it for five minutes?" I have to wonder what Charlie Merrill would think of today's financial statements and their complicated footnotes.

Another way things would change is that brokers would not give investment advice unless asked for it: "The financial business has been pouring so much advice at the customer that he no longer gives the proper value to good advice. If the customer is getting advice poured at him like a stream of water and he doesn't even have to ask for it, that raises a question in his mind: 'What are these fellows up to?'" Customers who asked for advice would be given "research reports of unexcelled quality," which they could use in making their own decisions. (Imagine if, a half-century later, CDOs, subprime mortgage-backed securities, and credit derivative swaps were explained according to Charlie Merrill's simple rules. I doubt if most people would have purchased them.) Then the shocker: Brokers would be paid salaries rather than commissions. "One of the troubles in our business," Merrill told the managers, "has been a potential conflict of interest between the customer and the customer's man, created by compensation practices which were fundamentally wrong. We're going to minimize, perhaps even eliminate, that potential conflict of interest. A real man doesn't want to be subsidized, and he doesn't want any favors. All he wants is a chance to demonstrate his ability and look to the boss to promote him and reward him if he does good work and makes regular progress. Therefore, every representative of this firm will be a definite-salaried employee—and it will be his duty to earn that salary." The minimum broker's salary would be $200 a month, which for many of them meant a substantial increase over their present earnings.

And there was more. In an idea unprecedented on Wall Street, Merrill Lynch brokers would be trained, CEM told the managers: "We are going to make you the strongest competitive customer's man in town. We are going to give you service, rates, support, help, to the end that you will broaden your base of customers, bring in more business to the firm. You will have more dollars in your pocket, though you may have fewer percents." Today both financial advisers at the national firms and independent financial advisers are getting back to this basic principle of not being in conflict with their clients by charging a fee on assets under advisement or management rather than earning a commission. It's too bad Wall Street moved away from Merrill's principle for so long.

Brokers also would be supported by vigorous advertising, and on this score he mocked current Wall Street practice. "If R. H. Macy [the department store] had the same approach to the important expenses, the business-getting expenses, that all members of the New York Stock Exchange have, I assure you R. H. Macy and Company would be out of business by next April first, and it wouldn't be April Fools' Day either." Merrill concluded his address in the afternoon of the second day by reading a set of principles that would be carried by every employee while doing ML business. Though there were only nine of them, they quickly came to be called "the Ten

Commandments." And though they seem tame by modern business standards, they were iconoclastic, bordering on insurrectionary, for Wall Street in 1940.

I

Our customer's interest MUST come first. Upon our ability to satisfy him rests our chance to succeed.

II

Our business deals with people and their money. This creates financial and ethical responsibilities which we accept completely.

III

Eliminating all expensive frills which do not make a direct contribution to the fundamental requirements of our customers, we offer simple offices, competent manpower and efficient, impartial service.

IV

When our relationship with a customer is other than that of a commission broker, the fact will be made known before the transaction. When supplying printed reports concerning a security in which the firm is not acting as principal, we intend to indicate the extent of the aggregate direct and indirect ownership, as of the date of the report by the firm and its general partners. The purpose of such disclosure is to help the customer estimate the possibility and extent of bias on the part of the firm in its presentation of facts relating to a particular security.

V

Salaries of our Registered Representatives (Customers' Men) are related primarily to their success in satisfying the service requirements of customers—thus eliminating conditions which indirectly create pressures to increase the trading of customers.

VI

Our managers and partners are available for consultation with all customers, large or small. And, upon request, we will assist our customers in working out their investment, speculative and hedging problems. However, we will not foist gratuitous advice upon our customers

*and all reports issued by our Research Department will
be limited to facts—impartially presented.*

VII

*During periods of extraordinary activity, no new ac-
counts will be opened on any day when the volume of
trading at any time indicates that the facilities of the firm
may be overtaxed.*

VIII

*Our working capital position will at all times exceed
the requirements of the law, the New York Stock Exchange
and other exchanges, and our financial statements will
be issued in a form designed for maximum clarity and
understanding.*

IX

*We heartily support the laws and other controls de-
signed to protect the investor by preventing manipulation
and fraud.*

"The customer may not always be right," CEM concluded, "but
he *has* rights. And upon our recognition of his rights and our desire
to satisfy them rests our chance to succeed." Charlie actually wrote
this simple thought in 1913 and never lost sight of it during his life.

My father was awed by Merrill's performance over those two days:
"[He] took the leading role and made a tremendous impression on
the visiting managers. He inspired them, put new hope into them,
and sent them home after the second day in an optimistic mood, full
of confidence and ready to go out and lick the world."

"I know that I just felt it was a new world for me," says Ned B.
Ball, manager of the Raleigh, North Carolina, office. "I thought Mr.
Merrill was the type—and Mr. Smith also—were the two type of men
I would want to be associated with the rest of my life." Except for
World War II service, Ball did stay with Merrill Lynch and rose to
president and chief operating officer before his retirement in 1973.

When the meeting had ended, Merrill and my father gave
the press a "Statement of Policy" that included the Ten
Commandments and ML's plans for advertising, promo-
tion, and cost control. The *Chicago Daily News* called it "the most

refreshing document that has come to LaSalle St. in years" and forecast a new day for the brokerage business. The *San Francisco Chronicle* said the policy statement was "the most forthright on record for a business of its kind." The *New York World-Telegram* said Merrill "brings to the Street with his re-entry a fresh perspective which has been badly needed."

This was just the beginning of years of favorable publicity, much of it personally orchestrated by CEM, that contributed immeasurably to the company's growth. Merrill liked to impress upon subordinates the importance of public relations with his "baby-on-the-track" story. "If a baby were on a railroad track," he would say, "and some fellow accidentally happens to come along and save it, and no one sees the baby being saved, the chap that does the saving doesn't get any Carnegie medals. But if a crowd has been assembled, and the baby is snatched from in front of the cow catcher—then there is some chance of getting some reward and appreciation." Years later I recall an ML training session where Merrill's philosophy was stated a slightly different way: "Never give an anonymous gift."

A few months after the Waldorf meeting a widow from rural Kentucky penned a letter to "Merrill, Lynch, E. A. Pierce & Cassatt." After the salutation, "Gentlemen," she asked for advice on investing $4,000 she had just realized from the sale of her land to the Tennessee Valley Authority. She received a reply ten days later—from Charles Merrill himself—apologizing for the delay and saying advice would be coming soon. The widow responded within a week, this time directing her letter to "Charles E. Merrill." She said her goal was to receive annual dividends totaling $300, which was all she needed to live on. Then she listed four stocks that had been suggested to her by a friend. Merrill was back to her in a week with a 1,500-word letter detailing different options, strongly cautioning against her friend's suggestions, and recommending a seven-stock portfolio that would meet her investment goals. Then he solemnly reassured her that "we have no service charges of any kind whatsoever and we rely entirely on commissions to pay our expenses and to earn us a profit." The widow wrote another letter thanking him effusively and saying she had bought the stocks he recommended from a local broker not affiliated with Merrill Lynch.

It was no accident that the exchange of correspondence found its way to the desk of Leslie Gould, the prestigious financial editor of the *New York Journal-American*, who quoted the letters verbatim in his widely read column. This included, of course, Merrill's 1,500-word missive, which served as a primer on investing that anyone could make use of.

More good press grew out of the decision to break with the ingrained practice of charging West Coast customers an additional fee for NYSE transactions. Although the putative reason for the so-called "Pacific override" was to cover the additional cost of leased communication lines, some of the surcharges were as much as 50 percent. Braun's Los Angeles survey had shown that Pierce customers resented this regional discrimination. Eliminating the fee cost Merrill Lynch about $230,000 in desperately needed revenue in the first year, and it angered brokers all up and down the Pacific Coast as well as their superiors back in New York. It also publicized the new company's principle of making the customer No. 1. Over the next few years, the other brokerages quietly dropped the override themselves, and any revenue lost to Merrill Lynch was more than offset by the additional business generated by the change. Thirty years later Don Regan ignited similar anger among Wall Street scions when he advocated doing away with fixed commissions because they were not in the customer's interest.

Even the most careful news management did not prevent a whiff of scandal, though. Less than a month after the Waldorf meeting, CEM learned that J. Chester Cuppia, a partner and very close associate of Pierce, was being investigated by the SEC for taking kickbacks from floor brokers on the Curb Exchange (predecessor to the American Stock Exchange). Acting on Braun's advice, Merrill insisted on full disclosure. A spate of negative publicity ensued, but that summer CEM wrote Braun and thanked him for his advice:

> The papers have certainly had a Field Day. I have tried not to let my resentment get the upper hand for the simple reason that it is gradually dawning on me that whatever concerns this firm is considered by the papers as news. Generally speaking, the papers have been very helpful on

the constructive side of our efforts and, therefore, I think it would be silly to resent too much the space that they have given to the troubles of Cuppia. I learn from Guenther that most of the fellows think that it is just tough luck for me individually, and, of course, that goes for many of our partners, to have to take it on the chin because Cuppia is alleged to have gotten mixed up in a split commission racket. In any event, there is plenty of consolation in the fact that the public did not lose any money.

A second Merrill employee revealed to be corrupt was a man named Waldorf J. Guttman, who had been serving as Pierce's head cashier and was elevated to partnership by CEM. Guttman was a close ally of Pierce and had gained some recognition in the thirties as a Wall Street reformer. However, shortages in his accounts soon were discovered. The suspect appeared in my father's office a few days later, pulled out a gun, handed it to the stunned managing partner, and told him to take it or he would use it on himself. He confessed to the misdeeds and eventually went to prison.

In a third case, a partner resigned after being charged with manipulating a stock in violation of SEC rules. It didn't help that his name was Joseph Merrill. Though he was no relation to the directing partner, he had been with CEM since shortly after World War I, and for most of that time he had been a full partner.

Despite the bad press emanating from these three men's transgressions, by early 1941 CEM had another PR coup. He announced that Merrill Lynch would open its books to the public by publishing an Annual Report. Once again Wall Street was startled, dismayed, and skeptical. Once again Charlie Merrill was setting an example that other brokerages did not want to follow. The Annual Report was a departure from custom and tradition to a degree that can scarcely be exaggerated. No private partnership had ever lay bare its balance sheets for anyone to see. Such action was not required, or even recommended, by the SEC or the New York Stock Exchange. And no one could accuse CEM of bragging, for the first report released would show a firm operating in the red. The report recorded a net loss for the period April 1, 1940, the date of the merger, to January 3, 1941, of

$308,621.31. However, it also called attention to the fact that during this period Merrill Lynch, E. A. Pierce & Cassatt had abolished the then-common practice of charging for services related to, for example, dividend collection, collection of rights and interest, coupon clipping, and the like; reduced commissions to the lowest level allowed by the New York Stock Exchange; and cut the interest rate charged customers on debit balances. And in case anyone had missed the initial gush of publicity the previous spring, the report contained a list of nine commandments.

Merrill was counting on his bold move of issuing an Annual Report to further earn the trust of the investing public and to garner more favorable, free publicity. And it did. Ralph Hendershot, financial editor of the *New York World-Telegram*, commented on March 25, 1941: "The novelty of the report is probably as important as the report itself. The firm is a partnership rather than a corporation, which means it has no outside stockholders. But it deals with the public, and the public has a right to know something about its financial affairs and policies. Mr. Merrill is to be congratulated on recognizing this fact, and he deserves any recognition he may get by being the first to do something about it." The Annual Report was similarly applauded by newspapers from coast to coast. Moreover, in subsequent years the Merrill Lynch Annual Report became a popular barometer for all of the securities industry—as Merrill Lynch goes, so goes Wall Street—and it was the single biggest source of positive publicity year after year.

Nevertheless, the bleak financial picture was very real. Michael W. McCarthy, who had been brought in from Safeway to streamline paperwork operations (and would lead ML seventeen years later), met with Merrill early in the life of the new firm.

"We both smoked very heavily at the time," McCarthy recalled, "and it wasn't long before all the ashtrays were filled. I almost had a heart attack when I saw the profit-and-loss figures. Believe me, they were pretty bad. In fact they were awful. The bottom line was in the red and it was bigger than the gross income figure at the top of the page. The expenses were so much higher than the income that I thought Charlie was holding the book upside down."

Using my father as his hatchet man, Merrill imposed stringent economy measures that were designed to cut overhead by $1 million.

Partners' salaries were cut. Account executives and office managers were required to pay for memberships in local fraternal, social, and service clubs. After a study found that 85 percent of a brokerage's business was done by telephone, branch offices were closed in favor of smaller, less expensive quarters. "It is perfectly damned nonsense to maintain a gilded palace to take care of 15 percent," CEM intoned. Thus the Atlanta Merrill Lynch branch was moved to a smaller third-floor office where the monthly rent was $85. To save the expense of a boy to mark a blackboard, the office listed stock quotations on a sheet of paper tacked to a board. Even Western Union clocks, which were leased for $1.75 a month, were removed from all offices. The home office set an example by moving from 40 Wall Street to 70 Pine Street, at an annual savings of about $50,000. Wire costs were slashed by $160,000 million through consolidation to eliminate duplication.

At the New York headquarters, many aspects of the old Pierce operation, bearing the unmistakable stamp of Ethel Mercereau, were eliminated. One of the first features to go was the tall desks, which required personnel to stand all day. Carpenters sawed part of the legs off the desks so employees could sit. Instead of a guard at the front door making sure arriving and departing employees punched time cards, they were allowed to merely sign in under the honor system. The entire accounting system was modernized so that the performance levels of every division and branch office could be measured instantly.

Meanwhile, Merrill ordered his branch managers to intensify their efforts to recruit new customers: "What we need is real salesmen to go out and sell stocks, men who will find these thousands upon thousands of new potential investors, men who are willing to work and who have confidence in the future of their country to sell the people on the idea that shares in American industry are more worthwhile than paper money." Merrill himself sought new customers by telephone and letter. On June 20, 1940, he wrote directly to Philip K. Wrigley, the chewing gum and baseball mogul from Chicago whom he barely knew, seeking him as an account. Wrigley declined the offer. CEM made sure everyone knew that neither family ties nor old school ties were going to carry any weight at Merrill Lynch, E. A. Pierce & Cassatt. "I hold no brief for the so-called country club boys," he said. "What we need is ordinary, straightforward, hardworking fellows who will follow the program and everlastingly stick to it."

Arthur Kerrigan, a partner who was in charge of floor brokers in the early days, often told the story of CEM and E. A. Pierce discussing a candidate for floor broker. Pierce thought there was a good man on the bond floor, but expressed reservations because the man had no college education and his parents were Italian immigrants.

CEM: "Does he have ability?"

EAP: "Best broker around."

"Does he have any money?"

"No."

"Does he owe any money?"

"No."

"Where does he live?"

"A small apartment uptown."

"Does his wife work?"

"Yes, does all her housework and has an outside job as well."

"Well, good God, what more background do you want?"

The man was hired.

But the immediate rush of cold calls and bell-ringings on the part of the sales force proved ineffective because they were inexperienced in the overall securities business. For example, in Chicago there were account executives who knew a lot about commodities but little about stocks and bonds. In other offices, the reverse was true. Merrill had sent his people home from the Waldorf conference with a bulky portfolio that held large-type renditions of those nine basic business principles for the new Merrill Lynch, and he'd issued the portfolios with these marching orders: "Every salesman will have a portfolio—and when I say salesman I mean every man in this organization, partner, salesman, or clerk, every representative of our firm—and when he goes to call on that customer, he must carry our principles to the public." Though well-intentioned, it was not one of CEM's better ideas. One of the branch managers who lugged the simulated-leather, zippered, twenty-four-by-eighteen-inch portfolio home recalled: "What we had to do—and I did it and I assume that all the other people did it, too—was we had to take that damn thing and call on our customers, sit it up on the desk and try to show it to them. I can remember feeling a little embarrassed about this thing, but we had to try to show them what we were attempting to do—there it was in black and white, and we abided by that."

Eventually, Merrill recognized the flaws in this approach and introduced a series of three phonograph records that were intended to train ML salesmen and ensure that they all were giving out the same information. The recordings include an imaginary conversation between a Merrill Lynch account executive and a prospective customer. An excerpt: "Now, we definitely don't think, Mr. Withered, that we are any smarter or better than anyone else in this securities business, but at least we have a plan for building a better product for some customers and we think this is the only way for us to proceed. That is the idea, as you see on this page, a kind of public utility slant—a recognition of the customers' rights and a determination on our part to satisfy them." Though the canned sales talk did no better than the portfolios in boosting sales, the two halting steps were the first shots in a revolution Merrill would bring to Wall Street in 1945.

Behind Merrill's early efforts to cut costs and boost sales was a damning statistic: The firm had an average income per transaction of $10.17 and an average cost of $14.29. According to Merrill, "When you figure that one of our clients, the Carnation Milk company, can content the cow, milk it, pasteurize the milk, put the milk in the can, put a label on it, put it in a box, advertise it, and ship it all over the world, and sell the can of milk for five cents, then you realize how perfectly frantic these figures make me feel." At first, the results of their efforts to change this were discouraging—the cost of a single transaction actually rose to $15.05 by the end of 1940. But one year later it had shrunk to $9.91—a one-third reduction.

The first, abbreviated year of the new company was difficult. It struggled with a new and complicated salaried reimbursement plan that replaced the easy-to-administer commission system, but by December 31, nearly 13,000 new accounts had been opened—most of them by individuals with $2,000 or less to invest who had never owned a stock or bond. Advertising and low commissions were beginning to pay off.

Merrill was always on the lookout for growth opportunities, and in the first year of the firm's business he acquired several small brokerages. Then sometime in early 1941 my father was approached by representatives of Fenner & Beane, the nation's largest commodity house and second only to Merrill Lynch, E. A. Pierce & Cassatt in securities: They were interested in a merger. Cofounder Alpheus C. Beane had died in 1937, and his successor was ailing. Charles E. Fenner, the other original partner, did not want the business to fall into the hands of Beane's son and namesake, Alpheus Junior, whom he felt was inadequate for the task. Fenner & Beane had been founded in New Orleans in 1916 and traded cotton. It expanded into securities in 1919, and as the firm grew, it gained CEM's attention for its advertising programs and its advocacy of Wall Street reforms. In 1923, Pierce had proposed a merger of his firm with Fenner & Beane; the deal was near consummation when it foundered on a single issue—what to name the new brokerage. Cofounders Alpheus Beane and Charles Fenner wanted their names on the door; Pierce would have none of it, and the deal collapsed.

Now, eighteen years later, Fenner was prepared to yield on the name issue and suggested that the combined firm be called The Merrill Company. Fenner's son, who was at the meeting, recalls CEM responding: "I prefer the full name of Merrill, Lynch, Pierce, Fenner & Beane. A name like that will be a challenge to anyone's memory, and everyone will make an effort to remember it." The negotiations at New York's Commodore Hotel took less than a week and resulted in the marriage of the two largest firms in the brokerage industry on August 18, 1941. The new firm had offices in ninety-three cities (including one in Havana, Cuba) and memberships on twenty-eight exchanges. Despite the long name, Charlie Merrill was the man in charge, with a 55 percent ownership in the firm.

It was a rough transition for many of the Fenner & Beane people, especially salesmen who had to accept the new salaried compensation plan. Two important F&B partners, Victor Cook and Norman Weiden, decided Merrill's grand plan was not going to work, and they made plans to go into business for themselves. When he heard of the mutiny, CEM asked the pair to come to his office for fifteen minutes, and they consented as a courtesy. "Well, here are the two renegades," CEM greeted them as he opened the meeting at three-thirty one afternoon. "What is it about the firm you don't like?" Merrill took up their objections one by one. Seven hours later the trio was finishing off dinner and drinks at the '21' restaurant—and Cook and Weiden were on the Merrill Lynch team. Charlie had persuaded them, as Cook recalled, that his plans for the new firm "were based on strong personal conviction and great knowledge of Wall Street." As for CEM's negotiating skills, Cook said: "It was impossible to talk to that man for ten minutes without realizing that he knew as much about your problems and was as honestly anxious to solve them as yourself." Cook was tapped to head Merrill Lynch's largest sales office, which was located at 70 Pine, and he managed that important office for the next twenty-five years. Weiden worked out of the same office and became one of the greatest salesmen in Wall Street history. Shortly after his meeting with Merrill, Weiden went into the Army for three years, but even there he managed more sales than most of his civilian colleagues. As a staff sergeant, he took customers' orders in uniform from a pay phone at Fort Dix, New Jersey. In the postwar years, he did so much business that he was assigned his own call letters on the Merrill Lynch wire system. He had a staff of four with thirty-five telephone lines, and generated as much as $2 million a year in commissions, an enormous sum in those days and still impressive seven decades later.

Both Vic and Norman played crucial roles in the development of the early Merrill Lynch, and both of them became close friends of my parents. Like so many at Merrill Lynch, after my father's death in 1961, they were a huge source of support to my mother and were incredibly nice to me, an eleven-year-old. By the time I knew "Mr. Cook," he was nearly blind, but that did not prevent him from running Merrill Lynch's largest and most profitable office. Many of the firm's future managers started with Vic in SD, which was the wire code for the New York Sales Department. Besides being a top-notch salesman, he was also a talented pianist. He couldn't read a note, but could play any tune by ear and was the life of the party in his penthouse apartment.

Norman Weiden could be rough, crude, and foul mouthed, but he had a heart of gold and was an incredible salesman, covering most of the New York City banks as well as other large institutional accounts, and generating tremendous revenue for the firm. And, after his meeting with Charlie Merrill, there was no greater believer and champion of this new firm than Norman. When Merrill Lynch went public in 1971, everyone was amazed to discover that Norman was the second-largest shareholder after the Merrill family.

As successful and wealthy as Weiden became, he lived unpretentiously, and on most days my father and one or two others would go to 70 Pine Street in Norman's personal car—chauffeurs and limousines were not their style. Often in later years, Norman would hear about an employee who through no fault of his own had encountered financial difficulty. He would write out a check and have it delivered to that person.

Victor Cook and Norman Weiden were noteworthy, but many others from Fenner & Beane played an important role in the development of Merrill Lynch, Pierce, Fenner & Beane as well. It was a game-changing merger that put the firm on the path to profitability and a leadership position in the postwar Wall Street. In fact, it was the first of several important acquisitions that Merrill Lynch made over the next sixty years.

O n August 18, 1941, the day the deal was finalized, the telephone operators at 70 Pine Street began answering the calls with, "Good morning. Merrill Lynch, Pierce, Fenner and Beane." It was the beginning of one of the longest-running gags in Wall Street history (e.g., a timid investor inquires whether the firm's recommendation was unanimous or a simple majority). At various times, the firm would be called "Charlie Merrill and His Merry Men," "The Bureau of Missing Persons," and "The Thundering Herd," but it was "We the People" that delighted CEM the most. He used it frequently in advertising and promotional materials, and it became the name of ML's in-house publication. Just a few weeks after the Fenner & Beane merger, the *New Yorker* magazine carried an item in its whimsical "Talk of the Town" section that began:

> Last week we felt dizzily like a party to some of Wall Street's deeper complexities when we called in at the offices of Merrill Lynch, E. A. Pierce & Cassatt the afternoon that firm amalgamated with Fenner & Beane to form the largest brokerage-and-investment house in the United

States—Merrill Lynch, Pierce, Fenner & Beane (please don't ask us what happened to Cassatt), ninety-three offices in ninety-one cities and membership in twenty-eight security and commodity exchanges. This merger was the culmination of a series of earlier ones, beginning in April, 1940, when Merrill Lynch consolidated with E. A. Pierce & Co. and Cassatt & Co., forming Merrill Lynch, E. A. Pierce & Cassatt, which last May absorbed Fuller, Rodney & Co., Banks, Huntley & Co., and three offices of Sutro Bros. & Co. The idea of people having to make out checks to Merrill Lynch, E. A. Pierce & Cassatt, Fuller, Rodney, Banks, Huntley, and three offices of Sutro Bros. & Co. was apparently too much for all concerned, so several of the names disappeared, like Cassatt. We never did find out what happened to Cassatt.

Despite the merger, 1941 was a grim year for Merrill Lynch. Market activity was at its lowest point since 1921, with some 171 million shares traded on the NYSE for the entire twelve months. Merrill was determined to end the year in the black, and in December he worked out an underwriting deal with Fisher Brothers, a Cleveland-based grocery chain, after which he sent a telegram to all salesmen stating that he expected each of them to sell 100 shares of the Fisher preferred, even if they had to sell them to their grandmothers. "Almost everybody performed," according to Winthrop ("Win") H. Lenz, a future ML partner, "and they didn't have to call on too many grandmothers." As a result of CEM's persistence, the firm ended the year with a profit of $459,258. That trend of profitability lasted until 1987 when Merrill reported its first annual loss since 1940.

Of course, 1941 was a grim year for America as well. A few weeks after the Japanese attack on Pearl Harbor, MLFP&B announced that it would aggressively sell Defense bonds. "These securities, by reason of the National Emergency, have become the number one consideration with our firm," said a company press release. The firm's nearly one hundred offices, its 24,000 miles of leased wire, and its growing advertising expertise were committed to the bond effort. Merrill's motivations were not wholly patriotic, though, for he still believed that the bond program would introduce millions of ordinary Americans to the wisdom of systematic investing.

Nearly four hundred employees departed to serve in the Armed Forces, including Bob Magowan, who left the firm in early 1942 to serve with the Navy in the Pacific. Beginning January 1, 1943, each of them received a monthly payment of $25 to supplement their military pay. Many of the departed employees were from the critical "backstage" operation, and Merrill's motivation was at least in part an attempt to stay in touch with them so they would return to the MLPF&B fold at war's end.

One of Merrill Lynch's least-known contributions to the war effort involved espionage. For several years before the war, President Roosevelt had worried about German influence in Central and South America, and in August 1940, he established a special office under Nelson Rockefeller, who enlisted the aid of some 1,700 companies that did business there. The British, who had the most experienced espionage apparatus, had always taken businessmen and trained them as spies, but the U.S. was in a hurry and figured it would be faster to take spies and train them as businessmen. A training school was established under the Federal Bureau of Investigation (this was before the creation of the Office of Strategic Services (OSS) and its successor, the Central Intelligence Agency), and several of the first graduates were assigned to Merrill Lynch. One of them was twenty-six-year-old Kenneth M. Crosby, who was then trained as a stockbroker at 70 Pine Street. He and the others were treated like any other employees. Only Merrill, my father, Pierce, and, later, Magowan, knew of their dual role.

"Everyone else," recalls Crosby, "was told this story: 'Charlie Merrill had a vision that Latin America would be the great growth area in the future for Merrill Lynch after the war and that he, at his own expense and at no expense to the partnership, was going to arrange to train a few young men to go down to Latin America, into the major countries, open offices and begin to develop contacts and business leads.'" Crosby was assigned to Argentina—officially neutral in the war but in fact a hotbed of pro-Axis espionage activity—and in March 1942 he arrived in Buenos Aires with his Merrill Lynch files, an FBI code book masked as a Spanish-English dictionary, and a Parker Ink bottle filled with disappearing ink to file his reports to J. Edgar Hoover. The cover worked well. Business was so brisk that Crosby had to hire a local broker to help out. His quest for intelligence information frequently took him to the most spectacular nightclub in Buenos Aires, the Tabors, a notorious hangout for European spies. One of the hostesses was an aspiring singer-actress named Eva Duarte. "She was one of many hostesses," says Crosby. "You could buy them drinks and dance with them." It is believed that this is where she met Juan Perón, whom she would marry in 1945. In later years she would come to be known as the nation's beloved Evita. Soon after Perón seized power in 1945, the dictator denounced Crosby by name, abruptly ending his assignment in Buenos Aires. Crosby met Perón many years later in Madrid, and the two reconciled their personal differences. After the war, Crosby cast his lot with Merrill Lynch rather than the FBI and became a partner in 1981.

Crosby's early adventures with Merrill Lynch in Argentina set the stage for the firm in later years to understand the potential of this market. As part of a South American tour, my parents and I went to Buenos Aires in the summer of 1956. Perón had just been deposed in a military coup, and my father visited the recently reopened stock exchange. Thirty-seven years later I stood on that same Exchange floor as trading began in the initial public offering of YPF, Argentina's privatized oil company and at the time the largest privatization every done. Our position as co-global manager established our credibility and opened up a decade of successes in leading privatization around the world. Ironically, our foray into espionage in 1942 ultimately led to a very successful and profitable private wealth, debt and equity trading, and investment banking business for Merrill Lynch in Argentina in the 1990s.

With so many of the firm's employees having left to serve in the military, CEM realized that many of the backstage jobs would have to be filled by women, and in anticipation of this, a program was set up in January 1942 in which female high-school graduates were trained to be clerks and teletype operators. On April 28, 1943, eighteen-year-old Helen Handelian walked onto the floor of the New York Stock Exchange wearing the yellow-tan gabardine uniform of Merrill Lynch, Pierce, Fenner & Beane, becoming the first woman to work on the floor in the 151-year history of the NYSE. Despite initial reservations about the program, many of the women turned out to be as good as or better than their male counterparts. However, at the end of the war, most of the women had to give up their jobs to the returning men. Thirty years later the Equal Employment Opportunity Commission would sue Merrill Lynch over its "discriminatory practices," and this regulatory action eventually opened Wall Street to women. While Merrill Lynch was singled out because of its size and leadership position, the truth is that every other firm had an equally poor or worse record.

Back in the summer of 1939, CEM had spent several weeks in Europe, and when he returned he decided to gear his personal investment strategy to the coming war. He ordered Milija Rubezanin, his research chief, to monitor radio broadcasts and inform him immediately upon the outbreak of war. Rubezanin telephoned CEM in Southampton early on the morning of September 1, 1939, and when the market opened later that day, a series of trades were executed on behalf of Merrill Lynch and Safeway. There is no record of the long-term results of these transactions, but one unpublished biography suggests "a substantial gain."

The following spring, as the Nazis were overrunning France, Merrill summoned the senior staff of the Research Department and, as one of them remembers it, said: "There is something very important that I want you to do for me, but I want you to be very sure that you understand what I do not want you to do for me. I'm not interested in your views as to what will happen to the French when France falls. I have already made up my mind on that, and I can tell you, France will fall. Secondly, I am not interested at all in what you think will happen to our stock market when France collapses. I have already made up my mind on that. The stock market will go to hell in a handbasket. What I do want you to do, very carefully and imaginatively, is prepare a list of not more than fifteen or twenty stocks at the outside, that I will be buying when France falls and the stock market collapses." As he left the meeting, he said, "Incidentally, the amount of money I plan to put out in the market is about $2 million." About a week later, the Nazis goose-stepped into Paris. My mother and father did not meet until after the war, but during the wars years, my mother was one of the nation's leading models for the Robert Powers agency and was the "poster girl" for a number of ads promoting war bonds. And thus in her own way she was helping her future husband's and his partner's business efforts long before they met.

Motivated by self-interest, America's newspapers (there was no television, and ML did virtually no radio advertising) looked favorably upon Merrill Lynch's pioneering effort in financial advertising, which was aimed at selling the firm as trustworthy rather than convincing investors to buy a particular product. It began with a $100,000 campaign put together by Rudy Guenther's firm. Other partners had objected to this large expenditure, but CEM insisted on it. Part of his motivation was to make inroads into the financial securities market, which until now had been dominated by the life insurance companies, which used extensive advertising that featured widows and orphaned children in emotional, vivid detail. One of the insurance firms, Equitable Life, would even sponsor a CBS radio program, *The FBI in Peace and War*, in an effort to identify with an icon of American security.

Although the NYSE had recently liberalized its advertising rules, up until this time most financial advertising consisted of genteel "tombstone ads"—routine, all-text announcements of a coming sale of stocks or bonds followed by the underwriter's name and a long list of the members of the underwriting syndicate. For the ML ads, Merrill demanded that illustrations be used, accompanied by "snappy copy" that "put color, human interest and romance into what is so often dry and uninteresting." The "opening gong" (in CEM's phrase) was a series of ads in *Time* magazine, which had a circulation of about 750,000, that began by outlining the company's nine principles and, in subsequent weeks, discussed each in detail. The *Time* ads covered two-thirds of a page and ran for twenty-eight consecutive weeks.

The ad campaign also targeted daily newspapers in cities that had Merrill Lynch offices. An early newspaper ad for war bonds ran a full page under the banner headline 50 DESTROYERS FOR ENGLAND! Most of the investment community was affronted and dismayed by the Merrill Lynch ads and considered them unseemly and improper. The October 26, 1941, issue of *Time* contained two deceptive Merrill Lynch ads that were carefully designed to appear as though they belonged in the news columns. Written in the breezy *Time* style, they even purported to quote a memo from CEM that was leaked and never intended for public use. In truth, all of the "news" was self-serving, unalloyed praise for the new firm.

One of the most effective early advertising campaigns was the brainchild of John H. "Jack" Moller, a senior researcher, who developed it over a weekend. It set up eight hypothetical portfolios, ranging between $2,000 and $100,000, using well-known stocks like General Motors and Paramount Pictures. CEM was delighted with the concept, and transferred Moller to the Sales Promotion Department. Not long afterward, Moller chanced to meet Merrill in the third-floor men's room at 70 Pine Street. As Moller recalls: "Merrill came in and greeted me very cordially, and said, 'Jack, I really want to compliment you most highly on the chemical industry survey that you did.' I'm standing there feeling no pain at all. Merrill is standing there, combing his hair. He finally looked over and said, 'Oh, Jack, let me add a little word of information and advice after the compliments I have been handing you on that survey.' I said, 'Yes, sir, what?' And he said, 'I have found it a very useful technique that you always follow a pat on the back with a good swift kick in the ass.' So, he said, 'Don't forget to duck.' I said, 'I'll remember.'" This was a line that Bill Schreyer paraphrased years later when he used to say: "Just remember that a pat on the back is only a few inches away from a kick in the ass."

While he left most operational details in the hands of subordinates, Merrill kept a hand in every phase of advertising and promotion. When one proposed ad came to his desk for approval, he sent it back with a scathing memo:

> This advertisement is an example of what not to do with advertising space. I would like to have it re-set as per the enclosed sketch, as a two-column ad. I would also like to have it rewritten so that all the words used in the ad itself will be as short as possible and as clear as possible.
>
> My objection to our ad is that it is ineffective because the illustration on our booklet is a Grade A illustration and it fights with the illustration of a dinner table which, to be most optimistic, is a Grade C illustration. Of course, the whole thing is a matter of taste. I think it is both poor taste and poor business to spoil a good illustration by making it compete with a poor one. I also think there is no excuse for having two illustrations in one financial ad.

Furthermore, I would recommend that we get back to first principles. The first principle to keep in mind in spending money for advertising is that we certainly have a right to expect the use of as much brains in the preparation of a $20,000 ad as a home owner would have the right to expect in drawing the plans for a $20,000 house. The only difference is that the architect gets a considerably smaller fee in percents than the agency gets for its services.

The ad as sketched by me is, of course, not drawn entirely to scale, but I hope I have made my point clear.

Wall Street had been brought to Main Street. For the first time, the small investor felt comfortable knowing that their interests came first and they felt comfortable coming into the offices of Merrill Lynch.

Win Smith and Bob Magowan in 1955 at the Merrill Lynch "How to Invest Show" in Manhattan. Considered the most ambitious attempt ever made to explain Wall Street, the show included mechanized dioramas, lighted tableaux, and a movie.

CHAPTER SIX

Investigate
Before You Invest

(1942–1957)

I t wasn't until 1957 that "Smith" became part of the firm's name. The recognition was overdue, for just as surely as Charlie Merrill's vision and capital make him the founder of the firm, it was my father's genius for organization and conciliation, as well as his ability to work with Charlie, that helped to build it into the nation's largest brokerage and ultimately one of the world's leading financial firms by 2001. And, of course, it was he who singlehandedly persuaded CEM to get back into the securities business in the first place—and then carried out their dream of bringing Wall Street to Main Street.

When my father returned to New York in 1940, he devoted most of his waking hours to building the new Merrill Lynch, but a couple of years later his life outside the office took a turn for the better when he was introduced to a beautiful Robert Powers model from Washington, D.C., named Vivian Gordon Linke, who went by the name of Carol Carter professionally.

My mother was born Vivian Gordon Brown on December 16, 1903, in Washington, D.C., and was the youngest of three sisters. Her father, a successful Washington attorney, was born and raised in Richmond, Virginia, and both her mother and father's lineage traced back to the early settlers of Jamestown. At the age of nineteen my mother married a career naval officer, Gerald Linke, and had two sons, Gerald and Gordon. Tragically, at the age of three, Gerald found some matches and set his nightshirt on fire. While he was burned badly, it was actually an overdose of Adrenalin administered to him by a nurse in the hospital that caused his heart to fail. It was an event that haunted my mother for the rest of her life.

My mother eventually divorced Linke. After her sister Marjorie's husband, Richard Buchanan, a young Marine, was killed while fighting the Sandinista guerillas in Nicaragua, the family's economic situation changed dramatically. Marjorie had three young daughters, Ann, Betty, and Aileen, and the sisters agreed that Marjorie would watch their combined four children while Vivian would find work to support the family. My mother was a classic beauty who had prematurely silver-gray hair, and this enabled her to land a job with the prestigious John Robert Powers modeling agency in New York, where she became one of Powers's "long-stem roses"—one of the top models of that day. With her youthful looks and gray hair she modeled the latest fashions and also became the poster face for the WAVES in World War II.

One day my father asked my mother to join him and some other Merrill partners, as well as two of Charlie Merrill's grandsons, Robin and Merrill Lynch Magowan, at a baseball game at Yankee Stadium. They sat in the Merrill Lynch seats near home plate and were enjoying the game and the sunny summer day. As Merrill Magowan recalled, "I was nine years old and short for my age. Yankee Stadium had a very graduated escalation in the lower deck where we were sitting, and it was hard for me to see. Around the fourth inning Vivian took pity on me and exchanged seats. On the very next pitch Dom DiMaggio, the brother of Joe who played for the Boston Red Sox, hit a line drive foul ball right at us. Vivian instinctively moved her face toward me to protect me, and the ball smashed into her nose." My mother, dressed in a white dress, fell unconscious into my father's lap. She was covered with blood.

Knowing that Robin and Merrill would be cared for by the other partners in attendance, Dad rushed my mother to the hospital. She recovered, but she lived with sinus problems for the rest of her life. Dom DiMaggio came to visit her in the hospital, but she was always bothered by the fact that no one from the Yankees ever contacted her. Much to my father's horror, she became a Red Sox fan after that. In these litigious times, some might find it curious that she never sued, but that was not her nature. I once asked her why she had not sued the Yankees, and she explained: "It was a foul ball, after all, and it wasn't Dom's fault that I didn't duck, so why would I sue?" As terrible as that moment was in 1947, I have often wondered what fate brought with it. Was it out of sympathy that my longtime bachelor father proposed to my mother shortly afterward. Perhaps I owe Dom DiMaggio thanks for my own existence.

Merrill Magowan mentioned to me years later that he had the same birthday as my father, and Dad always called him to wish him a happy birthday. While he was not at this game, Merrill's other grandson Peter Magowan went on to buy the San Francisco Giants after stepping down as CEO of Safeway Stores. Ironically, Ken Crosby was also at Yankee Stadium that day to witness the accident, and he told me about it: "I saw this woman in a white dress covered with blood being taken out of the stadium, and I thought she was dead. I had no idea at the time that it was your mother-to-be."

Ken Crosby was the manager of ML's retail office in Havana, Cuba, office at the time, and one day he received a teletype message from my father: "Ken, I am confidentially letting you know that I am getting married to Vivian Linke. I would like you to help me arrange a quiet three day honeymoon in Cuba, but I don't want anyone to know and don't want any fanfare. Thank you for your help. 73's, Win." ("73s" was a shorthand for "best wishes" used on telegrams and by ham radio operators.)

Ken and his first wife, Cricket, became very close friends of both my father and mother, and later Ken and his second wife, Peggy, became close friends of mine, and we shared many fine moments together when we both worked for Merrill Lynch in Washington, D.C.

Ken had joined Merrill Lynch as a "real" employee after his FBI assignment in Buenos Aires. No one ever knew whether Ken ever actually left the CIA, which took over from the FBI after the war. After artfully preventing Fidel Castro from seizing the assets of Merrill Lynch clients after he came to power, Ken closed the Havana office and moved to manage the Madrid, Spain, office and later moved back to head Merrill's main office in Washington, D.C. Over the years, Merrill Lynch's CEOs often had confidential conversations with the CIA and cooperated with them in a number of ways. During the time I served as chairman of Merrill Lynch International, I occasionally met with some CIA analysts to share information about the business and political climate in certain countries and I was always amazed at their lack of knowledge in those days when the CIA seemed to have lost its way prior to 9/11.

Shortly after my father and mother were married, they decided that even at their mature ages they wanted to have a child. My mother had not given birth for twenty-one years, but she became pregnant at forty-five and I was born when she was forty-six. My father was fifty-six and his first son, Bardwell, was twenty-five at the time. My mother's first son, Gordon Linke, was twenty-one at this time. After graduating from Bowdoin College and serving in the Marine Corps, he would begin a successful career of his own at Merrill Lynch. Gordon was a great friend and older brother and he also had a wonderful relationship with my father. Because my mother was in her mid-forties when she became pregnant with me, it was a risky pregnancy, but on a hot summer day, August 5, 1949, I was born without any complications in New York's Leroy Sanitarium. A few days later we made our way to Morris, Connecticut, in Litchfield County, where two years earlier my mother and father had purchased a 113-acre farm with a 1775 saltbox colonial that they restored. The farm was renamed Winvian for "Win" and "Vivian." Like my father, I was introduced to investing early in life when Charlie Merrill gave me a couple of shares of Safeway and Winn Dixie as a birth present. Twenty years later they had appreciated sufficiently to pay for the final two years of my Amherst tuition.

I have so many happy memories of Dad at the farm. We raised sheep, pigs, and pheasants in those days and I loved riding around our farm on the tractor with my father. Today the farm is still called Winvian but has been transformed into a spectacular Relais & Chateaux Spa Retreat and is owned by my former wife, Maggie, and managed by my eldest daughter, Heather. My son, Win III, is the director of Sales and Marketing. My mother and father's portraits, along with other family mementoes, are prominently displayed in the house, which is now the centerpiece of this exclusive retreat.

Coincidentally, just five miles away in Bethlehem, Connecticut, another rising star in the investment world, Bill Ruane, also purchased a farm a few years later. His young son, Billy, and his daughter, Lili, began riding at the Litchfield stable where I worked summers after my father passed away. I helped Billy learn to ride. When I was sixteen, I sold my pony named Rousty to the elder Bill Ruane as a present for his son and daughter. One August day in 1965, I delivered Rousty to their farm. Apparently, Lili (ten years my junior) had a crush on me and was eagerly waiting in the courtyard for my arrival. I clearly remember a cute little girl with shiny blond hair, and I think that was the last time I saw her until we had a chance meeting in Vermont at the Burlington airport forty-four years later. We were married on August 11, 2011, on the mountain at Sugarbush and now have a combined family of eight wonderful children and four grandchildren so far. Ironically, when I became chairman of Merrill Lynch International in 1992, Bill Ruane was considering an investment in Merrill Lynch for his Sequoia Fund. As was his practice, Bill was conducting extensive due diligence and interviewed me for some time about our international business. He never made an investment, however, because he did not believe that Merrill had great growth in its future. I have always thought that this was one of Bill Ruane's few investment mistakes.

My father died when I was eleven years old. I wish I'd gotten to have him longer than that. I think about him every day. However, I am fortunate to have worked with so many people who knew him and could pass on tales about how he influenced their lives and how he set the tone that established the culture that allowed our firm to grow and innovate and yet retain its basic principles and rock-solid foundation. My dad was and is my hero, and throughout my life has been my mentor in spirit.

In 1944, Charlie Merrill suffered a heart attack that left him disabled and unable to continue in an active role as directing partner. While my father took over the day-to-day direction of the firm, from that time until 1957 (when his name replaced that of Beane at the end of the partnership's name), he was virtually unknown to the investing public. Despite his power and prestige, my father lived very modestly and came to work every day in a four-man carpool from his Manhattan apartment on East Seventy-second Street. He was not interested in the pretentiousness of Greenwich or Southampton, and he preferred riding his tractor and farming on the weekends in Connecticut. His New England roots never left him. Win and Vivian are buried side by side at the Litchfield Cemetery.

Dad's perch in the managing partner's chair often teetered because CEM's participation was irregular, ranging from focused supervision to forced inattention. In the early years Merrill Lynch was not so much a unit as a federation of several firms, each of which brought its own cast of egos—Homer P. Hargrave in Chicago, Ferdinand C. Smith in San Francisco, Lyman McFie in Los Angeles, Edwin O. Cartwright in Dallas, Francis C. Hunter in Washington, Gus E. Ledbetter in Seattle, John J. Gurian in Portland, T. Johnson Ward in Philadelphia, the Fenners in New Orleans. These were all names I grew up hearing. Each ran a fiefdom that sometimes clashed with the others. Each fiefdom had its own strengths and weaknesses. There were old alliances and loyalties that predated the formation of Merrill Lynch, Pierce, Fenner & Beane. Wedged between this disunity and Charlie Merrill's wavering degrees of participation, my father managed to forge a dynamic enterprise that became the envy of its competitors and a model for them to follow.

And most remarkably of all, he achieved all this while becoming one of the best-loved executives in the history of American business. One of his successors, William Schreyer, put it best: "Some people get respect, some affection. Win Smith got both." Over the years, as I met more and more people who knew my father, I was increasingly amazed at the affection they had for him. My brother, Bardwell, also remarked that he never met anyone who did not like and respect our father.

Perhaps the unkindest words ever written about Dad came from Boris Polevoy, a leading Russian editor who accompanied a delegation of Soviet journalists that visited ML headquarters in 1955 as part of an American tour. Polevoy wrote a book about his experiences called *American Diary*, and in it he described meeting the managing partner: "Mr. Smith had the appearance of a kindly grandfather who on Sunday gives candy to his grandchildren and takes them to church or the circus. . . . But it was sensed he was accustomed to great power and his right to spit on the opinion of those around him."

By the time of Merrill's heart attack and disability in 1944, MLPF&B had been given a lean, efficient structure that was primed to move the firm into the postwar bull market. The firm's distribution network was second to none. Although for the final twelve years of his life, CEM would remain a powerful figurehead, insomuch as he was the principal owner of the partnership, the fact remains that by this point he was essentially a consultant. Though his participation was sporadic, there were periods of intense activity in company affairs, and in these times he tended to focus on advertising and promotion. This remote-control management from Southampton, Florida, and Barbados (where he eventually owned a home) could not have worked without the self-effacing temperament and leadership of my father and, to a lesser extent, Robert Magowan and Michael McCarthy.

One of the positive aspects of Merrill's absence is that it enabled him to focus on the big picture away from the distractions at 70 Pine. As my father said after Charlie's death: "He had a better perspective of what was happening to the business as a whole, and to our firm in particular, than he might have had had he been actually participating in the day to day events." CEM himself verbalized this in a 1946 letter to Dean Witter: "I have been out in the Gulf Stream a number of times sail fishing and playing quite a bit of bridge in the afternoon and am taking a renewed interest in business. In many ways I think I am much more helpful to the firm by not being engaged in the hurly burly of day-to-day business, for now I have the opportunity to look at matters objectively, to study the more fundamental and important aspects of both our own business and the industry in general." McCarthy also saw a positive side to the boss's infirmity: "Maybe from the standpoint of the firm it was better that it happened that way. It forced us to take ahold, rather than wait to the last minute, when sometimes you're not ready." Indeed, Merrill's absence from the daily scene paved the way for the development of new leadership.

On his better days, there would be a two-hour, late-morning telephone call to my father. James Merrill remembered his father peppering my father with questions. Why had he not received the monthly report? Why had he not been informed that a partner's spouse was ill? A grandson who spent summers at "the Orchard," Merrill's home in Southampton, described his telephone conversations as ranging from "ranting to tears." Along with the phone calls, Dad was on the receiving end of Merrill memos on every conceivable subject. For example, there was this complaint about the Annual Report in 1947:

> For the past four years I have been irritated because my instructions have not been carried out. These were to have it ready in draft form by November 1st and, with the exception of the statistical data, ready in final form by December 1st. Every year there has been some alibi offered for the lack of preparation and foresight. Frankly I am now tired of all this nonsense. I want you to make this clear and insist on sustained persistent effort so that it will be issued in January as planned and above all be a useful and praiseworthy tool for the entire organization. Kindly show this wire to Braun, Ruby, Mike, Bobby.

As I said, more than any other subject, Merrill focused on advertising and public relations during these years, as evidenced in this memo to my father:

> I am very much concerned about the apparent deterioration in the favorable relations that once existed between our firm and the publishers of newspapers and magazines.
>
> Another instance in which our firm was ignored is the issue of Holiday magazine containing picture after picture of Palm Beach business establishments with the name plainly showing, and yet when it took the picture of the interior of our office they didn't even do us the courtesy to mention our name.
>
> Another instance was an annoying story which appeared in a syndicated column in an Atlanta paper which was sent to me by Homer Hargrave; this story bewailed the fact that there were so many vacant pulpits in the country, and threw out a gratuitous remark to the effect that rewards obtainable by employment with "Fenner & Beane" beguiled men away from the Ministry. Why this columnist should have picked out a concern employing altogether about 3,000 people is just an example of what lengths some writers will go to to coin a phrase they consider interesting and devastating.

Sometimes it seemed that no detail was too small to be ignored by the absent chief. In 1952, Esther King, Merrill's secretary, wrote Dad:

This morning Mr. Merrill wanted to get in touch with an A/E in our Miami office, and when he could not find his name in the new directory, and his home address and phone number, he was upset.

He asked me to write you and suggest that the names of all the Managers, their home phones and addresses, as well as the Back Stage Managers be included in this directory in the future - Just so in case he wants to reach some of them on a Sunday or holiday, at their homes, he can do so.

Dad received complaints from Merrill about the volume of advertising in Miami newspapers, about not receiving his copy of the monthly *Investor's Reader,* and about a perceived lack of attention to smaller clients on the part of the account executives.

To keep Merrill abreast of what was going on, my father would send him, by courier, a daily log of important meetings and decisions. Periodically, he would lead a coterie of executives to Southampton or Palm Beach for meetings with Merrill. The guests usually arrived for a leisurely dinner, and then retired to their rooms for the night. Breakfast was served en suite, and then everyone gathered in the library with CEM. A frequent participant was James Corbett, a future partner who was then in the Research Department. "Merrill would ask us the most penetrating questions," Corbett recalled, "sometimes about our own departments, and sometimes about stuff way outside of our departments. But he'd listen very carefully to what you had to say. And the morning was so doggoned interesting that all of a sudden Merrill would say, 'Well, I think it's time we marked off and had a libation.' I instinctively looked at my wristwatch cause it seemed to me, God, it must be about only eleven o'clock. He'd say to me, 'Jim, it's perfectly all right. The sun is over the yardarm.'" Some four decades later, when Bill Schreyer was CEO, he would paraphrase Charlie and say, "It's time for a drink. The sun must be over the yardarm somewhere in the world."

To keep abreast of what was going on in the world, Merrill read several daily newspapers, especially *The New York Times* and *The Wall Street Journal*, and many MLPF&B partners and managers regularly received clippings from him with applicable comments penciled in. Several times over the years he telephoned a key figure in the firm at 4:59 P.M.–apparently to insure that he was still at his desk and working. During a visit to the San Francisco branch in 1948, he had each account executive describe his territory and then asked who covered the thirty-story Russ Building in which they were sitting. After a long silence, he quipped, "I think that one or a few of you ought to start calling and knocking on doors in the building, because you'll find that there is business right under your own noses." Just two weeks before his death in 1956, Merrill, as was his practice since 1940, read over the final draft of the MLPF&B Annual Report and made changes before it was sent to the printer.

Yet for all his reluctance to fully hand over the reins, Merrill held my father in unalloyed affection, and he lavished praise on him for his abilities at every opportunity. He wrote this letter to Dad in 1952:

> I want you to know how grateful I am to you for the job which you have done since the new firm started out on the long hard campaign which, except for your character, courage, capacity and infinitesimal fortitude might so easily have ended in disaster. To sum it all up, Win, I for one am determined that you shall not escape receiving the lion's share of the gratitude and pride that is in my heart.
>
> When next you see your mother, be sure to tell her that I love her very much and that I know the fact that her boy Winnie who works for Merrill Lynch is responsible for what Merrill Lynch is and hopes to continue to be.

I firmly believe that Dad had as great an influence as Charlie Merrill did on the firm—maybe, in many ways, a greater one. Yet were he alive today, he would never agree with that. It was remarkable how humble and self-effacing he was. His and Merrill's partnership was extraordinary, and is the subject of a chapter in *Co-Leaders: The Power of Great Partnerships* by David A. Heenan and Warren Bennis, who wrote:

> An executive whose light touch was the perfect foil for his boss's bravado, Smith understood the meaning of com-plementary leadership—and used it brilliantly. Look at

some of his more notable achievements. He engineered the company's major acquisitions and assimilated them into Merrill Lynch's innovative culture. He accelerated Merrill Lynch's overseas expansion. He led the push for incorporation and set the stage for the firm's public offering in 1971. He modernized its primitive office and administrative systems. He introduced fresh talent to the organization and trained them in its co-leadership culture. He identified and developed key executives, including several of his successors. Deep leadership and seamless succession were two of his highest priorities.

When Charles Merrill and Winthrop Smith entered Wall Street, Americans were wary stock buyers. At most, only 15 percent of households were in the market. Today almost half of the adult population has money socked away in equities—either directly or through a 401(k) retirement program. The financial world has changed, in large part because of these farsighted co-leaders. Investor confidence is at an all-time high. More people have money in the stock market than ever before.

Working together, Merrill and Smith made ordinary people bullish on America. Thanks to them, people's capitalism is a reality. Besides democratizing investing, they helped provide U.S. industry with much-needed capital for expansion. In tandem they were truly, in Merrill Lynch's famous catch phrase, "a breed apart."

With a round face and ready smile that made him look somewhat like actor Carroll O'Connor, Smith had qualities we sometimes fail to associate with effective leadership: a genial personality, unaffected naturalness, and unfailing optimism. One of Smith's premier skills as an executive was his ability to stand above the fray and disarm antagonists. Company executives report that Smith was the driving force behind the smooth functioning of the disparate elements that comprised Merrill Lynch. It was Smith who was able to reconcile the big egos and competing interests of the newly acquired brokerages. In doing so he was a "wonderful umpire," said Herbert H. Melcher, a partner at the firm. "He [would] listen to any opposing view and understand it." Whereas most big Wall Street houses were loose confederations of super egos with super paychecks, Smith turned Merrill Lynch into that rare outfit that was bigger than the sum of its parts. That kind of synergy is what co-leadership is all about.

There was debate after the financial crisis of 2007–08 over whether corporations should separate the roles of the chairman and the CEO. Maybe they didn't do it consciously, but Charlie Merrill and my father did just that: After his heart attack, CEM assumed the role of the non-executive chairman and my father became the CEO. Even though Charlie did not manage the day-to-day operations, his influence on my father was considerable, and together they became greater than either of them could have been alone. Their effective co-leadership has convinced me that the role of chairman and CEO should be separated for the benefit of all stakeholders. I also realize that what the banking and investment banking world desperately needs today are principled leaders like Merrill and my father, who not only know how to run a profitable business but also have a moral compass and an ability to connect to Main Street.

With Dad running things on a daily basis in New York and Merrill participating when he could from the sidelines, MLPF&B forged ahead and solidified its status as America's No. 1 brokerage in the years after World War II. Innovation continued to be the firm's strong suit, and nowhere was this more evident than in the establishment of a training school in 1945.

The long Depression and the general fall from grace of the securities business had left a vacuum on Wall Street. Since the 1930s, the most able young people interested in business careers had turned to banking, insurance, and other fields—anything but the seedy, greedy pursuit of profit in the stock market. The Street, literally, had lost a generation. As a result, as CEM and my father discovered near the end of the war, the average MLPF&B broker was in his early fifties.

No single individual was responsible for the establishment of the formal training program, which was the firm's most important development in the postwar years, but the experiences of many key people supplied a convincing rationale for its formation. Merrill himself, who was trained as a pilot by the U.S. Army in World War I and then turned the tables by instructing pilots himself, knew the flight-school value of combining classroom teaching with on-the-job experience. Robert Magowan had been enrolled in a training program at the R. H. Macy's department store chain in 1928 before coming to work for his father-in-law, and he was an influential supporter of the idea. And at least some of the impetus came from the program established by Merrill Lynch during the war to train FBI agents like Ken Crosby to go into the field as spies with a cover of being stockbrokers. Then there was Milija Rubezanin, who had come up with a plan as early as May 1941 for the training of account executives. And Ted Braun was a persuasive voice in implementing the concept.

Many other partners resisted the proposal, chiefly because of the expense, but CEM prevailed. It was a risky, bold move. Trainees would be paid salaries without producing any revenue for the firm. But it paid off. "The school was expensive, our business was down, and there was a feeling on the part of many that we could not afford such an expensive luxury," Dad recalled in 1953. "Of course, it wasn't a luxury—the future has proved that."

It was another revolution in the securities business. Until then, most brokers, including those at Merrill Lynch, had simply been hired into a kind of informal apprenticeship, perhaps after receiving a brief orientation. If you happened to live near New York, you could attend a course offered by the New York Stock Exchange, but no such advancement opportunity existed for the men and a few women who sold securities in the rest of the country.

Dr. Birl E. ("Doc") Shultz was hired to establish a curriculum and hire faculty. Class No. 1, which consisted of twenty-three young men, most returning veterans, gathered at 70 Pine Street on December 3, 1945. They were, my father said at the time, "of good education, coming from good families, who are earnest, serious-minded, and honest, and who will be, some ten, fifteen, and twenty years later, the partners and key executives of the firm." They studied economics, business, and finance. Students also were drilled in public speaking, and at Alpheus Beane's insistence, they were required to take a Dale Carnegie course on how to get along with people. Teachers were recruited from nearby colleges, and every top Merrill Lynch executive, except the ailing Merrill, was brought in to talk to the classes. One of the first students was George Shinn, later nicknamed "the Gray Ghost," an Amherst man who would one day become Merrill Lynch's president and chief operating officer. When he got out of the Marines in 1945, Shinn considered going to a graduate business school, but opted for the Merrill Lynch program instead, and soon after he started the class he said to himself, "My Lord, I'm getting paid for learning what I would have to borrow money to do." Class No. 2 included another returning Marine, Donald T. Regan, who twenty-five years later would become one of the firm's strongest leaders, a major figure first on Wall Street, and later in Washington. Interestingly, Doc Shultz was unable to convince his own son, George, an ex-Marine, to enroll. Instead, George Shultz pursued an academic career. Some thirty-five years later, he and Don Regan found themselves in President Reagan's cabinet—Regan as Treasury Secretary (and later White House chief of staff) and Shultz as Secretary of State.

The first courses lasted six months, but the duration was reduced to three months a few years later. While all of the early trainees were groomed to be account executives, in succeeding years and decades there would be additional programs for managers and operations supervisors. It was because of its policy of training its own personnel that the firm began to be called "Mother Merrill." Initially, there was a mildly derisive nuance to the term, but as the company grew and prospered, its rivals began similar programs. The training school became a binding force within the firm—what one writer called "the experience that binds one Merrill Lynch man to the same culture as the next Merrill Lynch man." Twenty years after the establishment of the training school, Regan would boast, "We could switch managers from Amsterdam to Tacoma and we wouldn't drop a stitch, because they've both been trained the same way." This emphasis on professional management development was truly unique on Wall Street, and was a major reason for Merrill Lynch's success over the years.

For many years on Wall Street, the people who handled personal accounts for brokerage houses were called "customer's men." Mary Ann Price helped make that phrase obsolete when she enrolled in the Merrill Lynch Training School in 1946—and for the next thirty years proved beyond a doubt that a woman's place is in the stock market. Just before graduating and becoming Merrill Lynch's first woman account executive, Price precipitated a minor crisis on the floor of the New York Stock Exchange when she arrived with her class after trading hours as part of her training.

"No women," said a guard, extending an admonitory palm.

"What harm can she do?" pleaded her instructor. "The place is closed."

Telephone calls leap-frogged up the NYSE chain of command all the way to president Eric Schram, and Price was allowed to join her class.

Price had grown up in Illinois and was the daughter of a grain dealer. Business and market news were part of the family dinner conversations. As a young woman she studied music and gave many piano recitals, and she was an outstanding athlete at the University of Illinois. After her graduation from the training school's third class in 1946, she worked in Merrill Lynch's Chicago office until her retirement in 1975.

In 1947 the training school was taken over by Art Tighe, a high-school dropout at fourteen who had vainly sought his life's niche as a railroad mail clerk, messenger boy, draftsman apprentice, bartender, freight handler, traveling salesman, typist, and stock clerk. He came to New York in 1924 and took a job as a reservations clerk with the New York Central Railroad, and five years later he joined E. A. Pierce & Co. as a runner, at which point he decided to resume his education. He attended the New York Stock Exchange Institute and the American Institute of Banking, received his high-school diploma in three years at the age of thirty-one, then went on to study philosophy, logic, and psychology at Brooklyn College and New York University. When he became director of the Merrill Lynch Training School, he told students, "Those who appreciate a formal education are those who get it after they have learned its value."

The training school won the firm more favorable press coverage, such as this item in *The New York Times*:

> Veterans with discharge buttons shining on lapels of business suits are making late reveille and burning midnight oil to learn the securities business under the tutelage of Merrill Lynch, Pierce, Fenner & Beane, and judging from the demanding scope of the six-month curriculum, it would seem that the erstwhile warriors will have little leisure in which to contemplate adjustment to civilian life. To borrow military lingo, they are "sweating out" the Academic Battle of Wall Street.

Some of the more promising graduates of the training school were picked for special duty in 1948 on the Sales Promotion Team, an eleven-member team of account executives that was an outgrowth of a series of visits to all ninety-five MLPF&B branches by groups of partners and executives in 1947. Merrill called for the creation of the team after reading the reports of these visits, saying, "If every manager could know what each other office has found successful, we could improve our business-getting strategy 100 percent." Bob Magowan was named to head the effort and picked eleven of the brightest stars among the account executives. Called "Whiz Kids," the team members were trained and then sent to every branch, where they helped managers devise specific sales strategies. When they completed their work in December 1948 it was obvious that team members had the inside track to the top of the company hierarchy. Magowan sent a memo to Francis C. "Bill" Hunter, head of the Washington, D.C., office, which had lent a promising AE to the team, saying: "It won't surprise you, I'm sure, to hear that Don Regan is one of the very best, and that he has handled himself exceptionally well thus far. I think he is destined to go far in this firm, and I thank you once more for relinquishing his services."

No account of the Sales Promotion Team would be complete without mentioning the man who organized it—Milija Rubezanin, who first came to Charlie Merrill's attention back in 1927 as he passed through the Research Department one day and spotted an unfamiliar face.

"Who the hell is he?" Merrill asked an aide.

"That's Ruby."

"How much are we paying him?"

"Nothing. He's working for nothing just to learn."

Merrill was annoyed. "Either fire him or pay him a salary. I don't want people working for me for nothing."

They hired him the next day, and more than any other individual, "Ruby" carried out Merrill's belief that if you took the mystery out of finance, people would be attracted to Merrill Lynch. Ruby was born in Montenegro, Yugoslavia, and as a teenager he was drafted into the German Army during World War I. He escaped and made his way to England, where he attended Oxford. He migrated to the United States in the 1920s and took a job laying cables for Consolidated Edison in New York. His first brokerage job was as a runner with Calvin & Co.

As soon as he began earning enough money, Ruby set out to correct what he regarded as a grievous flaw—his spoken English, which was accented heavily with his native Serbo-Croat tongue. He went to a tutor for private lessons, but after several months his mentor threw up his hands in despair. "Mr. Rubezanin," he said, "you can live in this country for ninety years and you'll never speak any better than you do right now. You're wasting money, and you're wasting my time—and besides, I'm beginning to talk like you."

After his impromptu hiring in 1927, Ruby stayed with Merrill Lynch during the Depression, helped launch *Family Circle* magazine, was elected a vice president in 1938, and became a full partner with the merger in 1940. But his signal achievement was putting together the Sales Promotion Team in 1948. Ruby was one of the most beloved Merrill Lynch executives, and his retirement dinner in 1965 drew eighty-four people who had worked for him. These were "Ruby's boys," and they included Don Regan and Bill Schreyer, both eventual chairmen and CEOs. The dinner program carried this tribute:

> We are here to pay tribute to a guy called Ruby.
>
> Ruby is many things—a bon vivant, a man of the world, a drinking buddy par excellence, a financial wizard, a wise counselor.
>
> But if in our hearts we remember him best for one thing, it will be—selfishly—for his warmth for us and his understanding of us.

It can be truly said that our winters of discontent were
made glorious summer by the sun of this guy called Ruby,
He was—and is—a "people" man.

In December 1945 it became clear that Merrill Lynch would realize
annual earnings of about $8.8 million (nearly double those of the
previous year), and it occurred to Charlie Merrill that the firm
had an obligation to protect and perpetuate the economic climate that
had made this success possible. With his characteristic spontaneity,
he sat down and dashed off a letter to each of the partners:

> Our successful firm may be measured not only in finan-
> cial terms but in terms of vitally useful financial service
> which we have rendered to our country's economy.
>
> We, in common with most Americans, may have come to
> take for granted the country's great growth and prosperity
> just as many of us take for granted the Constitution and
> the Bill of Rights. It is but pointing out the obvious to say
> that the United States is now at one of the major crossroads
> of its history. Political and economic systems which differ
> profoundly from ours are growing up throughout the world.
> Coupled with their challenge to our democracy is the need
> within our own country for a better understanding of basic
> principles in the light of current and future problems.
>
> I believe our firm has an obligation and an opportunity
> to make a contribution toward helping the American
> people make the right decision at this time through im-
> partial channels.

Whereupon Merrill asked the partners for a total of $1 million
through pro rata contributions for the establishment of the Merrill
Foundation for the Advancement of Financial Knowledge. The response
was immediate, enthusiastic, and complete, and in 1947 the foundation
was created. Its first gift was a $175,000 grant to Harvard University
for a study of taxes and their impact on business. In ensuing years,
the foundation financed studies at the University of Pennsylvania's
Wharton School, the Brookings Institution, and the Massachusetts
Institute of Technology.

The United States had emerged victorious and powerful from World War II, and for the first time in their lives, many Americans had steady jobs and money in the bank. But amid this sea of prosperity the memory of the Depression loomed like a dorsal fin, and there was much talk at coffee breaks and across the backyard fences of new homes of "another 1929." Americans were far more inclined to buy a life insurance policy than a stock or bond. Although the New Dealers had taken care of most of the abuses that led to the Crash, memories of foreclosures, breadlines, and joblessness were fresh and painful, and they produced thought-erasing fears that were beyond reason. Moreover, suspicious fingers still pointed toward Wall Street as the culprit.

Germany and Japan were defeated, but Merrill Lynch's battle to bring Wall Street to Main Street was just beginning. In a postwar survey of five thousand Americans by *Collier's* magazine, nearly two-thirds of the respondents still thought that cattle were traded on the Stock Exchange. Among 375 heads of household of middle-class families in the Los Angeles area, 328 did not know what a stockbroker did, and only seven could name a single brokerage house.

Merrill Lynch set out to change all of this.

Right from the beginning, the Merrill Lynch advertising budget kept pace with its rising revenues, and by the end of World War II, the firm was spending $1.5 million on research, surveys, and advertising intended to sell the stock market as a place to invest modest sums of money and itself as the place to strike that bargain. No other item of company business attracted as much personal attention from Charlie Merrill as advertising and its handmaiden, public relations. And no other Merrill Lynch activity shattered as many Wall Street rules.

Before MLPF&B came along, the standard of brokerage advertising was the tombstone, with its black border, separated by a moat of white space from a sober body of text that included the firm's name, some platitudes on its integrity and good intentions, and then the stark details of a particular stock or bond offering. Just after the war, *Time* magazine lamented "the deadly premeditated dullness of financial ads." And columnist Billy Rose mocked the tombstones with a suggested alternate: "Amalgamated Goulash—The Stock That Has Everything. Coming Soon to Bijou (formerly

E. F. Hutton, Inc.). . . $13 a Share Until 1:00 O'clock. Children Under 12 Half Price. Free Bubble Gum."

Meanwhile, Merrill Lynch was turning out iconoclastic, head-turning copy like this piece, which carried the headline WE THE PEOPLE and capitalized on the sobriquet originally applied with derision by the competition: "We like the name because today the security business must inevitably be a people's business. The day of the wing-collar broker, the glib customer's man, the corner-cutting insider, is gone—and good riddance. It is our business to help you put your money to work. It's the business of 'We the People' to help all the people all the time." Another offering was an Alice in Wonderland parable that included cautionary advice like "DANGER! INSIDE TIP AHEAD," "IT'S YOUR MONEY," and "INVESTIGATE. THEN INVEST." Merrill Lynch was selling itself, not a specific product—that was the job of the account executive.

The firm's early advertising was handled by Albert Frank Guenther Law, the agency founded by CEM's old pal Rudy Guenther, but something more was needed in those first postwar years. Help came from a familiar source—Ted Braun. During the California chain-store tax battle in 1935, Braun had met Louis Engel, a twenty-six-year-old reporter for *Business Week* magazine, and was impressed with Engel's clear writing style and professionalism; in Braun, Engel found a reliable source for his reporting, and the two struck up a lasting friendship. Braun's first overture to bring Engel on board at Merrill Lynch in 1945 was rejected by Engel, who had risen to become *Business Week*'s managing editor. But a short time later a top-level shakeup at the magazine forced Engel to move to a job with a new Kiplinger publication, *Changing Times*. It did not work out, and in early 1946 Engel made a spur-of-the-moment telephone call to my father from Grand Central Terminal during the afternoon rush hour to see if the job was still open. It was a story Engel loved to tell.

"I stuck my nickel in a phone, asked for Mr. Smith, and I said, 'Mr. Smith, remember we talked about that job as advertising and sales promotion manager about three months ago?' He said yes, and I said, 'Is it filled?' 'Well,' he said, 'this is very interesting. We expected to fill it tomorrow.' He asked, 'Are you interested?' I said yes. He said, 'Hold the phone.' He went away for five or ten minutes. I just barely made it on my nickel supply. I still don't know what he did. I guess he called Ted Braun out in Los Angeles. When he came back on he said, 'All right, you're hired. When can you report?'" When Engel reported for work as MLPF&B's advertising director on November 15, 1946, he had already warned Smith of a startling personal deficiency: He had no understanding or interest in stocks or bonds. As editor of a national business publication, Engel had always managed to avoid the subject by assigning it to others. But Engel's financial naïveté turned out to be his greatest strength, for he was the embodiment of the very person he hoped to reach.

Engel found it rough going during his first days at Merrill Lynch. His immediate superior was George B. Hyslop, director of the Sales Division, who had come to work for the old Merrill, Lynch & Co. during the 1920s. Engel complained that Hyslop insisted on supervising every detail of his work "even if it was for hog bellies in the *National Butcher* magazine." Engel bristled against his overseer, and when Hyslop protested about his insubordination in a memo to his supervisors, Merrill came in from Southampton to deal with the situation personally. After meeting with my father and again reading the memo, he picked up the telephone, called Hyslop, and said, "George, this is Charlie Merrill. I just finished reading your memo for the second time in the last twenty minutes. I just have one question that I'd like to ask you: How soon can you have your desk cleaned out?" Hyslop's duties were taken over by Bob Magowan, who not only gave Engel a free hand to develop a bold, imaginative advertising campaign but backed him up when his plans were opposed by other MLPF&B executives.

For the first ten years of his Merrill Lynch career, Engel was obliged to tiptoe around Rudy Guenther, who headed the firm's agency of record and had earned CEM's undying gratitude by helping out, often without remuneration, in the formative years before World War I. Engel felt strongly, though, that the agency did not fit into his plans for Merrill Lynch advertising. His first move was to tell the agency that it would continue to handle all mechanical work and get all commissions, but he would write all the copy and select the media where the ads would appear. The system worked well until about a year later when Engel found himself unable to handle the workload.

Still not trusting the available talent at Albert Frank Guenther Law, Engel persuaded them to hire Jack Adams, a gifted copywriter, and got him installed as a vice president at the advertising agency. This arrangement was successful, and Engel and Adams turned out all Merrill Lynch copy. Though nominally an employee of the Guenther agency, Adams worked exclusively on the Merrill Lynch account, and all but an inside few thought he was a Merrill Lynch employee.

When the U.S. Congress took up legislation that would have severely restricted trading in commodities futures, Engel was assigned to write a newspaper advertisement opposing the bill. First, he went to a neighbor's house in suburban Long Island and borrowed a basic economics textbook. Next, he read some of the testimony before the congressional committee considering the bill. Then, his education in commodities complete, he wrote the ad, which carried the headline COMMODITY EXCHANGES CUT BUSINESS RISKS; RESULT: LOWER COST OF FOOD TO CONSUMERS. The text explained, in layman's terms, the workings of the commodity exchanges and how they were important to everyone. The ad appeared in twenty-seven newspapers in January 1948. The bill languished in committee and died when Congress adjourned. What role, if any, Engel's ad played in its defeat is debatable, but the ad drew praise from Engel's superiors, and there was a favorable response to it from other brokerages. Its success inspired Engel to apply the same simplistic approach to the securities market. The result was a classic.

For months Engel immersed himself in a crash course on securities, reading books and articles and interviewing knowledgeable Wall Street hands. Finally, he took everything he knew and crystallized it in a single six-thousand-word advertisement that he entitled "What Everybody Ought to Know About This Stock and Bond Business." There were no photographs or artwork of any kind accompanying the text, which was broken up only by two subheads. Readers were invited to write to Merrill Lynch for more information. When Engel showed the ad to Merrill, my father, and Magowan, they were polite but not supportive of this unusual idea. When they took it to a partners meeting, reactions ranged from indifference to incredulity to outright opposition. There was no enthusiastic support. But Engel insisted that his innovative approach would work, and he was allowed to run the ad on a trial basis in the *Cleveland Plain Dealer*, which had space rates substantially lower than the New York newspapers. It was a modest success—enough for Engel to be permitted to risk $5,000 of his advertising budget by purchasing a full page in *The New York Times*. It ran on October 19, 1948, and the next day there were eight hundred requests for copies, and six thousand more over the next few weeks. Some of these requests came with unalloyed praise for the author and for Merrill Lynch.

"What was most amazing," Engel recalled, "was that we got hundreds and hundreds of long and thoughtful letters: 'God bless Merrill Lynch—I've been wanting to know this all my life'. . . 'I majored in economics in college, and frankly, I never understood'. . . 'I owned stocks and bonds and I never knew what I really owned.' Letters of this caliber." The firm continued to run the ad for years, and within ten years of when it first appeared, it had received 3 million responses—each one, of course, representing a prospective Merrill Lynch customer. Engel's work was included in Julian Lewis Watkins's 1959 book, *The 100 Greatest Advertisements,* alongside classic ads from Ivory Soap ("99 and 44/100ths Percent Pure"), RCA ("His Master's Voice"), and Coca-Cola ("The Pause That Refreshes").

Engel's responsibilities as the company's advertising director were far-reaching, and sometimes he was even pressed into politics. During his 1948 campaign, President Harry Truman condemned the greed of the "money changers" of Wall Street, and Merrill was offended by the remark. The morning after Truman's election, which surprised many political experts, CEM summoned Magowan and gave him some handwritten notes he had made in the middle of the night. He wanted Engel to put his ideas together and make them into an ad. The result ran in twenty-five large national newspapers under the headline GENERAL MCAULIFFE SAID NUTS—a reference to the World War II American general who declined a German demand that he surrender. The text showed Merrill and Engel at their best:

> One campaign tactic did get us a little riled. That was when the moth-eaten bogey of a Wall Street tycoon was trotted out. Mr. Truman knows as well as anybody that there isn't any Wall Street. That's just legend. Wall Street

is Montgomery Street in San Francisco. Seventeenth Street in Denver. Marietta Street in Atlanta. Federal Street in Boston. Main Street in Waco, Texas. And it's any spot in Independence, Missouri, where thrifty people go to invest their money, to buy and sell securities.

Whenever Lou Engel was asked to define advertising, he replied with this story: "There was a blind beggar in Central Park one day with a tin cup wearing the conventional sign, 'I am blind.' A man standing by noticed how few contributions the blind man received, so he went up to the beggar and said, 'Look here, you're not doing too well. I'm an advertising man, and I think I can help you if you'll just let me change your sign a little bit.' The beggar didn't have much to lose, and so the advertising man wrote a few words on the sign and left. Later that afternoon he returned. The beggar was doing much better. As he approached, the blind man recognized his footsteps and said, 'My friend, what have you done to help me? I've never had a day like this. What did you put on my sign?' The advertising man replied, 'I just wrote three additional words on it, and now it says, "It's springtime and—I am blind."'

"That," Engel would say, "is advertising."

Aside from how he handled the "big issues," Lou Engel also had a knack for pouncing on ordinary events and turning them into coups. In one instance, on April 17, 1951, Fern Lang, the wife of a Texas minister, wrote to the MLPF&B Shreveport, Louisiana, office seeking advice on setting up a small investment program for the couple's newly born daughter. "My husband and I have a lovely baby girl for whom we would like to buy some common stock," Mrs. Lang wrote. "Since my husband is a preacher, our income probably never will be very large, and since this baby is only the first of several that we hope to have, we are pretty sure that we will not be able to invest more than, say, $50 or $100 a year." Mrs. Lang promptly received a three-page reply from the branch manager giving detailed investment advice. Engel somehow learned of the letter exchange and turned it into a full-page national newspaper and magazine ad entitled "What Would You Buy for a Beautiful Baby Girl . . . If You Had Only $50 to

Invest?" Not only was the advertising campaign successful, it inspired newspaper feature stories on the couple and MLPF&B.

For the next several years, the firm's print advertising spread the gospel of the value and good sense of investing in the stock market and, incidentally, doing it through the services of Merrill Lynch. Each education effort smoothly segued into promotional material seeking inquiries and prospects, and always overseeing these efforts was Charlie Merrill. In 1947 the New York Stock Exchange decided to run a full-page ad in all of the nation's major newspapers urging investors to avoid tipsters and other unsound advice and instead consult an NYSE member with their investment questions. The ad showed a bearded man with earrings and a turban gazing into a crystal ball saying, "I see a great opportunity...." Merrill got an advance look at the ad, liked what he saw, and somehow arranged to have a small "Merrill Lynch, Pierce, Fenner & Beane" run in a strip directly beneath the NYSE ad. It was subtle, but the inference was clear: Merrill Lynch was the place to go for trustworthy investment advice. Not surprisingly, competing brokers cried foul, but their protests were in vain.

For the infant medium of television, 1947 was an important year: *Howdy Doody* and *Meet the Press* made their debuts, the World Series was televised for the first time—and on January 30, 1947, it is believed that Merrill Lynch became the first Wall Street financial house to advertise on television when Engel arranged for MLPF&B to sponsor a documentary film on the New York Stock Exchange that was carried on WCBS-TV. Dad appeared in a two-minute introduction to the documentary, and after stressing the importance of individual investors investigating opportunities for themselves, he intoned: "This is a point with which our own firm, Merrill Lynch, Pierce, Fenner & Beane, is in complete sympathy. For years, to all our three hundred thousand customers, through all our ninety-two offices, we have regularly repeated our watchword, 'Investigate—Then Invest.' And we have sought to make that advice as practical as possible by maintaining a Research Department of seventy-nine people, by furnishing our customers with objective reports with full disclosure of all factors affecting the outlook, both favorable and unfavorable." Dad then concluded his introduction by inviting interested viewers to telephone or drop by their local Merrill Lynch office. There were no ratings in those days, so no one knows how many people watched the program, but it was without doubt a bargain. Total cost of the sponsorship: $250.

It was the first in a series of ventures into new types of media by the company. Soon after the television appearance, my father went on an international shortwave station—WRUL in Boston—to launch a five-days-per-week program of business news and daily market reports aimed primarily at American investors in Europe, Africa, and Latin America. Later that same year, Merrill Lynch produced a twenty-minute slide program entitled *People and Their Money*, which was a historical account of the firm designed specifically for ML employees. The idea was based on a concept used successfully by the Armed Forces during World War II—that visual-sound training was more effective and took less time than other methods. In 1949 the company produced a twenty-five-minute film, *That Money Problem*, dramatizing "What Everyone Ought to Know About the Stock and Bond Business." Shown on local television stations across the nation, it told the story of a fictional secretary who has $5,000 in the bank and wants to invest about $3,000 of it.

The use of investment education became a powerful promotional tool. On April 18, 1949, just a few months before I was born, major newspapers in the San Francisco–Oakland area carried an advertisement addressed to "Women Who'd Like to Know More About Investments," offering them a series of eight weekly lectures. Ferdinand C. Smith, the local office manager who developed the program, rented a hall that would accommodate the fifty or so women he expected to reply, but some 850 women responded to the initial call, and Smith had to rent an auditorium that would hold five hundred of them. The rest were put on a waiting list, which soon grew to a thousand within a week. The San Francisco program came to the attention of Sylvia Porter, who wrote in her nationally syndicated column: "Merrill Lynch, Pierce, Fenner & Beane, the largest stock brokerage house in the world, is still gasping from the shock. It has discovered that the American woman has a lot of money and thinks enough about her money to care how it should be and is invested. And so, as you might expect from a firm shrewd enough to beat the competition and become the greatest of them all, Merrill Lynch is now doing something about the American woman and her money." Dad followed up with an announcement that there would be similar courses in all ninety-six MLPF&B offices, and by the end of the year some thirty thousand women had gone through the eight-week program. Other brokerages soon began offering similar educational programs for women, but only after Merrill Lynch had seized the attention of the nation.

Around this time, my father wrote a memo about the unexpected reaction from potential women investors:

> It has astonished us, I admit, to have so many women saying, "Information, Please," on the subject of stocks and bonds. We hadn't dreamed that so many would be interested enough to sit through eight lecture sessions to get it. Some of them even did "homework" in the form of reading the booklets we provided on "How to Invest," "How to Read a Financial Report" and similar literature.
>
> All we set out to do in these lectures was to make our women listeners more familiar with the kind of merchandise we and other brokers handled. At the end of the series we invited them to come in to see the mechanics of a brokerage office, but we expected little or no direct sales results. Again we were astonished. In each city where lectures were held there has been enough new business within thirty days to more than cover the costs of the courses.
>
> There was another highly satisfying development, too. Some of the women asked if we would give courses for their husbands. This meant that our merchandise was beginning to be discussed in a few homes where it had never been discussed before. It is a small step, admittedly, when you consider that only about 7% of the 52,000,000 families in this country own any common or preferred stock at all.
>
> We do not know accurately, of course, how many of the remaining 93% have available funds for investment in our country's industries, but we do know that there are tens of millions who could buy our products but do not. That is why there is no more challenging and necessary mass merchandising project than that which faces investment houses today.

The Merrill Lynch promotional efforts to bring Wall Street to Main Street reached dizzying levels in the 1950s. The firm's representatives held how-to-invest exhibits under tents at county agricultural fairs, sharing space with prize-winning hogs. They held seminars that provided child care so both husband and wife could attend. They set up exhibits at flower shows and furniture shows, where literature was distributed and brokers were on hand to answer questions. They even joined General Mills, makers of Wheaties breakfast cereal, in a contest where the top prize was $25,000 in stocks and bonds of the winner's choice, second prize was $10,000 in securities, and there were sixty other prizes—all paid in stocks. Entrants were judged on twenty-five-word statements beginning, "I Like Wheaties because . . ." The role of MLPF&B was to help the winners select their stocks and handle all the details. It was the first nationwide contest to offer securities as prizes.

Lou Engel's public-education efforts grew exponentially. On April 12, 1954, three silver-and-blue passenger buses, converted into Merrill Lynch mobile offices, moved out into Wellesley, Massachusetts; Paterson, New Jersey; and Hammond, Indiana, stopping in shopping districts and parking lots. These "stockmobiles," connected by two-way radio to Merrill Lynch branches, had a boardroom where stock prices were posted and two private offices where investors could open accounts on the spot. The buses moved around on a regular basis to different locations, usually spending one day a week in each spot.

In 1955, Engel organized a "How to Invest" show at Manhattan's Seventy-first Regiment Armory that featured displays by eight leading corporations and trade groups and explained the stock and bond markets both in principle and everyday operation. In what would be his last public appearance, Merrill himself was there for the ribbon-cutting ceremony and posed for a memorable photograph with eighty-year-old Ed Pierce and the sons of the three deceased name partners—Edmund C. Lynch Jr., Darwin S. Fenner, and Alpheus C. Beane. In seven days, the show attracted nearly a hundred thousand people—double the expectations—and its success inspired Engel to establish a more permanent operation. Thus on the morning of March 1, 1956, commuters getting off trains in Grand Central Terminal from places like Greenwich and Chappaqua were startled by unusual activity in what had been a quiet baggage-checking area. Striding across the creamy marble floor, they spied a phosphorescent sign proclaiming that the new addition was the "Merrill Lynch Investment Information Center." MLPF&B had set up shop in what at that time amounted to New York's town square, and for the next thirty years, a revolving team of account executives answered questions and offered easy-to-understand literature (but never advice) to interested passersby in a booth beneath the renowned constellated ceiling at the Lexington Avenue end of the upper concourse. At the height of its activity, some five thousand people came to the Information Center every week. A similar operation was opened across town at Pennsylvania Station five years later. These booths, especially the one in Grand Central, were a brilliant marketing strategy. As they waited for their trains, people could stop in, get a stock quote, and speak to a Merrill Lynch representative without getting a "hard sell." It led to many new accounts and also branded Merrill Lynch in a way that no other Wall Street firm had been. When I first started working for Merrill Lynch in the early 1970s, I used to drop by the booth myself as I waited for the train to Greenwich. The booth was never empty.

Lou Engel took on one other monumental task that was a great success. He wrote a book called *How to Buy Stocks: A Guide to Successful Investing*, which was published by Little, Brown and Company and was dedicated to Charlie Merrill, "who formed a new philosophy of investing to fit a new phase of capitalism." Written in simple language, it explained how "to make your money earn more money for you by investing it." Anyone could read the book and afterward have a great understanding of the stock market and how to invest. It was a hit and for years remained atop the best-selling list for business books. I still have the copy that Lou gave to my father with a personal note written on the inside: "To Winthrop H. Smith: Because this is a book that would never have been written if it were not for the fact that he symbolized in himself the character and integrity of a business about which I once had reservations."

Much of the mid-fifties promotional effort was spurred by the NYSE's Monthly Investment Plan, which was introduced in 1954 to encourage regular investing in small amounts by people with modest incomes. The MIP allowed investors to accumulate fractional shares of common stocks by monthly or even quarterly investments of as little as $40. Charlie Merrill must have been gratified that the institution that had disciplined him thirty-seven years earlier for breaking its advertising rules on Liberty Bonds now so completely embraced his vision of a people's capitalism. No one was surprised when Merrill Lynch handled nearly half of all MIP business in the first year, and within a few years it was doing nearly all the plans on Wall Street. These accounts were unprofitable for the most part, of course, but the firm was betting that enough of these tiny customers would grow into medium and large investors. No other brokerage provided this level of service to neophyte investors. On the first day that the MIP was available, five sea captains—commanders of tugboats, trawlers, and scows—showed up at an MLPF&B branch in Brooklyn to open pay-as-you-go accounts as a means of supplementing their pensions. In the ensuing weeks, the same office enrolled subway conductors, post office clerks, schoolteachers, housewives, and mechanics. The firm sold its 100,000th MIP account in 1958, and when it turned out to be to a secretary in the Moscow embassy, Engel seized the moment and had her flown to New York for photographs and interviews. After a few years, Merrill Lynch began offering a corporate version of the MIP that permitted employees to make regular small investments in their company stock through payroll deductions. After twenty years the firm converted the MIP into its own Sharebuilder Plan.

All of these postwar innovations—the training school, the highly visible promotions, the courting of the small investor, the opposition to higher broker commission rates—produced a dividend of incalculable value to Merrill Lynch, Pierce, Fenner & Beane: widespread, largely uncritical coverage in the media.

On January 10, 1948, the *Saturday Evening Post*, then one of America's most popular magazines, published the first of a two-part series entitled "The Thundering Herd of Wall Street," highlighting the moniker ML had been given because of the size of its partnership. The article did nothing to slow the rapid growth of the firm in this period. In fact, it is probably the most comprehensive, favorable, and widely circulated article ever written about a brokerage. Merrill Lynch was referred to throughout the long piece as "WE," as in "We the People." Some excerpts:

WE is not only a commission, or wire house handling stock and commodity orders for clients on stock and commodity exchanges, but an underwriter of new securities for companies which issue them, a retail distributor of new securities which it owns and itself sells, a trader in unlisted securities which are shipped around by telephone, and occasionally a broker in actual commodities like meat, flour, eggs and sugar.

. . . and some of its partners were active participants in the revolution that changed the New York Stock Exchange from an inviolate society to a public institution.

To Charles E. Merrill, the casualty list was simply more evidence that the brokerage business was the most poorly managed business he could think of. He once told his partners, "If R. H. Macy [the department store] had the same approach to the important expenses, the business-getting expenses, that all members of the New York Stock Exchange have, I assure you R. H. Macy and Company would be out of business by next April first, and it wouldn't be April Fools' Day either."

But it is still unquestionably a brokerage firm. Its ninety-five offices look like what they are—brokerage offices. Some are ultramodern; some are still old-fashioned, rather dim, chalk-board, hard-seat offices with cuspidors and board-room loafers. When the stock market is active and people are market-conscious, WE's offices are crowded. When the stock market is dull, they are empty.

Each office has a quotation board, a translux—a moving picture of the stock ticker—usually a news-service ticker and WE's own news wire. As befits a goldfish bowl, WE has torn out partitions in many offices, substituted glass or nothing, and removed brass bars.

Its main office here—four floors with private escalator—is a spectacle. The public board room is banked like an amphitheater, and the more distant account executive must pick their quotations off the electric board through binoculars.

WE's research department is massive. It employs sixty-eight people, maintains specialists in several fields like railroads, chemicals, utilities, and so on, and houses a half acre of reference works and its own files.

A judge once stopped into a WE office to let the manager know that WE had just decided a case for him. He had read a copy of a WE booklet entitled "How to Read a Financial Report," a simplified and instructive work on how to make sense of the jargon of accountants, and a point which had been worrying him about a case in his court was cleared up therein.

WE is highly employee-conscious. It gives employees free insurance, bonuses, and has a profit-sharing fund which in 1945 credited each employee with 15 percent of his annual salary. In its best year the firm put 20 percent of its net profits into profit sharing and other employee dividends. Music is piped into many departments in New York, and Win Smith is asking partners to consider a country headquarters for the firm, where employees can live a rural or small-town life and save the harrowing hours of commuting to Wall Street.

Almost two-thirds of WE's partners are in New York, and at weekly meetings of the New York administrative partners . . . someone listening at the transom would not be able to differentiate between the WE brass and a bunch of school kids at recess.

If the figures reported at a meeting show a slight profit instead of an expected loss for the latest month, the partners cheer, whistle and stamp their feet. Almost any report on any aspect of the business may draw wisecracks, argument, moans or applause.

While there is no question that all of this good press, the promotions, and the advertising helped Merrill Lynch expand its business, the firm also benefited from one other factor: a surging economy. By 1950 there was a new generation of Americans who knew about the Depression as children but were too young to have experienced it as adults. Despite a sharp drop in the stock market at the beginning of the Korean War in June, the Dow Jones Industrials closed out the year with a net gain of 17 percent and reached a post-Depression high of 235. Two decades of deprivation yielded to a pent-up desire for consumer goods, and the nation's factories, freed from wartime constraints, were eager to oblige. The victory of Dwight D. Eisenhower in the 1952 presidential election set off a bull market that would continue for fifteen years.

Inevitably, business picked up on Wall Street. More branch brokerages were opened and additional salesmen hired. Radio personalities were the popular figures of the day, and they began praising the market as a solid investment. One of them, Walter Winchell, made stock suggestions a regular feature of his nationally broadcast weekly show. For middle-class Americans, having a stockbroker became almost as important as having an insurance agent or a family doctor.

But it was Merrill Lynch, Pierce, Fenner & Beane, more than any other brokerage, that restored public confidence in the stock market. Its relentless educational campaigns easily made MLPF&B the best-known brokerage firm in America, and by mid-century it was a symbol of a newly respectable Wall Street. When members of the Soviet press came to visit New York City in October 1955, they stopped at two bastions of capitalism: the floor of the New York Stock Exchange and the headquarters of Merrill Lynch at 70 Pine Street. MLPF&B's rivals soon remade themselves in its image. Bache, Dean Witter, E. F. Hutton, Goodbody, and others began training programs, toned down hard-sell tactics, initiated advertising programs, and changed their attitudes toward smaller investors.

A s always, though, rapid growth created problems—and once again ML was Wall Street's guiding light.

During the early days of the New York Stock Exchange, when there might be a few thousand purchases and sales on a good day, transactions were recorded by bleary-eyed clerks with green eyeshades sitting on tall stools, writing into huge corduroy-covered ledgers. But with the industrialization of America came mass production, and with mass production came consumer demand, and with consumer demand came the need for capital to meet the demand. The NYSE volume of daily transactions rose steadily. The old bookkeepers first found help in typewriters, then in adding machines, bookkeeping machines, and other advances. Back in the 1920s progressive firms like E. A. Pierce & Co. and Fenner & Beane had begun experimenting with IBM electric tabulating machines, which worked fine through the Depression and the war years, but by the 1950s when prosperity was sweeping through America, and Wall Street was really finding its way to Main Street, Merrill Lynch couldn't keep up with its volume of business. Charles Merrill sounded the alarm at the 1953 Managers Conference:

> Wall Street is still hitched to the horse and buggy. While many advances have been made by our legislators and ourselves for the protection of the public, the basic manner in which we process our business is not very much different from the way it was done in 1865. A basic overhauling of the whole machinery for the marketing of securities, both on and off the Exchange, is the big challenge to this atomic age Wall Street.
>
> The existing machinery keeps bogging down under modern conditions because it was built to function in a world where the buying and selling of securities was of interest only to a handful of wealthy men. Merrill Lynch has pioneered in bringing Wall Street to Main Street, in selling the American economy to the butcher and baker and salaried clerk. And Merrill Lynch must pioneer in doing away with the antiquated machinery geared to selling securities to the few, and discover new methods and mechanics for selling them to the millions!

In 1954, Merrill Lynch officially adopted the name "Operations," replacing the traditional name, "Backstage," for the function that involved the processing of customer accounts and related matters. The Annual Report explained that "it was felt the old name implied a behind-the-scenes work force rather than an open and integral part of the firm operations." But a new name didn't change the fact that Merrill Lynch was still using IBM's electro-mechanical accounting machines. In the course of handling the business of an average day, some two hundred people guided some 1 million individual punched cards through 147 different computing and collating machines an average of fifteen times each, for a total of 15 million handles in all. Most of the work was done between the time the market closed and when it opened the next day. As the workload increased, there were more and more mistakes. The simple act of sending out monthly statements involved 3.3 million punch cards and took a week to complete. Operations employees worked twelve hours a day, six days a week to keep up. "We were in at eight o'clock in the morning, and our hours ended about eight o'clock at night," recalled one backstage veteran. "That's including Saturdays. Saturday, too, was required only because they were busy, it was the growing years in Merrill Lynch, these fifties and early sixties. As such, you had to put in these hours if you wanted to move with the job and move up the ladder. You made friends for life. Many of the men and women I worked with then eventually got married to each other. So it was a closeness. You got to know people."

My father came across a computer for the first time at the 1933 Chicago World's Fair, but he was told that the IBM machine could not be applied to the brokerage business. Nevertheless, he firmly believed that one day the machines would set off a revolution in the keeping of financial records. When the early mainframe computers, like the ENIAC, tried to tackle larger jobs they ran into trouble. They were temperamental monsters that frequently broke down and could take months to fix. They had 500 miles of wire, 300,000 electrical connections, 18,000 tubes, and consumed so much electrical power that they sometimes caused the lights to dim in nearby towns. Then IBM came up with a new kind of machine that worked electronically instead of electrically, had a built-in memory along with its ability to compute and calculate, worked at the speed of light, and used magnetized tape rather than punch cards. The machine was being used with great success on scientific projects, including tracking earth satellites and planning rockets to go to the moon.

And so in 1955 Dad set up an Electronics Feasibility Committee to study whether these new electronic data-processing machines were the answer to the growing bookkeeping problems. A few big businesses already were using the machines, including General Motors, Westinghouse, and Metropolitan Life. Merrill Lynch's needs were much greater that those of these other companies, but an exhaustive study by the committee concluded that computers would still work. The project overseers were Mike McCarthy, who had been elevated to the position of assistant managing partner, and James E. Thomson, who had joined Merrill Lynch as a runner in 1924 and had replaced

McCarthy as Director of Operations in 1948. "We put in the first IBM system ever on Wall Street," McCarthy said. "We had looked into it, but [Thomson] particularly had studied all the different systems. What we bought was a blackboard presentation. We never saw the machine. It has to work because otherwise Thomson's name was mud and so was mine."

In 1958, Merrill Lynch became Wall Street's most efficient firm with the installation of an IBM 705, a first-generation mainframe, affectionately known as "the Million Dollar Baby." It was a slight exaggeration—the rental for the machine came to $750,000 a year. Merrill Lynch's first computer was installed in a specially electrified, air-conditioned, dehumidified area of the third floor at 70 Pine Street. The 705 consisted of a bright-red, L-shaped computer, a yellow control panel, and twenty attendant machines. It took up nearly the entire floor, which had to be reinforced. A group of Russian journalists visited the site of the installation, and they were so fascinated by the IBM machine that they stayed on an extra hour to observe it and missed a scheduled luncheon. But even as the 705 was being installed, the company ordered another more transistorized IBM—the 7080. Operations work that used to take an hour was now performed in seven or eight minutes by the computer. The savings more than offset the monthly rental charges. As Merrill Lynch grew, its sheer size enabled it to afford the latest electronic equipment. Soon it gained a reputation for the fastest executions in the financial world, and from this point forward, the company led the way in technology among financial firms.

Although commodities trading seemed to run counter to the MLPF&B gospel of prudent investing, this division made an important contribution to the firm's profits in the postwar years. Merrill Lynch injected a measure of conservatism in suggesting investments in items such as coffee, cocoa, lumber, cotton, and copper, and it only worked with investors who were financially able to absorb the inherent risk in the long-maligned "futures" market. The Commodities Division had accounted for only 8 percent of the branch network income in 1943, but ten years later this figure had risen to 20 percent. Some of the success was an outgrowth of the educational advertising efforts of Lou Engel, who had made commodity trading one of his first projects. In addition, the company produced a brochure entitled "Handbook for Commodity Speculators" and ran seminars on sound commodity-trading practices in some forty cities. Merrill Lynch made agreements with local commodity firms in Europe to act as its agent, and the Commodities Division's role in developing overseas markets was at least as important as its contribution to company profits.

Despite the growing popularity of commodities, though, most of the foreign offices sprang from the securities business. After the war Merrill Lynch opened overseas offices to serve American military personnel. Most of its business was done by mail and cable. A small office was established in Geneva in 1951 as a contact point in Europe. Operations were begun in Paris and Rome in 1957 with the avowed purpose of serving American investors, but before long they had an international clientele. As recovery from the war took hold on the Continent, European investors became interested in the U.S. securities and commodities markets.

Amidst all this growth, there was one area where Charlie Merrill's vision failed him, though, and it was a big one. Mutual funds were becoming one of the investment business's fastest-growing segments, but MLPF&B adamantly refused to sell them—wholly because of the opposition of the founder. Merrill believed mutual funds ran afoul of the company credo that investors should make their own decisions, and he also felt the sales charges and management fees took away too much of the initial investment. Some mutuals were being peddled door-to-door by unqualified salespersons, and CEM considered these operations to be on an equal footing with penny stocks. One of the first Merrill Lynchers to see the potential in mutual funds was Donald T. Regan, who had become the firm's youngest partner in 1954 at the age of thirty-five. Soon after, he decided he could change CEM's mind on mutual funds.

"So I very carefully wrote out a paper," he recalled four decades later. "It took me weeks to fashion it and I got it down to where it was just a nub of four pages. And I gave them to Bob Magowan and he said, 'What do you want me to do with these?' He said, 'You know Merrill's not going to buy this.'" But Regan believed he had made an irresistible case, and he persuaded Magowan to take his proposal to CEM in Southampton over the weekend. The following Monday morning Regan waited impatiently for Magowan to arrive at his office at 70 Pine Street, and when he did, he gave him about an hour to get settled before entering his office. Regan recounts this exchange:

"Yep, what can I do for you?"

"Tell me the news."

"What news?"

"Well, you were in Southampton this weekend. Did you show my paper to Mr. Merrill and to Win Smith?"

"Oh, that. Merrill didn't like it, and he said Smith agreed with him. So I went along."

"Christ!" Regan exploded. "Shot down by the Father, Son, and Holy Ghost."

It would be another fifteen years before Merrill Lynch got into the mutual fund business.

During the postwar years, there was a tangible feeling among company workers that upper management really did care about their welfare and felt a sense of responsibility for them; this produced a staff of unusually dedicated and loyal workers—and reinforced MLPF&B's not-unflattering nickname of "Mother Merrill." Regardless of their position with the firm, the average MLPF&B employee by and large earned more than he or she would have for identical labor at a rival brokerage. For brokers, Merrill Lynch's large volume of business produced higher-than-average income despite the absence of the commission system, which helped immeasurably in enabling employees to be imbued with Charlie Merrill's values about honesty and customer satisfaction. As soon as business picked up at the new company, CEM resumed the pre-Depression policy of paying year-end bonuses in good years. In addition, Merrill never forgot James Cash Penney's lesson in earning employee loyalty through profit sharing, and in 1945 the company set up a profit-sharing fund. Unlike the earlier chain-store plans, which were restricted to middle managers, the Merrill Lynch plan included all full-time employees.

It is impossible to determine the extent to which this generosity paid dividends in management's efforts to preserve the company's good name, but one small example occurred in 1951 and was singled out by my father: "Let me tell you how proud I was to see how well this organization could keep a secret. We recently earned a substantial fee from W. R. Grace for acting as their agent in the acquisition of a large block of Davison Chemical. Necessarily some people in 70 Pine Street knew that Grace would make an offer for Davison stock some six points above the market. The stock remained inactive—static in price until the public announcement was made. From a lifetime of experience in Wall Street, I'm afraid that wouldn't have happened in many places."

Employee loyalty was reciprocated. During the 1950s, when Senator Joseph R. McCarthy whipped up anti-Communism to a frenzy, Lou Engel became embroiled in a hometown dispute over a group's claim that standard public-school textbooks were filled with Communist propaganda. Engel knew better, and he spoke out at a public meeting. In retaliation, the McCarthyites made him the subject of a pamphlet entitled "Who's Tarnishing Our Town?" As a result of this, hundreds of people wrote irate letters to my father informing him that Merrill Lynch was employing a Communist. Most of these missives were handled by Pierce, who wrote back and invited the complainant to meet in his office with Engel. No one ever responded, and instead of firing Engel, MLPF&B made him a partner in 1954.

The folksy, friendly Merrill Lynch employee magazine, *We the People*, debuted in January 1947. The first issue included a long feature on the Tabulating Department, a gossipy column called "On the Sunny Side of the Street," and a "Pinup of the Month," which was a facial photograph of Rosemary from Cash Accounts, who was described as "a vivacious little brunette with big brown eyes and no steady boyfriend."

Charlie Merrill's favorite company institution was the Quarter Century Club, which he set up so that longtime employees would be "fully recognized for their long service, loyalty and dedication to the firm." When the club began in 1945, there were 126 members nationwide, and by the end of the century membership had reached nearly five thousand. The charter members included fifty-four from the New York area, who met at the Waldorf-Astoria for the first annual Quarter Century Dinner.

Not all of Mother Merrill's ideas worked out. The partners and department managers who assembled at the University Club for the annual Merrill Lynch Christmas dinner in 1946 were startled by what my father had to say: Why, he asked in his address, couldn't we move most of our offices out to the country so that each employee would be "only ten minutes from his home, his garden, and relaxation"? Warming to his subject, he added: "Let's suppose our home office were located in beautiful, healthful surroundings in the country, say, fifty, seventy-five, or a hundred miles from New York. Why couldn't we function exactly as well as we do now at 70 Pine Street?" Then he drew thunderous applause when he said, "Please don't say it cannot be done. I remember back in 1933 hearing that the IBM machines were not adaptable to the brokerage business. Nothing is impossible.... It's only a question of working out the details." And work he did. Dad became Captain Ahab and the project became Moby Dick. Indeed, in its April Fool's issue for 1952, *We the People* ran this spoof:

> "Back to the birds and the bees," cried Win Smith for the thirteen hundredth time during the past five years, last month in his office. "We've got to move MLPF&B out to the country, where all Merrill Lynchers will get plenty of sunshine and fresh air—and where no one will live further than five minutes' drive from the office—and every bookkeeper can play nine holes of golf before dinner—and..."
>
> But right then he yawned mightily, fell sound asleep. He dreamed Charlie Merrill and he had set up a temporary headquarters in the middle of a wheat field, and were actually planning the wonderful Birds and Bees setup.

The *WTP* cover depicted CEM and my father doing just that. It was not until May 1957 that Dad put down his harpoon. "After many and expensive studies, we have decided that the Home Office should be centrally located in the heart of the world's financial district.... And so—farewell to the birds 'n bees." Nearly thirty years later, Bill Schreyer moved the headquarters of Merrill's private wealth business to Plainsboro, New Jersey, and I am sure my dad smiled, even though he would have preferred a New England site.

M y father rose from his chair as dinner was winding down at the Hotel Statler in Midtown Manhattan on October 20, 1953, and rapped a spoon on a glass for attention. "Gentlemen," he said in his usual understated manner, "Mr. Merrill is with us, and he's going to close the conference." A hush settled over the room.

A small, frail man stood up at the head table. Many of the assembled partners and top managers of Merrill Lynch, Fenner, Pierce & Beane had never seen Charlie Merrill before, and they found it difficult to believe that the slowly shuffling figure could make it to the speaker's dais, let alone that they were gazing on one of the giants of Wall Street.

The tension was broken by CEM himself, who gripped the lectern for support, flashed a sheepish grin, and said, "Well, here's the old son of a bitch. . . ." There was an appreciative roar of laughter.

In the nine years since his heart attack, Charles Edward Merrill had become a legend on Wall Street and assumed god-like proportions within his own firm. His place in history had been staked out in 1947 by *Forbes* magazine, which named him one of America's fifty foremost business leaders. Moreover, his near-total absence from the offices of MLPF&B, which was sternly demanded by his physicians, had given him the remoteness and intrigue of a figure from Olympus.

In the summer of 1953, a new, experimental treatment had given him respite from the pain of his ailing heart, and now, a few months later, he had come to New York to celebrate his sixty-eighth birthday. In a two-day spree, Merrill gave a pep talk to account executives from the New York metropolitan area, lunched with financial journalists, made a telephone address to all company personnel, and was the guest of honor at a gala birthday party the night before. Now he cleared his throat to address several hundred partners and top associates—the first such gathering since the now-fabled Waldorf meeting of 1940.

The laughter had barely died down when CEM launched into a scathing attack on the securities business for having a lack of vision, for failing to realize the value of its product, and for failing to promote and educate the public about that product. It was a clear admission that, in his eyes, his long-standing dream of bringing Wall Street to Main Street was far from reality.

"Why have we failed to sell this market? Why is the Federal Reserve Board able to report that one-third of the people with liquid assets of

$5,000 or more own no corporate securities? Why does it find that 54 percent of the people who earn incomes of $10,000 or more a year are not stockholders? Let me tell you candidly that I think part of the explanation lies in the fact that many of us who sell securities are not really sold on the product we sell. And because we have not been sold on stocks as investments ourselves, we have quite obviously done a bad job of selling others."

And he was only getting started: "I am not only shocked but downright disgusted to find how little change has taken place in Wall Street in the past ten years. I told every other firm we'd be glad to show them how it was done. Thirteen years ago I said—and I meant it then and I mean it now—'I do not want to be a partner in the only firm that makes money when everybody else in the same business is dying of starvation.' Actually, it isn't a case of starvation. It's just plain dry rot—old-fashioned inertia. Frankly, I can't think of a business that has changed less.

"Wall Street is doing business at the same old stand. Sure, here and there a face has been lifted, a hair changed, a few bulges and wrinkles cut away. But after all is said and done, most Wall Street houses are still the same old joints that they were—not just thirteen years ago but, even worse, thirty years ago."

Merrill went on for nearly ninety minutes, and he soon turned optimistic, saying ML eventually would lead Wall Street to a union with Main Street. "If we keep up with this program, I predict that in years to come we will not have to go out and seek the customers or prospects. People will come to us the same as they go now to doctors, lawyers, and other professionals. And the firm they will select is the firm that has a reputation, and gentlemen, our objective is to build that reputation so that there won't be any doubt."

Then he anticipated by nearly twenty years the dominant advertising theme of his firm: "Now do you understand why I'm bullish about the future of American business in general and the future of the securities business in particular?"

He then turned to my father, who was seated next to him. "I have been truly blessed—and in many ways. Perhaps the greatest blessing of all was to have Win Smith at my side when I was stricken; all of us owe him much—spiritually and financially. No words of mine can express the pride and gratitude I take in Win and the character and ability of the staff that surround him—every last one of you!" And he promised that after he died, the $5.5 million in his capital account would remain in the firm for at least five years.

By the time he finished speaking, Merrill was sobbing. "The audience was profoundly moved," Dad recalled, "and tears appeared in the eyes of practically everyone there." But the actual presence of the directing partner had fired up the troops and made them believe they were the very best team on Wall Street. "It was really an inspirational moment for all of us to see this legendary Wall Street figure come back on the stage and talk to all of us assembled Merrill Lynch sales and management people," said John Loughlin, a young account executive who would go on to become a top Merrill Lynch executive. "He was obviously in failing health at the time, but you could sense the force and the inspiration in the man's voice as he talked to us."

There was every expectation that this appearance marked Charlie Merrill's return to Wall Street.

But, in fact, it would be his valedictory.

It was an experimental treatment based on the use of a fission byproduct of atomic energy research that had granted Merrill the reprieve from angina pain that permitted him to return to New York in 1953. The treatment, which involved regularly drinking a glass of radioactive iodine, was prescribed by Dr. Samuel A. Levine, a renowned heart specialist at Boston's Peter Bent Brigham Hospital. It was called a "radioactive cocktail" by CEM and others. The dosages were begun in June 1953, and in about two months Merrill was relatively free of pain for the first time since his heart attack in 1944. "It's almost incredible now to realize that I was able to go through the past nine and a half years," he wrote to a friend in September. "I can play bridge, I can dance, I can swim, I can laugh and, above all, I can plan."

But eventually the palliative powers of the iodine treatment waned, and CEM gradually returned to a state of semi-invalidism. Nevertheless, he marshaled his strength for one more major business decision. A series of disastrous management steps had driven Safeway to the brink of bankruptcy, creating a pool of unhappy

investors that included Charles Edward Merrill himself, the founder
and largest single stockholder, with about 6 percent of the total. Lingan
Warren, whom CEM had installed as president in 1934, had instituted
autocratic rules that had brought the company to near ruin. Merrill
quickly determined that Warren had to go, but he could not decide
whether his successor should be McCarthy or Magowan. According to
one witness, Merrill used the same strategy he had in 1917 in Detroit
(see p. 71): He flipped a coin. "If it's heads, Magowan will run Merrill
Lynch," he said just before tossing the quarter. It was tails. Then CEM
summoned Warren to a meeting and told him he was through. "Who's
going to be my successor?" Warren asked. "Mike McCarthy's candidate
is Bob Magowan, Bob Magowan's candidate is Mike McCarthy," Merrill
replied, "and I've chosen Bob Magowan." Magowan rescinded most
of Warren's doctrinaire policies, introduced new retailing strategies,
and jumped into the new challenge with a hands-on approach. He
paid regular, unannounced visits to Safeway's two thousand–plus
stores, hustling shopping carts when he found them in the parking
lot and popping into offices, saying to stunned managers, "Hi, I'm Mr.
Magowan." Magowan engineered a turnaround in Safeway's fortunes
and turned it into a supermarket powerhouse.

Meanwhile, Merrill's personal life followed the familiar pattern
of marital disharmony and extramarital activity. He and Kinta were
divorced in December 1952—rounding out his marriage career with
a neat if unenviable symmetry: thirteen years per wife. After the
divorce, Merrill bought and refurbished a Caribbean country house
surrounded by sugarcane fields on Barbados. At the time the island
was a British possession, and the purchase was prompted in no small
part by CEM's long-standing Anglophilia. Called Canefield House, it
was widely held to be the most beautiful home on Barbados.

Merrill's relations with his sons continued to waver between
obligatory paternal affection and dissatisfaction, especially over
their failure to enter the business world. Charles Jr. was a disappointment first because of his choice to attend Harvard instead of
Amherst and then because of his liberal politics. There was an angry
clash in 1951 over Charles's sale of stock that CEM had given to his
grandsons. Merrill was proud of Jimmy's achievements as a poet,
but he was unable to acknowledge his homosexuality. Shortly after

CEM died, Jimmy published a novel, *The Seraglio*, which is a thinly disguised and unflattering account of his father's final years. Only with his daughter, Doris, did Merrill maintain a lifelong and strong bond. Even when she was an adult and the wife of Robert Magowan, Merrill addressed his letters to "Dearest Darling Doris" and signed them "Daddy." Magowan once said: "There's one person in the world that Mr. Merrill thought more of than all the rest of the people put together; it was his daughter."

Long before he died, Merrill provided generously for his family. His residual estate, which he called "my bundle," came to about $25 million and most of it went to "colleges, churches, hospitals and causes I love." In addition, his $5.5 million interest in Merrill Lynch was left in the partnership as a trust that would take its share of the firm's profits and donate them to worthy causes. Under this unusual arrangement, the trust's beneficiaries became, in effect, Merrill Lynch partners. Over the years, the profits were substantial, and when the Charles E. Merrill Trust closed out its books in 1981, it had distributed nearly $114 million. Five years before his death, Merrill gave his Southampton estate to Amherst for the creation of a "place where experts, living together informally, may probe, ponder and discuss" significant economic issues. It was called the Merrill Center of Economics, and it held regular sessions until it closed in 1972. In addition, CEM endowed a chair of medicine at Harvard University in 1954 in honor of Dr. Samuel A. Levine.

Merrill spent his final winter at Canefield House, where he continued to suffer from angina pains, which returned with increasing frequency between iodine treatments, plus a series of vexing skin ailments that plagued him for months. He had spent much of the summer of 1956 in a Boston hospital for an array of illnesses that had widened to include kidney disease. Finally, he developed uremia in September, lapsed into a coma, and died late in the afternoon on Saturday, October 6, a fortnight away from his seventy-first birthday. The following Monday—at 70 Pine Street, at the 117 branch offices, at offices in San Juan, Toronto, Geneva, Paris, and Rome, on the floor of the New York Stock Exchange, and in Grand Central Terminal—nearly six thousand MLPF&B employees were asked to observe a moment of silence. Then they returned to the firm's 440,000 customers in

Dubuque, Iowa; Baton Rouge, Louisiana; Homestead, Pennsylvania; Seattle, Washington. . . . By this point, Merrill Lynch was handling about one in every eight round-lot transactions on the NYSE, and one in every five odd-lot transactions. Much of Charlie Merrill's drive to bring Wall Street to Main Street lay in the future. Only about 8 million Americans—one in every twenty—owned shares of stock. But very few Americans still believed that cattle were bought and sold on the floor of the New York Stock Exchange.

Charles Merrill had set in motion the democratization of the investment world. Before he came along, most of Wall Street looked upon the public as suckers. Merrill refused to believe this, and instead set about to show them that they were competent to make investment decisions and could make money in the stock market. He was free enterprise's most eloquent and convincing spokesman. He advertised honestly and respectfully, seeking "the modest sums of the thrifty." His success is witnessed by the fact that by the end of the twentieth century, three in every four Americans owned stock directly or though mutual funds, pension plans, and retirement accounts.

In 1947, when *Forbes* magazine conducted its survey to name the nation's fifty outstanding business leaders, Charles Merrill was the only representative from the securities industry. Excerpts from the comments on CEM:

> Mr. Merrill is now 62. His organization dominates its own field. As an individual, he has done more to make the business of marketing securities respected than any other person.
>
> He has pioneered almost every new idea which has come to Wall Street in the last quarter of a century.
>
> He has been the most convincing spokesman Wall Street has had with respect to the importance to our system of free enterprise of a free capital market.
>
> A master salesman and keen student of economics, Merrill has outguessed the best. More than any other individual, he has made Wall Street what it is today. Always ahead of the time, he was the first to realize in a practical sense that the crash of 1929 and the decade of depression

which followed called for complete reorientation on the part of the commodity and security dealer, and of the investment banker.

In his book, *Wall Street: Men and Money,* published in 1955, Martin Mayer said of CEM: "He is the first authentically great man produced by the financial market in 150 years. Merrill brought in the public, not as lambs to be fleeced but as partners in the benefits. Today a man who loses his shirt in the market is the victim of his own stupidity or greed, not of the machinations of insiders. The climate of the 1930s helped, the New Deal laws helped, and many individuals helped, but the prime mover was Charlie Merrill." In his 1999 biography, Edwin J. Perkins gave this assessment: "In democratizing the stock market, Merrill created an enterprise that gave middle-class households access to a far wider range of investment opportunities. He truly brought Wall Street to Main Street. Because of his many contributions, Charlie Merrill deserves recognition as the nation's premier entrepreneur in the thriving financial services sector."

Mom, aka Carol Carter, was one of the leading fashion models of her time.

Mom and Dad on their wedding day. It was the second marriage for both of them.

In 1947, my mother and father purchased a 1775 saltbox and 113 acres of farmland in Morris, Connecticut. It is still named "Winvian" after Win and Vivian.

Ken Crosby, manager of ML's Havana office, arranged Win and Vivian's honeymoon in Cuba.

This is my favorite picture of us together and was taken at Merrill's Landing in Palm Beach, Florida, while my father was still healthy.

My dad loved nothing more than spending time at his Connecticut farm. Both my mother and father are buried in the Litchfield cemetery.

The Knickerbocker Greys had an annual father/son dinner and, despite his busy schedule and early complications from Parkinson's disease, my dad was by my side and still is.

In April 1940, Charlie Merrill and Win Smith brought together their new partners at the two-day Waldorf Conference to teach them about the new strategy of bringing Wall Street to Main Street. My father called it "probably the most important thing that has ever been accomplished in our entire history."

In 1955, my dad cut the ribbon at the opening of a week-long "How to Invest" tradeshow in Manhattan that attracted thousands. From left to right are Charlie Merrill, Eddie Lynch Jr., E. A. Pierce, Darwin Fenner, and Alph Beane, Jr.

CEM and WHS held many intense planning sessions together. This was at Charlie's New York City Sutton Place home.

After Charlie's heart attack, my father and other partners would often visit him at one of his homes to seek advice. Here is Merrill (second from left) and Dad (center) with Milija Rubezanin, Don Regan, and Lou Engel.

In December 1945, ML started their first Account Executive Training School, a six-month course of study that included classroom sessions on the floor of NYSE. Six years later, the sales staff included over four hundred graduates, and many went on to join Research, Commodity, and Underwriting.

Merrill Lynch partners were also good friends. Here my mother and father are playing bridge with Doug Findlay and Ted Braun at the farm.

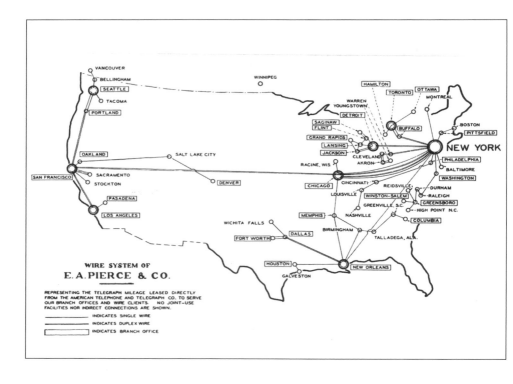

WIRE SYSTEM OF
E. A. PIERCE & CO.

REPRESENTING THE TELEGRAPH MILEAGE LEASED DIRECTLY FROM THE AMERICAN TELEPHONE AND TELEGRAPH CO. TO SERVE OUR BRANCH OFFICES AND WIRE CLIENTS. NO JOINT-USE FACILITIES NOR INDIRECT CONNECTIONS ARE SHOWN.

————————— INDICATES SINGLE WIRE

————————— INDICATES DUPLEX WIRE

[ ] INDICATES BRANCH OFFICE

In the 1930s, E. A. Pierce & Co. became the number one "wire house" in the U.S. My father managed to convince Merrill of its huge potential and acted as chief architect of the merger between the two companies.

Lou Engel was a genius in communication and advertising, enabling the average person to understand how to invest in stocks.

In 1958, the partners at Merrill Lynch voted to replace "Beane" with "Smith" in the firm's name. My father was surprised and touched. Company signage throughout the USA made the switch.

CHAPTER SEVEN

Good-bye, Beane
Hello, Smith

(1957–1970)

T rembling visibly, my father rose before a regular Monday partners meeting in October 1957 and announced to the gathering that he was suffering from Parkinson's disease. It was a poignant moment, even though most of the partners already knew of his affliction. However, no one was prepared for the high drama that would follow a few minutes later. Since Charlie Merrill's death a year before, Dad had been serving as both managing partner and directing partner, but his illness had progressed to the point that he'd decided it was time to choose a second in command, who would play much the same role for him that he had played for CEM.

"As is my privilege and responsibility under the Articles of Partnership, I have the power to appoint my successor," Dad began. "And I shall, of course, name as my successor Michael McCarthy." After a seemingly unanimous chorus of approval from the partners, McCarthy got up and said a few words of acceptance, and then Dad was ready to put his choice to a vote. But first he followed past procedure by asking if any partner wanted to speak. Unexpectedly, a hand shot up, and my father recognized Alpheus C. Beane Jr.—son of one of the founding partners. Beane stood, reached in his pocket for a sheet of paper, and began reading what most of his audience assumed would be a warm endorsement of McCarthy. They couldn't have been more wrong.

"I do not believe that Mr. McCarthy is capable of running this firm," Beane began, his voice high with nervousness. Lou Engel was sitting next to Beane and could read from the sheet of paper; he said there was a space left in the text that Beane filled in verbally with "Mr. McCarthy." Beane went on to say that he believed the partners had overlooked his own qualifications, which he proceeded to list in detail. Ironically, one of the reasons that Fenner had wanted to merge with Merrill Lynch in 1941 was the family's concern that the younger Beane generation was not capable of managing the firm. For a moment after he finished and sat down, the room was prickly with tension. McCarthy stood and said he had not sought the No. 2 job and wanted the decision to be made by the partnership. My father said that was fine with him—but if McCarthy was not acceptable, he would step down. Dad, the compromiser, did not often issue ultimatums. However, he knew that Mike McCarthy was the most qualified partner to lead Merrill Lynch and that he totally embraced the culture of Mother Merrill. Finally, someone asked for a vote on McCarthy. It passed overwhelmingly with only one dissenting vote. After the meeting, Beane announced that he was resigning from the firm and taking with him his money and his name. In subsequent negotiations, Beane asked for $100,000 a year over the next five years for the continued use of his name. "The hell with him," said McCarthy, the new managing partner. "We'll put Win Smith's name in there. It'll just fit." This was done without my father's knowledge. A wise move because he likely would not have wanted the recognition.

McCarthy got approval from the top partners, and a few days later, he telephoned my father, who was vacationing in Florida and not well. "I told him that his partners wanted to honor him by adding his name to our firm name," McCarthy recalled. "As a rather lame joke I said that we found that there were the same number of letters in each name and that the firm would save quite a bit of money in changing our signs, rubber stamps, stationery. I am sure that Win was surprised and overcome by the news because there was dead silence for a moment and when he came back on the phone I detected a catch in his voice." It was estimated it would cost $250 per sign to have painters scratch out "Beane" and replace it with "Smith." Fortunately, the firm's old name was not etched in stone or cast in bronze anywhere—though the Chicago office had a neon sign that would cost $5,000 to replace, and there were twelve metal signs that had to be recast. In all, there were some 750 signs affected at the 122 offices. Company lawyers decreed the changes couldn't be made until Beane's last day, February 28, 1958, but at that point the entire name conversion was accomplished in a single day. The new letterheads were an equally minor matter, and the old "Beane" stationery was downgraded to interoffice memo duty. On the day of the change my mother drove Dad by the Delray Beach, Florida, office so that he could see the new sign. Dad was not well that February and was taking time to rest. My mother later told me how touched he was by this honor bestowed on him by his fellow partners. The change provided abundant grist for the mills of the nation's newspapers, and there were tongue-in-cheek editorials asking, "What happened to the Beane?" Beane ended up joining the firm of J. R. Williston & Co., which was renamed Williston and Beane, and capitalized on the moment by running an ad in the *New Yorker* magazine headlined "Who has the BEANE? We have the BEANE!—J. R. Williston & Beane." Charlie Merrill would have been delighted, not only because of the recognition of my father, but also because of the tremendous publicity the name change received. What great "free" advertising!

While my mother was thrilled with the recognition, she was nervous about the publicity, and her worst fears came true one day when the Buckley School, on Manhattan's Upper East Side, received a call from someone with a Spanish accent. "Mr. Smith has been in a serious car accident and Mrs. Smith is rushing to the hospital," the caller said. "Would you get their son ready. We will pick him up shortly." The school was only two blocks from our apartment. They immediately called home and my mother answered the phone. "Oh my God, keep Winnie there," she told them. "I'll be right over. This is a kidnap attempt." My mother, who had lost her first son tragically, was overly protective of me, and this episode put her over the edge. She hired private detectives to take me to school each day and sit outside the apartment at night. And for a few weeks, we actually moved several blocks away to my Uncle Frederick's apartment. I was only eight at the time, but I do remember this event clearly. While no one likes to live in fear, leaders of firms like Merrill Lynch have always been the target of criminals and others. Beginning with Don Regan, all chairmen and CEOs were provided with security guards when they traveled, their homes were alarmed and monitored, and they were given a car with a driver who was trained in evasive driving skills.

W hen Michael William McCarthy came to New York to work for Merrill Lynch in 1940, his easygoing, Midwestern manner and rural folksiness intrigued the older Pierce partners, who regarded him skeptically from behind dark suits and white shirts. After a few weeks one of them came up to him and asked, "You're Mr. McCarthy, aren't you?" McCarthy affirmed he was with a nod and the inquisitor proffered his hand, introduced himself—and added as further identification, "Yale, 1918." McCarthy shook his hand and replied, "I'm glad to know you. I'm Beach High School, 1919."

Mike McCarthy finished his formal education when he graduated from Beach (pop. 1,500) High School in the wheat country of North Dakota, a few miles from the Montana border. All four of McCarthy's grandparents had arrived in America from Ireland just before the Civil War. Mike McCarthy was the youngest of the six children in his family. His father was a "sidewalk farmer"—meaning he lived in town rather than on the farm. In addition to wheat farming, the elder McCarthy taught school, sold farm equipment, and served as auditor for Golden Valley County. After he graduated from high school in 1919, the sixteen-year-old McCarthy went to work in his father's office and then took a job with the county treasurer as his deputy. Right after the 1920 statewide elections of county officers, McCarthy wired all of the incoming auditors and treasurers to tell them that he was available for employment. He landed a job in Stanley, North Dakota, near the Canadian border, as deputy auditor for Mountrail County. As he recalled: "My new boss came down to meet me at the train and his first question was, 'When did you get out of knee pants?' It was a terrific job I had, although one thing I didn't like very well was that there was a bounty on coyotes and we had to bring in their pelts. We punched their ears and it smelled to high heaven. I don't know what they got—something like five dollars a pelt. But that was one of the chores of the deputy county auditor."

Winters were mean and unaccommodating in northern North Dakota, so in 1924 the twenty-one-year-old McCarthy, along with his older sister, Mary, set off for California in a Model T Ford. They made it to Oakland, where an employment agency found a job for McCarthy as a bookkeeper at Mutual Stores, a grocery chain of some one hundred retail outlets in the Bay Area run by Emil Hagstrom, an innovative and expansion-minded enterpriser. Within a year, McCarthy was made office manager. Hagstrom had installed an electric punch-card system to handle the chain's accounting and billing and to keep track of inventory, and according to McCarthy, "the system also provided a great deal of statistical information that was helpful to management." When Charlie Merrill came out in 1928 to bring Mutual Stores into the MacMarr chain, he was "quite impressed with the information we could give him. As a result, I got to know him quite well." McCarthy ended up manager of Safeway's Los Angeles region, and when Merrill needed someone to streamline the "backstage" operations—the accounting, administration, and paperwork—of his new firm in 1940, he recruited the bright young man from North Dakota, who had never seen the inside of a brokerage office.

"I thought I was going to take over the accounting end," McCarthy said. "When I met with Charlie the first day, I found out he was handing everything over to me except sales and underwriting. Most of Wall Street couldn't understand it. They had never heard of me. I came out of the blue. I was told that I would have a two-week training program to learn the operation of a brokerage business, but there really was no training program, so I wandered around for two weeks to find out where the doors opened and spent some time visiting each department." McCarthy flourished in his new career, and in 1944 Merrill invited him to become a partner. To come up with the $10,000 for his capital contribution, McCarthy had to borrow $7,500 from Merrill. He went on to become assistant managing partner in 1948, and in December 1957 the former deputy auditor for Mountrail County, North Dakota, became managing partner of Merrill Lynch, Pierce, Fenner & Smith. The firm seemed to be in robust health, but there was an immediate crisis that confronted him.

R. Leslie Nicol, the son of a British civil servant, was born on the Caribbean island of Barbados in 1895, educated on Trinidad, and in 1918 came to New York, where he found work as a businessman's all-purpose problem-solver. He moved on to Wall Street in 1921 with the old A. A. Housman and Co. firm as a stenographer, but he quickly displayed an aptitude for handling difficult personnel situations. When the Housman firm became E. A. Pierce & Co. in 1927, Les Nicol was appointed personnel manager, and when Charlie Merrill and my dad engineered the formation of the modern Merrill Lynch in 1940, Nicol seemed the best choice for one of the new firm's most taxing tasks: partnership relations. For the next two decades, Nicol's clipped British accent and lucid prose were employed to placate, inspire, cajole, inform, chastise, reassure, and muster the men and occasional woman who had invested money in MLPF&B.

It was demanding, time-consuming work, for the rules of partnership were cumbersome. The task was manageable for most brokerages because they had fewer than ten partners, but Merrill Lynch was another story. Every year Nicol and his assistants were obliged to obtain new articles of agreement signed by every partner—this after getting the articles approved by the NYSE and dozens of smaller exchanges. Partners had to be tracked down as far away as New Zealand, and if they happened to be on vacation, the difficulties were magnified. When a partner died, his money was withdrawn from the firm. Whenever the firm needed additional money to finance its growing business, Merrill and my father were obliged to ask each partner to increase his contributions. When a partner refused to provide more capital, the firm had to take in additional partners to fill the gap. When Nicol began his work in 1940, there were forty partners and his job was very difficult. By 1955 there were more than a hundred partners, and it was nearly impossible.

Like so many rules and traditions on Wall Street, the partnership requirement was based on once-valid reasons that no longer existed. Some 250 years earlier, when New York City was still part of an English colony, sales in cotton, sugar, and spices were conducted near the riverfront at the foot of Wall Street. During the American Revolution, the states and the Continental Congress issued bonds, which were called stock, to finance the war. By the end of the war, these securities were practically worthless, so Alexander Hamilton proposed that the new United States government assume these obligations. Because news traveled slowly in those days, a few insiders—sharp businessmen and members of Congress—went around the thirteen states buying up the war bonds before the owners realized that they were now worth something. These securities began to be traded right along with cotton, sugar, and spices on Wall Street about 1790.

As banks and insurance companies were formed, they, too, issued securities—and the need for an organized market to trade in them developed. A central auction was set up at 22 Wall Street, and the securities were traded every day at noon. But some traders came to the auctions solely to listen to prices, and afterward they would offer the same securities at reduced commission rates. To thwart these early insiders, twenty-four men signed a document on May 17, 1792, in which they agreed to trade securities only among themselves, to maintain fixed commission rates, and to avoid other auctions. The signatories did business as individuals, and their relationship with their customers was personal, like that of doctor and patient or lawyer and client. As brokerages grew larger, the individuals took on partners. Because this arrangement preserved the personal relationship aspect of the securities business, the partnership form of management became the norm for Wall Street. Well into the twentieth century, the rules of the New York Stock Exchange forbade corporate members—and the joke was that MLPF&B had to hire a hall to hold partnership meetings. The truth was that all of the firm's partners had never sat down together.

Charlie Merrill had seen right from the beginning that partnership posed serious difficulties for his firm. He called it an "antique" way to do business in 1940, and in subsequent years he often wished aloud that MLPF&B would be allowed to incorporate. Other securities dealers joined the chorus, and the NYSE governors finally approved the rule change, by a vote of 594 to 538, in 1953. A small firm, Woodcock, Hess, became the first corporate member a few months later, but Merrill Lynch faced a catch-22: It needed to throw off the yoke of partnership and become a corporation to streamline its operations, but being a hydra-headed partnership made such a major change difficult to achieve. Moreover, before the intricacies of incorporation could be worked out, CEM died in 1956, and his will left a substantial financial interest in the firm—thus further complicating the incorporation process.

The overriding impetus for incorporation was always the same: It would allow MLPF&B to retain its earnings year after year and thus build a solid capital foundation to finance its growing business. The inability to do this had serious implications. For example, since the firm started each year with zero reserves, it had to wait until well into the year to predict how much money it would make that year. Thus expenditures for advertising and promotion tended to come at the end of the year, which often was not the best time for it. While CEM was on the scene, there was a patchwork solution to this problem. According to Bob Magowan: "He wouldn't let us take our money. When we finally made some money, we couldn't take it out of the firm because we were undercapitalized and he made us leave it in there. He was the boss if there ever was one."

After Merrill's death, Dad managed to use the force of his personality to "pass the hat" among the partners for additional contributions to the firm, but as his illness deepened, his capital-raising activities waned and the incorporation movement fell by the wayside.

An early and vigorous incorporation proponent was Edwin O. Cartwright, manager of the Dallas office, who became a general partner in 1949. Cartwright made a statistical study that showed the financial advantages of incorporating MLPF&B and sent it to all the partners. He figuratively held his breath until nothing happened, then wrote to my father and asked him if the issue was completely dead. "I don't think it's completely dead," Dad responded, "but it's pretty dormant."

When McCarthy was handed the reins of leadership in 1958, he realized he would not be able to pull together the capital needed to nurture the growth of the newly named MLPF&S. "After Charlie passed away, and Win was not well, I felt a heavy burden of capital requirements," McCarthy said. "The general [working] partners could not make much of a capital contribution each year because quite a few of them were young and raising families—they had kids going to college or were building homes. But probably the biggest reason was that the IRS was taking a big bite out of their incomes at that time, as much as ninety percent. The firm distributed all profits to the partners each year, leaving the cash box empty. I was always fearful that if we ever had a loss year, some of the money partners would come knocking at my door at the end of a partnership year and tell me they wanted out, and withdraw all of their capital."

In the spring of 1958, McCarthy arranged a meeting with my father, who by this time was bedridden in his Connecticut home. McCarthy brought along two partners—George Leness, who supported incorporation, and Earle English, who strongly opposed it. After each presented his case, English excused himself, apparently to use the bathroom. McCarthy seized the opportunity to get Dad to agree to the appointment of William A. Forrester Jr., a talented underwriter who worked for Leness, as head of a special committee to pursue incorporation. Leness seconded Forrester, and Dad went along with it. In later years, McCarthy would recall with laughter that once my father had given his blessing to Forrester, the absent Earle English "was pretty well locked in—there was nothing he could do about it." Forrester's group, which included twenty full-time lawyers, then set out to find how best to maneuver the new form of management through the laws and regulation of federal agencies, some forty states, a dozen foreign countries and forty-six exchanges in which MLPF&S was a member. By this time, fifty-one of the 635 NYSE member firms were incorporated—though none of the bigger houses had taken the step. Five months later, Forrester presented McCarthy with a precise plan for incorporation. But a map is not a journey, and the difficult part had just begun.

The task was to sell the idea to the partnership, which was composed of two distinct wings: the fifty general partners, who actively worked for the firm (many of whom were still paying off loans originally granted by Charlie Merrill that enabled them to buy their interest), and the sixty-seven limited partners, who were mostly out-of-town, non-active investors in the firm. McCarthy planned his strategy carefully and proceeded slowly. First, he called in a handful of the most powerful general partners who worked with him in New York, persuaded them that incorporation was essential, and asked them to work on the other general partners. Once the proselytization was complete, he called a meeting of all the general partners, who, after spirited debate, approved the proposal. Because voting power was weighted by interest in the firm, the general partners could control any firm-wide vote. "Then I called in the out-of-town partners," McCarthy said. "All they could do was bless it because we already had the votes." Even so, there was a last-minute holdout: Harold Johnson, a limited partner who was a lawyer from Florida. The problem was resolved in a way that would have pleased Charlie Merrill. "Harold was very upset that his interest in the firm had been substantially reduced," according to McCarthy. "As we got closer to D-Day, we were afraid he might bring suit, which would delay incorporation, and we could be in the courts for a long, long time. We finally heard from Harold that he would sign off from the partnership if we contributed $50,000 to Amherst. Jim Thomson got a group together and we all personally wrote out checks of $1,000 to $32,000. After he signed all the necessary papers, instead of giving him one check from Merrill Lynch, Jim handed him all the checks from his former partners. He was a bit chagrined, but it all ended up on a good note." Immediately after the vote, McCarthy turned to Cartwright and said, "If this doesn't work, we're going to blame you."

The last partners meeting of Merrill Lynch, Pierce, Fenner & Smith was held on October 24, 1958, and on January 12, 1959, the 117 partners became shareholders in Merrill Lynch, Pierce, Fenner & Smith Incorporated. For many of these former partners, there was a onetime financial sacrifice because they had to pay extra taxes to effect the change, but they benefited in the long term. "Now," said my father, the newly elected chairman of the board, "we will be able to sleep nights." As the corporation's new president, McCarthy for the first time could confidently plan the firm's future beyond the next annual expiration date of the partnership agreement. He called incorporation "among the most significant events in Merrill Lynch history." Freed from the harness of partnership, the firm was able to make acquisitions that would broaden its offerings to investors and even, in one spectacular move a decade later, rescue the Street itself from possible collapse. It also allowed the firm to reward senior employees with share ownership. Within two years, the roster of stockholders would grow from 117 to 255. Ed Cartwright had had no cause for concern. Ten years after incorporation, the firm's net income had more than tripled, from $13.5 million to $40.7 million. Incorporation also paved the way for the longer-range goal: going public and raising capital the same way other American businesses had been doing since 1792.

V ery early in the life of the firm, Charlie Merrill had turned his attention to his first love: investment banking. He was, however, severely hampered by the distrust many other partners held for underwriting, which they viewed as unnecessarily risky and too dependent on personal contacts. Moreover, most of CEM's own contacts, dating from the 1920s, had dried up. Thus it is not surprising that in 1943 the Underwriting Division contributed a puny $129,250 to the firm's earnings—largely through the efforts of Merrill himself. A year earlier, CEM had failed in his attempt to persuade George Leness, who at that time was a vice president of the First Boston Corporation, with a reputation as a talented, honest investment banker, to join MLPF&B as chief of its underwriting operation. Leness had told Merrill that he didn't want to risk involvement with a "shaky" company. According to Leness, that first conversation ended like this:

Leness: "I take it you think I have made a mistake."

Merrill: "Yes, I most certainly do. I am willing to bet a substantial sum, with odds of two to one, that when activity does come back to the markets, our firm, which has only one-half the capital of your corporation, will earn twice as much money. Considering the capital ratio, this makes the odds I am offering four to one and not two to one."

Leness didn't take the wager, and Merrill's prediction wouldn't come true for many years, but when CEM saw the 1943 underwriting figures, he tried Leness again; this time he succeeded—and in future years Leness would reflect gratefully that "opportunity knocked twice." When Leness took over the Underwriting Division on January 1, 1944, he inherited two small rooms, four employees, very little business—and a No. 43 ranking among the nation's investment bankers.

Leness, an outstanding middle-distance runner who had won the gold medal in the 600-yard run at the famed Millrose Games in 1926, got off to a fast start at Merrill Lynch, and by 1946 the firm was ranked fifteenth in underwriting. Most of the early gains came in public utility issues, which had been Leness's specialty throughout his Wall Street career. Merrill Lynch was helped greatly by a 1941 ruling requiring utilities to submit their security offerings to competitive bidding. Until this time, the utility securities field had been dominated by a handful of big New York banks led by J. P. Morgan. With the field wide open, Leness was able to make maximum use of Merrill Lynch's strongest asset as an underwriter: its national distribution system.

Charlie Merrill had always viewed brokerage and underwriting as related responsibilities, but at the same time he had always approached the connection cautiously, and so he turned the Merrill Lynch underwriting arm over to George Leness with explicit orders to tread softly and be certain that the firm's underwriting activities did not conflict with the best interests of its retail customers. The firm's 1944 Annual Report set ground rules for the underwriting operation: "On the one hand is a host of potential investors with the necessary capital, and on the other is industry needing capital. Some of the funds needed will be of a risk nature, and some of it will be of investment type. It will be our duty to see that funds of each of these types of enterprise are raised from the proper sources so that those who cannot afford to risk their savings are not diverted to ventures too speculative in nature." Merrill and my father also insisted that the Research Department remain independent of Investment Banking. This was not the case at other investment banking firms.

From Merrill's early safeguards, there evolved a set of house rules that were the strictest on Wall Street and went far beyond any legal requirements. Any hint of taint would drive Merrill Lynch away from backing an issue, and all doubts were resolved in favor of the individual investor. Thomas Chrystie, who worked under Leness, said there was "a feeling that if anybody doing business with a prospect or client of the firm—even a very lucrative client—somewhere along the line didn't feel comfortable developing that prospect or doing a specific transaction, he should just back away." In 1969—a quarter-century after CEM set down the underwriting edict—Merrill Lynch was among a dozen major firms invited by First Boston to join an investment-grade offering by the new Penn Central Railroad, which was a hasty marriage of the old New York Central and Pennsylvania Railroads. Other major firms accepted eagerly and quickly, but a Merrill Lynch researcher raised a yellow flag after reviewing the company's financials and cash flow. Ultimately, Merrill Lynch declined the invitation—and a few months later Penn Central revealed it could not meet its commercial paper payments.

Such discretion stunted the growth of the Underwriting Division for many years. In fact, postwar activity was so lean that when the U.S. Department of Justice filed antitrust charges against seventeen major investment banking firms in 1947, Merrill Lynch didn't even warrant a mention. Because of its unmatched retail distribution network, the firm was frequently invited to join the syndicates of leading underwriters during the 1950s, but it remained outside of an almost closed club of major originating underwriters. When Leness took over, he built the business painstakingly, basing it on his own personal reputation on the Street. "George Leness deserves every credit for having made the Investment Banking Division at Merrill Lynch," says Winthrop Lenz, who would succeed him in 1961. "He had tremendous standing in the industry and with the corporations, and everybody knew he had complete integrity. As a result, he was completely trusted by the companies he did business with, the institutions and his competitors." Chrystie recalled turning in a report on a proposal that ended with an estimate of the amount of money the firm would realize from participation. "George Leness turned to me and said, 'That is not a consideration.'"

The big breakthrough came in 1955 when Merrill Lynch was asked to participate in the hottest underwriting event of all time up until then: the Ford Foundation's offering of 10.2 million shares of Ford Motor Company stock. With a value estimated at $660 million, it was easily the largest underwriting in history up to that time. When the Ford stock went up for sale on January 18, 1956, thousands of first-time investors placed their orders, and all 10.2 million shares were sold out in a matter of hours—including the 236,000 allotted to MLPF&B as one of seven co-managers of the underwriting. The Ford financing was the major contributor to Merrill Lynch's first billion-dollar underwriting year, and as a result of it, the firm reached a No. 5 ranking in the underwriting sweepstakes.

One less-publicized activity of the Underwriting Division involved Howard Hughes, the mysterious, eccentric millionaire and aircraft pioneer. In December 1954, Hughes was in deep trouble with the Internal Revenue Service, and he turned to MLPF&B for help. A plan involving the sale of 25 percent of the stock of the Hughes Tool Company was drawn up, apparently by CEM himself. Hughes then wanted Merrill to come meet with him in Los Angeles, but CEM's doctors summarily vetoed the trip. Soon afterward, my father, Leness, and Courtney J. Ivey, an outside attorney representing the firm, were summoned to a meeting with a "Mr. X" in his suite at the Beverly Hills Wilshire Hotel in Los Angeles. After waiting for five hours beyond the scheduled appointment time, the MLPF&B trio was ushered in, only to learn that Hughes was indecisive and unable to make a commitment to the plan. Leness wrote to Merrill a few days later to fill him in on the meeting:

> "Mr. X" is unquestionably a very brilliant, original person. However, one of his failings, or perhaps one of his great virtues, is the fact that he cannot seem to make up his mind to part with any of his property. We are told that the only item of property which he has ever sold happened back in 1928 when he sold a 1912 Buick. A number of people have tried to buy some of his other assets and have hired expensive lawyers and have worked long and hard on it, only to get up to the day of signing and find that "Mr. X" had changed his mind. When he starts one of the proposed sales of assets, he sincerely believes he should do it and go forward with it and he will spend an unlimited amount of money to bring the proposed sale about. At the eleventh hour, however, he always has some good reason for changing his mind and it comes to nothing.
>
> This is a fascinating piece of business and we are going to keep after it. There is no question that the provisions in the new tax law, which provide that he can liquidate his assets on a long term gain basis are of tremendous value to him and sooner or later he is going to be forced to sell them. We are going to keep eternally after him.

Leness ran the underwriting operation for eighteen years, and left in a blaze of glory. Among his finest achievements in his final days at the firm was a mammoth $200 million municipal bond offering to finance the Chesapeake Bay Bridge and Tunnel, the 17.5-mile connection between Cape Charles, on the tip of Virginia's eastern shore, and Chesapeake Beach, on the Virginia mainland. This was the centerpiece of five underwritings headed jointly or solely by Merrill Lynch in 1960.

During the first half of the twentieth century there had been a pervasive belief that investment bankers shouldn't solicit business. Like a doctor or a lawyer, you established a reputation and then waited to be asked for your services. But when Win Lenz took over for Leness in 1961, the Merrill Lynch Underwriting Division became more aggressive in seeking business. "I was anxious to try making calls on companies," Tom Chrystie says of those days in the early sixties, "so I would write letters to companies and put copies of them in Win Lenz's in-box, and if I didn't hear from him for a couple of days, I would mail the originals and then go make the calls." Under Lenz, Merrill Lynch won a role in the biggest deals of the decade and in the process became a founding member of "the Fearsome Foursome," an underwriting partnership with Lehman Brothers, Salomon Brothers, and Blyth & Company that was formed to challenge the established syndicate leaders, Morgan Stanley and First Boston. As a result, Merrill Lynch averaged $2 billion a year in managed or co-managed offerings between 1964 and 1968—nearly triple the totals for the preceding five years.

Just as Leness had promised Charlie Merrill in 1954, the firm kept after the "fascinating piece of business" known as Howard Hughes, whose financial empire continued to teeter on the edge of calamity. Secluded at the Beverly Hills Hotel, Hughes stayed in touch with the Merrill Lynch Underwriting Division by telephone during the 1950s. Hughes's biographers report that he usually called from a darkened room, sitting naked in a white leather chair, his uncut hair cascading down his back, his unshaven face bristling with beard, his untrimmed fingernails and toenails grotesquely long. When he asked the company to develop a plan for the public sale of the Hughes Aircraft Company in 1958, a Merrill Lynch team headed by William Forrester moved into a suite at the hotel and began talking to Hughes by telephone. The financier was less than a hundred yards away in his bungalow, but no one from the firm ever saw him. The Forrester team faced a daunting task, for Hughes had already given the stock to a tax-exempt medical institute—supposedly to "benefit mankind" but in fact to avoid taxes. Thus the deal collapsed, but Lenz stayed in touch with Hughes's top aides.

The persistence paid off in 1966 when Hughes, trapped by cash-flow difficulties and legal problems, decided to sell his massive stock holdings in Trans World Airlines. This time, the Merrill Lynch effort was headed by Julius H. ("Dooley") Sedlmayr, who had just succeeded Lenz as the director of investment banking. It was a very secret deal, and Hughes had a special telephone installed on Sedlmayr's desk at 70 Pine Street so that only he would answer it when Hughes called. Merrill Lynch led a syndicate of 404 investment bankers that sold Hughes's 6.5 million shares of TWA on May 3, 1966, at $86 a share. All of the shares were sold to the public in less than one hour. The sale was the largest underwriting managed by a single investment firm in Wall Street history, and it also was the largest offering made by any syndicate since the $660 million Ford Motor Company sale in 1956, which Merrill Lynch also co-managed. The firm took a $2.9 million management fee and handed Hughes a certified check for $546,549,771.

Six years later, Hughes's aides came to Sedlmayr to sell the foundation of his family fortune—the oil-tool division of the Hughes Tool Company. There was, however, a serious problem, for Hughes had increasingly come under the control of his aides, and there was even some doubt that he was alive. Before it would approve the sale, the Securities and Exchange Commission wanted conclusive proof that Hughes was alive and mentally competent to make this decision. Thus Sedlmayr's most pressing task was to ascertain that the firm actually was dealing with the reclusive Hughes himself. He would have to see the man in person. To that end, Sedlmayr and attorney Ivey flew to Managua, Nicaragua, where Hughes had sequestered himself in the Intercontinental Hotel, spending most of his time taking drugs and watching movies. A meeting was scheduled for September 24, 1972, at two P.M., but as the hour approached, Hughes—despite massive doses of tranquilizers—was unable to bring himself to meet with the

Merrill Lynch officials. The meeting was delayed until five P.M., then eight P.M. and then ten P.M. When the ten P.M. meeting failed to materialize, Sedlmayr angrily told Hughes's aides that the deal was off unless he and Ivey could personally meet with Hughes immediately. Finally, about four A.M. on September 25, Sedlmayr and Ivey were ushered into Hughes's hotel room. The sixty-six-year-old tycoon had shaved and showered and appeared nostalgic about selling part of the tool company. Both men were sure it was Hughes because he looked very much as he had when he was last seen in public some fifteen years earlier. The meeting lasted about thirty-five minutes, and when it was over Hughes signed the necessary papers. The oil-tool division was sold to the public on December 7, 1972, for $150 million. Merrill Lynch earned $1.5 million in a management fee plus another $1 million in commissions on the sale of the stock, and Sedlmayr nailed down his reputation as one of the Street's shrewdest investment bankers.

After Hughes's death in 1976, there was great controversy about where he had actually died and if he had a will. Texas was ultimately given jurisdiction, and despite the fact that many purported wills were presented, the courts never recognized any. Will Lummis, a Dallas attorney and Hughes relative, was made the executor, and he hired Merrill Lynch to value the estate for tax purposes. Dooley was no longer running investment banking, but he oversaw the team that worked on this project. Trey Fitzgibbons led the effort and John Otto, Frank Weisser, and I did the lion's share of the work. It was a fascinating assignment, and one of my most interesting projects ever.

Our first meeting was near Las Vegas at the headquarters of the Summa Corporation, which was the holding company for all of Hughes's business assets. We walked into the building and rode the elevator down from the lobby to the basement offices, where none of the desks had papers on them, and there was only one oil painting in the conference room: the famous one of Jane Russell, one of Hughes's paramours, from the movie *Outlaw*. The Summa directors were uncommunicative and unhelpful, and it was clear they were there only because they had been ordered by the court to cooperate. Hughes's fortune had been rumored to be as much as $2 billion, but when we turned in our report after a year of work, we valued Summa as a "going concern" and presented an estate valuation to the executor of about

$115 million. Hughes had spent years assembling varied assets like casinos, land, a regional airline, radio stations, and trailer parks, but as his faculties deteriorated, it was obvious that those managing his business were incompetent at best and likely taking total advantage of Hughes's mental state. Virtually none of the businesses were making money, and years earlier Hughes had contributed Hughes Aircraft to the Hughes Medical Foundation, so this asset was not in his estate. Yet the Summa officers were being handsomely paid. The brilliant aviator who had once amassed a fortune that was worth more than a billion dollars died a broken man and left a mess behind. It really was an amazing look into this secret world of Howard Hughes.

For the first dozen years of its existence, the Merrill Lynch international operation consisted of a single office in Havana on the then-friendly island nation of Cuba, just ninety miles from Miami. The Havana office was an anomaly that had opened in 1941 with the acquisition of a sugar brokerage firm. During World War II, it was probably the smallest, least-sophisticated facility in the Merrill Lynch galaxy—consisting of four desks in the middle of a small room and a chalkboard listing some three hundred stocks. Kenneth M. Crosby, the American spy who worked under a Merrill Lynch cover during the war, opted for a peacetime career as a stockbroker and took over the Havana operation in 1946. One of his first moves was to install an NYSE ticker, which soon proved to be a boon to business. Among the world's biggest postwar commodity brokers were the Chinese, and when the nation fell to the Communists in 1949, most of them headed for Havana. The reason: They had developed an interest in equities, immigration quotas kept them out of the U.S., and Cuba was the only place in the world outside the U.S. that had an NYSE ticker. The office blossomed and soon moved to larger quarters. Most of the clients were super-wealthy, and as Cuba had no capital gains tax, they were active traders in large lots. There were never odd-lot orders. In fact, there were very few 100-share orders. The main denomination was 1,000 shares.

Crosby's career blossomed, too. One reason was that Havana remained the only Merrill Lynch international office, and so it became a popular vacation spot for many partners, thereby giving the young manager an opportunity to develop personal relationships with all of the top executives. Moreover, under Cuban law all of the partners had to file personal income tax returns in Cuba, which Crosby had to handle. With such access to the confidential data revealing the capital position of each partner, Crosby soon knew the pecking order inside the company. One of the account executives hired by Crosby was Jack Hemingway, son of Ernest Hemingway, who lived in Cuba. Crosby became friendly with the author, and sometimes would drink daiquiris with him at the Floridita, a favorite Hemingway watering hole. In 1959 and 1960, Crosby came to know Fidel Castro on a personal basis. "I was a director of the Havana Rotary Club," Crosby recalled, "and I once helped arranged a benefit luncheon for him at the Hotel Nacional." Crosby also served on the banking committee that organized a special dinner for Castro to address the financial community. After Castro took over in 1959, the office remained open until about a year later when the U.S. and Cuba broke off diplomatic relations. Because the break required the cancellation of all the necessary insurance coverage for the office, it had to be closed. Later, Cuban exiles would thank Merrill Lynch for having had an office in Havana because it encouraged them to invest outside Cuba, and when they were forced out of their homeland, the only money they had was in their Merrill Lynch accounts in New York.

Charlie Merrill had always believed that the same sales techniques that worked well with the American middle class would work equally well in foreign markets, but he died before there was any concerted effort to develop a global presence. Other firms, such as Bache and Fahnestock, were well down the international track before Merrill Lynch left the stating gate. One of the earliest and most earnest advocates of overseas expansion was Ken Crosby himself, and he believed that Merrill Lynch's reluctance to go international had roots in the Cuban experience. Contrary to the Merrill Lynch tradition, the Havana office catered to a few wealthy clients who were constantly manipulating their portfolios and causing endless problems for the New York office in general and Earle English, the administrative director, in particular. "I was promoting the idea of going into Caracas, Venezuela," Crosby said. "I remember sitting with Earle and making this tremendous presentation. Earle listened to it all very quietly. He says, 'Do you see that map of Manhattan on the wall? I want to tell you why we're not going to open an office in Caracas. Out of Havana, you give us one percent of our business, but you give me ten percent of my headaches. You can blindfold me and I can stick a pin in that map anywhere and I'll open an office there tomorrow and we'll do as much business there as you'll do in Caracas, and I won't have one-tenth of the headaches.' That's why it took a long time to expand the international operation." Over the years, many in Merrill Lynch shared English's skepticism, and it took the persistency of people like my father, Mike McCarthy, Tom Chrystie, Bill Schreyer, Harry Anderson, Bill Arthur, Archie Urciuoli, and later Dan Tully, Dave Komansky, Jerry Kenney, and myself to champion the overseas growth.

Right after World War II, Merrill Lynch had opened European offices to serve American military personnel stationed abroad. As the Marshall Plan brought recovery to the war-ravaged continent, Europeans began investing, and within a few years, these Merrill Lynch offices had picked up a substantial international clientele. The firm established itself in Europe in October 1951, with an office in Geneva. Operations were opened in Paris and Rome in 1957. The commodities business contributed to the early international activity because Merrill Lynch retained agents in many cities that, like Hamburg and Amsterdam, would become the nucleus to future offices. When Mike McCarthy became managing partner, there were only six offices in operation outside the United States (Toronto, Havana, San Juan, Paris, Rome, and Geneva). He quickly ordered a major expansion. Four new offices were added in 1960 alone—London, Hong Kong, Cannes, and Panama City. Between 1962 and 1970 revenues from the international operation quadrupled to $20 million. This global expansion was not accomplished easily, though, for while many nations were naturally eager to accept investment by American manufacturing firms and venture capitalists, the value of permitting a U.S. brokerage firm to operate freely on their soil was not so apparent. McCarthy's strategy was to get a foothold in the form of whatever Merrill Lynch representation was permitted and proceed from there. Often the opening wedge was a Merrill Lynch facility to accommodate the wishes of foreign investors to speculate in commodities. This happened in Beirut, for example, where the first customers pulled up in Mercedes and waded through herds of sheep to reach the office door. Within a year, Merrill's Beirut office had become an extremely profitable operation, and Merrill was the only American financial firm to continue doing business throughout the brutal civil war, even though it sometimes operated from the basement of a hotel.

On October 9, 1951, Charlie Merrill had sent a memo to my father: "I think we should have a model office in Tokyo. The opportunities in Japan, in my opinion, are comparable to the opportunities that existed in the southern states after the Civil War. The biggest fortunes were not made by carpet-baggers, but were made by high-class, responsible businessmen who were attracted to the South by cheap labor. For years to come Japan will be able to compete, fabricate and exchange manufactured articles at prices lower than they can be made in the US." Once again, CEM had seen opportunity before anyone else. When McCarthy and his top assistant, Jim Thomson, touched down at Tokyo International Airport eight years later, there were more stockholders in Japan (10 million) than in the United States (9 million). McCarthy and Thomson were hosted by officials of Nomura Securities, which had copied Merrill Lynch methods (they even published an employee magazine whose title translated roughly into "We the People") to build a network of nearly fifty branch offices. It was a friendly meeting, but there were strictly enforced laws against foreign securities firms doing business in Japan. Nevertheless, in 1961, over the complaints of many stockholders who could see no reason for the expense, McCarthy sent Donald P. Knode, who had just set up an office in Panama, to Tokyo to operate a Merrill Lynch "subsidiary." Knode's first office was a listening post in his home.

The following year it seemed briefly like a brilliant move. Sony became the first Japanese firm to make a public offering in the United States, and dozens of Wall Street firms sent representatives to Tokyo to help Japanese firms tap into the U.S. money market. The Americans established themselves in the city's Marunouchi financial district, which came to be called "Wall Street East." Back in Washington, however, Congress saw an unfavorable balance-of-payments getting worse and slapped a tax on all purchases of foreign securities by U.S. citizens. Most of the Americans in Tokyo saw their market dry up almost immediately and said "sayonara," but Knode stayed as the lone American presence, steadily urging the Japanese government to allow Merrill Lynch to do business there. Back home McCarthy helped matters along by opening the vaunted Merrill Lynch training program to Nomura Securities' salesmen. MLPF&S did business in Japan anytime it was possible, usually working with Japanese firms and helping them underwrite Japanese securities in Europe. It paid off in 1964 when Merrill Lynch became the first foreign securities firm to open a representative office in Japan, where they were allowed to dispense market information, though not solicit business. By 1972, Japan was awash in unwanted American dollars, and Merrill Lynch became the first foreign securities firm to be granted a full securities business license. Our new branch office was opened in Tokyo's new Mitsui-Toranomon Building, and the sign on the door read MERIRU RINCHI SHOKEN KAISHA TOKYO SHITEN–MERRILL LYNCH STOCK MARKET COMPANY, TOKYO BRANCH. Twenty-one years after Charlie Merrill's memo to my father, Merrill Lynch was here to stay.

A Merrill Lynch overseas branch was an exciting place to be as the firm flexed its global muscles. Every situation was different and demanded special skills. There were local politics to be mastered, ingenuity was needed to speed up communications worldwide, and there was glamour because some of the early clients were jet-setters. No place was more exciting than the Merrill Lynch Beirut office when civil war broke out in April 1975. William R. Arthur was president of Merrill Lynch International at the time, and he monitored the action from his office in New York. As he remembered it: "Every morning at six o'clock New York time, which was two in the afternoon in Lebanon, I'd get a phone call from Makram Zaccour, our manager there, advising me on their transaction status and asking me to please tell our wire room they'd have to close for the day. Often he'd add something like, 'They're shooting near our window.'" Then came the frightful morning when the phone call didn't come. "I turned on the TV," Arthur remembered, "and there was the St. George Hotel going up in flames and sniper fire all around the square where our office was located. We tried frantically to get through to Zaccour and his people but could get no word about them. A week or so later I was at a managers' meeting in Geneva, and right in the middle of it, Zaccour walked in and said, 'Sorry, boss, I'm late.' He had spent several days in the hotel basement while they were fighting all over the place, and got out during a brief truce, switching identity papers from checkpoint to checkpoint."

As the only U.S. firm to stay in Beirut, Merrill Lynch was later rewarded by winning investment banking mandates in the 1990s from both the Republic of Lebanon and several of the banks. I was chairman of Merrill Lynch International at the time, but as an American citizen I was prevented by our government from visiting Lebanon until 1993. When I finally got there, we had established a new Private Client office in downtown Beirut. Our former client Rafik Hairi was now the prime minister, and the head of the Central Bank was Riad Salame, formerly Hariri's Merrill Lynch broker. In my visits to Lebanon, I was struck by both the devastation of portions of the city and the strength and optimism of the Lebanese people. On one visit Makram took me to his former home, which had been reduced to rubble. In the debris was a plaque honoring his father, Michel Zaccour, who had died at the young age of forty-one in 1937. As a journalist, member of parliament, and minister, he was one of the major figures in the history of Lebanon. The plaque said he was being honored "because his principles were those of a fervent Lebanese attached to the independence of his country and against unionist projects or pan-Arabic division which existed in the region." A recent book by the esteemed Lebanese writer Alexandre Najjar, *The Rebel*, chronicles the life of this extraordinary man.

In Europe, Merrill Lynch faced the same basic problem it was working on at home—educating middle-class citizens about the value of investing in stocks and bonds. But there was more to it than simply taking advertising that had succeeded in the United States and translating it into French, German, Spanish, and Italian. Local creative talent needed to be hired in each country to reconcile advertisements with national standards. The exuberant advertising that worked so well in America often didn't survive the transatlantic journey, and tamer alternatives had to be substituted. At first, Great Britain, Switzerland, and the Netherlands forbade advertising, and Germany looked on it with disdain. Each country presented a different set of problems, and many of them required brokers to go through local banks rather than deal directly with customers. As a result, much of the early overseas business was with expatriate Americans who could be approached directly. Despite the hurdles, though, by 1966 MLPF&S had nineteen offices with some six hundred employees outside the United States—and the foundation had been established for making Merrill Lynch a force in international banking.

On September 5, 1962, the firm participated in a historic experiment: the transatlantic relay of financial news and actual brokerage orders via the Telstar satellite. It was a cooperative effort with the U.S. government, the French government, and American Telephone & Telegraph. At the time, Telstar was 3,300 miles in space and traveling 16,000 miles per hour. The event earned headlines around the world. McCarthy spoke with Frederick J. Sears, an ML vice president and manager of the Paris office, and said with prescience even Charlie Merrill would have admired, "Eventually this system will tie together the financial capitals of the globe and create one world of finance."

J ust before Charlie Merrill died, his old friend Ted Braun began a "self-analysis" of the company that focused on a single branch, Cincinnati, hoping to use this office as representative of all offices. It was the most thoroughgoing examination since the 1939 Braun & Co. survey that provided the foundation for the company. When it was delivered to New York in 1957, the fourteen-month study was twenty inches thick and arranged in twelve volumes. Perhaps the most important finding was a change in customers' attitude since 1940: Back then, most people wanted only the facts and figures on a given security and preferred to make up their own minds about whether to buy or sell; by 1957 they still sought the straightforward information, the survey showed, but now they also wanted some opinions and guidance from their brokers.

From the very beginning, the Merrill Lynch Research Department had been critical to the company's success. Understandably, savvy traders turned to the house with the most comprehensive, up-to-date information. But Research did more than provide convenient, timely information for clients, for it was Charlie Merrill's radical idea that the fruits of Merrill Lynch research should be shared with anyone who asked for it. Among the most frequent users of this resource were financial journalists, who passed on the information—with suitable attribution—to millions of readers. The mere publicity value of this arrangement is incalculable. But by 1957, Braun had found a festering problem, and there was an immediate attempt to strengthen the department with special emphasis on providing more information on individual securities.

Despite these efforts, by the end of 1959 Research was in trouble. Budgetary restraints were hampering its effectiveness and causing defections of top personnel to other firms. Moreover, its recommendations were widely criticized as too conservative and too general in nature to be of much value to specific investors. On New Year's Day 1960, Jack Moller, the man who, over a single weekend in 1942, had developed a hugely successful campaign using hypothetical portfolios, was brought in to take over the research operation. Moller had left Research in the postwar years and gone on to manage the Fifth Avenue office in New York City, and to establish an office in the Time-Life Building. When he returned to assume his new post, he found—in his words—"turmoil" and "a constant barrage of complaints" against Research. Within six months of Moller's takeover, the department was recommending more speculative stocks and encouraging commodity trading for those who could afford it.

Along with making these big-picture changes, Moller also moved to resolve operational problems as well. When he found there were inexcusable delays, sometimes as long as several days, in his department's replying to research inquires from customers, he turned to Robert ("Rocky") O'Connell, Merrill Lynch's longtime operations genius, for help. Upon reviewing the situation, O'Connell found a cumbersome system of card files that relied heavily on handwritten information for input and output. The solution was obvious to him: Use the data distribution system that he had developed jointly with AT&T and that had been in operation since 1961. The result was called QRQ, for Quick Retrieval Query, and in later years O'Connell would label it "the most significant development in our firm's operational history." Under QRQ, account executives could receive in a matter of minutes the Merrill Lynch research opinion on any of 3,500 stocks. The latest opinions of industry specialists were stored in a computer, and a request from any office was automatically transmitted to the computer, which instantly located the investment opinion and then transmitted it over the private wire system to the office that made the request. It sounds simple by today's technology, but in 1964 no other brokerage had such a powerful sales support tool.

The firm's most notable venture into independent research grew out of Lou Engel's frustration at being unable to advertise common stocks as a good investment. The NYSE had veto power over all advertising by its members, and over several years Engel was told that he couldn't make such a claim in an ad unless he could prove it. After yet another rejection in 1960, Engel turned to his alma mater, the University of Chicago. The firm put up $50,000 to establish the Center for Research into Security Prices, headed by James H. Lorie of the university's Graduate School of Business, which was supposed to complete the study in six months. As it turned out, the study required three years and another $100,000 from Merrill Lynch to complete. Lorie and his colleagues considered all 1,715 stocks listed on the NYSE and all capital changes in those stocks. They took into consideration not only commission charges but capital gains and income taxes as well. They assumed that equal dollar amounts of all listed stocks were bought in 1926 and sold in 1960, and similarly for twenty-one other time periods within the thirty-five-year span. Computations were made not only for twenty-two time periods but for three different tax brackets: no tax, as for a tax-exempt institution; that of a married man with an income of $10,000 in 1960 or its equivalent in earlier years with standard deductions; and that of a married man with an income of $50,000 in 1960 with standard deductions. Thus the time periods included boom and bust and war and peace, and the income brackets also covered a variety of circumstances. The conclusion was that the overall return on all the stocks would have been 9 percent a year for tax-exempt institutions and 6.84 percent for individuals in the $50,000 income bracket. Both returns were substantially higher than for other types of investments. It was another public relations coup for Merrill Lynch as well as the rest of Wall Street, and it was front-page news in hundreds of newspapers and magazines.

COMMON STOCKS GIVE BEST RETURN
—*The Boston Globe*
CHICAGO PROFS CONFIRM CLICHÉ: "HARD TO GO BAD WITH STOCKS"
—*Houston Chronicle*

DOES IT PAY TO INVEST IN STOCKS? STUDY SAYS YES
—*Chicago American*
UNIVERSITY OF CHICAGO STUDY PUTS COMMON STOCKS IN
ILLUSTRIOUS CLASS—*Chicago Tribune*
COMMON STOCKS WIN A ROSE FROM CHICAGO STUDY
—*Business Week*

The study went on for another six years, and among its final conclusions was one that left the Merrill Lynch Research Department, as well as its counterparts in other brokerages, perplexed: "The most ignorant investor, speculator, or outright gambler, buying any common stock listed on the New York Stock Exchange at any time, would have had more than a three-to-one chance of making an eventual profit."

In his 1957 study, Braun also concluded that the company had neglected the institutional sector—insurance companies, college endowment funds, labor pension funds, bank transactions, and others with big stakes in the market. As a result, there was a general upgrading of all departments that serviced institutional accounts, and then in 1964 the firm took a gigantic step in expanding its business.

A sweeter deal could scarcely be imagined," proclaimed Time magazine. "It was a little like Macy's acquiring Tiffany's." The metaphor was extraordinarily appropriate. Merrill Lynch, Pierce, Fenner & Smith Inc., the department store of finance, had acquired the business of C. J. Devine & Co., the biggest and best-known of the handful of gilt-edged Street firms that dealt in government securities. It was a coup for Merrill Lynch because most of its competitors were covetous of the lucrative market in U.S. Treasury and tax-exempt bonds, but they were deterred by the difficulty of building the necessary organization from scratch. So for years these two specialized financial families—government securities dealers and corporate stock and bond brokers—lived on opposite sides of Wall Street. With the acquisition of Devine, Merrill Lynch bridged that divide and gained entry into this market without paying anything. The Devine group simply became the Government Securities Division of MLPF&S. It continued to operate out of its old offices at 48 Wall, and it even had the same telephone number—HAnover 2-2727.

Merrill Lynch could thank an old adversary, federal tax laws, for its good fortune. Christopher Joseph Devine, the son of a New Jersey fireman who founded the firm in 1933, died in 1963. Mindful that his heirs would have to pay estate taxes on his three-quarters share of the assets of the partnership, Devine had left them the money, estimated at $12 million, but willed the firm's name and good will to a charitable foundation with instructions that it dedicate itself to the support of schools that did not teach Communism. This left the surviving partners with the remaining assets—about $4 million—but no name to call their own. Their chief asset, however, was their skill and experience in a part of the market that few on the Street understood except as customers. The old Devine partners made the first move. George Raskin, a personal tax adviser to Devine himself, contacted Victor Cook, the longtime Merrill partner, and suggested that the former Devine people swap their shares for Merrill Lynch shares at existing book value. Cook took the proposal to Mike McCarthy and George Leness, and within three weeks the thirteen Devine partners had become MLPF&S shareholders. The new Government Securities Division quickly developed a 25 percent annual growth rate, and within a decade the firm had the biggest share of the government securities market, about 15 percent, among all Wall Street firms. The larger significance of the Devine deal was that it was the firm's first successful move outside the commission business, and it would be a stepping-stone into other financial fields in the seventies, including the development of Merrill Lynch's Capital Markets business.

Back in 1947, Kenneth W. Martin and Jim Thomson were made full partners—even though neither of them had ever sold a share of stock. They had ridden to prominence for their skills in operations, the processing of orders and the maintenance of customer accounts, which used to be called routine but had grown in prominence along with the firm itself. When the promotions were announced, Charlie Merrill sent a note to McCarthy (who had never sold a share of stock, either) saying that inviting Martin and Thomson into the inner circle would "show the organization the importance we place on backstage operations" and that men like them will not be "overlooked by the firm or overshadowed by fellows in the more spectacular jobs." One of McCarthy's earliest tasks as managing partner was to oversee the installation of the IBM 705 computers, and once this was achieved, many of those "more spectacular jobs" were in the operations end of the business. Following incorporation in 1959, the firm ordered the first of the IBM 7080s, which were said to "run cooler" because they used transistors rather than vacuum tubes. McCarthy was ideally suited to steer the firm into the burgeoning field of operations technology. His background consisted almost entirely of managing merchandising operations, first in chain stores and then in overhauling accounting and data-processing technology in the early days at Merrill Lynch. He did not need to be persuaded of the importance of seeking ever-better ways to keep track of ever-more numerous transactions occurring simultaneously over great distances.

MLFP&S was the world's largest brokerage, and the growing burden of business could have staggered the entire operation. On a single busy day in April 1961, for example, trading exceeded 7 million shares, and switchboard operators plugged in 9,102 times and said liltingly, "Merrill Lynch, Pierce, Fenner and Smith." That week the firm executed some 50,000 orders, gave about 121,000 price quotations, and answered around 41,000 queries from customers about specific stocks. In the process, its 100 teletype operators sent and received more than 12 million words of traffic over a 115,000-mile network of wires connecting its 129 branches in the U.S. and 12 overseas. The firm was the largest single stockholder of record of nearly every publicly traded corporation in the United States. The Merrill Lynch vault three floors under 70 Pine Street held some $5 billion worth of securities for its customers—including, for example, more than 10 percent of the outstanding common stock of RCA.

By the mid-1960s, the Merrill Lynch backstage was the most highly automated and most economical operation on Wall Street. But even that would not be enough for the years ahead.

One of the company's most unusual efforts to keep spending in check took place in 1969 after the firm's insurance companies began requiring that U.S. Treasury bills be stored in a Federal Reserve bank vault. Until this time, T-bills had been kept in the vault beneath company headquarters. As the head of General Services, William

Emerson was responsible for the transfer. Inquiries were made to Wells Fargo and Brink's about how much a transfer would cost. The estimate was $30,000—a sum Emerson found excessive since there was a Federal Reserve bank just two blocks away. So one morning Emerson put the T-bills—all of which were negotiable—into two laundry carts and had workers push them down Cedar Street to the bank. Emerson walked along one side of the carts with a loaded pistol under his trench coat. Jerry McDevitt, ML head of security and a former FBI agent, was on the other side. Two New York City policemen, armed with rifles, watched the transfer from a nearby rooftop. Afterward, Emerson gave each of the policemen a fifth of scotch—and that was the total cost of transferring millions of dollars in negotiable Treasury bills.

C harlie Merrill and my father had established a series of safeguards designed to shield the public from fraudulent dealings and simultaneously protect the firm's integrity. These protections were continuously refined and updated, and by 1960 Merrill Lynch was operating under a self-imposed set of rules that went way beyond any requirements of the law or Wall Street ethics. The firm still issued a candid and thorough Annual Report (addressed to "Our Customers")—even though there was no mandate to do so. There were also extraordinary limitations on Merrill Lynch employees. An extravagant lifestyle or a large personal debt could lead to dismissal, and no Merrill Lyncher was allowed to sell stock short on his own account. To enforce the rules, there were roving teams of inspectors, some of whom might be top executives. These safeguards, coupled with our rigid training program for account executives and our vast research facilities, won the respect of investigators for the Securities and Exchange Commission.

But bull markets often breed excesses, which was the case during the late 1950s and early 1960s when NYSE member firms used get-rich-quick themes in their advertising. Abuses piled up, regulatory concern heightened, and the world's largest brokerage, Merrill Lynch, did not escape unscathed. The SEC found in 1963 that Merrill Lynch brokers in the Los Angeles area had engaged in "questionable merchandising techniques" by selling shares of the Aquafilter Corporation, a firm that manufactured a water-impregnated filter for cigarettes, on the basis of such representations as "Aquafilter production could not keep up with demand" and "a favorable Dun and Bradstreet report had been obtained on [Aquafilter's] president." In addition, the salesmen violated several internal rules, including one that they consider the suitability of high-risk securities customer by customer, and another that they consult the Research Department before recommending high-risk securities.

Mike McCarthy, who was CEO at the time, moved quickly. "When the Aquafilter situation came to my attention," he remembered, "I recommended to my partners that we contact each customer and offer to make good any losses they had suffered in buying this highly speculative stock. [Earle] English and some of the others were opposed to the idea because they were very fearful that we were setting a dangerous precedent—[one] that might haunt us later. We decided, however, to make our customers 'whole' and it cost our firm around $150,000. However, we received a million dollars in favorable national publicity and editorials, because the story reported that ML paid their investor losses in full. It was a very unusual thing to do at that time on Wall Street." The company also fined the errant salesmen.

The Aquafilter incident also provided a memorable moment in the career of Donald T. Regan, the up-and-coming administration division director, who had a reputation for saying much in very few words. Regan drew the unhappy assignment of testifying on behalf of the company at SEC hearings in Washington. After thoroughly reviewing the firm's internal safeguards and their failure to stop the Aquafilter incident, the SEC interrogator asked Regan, "How, then, could this instance happen?" Regan shot back: "Let's face it. This time we goofed." The story, which included a photograph of Regan, made Page One of the next day's *New York Times* under the headline WE GOOFED. Regan's admission that Merrill Lynch had erred but moved to correct the situation and learn from it grew into legendary status. It was a story that resonated around the firm for decades and reinforced the principles that guided our firm.

ML had a far more serious and damaging clash with the SEC in 1968, one that went to the heart of its treasured reputation for integrity and for championing of the small investor. The case involved a

$75 million convertible debenture offering by Douglas Aircraft, and the government charged that Merrill Lynch distributed damaging information about the bond issue to its institutional customers but not to its individual customers, in violation of insider-trading rules. On June 7, 1966, Douglas Aircraft had reported profits of 85 cents per share, but by this time it was running into production and cost problems that threatened its earnings outlook. On June 24, Douglas disclosed that its profits had fallen to 12 cents a share and predicted poor earnings, at best, for the entire year. The bad news shoved the price of a Douglas share on the New York Stock Exchange down from 90 ½ to 64 ¾ within a week. The SEC alleged that between the two announcements Merrill Lynch had warned fifteen institutions, including such star customers as the Dreyfus Corp. and Investors Management Co., but had not informed its other 1.1 million customers, and, indeed, that the firm's brokers had kept on selling Douglas stock to some of their smaller customers. Meanwhile, the institutions had sold their Douglas stock, thereby contributing to the drop in its price.

This was a serious charge and the kind that my father and Charlie Merrill had dreaded. In effect, the SEC said, the world's largest brokerage house had misused inside information to take care of its biggest customers at the expense of its smaller customers—and, in the process, partially caused Douglas stock to plunge 26 points in one week. There were hearings into the charges and widespread media coverage. An agreement was reached under which Merrill Lynch neither admitted nor denied the charges but accepted penalties, including suspension of two of the brokerage's offices for several weeks, resulting in a loss of business estimated on Wall Street to be about $1 million, and suspension for a brief period without pay of seven executives and the censure of several others. In addition, the firm agreed to adopt certain formal procedures, including the erection of a "Chinese wall" between investment banking and securities research to prevent the exchange of confidential information. This case was precedent-setting for Wall Street and a deep embarrassment to all at Merrill Lynch. It showed that a growing and expanding firm not only required good intentions, it needed to improve controls continuously and be ever-mindful of potential conflicts of interest.

In 1966, Mike McCarthy stepped down from the No. 1 post and returned to Southern California, where he served as Executive Committee chairman until he reached the mandatory retirement age of sixty-five in 1968. In his decade at the helm—first as managing partner when my father was ailing, then as the president of the newly incorporated MLPF&S—he had directed the new colossus of Wall Street from the tenth floor of the now-grimy building at 70 Pine. He modernized the company's paperwork systems, accelerated international growth, oversaw the vital transformation from partnership to corporation, and prepared his top subordinates for future leadership. He never lost his zeal for supermarket efficiency, and he never stopped calling Merrill Lynch branch offices "stores."

McCarthy's semi-retirement cleared the way for George Leness, the firm's original underwriting genius, who was sixty-three years old, to become chairman and chief executive officer. Replacing him in the presidency was Jim Thomson, sixty-one, whom Charlie Merrill himself had hired as a runner in 1924 at $14 a week. Thomson had gone over to the Pierce operation in 1930, where he distinguished himself in Cleveland and Detroit by steadily improving backstage operations. Even so, in the worst days of the Depression, he was sometimes paid in scrip rather than cash. When the modern Merrill Lynch was formed in 1940, Thomson came back to New York and worked under his long-time friend Mike McCarthy, whom he succeeded as head of operations in 1948. Two decades later he would become CEO. Thomson was a strong administrative executive, but he lacked the personality and charisma of his predecessors. A story circulated for years of his first speech as CEO to the training class. Nervously reading his prepared remarks, he began: "When I returned from World War Eleven . . ." The trainees snickered, but Thomson droned on, unmindful of the fact that he had confused Roman and Arabic numerals.

The firm was now a quarter-century old, and there was considerable reason to look back with pride. Merrill Lynch, Pierce, Fenner & Smith was, by far, the single most important seller of common stocks to the common man. Its very name had found its way into American folklore. By 1966 it had 165 offices in the United States, plus operations in London, Paris, Madrid, Hong Kong, Tokyo,

Geneva, Beirut, and other cities. It held membership in forty-one stock exchanges. Its capital totaled $148 million, about three times that of its nearest competitor, Bache & Co. There were $13 billion in negotiable securities in its vaults under Pine Street. There were 2,800 Merrill Lynch salesmen who were products of a training program that rejected fourteen of every fifteen applicants. There were 210 crack researchers who kept abreast of some 3,600 companies. Its commodities operation made it one of the biggest brokers on the Chicago Board of Trade. In the underwriting derby it had moved from forty-third place to third place and had just scored a major coup with the sale of Howard Hughes's TWA stock. The firm had served its customers and stockholders well.

However, just beneath the surface of the glowing Annual Report facts and figures, there were deep-rooted problems. The early policy of paying salesmen a flat salary instead of putting them on a commission basis had worked fine at first because it helped overcome the public's fear that brokers were out simply to turn over shares, but the policy began to lose some of its effectiveness as trading increased in volume and salesmen in competing firms began earning larger and larger remunerations. To offset employees' temptation to jump ship, in 1942 the firm had added an adjusted compensation plan that was calculated twice a year on the basis of a salesman's intake. As further incentives to hold on to employees, it had established its profit-sharing plan (1945), a pension plan (1959), and finally the opportunity to become a stockholder (1960). But the drain of salesmen, who were held at a premium precisely because of their Merrill Lynch training, could not be plugged as competitors dangled promises of bigger rewards in money and position and a more varied mix of products to sell.

There were other problems as well. All divisions, notably Research and Underwriting, were suffering from cost-cutting restraints, and the scope of operations had exceeded the firm's ability to manage it. The firm needed new and bigger office space. After twenty-five years, the firm had outgrown its original facilities at 70 Pine Street (also known as the Cities Service Building and 60 Wall Tower). Indeed, anyone determined to make a complete tour of Merrill Lynch, Pierce, Fenner & Smith in New York would be obliged to visit no fewer than sixteen different locations, ranging from Midtown to the Battery. The sprawl was inherently wasteful.

A decision was made in 1966 to move to larger quarters. A group was formed to study the idea, and it ultimately recommended constructing a fifty-four-story building on lower Broadway. The projected cost was $100 million, but when it was finished the price tag was $125 million. The firm began moving into the new quarters in May of 1972, and it took until October to complete the transition. Don Regan named it One Liberty Plaza because Liberty Street was on one side of the building and because it had a patriotic ring. During the five years it took to complete construction, the firm's projected space needs tripled from 250,000 square feet to 750,000 square feet, and One Liberty Plaza was too small before it was even occupied. The mailroom had to be shunted off to a group of warehouses along West Street to make way for new computers.

Aside from all these internal problems, the firm was also at risk of not keeping up with changing conditions. Richard B. King, a young vice president who managed the Detroit office, offered this assessment: "We had a very serious problem in the firm, and it stemmed from the fact that Messrs. Thomson and McCarthy had come up from the operational end of the business. They had built up a very fine processing plant. . . . But as they got further up in the firm and away from it, they did not realize that it was stagnating and falling behind technologically."

Probably most significant, the market had changed as insurance companies and big pension funds bought huge blocks of stock, but the firm had been slow to respond to the growing importance of this institutional business. In fact, it was about a decade late in doing so. The firm's share of the institutional market lagged woefully behind what it should have been, but the numbers were deceiving because institutional activity was nevertheless growing year by year. John A. Fitzgerald, who had just been named head of the Sales Planning and Development Division, recalled this problem: "The general point of view was that we had a good institutional effort. We were kind of an inbred, insulated firm. Bear in mind that back in the forties, we embarked on a course of training our own, and there were no new people coming into ML. For two decades we rarely went out and hired anybody. Everybody who went through the training program came up the ML ladder. So there was a sort of inbred thinking. There was also a feeling that we were terrific and we could do no wrong. The results were outstanding during the fifties and most of the sixties. It was due overwhelmingly to the retail business. The institutional business got carried along simply because it was growing outside us, and we were growing. But our market share was never what it should have been."

The early partners' reservations about the commodities business had been overcome and commodities had emerged as an important source of profits in the postwar era, but by 1960 the old doubts about speculation and instability had set in. Thomas J. Cassady was manager of the Fort Wayne office in 1964 when McCarthy asked him to take over the Commodities Division—and gave him thirty seconds to make up his mind. Cassady accepted, even though he knew that "being head of the Commodities Division was considered one of the worst jobs in the firm." He found "unbelievable opposition to commodities. McCarthy was lukewarm, but Leness and Thomson were dead set against them." Leness "couldn't even stand to say the word *commodities*. To them it was strictly speculation and everybody in commodities lost money."

By the late 1960s, it was time for change. It was time for the leadership of Merrill Lynch, Pierce, Fenner & Smith to be passed on to those who much later would be called "the Greatest Generation."

For the latter part of 1960, my father was in a rest home in Litchfield, Connecticut. His mind was still sharp, but his muscles had deteriorated, he had difficulty speaking, and he was growing weaker and weaker. During these days his partners would visit, still seeking his advice and keeping him up to speed on Merrill Lynch matters. My mother later told me that they had decided not to ask him to retire, but to have him remain as board chairman and treat him much the same way Dad had treated Charlie Merrill in his final days. When Arthur Levitt, the former chairman of the Securities and Exchange Commission, said, "Merrill Lynch is the only firm on Wall Street with a soul," it was gestures like this toward my father that he was talking about. This was the essence of Mother Merrill.

While my father remained mentally alert until the day he died, it broke my heart to see him less and less mobile and eventually bed-ridden and having to be fed. I really didn't comprehend the terminal nature of his illness because my mother kept it from me. I was always hoping that when he went to the hospital he would be cured and that we would play together again. Our wonderful Roman Catholic housekeeper, Florence Regosia, took me to church, we lit candles, and she taught me to pray to St. Jude. On the afternoon of January 10, 1961, I came home from school and saw my mother sitting in the living room, and knew instantly that my father had passed away. I ran into my bedroom sobbing. It was so unfair. St. Jude and God had let me down.

At his funeral service at the First Congregational Church in Litchfield, the pews were filled with his Merrill Lynch colleagues, Amherst classmates, and personal friends. My mother had been asked how one should eulogize him, and she said, "Win doesn't need and wouldn't have wanted a eulogy. Anyone who knew him knew what a wonderful person he was and nothing more can be said about him."

I came to know that Dad was a man who was admired, respected, and loved. He was a man who was modest, generous, caring; a man who could be tough and at times earthy in his language in the privacy of his home; a man who existed in the tough environment of Wall Street and yet was called a "sweet man." Until I learned more about him in later years, I could not envision my father as "sweet," but I now understand that this is maybe the nicest compliment he could have received from a fellow Wall Streeter.

Aside from the personal tributes, it was also nice that by this time he had finally achieved national recognition: In 1957 *Forbes* magazine identified my father as one of America's fifty top business leaders—just as it had designated Charlie Merrill ten years earlier.

To this day I miss him enormously but I am so lucky to have wonderful memories of our times together and fortunate to have gotten to know him better over the years through the eyes of fellow Merrill Lynchers. Even today, faced with a tough situation, I often ask myself what he would have done. I also cherish my twenty-eight years of working for his firm and experiencing firsthand the values that he had and passed along to the future generations. I had hoped to work at Merrill Lynch until I was sixty-five and retire in 2014, which will be the centennial of the founding of Merrill Lynch & Co. But fate led in another direction.

June 20, 1956

To All New York Partners:

This year will celebrate Mr. Winthrop H. Smith's 40th year with Merrill Lynch. Mr. Smith's birthday is on June 30th.

After talking with a number of the partners it was generally agreed that we would like to do something to commemorate this occasion. Therefore, on Wednesday, June 27th we are going to have an informal dinner for him which will be held in the Entertainment Suite of the River Club, 447 East 52nd Street. Cocktails will be served at six o'clock, followed by dinner.

M. Rubezanin

Bernard B. Ramsey   William H. Culbertson   Michael W. McCarthy
Winthrop H. Smith   M. Rubezanin

George J. Leness   Robert C. Rooke   Richard A. Woods

E. A. Pierce   Winthrop H. Smith

Earle W. English   John H. Moller   Louis H. Engel, Jr.

George J. Leness   Robert O'Connell   Manuel Weisbuch

Caryl H. Sayre   Arthur S. Laundon   James E. Thomson

Herman Belth   Harry B. Anderson

George J. Leness

Winthrop H. Smith

Winthrop C. Lenz   John L. Julian   Anthony D. Cassatt

CODE 822R 4-48—(1-55)
PRINTED IN U.S.A.

MERRILL LYNCH, PIERCE, FENNER & BEANE

OFFICE CORRESPONDENCE

To: At   Date

From: At

Subject: WIRE TO BE SENT TO

PARTNERS OF MERRILL LYNCH, PIERCE, FENNER & BEANE
RIVER CLUB
447 EAST 52nd ST
NEW YORK CITY, N. Y.

NEVER IN MY LIFE HAVE I FELT MORE UNHAPPY AT MY INABILITY TO BE WITH MY

FRIENDS AND FELLOW PARTNERS THAN TONIGHT. FOR PERHAPS MORE THAN ANY OF THE REST

OF YOU I KNOW WHAT A DEBT WE ALL OWE WIN SMITH AND LIKE ALL OF YOU I SHOULD

LIKE TO HONOR HIM ON THIS OCCASION, CELEBRATING NOT ONLY HIS BIRTHDAY AND

THE ACADEMIC DISTINCTION HE HAS JUSTLY RECEIVED, BUT MOST IMPORTANT OF ALL

HIS 40TH ANNIVERSARY WITH MERRILL LYNCH, PIERCE, FENNER & BEANE. I CAN

THINK OF NOTHING MORE FITTING TO SAY THAN TO PARAPHRASE WINSTON CHURCHILL'S

FAMOUS REMARK: SELDOM HAVE SO MANY OWED SO MUCH TO ONE MAN -- WINTHROP

H. SMITH. DUE TO HIS HELP AND HIS COUNSEL, TO HIS UNFAILING GOOD JUDGMENT,

HIS INHERENT SENSE OF JUSTICE AND ABOVE ALL THINGS HIS WARM AND HUMAN

UNDERSTANDING, WE HAVE SUCCESSFULLY WEATHERED EVERY STORM WE HAVE MET.

ALL I CAN SAY IN THE DEEPEST HUMILITY IS GOD BLESS YOU WIN -- MY FRIEND,

MY PARTNER.

OK - CEM

CHARLES E. MERRILL

In 1971, CEO Don Regan and president Ned Ball saw "MER" on the New York Stock Exchange ticker tape for the first time. Going public was one of Regan's many bold moves as head of the firm.

CHAPTER EIGHT

Bullish on America

(1970–1980)

I n 1948 a group of Merrill Lynch account executives were summoned to New York for a discussion of advanced sales techniques, and at one point they sat in a room at 70 Pine Street listening to a very senior partner make a very long-winded presentation. One of the listeners was Donald T. Regan, a former Marine who had graduated from the training school two years earlier and was now assigned as an account executive in the Washington office. He was twenty-nine years old. The partner rambled along, and boredom hung over the scene like a haze. Finally, Regan raised his hand. "What firm, what securities, what customers are we talking about?" he asked. "I don't recognize anything you've said. That's not life as it's lived in Merrill Lynch's branches today." The speaker glared at the upstart as Patton might have appraised a malingering corporal. A bare-knuckles discussion ensued, but Regan refused to give ground to his elders. ("My father had taught me never to back down when I thought I was right, so I didn't," Regan said forty years later.) Regan was unaware that just before his outburst, Charlie Merrill and my father had slipped into the back of the room and were auditing the proceedings. After the meeting, Merrill told Bob Magowan, "That Regan is a fresh little SOB, but by God, I admire his guts in speaking up when he thinks something isn't right." When told of the remark years later, Regan said, "I'm not little." In fact, there was nothing little about Don, and you either loved or hated him, but my father,

271

Charlie, and Bob saw in Don a natural leader who had the courage to speak his mind and swim against the tide. Beneath the bark and his enormous ego was also a sensitive man whom few others than his immediate family recognized.

Donald Thomas Regan was less than nine months old when his father, a police officer, was fired by then–Massachusetts Governor Calvin Coolidge as part of the Boston police strike in 1919, leaving the thirty-three-year-old jobless with a wife and two young boys for more than a year. "To my father, his dismissal was a dark cloud hanging over his reputation," Regan wrote in his 1988 autobiography, *For the Record*. "To this day, although I cast my first vote for Wendell Willkie and spent most of my working life on Wall Street, I have great difficulty in crossing a picket line." However, Regan never had trouble speaking his mind. He was briefly expelled from his kindergarten class after informing the teacher that she was doing everything wrong and insisting that she reorganize the class along more sensible lines. His brother died of peritonitis in 1929, and after the funeral his parents informed their nine-year-old son, "You're going to have to take Billy's place. From now on you're going to have to be two sons to us."

Regan went to Harvard University on a scholarship and worked as a tour guide during the summer months. Occasionally he would pass a classmate named John Fitzgerald Kennedy in Harvard Yard. They would nod at each other, but never became friends. In fact, when both ran for president of the Neuman Club, it was Don who beat out young Jack Kennedy. This was the last election that Kennedy ever lost. When Regan graduated in 1940, he had money in the bank and bought the tour guide business. "There's no doubt that this early experience left me with a taste for entrepreneurial life and a belief that good ideas plus hard work equals profits," he recalled in his book. But while Regan completed his senior year in college, the Nazi war machine rolled across Europe. He volunteered for the Marine Corps, and while training to be an officer at Quantico, Virginia, he met and fell in love with Ann Gordon Buchanan, my mother's niece. Ann was the daughter of my mother's sister Marjorie, whose husband, Richard, had been killed fighting the Sandinistas in Nicaragua. Ann and Don were married in 1942. Regan served for thirty-three months in the Pacific and took part in five major campaigns—Guadalcanal, New

Georgia, the North Solomons, Guam, and Okinawa. Don's Marine career had a profound effect on him. He was comfortable with fellow Marines and the motto "Semper Fi" stood with him at Merrill Lynch. To him Merrill Lynch was the best, and those who followed him into battle deserved his loyalty, but for those who didn't pass muster, he cut them no slack. He returned to the U.S. as a major just before the Japanese surrender, and Ann met him in San Francisco. In *For the Record*, he recalled:

> After our reunion in San Francisco, Ann and I traveled by train across the country to Washington. We arrived at Union Station on July 10. There we were met by Ann's mother, Marjorie. Accompanying Mrs. Buchanan was a small blue-eyed girl with blond ringlets, my daughter Donna Ann, who had been born during the Battle of New Georgia. Donna Ann was wearing a beautiful dress. She curtsied and said, "Hello, Daddy." She was two years, three months, and two days old, and this was the first time she had ever seen me or I had ever seen her. When I remember the war, it is this last moment that I remember first.

I chuckle at this image of Donna curtsying, because my early memories of my eldest cousin were of her chasing her younger brothers and me around the house trying to kiss us with her ruby red lipstick, which she had "borrowed" from her mother. To us this blue-eyed girl who no longer had blond ringlets was affectionately known as "Poison Lips."

After he left the military, Regan had job feelers from three companies—Mobil Oil, the Muzak Corp., and Merrill Lynch, Pierce, Fenner & Beane. My mother, who had just started dating my father, had arranged for Don to get an interview. "He is a terrific young man, and I think you should get him for Merrill Lynch," she told Dad. Don would later dispute that anyone had helped him get any job or even an interview. A reporter later erroneously said that Don got the job because of my father's affection for Ann, who supposedly called my father "Daddy." The fact is, Don had a chance to interview because Ann's aunt was married to my father, but Don got everything on his own merits and Ann never called my father anything other than

"Win." In considering the three companies that were interested in him, Don must have acknowledged to himself that he knew nothing about oil, music, or investments, but in the end he chose Merrill Lynch because it had a new training program for account executives. "For the third time since leaving Harvard six years before," he wrote, "I felt the exhilaration of having made the right choice in life—first the Marines, then Ann, and now my lifework." His career path surprised his parents. "My thrifty grandfather Regan had lost a lot of money when a Cambridge bank failed in 1933, an experience that blackened the name of investment in our family for a long time after." Regan graduated in the second training school class in 1946, and two years later he was one of ten account executives—the aforementioned "Whiz Kids"—chosen to work for Bob Magowan on a new sales promotion team that went to every branch office in the nation to teach new sales techniques. When a kickback scandal was uncovered in the Over-the-Counter Trading Department in 1951, Regan was asked to take over. It was a major department with more than a hundred employees, and Regan, now thirty-two years old, wasn't sure he could handle it. Charlie Merrill either sensed or heard about Regan's misgivings, and he sent him a letter from Barbados:

> Dear Don:
>
> While it will be difficult for me to associate [sic] our Trading Department without Johnny Wark, I am very pleased that his mantle will fall on your shoulders. I know as well as you do how little you know about the technical workings of the over-the-counter market, but that is a situation that can be remedied with each passing day if you give to the job the same devotion you have given to the other tasks that have been assigned to you up until now.
>
> I hope you will remember a remark I made to you and the other boys on that Sales-Promotion Team a few years ago to the effect that there was no job in the firm that an alert, able, ambitious young man of thirty could not fill. You need not be discouraged by your lack of years, for God will take care of that in due time.
>
> I wish you great success in your new and very important job.

This philosophy of Charlie's, which was also shared by my father, was unique to Wall Street and set Merrill Lynch apart from other firms. Good leadership and management practices could allow one to manage an area even if it wasn't one they had worked in previously. The practice of moving talented managers around into different departments prepared them to become better senior executives of the firm.

After succeeding—as Charlie Merrill knew he would—at managing the Over-the-Counter Trading Department, Regan's rise was meteoric. At the age of thirty-five he was asked to become a general partner, the youngest ever up to that point, and the first training school graduate to do so. Regan didn't have all of the $10,000 in required capital, so Merrill lent him the difference, as he had done before for new partners who oftentimes couldn't come up with that amount of money on their own. Regan spent five years in charge of the Philadelphia office, returned to New York in 1960 to head the administrative divisions, and then launched Wall Street's first planning department.

After my father passed away in 1961, my mother and I visited the Regan home on the Main Line outside of Philadelphia a number of times. As a young boy I always liked and admired Don. He and his family visited our farm in Litchfield often, and while I played with my cousins, Dad and Don and a few other partners discussed business on the veranda. Don was devoted to his family and they to him, and he always made a point of getting home at night whenever possible, even when his career moved him to a New York job and his family home remained in Philadelphia.

In 1964 he was named Executive Vice President for Marketing. Four years later, it was time to select the next president of Merrill Lynch. Regan had the backing of the then-chairman and CEO, Jim Thomson, and Mike McCarthy, who was retired by then. But George Leness and Win Lenz, both from investment banking, were supporting George L. Shinn, the genial, laid-back executive who had succeeded Regan in several top posts and then set ML on a course that would make it a top institutional brokerage several decades later. George, an Amherst graduate and later chairman of the Board of Trustees of Amherst, was a real gentleman and somewhat more refined than Don, lacking Regan's fiery temper. McCarthy had enormous respect for Shinn, but "I felt that Regan had more experience and I thought he was a better leader than Shinn," he said years later. "So when George [Leness] told me that he was going to make Shinn president, I said, 'Over my dead body. If you want a proxy battle, I'll give you a proxy battle. I'll beat your ass off on it.'" McCarthy backed up his boast, and at the age of forty-nine, Regan became president. It was controversial because many ML executives thought he was too young and found him too brash, but in later years, Leness would concede that Regan had been the right man for the job.

There was an internal effort to block Regan from ascending to the No. 1 spot, but by this time he was too powerful, and on January 1, 1971, he became chairman and chief executive officer of the world's largest brokerage, succeeding Jim Thomson. Ned Ball, who had been chairman of Merrill Lynch International and was a genial gentleman from North Carolina, became Don's president and COO. The two of them made a great team. A couple of years later after Ball retired, George Shinn became president of the newly formed Merrill Lynch & Co. for a couple of years. It was an appropriate time for strong leadership. Don would later boast to a successor that if one ever needed to learn Machiavellian techniques, he would be glad to teach them. While this was said somewhat tongue-in-cheek, there was a lot of truth to his remark. Years later I met George Shinn at an Amherst athletic event. I mentioned Don's name, and George, whom I liked and respected greatly, went into a tirade about him. "He was unethical," George said with a reddened face. I had heard many people throw barbs at Don, but I had never heard the word *unethical* used. There was clearly bad blood between the two, and I surmise it had something to do with the elevation of Don over George. George was president when I joined the firm in August of 1974, but shortly thereafter he unexpectedly resigned to become president of First Boston. Interestingly, even though George despised Don, he never recruited anyone from Merrill Lynch, which speaks to his character and his lasting affection for his former firm.

To consolidate power, Don employed a strategy that he must have learned from Sun Tzu's *The Art of War*—namely, "Keep your allies close and your enemies even closer." Regan brought several of Merrill's powerful branch managers onto his team in New York, thereby breaking down the old partnership form of decentralization. Dick King from Detroit became EVP Service, John Orb was named EVP Sales, and Dakin Ferris out of Atlanta became group vice president for customer sales. Win Lenz was named Vice Chairman of the Board, and George Shinn, who'd been working in Boston at the time, was also named a Vice Chairman of the Board and put in charge of long-range planning. Within a few years all but Dakin had left the firm. Orb went on to become CEO of Smith Barney, Shinn became CEO of First Boston, and the others retired.

Don clearly understood the corporate politics of gaining and holding on to power, and he truly believed that he was the most capable person to lead Merrill Lynch into the next era, but at the same time he wanted to preserve the principles of Charlie Merrill and my dad, and make Merrill Lynch a better firm for clients, employees, and shareholders alike. In the 1970 Annual Report, his first as chairman and CEO and ML's last as a private company, he wrote:

> We will carry our principles with us, for they have withstood the tests of time and radical change. They were never put to a harder test than in 1970, and they came through splendidly. We are, of course, in business to make money. But if adherence to this careful philosophy of Merrill's had benefitted only Merrill Lynch, those of us who direct the firm would have a sense of incompleteness. In a time when our interest and some broader interests of the public coincided more clearly than ever before, we were gratified by the knowledge that our policies served other people besides ourselves and served them well. It was a year when wrenching changes proved again the worth of constant principles.

In 1971, Merrill Lynch's first year as a public company, Don's year-end letter to the shareholders once again spoke of the firm's values, emphasizing the clients' interests, acknowledging that the firm's people were its primary assets, and underscoring Charlie Merrill's caution on being well capitalized and not becoming over-leveraged. All subsequent chairmen and CEOs with the exception of Stan O'Neal spoke about these fundamental principles in their annual messages.

W hen the modern Merrill Lynch opened for business in 1940, the daily volume on the New York Stock Exchange ranged from 250,000 to 400,000 shares, and it was said that a floor trader could easily cram an entire day's ticker tape into his pocket—without squashing his peanut butter sandwich. However, over subsequent years, led by Charlie Merrill's upstart new firm, Wall Street succeeded in attracting millions of small, first-time investors, and twenty-five years later, daily volume reached 5 million shares. From this point, the pace picked up steadily, and a speculative splurge at the end of 1967 pushed the average daily figure to about 10.1 million shares. The following year President Lyndon Johnson announced that he would not seek reelection, and the bulls surged; on April 10 the NYSE broke the 20-million-share trading barrier.

Every one of these trades required paperwork as they made their journey from the salesman, to the brokerage office, to the home office, to the trading floor, and then back again. But neither Merrill Lynch nor any other brokerage had the people, the space, or the equipment to cope with it all—and the financial community was in danger of choking on its own success. The worst technical failure the free-enterprise system had ever known, it was variously called the Paper Crunch, the Paper Blizzard, the Backstage Crisis, and, by the *New York World-Telegram & Sun*, "the Paper Potamus."

This was the situation as Regan took command. "The Street was dizzy with prosperity," he reflected later. "Greed replaced good judgment. Brokerage firms took on more business than they could handle—and choked on the paperwork the new business generated." In his first days as president, Regan accidentally discovered an employee in the Merrill Lynch back office whose base salary was $7,200 but who was taking home $18,000 because of overtime. He was working from nine A.M. to eleven P.M., seven days a week. When Regan questioned this seeming anomaly and expressed amazement, he was told that the case was typical of the entire department. Brokerage back offices were known as "the Cage" and they were a favorite target of cost-cutters. The work performed there was so compartmentalized that the job could be mastered by any high-school graduate in a day or two, though many of the workers on Wall Street were high-school dropouts, and it took them a little longer. They sat on chairs with missing casters and pecked at typewriters with missing keys. Pay and morale were low, and the annual turnover rate approached 60 percent.

By June 1968, the clerical errors, discrepancies, and oversights had built up to a point where an estimated $4.5 billion worth of undelivered stock was caught in the clotted pipelines. Various emergency measures were taken in 1969. In January the NYSE moved its closing time up one hour to two P.M. In February the settlement time was extended from four days to five days. In June the major exchanges went on a four-day week, and the amount of cash needed to buy stocks was raised to 80 percent of the stock's price. Nevertheless, the trading torrent continued. In the first five months of 1969, Merrill Lynch alone opened some 200,000 new accounts. Charles Napolitano, a back-office supervisor, recollected: "You could probably not even see me over the piles of paper on my desk. As the day progressed, the piles just got higher and higher." Wall Street, that carping critic of the management practices of other American companies, did not even have a clerical apparatus capable of handling its own volume of business.

The Federal Reserve Board made a long-term step toward resolving the paper blizzard by updating its forty-six-year-old bank wire system, and a central depository was created to eliminate much of the physical transfer of paper. The system dispensed with certificates altogether, and substituted a network of computers to record transfers of ownership, to pay dividends on stocks, and to pay interest on interest-bearing securities. Merrill Lynch weathered the crisis better than its competitors because—largely due to my father's and Mike McCarthy's foresight—it had more capital and better computers to deal with the problems, and it was ready to take advantage of the new systems. Elsewhere the crisis continued largely unabated. Brokerages lost track of the trades they made, the certificates involved in the trades, and the status of their customers' accounts. All available resources went toward coping with the mess, and very few NYSE members made a profit in 1969. About eighty firms went bankrupt or merged with other firms. A disastrous collapse loomed just ahead in 1970, and only one firm had righted itself and had the resources to prevent it.

On November 4, 1970, Robert ("Ritt") Rittereiser, service director for the Northeast region of Merrill Lynch, Pierce, Fenner & Smith, was in Rochester, New York, on routine business when he got the most important telephone call of his career. *Come back immediately,* he was told by Roger Birk, director of the Operations Division, *and report tomorrow morning at the offices of Goodbody & Co. We have twenty days to examine their operation and determine how we will manage them when we take them over on Day 20. You're in charge.* Rittereiser was thirty-two years old. "I was too young and inexperienced to figure out how not to wind up in such a job," he reflected later. "I also was young and idealistic enough to think I could do it. If I realized what I was getting into, I might have choked." Goodbody would occupy most of Rittereiser's waking hours for the next year and a half.

Goodbody & Co., the fifth-largest NYSE member, had been brought to its knees by the paper crunch and was on the verge of bankruptcy, and its 225,000 customers were in serious and immediate financial jeopardy, without any insurance to cover the value of their securities. A collapse of this magnitude would inevitably frighten shareholders at other brokerages into selling out, thereby triggering a panic and crumbling the foundation of public confidence on which all of Wall Street rested. "We would have had a panic the likes of which we have never seen," said Robert Haack, the NYSE president. Haack and Bernard Lasker, chairman of the Big Board, looked around frantically for someone to come to the rescue by acquiring Goodbody. There was only one firm with the resources to do it. Besides, hadn't E. A. Pierce & Co. done the same thing during the Depression for foundering firms? As Regan recounted in Merrill's 1970 Annual Report, "A couple of abortive attempts to save Goodbody were made by corporations outside of the securities industry. But it soon became apparent that no one but Merrill Lynch could combine the financial strength, the managerial expertise and depth, and the desire that were needed to mount a successful rescue operation. There was a confluence of the interests of the public, the industry, and our firm. Our intervention suddenly became inevitable." There was really no choice. As Regan put it, Merrill Lynch found Goodbody "dying on our doorstep."

Under the rescue plan, Merrill Lynch would immediately supply $15 million for the ailing Goodbody operation and eventually acquire the firm, and the NYSE members would indemnify Merrill Lynch for up to $30 million for liabilities that might arise from the merger. "Before we stepped in," Regan said later, "we sought from the members of the New York Stock Exchange an indemnity against certain kinds of damage that we might suffer as a result. The total indemnity came to $30 million. We believed at the time that insistence on this prudent condition was the better part of valor. In those confused days of urgent decision, no one could be sure exactly how desperate Goodbody's internal situation was—not even Goodbody's management." Nevertheless, the agreement left ML exposed to substantial risk.

George Shinn, who had spearheaded the firm's institutional effort and was now its chief long-range planner, was made president of the new Goodbody subsidiary. It probably was not the best use of Shinn's skills, and he soon earned the nickname "the Grey Ghost." People at 70 Pine Street, ML's headquarters, would ask, "Where's George?" "Oh, he's probably over at Goodbody." People at Goodbody would ask, "Where's George?" "Oh, he's probably over at 70 Pine Street." Shinn did spend a lot of time at both places, but in doing so he was wearing himself thin. Regan knew of his nickname and this likely caused more friction in their relationship. Roger Birk, a newcomer to the home office from Kansas City with great technological skills, assumed a key role in the untangling process. Goodbody's computers had been set up willy-nilly by technicians who were not familiar with the securities industry, and there were several different types of computers that were incompatible with one another. Robert O'Connell, the director of ML operations, called it "an electronic Tower of Babel." Many tasks that were routinely performed by computers in other brokerages were still done by hand at Goodbody. O'Connell found the results predictable: "When the differences piled up between floor transactions and customer accounts, they couldn't strike a balance, so they'd just kind of wash them out by setting up separate accounts arbitrarily. They had changed general accounts so often that you couldn't track them down. They had shipped securities out to people who hadn't bought the stuff, but you could never trace the orders. Nobody knew what the losses were."

In addition, as Shinn's operations chief, Rittereiser found Goodbody's books in extreme disarray—partly because of its makeshift efforts to dig out of the paper blizzard in its early stages. When ML took control of Goodbody's affairs on December 10, 1970, the books showed net assets of about $21 million, but when the Merrill Lynch auditors completed their examination ninety days later, they found a deficit of $28 million. This was a disastrous swing of $49 million between what was assumption and fact, and it fell to Rittereiser to convey the bad news to Goodbody partners. "I literally sat there and told people that securities in their accounts had been sold out. They didn't realize that when they signed the partnership agreement that their personal assets had been assigned. In at least two of the cases, the people did not even understand what they had done, what situation they were in. Most of them went into personal bankruptcy. One guy had pledged a lot of assets of his wife, and he had never really told her. It was a tough time for them."

In moving to save Goodbody, our firm had placed its reputation as the leader of Wall Street on the line. It succeeded, but as Rittereiser put it in basketball terms, it was no lay-up. While it was a gigantic risk, Goodbody turned out to be one of the better acquisitions in ML history and allowed an expansion of the retail network, especially in municipal bonds and unit investment trusts. Roger Birk looked back on the Goodbody affair in 1981 as Regan's successor: "It was a costly affair. However, we also realized some fruitful results. We acquired a great many talented people, a number of good branch offices, and we gained early expertise in unit trusts and options trading, both of which we developed into major activities during the 1970s." Despite the indemnity, which did not cover operating losses, Merrill's financial statements for the next couple of years reflected the losses that Merrill bore in saving the industry from potential calamity. That American history textbooks do not today carry "Panic of 1970" in their indexes is mostly due to the response of MLPF&S to the crisis.

While Merrill Lynch's Goodbody rescue proved to reap many benefits for the company, at the same time it caused yet another delay in the firm's next big step toward growth: public ownership. Ever since the firm became a corporation in 1959, its leaders had sought access to additional money from outside investors to meet the ever-growing demand for investment services, but events had conspired against this. The NYSE appointed a committee to study the issue for all member firms in 1964, but there was no forward movement. Finally in 1969, a small member firm, Donaldson, Lufkin & Jenrette, said it would register a stock offering with the SEC with or without Exchange approval. In March 1970, the NYSE adopted rules for public ownership.

But Wall Street was reeling in the aftermath of the paper blizzard, and its resident firms did not look like good bets to most investors. Earnings were poor everywhere, including at Merrill Lynch. The Penn Central Railroad had just derailed into bankruptcy by defaulting on its commercial paper and this almost brought down the venerable Wall Street firm Goldman Sachs. Nevertheless, Don Regan ordered the preparation of a prospectus just in case, and in March of 1971, a patch of blue sky suddenly appeared. Most significant among the promising signs: The Government Securities Division was going to rack up a spectacular first quarter, Rittereiser had a handle on the Goodbody problem, and the annual audit had just showed a record capital base of $280 million. A summit meeting was held over Easter weekend, and the decision was made to go public immediately.

On July 27, 1971, a few minutes after the opening bell on the floor of the New York Stock Exchange, the new MER symbol crossed the tape at 28¼. Regan placed an order to purchase the first 100 shares of his firm's stock to trade on the Big Board. The 4-million-share offering was issued at $28, quickly jumped to $41, and by the weekend had settled in at $37. About half of the shares came from existing stockholders, but the rest (about $55.7 million) was new capital. In order to have a sufficiently sized offering, a number of Merrill Lynch employees and their families participated in the offering. At the time, Don was one of my mother's trustees and almost all of her net worth was in Merrill Lynch stock, which paid a modest dividend. While a concentration like that was not prudent, my father had said to my mother, "Vivian, don't let anyone sell your Merrill Lynch stock. It's going to be worth a lot more in the future." My mother was furious that some of her shares were included in the offering without her permission, and she called Don. "Vivian, you don't seem to realize that you don't own anything," Don told her. "The stock is in trust and we, the trustees, make the decisions." Don's blunt statement was factually correct, and he actually did the right thing from a fiduciary responsibility, but interestingly, it was this same display of impatience and lack of sensitivity to a woman that would ultimately cause him to fall out of favor at the Reagan White House many years later.

One of the biggest surprises in the offering prospectus was the fact that Norman Weiden, the former Fenner & Beane salesman whom Charlie Merrill had convinced to stick with Merrill Lynch, owned more shares than anyone other than the Merrill family. Weiden had constantly reinvested in the firm and had accumulated 500,000 shares. By 2001, when the stock traded at $80 per share, his post-split share would have been worth $640 million. When Merrill went public, I wanted to buy 100 shares, but as the son of a selling shareholder I was not permitted to do so. A couple of months later, I received my monthly brokerage statement and was surprised to see that it included 100 shares of Merrill stock. Apparently, Norman Weiden had heard about my interest in buying shares and transferred some of his shares to my account because, as he said to my account executive, Don Rundlett, "Young Win should be a shareholder of the firm his father built."

One consequence of the public offering was a suit brought by the Bitting family. Ken Bitting, a retired partner of the firm, had sold his stock back to Merrill Lynch at book value shortly before the public offering. After the stock went public, he sued Don Regan and Merrill Lynch, alleging that they had purposely defrauded him by not telling him of the intention to go public. Don hired Rogers & Wells, a prominent law firm, to defend ML. After he left his post as President Nixon's Secretary of State, Bill Rogers took on the case personally and was successful in defending it. This began a close personal friendship between Don and Bill, which eventually led to Don's introduction to Ronald Reagan and his appointment in 1980 as Secretary of the Treasury. While Reagan's first choice for the Treasury job was Walter Wriston of Citicorp, after he turned it down the job was offered to Don thanks to Rogers's close connection with Bill Casey, Rogers's law partner. Rogers also joined Merrill's board and became an invaluable adviser to Don, Roger Birk, Bill Schreyer, and Dan Tully, and helped greatly with our international expansion.

Merrill Lynch had once again broken tradition and become the second firm to achieve the dual status of member firm and listed company on the Big Board. More important, the firm had gained access to a vast sea of capital that it might use to develop its existing programs, finance new acquisitions, or strike out in new areas. As it turned out, it did all three.

Edwin J. Perkins, Merrill's biographer, gives this interpretation of the action:

> Going public was perhaps the ultimate realization of Charlie Merrill's vision. The democratization of the stock market reached another milepost; customers and owners were no longer distinct categories but potentially overlapping groups. Customers could still obtain outstanding service at reasonable prices and, in addition, by acquiring just a few shares of stock in Merrill Lynch itself, they could become part owners of the enterprise launched in 1914 by the nation's preeminent entrepreneur in the financial services sector.

At the same time, though, going public also had other consequences that were not so positive. For one thing, maintaining a long-term view became far more difficult as quarterly earnings were scrutinized by analysts and ownership was increasingly transferred into the hands of institutions. In fact, so important were quarterly earnings that there was one quarter in 1974, only a few years after the firm went public, when Don frantically searched for ways that Merrill Lynch could report earnings of a penny a share instead of reporting its first quarterly loss since 1941. Being a public company also meant that additional disclosure was required and that the compensation of Merrill's top executives needed to be disclosed. When Regan and a handful of other senior executives received stock options after Merrill went public, many throughout the firm were outraged. However, the 1971 proxy statement showed that the top executives were not highly paid compared to many on Wall Street, a mixed blessing, since for certain types of staff, like those in investment banking, that created another concern: Was their pay going to be capped so as not to exceed what the chairman and CEO made?

Shortly after the firm went public, Don was given a chauffeured limousine to commute to work, and many top ML people, including former partners like Norman Weiden, were highly critical of this. None of his predecessors had needed this perquisite. What most were unaware of, however, were the death and kidnapping threats that Regan received. As Merrill Lynch and Don himself became more prominent, he became a target for certain terrorist and criminal groups. At one point when his youngest son, Richard, was a student at the College of William & Mary, a roommate returned to their room to find this message written on the bureau mirror: "We have your son." The Regans frantically tried to find Richard to no avail. The FBI was contacted, and everyone feared the worst. When Diane, the youngest of the family, was finally reached, she said, "Oh, Richard is on a camping trip." The threat proved false, but it suggested that Don's prominence had made him a target, and that was not to be taken lightly.

By the 1970s, Merrill Lynch had developed a reputation for managerial expertise unmatched on Wall Street. Here is a cross section of journalistic comments:

> In the hung-over, run-down, blah-feeling securities business, one firm still is bounding about with the healthy vigor of a 10-year-old boy in summertime. It is Merrill Lynch, Pierce, Fenner & Smith Inc.—*The Wall Street Journal*, July 23, 1970

> During the economic crunch of 1969–70, more than a dozen large U.S. brokerage houses foundered, about the same number hurriedly merged to avoid disaster, and well over 100 smaller brokers went out of business altogether. The largest of them all, however, Merrill Lynch, Pierce, Fenner & Smith Inc., emerged larger and stronger than ever.—*The Exchange*, July 1971

> Amidst all the shouting, the bickering, the political chaos, the reforms, the counter-reformations, the recriminations, all attendant upon the now-accepted fact that the securities industry will never be the cosy place it used to

be, one firm, one large brokerage company, stands out as an expression of order, symmetry, rationality and good management. That firm is Merrill Lynch, Pierce, Fenner & Smith.—*Management Today*, February 1973

The big firm is working toward that goal by a process seldom thought of, much less attempted, on Wall Street: management by objective. That process, more often found in the savviest industrial corporations, involves setting specific long-term and short-term goals—in an endless succession of one-year, three-year and five-year plans—for every operating unit and every executive in the company. . . . With that eye-opening performance in volume and profitability, 1975 is the year in which Merrill Lynch's master strategy has really paid off—putting it in the select company of the U.S.'s five best-managed companies.—*Dun's Review*, December 1975

Indeed, three decades after Charlie Merrill was mocked on Wall Street for his idea to create a new kind of brokerage, no one was laughing. The May 1972 issue of *Fortune* magazine carried a cover article entitled "The Merrill Lynch Bull Is Loose on Wall Street." It began:

Competitors of Merrill Lynch, Pierce, Fenner & Smith must have a sense these days of never being able to get away from that giant firm. There are, for one thing, those "damn bulls," as one Wall Streeter describes them, filling up the television screen. Offscreen, there is Donald T. Regan, the company's forceful and outspoken chairman, calling at every opportunity for the complete abolition of his industry's fixed commission rates, which keep, he says, "a security blanket over the inefficient." And, in the everyday world of Wall Street, there is Merrill Lynch itself, roaming these days over the entire securities business, and casting a far larger shadow over the Street than any company ever has.

The article ended with this anecdote:

Think, for example, of the major difficulty facing Bill Crawford, the branch manager in Atlanta. Reflecting recently on what firm might be his biggest retail competition, he seemed honestly perplexed to come up with a name. Finally, he said, "I guess you'd just have to say it's the Merrill Lynch office half a mile away. They're really tough."

Years later Bill Schreyer would often joke to internal audiences, "Just remember that we are the only ones who don't have to compete against Merrill Lynch!"

When I was a boy I never really understood what my father did for a living, and I certainly never appreciated his status in the business world. We lived very comfortably in an eight-room cooperative apartment on Seventy-second Street between Park and Lexington Avenues in Manhattan, and I attended the Buckley School, one of New York's finest private day schools, but I never thought of us as really wealthy. In fact, most of my friends lived in larger apartments than ours, and some of them had chauffeurs and beautiful country estates in Greenwich, Connecticut, and the Hamptons. One even had his own squash court. Only later did I come to understand my father's Yankee roots and appreciate how unassuming and unpretentious he was.

After my father's death when I was at Deerfield Academy, some of my fellow students used to tease me about being wealthy and a stuffed shirt. They seemed to think that my father must have been a multimillionaire and that I must have been just a spoiled rich kid from New York City. Little did they realize that my dad's estate consisted primarily of stock in the private firm Merrill Lynch, Piece, Fenner & Smith, Inc. He had previously given ownership of the apartment in New York and the farm in Litchfield to my mother, and he also had been very generous to Amherst College. His estate was valued at around $1 million, which, of course, was a lot of money in 1961 but nowhere near what many thought. One of the things that Merrill Lynch did in 1940 was to diversify the ownership among the partners and the employees, so with the exception of the Merrill family, no one owned a significant percentage of the firm, but many became wealthy through their ownership.

After my father became ill when I was seven years old, and as his Parkinson's disease progressed, I vowed to someday become a doctor so I could help people get well. One Christmas my mother gave me a learning toy called the Invisible Man, and I really enjoyed getting to understand the human body and learning the different functions of the organs. Even when I enrolled at Amherst College in 1967, I was still thinking I would be pre-med. It wasn't until I took my first chemistry class that I realized that this was not my strong suit, so I became a political science major. After graduating from Amherst, I moved on to the Wharton School at the University of Pennsylvania to get my MBA. It was only in my second year that I decided to pursue investment banking, but I was reluctant to go to Merrill Lynch. Even though my father had been gone thirteen years by then, I worried about having the same name, and I wanted to prove myself on my own.

In the fall of 1973, after beginning my final year in business school, I visited Don Regan. Sitting in his new office on the forty-sixth floor of One Liberty Plaza, he listened to my rationalization for getting a job at another Wall Street firm. Then he said in his usual blunt manner, "Who are you kidding? Do you think anyone would really hire you knowing who you are? They would just think you were going there to learn about them and then leave for Merrill Lynch. I've just put a really bright young guy by the name of Tom Chrystie in charge of investment banking, and he's going to build up that business and make us a leader. You should apply for a job with him." Then he added, "If you're worried about being treated preferentially here, don't be! If you don't perform, I'll fire you myself." That hit the spot. After all, when he became CEO he fired Eddie Lynch Jr. because he wasn't performing. Yes, Mother Merrill looked after her employees, but the firm still always had high standards that didn't allow for nepotism.

After meeting with Don, I interviewed with Merrill Lynch on campus as well as with a host of other firms—Goldman, Morgan Stanley, Kidder Peabody, Dean Witter, Lehman, JP Morgan, Brown Brothers Harriman, Blyth Eastman Dillon, Citibank, and the Irving Bank and Trust. After meeting with these firms and being invited back by several of them for second interviews in New York, I quickly realized how different each culture was. When Morgan Stanley arrived on campus, for example, they came with two associates who were just out of the Harvard Business School. They were tall with dark hair, and they each wore blue suits, white shirts, and club ties. It was hard to tell them apart. They were humorless and clearly impressed with themselves. "Do you read the Sunday *New York Times*?" one asked as I sat down. "I do," I responded honestly. "Which section do you read first?" the other quizzed. "I start with the sports section," I said, "and—"

But before I could finish, the first associate, who looked like he was sitting with a pole up his butt, said, "Well, at Morgan Stanley we choose to do the chess puzzle first." I did not get invited back to New York for a second interview.

When Merrill came to campus, I signed up for the first interview of the day, and much to my shock, the interviewer was dressed in a plaid suit. He was from the Personnel Department and usually interviewed people applying to be an account executive, as brokers were called in those days at Merrill Lynch. As we discussed the firm, it became apparent that he knew very little about investment banking. Fortunately, about ten minutes into the interview, Mike O'Neil walked in. Mike was a second-year associate. His train from New York had been delayed, which is why he was late, and the Personnel Department guy had just been standing in for him.

I immediately liked Mike and we had a great interview. He was smart and asked good, probing questions, but was also very easy to talk to. He had no air of self-importance about him and was really enthusiastic about working for Merrill Lynch. "We're on the rise and building investment banking, and we're going to overtake Morgan Stanley in a few years," he told me. After my meeting with the Morgan Stanley associates, Mike was a breath of fresh air, and I felt I would put my money on people like him instead of the creeps from Morgan Stanley. When Mike returned to New York and told Rad Lovett, the assistant director of Investment Banking, that I was one of the students he wanted to bring back for further interviews, Rad said, "Good choice. Do you have any idea who he is?" Mike did not.

When I arrived at Merrill Lynch for my second round of interviews, I was again met by Mike O'Neil, and he gave me the schedule for the day. It consisted of eight interviews with people ranging from associates to Rad Lovett. My first interview was in the bullpen (the name of the room where first and second associates had their desks) with Will Elting. Will was a bit imposing, with his suspenders and receding hairline and wire-rimmed glasses, and he started asking me some technical questions about finance, but then Mike walked over and whispered something in his ear, at which point Will's questioning changed, and we ended up having a very pleasant conversation. (After I was hired I learned that Mike had said, "Take it easy. Do you know who he is? He might be your boss one day.")

My next interview was with Milan Kerno, the general counsel of Investment Banking, who had just been hired from Lehman Brothers. Milan was German and sounded like Henry Kissinger. He took a long look at my résumé, looked up, and said, "It is a very precise résumé." What he meant was: *You don't have a lot on it, do you?* Fortunately, I had my interview with Milan early in the day, and everyone I met after that was like Mike O'Neil. They were bright, enthusiastic, and totally committed to making Merrill Lynch into an investment banking powerhouse. In many ways they were like the hapless Mets baseball team. They were in last place and no one gave them any respect, but "they believed" that one day soon they would win the World Series.

I lunched with Rad Lovett, who spoke to me directly about the challenges of being the son of Win Smith were I to come to work at the firm. Rad's family owned Piggly Wiggly stores, among others, and they had been close friends of Charlie Merrill's, so he understood some of the challenges when you come from a family with connections. He told me I would have to prove myself more than others and that many people would still think I was there only because of my father. That would be the reality, he said, throughout my career, and I just had to deal with it and earn their respect through performance. Rad shared many fond memories of my father and told me stories I hadn't heard before, including about Dad's interactions with Howard Hughes when Merrill underwrote the TWA stock sale. In addition to being a very competent banker and executive, Rad was one of the nicest gentlemen I'd ever met, and he was held in great respect by everyone who worked with or for him.

My final interview that day was with Joe Low, who headed the Southwest Region for investment banking. A Williams College graduate, Joe immediately made fun of my Amherst background, and we parried back and forth about this for a while. Joe was the ideal person to end the day, and I left feeling that I had really enjoyed the experience, that I could work well with these people, and that this culture was one I would love being a part of.

I came back another day and then a third, and it was only after three days of interviewing that Rad offered me a job starting at a salary of $17,000 a year. He told me that he had scheduled me to interview with more people than other applicants because he wanted to make sure that I was up to the job and that everyone supported hiring me because of my ability and not my name. That made a huge impression on me. (I later found out that he also paid me $1,000 less than everyone else.)

I phoned Rad the next day and accepted his offer, and started working on August 5, my twenty-fifth birthday, during a particularly slow period. Nothing was happening in investment banking at that point. The market had gone through a few years of stagnation. Watergate was the main news of the day and hardly any investment banking deals other than for public utilities were being done. As a first-year associate, I spent most of my time doing debt covenant analyses for more senior bankers, and retail information memorandums for the various utility underwritings managed by Merrill Lynch. Our bullpen was quite diverse. We had several white male Americans, a Frenchman, a Dutchman, an African-American, and a woman. Most were graduates of Harvard, Columbia, or Wharton, with the exception of probably the smartest in the group, Frank Weisser, who had gone to the University of Michigan.

Joining Merrill Lynch in 1974 was the beginning of a twenty-eight-year career that I have never regretted. Being there while Don was chairman and CEO and watching his leadership style and his courage as well as his intensity for winning and doing the right thing was something I will always appreciate. Knowing him as an employee was different from knowing him as a relative.

When Don Regan rose to leadership, much of Wall Street still looked upon the institutional and investment banking side of Merrill Lynch as an upstart, run by callow, unsophisticated "salesmen" who were unschooled in the finer nuances of the Street and disrespectful of its traditions. The firm was not run by Ivy Leaguers and didn't have MBAs from the likes of Harvard or Wharton.

"The Thundering Herd" was not a term of endearment in those days but rather one of derision. Merrill Lynch, said its detractors, made its money selling odd lots to grubby middle-class investors, all the while wallowing in the gutter with the use of such base techniques as mass advertising. Competitors made fun of Merrill's small investors, some of whom would bring their lunch in paper bags to ML brokerages and watch the ticker tape and maybe place an odd-lot order. In today's world, these investors would be called "the 99 percent." And yet for all the disparagement, amid all the upheavals in the securities industry during the economic squeeze of 1969–70, ML emerged almost alone in vigor and health. Charlie Merrill had recognized the weaknesses of the traditional, laissez-faire Wall Street management processes, and he had made management a priority. It started with the training school, which by 1970 was turning out a thousand account executives every year, and extended to a disciplined approach to management selection and development, with a process created to assess managerial talent. If one passed, he was sent through a formal management training program, and rarely were the trainees allowed to return to the office whence they had come. They apprenticed as sales managers under experienced branch managers before getting an office of their own. Almost all started as account executives, but it was rarely the highest-producing account executives who were chosen for management positions—a radical notion in a business where producers ruled. Unlike the competition, ML managed carefully by setting long- and short-term goals and reviewing them periodically to be sure they were on target. Like Merrill and my father, Regan made long-range planning a priority. Two of the most obvious results of this process were advanced computer technology and diversification. Even for the Street's most hidebound traditionalist, the efficacy of the ML approach was getting hard to ignore.

To prepare the firm for the survival-of-the-fittest conditions that would follow the end of negotiated commission rates (an event that was looming on the horizon), Regan imposed a cost-cutting regimen in mid-1972 that he called "PIP," for Profit Improvement Program. Without harming such essentials as customer service and the training school, PIP helped ML regain control of costs, which had shot up in the effort to cope with the paper blizzard, and it made the firm lean and ready for the coming competitive wars. PIP was still in place when I joined the firm. While it wasn't pleasant and sometimes went to an extreme, it did allow Merrill Lynch to remain profitable at a time when other firms were failing left and right. Nothing was sacred. I remember one young colleague of mine in Investment Banking, Clay Rohrbach, who was very resourceful in dealing with PIP. Some accountant had determined that the new push-button phone was more expensive than the old rotary-dial one, so an edict went out to replace the new phone with the dial phone. Clay brought in a dial phone from home, and whenever he was alerted that one of the "accounting police" was on the floor, he put his rotary phone on his desk and hid the other in one of his desk drawers. His preferred phone then came out when the all clear was given.

Don's PIP program was not the last cost-reduction program I saw during my almost twenty-eight years at Merrill Lynch. The securities business is a cyclical one and downturns almost always occur more suddenly than expected. People in most businesses love to grow, but only a few masochists enjoy downsizing and cutting expenses. While Don and all of his successors had years when tough decisions needed to be made, all of them did it with an understanding that the employees of the firm were its most important asset, and so they were mindful to cut fat and not muscle. All of them felt badly when payroll needed to be trimmed, and only did what they felt was in the best interests of the majority of the stakeholders of the firm. One of Regan's successors, Dan Tully, summed this attitude up best when he told us, "You never throw a fellow employee down a flight of stairs. You always preserve one's dignity."

During this time, Don also realized that the firm needed to diversify its funding sources. Up until then it relied, like all other investment firms, on overnight call loans from banks. This put the firm in a precarious position, so Don asked his young director of Investment Banking, Tom Chrystie, to develop a new funding strategy along with his treasurer, Ed Ryan.

Ryan, an ex-Marine like Don, was a Regan protégé and a devoted disciple. He had succeeded him as manager of the Philadelphia office and would later come to New York, at Don's request, to become Merrill's treasurer (there was no chief financial officer then). Ryan was a wonderful person, a devoted Merrill Lyncher, and a successful office manager, but in finance he was out of his core competency. Yet he was smart enough to recognize that he needed to rely upon someone like Chrystie, a Columbia University graduate, to develop a funding strategy for the firm. Years later Ed was thrilled when his son Mike was recruited into Merrill's Investment Banking Division and ultimately became the head of our Global Capital Markets Group.

In their efforts to diversify the firm's funding sources, Tom realized that they needed to tap the commercial paper market to reduce its dependency on the banks, and he also knew that Merrill needed to term out its debt and improve its balance sheet by substituting long-term debt for short-term bank loans. The first step was to achieve an investment-grade rating from either Moody's or Standard & Poor's. Finally, On October 8, 1975, after two years of work, which included some legal and regulatory maneuvering, Merrill Lynch & Co. became the first securities-related firm to issue its own commercial paper with a rating of A-1 from Moody's. This was a terrific coup for Don, Ed, and Tom, and opened the door for Merrill to fund its future growth and diversification. Five years later, ML issued its first long-term public debt, a milestone for a securities firm. Once the firm achieved an investment-grade rating, Chrystie impressed upon his colleagues the importance of continuing to seek a higher rating—and thus lower funding costs—by carefully watching the amount of leverage that Merrill took on and also by generating a more stable stream of earnings and reducing the dependency on volatile commission revenue.

Back in the 1920s, Charlie Merrill had warned both customers and his partners about excessive leverage, and his focus on being properly capitalized was passed along to his successors. Regan knew that ML came through the crisis of 1969 largely because of this, and he personally watched the regulatory capital of the firm daily. In the 1971 shareholder letter he said, "As it [the new world] unfolds our constants remain. We shall always manage our capital conservatively." This goal was passed along to all of us and became our guiding objective over the subsequent three decades. What a shame that this was not appreciated by those who were accountable for the firm in 2007.

Don subsequently asked Ed to become chairman of Government Securities when Bill Schreyer was named EVP of Capital Markets,

Tom Chrystie, a brilliant and creative visionary, was one of Regan's most important promotions. He grew investment banking, professionalized Merrill's finances, and expanded international. Perhaps most important, he led the development of CMA.

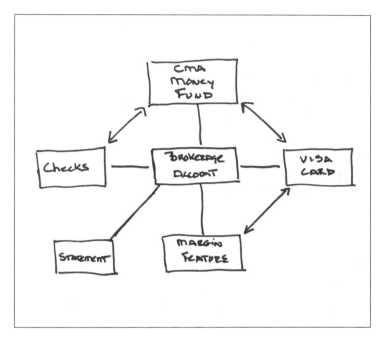

Paul Stein came up with a simple but brilliant way to explain the new Cash Management Account to Merrill's financial consultants. This is my version of Paul's original sketch (I drew it many times). It shows how a brokerage account, Visa card, and checking account would all be tied together into CMA, and the client would only receive one statement each month. After opening my own CMA account, I never set foot in a bank again. CMA is the reason Citicorp Chairman Walter Wriston referred to Merrill Lynch as the "bank of the future."

and he made Chrystie senior vice president and chief financial officer. Don made many excellent executive appointments, but putting Tom into this position may have been one of his best, as it made perfect use of Tom's talents. Tom knew that he needed to improve the talent in the financial area. As he said to me in 1977 when he was recruiting me to join his team, "I don't need bean counters, I need people who can think and who have strong analytical skills." I joined Tom's team as manager of financial analysis and budgets.

Working for Tom Chrystie was one of the highlights of my career. He had a brilliant and creative mind and was always thinking about ways that Merrill Lynch could innovate and grow. Having come from investment banking rather than the brokerage side of the business put him a bit at odds with his other senior executive peers, who often challenged his ideas. At a young age (I was twenty-eight years old at the time), I had the opportunity of providing financial analysis reports for Don, Roger Birk, and Tom, and participated in the quarterly review and budgeting session for all the business units. I worked hard to put these reports together, and when Tom approved them they were sent to Don. While I'm sure he read them, during meetings Don always relied on his own analysis and asked hard and probing questions, which his executives often didn't have answers to. These reviews were taken seriously by all, and Don loved to play "Gotcha!" with a question. Don's style was intimidating and not everyone liked it, but it kept us sharp.

Naturally, Tom reached into the Investment Banking Division for talent, making Greg Fitzgerald his treasurer and Steve Warner and Dennis Hess his strategic thinkers. Others from Investment Banking were brought in to help Regan's team. Bob Arnold became assistant to Regan and then treasurer. Herb Allison became Roger Birk's assistant and ultimately president of Merrill Lynch & Co. for a brief period. Arthur ("Archie") Urciuoli was an adviser to Bill Schreyer and then president of Merrill Lynch International. Nassos Michas, a bright young research analyst, was also identified as a person with great potential. Under Regan one did not have to come from the brokerage side of the business anymore to move up the management ranks, but one still did have to understand and appreciate the values of the firm.

A mong the most pressing management issues at the dawn of the Regan Era was inventory control. A hodgepodge of incompatible computers and machinery, purchased at different times for different purposes, was being used to keep track of the billions of dollars' worth of stocks and bonds on deposit with ML. Despite the fact that there was some computer support, this was basically a manual operation. Although it was an inefficient system, ironically it was still way ahead of anything else on Wall Street. The main impetus for establishing better inventory controls was the rise of institutional trades, because on a large trade even a one-day delay in delivery could mean heavy interest charges. Regan, who at this time was one of the few top executives in America to have a computer terminal in his office, wanted a better system. While the chairman kept his PIP zealots at bay, the ML computer center was reconfigured and every computer was replaced. The firm built its systems capacity at a time when the market was in the doldrums, so that when it took off—as it would in 1980—Merrill Lynch would be ready.

Don was a salesman at heart and often followed the principle of "selling the sizzle, not the steak." He had a handsome mahogany credenza built behind his desk in his corner office on the forty-sixth floor of One Liberty Plaza. When a CEO from another company would come to visit Don, he would say, "Let's see how your stock is doing." Turning around in grand fashion, he would open the panel displaying his computer screen and type in the company's stock symbol. Up would come a screen showing the price. Then another screen would appear with some facts and analytics about the company followed by Merrill's QRQ (the research opinion) and some other news. His visitor was always impressed by Don's facile ability with a computer and the seemingly real-time information he had at his fingertips. Undoubtedly, the visitor went back and asked his own IT department why he couldn't have what he had seen in Regan's office. What the visitor didn't know was that Don would have the IT department notified of the visit ahead of time and a young programmer would put together the information and feed it into Don's computer, so that all he had to do was open the panel and punch the button. Don loved to put on a show.

One of the most important lessons that Don learned from Charlie Merrill was that advertising and public relations were critical. Regan built upon efforts begun before his time and took them to new heights.

Grand Central Station seemed to bring out the impulsive side of Lou Engel. It was here in 1946 that he had made his spur-of-the-moment call to my father and was promptly hired to direct Merrill Lynch advertising. Twenty years later he was back there in a phone booth spontaneously thumbing through the telephone directory to find the address of Ogilvy & Mather, the famous advertising agency that created the Hathaway shirt man and proclaimed that Maxwell House coffee was good to the last drop. The agency's offices were located just a few blocks away, at Forty-eighth and Madison, and a few minutes later Engel walked in the door and said he would like to see somebody about an account. . . .

Though Rudy Guenther's ad agency had not performed well for Merrill Lynch during the fifties and sixties, it retained its position as the firm's go-to agency out of a sense of loyalty to Rudy for his early support of Charlie Merrill. However, when Guenther retired in 1966, Engel was at last free to seek a new agency. He had read David Ogilvy's 1963 book, *Confessions of an Advertising Man*, and had been impressed. Now he was being ushered into the office of David Ogilvy himself, who was having difficulty believing his good fortune.

Over the next few weeks, Engel met with various people at Ogilvy and his respect for the agency grew. Though Ogilvy & Mather had a policy of not making formal presentations to prospective clients, Engel's first job was to convince the agency that it had to make an exception in this case and go before a Merrill Lynch selection committee. After six agencies pleaded their cases with pasteboards and mock-ups, the committee became deadlocked between Ogilvy & Mather and a second major firm, Foote, Cone & Belding. George Leness favored the latter because Merrill Lynch had underwritten its initial public offering a few years earlier, while Engel and Regan wanted Ogilvy. Neither side would budge, and finally Mike McCarthy, semiretired but still a "respected elder" of the firm, came in from California and effected a compromise: Foote would handle direct mail; Ogilvy would handle print and television. Engel called McCarthy's solution "a genius of management."

Ogilvy's first efforts carried the theme "We look for the trends." One trend spotted by Merrill Lynch was growth in the office maintenance industry, and to illustrate this, Ogilvy showed a cleaning lady with her mops and rags and the headline "We Saw Her as a Glamor Stock." It was a good campaign, but it failed to register an overall favorable impression. "We decided the problem was one of dimension," said Richard G. Evans, Ogilvy's creative director. "We were depending on mastery of the peashooter to stop a tank, when what we needed was a 155mm cannon, something so big, it would be explosive. And instead of print, we'd try television. We flailed away in this direction for a few days without getting anywhere. Finally, an idea. Instead of a memorable line, suppose we tried for a memorable visual? Something that conveyed the idea of a trend. We thought of geese flying south. No good—too poetic. And, besides, what did geese have to do with the stock market? On the other hand, what about bulls?"

Since the early days of Wall Street, the bull, probably because it thrusts its horns upward, had been a symbol of optimism and rising prices. The association was even stronger for Merrill Lynch, which had come to be known very early as "the Thundering Herd of Wall Street" because of the size of its partnership. It was Roger Butler, the head of Ogilvy's copy group, who honed the idea. In a 1971 memo to Evans, he said the bull should be exploited as fully as possible:

> It should symbolize some mammoth generality, not some two-bit promise of personal wealth. . . . The image of the bulls is worth more than just suggesting you're going to tell [sic] me a little stock that will grow. . . . The correct idea, not words, in my opinion, would be that Merrill Lynch had unbounded faith and confidence in the future of America and its industrial might—and is quite willing to let you share in the long-term BRIGHT FUTURE.

Butler offered six possible sell lines, one of which was "Merrill Lynch: We're Bullish on America." Then he closed his memo: "These are, admittedly, broad and corny sentiments. But I think they're the kind of sentiments that are the essence of this client. . . for a lot of sophisticated psychological reasons, they might just work."

One formidable hurdle remained. "After weeks of work, we had finally succeeded in compounding a questionable visual with an even more questionable line," Evans recalled. "It was the summer of 1971 and the stock market was on its knees. The country had just gone through a severe recession—and no one was sure the worst was over. How could ML proclaim they were bullish on America? We knew, of course, that ML was bullish on the long-term future of the American economy. What we didn't know was that ML had turned bullish on the short term. The [Merrill Lynch] economists said the 1971 gross national product would soar to $1.1 trillion, the highest in U.S. history. Supported by this forecast, the campaign got all the way up to Donald T. Regan, chairman of ML. We braced ourselves for a 'no.' But Mr. Regan was bullish."

This was reinforced at a management meeting that took place right around that time. To learn more about the firm, Ogilvy was invited to sit in on these sessions, and at one of them, Merrill's chief economist, Gary Schilling, was offering his usual dour view of the world. As Regan doodled through the presentation, as he often did when was he was bored or irritated, those in the room could sense that something was about to occur. When Schilling concluded his presentation, Regan looked up, pounded the table with his fist, and snapped, "Goddammit, I don't care what anyone thinks, I am bullish on America." Thus began one of the most successful advertising campaigns of the twentieth century. A postscript: Regan soon fired Schilling.

I was still a student at Amherst College when Don slammed his fist on the boardroom table at 70 Pine Street, and in those days we used to gather in the Chi Psi fraternity TV room after dinner to watch Walter Cronkite and the *CBS Evening News*. Mesmerized by the coverage out of Vietnam and personally interested in the draft lottery, I distinctly remember one fall evening when a commercial came on showing bulls running across the screen. As the thundering of their hooves grew louder, the voice-over proclaimed that "Merrill Lynch is bullish on America!"

The first spot ran on October 6, 1971, between innings of the World Series between the Baltimore Orioles and the Pittsburgh Pirates. "In the years ahead we see this country growing in many different ways," the announcer said. "Merrill Lynch has a lot of different ways to put your money to work. Merrill Lynch is bullish on America," thundered the announcer as the herd of raging bulls roared across the screen. The Series went seven games, and the sixty-second spot ran eighteen times in all. Print ads in twenty-five top markets, going into more detail about Merrill Lynch's bullishness, followed soon afterward. The dividends came almost immediately. Within eight weeks awareness of the theme among upper-income men jumped by 140 percent, and the perception among them of Merrill Lynch as "the best firm for handling a wide variety of investments" rose from 19 percent to 28 percent. The media picked up on the bull theme, and comedians worked it into their routines. President Richard Nixon even mentioned the commercial in a news conference. The ad campaign helped the firm increase its average-size order from $3,630 at the start of the 1970s to $4,604 in the middle of 1972. It was one of the most famous and successful campaigns in advertising history, and the bulls would be associated with Merrill Lynch for the rest of the twentieth century and beyond. (The bulls used originally for the commercial were from Mexico. When someone discovered this, it had to be shot all over again, this time using bulls from Texas.)

To complement the "Bullish on America" ad campaign, Regan also had the Merrill Lynch logo redesigned to integrate the new Merrill brand. The old logo was a mixture of the letters MLF. Nice but not very distinctive or memorable. A visual of a bull was designed to precede the words *Merrill Lynch* on all stationery, business cards, collateral, etc. The original design seemed a bit effeminate, and as two creative designers from Ogilvy were thrashing this about over a two-martini lunch, one of them took out a pen and drew a jagged penis on the bull. "That's it," they both slurred. The new addition looked like a bolt of lightning, and the Merrill Lynch bull was thereafter named Lightning.

After more than a decade as Merrill's agency of record, Ogilvy was abruptly fired in 1978 when it chose First Boston—not Merrill Lynch—to underwrite a stock offering. ("What the hell do you think you're doing?" Regan fumed to an Ogilvy executive. "You had a full-page ad for us in *The Wall Street Journal* today saying how terrific we are at issues like this. You must be out of your mind." No question, this was one of the great business screw-ups of all times.

Ogilvy lost the account to Young & Rubicam, which developed a campaign around a single bull, intending to communicate individuality and self-confidence (as well as what people wanted in a financial institution: size, strength, and stability), with the theme "Merrill Lynch: A Breed Apart." In various commercials, the lone bull was seen wandering through the canyons of Wall Street, running on a beach in Northern California, trotting in a redwood forest, snorting on a dry river bottom in Wyoming, cavorting in an Idaho wheat field, and crossing a bridge in Taos, New Mexico. But the most famous spot showed him delicately picking his way through a china shop. This was before computer-enhanced graphics, so first Y&R had to train the bull to walk through a maze before they let him loose in the set they had built, which included shelves of Waterford crystal. In the final ad, the bull made his way through perfectly. The only loss came when a crew member dropped a crystal bowl. The "Bull in the China Shop" ad was a classic and demonstrated a more agile and sophisticated Merrill Lynch than the original bulls of Ogilvy rushing across the plains.

The star of most of these commercials was a 1,700-pound longhorn named Native Texan, who traveled with an entourage that included his owner, four ranch hands, four horses (to lead him through his paces), and two steers named Snowflake and T-Bone (to lure him when the horses couldn't handle him). Native Texan was not a quick learner. He had to navigate the shop many times and took down a lot of inexpensive props before the final take with Waterford Crystal. Years later, at Don's retirement dinner at the River Club, we got ahold of the outtakes from the commercial showing the bull starting to walk through the china shop. Everyone expected the actual commercial of Native Texan's perfect walk-through, but suddenly the bull went wild and destroyed the entire shop. It was a hilarious moment and Don roared laughing! No one in the room had seen the outtakes before, including Don.

Not since Charlie Merrill thumbed his nose at clubby Wall Street tradition in 1940 had anyone been as disliked by the financial establishment as Don Regan was soon after he took control of Merrill Lynch. He fumed at the monopolistic specialist firms: "They stood there at their post, allowed to trade for their own account, and made a fortune! The bastards!" He demanded repeal of the Glass–Steagall Act, the federal law passed in 1933 to address practices that were believed to have brought on the stock market crash. Basically, it barred banks from doing business on Wall Street and vice versa. But Regan fumed: "What the hell happened to competition? There is no God-given right that Wall Street firms should all succeed or that banks shouldn't have competition." There were times in the seventies when it appeared there were two warring camps: Merrill Lynch versus the rest of Wall Street. Behind all the battles, though, was Regan's belief that ML couldn't continue to grow until the securities industry reformed itself. He also firmly believed that if he was going to place the clients' interests first, he had to fight for regulatory reform. After all, Merrill Lynch had brought Wall Street to Main Street. Now Main Street's interests had to be brought to Wall Street.

Regan's most withering criticism was leveled at the NYSE's monopolistic rule that fixed commissions on all trades, thereby preventing brokerages from competing vigorously with one another and keeping commissions artificially high. "Why should our industry be any different from any other?" he asked scornfully. Certainly Regan and ML had an interest in deregulating commission rates, for as the Street's biggest brokerage (10 percent of the round-lot business, 25 percent of the odd-lot), it stood to gain the most from competitive rates. Again in this case, though, what was good for Merrill Lynch was good for the average investor, too. Pressure for change also was coming from institutional investors, whose business was especially lucrative for the brokers because of high activity and high volume. But now some institutional clients were demanding seats on the Exchange in order to bypass regular brokers entirely—and, ominously from the brokerages' viewpoint, both the SEC and Congress appeared amenable to the idea.

Regan fired his opening salvo before the Rotary Club of Dallas in December 1970. "Wall Street is hiding behind a protective pricing system while it preaches free competition and free markets," he said. "That is like catching Carrie Nation tippling in the basement." The fixed-commission battle was bitter, and at first ML was alone among the brokerage houses in seeking change, but the firm was the unchallenged leader of Wall Street, and its lone voice was a powerful one. Just how powerful was driven home on January 16, 1974, when for the first time in history the NYSE delayed opening because of an order-processing problem at ML. If it had been any other firm, the problem wouldn't even have made a ripple, but this was Merrill Lynch, Pierce, Fenner & Smith, and the opening was held up for fifteen minutes beyond the ten A.M. bell until the problem was corrected. Regan was furious, but the incident underscored ML's influence. Before long other securities industry leaders began joining the move toward negotiated commissions, and eventually, in 1975, the SEC ordered that brokerage commissions were to become fully competitive. "After 183 years of doing business under fixed commissions," Regan exulted, "Wall Street will have to respond to the challenges of the free-enterprise system." While Regan was a firm believer in capitalism and free markets, he also understood, as had Charlie Merrill and my father, that appropriate regulation was needed. As the new chairman of Merrill Lynch, he said, "In hearings before the Congress, the Securities and Exchange Commission, and the various self-regulatory bodies, we raise our voice in favor of regulation that enhances competition—the greatest and most efficient regulator of all—and in favor of regulation that aims to govern not what the industry was a decade ago, but what it is becoming, what it will be in five more years." After the Goodbody crisis, Regan was also a strong supporter of the creation of the Securities Investor Protection Corporation (SIPC) even though it came at a significant cost to ML, and he became one of its first appointed directors. SIPC, funded by the industry and supported by a guarantee of loans from the U.S. Treasury if required, insured individual customers against losses up to $50,000 they might incur as a result of their broker's failure. This amount was later increased to $500,000. As Regan said, "The legislation will be costly to Merrill Lynch, but its passage bolstered public confidence and added to the spreading sense that the crisis on Wall Street was ending."

Despite the doomsday warnings of standpat supporters of fixed commissions, "Mayday" came off smoothly. May 1, 1975, was the beginning of Wall Street's competitive era, and what followed justified Regan's beliefs about the importance of competitive trading. The initial beneficiaries were the insurance companies, pension funds, and other institutional security buyers. Indeed, initially, most small investors experienced a slight increase in the commissions they paid. But slowly free enterprise took hold. Some firms sought individual investors for the first time ever. Those that failed to adapt to the new way disappeared, and others rose up to take their place. One of the key ML executives involved in the changeover, Dan Tully, who would one day sit in Regan's chair, summed up the impact on Merrill Lynch: "Once the fixed-price environment ended in 1975, you had to provide value-added service to gather and retain customers. You had to turn from sales—what do we have to sell?—to marketing—what do customers want to buy?. . . Sales is a one-shot deal. Marketing is a much longer-term approach. It's the development of a customer relationship, so the customers, whenever they come back to the market, will want to do additional business with you. And, you know, that's just what Charlie Merrill kept pounding into the heads of his people seventy years ago."

Edwin J. Perkins said the new order played into ML's strengths:

> After 1975, a range of financial inducements undermined the longstanding gentlemanly relationships among the elite investment banking houses and their clients. Suddenly, vigorous competition ruled the day. Even formerly staid firms like Morgan Stanley joined the fray. Merrill Lynch was one beneficiary of this fresh start because it was often in a position to offer clients and customers the most attractive deals on the basis of service and price. The expertise of the research staff, which had been one of the firm's hallmarks since the early 1940s, was an important element in moving Merrill Lynch into a leadership position in underwriting, mergers, and acquisitions in the 1990s.

Don Regan had been in the CEO job only a few months when he began the final phase of my father and Charlie Merrill's grand plan: the creation of a department store of finance. "We understand the chain-store concept," he told an interviewer. "This is what the consumer wanted—first in groceries. Then we had Macy's, where you could buy a $5,000 diamond or a five-cent thimble, all under one roof." But Regan was not merely planning to offer additional services to investors, he was going to transform Merrill Lynch from a simple brokerage to a vast financial superpower operating well outside the traditional securities business, offering options trading, commercial paper, real estate, insurance, precious metals, and, at last, mutual funds. To some, this was heresy, but Regan pushed on with a single-minded intensity. The magic word was *diversification*, and Regan preached as fervently as an evangelist with a full tent.

Behind the change was the need to get away from total dependence on the vagaries of volume on the New York Stock Exchange. Bear markets hit the commission business with a double whammy: Not only were there fewer transactions, but what transactions there were were worth less because they were based on market value. Diversification would enable ML to ride out periodic downturns in the market. "We were subject to the whims of the marketplace," Regan wrote in his memoirs. "We were not setting our own destiny. To me that was wrong. That's not the way management tries to do things. Management should have control over what it is doing. So, if it's losing in the apples, it makes it up in the oranges. You've got to have a diversified product." The firm's ensuing freedom from the boom-and-bust environment of the stock market was one reason it was able to sell its stock to the general public with such confidence in 1971. By 1976, Merrill Lynch was not only the world's largest stockbroker, it also led Wall Street in mutual funds, commodity trading, and municipal bonds, and it was a growing influence in investment banking. Its utility underwriting prowess was respected by all, and under the leadership of Tom Chrystie, Merrill was beginning to gain credibility in the investment banking world.

Chrystie understood the power of Merrill's foray into retail distribution, and he pitched prospective investment banking clients with the simple argument: You need Merrill Lynch as a co-manager to get its retail distribution. This had particular appeal to electric utilities, which were financing frequently, but it also began to resonate with other industries as well. Chrystie recruited a number of seasoned investment bankers like Hal Berry from Harriman & Co., but he was particularly keen on bringing in young talent from the top MBA programs, knowing that they would better understand the culture of the firm if they grew up within it from the start of their careers.

George Leness, Win Lenz, Dooley Sedlmayr, and now Tom Chrystie understood that Merrill would only underwrite and distribute securities to its individual clients if it believed it was in their best interests and if an independent research report blessed the issue.

ML had made the first big step toward diversification in 1968 with the acquisition of Hubbard, Westervelt & Mottelay, a commercial real-estate financing firm that specialized in finding money for chain stores. Though Ted Braun, the veteran management consultant who had worked with Charlie Merrill years earlier, had fallen into disfavor with Regan and other top executives, the idea of getting into real estate had originated with him. Braun reasoned that most of ML's brokerage customers were also potential real-estate customers. Win Lenz, the underwriting chief, set the deal in motion by calling his old friend G. Morrison ("Morrie") Hubbard, to ask some advice on entering the real-estate business. "Why don't you think about acquiring us?" Hubbard responded. The negotiations dragged on for eight months, but Hubbard was eager to sell because neither his nor his brother's children were interested in taking over the business. The Hubbard acquisition brought Merrill into the investment side of the real-estate business, but Regan envisioned a retail presence as well. When the deal was closed in October, Regan was ecstatic: "Here we have a real-estate division where we can either build you a shopping center or rent you a store or find you a home. Name what you want!" Indeed, Merrill Lynch would now not only be selling Wall Street to Main Street, it would be selling Main Street to Main Street.

In fairness to CEM, his intractable stand against mutual funds was formulated at a time when they were akin to penny mining stocks—in other words, they were hardly considered a respectable investment. The first modern mutual fund showed up in 1924, but it and its immediate successors were overshadowed by the big glamour issues that ruled in the years before the Crash. In the forties and fifties many mutual funds carried larcenous fees and were peddled door-to-door by untrained salesmen, including college students, or moonlighting barbers and house painters. But over time the funds evolved into a friendly tool for investors, and when Regan took over, mutual funds held some $50 billion in assets; indeed, nearly one in every three ML clients already owned funds—meaning they had gone to another broker in order to buy them. Regan made entering the fund business one of his top priorities, and he firmly believed that CEM would have supported the move. In May 1969, ML acquired Lionel D. Edie & Co., one of the Street's top three investment advisory firms and manager of two mutual funds. Almost immediately, ML began selling mutual funds from an approved list that included Massachusetts Financial Services and other respected groups. All branch managers were summoned to New York and told that a concerted effort was expected from each of them to sell the new product. Two years later the firm led the entire fund industry, with sales of $217 million. While most of Lionel D. Edie was sold to its employees for legal reasons in 1976 after the enactment of the ERISA legislation, its main mutual fund functions remained at ML and helped give birth to the Merrill Lynch Asset Management (MLAM), which would turn out to be one of the company's greatest success stories.

Regan promoted Charles Ross, a young executive, to lead this new asset management subsidiary. Ross, who began his career as a commodities broker in Orlando, Florida, was a hardworking and aggressive salesman, and tenacious as a pit bull. After he became manager of a branch office, Roger Birk brought him to New York as an Assistant Division Director of Operations.

When Ross received the job to lead Asset Management, he realized that his first and last task was to find a professional to succeed him. When after sixty interviews he still hadn't come up with someone, Regan's patience ran thin. Then Ross interviewed Arthur Zeikel from Dreyfus, and knew he had the right person for the job. Ross told me later that he was tired of interviewing and had decided he was going to hire the next person he brought in. "Thank God it was Zeikel," he said. On his first day of work, Ross took Zeikel up to meet Regan. Talk about Don meeting his match! Regan finally had someone who was smarter than him, not intimidated by him, and controlled the conversation. Shortly after Ross returned to his office, Regan called him and asked, "Where the hell did you find that guy?"

"Don," Charles answered, "a month from now you'll think I was brilliant." Ross was correct. Arthur Zeikel was a very different Merrill Lyncher, but he quickly gained the respect of Regan and the retail sales force, and built an incredibly successful and profitable asset management business. In addition to his running Asset Management, future chairmen like Birk, Schreyer, and Tully often consulted Arthur for his views about the markets and business and he became an invaluable member of their inner circle. Arthur also proved to be very popular with the financial consultants and his presentations at Chairman's Club meetings were eagerly anticipated. Ross soon was promoted to become director of the Human Resources Division.

I n 1973 the company had recorded another "first" for the securities industry by adopting the holding company format, an important structural step that facilitated its diversification effort. The parent company was named Merrill Lynch & Co., Incorporated, while the main operating subsidiary remained Merrill Lynch, Pierce, Fenner & Smith, Inc. Even with the change, the firm was having difficulty adjusting to a world of new ventures, negotiated commissions, increased government regulation, and rising competition. The company didn't always know which of its activities were profitable and which were not. A massive overhaul was needed, and it would take time. Regan likened it to a huge ocean liner changing direction: "You only turned the *Queen Mary* around slowly. You don't try to flip the helm over and expect it to turn on a dime."

Initially the new holding company had only two direct subsidiaries: Merrill Lynch, Pierce, Fenner & Smith, Inc. (MLPF&S) and Merrill Lynch Government Securities (MLGSI). Regan explained the new structure in the 1973 Annual Report:

> Some immediate advantages such as less restrictive policies for Merrill Lynch Government Securities have resulted from this reorganization. But the principal reason leading Merrill Lynch to become one of the first securities firms to structure itself as a holding company relates more to the future than the present. We are now positioned through acquisition or internal growth to become a diversified corporation that will offer a complete range of financial services to our customers. That is our long-range corporate objective.

For the next seven years Regan moved aggressively to fulfill this vision.

International expansion was a particularly important priority for Don, and he had Harry B. Anderson installed as chairman of Merrill Lynch International. Although Harry and Don both began working at Merrill Lynch in training class No. 2, Harry was a couple of months senior to him in the Marine Corps and never let Don forget it. They had mutual respect for each other and were great friends who shared a sense of humor that made them even closer. After the holding company was formed, some clients were a bit confused about who did what. Regan was chairman of Merrill Lynch, Pierce, Fenner & Smith, and Anderson was chairman of Merrill Lynch International. When asked how their roles and responsibilities differed, Harry gave a simple explanation. "Well," he would respond in his slow Southern drawl, "Don runs the U.S., and I run the rest of the world." Only Harry could get away with that.

To prepare for the new direction by reorganizing the management structure, in May 1976 Regan summoned top management to three days of strategic planning on John's Island, an enclave of executive mansions near Vero Beach, Florida, where he had a winter home. A working paper for the sessions defined Regan's plans for Merrill Lynch: "To become a leading international financial services corporation by developing and marketing a diversified array of securities, insurance, banking, tax, money management, financing and financial counseling products and services which are combined and tailored to meet the demands of individuals, institutions, governments and corporations in the U.S. and throughout the world." Though it would be refined and redefined periodically, the course of the company for the balance of the century was established during this meeting. The work that was done there was critical. "We had to get control," Regan said. Indeed, John's Island was the most important meeting since the modern ML was launched at the Waldorf-Astoria thirty-six years earlier.

The participants in this pivotal meeting were Don, Roger Birk, Dakin Ferris, Ross Kenzie, Howard Sprow, Harry Anderson, and Tom Cassady. Knowing Don's love of golf, they knew that in between meetings they would need time for a round of golf. Kenzie was in a panic when he was invited to the sessions since he didn't play golf. "I was dammed if I was going to be left out and have them make decisions when I wasn't present," he said. So Ross took some golf lessons, bought some clubs, and joined everyone on the links.

One of the basic managerial concepts to emerge from the John's Island sessions was that operations were to be arranged according to customer orientation, from individual investors to large institutional clients, rather than product lines. Nowhere was the need more urgent than in investment banking.

After the John's Island meeting, Regan named Bill Schreyer, a future chairman, to head the Capital Markets Division of Merrill Lynch, Pierce, Fenner & Smith and ordered him to build a top-tier investment bank. "I took a look at it and told him the solution was an easy one," Schreyer said. "Just give me control of all sales, research, and trading." Regan chuckled at the jest and called it "a good idea whose time hasn't come." One of the things Schreyer did after taking over the division was to set up an informal breakfast group of ML leaders from the different functions that served large institutional clients. The goal was to coordinate these activities, which were now scattered throughout the organization. About a dozen executives took part in this exchange of ideas, and eventually Schreyer dubbed the gathering "the Capital Markets Group." One of Bill Schreyer's great skills was to surround himself with smart and talented people who became fiercely loyal to him. He used Archie Urciuoli, a lawyer and a member of the Investment Banking Division, to put together his Capital Markets plan.

When the restructured operation was placed on the ML organization chart in 1976, the name stuck. The new Merrill Lynch Capital Markets Group brought under one roof underwriting, mergers and acquisitions services, and institutional sales, trading, and research. Schreyer was placed in charge and promoted to executive vice president. Urciuoli was later promoted to president of Merrill Lynch International. However, in 1976 Merrill Lynch was still a fledgling, second-string investment banking operation playing catch-up with the elite firms that dominated the very profitable activity of underwriting America's corporate stock and bond issues and managing lucrative mergers and acquisitions. Regan contemptuously labeled these bigger investment banking competitors "white-shoe firms," but there was a hint of envy in his voice when he said it. "Merrill Lynch was tolerated by the white-shoe firms because we could distribute for them if they had a tough stock issue," Regan said. "But if it was a deal that was easy to sell, they didn't want any part of us. They'd just wave the old school tie and take care of each other."

I don't think Don ever really fully understood investment banking. He was reluctant to allocate very much time soliciting this business personally, but he was wise enough to understand that it was profitable and that Merrill Lynch needed to establish a strong presence in the field. Schreyer, on the other hand, and his successors Dan Tully and Dave Komansky spent significant efforts originating investment banking business throughout the world. After Tom Chrystie had run Investment Banking for several years, Regan promoted him to be the firm's CFO and head of strategy. In my opinion, this proved to be one of Don's most important appointments. Tom's strong suit was not communication, but he had a brilliant and creative mind, and he could be tenacious if he believed he was correct about something. I think Don saw in young Tom what Charlie Merrill and my father had seen in young Don.

In addition to Schreyer, Regan named two other executive vice presidents reporting to Tom Cassady, the president of MLPFS. Ross Kenzie took over marketing and sales and was responsible for all domestic branch offices and their marketing support. Alan Sher was named EVP of Operations and had all the administrative staff, with the exception of finance, reporting to him. Don consciously set up a three-way horse race to succeed Tom Cassady. While this motivated the three EVPs to set high standards for their operations, the arrangement was at times very dysfunctional. People had to be perceived to belong on the team of one of the three, so everyone began to try hitching their wagon to the executive they thought would ultimately win out. Kenzie was tough and disciplined. Sher was focused on cutting costs to prove his worth. Schreyer, on the other hand, was a real people person and had the ability to get along with everyone and have them feel good about themselves. The only rap on Schreyer was that he liked to spend money, and Kenzie and Sher did their best to point out that he might generate revenue but he couldn't bring it to the bottom line. The competition got to a ridiculous extreme at one point when all presentations made by the three had to be color coded.

Kenzie's were bound in green, Sher's in blue, and Schreyer's in red. Kenzie was the first to pick a color, and since green was the color of money, he hoped to give the impression that he knew best how to run a profitable business. The race really came down to Kenzie and Schreyer, and in the end the decision was mainly about Regan's vision for the future of Merrill Lynch. Kenzie would have been a very able CEO, but his focus would have been on the traditional U.S. brokerage business while Schreyer would turn his attention to the growth of the investment banking and institutional side of the business, as well as growth internationally. And so Bill Schreyer was named president of MLPFS. Kenzie left to become the CEO of Buffalo Savings, an appointment Schreyer helped to arrange, and Alan Sher moved over to Bear Stearns. Had Bill not been the choice, Merrill Lynch would have become a very different firm.

Regan was not going to allow Merrill Lynch to sit on the sidelines with the research side of the business, either. When *Institutional Investor* magazine began publishing its annual lists of "All-America" research teams in 1972, ML was not represented on the squad. Regan was disappointed and dismayed. Nor was there anyone from the firm on the 1973 team. Regan was appalled, and he ordered an immediate effort to beef up ML's institutional research capabilities—including the hiring of some of the all-stars from other firms on the magazine's list at substantial salary increases. Just two years later, in 1975, the company was ranked eleventh overall, with eight team members, and the following year the company was No. 1. With only a few exceptions, Merrill retained the No. 1 ranking for more than three decades, and this proved to be invaluable to the development of the firm's retail and institutional businesses.

Anyone who ever underestimated Don Regan's competitive nature made a big mistake. Certainly those of us who worked with him never did.

I n early 1978, I had just become ML's Manager of Compensation and Benefits, reporting to Charles Ross. Tom Chrystie's secretary, Jane Roundtree, called me one day and asked me to stop by his office at one P.M. No reason was given for this summons. When I got there, a dozen people were in the room. "I've asked you to be part of the White Weld acquisition team," Tom said to the group to start the meeting. "This is totally confidential, and other than Don Regan and Roger Birk, no one outside of this room is to know anything about this. We have less than two weeks to conclude the deal and create a transition plan. We're concerned that the Justice Department will not look favorably on this deal, so our strategy is to make White Weld disappear two Fridays from now so that there is nothing to divest on the following Monday. All the White Weld employees will be employees of Merrill Lynch, and all the assets will be integrated with Merrill Lynch."

White Weld & Co., an old-line investment bank founded in 1895, had twenty-six offices nationwide. White Weld was one of Regan's "white-shoe firms," but it hadn't been doing very well in recent years and had put itself up for sale. Charlie Merrill would have loved it, for White Weld had been one of the many established firms that had turned him down when he was desperately seeking financing for the McCrory deal in 1914.

Tom proceeded to give everyone their instructions. My responsibility was to look at all of White Weld's compensation and benefit plans, figure out how to get all their employees on the payroll by the following Monday after the acquisition was announced, and prepare statements that we could give to each employee to explain our benefit plans. And I couldn't tell my boss, Charles Ross, the Personnel Division director, what I was doing until Tom briefed him later in the week. We had planned to announce the acquisition after the close of business on that fateful Friday, but by three o'clock word started to leak out, and all White Weld managing directors were told of the deal and invited to join a reception in the executive ML dining room at One Liberty Plaza. It was as though a cement block had dropped on White Weld. Everyone there felt betrayed, but the reality was that their firm was going out of business and Merrill was coming to the rescue. Nevertheless, the idea of working at a "blue-collar" firm like Merrill Lynch did not sit well with many of these elitist investment bankers and brokers.

Tom Chrystie, operating on three hours of sleep a night, completed the complicated cash deal in fifteen days. The speed of the transaction came as a shock to many White Weld employees, and there were plenty of problems with the transition. One involved, of all things, executive washrooms: White Weld executives were used to individual soap bars and linen towels, and there was grumbling when Merrill Lynch replaced them with soap dispensers and paper towels. In general, there was widespread dissatisfaction among former White Weld employees, many of whom felt they had gone from working for Tiffany's to working for Kmart.

Don saw two values in White Weld: its investment banking business and its international partnership with Credit Suisse (while it had a good brokerage operation, this was secondary). Merrill paid $50 million cash for White Weld. However, Credit Suisse insisted that Merrill fold all of its international operations into the joint venture. Regan refused, so Credit Suisse bought the White Weld portion of the joint venture for $25 million and later allied with First Boston. Thus, Regan paid only $25 million in cash for the U.S. assets of White Weld, and as they were merged into Merrill's operation, $25 million of excess cash was discovered, so essentially Regan paid nothing for what was a transforming acquisition.

There was a large number of defections in the early days as people responded emotionally rather than giving the acquisition a chance. In one instance, Dave Palmer, who managed the Northeast Retail Sales Division of Merrill Lynch, took all the brokers in the Philadelphia White Weld office to dinner one night, where he spoke at length about his career and himself. A few left in the middle of dinner "to go to the men's room" and never returned. The next morning the entire office resigned, and Merrill Lynch was left with a beautiful empty new office carrying a long-term lease on Market Street in Center City Philadelphia.

As part of the transition, I was dispatched to the ML offices in Wilmington, Delaware, New Haven, Connecticut, and Boston to speak to former White Weld employees about Merrill Lynch's benefit programs. After my presentations in Wilmington, I was bombarded with questions that had nothing to do with benefits. "What does Merrill Lynch know about investment banking?" "How does a big bureaucracy like Merrill Lynch get anything done?" "Does Merrill Lynch have any wealthy clients?" "I hear that brokers are given quotas and have to sell whatever the product of the day is." Fortunately, because of my father and my role in working with Tom Chrystie, I had a deep knowledge of the firm and its history and strategy and was able to address a lot of their concerns. After about two hours in front of the staff of the Wilmington office, one of the stuffiest of the brokers said, "Okay, we've pounded you enough. Let's go to my club for some drinks." The entire staff remained at Wilmington, and this became one of Merrill's flagship offices. I later became good friends with most of the brokers who worked there. New Haven also stayed largely intact, but Boston did not fare as well because their office manager moved on to another firm and took many of his staff with him.

In the wake of the White Weld acquisition, Bill Schreyer made the decision to rename the Capital Markets Group the Merrill Lynch White Weld Capital Markets Group, and he appointed Nigel McEwan, the president of White Weld, as director of the Investment Banking Division. It was believed at the time that the addition of the White Weld name would provide cache and credibility to our capital markets activities, but in hindsight I think it was a big mistake and, in fact, the name White Weld was dropped a few years later. Merrill had many good investment bankers, but those from White Weld had the attitude that "if you worked for Merrill Lynch, you had to be second rate." With the fortunate exception of Dan Bayly, McEwan purged most of the Merrill Lynch investment banking team hired by Tom Chrystie—many of my former colleagues, who were also friends— though almost all of those who departed had successful careers at other investment banking firms. (McEwan was also pompous enough to refuse to use the designated Merrill Lynch calling card. He thought the bull looked "tacky," and he had his own made up.)

While the integration of White Weld was difficult, and it did not achieve the short-term results we had hoped for, over time it proved to be a valuable acquisition. A number of White Weld bankers, including George Leness's son, Tony, stayed with us and contributed to the further development of Merrill's investment banking business. Likewise, we gained three particularly talented but controversial bankers—Tom Patrick, Chuck Lewis, and Jeff Neal—from White Weld's Chicago investment banking operation. Neal and Patrick would later seek broader managerial roles in investment banking and in the broader firm. Patrick, in particular, had aspirations to climb the corporate ladder and believed that he was smarter than anyone else, though his ambition would have both positive and negative consequences. Perhaps the best part of the acquisition were two people who would contribute enormously to the firm's success over the next three and a half decades, Jerome P. Kenney and Stephen L. Hammerman. A Yale graduate and analyst by training, Jerry Kenney took Merrill's emerging research division to an even higher level, contributed enormously to the global development of the firm's investment banking and institutional businesses, and ultimately served as Merrill's top strategic thinker under CEOs Schreyer, Tully, and Komansky. Hammerman was a tough—and occasionally rough—lawyer who was a master at crisis management and negotiation with the various regulatory authorities. He was feared throughout the firm and yet respected for his ability to protect the firm's reputation. Ironically, many years later, both he and Tom Patrick would contribute to the rise of Stan O'Neal and the destruction of the firm's culture.

Aside from the people, another positive to come out of the White Weld acquisition was the fact that the wholesale defections of their salespeople forced Regan to acknowledge that the salary system for account executives put in place by Charlie Merrill in 1940 was no longer tenable. CEM's strategy to regain public trust in the aftermath of the Depression and Wall Street scandals had worked stunningly, but it had been diluted very early on by a bonus system under which office managers rewarded high-performance salesmen. This salary-plus-bonus system worked for many years because Merrill Lynch's clear advantage over its rivals in research, training, and advertising made its salesmen more productive and therefore placed them on more or less equal footing with their commission-paid rivals. Until the late 1960s, ML's annual turnover rate for account executives was an acceptable 8 percent, but then it began rising as competitors caught up in research, training and advertising, and by the early seventies the turnover rate reached 18 percent. ML responded by fiddling with the compensation formula, but the talent drain continued. Between 1973 and 1977, some 2,200 salespeople left the firm, and below-average commission payout was the clear culprit. In the wake of the White Weld defections, Regan raised the payout structure to more competitive levels. Subjectivity was eliminated. Brokers produced and were paid a commission. It was the end of what Charlie Merrill had done on Ted Braun's advice in 1940.

Meanwhile, the deregulation of commissions had hit the retail end of the securities industry hard. Discount brokers began appearing, and banks began offering traditional brokerage services. The introduction of money market funds, which offered liquidity but paid more than bank accounts, provided an opening, and ML rushed in with its first money fund—the Merrill Lynch Ready Assets Trust—in 1975. In addition, the firm moved aggressively into real estate, which for the average American was proving to be a far better investment than stocks or bonds, and it made more selective acquisitions that carried over into such fields as employee relocation and specialty insurance. The boundaries between different types of financial firms were blurring rapidly, and there were battles among big brokerages, insurance companies, and banks to win over customers. Other wirehouses had followed ML's lead in diversification, but only Merrill Lynch had come up with what would be the crown jewel of its diversification.

The setting was a meeting between Regan and some of his top advisers in early 1977. Over and over again, Regan's fist crashed down on the tabletop. "There are several ways you can do this," he thundered. "One is over my dead body!" His outburst was in response to the suggestion that management throw in the towel on a revolutionary new product that wasn't working out, one that even many of the company's own executives and employees vehemently opposed. "Absolutely not! We continue," Regan insisted. And with that he rescued what would become the key to Merrill Lynch's success for the balance of the twentieth century, and, indeed, one of the most successful retail financial products in Wall Street history.

Like the automobile and the computer, the Cash Management Account (CMA) seems deceptively obvious and simple in retrospect, but it must be considered within the context of the marketplace of 1975 to understand just how radical it was. For starters, there were no ATM machines then, and when people bought stock, they received actual certificates, which they'd then store in safe-deposit boxes or with brokerage firms. To meet their basic savings and investments needs, the average middle-class American dealt with three or four different financial institutions. They might use their local bank for checking, the savings and loan for their mortgage, a regular broker for stocks, and a mutual funds group for money market funds. With the Cash Management Account, all of this could be consolidated in one place—the ultimate one-stop shopping. The CMA offered Merrill Lynch brokerage customers a comprehensive menu of financial services—stocks and bonds, money market funds, customized portfolio management, estate planning, mortgages, insurance, and, most controversially, a checkbook and a credit card. Brokerage balances would be invested automatically in money market funds that paid interest daily. In other words, Merrill Lynch would handle its customers' entire financial lives in a single all-in-one account with one monthly statement. Wall Street had never been known as a hotbed of innovation, but this was breathtaking. So unique was this idea that ML would one day patent it.

That Merrill Lynch was able to even consider such a concept was the result of its having gone public. In the five years since then, the firm had built up excess capital, and now it was ready to put it to work in a single bold gamble. The impetus came from commission deregulation, which opened the door to discount brokers and posed a distinct threat to Merrill Lynch and other traditional houses. Regan ordered research by the Stanford Research Institute, a California think tank, into what ML could offer as an alternative to the discounters, and it showed strong customer interest in an integrated financial product that would provide both convenience and advice. Tom Chrystie went out to Stanford for a ten-hour meeting at which the idea of a brokerage account with check-writing privileges came up. They didn't pursue the idea there, but the idea stuck with him.

"I took the red-eye flight back, and I couldn't get the concept out of my mind," he said. By the time he landed at LaGuardia, Chrystie was ready to explore the idea fully. There were more meetings with Stanford Research. Other ML executives—Roger Birk, the company president, and Dennis Hess, vice president for product development—got involved. They labored in secret, and when they showed their conclusions to Regan, he jumped at the idea. Indeed, Regan ordered a researcher to the New York Public Library to find what color would work best for the monthly customer statements; he ultimately chose green. Meanwhile, Chrystie wrestled with a name for the new product. "Ready Asset Money" drew a lot of attention, but then it was pointed out that the acronym, RAM, would clash with the Merrill Lynch bull. The product was born without a name in 1976, and only later was it given the name it carried during the development stage: the Cash Management Account.

Once all the details had been worked out and the idea was ready to be presented, it faced a massive selling job—not to the public, but to Merrill Lynch itself. Operations leaders saw the CMA as a technical nightmare that would be difficult to set up and run because it involved many functions not related to traditional brokerages. Ultimately, a solution was found after some one hundred people, putting in the equivalent of thirty years of man-hours, set up the proper computer systems to handle CMA transactions smoothly. The most intense opponents were the account executives, who could not see how the new product would sell or how it would increase their commissions. Then there was Regan's fist-pounding meeting with ML's top managers in early 1977, during which many voiced strong opposition to continuing the CMA project, which was incurring huge fees and other expenses. The consensus was that the firm would be better off expending its time and money elsewhere. Regan called for a vote, and the result was lopsidedly negative. He then hunched forward, turned and looked out the window at the panoramic view of New York Harbor, and said, "I appreciate your concern, but there's been a vote taken here today, and it's one to nothing. I'm the one, and you guys are out of here. We go forward, and if any of you ever says anything bad about this again, I'll throw you out the window! This concept is going to be the salvation of this firm, and it will also be widely regarded on Wall Street and accepted by other firms. Anybody in this room who is not totally behind the CMA can get up now and walk out." Nobody moved.

Paul Stein, who was in charge of marketing the CMA, fretted about how best to sell the new product until inspiration struck one spring evening. "It came to me we didn't have a marketing problem, we had an education problem," he recalled. "We had to stop trying to sell this to the public before we educated the account executives on what the account could do, so that they could then educate the public. The CMA will sell itself, but it can't present itself." Stein drew a diagram showing how the CMA would work, continuing to refine it by sketching it over and over until he had it right. The rough sketch turned into one of Merrill Lynch's greatest marketing tools, and was used both to show account executives how the CMA would work and then to launch more than a million accounts. The CMA was announced to the public on June 21, 1977, by Regan, who was joined by John G. McCoy, chairman of City National Bank of Columbus, Ohio, which had been designated to handle the banking and credit card transactions. (It was actually a debit card, but that technicality didn't make a difference, because people understood better what a credit card did.)

From its early days, the CMA was a hit. *The New York Times* said the Cash Management Account had "propelled the firm into the leading edge of the revolution in financial services that is transforming Wall Street" and was "the envy of most of the financial services community and has spawned a host of eager imitators." Indeed, ML was obliged to continually deny charges that it was intruding into the banking business, as the CMA came up to the very threshold of the Glass–Steagall Act. To many, the CMA seemed like banking rather than brokerage, but ML lawyers had carefully crafted arguments contending that it didn't stray into forbidden territory—Merrill Lynch was not taking deposits like a bank. Not surprisingly, the banking industry was in an uproar and viewed Merrill Lynch as a modern-day Jesse James bullying its way into banking's comfortable and protected domain. David Rockefeller of Chase Manhattan Bank called ML "a bank in disguise." And Walter Wriston, chairman of Citicorp, the nation's second-largest bank, said: "I have seen the bank of the future, and it's called Merrill Lynch, Pierce, Fenner & Smith." When the first CMAs were offered in Denver, the banking industry filed a suit that touched off a long legal wrangle, a dispute that indirectly helped Merrill Lynch by deterring its competitors from developing similar products and giving ML a huge head start.

From this point, the CMA gathered momentum. And yet there were dozens of legal battles plus hundreds of lesser skirmishes in the formative years of the Cash Management Account as banks and savings and loans tried desperately to thwart it. None was as astonishing as what occurred in the Utah House of Representatives on March 11, 1981. Just a week before, legislation that would have banned the CMA had been overwhelmingly approved in the State Senate by a vote of twenty-six to three. Utah banks were a powerful lobbying force, and no one expected any problems for the bill in the House of Representatives. Merrill Lynch lawyers considered conceding defeat, but instead Paul Stein decided to launch a letter-writing campaign to CMA customers. It paid a big dividend when the bill came up for a vote. Just before the roll call, seventy-three-year-old Afton Forsby, a highly respected former schoolteacher, made her way down from the spectators' gallery to speak on behalf of the right of the retired to make investments. In her brief remarks, she pleaded with the lawmakers not to take away one of the most reliable forms of investment available to her: her CMA account. Many of the legislators were her former students, and they were glued to every word she spoke. The bill was defeated by a vote of thirty-nine to thirty-six, and the CMA remained legal in Utah.

"This was one of the most dramatic turning points in the history of the CMA," said Roger Birk. "We could scarcely believe it in New York." The CMA proceeded to get approval in all fifty states and eventually made its way around the world and became available to all Merrill Lynch clients.

One by one, state legal barriers were overcome. As account executives signed up CMA customers, they discovered assets they didn't know existed. Suddenly brokers knew much more about their clients' financial lives than the clients did themselves, and their resistance melted. Word of the CMA's convenience spread, and by the end of 1980 there were 190,000 CMA accounts; by the end of 1981, there were 580,000, with combined assets of $33 billion. The CMA fomented a Wall Street revolution, and Merrill Lynch left its competitors in the dust. By the end of the twentieth century, the Cash Management Account was the foundation of ML's worldwide retail investment business and held $662 billion in 2.5 million accounts.

Though Regan saw the potential in the CMA, he also understood that Merrill Lynch needed to grow internationally. Despite the disappointment of not getting the international assets of White Weld and a partnership with Credit Suisse, he pushed forward globally.

By the early 1970s, Merrill Lynch International was unique on Wall Street. Very few of the 569 NYSE member firms had an overseas operation at all, and those that did had no more than a dozen offices. Merrill Lynch had nearly fifty. Moreover, many American brokerages went abroad mainly as a gimmick to provide tax-deductible vacations for their top executives. First under McCarthy, then under Regan, Merrill Lynch was a serious international player. Most of the international offices began in modest circumstances by providing services for Americans living overseas—essentially, they were there to sell U.S. stocks to American expatriates—but they then evolved into offices selling U.S. stocks and commodities to local citizens. While this generated short-term commissions, 97 percent of all people who speculated in commodities lost most of their money, which created a terrible image for Merrill Lynch in many parts of the world that took years to erase.

Still, Regan had a vision of ML as a worldwide financial organization, and in the seventies he pursued vigorous overseas expansion focused on investment banking and institutional sales and trading. This activity was all the more appealing because there were no Glass–Steagall restrictions to deal with overseas, so ML could function as a bank without legal complications. The drive toward leadership in global private banking began in 1972 with the acquisition of Brown Shipley & Co., a London merchant bank, which was renamed Merrill Lynch International Bank. Next the firm acquired an interest in Trident International Finance Ltd., a merchant bank in Hong Kong. Barclays Bank International Ltd., in London, and Nomura Securities Company Ltd., in Tokyo, were Merrill's partners in this venture, but it was short-lived, so Merrill opened its own investment banking offices in Hong Kong and Singapore in 1974.

Don was eagerly looking everywhere in the world for opportunities, and one place he looked to develop relationships was the emerging oil nations of the Middle East. He had Tom Chrystie negotiate a partnership with the Alireza family in Saudi Arabia, but sadly nothing ever materialized. Before we acquired it, White Weld had had an assignment to provide advice to the Saudi Arabia Monetary Authority (SAMA), but Merrill was never really able to leverage this into more.

Then with Bill Rogers's assistance, Regan traveled to Iran in 1974 and met with the Shah of Iran, who gave him permission to develop a joint venture along with two Persian partners, Bank Melli and the Iran Mining & Development Bank. A young banker from Paris, Herbert Allison, was assigned to this venture and part of his mission was to help Iran develop their capital markets. Herb was a perfect choice for this assignment—cerebral, diligent, and meticulous.

When I joined Merrill Lynch, Archie Urciuoli, the head of our international investment banking group, asked me to be Herb's liaison in New York as part of my assignments. In 1975 when Chrysler was going through the first of their many financial crises, Tom Chrystie proposed to them that they approach the Shah with the idea of receiving a loan in consideration for providing technical assistance to Iran's fledgling government-owned automotive company. A proposal was crafted quickly, as everyone was lining up to get Iran's petrodollars, and I was designated to personally carry the proposal to Herb so that he could present it to the Shah. In the spring of 1975, and only a few weeks before the birth of my first daughter, Heather, I boarded a Pam Am flight to Tehran that stopped in Beirut, where the airport had just reopened after a pause in the Lebanese civil war. It was bedlam, and the airport in Tehran was not much better. The passenger terminal was a small Quonset hut, and it looked like Walmart on Black Friday when I deplaned and attempted to claim my suitcase. I stayed with Herb and his new wife, Simin, and was treated to Persian hospitality. As I had arrived just before the Muslim weekend, Herb said that we would probably not hear back from the government for several days and that I should remain until we did. He suggested that I visit Isfahan, the site of some of the most beautiful mosques in Iran, and stay at the Shah Abbas Hotel as my mother had a few years earlier. It was a great excursion, but as I walked around the bazaars in my running shoes, blue jeans, and polo shirt, with a camera slung around my neck, I felt very uncomfortable. The Shah's security police with their submachine guns were visible and so I felt physically safe, but the eyes of the merchants whom I walked by told me that I was not welcome. There was revolution in their stares. Though our proposal was not accepted, this joint venture lasted a few years longer until the Shah was overthrown.

Don also saw Asia as a theater of opportunity. Ever since ML opened its Hong Kong office in 1960, the firm had looked toward the People's Republic of China with the knowledge that one day it would resume its historic role as a center of world trade. Regan began sending feelers out in 1975 hinting that Merrill Lynch executives would like to visit Beijing, and two years later the Chinese government expressed interest in knowing who would come and what they would want to discuss. There was an exchange of information in which ML set down one condition: that its representatives go as a company and not as part of a larger group. "We wanted to go as Merrill Lynch because we have so many types of businesses," Regan said. "We are unique in many respects. We are not a bank, and we're not a manufacturer, but we represent aspects of both." In the summer of 1978 visas were approved, and we were invited to come to the Chinese capital in the fall. In November, just a month before the U.S. announced the normalization of diplomatic relations with the People's Republic, a delegation headed by Regan met with high-ranking Chinese government and trade officials. That Beijing chose to meet with Merrill Lynch during the normalization negotiations was an indication that it held the firm in high esteem. Regan was accompanied by Bill Rogers, the former Secretary of State who by this time had become an ML director; William R. Arthur, chairman of Merrill Lynch International; and Karl Gelbard, Far East Regional Director and manager of the Hong Kong office, who coordinated many details of the trip. As it had been with Japan, progress in the People's Republic was slow, and there were a number of false starts. But in 1993, when I was chairman of Merrill Lynch International, we managed the initial public offering for Shanghai Petrochemical, the first Chinese company listed on the New York Stock Exchange. A year later we advised the People's Republic and helped it achieve investment-grade ratings from both Moody's and Standard & Poor's. Then we solely managed its first $1 billion global bond offering.

D on's vision for the CMA, the growth of Research, the push into the major leagues in investment banking, and his emphasis on global expansion set the stage for Merrill's success over the next two decades. However, his concept of becoming a diversified financial services institution that included residential real estate and insurance did not pan out. His push into these areas began with the acquisition of Family Life Insurance, a company in Seattle, Washington, run by Fen Crane that sold mortgage life insurance. It was a profitable company, but it had no synergies with the rest of Merrill Lynch, and getting Merrill Lynch retail account executives interested in selling this type of insurance was like pushing on a string.

Regan next acquired a company called TICOR, which was in the business of helping business executives who were relocating, and renamed it Merrill Lynch Relocation Management. The company would appraise the value of the home the employee was leaving, then buy it, usually guaranteeing that there would be no loss to the employee on the sale. Regan thought that because it had relationships with the Human Resources departments of the largest employers in the United States, TICOR would help in the development of investment banking relationships. This was flawed thinking. Relocation Management was run by Weston Edwards, who convinced Don that Merrill Lynch should get into the residential realty business. Edwards started buying Realtors all over the United States, and account executives were told to get registered as real-estate brokers so that they could receive a finder's fees on real-estate development. By the early 1980s, there were more ML realty offices around the United States than security branch offices. Many ML traditionalists worried about Merrill's brand, but while Regan was in charge, one was not going to question his ideas on diversification.

Unknown to most at the time, Regan was also looking at game-changing mergers and acquisitions. For example, he and Jim Robinson of American Express spoke very seriously about merging their two companies. This was actually the second time such a union had been discussed, as Mike McCarthy nearly purchased a much smaller American Express after it had come close to bankruptcy with their exposure to "the Salad Oil Scandal" in 1963, but the talks broke off because of the partners' concerns about unknown liabilities they might absorb. This time, however, discussions ended when neither Regan nor Robinson could agree on which of them would be the boss. Don strongly believed that the successful financial firms of the future would need to be bigger and more diversified. Had he not left for the Reagan cabinet in 1980, I think we likely would have merged with some firms that his successors rejected.

W hile Regan envisioned a future where mergers and acquisitions would play a large role, it was during his tenure that the firm took the opposite view on commodities, and a lot of this can be attributed to one especially disastrous event.

Beginning in the early 1970s, three brothers in the Hunt family of Dallas, Texas, launched an audacious plan to corner the world's silver market. By 1980 they had amassed about half of the world's deliverable silver, and the price of silver leapt from about $11 an ounce to more than $50 an ounce. The Hunts didn't own the silver outright, though, as they kept borrowing against it to buy more. One of the brokerages they borrowed from was Merrill Lynch—indeed, ML's exposure was the largest on Wall Street, some $263 million. As long as the price of silver kept rising, it didn't matter, but once it started falling, as it did in January 1980, the pyramid collapsed and the money had to be paid back. The margin calls began mounting up, and ultimately the Hunts had to be bailed out by their bankers at a loss of some $1 billion, threatening the stability of the American banking system.

"The Hunts had about one billion dollars in paper profit with Merrill alone," Roger Birk recalled. "That amount exceeded our capital at the time. When gold and silver crashed, the profits were gone and so were the rest of their assets. We were one of the few firms who had a 'cross collateral' agreement, which meant that if they didn't put up margin, we could sell their stocks. And we did." Birk added that as a result of the bailout the futures exchanges wanted to close, but ML persuaded them to remain open. "This episode almost wrecked the whole system."

Regan, Birk, and Schreyer, along with Charles Ross, the CAO of Merrill Lynch, Pierce, Fenner & Smith, Bob ("Ritt") Rittereiser, the Division Director of Operations, and John Conheeny, the Division Director of Commodities, gathered in Merrill Lynch's Essex House suite on Central Park South to develop a game plan to save the firm. Don barked orders and assigned tasks. He was clearly worried. For the first time in his career and on his watch, Merrill Lynch was in jeopardy. Nelson and William Hunt were shrewd and greedy Texans, and it took days of face-to-face hardball negotiation before a solution was reached. At one point Nelson called Regan and said, "Keep that little prick Ross away from me." I was working directly for Charles in those days, and he kept me up to date on his discussions with the Hunts. Charles had essentially delivered an ultimatum to the Hunts in their presence that they didn't like. He was like a pit bull, and the Hunts had never been treated with such "disrespect." However, playing hardball with these villains was the only language they understood. When told by Regan of his conversation with Nelson, Charles beamed with pride. He had won.

Eventually, Merrill was able to obtain additional collateral in the form of listed equity securities and through their forced sale succeeded in unwinding their silver position. The sale of these securities drove the market down, but the crisis was ended. After this, Merrill's Commodities Division was reorganized into a separate subsidiary, and within a few years, commodities were de-emphasized and few retail brokers bought or sold them anymore. Thus an area of Merrill Lynch that once was an important part of the firm's portfolio was no longer seen to be in the best interests of our clients and was deemed too risky for the firm itself. This impacted revenues short-term, but it was the correct long-term decision. In many ways, this silver manipulation crisis was a wake-up call to a firm that was growing and evolving more and more into an institutional and global brokerage and investment banking firm. Risk was rising, and the risks were different from what the firm was used to.

On a completely different front, Regan was confronted with a tough decision when in 1977 the federal Equal Employment Opportunity Commission brought a suit against Merrill Lynch for discrimination against women. Merrill was not operating any differently from all the other firms on Wall Street, but being the largest firm on Wall Street, Merrill was the logical target. In those days, if you walked into any branch office of any firm, you would see that the brokers were almost always men and the sales assistants were almost always women, and the difference in pay was enormous. There is no question that Wall Street's male managers did not think that women could be as effective as brokers as men. Regan quickly realized that settling with the EEOC was the right thing to do, and the subsequent agreement established hiring quotas for women, African-Americans, and Hispanics. By the mid-1980s some of the most successful financial advisers throughout the firm were women, and by the 1990s a number of women had moved up into executive management roles. Don and Roger Birk took the EEOC settlement seriously, and despite significant resistance within the firm, pushed to make Merrill a more accepting and diverse employer. Regan asked Jill Conway, the president of Smith College and an Australian scholar, to join the ML board, and she became ML's first female director. Conway ended up serving almost three decades and was the watchdog for diversity during those years, but unfortunately in her final years she failed to be a proper watchdog for the firm's principles.

W hile Don was an imposing executive and a fearsome figure to many people, he had a great sense of humor that came out on the golf course and at the annual Chowder and Marching Society luncheon, held on the last Friday in January. This lunch began in the pre-corporate days of Merrill Lynch when groups of partners would gather informally at Massoletti's restaurant in the lobby of 70 Pine Street to have lunch and drinks and reminisce about the previous year's events. As the alcohol flowed, the truth flowed as well, and partners would often gibe one another about mistakes of the past months.

The Chowder and Marching Society's founding fathers were Harry Anderson, E. A. Pierce, Sam Fuller, Ruby Rubezanin, Lou Engel, and Mike McCarthy. A group of partners, including my father, would gather for these luncheons with the mantra "Let's have fun." The only "outsider" was Doc Campbell from Rudy Guenther's firm. As more people were included, the session became more formal, and the event moved from 70 Pine Street to the City Midday Club and eventually to Windows on the World at the World Trade Center. There were no formal rules of membership. One was simply asked, "Would you like to join the luncheon?" In 1972, Lee Roselle, a young member of the Audio Visual Department, caught the eye of Don Regan and became the master of ceremonies.

Each year a small subcommittee would meet with Lee and decide which new executives would be asked to attend the lunch, what the theme of the luncheon would be, and what award would be given out. A day before the session, the new attendees were given a topic and told to prepare a five-minute speech for the event, and current members would vote on them immediately afterward. Needless to say, after they got that invitation, the newcomers spent the next twenty-four hours preparing their remarks, knowing their careers might be on the line. One by one the initiates were asked to deliver their speech. Rarely more than a few seconds passed before they were interrupted, hit with dinner rolls, or rudely taunted. Afterward a vote was taken and often the thumbs-down was given to the speaker. Eventually, however, a unanimous vote welcomed them all in. While the tales of this luncheon would not play well on YouTube today, it was a few hours when a group of the firm's most senior executives let their hair down, had some great laughs, and bonded as a team. Was it a fraternity? Surely that's one way to describe it, but as Don Regan used to say, "I learned more about my executives at the Chowder and Marching Society than any other time."

Another "fraternity" Regan appreciated was one he started himself, called the Chairman's Club. Don loved visiting with account executives and was most comfortable with them and their branch managers, and under his watch, he started the Chairman's Club to recognize the most successful ones. Don understood that while account executives were motivated by money, recognition was equally important. The first Chairman's Club event was a trip to Bermuda with the top thirty retail and institutional salesmen. While there was some business conducted, the real benefit was the opportunity for the top account executives and their spouses to mingle with one another and dine with the chairman of the board and give him direct feedback on the business. Such recognition programs became a critically important part of the culture of the retail side of Merrill Lynch. People from around the world came together and bonded, and every senior executive who attended realized that these were some of the most important moments of the year. I attended scores of them and as a result got to personally know our top advisers and their spouses and speak with them directly about the issues they faced. As the Chairman's Club grew in size we added more substantive business sessions and communication forums, but we also made the experiences unique and fun. Often when an adviser was being heavily recruited and offered a lot of money to jump to another firm, the thought of missing next year's recognition trip won the day in keeping him at the firm. I'm not sure that even Don understood the power of the club that he began with only thirty account executives.

One Monday in late November 1980, Don had just started out the weekly Executive Committee meeting when his secretary, Betty Lehrmann, walked in and whispered something in his ear. Regan turned the meeting over to Roger Birk and disappeared to take a phone call from Ronald Reagan, the new President, who offered Don a job. A few days later he announced his resignation as Merrill Lynch's sixth presiding officer to become Secretary of the Treasury. Suddenly the Regan era came to a close. As director of Human Resources at the time, I was responsible for organizing Don's farewell dinner. Lee Roselle worked with me on planning it, and Bill Schreyer also took a personal interest in the details. Bill wanted it to be "first class and the best send-off ever," as he knew that Don's shadow would loom large over Merrill Lynch for as long as he lived.

Bill had a membership at the River Club, which is where we held the dinner, and just as he wanted, this black-tie event *was* first-class. The members of the Board of Directors, the senior managers of the firm, Don's family, my mother and my half brother, and Gordon Linke and his wife, Jocelyn, were invited. The dinner was a combination of some good-humored roasting and a serious tribute to Don's leadership, and it was at this dinner that we announced that our new training program would be called the Donald T. Regan School of Advanced Management. When it was Don's turn to speak, he surprised us by focusing on the challenges the new Reagan administration would face and what its agenda was. Don was a great speaker and the content was interesting, but it was devoid of any sentiment about the firm that he was leaving or any mention of the man who'd been chosen to be his successor, Roger Birk. As much as I admired Don, I was often struck by his lack of sensitivity to those around him.

Along with overseeing the dinner, I was also in charge of Don's official portrait. The artist I hired was named Bob Templeton. He lived in Southbury, Connecticut, and had recently done my father-in-law's portrait for the bank he founded, Webster Financial. Bob had painted many famous Washington personalities, so I thought he was perfect for the job. His first sitting was at the Regan home in Mt. Vernon, Virginia. One Sunday he spent several hours in Don's home office and a couple of weeks later came by to show me the first sketch. It was perfect and captured Don's imposing presence and steely eyes, which also had a twinkle. "How did you enjoy Don?" I asked Bob. "Oh, he's a very nice, smart, and impressive man, but my, he does have a lot of pictures of himself, doesn't he?" That diplomatic artist had captured the true Don Regan.

In his first months in Washington, Regan would guide the new President's tax-cut bill through Congress and confirm his status as the President's chief economic spokesman. When Reagan was elected to a second term, Don swapped positions with Jim Baker and became White House chief of staff while Baker assumed Don's position as Secretary of the Treasury. This was unfortunate. Don was not one to pander to anyone, and he hated indecision. While he admired the President greatly and the two of them shared a great bond, Don had no time for Nancy Reagan, who'd often call Don at home in the evening to tell him to rearrange her husband's schedule. "My friend," she'd say, referring to her astrologer, "doesn't think this is the right day for the summit with Gorbachev" or for whatever had been planned. One evening, Don had had enough. "Goddammit, Nancy, this has been arranged for months. We can't change it." And he hung up on the President's wife. That was the moment that Ronald Regan hung up on Don. Shortly thereafter, during the Iran-Contra investigation, Don became the scapegoat for the administration, and he found out through the press that he had been fired. The President never spoke to him again, and Don never spoke to either of the Reagans again, either.

D on Regan left Merrill Lynch in far better shape than he had found it. During his tenure as CEO, revenue rose from $473 million to some $3 billion, and total assets quadrupled to nearly $13.25 billion. Three in every four Americans lived within twenty-five miles of one of the 476 ML branches, where one of some 8,600 account executives could help them pick and choose from multiple ways to invest their money. On a single day in Regan's final weeks, there were 81.6 million shares traded on the NYSE—and fully 15 million of them were handled by Merrill Lynch. More important, every one of those trades had been entered into ML computers by 9:30 P.M. the same day.

Regan straightened out the firm's internal paperwork problems well before the rest of the industry straightened out theirs, so when the demise of fixed commissions ignited cutthroat competition in the brokerage business, Merrill Lynch was ready. He focused on ML's long-term growth through diversification into insurance, real estate, and mutual funds. The firm moved aggressively into international markets and rose to the top in investment banking, research, and institutional services. As industry leader of the stock exchange, a role he assumed in the realization that Merrill Lynch couldn't grow and prosper until the NYSE itself shaped up, Regan championed protection for investors from defaulting brokers and helped to set up the Big Board's Central Certificate Service to break bottlenecks in the processing of trades.

Like Charlie Merrill and my father, who saw opportunity where others did not, Regan was a new kind of Wall Street leader—a professional manager, dedicated to the proposition that if something was going to run well, it had to *be* well run. Of course, there's no denying that Regan made a lot of enemies on the Street—even years after the CMA had been introduced, bankers were still smarting over how it had shattered their comfortable world, and some traditional brokers were deeply resentful of his leadership in bringing about competitive commissions. And the animosity didn't just come from the outside; his autocratic style had left him some detractors within Merrill Lynch as well. But nearly all his detractors, from without and within, gave him at least grudging respect, for Donald Thomas Regan had revolutionized the way business was done on Wall Street, and in doing so made Merrill Lynch bullish on America. But now more than ever, even more important, America was bullish on Merrill Lynch.

*By 1980, an average of four thousand people entered
the Merrill Lynch information booth at Grand Central
Station every day. The booth was the inspiration of Lou
Engel who also wrote the classic book* How to Buy Stocks.

CHAPTER NINE

Mr. Integrity

(1980–1985)

I n 1984, nearly four years after he left the spacious ML executive office on the forty-sixth floor of One Liberty Plaza to become Ronald Reagan's Treasury secretary, Don Regan was making a routine speech to a group of securities industry leaders at Washington's Mayflower Hotel and noticed that one of his listeners was William A. Schreyer, the new CEO of Merrill Lynch. When he finished with his prepared remarks, Regan threw the gathering open to questions—from anyone except his old colleague Bill Schreyer.

"Instead," Regan barked, "I have a question for you, Bill. What the hell went wrong?"

Regan got a big laugh, but his words knifed through the air to Schreyer, who was acutely aware—along with nearly everyone else in the room—that, yes, something had gone wrong at Merrill Lynch. While Regan was establishing himself as the chief economic spokesman for the Reagan administration, his old company had foundered. Indeed, at the time Regan chided Schreyer in early 1984, the firm had just suffered a 67 percent drop in third-quarter earnings, its stock was worth about half of what it had been just a year earlier, and there had been some egregious misadventures at home and abroad. The Bull, it seemed, was out of control. Around the same time, a critical article in *Fortune* magazine quoted Regan criticizing the management of his former firm. It took a while, and the intervention of Dan Tully, before Schreyer forgave Don for these events, and would even speak to him.

When Regan left for Washington in early 1981, there was little suspense about who the board would choose as his successor: Roger E. Birk. With the exception of Bill Schreyer, most thought this was the logical move. After all, Roger was the president and chief operating officer, was highly competent, and embodied the firm's values. Bill, however, viewed Roger as a manager and not a leader and thought that he himself was ready to take over for Regan. However, unlike Alf Beane Jr., nearly a quarter-century earlier, Bill bit his tongue. His day would come.

Birk had been groomed for the job by Regan since he made his mark in the Goodbody rescue; he and Regan had been a formidable team. Birk joined the firm in 1954 as a twenty-four-year-old margin clerk in Minneapolis. He attended the training school in 1956 and returned to Minneapolis as an account executive. He was named manager of the Fort Wayne, Indiana, office in 1964, and in 1967 he became a vice president and manager of the Kansas City branch. He arrived in New York as assistant director of the Operations Division in 1968—just in time for the paper crunch.

By this time, he had earned a reputation for quiet diligence, impeccable integrity, and a visionary concern for the technology of the brokerage industry. As Regan's top aide, Birk distinguished himself in the late 1970s by pressing for decentralization to the Princeton campus (overcoming substantial opposition from within the firm), introducing a more formalized system of management to Merrill Lynch, and, of course, helping to unravel the Goodbody mess. Birk rose rapidly to president of the brokerage unit in 1974 and then to president of the parent company in 1976, making it clear that he would be Regan's successor upon his expected retirement a decade later. In explaining his selection, Regan described Birk in these words: "steadiness, honesty, straightforward, a good thinker, decisive, and technically trained in the electronics applications that would be the thing of the future." Birk became the firm's seventh presiding officer in 1981 and, at the age of fifty-one, the youngest ever. Because Don could be difficult, I once asked Roger how he got along with him so well and actually survived. "I knew never to challenge Don in public," he told me. "Those that did got their head chopped off. I would always disagree and argue with Don privately. He would listen and often change his opinion. I do think I prevented him from doing some really stupid things." Roger was the perfect COO for Regan.

I first met Roger Birk a few weeks before officially joining Merrill Lynch, at Don and Ann Regan's daughter's wedding. I already knew several Merrill Lynch executives who were there, but this was the first time I'd met Birk, who at the time, in the summer of 1974, was the director of the Operations Division. He was in his forties and prematurely bald, but athletically fit. Unlike many other executives, Birk was careful to eat healthily. I recall him introducing himself to me, wishing me good luck at Merrill, and speaking fondly of my father, whom he had gotten to know as an office manager. He seemed like a gracious gentleman, though not as charismatic as the other ML people, who seemed to enjoy a party more.

After George Shinn left Merrill Lynch suddenly to go to First Boston, Birk became president and COO; he was a great second-in-command to Regan—disciplined, hardworking, and very organized. Roger was a student of the management process, and I think Don put him in place knowing that as Merrill Lynch evolved from a partnership to a private corporation to a publicly owned company, it had to be structured differently and run with more formality. To that end, Roger hired a firm called Lewis Allen to introduce a new management system whose buzz words were "Planning, Leading, Organizing and Controlling." While the thoughts behind this system were sound, it was an incredibly complex and bureaucratic system. Every manager had to go through training and then write a job and accountability statement using a numerical system. Special mandatory training classes were held for all supervisors. It drove everyone crazy, but Don Regan supported it, and I do think it brought a discipline to Merrill Lynch that the firm needed.

Birk began his term several years earlier than he might have expected to and inherited one substantial handicap. Representatives of banks and savings and loan associations saw a plot in Regan's step up to head the Treasury Department, charging that he and Birk planned to devise a scheme to put them out of business. The CMA was taking deposits that otherwise would go to banks and savings and loan companies, and most of these institutions were hampered by uninspired and bureaucratic management as well as dated regulatory constraints. To ward off any controversy, both the government and ML lawyers advised that Birk and Regan should have no contact whatsoever for at least the first six months of Regan's term as Treasury secretary. While the move helped the firm avoid further charges, it deprived Birk of an important source of counsel for his first days as CEO. "There were many times in those early days that I wanted to touch base with Don," Birk said. While Roger was Don's obvious successor, I think the timing caught him by surprise, and I always felt that he didn't really aspire to the No. 1 position. Roger often worried about whether he was up to the job, and that weight on his shoulders was heavy. Unlike Bill Schreyer, who always wanted to be CEO, Roger probably would have been content staying within his zone of competency. He was a humble man who just wanted to do the best job he could for Merrill Lynch.

When Birk assumed the top post, Merrill Lynch was the unchallenged leader of the retail American securities business. While its competitors struggled through the 1970s, ML cruised at full steam without a single losing quarter. It was miles ahead of the competition, prompting *Newsweek* to offer a wry observation: "When E. F. Hutton speaks, people may listen—but Merrill Lynch's pronouncements can move them to dramatic action. What action was this? Simply that a Merrill Lynch announcement to its clients over the Dow news ticker to buy common stocks aggressively produced an 'electric' effect: Within twenty-five minutes the Dow gained 8 points. When Merrill Lynch speaks, people listen and act." The *Christian Science Monitor* noted that on an average day, four thousand people entered our booth at Grand Central Station. But it was much more than that. Charlie Merrill and my father's brokerage partnership had become a huge, publicly owned conglomerate in the high-stakes world of investment banking and corporate finance. The company liked to call itself a "total diversified financial services company"—though it still had a ways to go to reach that goal.

During Regan's final year at the helm, net earnings reached a record of just over $200 million, and the firm had increased its market share in securities, options, and commodities trading. Total assets stood at $13.25 billion, a 400 percent increase over 1970.

During Birk's first two years, the company saw improving results and in 1982 Merrill's net income hit a record $308 million, our return on equity was 24.7 percent, we signed up our one-millionth CMA client, we had 800,000 IRA accounts, and we launched the innovative Equity Access account that used the CMA concept to allow clients to monetize the equity in their home. After the CMA was introduced in 1977, I and so many others never set foot in a bank again. With products like the CMA and Equity Access there was no need to. A new bank had indeed been created and it was a win-win for Merrill and for its clients.

R oger moved quickly in his first year to appoint Bill Schreyer as president and chief operating officer of Merrill Lynch & Co. in addition to his remaining CEO of Merrill Lynch, Pierce, Fenner & Smith. At this time I was the director of Human Resources, and one day Bill called me into his office and asked me to chair a study team to look at the firm's organizational structure. He appointed several smart rising young executives like Joe Grano, Nassos Michas, Mel Taub, Bob Arnold, and Steve Warner to work on this with me. "Win, the time has come for us to move forward as a major investment banking firm," Bill told me. "Don did not allow me to do this a few years ago, and I think he was right about the timing, but now the time has come to put all the investment banking and institutional departments together under one leadership. I want you to look at this totally objectively with your study team." He then pulled out a piece of paper. "But I won't mind it if your recommendation looked like this." That was classic Bill. He had already decided what he wanted to do, but he wanted an "objective group" to recommend it.

So over the course of several sessions I guided our discussion to Bill's recommendation, and he accepted our "recommendation" to create a fully integrated Individual Financial Services Group led by Dan Tully and a Capital Markets Group led by his longtime friend and colleague Ed Moriarty. While Ed had been an account executive and office manager, he had also managed the Municipal Bond Department, so Bill thought he had the requisite skills to manage the Capital Markets Group (plus he wanted to make sure that someone who grew up in the Merrill culture was in charge of investment banking and trading). Both Dan and Ed were given their own CFOs and operations and information technology groups, which was a radical departure from the past. Bill also appointed me as the director of Strategic Development and Marketing for Capital Markets, and I joined Ed's new team, which included Jerry Kenney running Institutional Sales and Research, Nigel McEwan heading investment banking, Sam Hunter leading equity trading, and Roger Shay running debt trading.

Meanwhile, Bob Arnold became Ed's CFO, Mike Reddy ran operations, and a recent recruit from Salomon Brothers, Hank Alexander, was put in charge of building a new IT platform for the Capital Markets Group. Tully promoted Launny Steffens and put him in charge of marketing, Herb Ruben took over the sales force, and Jay Conefry became Dan's CFO. Dan and Ed reported directly to Bill while Dakin Ferris, who headed the Diversified Financial Services Group, reported to Roger. Birk also promoted his two protégés, Bob Rittereiser, who became EVP of Strategy, and Charles Ross, whom he named EVP and Merrill Lynch & Co.'s Administrative Officer. Birk relied heavily on advice from these two executives and rarely made a decision without their input. He also placed Wally Sellers into a role overseeing the ongoing diversification of Merrill. When I was director of Human Resources, I reported to Charles Ross and thus attended many such discussions with him and Roger and was always flattered when Roger would ask for my advice. I gained great respect for him and to this day believe that he was one of the most underappreciated of Merrill's CEOs. Roger was self-effacing and always wanted to do the best for Merrill's stockholders, and I never once heard of him seeking more compensation or extra perks of any kind. However, it was clear that Roger felt uncomfortable making certain strategic decisions, and he would often fret before and after he made one that it was the wrong choice.

As I said, Roger's first two years brought improving results at the firm, and yet there were some hidden thorns in this bed of roses. One was a lack of strategic direction. There were other more generalized problems as well, chief among them that the brokerage business was being invaded by outside giants like Sears, Roebuck, Prudential Insurance, and American Express. Whether it was true or not, to the rest of Wall Street Merrill Lynch appeared to be on the defensive. ML brokers were being lured away to other firms, who offered better pay packages and straight commissions. Herb Ruben had made a terrible decision to fire all brokers not producing at least $250,000, and while he intended to improve productivity and weed out non-performers, the move also drove some of the firm's more productive advisers to accept offers from the competition. Morale sank throughout the firm. Certain parts of Don's diversification strategy were being questioned, particularly the move into real estate, and the world outside of Merrill Lynch appeared to be in chaos. Perhaps worst of all, the firm's cherished reputation was tarnished by a series of missteps.

Wall Street experienced two major investment disasters in 1983—the bankruptcy of the Baldwin United Corp. and the default of the Washington Public Power Supply System (WPPSS)—and Merrill Lynch was intimately linked to both.

The firm had established the Merrill Lynch Life Agency in 1975, and through it the life insurance products of various insurance underwriters were made available to customers at ML branches. Launny Steffens, one of Merrill's most strategic thinkers, understood the role of insurance as an investment product and was single-mindedly focused on creating innovative insurance products for Merrill's clients. One of these products was Baldwin United's single-premium deferred annuities, which ML account executives had sold as safe, high-yield investments. Under the arrangement, investors made a single payment, and interest was to accumulate tax-free until withdrawals began at the policyholders' retirement. Baldwin United sold 163,000 of these policies, worth an aggregate of $3.7 billion, through some forty brokerage houses in all fifty states. ML alone sold some $700 million in these policies. But Baldwin United didn't invest all of its customers' money in marketable securities; about 20 percent was pumped back into company loans to its subsidiaries. When Baldwin United faltered and filed for bankruptcy in September 1983, the policyholders' investments were in peril. Though it was under no legal obligation to do so, Merrill Lynch took the lead and together with other brokerages formulated a plan to reimburse these clients partially for their losses. It cost ML $83 million after taxes, resulting in a fourth-quarter 1983 loss of $42.1 million—the first quarterly deficit in its thirteen-year history as a public corporation.

Ironically, I had an inside look into Baldwin United because my father-in-law, Harold W. Smith, was a director of the company. Hal Smith was like a father to me, and I had great respect for his business acumen as well as great affection for him as a person of the highest integrity.

Hal had grown up in Waterbury, Connecticut, in an Irish-Catholic family. His eldest brother, Fran, was a force in Connecticut Democratic politics until his early death. The second brother, Joe, became a congressman and then a federal judge. Another brother went into the construction business and ran the local lumber business. Hal's family assignment was to start a federal savings and loan during the Depression to round out the family enterprises. Hal was a Phi Beta Kappa graduate of Dartmouth, and after service in the Navy in World War II, he returned to Waterbury with his new bride, Elizabeth "Copey" Smith, to begin a career in banking. Hal was really a local "homebody" and rarely ventured far from Waterbury, but he joined the Board of Directors of United Corporation, a closed-end investment fund, at the behest of his good friend and Dartmouth classmate Bill Hickey. United later merged with Baldwin, a well-known piano-manufacturing company whose new CEO was an energetic and charismatic man named Morley Thompson. Morley kept the piano business but saw the future of Baldwin United as an innovative financial services organization, and he used the cash from United to fund this venture. He soon became the darling of Wall Street.

When I joined Merrill Lynch in 1974, I knew that Baldwin United was growing and in need of an investment bank, so through Hal I arranged for Morley to visit Merrill Lynch in early 1975 and have lunch with Don Regan and Jack Morehouse, a managing director in our Investment Banking Division. Regan was taken with Morley, and the dynamics of that meal were intriguing as Don sparred with someone of equal ego. After lunch on his way back to the office he passed Dakin Ferris and told him, "I think I just met the second smartest guy in financial services. He's just what we need as my successor." This comment was made just outside of Roger Birk's office, and I often wondered if Roger overheard it.

Meanwhile, Jack Morehouse assigned one of our smart investment bankers, Trey Fitzgibbons, to do due diligence on Baldwin, and he came back a few days later and said that Baldwin was "a house of cards," and that we shouldn't touch anything they did. I was embarrassed and told Hal that we were not the right investment bank for

Baldwin, and in fact we never did any investment banking business with them. Over the next couple of years, Baldwin grew impressively and its stock soared and some other investment banks earned impressive fees, but Fitzgibbons's dire assessment of the firm had been sound. Unfortunately for Merrill Lynch, though, that assessment was never delivered to the retail side of the firm. To make matters worse, Carol Neves, the Merrill Lynch analyst following Baldwin, lost her objectivity and continued to assign a strong buy recommendation to the stock even when the rest of Wall Street was beginning to figure out what Morley was really up to.

Much like the directors of Merrill Lynch thirty years later, the directors of Baldwin United had no clue what the CEO was doing. Morley wined and dined them and included them in lavish recognition trips. They applauded his results but never challenged them and really did not have the expertise to fully understand the house of cards he'd created. Carol Neves also did not do sufficiently detailed analysis and chose to believe the words of the CEO. Once the company failed, my father-in-law suffered years of shareholder derivative suits and embarrassment, and it was sad to see him go through this. Although he was a very intelligent person, his experience running a small savings and loan did not prepare him for the shenanigans of a financial engineer like Morley Thompson. In my opinion, this also was true of many members of the Merrill Lynch Board of Directors in 2007.

The cost notwithstanding, I have always believed that Birk's finest moment at Merrill Lynch was his resolution of the Baldwin United crisis. He clearly put the clients' interests first and also did everything possible to salvage ML's reputation for integrity.

In the second major disaster, thousands of Merrill Lynch clients, along with customers of most of the other big brokerages, bought bonds issued by the Washington Public Power Supply System, or WPPSS (ironically called "Whoops" in Street vernacular), to finance two nuclear power plants in the Pacific Northwest. Merrill Lynch was the principal underwriter for the deal. The plants boasted state-of-the-art engineering and were built to withstand every disaster—plane crash, earthquake, tornado, you name it—save one: a shift in the political climate. In June 1983 the Washington State Supreme Court abruptly invalidated the contracts between Whoops and the electric utilities sponsoring the plants, and overnight the bonds held by some 78,000 people were rendered worthless. The $2.25 billion default was the biggest municipal bond collapse in American history, and many of the burned investors blamed their brokers. Fourteen brokerages agreed to pay a total of $135 million to compensate their customers for some of their losses. ML's share was the largest: about $44 million. Obviously, neither Merrill Lynch nor the other underwriters could have foreseen the unprecedented court action, but this was nevertheless a costly and embarrassing episode that tarnished the ML brand. However, once again Roger recognized the right thing to do despite the cost to the bottom line.

Meanwhile, some of the firm's efforts at diversification didn't work out, either, such as the 1979 acquisition of AMIC Corp., a North Carolina firm that insured lenders from losses on real-estate loans. AMIC did poorly under the ML umbrella, and one general reason was that record-high interest rates were slowing housing and mortgage activity. But the predominant cause of the failure was that AMIC's chief customers were savings and loan institutions, who, as I've mentioned, were infuriated by what they considered to be ML's invasion of their turf with the Cash Management Account. AMIC's association with ML proved to be an insurmountable burden, and just two years after its purchase, ML sold it.

Yet another failure involved a joint venture with IBM, called International MarketNet ("Imnet"), to provide information to brokers. The hope was that Imnet would siphon business away from Quotron Systems, Incorporated, and other leaders in the financial information industry. To get off to a flying start, ML and IBM tried to sell the hardware to the ten thousand Merrill brokers, but very few of them signed up and the whole project was dropped in less than two years. It was another public relations disaster—called "Imnot" by Wall Street cynics. Bob Rittereiser and Wally Sellers, whom Roger had put in charge of diversification, were the advocates of Imnet—much to the horror of Bill Schreyer, Dan Tully, and Ed Moriarty. Ritt had a perverse view that Merrill's future lay in its becoming a technology company rather than a securities firm, and this ultimately alienated him from most of his peers.

And then there was the Sun Hung Kai Securities embarrassment in 1982, when Bill Arthur, the chairman of Merrill Lynch International, and Greg Fitzgerald, Merrill's CFO, convinced Roger to make an investment in the Hong Kong financial services firm. Merrill purchased 25 percent of Sun Hung Kai Securities and 15 percent of Sun Hung Kai bank. Arthur properly saw the Asia Pacific region as a huge opportunity for Merrill in the decades ahead, and like so many people who visit Mainland China for the first time, he and Fitzgerald both developed China Fever ("Someday China will open, and just imagine a market of a billion people"). The principal owner of Sun Hung Kai, Fung King Hey, was known as "the King of the Securities World" in Hong Kong and had great relationships with the Chinese government. Arthur believed that an investment in his firm would give us access to this future market. When Don was still CEO, Bill Rogers, then a director of the firm, arranged for Regan, Harry Anderson, Arthur, and himself to visit Beijing and meet with Premier Chou Enlai and other senior officials. The Chinese held Rogers in high esteem from his days as Nixon's Secretary of State. Even though most people think that Henry Kissinger was the sole architect of Nixon's historic trip to China, the fact is that Rogers played an equal role, and his deft negotiating skills crafted the final subtle words that allowed both nations to sign the Shanghai Accord, which opened relations between them.

On Don's visit some memorandums of understanding about doing commodities business and training were signed, but they came to naught. Thus, having an ally like Fung was viewed in 1982 as the right way to build a China strategy. Unfortunately, though, when it came to Sun Hung Kai, our due diligence was lacking and we did not realize what an unprofessional bucket shop their securities business was; our Hong Kong retail professionals wanted nothing to do with them. We also failed to understand that the bank had a huge exposure to the Hong Kong real-estate market, and when China announced that they would not renew the lease of Hong Kong to the UK when it expired in 1999, the property market collapsed, Sun Hung Kai's assets were largely erased, and a capital infusion was needed from all owners. Birk was not at all willing to throw bad money after good, and after months of strained negotiations, Merrill and Sun Hung Kai went their separate ways with a loss of face to both in the Asia markets.

Considering all of the above, not surprisingly Merrill's financial results in the mid-1980s were grim. In 1984, for example, although revenues remained the same as the year before, about $6 billion, earnings dropped to $95 billion from $230 million the previous year. The company's 4.8 percent return on equity was far below the norm for the securities industry, and this is what led to Don Regan's question to Bill Schreyer that one afternoon in Washington, D.C.

Mergers were the rage on Wall Street during Birk's years as No. 1, but he steered the company through the frenzy and kept it independent. There were offers from Traveler's Insurance, Prudential, and American Express, but it was Sears that pressed most intensely. Sears wanted to dominate the emerging financial marketplace the way it had once dominated the sale of consumer goods, and no target was more tempting than Merrill Lynch, which controlled 12 percent of the securities brokerage market—more than three times that of its nearest competitor. The Merrill Lynch project even had a code name, Vermillion, which was the name of the Illinois county where Edward R. Telling, the Sears board chairman, was born. Early in the summer of 1981, Birk received a telephone call from Roderick M. Hills, a top Sears attorney, asking for a meeting to discuss a possible merger. Birk agreed to preliminary talks between Wally Sellers, ML's strategist, and Philip Purcell, the Sears president. Ultimately, Sellers and Purcell recommended a merger. A few weeks later, a secret luncheon was held at ML headquarters that included Telling and Purcell from Sears and Birk, Bill Schreyer, and several other top Merrill Lynch officials, during which Birk concluded that there was no coherent plan to merge the two firms, and the deal was vetoed. Afterward Sears purchased Dean Witter, a respected firm with origins in California, and this was lauded as the "socks and stocks" merger. American Express purchased Shearson, and Prudential Securities bought Bache. When Don Regan later learned that Birk had turned down these suitors, he was furious. Regan saw bigger as better and wanted Merrill Lynch's strategy to be a "three-leg stool": securities, insurance, and real estate. All of these mergers were unsuccessful in the long run, though, and in my and most of my colleagues' opinion, Roger made the correct decision to remain independent. Fortunately, his successors, Schreyer and Tully, carried forth that same belief. In many ways, Roger's most important fingerprint on the firm during his four years at the helm was saying no to the several suitors.

B irk focused on technology long before many other leaders on Wall Street, and it was due to his technical acumen that the company entered into a partnership in 1983 with Western Union, the City of New York, and the Port Authority of New York and New Jersey to form Teleport Communications, the world's first satellite communications center. The operation, which was located on Staten Island, some ten miles southwest of Wall Street, was a high-tech alternative telecommunications network mainly for corporate customers. Merrill Lynch spent about $125 million on the operation, and it became one of Teleport's best customers. After five years of losses, Teleport started turning a profit in 1988. The idea spread to other cities, including San Francisco, Chicago, and Houston, where other operations were established to compete with the phone companies. As part of a plan to drop non-core businesses, ML divested itself of Teleport in three stages in 1991 and 1992 at a substantial overall profit.

Almost immediately after Birk took over, the company began planning to move some of its operations to New Jersey. Some four years later, ML had opened its Somerset Operations Complex and its 275-acre Corporate Campus and Training Center in Plainsboro, New Jersey, near Princeton. One of the biggest supporters of the Princeton move was Bill Schreyer, who coincidentally lived only a few miles away. There is often a strong correlation between a headquarters move and the residency of the CEO. Yet most ML executives were not thrilled with the idea, and only Arthur Zeikel, head of Asset Management, volunteered to move his division there. Investment banking and the institutional business argued that they needed to stay in the heart of the financial community and that a move to the "cow pastures of New Jersey" would put them at a competitive disadvantage. However, Merrill had committed to the square footage and decided that the Private Client home office operations along with Asset Management would share the space alongside the new training center and company hotel. Other Manhattan-based companies had already made similar

Charles Ross was a tough, no-nonsense executive with a heart of gold and one of my important mentors. Despite Regan's disapproval, he appointed me as Director of Human Resources at age thirty. However, his most important contribution was hiring Arthur Zeikel to build and lead Merrill Lynch Asset Management.

Arthur Zeikel was a one-of-a-kind executive and one of the few who could intellectually challenge Regan. In addition to growing MLAM into one of the company's most important and profitable businesses, he served as a trusted advisor to several of Merrill's CEOs.

cost-cutting shifts to the suburbs, but this was Merrill Lynch, and when the actual transfer of personnel began in 1985, it attracted this worried speculation in *The New York Times*:

> Merrill Lynch, the nation's largest securities concern, is certainly not the first company to move a large group of workers outside the city. Dozens of manufacturers have moved their headquarters from New York to the suburbs, and many financial-services companies have sought less costly suburban offices for their check processing, record keeping and other so-called back-office operations. But the move by Merrill Lynch is unusual, and could set a precedent, in an industry that has always been as closely tied to Wall Street as the American theater has been to Broadway. Manhattan's securities and commodities concerns, employing 122,000 in the city, have been growing at a rate of 10 percent a year and are under intense pressure to find additional office space.

Michael Woodford, the Merrill Lynch vice president who directed the move, allayed such fears, though, pointing out that the core of the company—the top executives, traders, and financial analysts—all remained in Manhattan. "We have come to an era in which technology is allowing firms like ours to make the most cost-effective real-estate choices," Woodford added. "In some cases that means Manhattan, in others it doesn't."

Roger was especially worried about who would succeed him. While it seemed apparent to most that Bill Schreyer as chief operating officer was the obvious choice, Roger had two major concerns that he discussed often with Charles Ross and several times with me as well. It seems Roger had great respect for Bill's charismatic leadership style, his unbridled optimism, and his success in leading many different areas of the firm, but he was concerned because Bill had a selfish side and was often preoccupied with his personal image and compensation. Bill constantly pushed for more pay and perks, and Roger hated these conversations and often felt pressured to accede to his demands. Also, Roger as well as several members of the board worried about Bill's lavish spending style and wondered if he could be tough on expenses. (Because of these two concerns, both Ritt and Charles felt that they were better choices to succeed Roger when the time came.) Roger was also concerned about Bill's new organization. While he agreed that the Capital Markets Group needed to be pulled out from under the shadow of the retail side, he worried that costs would grow and that redundancies would occur. But he acceded to Bill's wishes after our "independent" study team made its recommendation.

Roger's difficult tenure came to an end on July 1, 1984, when he stepped down as chief executive officer; he remained chairman until April 1985, when he was named chairman emeritus. During his leadership, ML expanded its existing products, grew aggressively overseas, resisted the merger mania that was sweeping Wall Street, and engaged in a personal, hands-on upgrading of the critical back-stage operations. At the same time, Birk served as an effective and articulate spokesman for the entire securities industry. Perhaps his most important achievement was to expand the reach of the CMA, which became so popular that Merrill Lynch obtained a patent on it in 1981 and demanded that other brokerages pay license fees to operate similar systems. Whenever competitors unveiled what appeared to be clones, the firm sued for patent infringement. "We developed the process, it is unique, and we received a patent," said Birk. "Those who want to use it ought to compensate us. We have to respond to protect our rights and we are very serious about it." Dean Witter Reynolds ignored the warnings and ended up paying $1 million to ML in compensation.

Following a dynamic leader like Don Regan could not have been an easy job. While Roger only served four years and had to deal with many issues not of his making, he served an important transitionary role. It was my good fortune to work directly with Roger. He was a workaholic who never went to sleep until he had finished reading what he had taken home for the day. Roger was respected by most people at ML and in the industry, but he was not close friends with many and to some he seemed aloof. The consensus, however, was that he was an excellent manager, a great No. 2 man—but not a great leader.

In my opinion Roger never received the recognition that he deserved both as Regan's No. 2 and as the successor to Don who allowed Merrill Lynch to emerge and evolve from the Regan era and, indeed, set the stage for the great success that would follow under the leadership of Bill Schreyer and Dan Tully.

*This October 1987 Pittsburgh Press cartoon of U.S.
President Ronald Reagan depicted the rising influence of
Merrill Lynch after the market crashed earlier that year.*

CHAPTER TEN

The Eternal Optimist

(1985–1993)

B ill Schreyer had many memorable and pithy sayings: "I never met a rich pessimist," "Don't sweat the small stuff," and "The sun must be over the yardarm somewhere in the world—let's have a pop" are three good examples. And he had a genuine love and affection for Merrill Lynch, its history and its culture. Bill also had two great visions that he passionately championed: the growth of our investment banking and institutional business, and our global expansion. Bill was devoted to his wife, Joan, their daughter, Drueanne, and his grandchildren in later life, as well as to his beloved Penn State. Bill was also a deeply religious Catholic and visited the Vatican several times. While ever pious and respectful, he also used those visits to solicit the business of Pope John Paul and got him to open a special CMA account with a gold credit card. Bill was ever the salesman.

I first met Bill Schreyer when I was a second-year associate in investment banking. He had recently become the executive vice president of the newly formed Capital Markets Group and was walking down the hallway at One Liberty Plaza after a meeting with Bob Trone, the director of the Investment Banking Division. As he passed my office he noticed the name plate on the door and he stopped in to introduce himself. "Hi, I'm Bill Schreyer. I knew your dad and he was a great leader, and he would be thrilled that you are now part of our team." Schreyer was a warm and affable man, and it was personal gestures like this that made people want to follow him, remain loyal to him, and work hard for him. He in turn was loyal to his friends and supporters, sometimes to a fault. Bill could also make the tough personnel decisions when necessary, but he never got rid of anyone in a mean-spirited way.

"Don't sweat the small stuff" wasn't just one of his favorite expressions, it was often his modus operandi. Bill's optimism could be infectious, and those around him could get caught up in believing we could achieve anything even if he didn't have an exact road map on how to get there. That was for others to figure out. Bill was one of my main mentors over the eighteen years that we worked together at ML, and it was over the objections of most everyone else that he appointed me as chairman of Merrill Lynch International in 1992.

I n 1936, when William Allen Schreyer was eight years old, his father made a career switch from banker to stockbroker and became manager of the Williamsport, Pennsylvania, office of Granberry & Co., which five years later would become part of Merrill Lynch. Young Schreyer immediately began hanging around the brokerage when a group of regular board watchers convened for the market close. Sometimes he filled in as a board marker. "I got the feel, the excitement of the business early on," he recalled years later. The topic of his senior class paper in high school was the New York Stock Exchange, and by the time he went off to college at nearby Pennsylvania State University, "I knew exactly what I wanted to do—I wanted to come to Merrill Lynch."

He finished college in three years, and in 1948 applied to the Harvard Graduate School of Business, which rejected him on the grounds that, at the age of twenty, he was too young. Instead he joined Merrill Lynch in June 1948 as one of three charter students in a new management training program. (This was the forerunner to the firm's Junior Executive Training course for college graduates, known affectionately as the JET program.) That summer he befriended another young ML employee, Edmund Lynch Jr., son of the original partner. Later fired by Don Regan, Eddie Lynch was a member of the Underwriting Department and a bit of a dilettante who spent more time playing tennis and keeping up on the affairs of his Chi Psi fraternity than anything else. But he liked Schreyer and one weekend invited him to the family home in Southampton. There Bill was introduced to an elderly Charlie Merrill. Characteristically, CEM had taken the trouble to learn young Schreyer's background—and even asked about the health of his father, who, like Charlie, also suffered with heart problems at this time. He also met my father. "I hear that you're doing a fine job," my father said to him. "Your father would be proud of you. Do you have any idea of what you'd like to do in the firm once you're through with the training program?" Without a pause, Bill smiled impishly. "I want your job one day," he told him. Dad responded, "Go for it." Despite the smile, Schreyer was dead serious and kept a laser focus on that goal.

After completing the training program and doing a brief stint in the ML Pension Department, Schreyer was sent to Buffalo, New York, as an account executive under Howard Roth, the longtime resident partner. After several months Schreyer's performance there was top-notch, but Roth summoned the rookie broker to his office. "You know what's wrong with you?" Roth asked without expecting an answer. "You talk too damn much." Roth put an egg timer on Schreyer's desk and ordered him to limit his calls to three minutes. Schreyer later was named manager of the Trenton, New Jersey, office in 1963, and two years later he returned to Buffalo as manager and was elected a vice president of Merrill Lynch, Pierce, Fenner & Smith. Bill progressed through the management ranks. He served as the regional director of the Metropolitan Region, and when Don Regan bought the brokerage firm C. J. Devine, he installed Bill as chairman of this new subsidiary. It was a curious move in the eyes of many, especially the former partners of C. J. Devine. Here was this "glad-handing salesman" who knew nothing about trading, and he was now supposedly their boss. However, Don understood that integrating C.J. Devine into Merrill Lynch would be tricky—Devine concentrated on government securities, virgin territory for Merrill at the time—and he needed somebody there whom he could trust and who would look out for Merrill's interests. After all, acquiring Devine was a risky move that was not widely supported by many of the "old guard."

I remember Norman Weiden, the veteran all-star salesman, bemoaning the fact that Don was getting us into areas that placed the firm at risk. When Don became CEO, Norman walked into Don's office unannounced and said, "Don, your job is to keep the train on the tracks." Like many others, he worried that initiatives like Devine would derail this fast and smooth-running train. As part of the acquisition agreement, the Devine principals were guaranteed annual cash compensation of $500,000, a huge sum in those days and far more than anyone else made. Bill was paid a fraction of that, and when he lobbied Don for more money, Don characteristically said, "You're not worth any more. You're there to mind the store." While Bill bristled over that, he used his calling card (Chairman, Merrill Lynch Government Securities, Inc.) to visit institutional and government clients throughout the world, and his salesmanship proved to be a valuable asset to the firm. Later, when Regan decided to form the Capital Markets Group, Bill was its first executive vice president, and this put him in position a few years later, in 1984, to beat out rival Ross Kenzie to become president of Merrill Lynch, Pierce, Fenner & Smith. A year later, upon Roger Birk's retirement, he assumed my father's old job as chairman and CEO, and no doubt my father must have smiled down on him that day, recalling the conversation he'd had decades earlier on Long Island with that young upstart from Williamsport.

I should note that in the brief time that he was chief operating officer, Bill had no intention of waiting years to succeed Birk. He believed that Roger was a "bean counter" and not a great leader and thought it best for him to take early retirement at age fifty-five. In his 2009 memoir, *Still Bullish on America*, Schreyer claimed that Birk worried about dying at age fifty-five like his father had, and that the stress of running Merrill Lynch was too much for him. Roger has always denied this. While Roger had bridged the post-Regan era effectively, Bill believed that a change was needed and that only he could fix what was ailing Merrill Lynch. At the time, I was director of Human Resources and later Bill named me director of Strategic Planning and Development for the Capital Markets Group. I worked very closely with both Roger and Bill in both of those positions, and there were many uncomfortable times when Roger would press me about my and others' opinion of Bill. "Is he smart enough for the job? Can he be tough on expenses?" Roger fretted about Bill, but also recognized his strengths as a leader. Meanwhile, Bill knew that he had to convince the Board of Directors, who in that era were no "shrinking violets," that he had the "right stuff" to succeed Roger. Bill had a reputation as a spender, and he knew he had to convince Roger and the rest of the board that he could be tough on expenses.

And so in January 1984 he formed the Schreyer Working Team and asked me to be his "chief of staff" in addition to continuing my role in Capital Markets. Archie Urciuoli, another competent executive and Schreyer loyalist, also played a key leadership role in this effort. Earlier Arch had helped Bill draft the initial proposal that recommended the formation of the Capital Markets Group. With the help of McKinsey, the management consultant firm, the team set about to find ways of reducing expenses by between 5 and 10 percent. McKinsey introduced a process called Overhead Value Assessment (OVA), which made all offices identify cuts of that magnitude for discussion. Needless to say, it was not a very popular exercise, but Bill put his full weight behind it and gave Roger and the board regular updates. I think that most everyone was surprised by Bill's tenacity at cutting costs. While everyone knew about the tasks of the Schreyer Working Team, Carter Bales of McKinsey and I were aware of a side project: reorganizing the firm and moving Bill up to be CEO. Bales saw this as an opportunity to design a role for himself, and he convinced Bill that Merrill's existing executive team was not "world class," and that he needed to go outside to recruit talent. According to Bales, Bill needed a new CFO, a new head of technology, a new general counsel, and a new director of Capital Markets. Carter was angling for the CFO job. Then Bill could decide who should succeed him as president when he moved into the CEO job.

Bill partially took Carter's advice, agreeing that he needed a new head of Capital Markets. At the time the group was jointly directed by Ed Moriarty and Charles Ross. Both had had very successful careers at Merrill Lynch and were capable executives, but they were dysfunctional together and were not respected by the employees within Capital Markets, who saw them as retail brokers who didn't understand the institutional business. Ed was reluctant to make decisions quickly and Charles often shot before he aimed. If Ed said, "Let's turn right," Charles said, "Go left." During this time I reported directly to Ed and Charles and liked them both immensely. They were both wonderful human beings and always had the best interests of Merrill Lynch in mind, but I was placed in a very uncomfortable position, as they would each call me into their office and express to me their frustration with the other and bemoan the fact that they were not the sole leader of Capital Markets.

Bill was beginning to understand that Ed and Charles were not working out as he had hoped, and one evening he hosted a dinner at the River Club and invited "candid conversation." As he was wont to do, Sam Hunter, the head of the Equity Trading Division, after a drink or two, ripped into his bosses and everyone else piled on. It was a massacre, and I knew that Bill had to make a change after that dinner. Bill liked and respected Ed and Charles and didn't look forward to making the change, but he knew it had to be done in the best interests of Merrill Lynch. When Bill asked who I thought should run Capital Markets, I recommended Jerry Kenney, but Carter convinced Bill that he needed someone with more "stature and industry credibility." Bill was reluctant to use a headhunter, so he personally took the initiative and reached out to Peter Buchanan, the CEO of First Boston. His thinking was he would bring Peter in to lead Capital Markets and position him to become a candidate for president of the firm when Bill rose to chairman. Bill knew and liked Peter and thought he would make a "good Merrill Lyncher." So Bill and Peter had lunch. "It was really a bizarre lunch," Peter told me many years later. "Bill said he thought I should join Merrill Lynch in some undefined role. I really wasn't sure what the conversation was about, but I asked him, 'Why would I work for you? I already make a lot more than you do.'" Peter went on to say: "Even though it was a strange lunch, Bill and I became good friends, and when I retired from First Boston, he threw me a retirement party and even had people flown in from out of town. Bill was really a great gentleman." Schreyer came back from that luncheon and said, "I don't think Peter is ready to leave First Boston." I think Bill had assumed that if George Leness had come over years earlier from First Boston and become chairman of Merrill Lynch, then Peter Buchanan would have the same aspiration. But nothing gets Bill down, so he next set his sights on a notable Wall Street lawyer by the name of Sam Butler. He, too, turned Bill down.

At that point Bill decided he couldn't wait any longer and promoted Jerry Kenney to EVP of Merrill Lynch Capital Markets. It was the right decision.

Meanwhile, Carter had convinced Bill that he needed to put his personal imprint on the firm's structure and that Merrill Lynch should be organized around key markets, so he recommended that Bill create fifteen market-centered business units that would be placed within three business sectors: Consumer Markets, Capital Markets, and Real Estate and Insurance. A new Information Services Sector would also be formed "to be responsible for managing services and support for the market units and directing the company's wholesaling efforts." The Teleport and IBM joint venture were also part of this sector. In addition, a new position of chief administrative officer overseeing finance and human resources would be created.

Armed with this reorganization plan, which Carter and I put into a succinct presentation, Bill paid a weekend visit to Roger at his home in Red Bank, New Jersey. He essentially told Roger that this was how Merrill needed to be organized and that it would be best if Roger retired and turned the reins over to him. Later than day Bill called me at my home in Greenwich to say that Roger had accepted his recommendation. Bill became the designated CEO, with Roger scheduled to remain as chairman for a year. With the work completed, Bill realized that Carter Bales was becoming a liability with his new team in place, and the work with McKinsey came to a close.

Dan Tully was the clear choice to lead Consumer Markets, and Bill let Dakin Ferris continue overseeing Real Estate and Insurance, though he planned on retiring Dakin within two years. He was not a Schreyer loyalist. Bob Rittereiser was named chief administrative officer and the interim head of the Services Sector and was also asked to lead strategic planning for the firm.

Bill modified Bales's organizational recommendation slightly in order to save face for both Ross and Moriarty. He moved his longtime friend Ed Moriarty to have a new role, overseeing Merrill Lynch's facilities planning operations, including the relocation of Merrill Lynch's headquarters in Manhattan and the construction and start-up of the Princeton and Somerset facilities in New Jersey. "The magnitude of these pending real-estate projects demands the full-time attention of a member of senior management," he explained. While Carter had envisioned that Merrill's international activities be integrated within Capital Markets, Bill disagreed fundamentally and also saw a way of keeping Charles Ross as an executive vice president and member of his newly former Corporate Office. "Since we have recently concluded a specific review of our international activities and will be increasing our emphasis and commitment to that area, I have re-assigned Charles Ross to become chairman of Merrill Lynch International, to which he will devote one hundred percent of his time," Bill announced.

Both Ed and Charles accepted their new assignments but were not pleased. Ed rarely spoke to Bill again and always thought he had been betrayed by his old friend. Charles was shocked but he reacted very differently and threw himself into the new role. His wife, Beth, however, was furious and she phoned me shortly after Charles called to tell her the news. "What have they done to my Charles?" she asked. I felt horrible, for as much as I loved and respected Charles, and as much as I owed him for giving me an incredible opportunity at a young age, I knew that leading Capital Markets was not the right role for him and was not in the best interests of Merrill Lynch. At the same time, however, this new role was not right for him, either. While many people at the firm appreciated Charles's work ethic and integrity, his blunt American style did not play well overseas.

Charles had been diagnosed with multiple sclerosis but refused to slow down, and he traveled furiously around the world until the disease forced him to retire. A few years later while lying in bed alongside Beth, he fell asleep and dropped a cigar he had been smoking. Beth awoke to find the bed in flames, but she wasn't strong enough to drag Charles to safety. She ran next door to get the neighbor to help her, but it was too late. At the time I was chairman of Merrill Lynch International, and later that night Beth called me. "Win, this is Beth. Charles is dead. Can you get the Merrill Lynch jet to fly out to pick up Megan [their daughter] in Idaho? A friend will fly along to pick her up. I want someone with her when she finds out." I will never forget the shock of that call. Charles had a tough exterior but a heart of gold. He was a loyal Merrill Lyncher and had been successful in so many roles before the Capital Markets job. A few years earlier, Charles's son, Charles Jr., had perished in a car accident while we were at a Merrill Lynch retreat in Palm Springs. In the span of just a few years, Beth had lost both her son and her husband.

My family, too, lost a dear friend and I a mentor who had made me the director of Human Resources at age thirty. "What a stupid move," Regan had told him at the time. "He's too young to be a division director." But Charles held his ground and Don reluctantly accepted me. I will never forget Charles and what an inspiration he was to many of us who worked for him.

On June 27, 1984, Bill Schreyer, the newly designated Chief Executive Officer of Merrill Lynch & Co., issued under his name alone a press release with the headline "Merrill Lynch Reports on Cost Control and Restructuring Programs." It announced the organizational changes and executive appointments as well as "the first phase of the company's structural cost control program. It will include total personnel reductions in 1984 of 2,500 people and total savings of $200 million from budgeted amounts for the year." The release went on to report that while personnel reductions were occurring, "more than 350 account executives and other producers have been added." Bill wanted to make sure that Merrill was tightening its belt but still growing.

Shortly afterward, the new business unit heads were announced, and I moved over to work for Dan Tully as senior vice president of Emerging Investor Services, while Arch Urciuoli became SVP of Business Financial Services. Launny Steffens was named SVP of National Sales, Joe Grano became SVP of Individual Investor Services, and Bill Sullivan was named SVP of Investment Product Services. Arthur Zeikel, as president of Merrill Lynch Asset Management, also came to report to Tully.

In Capital Markets, Jerry Kenney named Barry Friedberg as SVP of Investment Banking, Sam Hunter as SVP of Trading, Brian Barefoot became SVP of Institutional Services, Jack Lavery was named to lead Research, and Jean Rousseau became SVP of Municipal Markets. The old Commodities Division was repositioned under Trading. John Heimann, the former Comptroller of the Currency, became vice chairman. Both he and Barry Friedberg came to Merrill when we purchased the failing Becker Paribas. The appointment of Barry was particularly significant. As an established banker himself, Barry recognized the institutional equity strength that Merrill Lynch had built, and rather than pitching our "retail strength," Barry focused on the unique and broad institutional presence we had in sales, trading, and research. He culled the weaker bankers and recruited talent from other firms, and by the 1990s had established Merrill Lynch on a par with Goldman Sachs and Morgan Stanley in debt, equity, and mergers and acquisitions. The other member of the team who was critical to Merrill's global growth was Roger Vasey. Originally hired by Sam Hunter from A. G. Becker to build Merrill's growing commercial paper business, Roger ultimately came to run all of Global Debt and arguably built Merrill into the dominant debt firm in the world. While he and Barry often clashed over who was responsible for a client, they were both strong executives who had an enormous impact on Merrill's success over the next two decades.

Clearly, Schreyer's organizational fingerprint indicated that Capital Markets was going to become an equal partner with Consumer Markets, and that International would receive far more focus than it had previously. Bill was off to a fast start as CEO.

However, a few months later, physicians informed him that he would need to have coronary bypass surgery. He called me into his office one day and asked me to look after some of his personal affairs if the surgery did not work out well. "But it will!" he added. He also told me that with the exception of his wife, Joan, his doctor, and his attorney, no one else knew about this yet, but that he would soon inform Roger and the board. Bill did not designate anyone to be the interim CEO in his absence and expected his new EVPs to operate as a team, and of course, Roger was still the chairman for a few more months. Bill left for his surgery confident that everything was in place for his absence, but while he was recuperating, Bob Rittereiser tried to organize a "palace coup," speaking openly to anyone who would listen about Bill's shortcomings. Ritt really believed that he had the vision to lead the firm in a different—and to his mind, better—direction and that Bill was incapable of doing that. He was counting on his longtime relationship with Roger Birk to help him gain control. Ritt had a very different vision than Bill, believing that Merrill should be more of a technology company than a brokerage firm. Needless to say, the many Schreyer loyalists reported this to Bill when he returned to work, and he realized that changes were needed. When Bill moved up to be chairman as well as CEO upon Roger's retirement in 1985, Dan Tully became president and COO and Launny Steffens was promoted to EVP of Individual Financials. Ritt eventually left to become Bob Fomon's successor as head of E. F. Hutton, and a few years later, after Hutton was involved in a check-kiting scandal that weakened the company to the extent that it was looking for a buyer, Schreyer told his team to make it appear that Merrill was interested in purchasing E. F. Hutton so that the price would get bid up. The truth was he never had any intention of purchasing the firm run by Ritt, but he enjoyed bidding up the price so that American Express, the eventual buyer, paid more than it needed to. Bill often told that story and laughed heartily about it.

B ill achieved a lot in his early months, but probably his greatest move was to quickly name Dan Tully to be president and COO. His chose Dan "primarily because he is a natural leader." Perhaps Bill's foremost strength was an ability to select the right person for the right job, and he and Tully would become one of the most successful executive teams in modern Wall Street history. In fact, in many ways their partnership resembled the one that my father and Charlie Merrill had decades earlier. Dan effectively ran the day-to-day business, but he always made sure to recognize Bill as the ultimate boss. Bill also relied heavily on the advice and counsel of Steve Hammerman, who, as the firm's general counsel, was exemplary at crisis management and was a tough enforcer of ML's principle of integrity. And Bill carefully crafted the Board of Directors. He selected people of ability but also people he knew would be loyal to him, and he spent a tremendous amount of time cultivating these relationships. It was clear that they were Bill's good friends as well as board members, but they took their jobs seriously and were effective directors.

Schreyer and Tully took over a company with $2.3 billion of equity capital, some 42,000 employees, and slightly more than a thousand offices around the globe. But despite all of this, the Street's perception of Merrill Lynch was that of a slow-moving giant, lacking a clear sense of purpose. While net earnings in 1985 had rebounded from the prior year's dismal $95 million, the firm's return on shareholder's equity was still a dismal 10.2 percent. Merrill was also facing tougher competition from conglomerates such as American Express (Shearson, Loeb Rhoades), Prudential (Bache Group Inc.), Sears, Roebuck & Co. (Dean Witter Reynolds), and General Electric (Kidder, Peabody & Co.). Discount brokers like Charles Schwab had gathered strength on Wall Street as well, and some began to question whether firms like Merrill Lynch were becoming dinosaurs.

Schreyer and Tully believed the firm was overextended and they directly questioned the wisdom of providing cradle-to-grave financial services that were not only unprofitable, but unrelated to the basic businesses of stock brokerage and investment banking. They resolved that ML would return to those two core operations, while expanding and diversifying them. They believed in the traditional retail client business but also saw growing opportunities in investment banking, debt and equity trading, and newer products such as derivatives and swaps and private equity; they also recognized the global nature of the investment banking and institutional businesses.

The sweeping overhaul of the institutional operation paid immediate dividends in 1985 when *Financial World* magazine, in its annual survey of the 150 top money managers in the United States, chose Merrill Lynch as the brokerage firm that best satisfied its clients' wants and needs. In moving to the top rung of the rankings, ML overtook Goldman Sachs, which had been ranked No. 1 for the two previous years. The survey placed ML first in research and second or third in other individual groups—most improved, best order execution, and best block trading. Survey respondents depicted Merrill's staff as "readily available at all levels—research analysts, traders, top executives." Despite all the problems of the early 1980s, ML had muscled its way into the top echelons of investment banking and become a major force in corporate finance. But its strength still lay in distribution rather than origination and mergers and acquisitions.

If there were any doubts on Wall Street about the sincerity of the restructuring effort, they were dissipated by the company's stunning announcement a few years later that it was getting rid of its $500 million-a-year real-estate business, which had been launched in 1979 and had once been viewed as the keystone of the financial supermarket.

From the start, though, the real-estate operation had problems, since in most areas of the country, it had been unable to acquire the top firms and was forced to settle for the second tier. Bright red Merrill Lynch real-estate signs began appearing in low-income neighborhoods, and ML financial consultants complained that they didn't fit with the overall company image. Soon after becoming chairman, Schreyer named David Komansky, a rapidly rising former broker who now headed the New York sales region, to take over Merrill Lynch Realty and decide whether it should be jettisoned.

In *Still Bullish on America*, Schreyer recalled the day in 1986 when Komansky was scheduled to make his report to the ML management committee. "We had other business to conduct in the morning; he was going to present his report in the afternoon. As we were breaking for lunch, about to go our separate ways, I said to him, 'Dave, I'm really looking forward to your report this afternoon. I can't wait to hear what you think we should do with this piece of crap.'"

Komansky recommended that ML get out of the retail end of the real-estate business because the uncertainties of real estate, not just fluctuating home prices but fluctuating mortgage interest rates, tended to magnify the firm's dependence on the ups and downs of the economy. Komansky also concluded that the 18,000 independent contractors who made up the real-estate sales force could not be fitted comfortably into ML's corporate structure. The unit was sold to Prudential Insurance Co. of America in 1989. Around this time, the firm also withdrew from European commercial paper markets, sold a telecommunications business, and closed its retail brokerage network in Canada.

Schreyer also challenged the hidebound tradition of promoting exclusively from within by bringing in professionals from outside the firm to run some of the increasingly complex support functions. Among the more prominent hires, Courtney F. Jones came over from General Motors and was made chief financial officer, Richard B. Stewart Jr. came in from the Kidder Peabody Group to be the firm's treasurer, and DuWayne Peterson was hired away from Security Pacific Bank to head operations. While these executives brought in some fresh perspective, they lacked the Merrill DNA and never really fit into the culture. They brought technical skills, but they never understood what Mother Merrill really was about. Jones in particular lacked the human skills to gain respect from his peers. Tully was never enthusiastic about them and eventually replaced Jones with Herb Allison and Peterson with Ed Goldberg.

Schreyer always had a deep love of the history and culture of Merrill Lynch, and he believed that future generations should appreciate the heritage of the firm. In 1985 he came up with a clever idea to restore pride throughout the organization after what had been a tough previous year. "Let's celebrate the one-hundredth anniversary of the founding of Merrill Lynch," he said. Of course, there was one small problem with this idea: Since Charlie Merrill opened for business on January 6, 2014, it would be another twenty-nine years before this celebration could occur. But someone discovered that a predecessor firm of E. A. Pierce by the name of W. W. Gwathmey of Richmond, Virginia, had begun in 1885, and thus Merrill could mark its one-hundredth anniversary. On May 1, 1985, the anniversary began when the NYSE sent a congratulatory message over its ticker at 9:59 A.M. and hung an ML banner over the trading floor. At four P.M. Roger Birk, chairman emeritus, rang the traditional closing bell.

To help with the celebrations, Bill commissioned journalist Henry Hecht to write an abbreviated history of the firm, which ended up being called *A Legacy of Leadership,* and we began a project under the careful tutelage of Lee Roselle to build a museum about Merrill's history in its new Executive Offices at 4 World Financial Center. The celebration culminated with a black-tie dinner at the New-York Historical Society on October 21, 1985, with a guest list that included senior Merrill executives, members of the board, former partners like Harry Anderson and Ed Ryan, and members of the founding families. My mother attended, as did my wife, Maggie, and I. It was a special evening and in my opinion one of the highlights were remarks made by Charles Merrill, Charlie's eldest son. Both his sister, Doris Magowan, and his brother, James Merrill, were also there. It was a grand birthday party even if it wasn't the real one-hundredth. But it did accomplish what Bill wanted: The heritage, the values that were the foundation of the firm, were to be honored and respected even as Merrill Lynch moved into the twenty-first century. We were proud to be part of Mother Merrill "one hundred years" after its founding, and we related to those on whose shoulders we now stood.

What also made us proud to be part of Mother Merrill were a number of philanthropic initiatives begun by Bill and Dan. Several first-grade inner-city classes were adopted with the promise that if the students finished high school, Merrill Lynch would pay for their college educations. Numerous Merrill Lynch employees around the United States mentored these students and encouraged them to finish their studies. Another widely acclaimed initiative was the Christmas Calling Program, where Merrill Lynch offices were opened nationwide for seniors to make free phone calls to their relatives back home in countries around the world. One caller, eighty-six-year-old Ruth Rose, spoke to her sister-in-law in Jerusalem. "I think it's beautiful," Rose said about the program, because calling to Israel was too expensive for her. Many Merrill Lynchers eagerly volunteered to help in this effort, giving up a Saturday during the holidays.

W hen Charlie Merrill decided in 1940 to start calling his salesmen "account executives" as a way of getting around the unsavory term "stockbroker," he was never entirely satisfied with the change. After all, he had borrowed the term from the advertising industry, and Madison Avenue was held only slightly higher in public regard than Wall Street. For the remaining sixteen years of his life, he toyed with alternatives like "securities representative" and "commodities representative," but he could never make up his mind on a change. By the time Schreyer became chairman, the need for a new name had become acute, for the days of brokers simply booking buy and sell orders for stocks and bonds were over. No longer could ML brokers spend their days offering their wisdom on the financial markets (most of which they gleaned from the Research Department). The new goal at Merrill Lynch was to be "all things to some people"—namely, the wealthiest 20 percent of the population. Don Regan had brought the company into the broader world of financial services, and now Schreyer was about to complete the job of transforming the company from a brokerage firm to a financial-planning giant.

Thus, in 1985, ML began calling its brokers "financial consultants," because they were expected to learn how to sell other financial service products, such as mutual funds and life insurance, partnerships, credit, and structured products, that were now receiving large doses of company money. The goal was to create broader, deeper relationships with clients and thus be able to generate fees, freeing the company from the spiking cycles of commission-based business. The change was a difficult one for the old account executives because the skills required to stay in daily contact with investing customers are different from those needed to sell a single, lifetime product like a life insurance policy or a trust. To educate its brokers for their new roles, the firm created an internal television network called the Direct Broadcast Satellite system ("DBS") that reached all branch offices, and opened its new state-of-the-art training center in Plainsboro, New Jersey, where new financial consultants went for their initial training and seasoned financial consultants and office managers returned for continuing education. Financial consultants could also benefit from offerings remotely since under the leadership of Madeline Weinstein, the center placed emphasis on computer-assisted education that could be delivered directly to them in their offices. Meanwhile, establishing these "total financial relationships" had one important advantage for customers that would have pleased Charlie Merrill: In offering such a fee-based financial supermarket, brokers were far less likely to "churn" accounts—buy and sell without justification—to generate commissions.

The point man in this effort was John ("Launny") Steffens, who was a Dartmouth math major and had joined ML in 1963 in the JET program. After tours in various departments, Launny ended up working as an account executive in Cleveland for Ross Kenzie, who immediately tried to convince Launny that to be successful he needed to wear long socks, a hat, and a white shirt. Steffens, always the individualist, did none of this but earned Kenzie's respect even so. In the summer of 1970, Kenzie invited Launny to "become part of management" as his sales manager. A few years later, Kenzie told Launny that he needed to go to the Assessment Center, where prospective managers went through a rigorous interview and a number of tests before they could become "official" managers. This didn't sit well with Steffens, and so he asked Ross, "What if I flunk?" Kenzie dismissed Launny's concerns and insisted that he take the test, which Launny passed with flying colors, and it became clear to many that

Launny Steffens was Dan Tully's protégé and led the private wealth side of Merrill Lynch for nearly two decades. He was responsible for the many innovations that occurred in those years. He was Tully's choice to succeed him as CEO but Launny withdrew from the race, preferring to stay as the head of private wealth.

Launny was one of the future "Whiz Kids." After a brief period of managing the Birmingham, Michigan, office, he was brought into the Operations Division in New York City to work for Charles Ross, who was the Assistant Division Director when Roger Birk ran the division. When Ross was promoted, Launny took his job and performed successfully until Tully pulled him into his Marketing Division to head a new-products group. Dan and Launny had a great working relationship. Dan recognized Launny's intelligence and creativity and gave him great latitude to move ML from a traditional brokerage operation to a private wealth management firm over the next two decades. While Bill was never as fond of Launny because of his often brusque manner, Dan recognized his intellect and also believed that Steffens should be his successor.

Over two decades, Launny had a profound impact on the success of this portion of the firm's business and was one of the real visionaries of the modern Merrill Lynch. One of the things he did was to encourage the firm to focus on the needs of specific client segments. For individuals, they were savings, investment, taxes, insurance, and financing. For small companies, they were cash management, investment, financing, and employee benefits, including 401(k) plans. Launny's priority was to build long-term relationships with clients by helping them meet their own goals and by focusing financial consultants on gathering assets. He recognized that there was a direct correlation between the amount of assets that a financial consultant had and the revenue he produced. The new role of the ML financial consultant in Launny's eyes was to become an asset gatherer, an asset allocator, and an asset manager. This "AAA" Strategy recognized the power of the Cash Management Account and the Individual Retirement Account as key ways of gathering assets, and each year, Launny oversaw a contest whereby the financial consultants who opened the most accounts were rewarded with trips to exotic locales. This motivation worked. Assets in all the accounts grew significantly, and those financial consultants who participated not only got a nice trip but their business grew and their clients benefited as well.

Though the CMA had proved very popular, to his amazement Launny discovered that it was losing money year after year. While the losses were immense—perhaps as much as $100 million over the life of the program—they were stanched by a series of measures: The annual fee was raised from $65 to $80; inactive accounts were issued quarterly instead of monthly statements; and a one-day delay in giving customers credit from securities sales yielded $10 million per year in extra float. Customers hardly noticed the changes, and before long the CMA was out of the red. Then, in 1986, the Working Capital Management Account (WCMA) was created, offering small businesses interest-bearing checking, a securities trading account, one or more credit cards, a commercial line of credit of $100,000 to $2 million, and the electronic transfer of funds from one account to another. Once again, just as they'd done with the CMA, the banking industry protested that this innovative product was an invasion of their turf. ML responded by increasing its direct loans to consumers and infiltrating the bankers' trillion-dollar trust business by founding the Merrill Lynch Trust Co. and introducing the Trust Management Account.

Launny realized that Depression-era regulations were holding banks back from delivering the products and services that individuals and small businesses needed and wanted. While products like the CMA creatively found their way past regulatory restraints, Launny knew that Merrill also needed to be a bank. The 1933 Glass–Steagall Act had defined a bank as an organization that made commercial loans and took deposits, but Launny wanted Merrill to be the type of bank that took deposits but didn't make commercial loans.

Toward that end, one Monday morning, he walked into the weekly Executive Committee meeting and announced that he had purchased a small bank in Utah. "You did what?" Steve Hammerman screamed. "You can't do that!"

"It's too late, I just did," Launny said calmly. That was Launny—always confident and never lacking the courage to move forward aggressively. The bank acquisition was approved by the regulators and Merrill was on its way to becoming the blueprint for the modern bank.

Meanwhile, the CMA program was steadily upgraded. With the passage of the Tax Reform Act in 1986, the monthly statement was revised to show nontaxable income. By 1988 it had grown into a vast repository of clients' assets and totaled some $170 billion. It was four functions in one: a money market fund, a margin account, a checking account, and a credit card. By putting all their money under Merrill's care, customers gave Merrill fees that were small but reliable compared to the commissions in a volatile market.

It was during the 1980s that ML stepped up its attempts to enroll America's most affluent individuals as customers. Perhaps the kickoff event was its sponsorship of the ninetieth-anniversary celebration of Carnegie Hall, one of New York's most cherished cultural institutions and a magnet for wealthy patrons. The highlight of the 1981 program was a re-creation of a concert at the hall's opening followed by a glittering 1890s-style supper. Some four hundred of the New York area's wealthiest individuals attended the event and mingled with ML executives.

The fact that the Consumer Markets area of Merrill Lynch was in good hands with Launny Steffens allowed Bill to devote most of his efforts to Capital Markets and International. Bill loved pitching business. He was good at it and he spent a great amount of his time during his eight years as CEO flying both around the USA and the globe helping bankers win investment banking mandates from corporations and governments.

While he was still head of the Capital Markets Division in 1979, Bill Schreyer happened to share a brief cab ride with John Whitehead, the managing co-partner of Goldman Sachs, one of the "white shoe" powerhouses of investment banking. Whitehead noted that Merrill Lynch was "coming along" with its budding investment banking program and then said to Bill: "With your incredible distribution strength we could be a great team. You would be a terrific co-manager of our deals. That would make you the largest co-manager of securities offerings." But Bill would never accept sharing power and shot back, "First of all, that wouldn't be any fun. Second, we plan on being the largest lead manager." So much for Whitehead's proposal.

Of all the Wall Street professionals I have known, none have I respected more than John Whitehead, whom I got to know well through several Outward Bound expeditions. Not only was he a brilliant investment banker, but he was a class act in every sense and a man of the highest integrity who also served as Assistant Secretary of State for Ronald Reagan. Furthermore, John has been incredibly

Jerry Kenney came to Merrill from White Weld. He built the Research Division and made it the best in the world, led investment banking and then the entire Corporate Institutional Client Group. Dan Tully promoted him to become the firm's chief strategist while continuing to direct research. Jerry was the primary force behind Merrill's successful acquisitions around the world.

generous to many charities over the years. Because of the man he is, I was especially touched when he spoke to me of his respect for Merrill Lynch and its leaders, like Bill Schreyer and my father. It wasn't often that someone from Goldman Sachs would admit that Merrill Lynch was indeed a formidable competitor.

T hroughout its history, Merrill Lynch had always been involved in investment banking, though usually as a big distributor of stocks and bonds underwritten by others. Its first expansion into direct underwriting activities in the 1970s began with utility issues. Utility companies wanted their securities sold to as many individuals in their service areas as possible, and therefore they favored the big distribution network that only a firm like ML could offer. When ML acquired White Weld in 1978, institutional trading was growing and there was money to be made in investment banking, but Merrill Lynch wasn't organized to take advantage of the opportunity. Even though the two types of investors are vastly different, Merrill Lynch brokers were simultaneously selling to individuals and to institutions. It wasn't working. Finally, the salesmen were given a choice of which of those two groups of clients they wanted to sell to. Because they found institutions intimidating, most of them chose individuals, thereby temporarily worsening ML's position in investment banking. It wasn't until Schreyer took over in 1984 that the firm got moving in this area.

Schreyer's first important step was to install Jerry Kenney, who had come over to ML from White Weld, to direct the firm's investment banking activities. At this time, the Merrill Lynch Capital Markets Division had about 9,000 of ML's 42,000 employees, but produced about one-third of its $5.7 billion in annual revenues. Kenney had already directed the acquisition of A. G. Becker, which solidified ML's presence in the fast-growing short-term finance market and brought into the fold some two hundred professionals who were experts in mergers and acquisitions, international finance, and private placement of securities. This was critical because Merrill's long-range goal here was to improve its high-level corporate contacts.

The firm was now ready to exploit its three strengths in capital markets: distribution, research, and trading. One of the first to see the advantages of ML was the Dutch government, which in 1986 financed the expansion of its airline, KLM, by selling off part of its holdings in the carrier. Merrill Lynch was chosen to place 15 million shares of stock that would raise $307.5 million. By 1988 the firm had stunned its "white shoe" brethren by shooting to the top of the underwriting charts in eight of eleven categories—and placing No. 1 in overall underwriting. This run continued uninterrupted until 2002. Merrill had become an underwriting powerhouse, and firms that once looked down their noses at this upstart were now gazing upward. ML Capital Markets began the 1980s as an investment banking upstart and ended the decade in the top tier of Wall Street. The firm was at the center of the era's biggest deals—raising equity and debt capital for corporations, advising on mergers and acquisitions, and financing the operations of towns, cities, states, and even nations.

And yet at the same time Merrill Lynch was making inroads into the investment banking business, it continued to serve the small investor, consistently leading Wall Street in packaging innovative financial products usually offered only to large investors and making them available to ordinary individuals as well. Take, for example, TIGRS.

In the late 1970s interest rates were extremely high due to the level of inflation, and individuals were looking for ways to lock in high yields on their savings. Joe Wilson, who ran Merrill's Canadian investment banking operation, was smart and independent and often clashed with management, but everyone knew that he ran one of the most profitable departments within the Investment Banking Division. Joe came up with a unique concept called Treasury Investment Growth Receipts (TIGRs), which effectively were synthetic Treasury bonds. Treasuries paid interest to investors semiannually, and the investor had to reinvest those proceeds. Thus, if an investor bought a thirty-year Treasury bond at 9 percent and the rate fell, he had to reinvest at a lower rate. TIGRs eliminated that reinvestment rate so that one could buy a security that had a compounded rate of growth of 9 percent for the entire thirty years. This was a particularly attractive investment in a tax-deferred account like an IRA or a pension plan. As with most new ideas, Joe faced battles externally as well as internally, but with the support of Tom Chrystie, Merrill launched its TIGRs only weeks before a similar product came out of Salomon.

Another product to emerge during this time was the LYON—"Liquid Yield Option Note"—one of the most successful corporate finance products in the history of American business.

In the early 1980s, many of ML's retail customers were wary of the stock market and unwilling to buy stocks outright. Instead, they wanted to hedge their bets and showed a strong preference for combining low-risk cash equivalents with call options on favored stocks. This strategy enabled them to avoid the risk of stocks while gaining the potential to share in their possible growth. Lee Cole, an ML vice president, watched this trend for several years, and in 1983 came up with an idea for a product that catered to such investors. It was a zero-coupon convertible—a fixed-income instrument that could be converted into the equity of a company.

Cole quickly sold the idea to Tom Patrick, managing director of investment banking. The next step was more difficult—finding a client to be the first to try a LYON. Cole and Patrick spent eighteen months searching the American business community; nearly all of the chief financial officers liked the concept, but they wanted someone else to be the first to offer it. Finally, they persuaded the firm Waste Management, which had rejected their entreaties twice before.

The LYON gave Merrill Lynch an important entree into the investment banking world, and within ten years it was a popular investment tool; moreover, it made it so the firm had a virtual monopoly on the zero-coupon convertible market because of its dual presence in the retail and investment banking communities. Not only was the LYON a good product for the investor, it also provided capital at a lower cost for the issuing corporation. This, in turn, allowed Merrill Lynch to secure business from corporations that had typically been served by other investment bankers. Perhaps the most notable was the Disney Corporation, a long-standing client of Morgan Stanley, which issued a LYON through ML. (Disney, incidentally, allowed Mickey Mouse and the Merrill Lynch bull to appear on the marketing material together.)

Yet another new venture during this time was the result of a team effort between Launny and Roger Vasey to market certificates of deposit for banks and savings and loan associations. Previously, these financial institutions obtained deposits from their own market areas, but now Merrill Lynch was raising deposits for a savings and loan in Ohio, for example, from all fifty states. The institutions were usually willing to pay a bit more for these funds, and thus our clients received a better rate on their investment.

Merrill was not a leader in merchant banking, but in the 1970s Tom Chrystie believed that the firm's strong capital base gave it a competitive advantage that could be used to help corporate clients raise money by ML committing its own money and taking ownership positions in those corporations. (Of course, this did have a precedent, as Charlie Merrill had made a fortune in the 1920s as a merchant banker by buying the stock of his own underwriting clients.) In the 1980s, merchant banking referred to the lucrative though hazardous practice whereby the major financial houses, rather than merely advising their clients in takeovers or buyouts, actually put up their own capital to facilitate takeovers specifically by investing their own equity through "bridge loans." Despite criticism from both outside and within about the inherent risks, ML Capital Markets persisted and became a formidable merchant banker on Wall Street, participating in many major leveraged buyouts of the 1980s, including the $4.23 billion Borg-Warner deal and the $25 billion RJR Nabisco agreement. ML even took clients way from competitors like Goldman Sachs and Kidder Peabody.

All in all, ML Capital Markets had taken Wall Street by storm, propelling itself into the top ranks of underwriters in some of the hottest areas of the time. Some thirteen years after their 1979 conversation in a cab, Schreyer and John Whitehead met again, and Whitehead asked, "Aren't you glad you didn't listen to me."

At nine A.M. on February 1, 1986 (it was seven P.M. the previous evening in New York), a buzzer sounded the opening of the Tokyo Stock Exchange, and down on the floor a team of Merrill Lynch traders went to work. "There we go," exulted Walter Burkett, general manager of the firm's Tokyo office. "We're off and running." For the first time in the 107-year history of the Tokyo Stock Exchange, a foreign firm was conducting transactions on the floor.

It was exactly thirty-five years after some of the Merrill Lynch partners had become angry with Mike McCarthy for the extravagance of opening an office in Japan, where government regulations prohibited the firm from trading. But McCarthy had insisted, reminding his detractors that none other than Charlie Merrill had predicted in 1951 that Japan was likely to become "important economically." And so, in 1961 McCarthy dispatched Donald P. Knode to Tokyo and began urging the government to give ML trading power. In 1964, the year that Tokyo hosted the Olympic Games, the firm opened its first representative office there. The Tokyo branch was licensed in 1972, making ML the first foreign securities firm approved for integrated securities business in the Japanese financial markets, but ML still had to pay commissions to Japanese brokers to trade on behalf of its clients. Persistence was finally rewarded in 1986.

For the first two years of his chairmanship, Bill Schreyer wondered how he could put his own stamp on Merrill Lynch. He was well aware of the legacies of his predecessors: Charlie Merrill came up with the idea of bringing Wall Street to Main Street; my father had executed that idea; Mike McCarthy brought in the modern back office, and Don Regan had emphasized growth and diversification. Schreyer remembered that during a one-year tour of duty with the U.S. Air Force in the mid-1950s he'd seen numerous signs pointing to the inevitability of a global marketplace, and in 1986 he made up his mind that this would be his legacy: "I decided ML had to become a global financial firm, doing business twenty-four hours a day in all corners of the world. And I decided it had to be done immediately."

ML's move to achieve a top-tier position in global private banking had begun back in 1972 with the acquisition of the Brown Shipley Bank, but the entire worldwide expansion effort stalled as the company suffered a series of international embarrassments. For one, Merrill bought into Sun Hung Kai Securities just before the Hong Kong real-estate crash. Then, in 1980, it tried to buy a British merchant bank, Hill Samuel, but was forced to abandon the idea less than a year later under the threat of a mass walkout by top executives and professionals that would have left Hill Samuel an empty shell. ML's international earnings record during the early 1980s was dreadful.

But now Schreyer breathed new life into global expansion and began broadening the firm's vision to a worldwide perspective by personal example. "You can't expect employees to believe in your ideas unless they see you getting involved," he says. "If you're thinking of a one-world market, you have to go out and make yourself visible." In 1986 alone, Schreyer traveled to Paris to address a meeting of world financial leaders; to London twice to prepare for deregulated trading; to Portugal to establish a Merrill presence; to China for the creation of its first securities markets; to Argentina, where Merrill had a remarkably successful private banking business; and to Korea and Japan, where, as just recounted, Merrill had just become the first foreign brokerage firm to trade on the floor of the Tokyo Stock Exchange.

One place Schreyer could not travel to was Beirut because the United States prohibited its citizens from going to Lebanon after the kidnapping of Americans during the civil war there. This was disappointing to Bill because one of his favorite colleagues was Makram Zaccour, the director of Merrill's Middle East Region. As I mentioned earlier, Makram was the son of Michel Zaccour, who before his death at an early age had been one of Lebanon's most respected journalists and politicians. Makram was well known throughout the Arabic community and introduced Bill to many influential people, including Rafic Hariri, a substantial client of Merrill's who later became Lebanon's prime minister and was responsible for rebuilding downtown Beirut after Lebanon's civil war. Bill later became a member of the board of the Hariri Foundation, which was founded in 1985 to further humanitarian causes. Sadly, Hariri was assassinated in downtown Beirut in 2005, allegedly by allies of Syria.

Unique among American securities firms, ML moved into the London stock market well ahead of "the Big Bang"—the deregulation of British securities markets in October 1986. When it first established a presence in Great Britain in 1960, the firm had carefully adhered to the conservative practices of London brokers and members of what was known as the Association of New York Stock Exchange Member Firms Having Representation in the United Kingdom. In those days, American brokers were prohibited from doing any European advertising, and direct-mail campaigns were frowned upon. The firm could not join the London Stock Exchange, since to become a member, a firm could not have an office outside London's financial district, which was known as "the City." But in its effort to establish a foothold in London, the ML office had two sets of doors—the regular front entrance, and a side door to allow clients to enter after the building was closed. It was an important architectural consideration because of the time difference between New York and London.

As always, technology was tugging at history. For Merrill and its major competitors, the trading day now began in Tokyo and other Asian markets. ML traders were at their desks at seven A.M. in London. Five hours later, as the sun rose over Wall Street, the company braced for the opening of the New York Stock Exchange. And when the Big Board closed, it was nearly time for Tokyo to open again. As technology enabled money to move in and out of markets instantaneously, these markets and their money became open to foreigners. Augmenting the technological advances were improved economic data and the relaxation of foreign exchange restrictions and securities market rules. More and more investors were thinking internationally, and they were naturally attracted to global networks like Merrill's. From New York to London to Tokyo, the world's financial centers were knit into a twenty-four-hour-a-day global market trading stocks, bonds, and currencies, and settling their accounts in dollars, yen, deutsche marks, pounds sterling, bahts, francs, pesetas, lira, rubles. By 1990, a half-century after Merrill Lynch, E. A. Pierce & Cassatt opened its first international office in Havana, the company was positioned to become the only financial institution in the world with the ability to serve both individual and institutional investors globally.

And yet even though our global expansion was progressing well, Bill thought we needed a "rainmaker"—someone to help us land foreign corporate and government accounts—and so in 1986 he hired Michael Von Clemm from Credit Suisse First Boston. Jerry Kenney had introduced Bill to Von Clemm, who was a talented banker and in many ways a "legend in his own mind," but he had a remarkable presence, had been responsible for the development of the Eurobond market, and was well known throughout the financial world. To get him to come to ML, Bill not only paid him significantly but he also made him a member of the Merrill Lynch & Co. Board of Directors— much to the irritation of most of the ML establishment. Von Clemm was arrogant. His expense account was enormous and was dwarfed only by his ego. But initially Bill supported him because he thought Von Clemm was just what Merrill Lunch needed to establish our credentials globally.

Von Clemm and I got along well, for while I, too, saw his flaws, I recognized the strengths that he brought to Merrill Lynch. The day Bill changed his mind about him was during a 1992 board meeting in Europe that had begun in London and moved to Paris for a second day. Bill liked bringing the directors overseas to educate them about our global presence and to show board support to our overseas employees. After the London meeting all the board members and their spouses flew to Paris and were greeted by a car service that brought them to the Plaza Athénée in downtown Paris. Von Clemm, on the other hand, was met at the airport by his chauffeur, who was driving his Rolls-Royce, which—courtesy of his ML expense account—had made the trip across the English Channel on the train ferry. This was the final straw for Bill, who was more tolerant than most, and he made the determination that Von Clemm had to go.

A few months later, Bill asked me to have lunch with him. At the time I was a senior vice president in charge of the Eastern Sales Division of Consumer Markets, reporting to Launny Steffens. It was a job I really enjoyed. After I had managed the Emerging Investor Market Group from 1984 to 1985, Dan Tully suggested that I needed "real line" experience, so he sent me to become the regional director of the Mid-Atlantic Region in Washington, D.C. Until now, nearly all regional directors had started out as financial consultants, and so my appointment was not universally popular. Fortunately, a few regional directors, like Ed Toohey and Larry Biederman, treated me as a colleague, rather than just the undeserving son of Win Smith Sr., and gave me some solid advice. Launny promoted me several years later to be one of his three national sales directors, and I had responsibility for one-third of Merrill's U.S. Private Client business. As I said, when Bill asked me to lunch that day, I was enjoying my job tremendously. I had moved back to New York City, our group was performing really well, and I liked working with our office management team and the many great financial consultants in the Eastern Division.

"Win," Bill said after we ordered, "I'll be retiring in a year, and I need someone to carry on with our global vision. We've laid out a great footprint, and I think you're just the guy to carry it forward after I retire." It took me a moment to realize he was offering me the job of chairman of Merrill Lynch International. I told him how flattered I was—but why me? "You've proven yourself in Private Client," he said, "and I think you have the leadership strength and the sophistication to do what needs doing. This is the job that we have been preparing you for." I asked Bill what the next steps were, and he suggested that I speak with Dan Tully, who he said was fully supportive. I asked if I could also speak with Launny since I reported to him, and Bill said that Launny already knew and was in favor of the move, as was Jerry Kenney.

But when I sat down with Dan, I got a less-than-enthusiastic reception. "Bill thinks this will work," he told me. "I'm not convinced, but he wants it done, and if you want to take the job, I'll support it." Leaving the room, I thought, *Great! Bill will be gone in a year, and his successor isn't sure this makes sense?* Launny was equally dismissive, saying, "This really doesn't make any sense. We don't *need* a chairman of Merrill Lynch International. All the product areas are organized globally, so what's the need for this position?" As always, Jerry Kenney was thoughtful.

So I went back to Bill and related the conversations to him. Bill just smiled and shook my hand, and a couple of days later he and Dan announced jointly that Michael Von Clemm would be retiring and I would replace him as MLI chairman, as well as become an executive vice president of Merrill Lynch & Co. and a member of its Executive Committee. One of the first people to congratulate me was Von Clemm himself, and I will always appreciate his graciousness. For the next several months he fully briefed me on everything he had been doing. "You may not want to continue what I have done," he said, "but at least understand it and make your own decision on what you want to do."

Becoming an executive vice president of Merrill Lynch & Co., chairman of Merrill Lynch International, and a member of the Merrill Lynch & Co. Executive Committee at the age of forty-two was an incredible thrill. My family was excited, and Maggie took us all out to dinner to celebrate. I had twenty-three years left until retirement, and now Bill Schreyer had positioned me to one day rise to the top of the firm. However, even after eighteen years at the company, I knew that many would think that I'd received the promotion only because I was the son of Win Smith and a "major" shareholder. (There was a lot of speculation about how much stock I owned or was held in trust for me. The reality was that the only stock I owned was what I bought personally or was paid as part of Merrill's compensation program.)

I had dealt with these issues all of my life. Being the son and namesake of someone like my father certainly had its benefits but there were also drawbacks. As I mentioned earlier, when I first interviewed for a job at ML in investment banking, I was brought back more times than the others before I was given an offer, and then I was started at a salary lower than the others. Rad Lovett, the assistant director of the Investment Banking Division, knew that I would be viewed skeptically by peers and others at Merrill Lynch, so he wanted to make sure that I earned my stripes and was not hired just because of who my father was.

Rad helped me realize that I was going to have to work harder than anyone to overcome the "handicap" of being Win Smith Jr. I tried to be the first to arrive each morning in the bullpen, where all the new associate investment bankers sat, and was among the last to leave. I worked weekends and took fewer holidays than was permitted. Apparently, this did make the right impression since I caught the attention of Tom Chrystie, who asked me to become the manager of the Financial Analysis and Budget Department when he was promoted to become the firm's CFO. Once again, the other managers who did not know me viewed my promotion as unwarranted, and I had to prove to them that I had the intellect and the financial acumen as well as the managerial skills for the job.

Eventually, I think I won them over, too, since I caught the attention of Charles Ross, the director of Human Resources, who brought me in as the manager of Compensation and Benefits and then promoted me a few years later to succeed him. And there again I found another group of Merrill Lynch professionals to win over. This continued throughout my career, and I came to accept it as the given reality.

Being the son of Win Smith, I had been sent to the finest schools, had been exposed to many interesting people, and had traveled to

Europe and South America, and as the only child of older parents, I had been doted upon and given privileges that few others were granted. Throughout my life I came to know that many would initially view me as someone who did not earn things on my own merits. Early on, that really bothered me, but over time I came to recognize that I would just have to work hard and earn other people's respect.

As I accepted Bill's offer, I understood that this job would be no different. What was interesting, though, is that as I traveled the world helping our investment and private bankers win mandates, it became clear that my heritage was a greater advantage outside of the United States than it had been within. Clients liked to be called upon by the chairman of Merrill Lynch International, who was also a member of the "founding family." It gave me greater credibility than I might otherwise have had as a young forty-two-year-old executive at Merrill Lynch. And so even though being Win Smith Jr. was difficult at times, I would never have wanted to be anyone else, and I think it would have made my father proud that I carried his name and understood and honored his values.

Working as I did was great for my career, but it took a toll on my family relationships. My wife, Maggie, and I drifted apart and were eventually divorced. She is a wonderful person and mother, and while we are both to blame for our separation, I fault myself for not recognizing what was happening to us. I spent a lot less time with our four wonderful children than they wanted. I missed their games, recitals, and other events. These can never be reclaimed, and yet despite my absences at important times of their early lives, they have continued to give me their unconditional love. Like my father, I was "married" to Merrill Lynch. I felt an obligation to him to do the best job I possibly could and strive to one day lead the firm that he was so instrumental in building.

All in all, I couldn't have served as chairman of Merrill Lynch International at a more exciting time, and in fact much of the global progress the company made came while I was in this job. We expanded our footprint in Europe, Asia, and Latin America, and we played a major role in helping Latin American nations with volatile economics regain their footing in the international financial markets.

It was a remarkable transition, especially considering that back in 1983 we had almost decided to shutter our Latin America operations.

At that time I was working for Ed Moriarty and Charles Ross, and Bill asked to me travel to Latin America to see if we should close everything down, as the offices were small and only marginally profitable. What I discovered in Buenos Aires was an incredibly talented and dedicated group of professionals. The top financial consultants there were Francis Verstraeten and his partner José Malbran, former commodities brokers who had matured into sophisticated financial advisers. They had been jailed in the Falklands-Malvinas war in 1982 after Merrill's office was raided by the Argentine police because of U.S. support for Great Britain. Despite the solid record of achievement, no Merrill Lynch senior executive had visited Buenos Aires since my father in 1956. I saw a group of professionals loyal to Merrill Lynch and with no real competition. But when José had asked to become Buenos Aires manager, he was deemed "too young and inexperienced" by Francisco Granados, the Latin American regional director.

Over lunch, Verstraeten told me, "José is your man, and because he is my friend and my partner, I'll do everything to make him successful." José became the manager of Buenos Aires, making it at one point the most profitable Private Client office in the world, and was later promoted to lead all of Latin America and subsequently the private wealth business in Europe and the Middle East. José was one of Merrill's most effective leaders. Verstraeten became Merrill's number one financial consultant globally. Both Francis and José have remained close friends of mine to this day, even though neither of them remained at Merrill Lynch.

By the time I became chairman of Merrill Lynch International, we had entered an age of privatization as nations turned longtime government-run industries over to entrepreneurship. Margaret Thatcher began it in the United Kingdom, and U.S.-educated Pedro Aspe continued it in Mexico with the privatizational of Telemex, the state-owned telephone company. Goldman Sachs led that initial public offering as well as the British Telecom deal and seemed invincible. After Goldman managed such successful offerings, why would any government risk going with someone else? But Goldman underestimated our Argentine roots, and we were successful in winning the mandate to privatize the Argentine state-owned oil company, Yacimentos Petrolieros Fiscale (YPF), in 1993.

Around the same time, we had also managed the first initial public offering of a Chinese company, Shanghai Petrochemical (SHK) on the New York Stock Exchange. While significantly smaller than YPF, in many ways SHK was equally important in establishing Merrill's global underwriting credentials. And as with YPF, we entered the competition as an underdog to Goldman, only to emerge victorious. I again was fortunate to lead our team. The challenges were different from those involved with YPF, but equally great. When I first visited SHK in 1992, it was hard to understand what was the municipality and what was the company that we were going to take public. China had no Generally Accepted Accounting Principles, and the manager of the company knew nothing about marketing an IPO. Furthermore, SHK was the first Chinese company to be approved for a listing on the NYSE, and therefore had the full attention of the senior leadership of the People's Republic of China. Success would establish us in this important market, but failure would likely doom us there. So when the offering approached, everyone involved in the deal, including Dave Komansky and Dan Tully, was watching closely and making sure that all areas of Merrill Lynch were supporting it fully. Fortunately, the deal went well.

In a single year, Merrill had successfully pulled off two major privatizations and had established its global credentials. This led to other successful mandates in countries like Indonesia, Spain, Italy, Brazil, Peru, Taiwan, Japan, and elsewhere. While Bill had just recently retired, his 1993 trip to China to celebrate the opening of our Shanghai representative office had certainly been an important step in winning the mandate, and his support of our Argentina presence, including his several trips to Buenos Aires, enabled us to be in a position to win YPF as well.

As Merrill Lynch expanded globally, so, too, did its operations and facilities at home. This process had begun with the move of various facilities to New Jersey. One of those was the training program.

When Merrill opened Wall Street's first training school in 1946, classes were held in dingy rooms where the acoustics were poor and cleanliness was next to impossible. Students were housed in Manhattan hotels and at the St. George in Brooklyn. They took their meals in local restaurants and often partied late into the night at local bars. They used stubby pencils to fill out exams that were hand-graded by their instructors. When they graduated, they became account executives and sold stocks and bonds. In some ways it was like Marine boot camp, but that allure had faded and Merrill was in need of new training facilities.

Four decades after that first training class, the 310th class was assigned to the 275-acre Corporate Center and Training Center along the banks of Bee Brook and Mill Ponds near Princeton, New Jersey. The 121 class members listened to lectures from high-backed seats in a large, comfortable amphitheater, each seat equipped with a keyboard on which they signed in and gave their answers to questions. They stayed on campus in a modern hotel in their own rooms, dined in company restaurants, and in their free hours used a swimming pool, exercise rooms, and tennis and racquetball courts. And when they graduated, they became financial consultants with responsibility for a wide array of products.

Many administrative and support facilities "went west" in the mid-1980s, following the opening of the Princeton Center, which, along with the training center, housed Consumer Markets operations and Arthur Zeikel's rapidly growing asset management business. In addition, an Operations Center opened in Somerset, New Jersey. However, most of the senior executive team, with the exception of Launny Steffens and Zeikel, remained in Manhattan, as did all the professionals in the Capital Markets Group and Research. By the early 1990s, the bulk of the work force, including top executives, traders, investment bankers, and financial analysts, were in Manhattan, scattered around eleven different office buildings. Yet despite the number of facilities, operations were still being hampered by cramped quarters.

The problem was especially acute at One Liberty Plaza, the headquarters building, where the trading floor was so crowded it was impossible to route even a single additional cable to cope with the rising tide of business. Files spilled into the hallways, and temperatures in the crowded rooms made conditions nearly unbearable. The solution was the World Financial Center, which consisted of four glass-and-granite towers of varying heights near the Hudson River. The irregularity of the towers was designed to soften the impact of its neighbor, the World Trade Center, with its oversized twin towers. Merrill Lynch leased two of the towers at the World Financial Center, and when the company began moving to the new quarters in April 1987, it was taken as a clear sign that more expansion was just around the corner.

As far as the Princeton and Somerset campuses, though, an important catalyst for the ability to shift to more cost-effective real estate was ML's continued leadership in communication technology. Computers and other technological advances had made physical proximity far less important for many functions, and the two suburban complexes were designed to take advantage of real-estate prices considerably lower than those in Manhattan. Years earlier, of course, my father had started to push for a move to the country, but his partners were not in favor of it, so it never gained any traction. Three decades later, I think he would have loved the beauty of the Princeton and Somerset operations. However, actions always have unintended consequences. I was never a fan of the move to Princeton because I felt it would begin to separate the firm into two sectors. Both at 70 Pine Street and One Liberty Plaza, executives from both the retail and the institutional sides shared a common executive dining room, and many informal meetings and decisions were made in the hallways. Such ongoing contact helped employees develop personal relationships and trust, with the result that even people who worked in different areas of the firm felt that they were on the same team. Now, though, with everyone split up, that began to change in subtle ways despite efforts to keep everyone working for the greater good of the firm.

In the 1980s, Merrill Lynch was the trailblazer for all of Wall Street in the field of business communications and advertising. The idea of producing business reports for broadcast came from the fertile mind of Lou Engel, who in 1947 persuaded my father to present daily international shortwave radio reports on Wall Street activity. In 1975, Don Regan authorized the installation of broadcast-quality equipment in a studio at One Liberty Plaza. The firm embraced satellite communication in 1984 with its first teleconference to simultaneously provide immediate information to thousands of employees. Sixteen offices across the nation were hooked up with one-way video and two-way audio to receive "Action Line," a program of information for individual financial consultants, and sales at all sixteen offices quickly shot up by 40 percent. "Action Line" became a Merrill Lynch staple, and by 1987 it was broadcasting 160 live programs a year to nearly 500 branch offices. Improved sales followed the programming wherever it went. Others made use of the new technology as well, in particular Launny Steffens, who held live town hall meetings with the entirely financial consultant community. However, its most severe test was just around the corner.

A nother early focus for both Bill and Dan was advertising strategy. Bill had never really related to Ed Ney of Young & Rubicam, who was in charge of the Merrill account, and so he put the firm's advertising out to bid. For the first two months of 1986, Madison Avenue focused on Wall Street, as some five hundred top advertising executives from five leading agencies zeroed in on one of the sweetest plums to come along in years: the $50-million-a-year Merrill Lynch account. They ate lunch at their desks, took work home with them, and sometimes returned to their offices the next day without having slept. More than anything else, they thought about a single animal and its symbolism, its power, its visual impact. One fact had been made clear to them: After a three-year absence, the bull was coming back to Merrill Lynch.

The original "Bullish on America" campaign, fashioned back in 1971 by Ogilvy & Mather, was one of the signal triumphs of American advertising. When Don Regan yanked the account from Ogilvy in 1978 and gave it to Young & Rubicam, the new agency reduced "the Thundering Herd" to a single bull and changed the slogan to "Merrill Lynch: A Breed Apart." Then, in 1982, the bull was dropped entirely in favor of a series of real-life mini-dramas that would drive home the idea that Merrill was not just a group of stockbrokers, but a larger, problem-solving organization. The no-bull ads didn't work very well, and there was an outcry from the branch offices. And so the search for a new agency began in 1986.

The winner was Bozell, Jacobs, Kenyon & Eckhardt, which promptly restored one of the best-known corporate symbols in all of advertising. The new motto was "Your World Should Know No Boundaries," and it was intended to herald ML's move into global markets. To launch the new campaign, the firm bought out all of the advertising pages for the January 5, 1987, issue of *Fortune,* marking the first time in the illustrious history of the magazine that a single advertiser sponsored an entire issue. Chuck Peebler, Bozell's leader, was also a Schreyer type of guy, and even though Bozell was a less prominent firm than many of the others that competed, I think that personal dynamic won the day.

With a new company image, things appeared to be on an upswing. But three months later, in April 1987, there came one of the darkest moments in ML history, one that Schreyer called "my Chernobyl"—a reference to the infamous accident at a Russian nuclear power station that had occurred just twelve months earlier. Through unauthorized antics by a senior trader in mortgage-backed securities, called IO/POs (interest only/principal only), the company absorbed a loss of some $377 million and earned a dubious distinction in Wall Street history: the largest one-day trading loss ever by one firm. Schreyer remembers the moment he learned of the disaster: "My first feelings were anger. I felt betrayed. Then I had a sense of total frustration. I thought: How can you control 50,000 employees? Then, I don't really know why, I thought of Gorbachev and the call he got on the meltdown at Chernobyl. This was my Chernobyl. I sat there and thought, *Why me, Lord, why me?"*

Most employees were shocked and dismayed, but the Private Client people were furious. This confirmed all their fears about the Capital Markets Group. Merrill Lynch had grown up as a retail powerhouse, and they feared that investment bankers and traders were taking over the firm. It was felt that they were paid too much, they didn't respect the financial consultants, and they were taking too much risk. Howie Rubin, the rogue trader responsible for the loss, was everything they feared. Moreover, since most of the senior office managers and financial consultants were shareholders, their personal pocketbooks were affected. Bill and Dan hosted a direct satellite broadcast town hall meeting for all of the offices, and it had

100 percent attendance. After they reported what had happened, they opened the meeting up for questions, and the first was, "Who the hell is accountable for this? Who's in charge?" Unfortunately, the caustic tone of the question caught Bill and Dan by surprise, and they looked quizzically at each other to see who would answer. The second or two it took them to respond seemed like minutes, and it gave the impression that they were confused and *not* in charge. The broadcast was a disaster and the field was up in arms. Some referred to Bill and Dan as "Bartles and James," a reference to two goofy guys in a TV commercial for wine coolers. At the time I was Mid-Atlantic regional director and spent weeks defending the firm's leadership and assuring everyone that we would come out of this stronger. In fact, we did, and Dan in particular emerged as a strong and effective leader.

To prevent another meltdown at the World Financial Center and tighten up on its mortgage-trading operation, these activities were temporarily placed under the direction of Dan, who set up a crisis head-quarters just off the trading floor. Bill then enlisted former Secretary of State William P. Rogers and former SEC Commissioner Irving Pollack to conduct an intensive review of the entire trading operation. Dan quickly discovered an out-of-control risk management system operated by arrogant traders. Records of misdeeds had been stashed away in desk drawers by traders who bet the wrong way on the direction of interest rates. Some of them inflamed Dan's Irish temper by asking for reassurances that the losses wouldn't affect their bonuses. Dan's response: "This is not gambling. I'm setting up parameters here. If you go outside them, I'll break your legs." One senior executive in the Debt Division asked Dan to protect the bonuses of his group who had performed well. "Get the f— out of here," Dan yelled.

The outgrowth of the Rogers–Pollack investigation was the establishment of a risk management department that set the standard for the rest of Wall Street. Originally Gene Rotberg, the former head of the World Bank, was recruited to head Risk Management and reported directly to Dan. However, after a while Dan realized that a better person from within the firm existed, and he promoted Dan Napoli, the director of the Government Securities Division, to replace Rotberg. Dan was made a member of the Executive Committee and did a remarkable job. The new Risk unit had broad powers to set standards and monitor risk in every security, and to order the trading desk to retreat from a position it judged improper. Dan firmly believed that flesh-and-blood sources were the keys to successful risk management. He cultivated relationships with junior accounts. "They see things first," he liked to say. "Almost every trading debacle was sitting on some accountant's desk." Until Stan O'Neal became CEO, Risk Management reported to the top of the firm. ML also signaled the importance it placed on its own reputation by making its chief counsel, Steve Hammerman, a vice chairman of the board.

The mortgage loss, embarrassing though it was, had positive side effects in that the reassessment of its internal procedures enabled the firm to avoid a series of costly and damaging blunders that plagued most of its competitors in the 1990s, and it was used by executives for years as an example of the need for constant vigilance against wrongdoing. The firm's basic commitment to the commandments laid down a half-century earlier by Charlie Merrill was restated by Schreyer: "No one's bottom line is more important than the reputation of the firm." That dictum, along with the efforts of a tough Compliance Department to actively protect its integrity, kept ML out of stormy waters that hobbled and in some cases destroyed competitors like Drexel Burnham Lambert, Bache, and Salomon Brothers. During this period, the days of the Levine-Milken-Boesky scandals, it seemed as though Merrill Lynch was one of the few major Wall Street firms that didn't have a book written about it (with titles like *Den of Thieves* and *Barbarians at the Gate*). In fact, to the contrary, ML even got favorable publicity because its Compliance Department provided important leads in helping the Securities and Exchange Commission investigate those scandals.

In *Den of Thieves*, the Pulitzer Prize–winning account of the insider-trading scandals of the 1980s, James B. Stewart of *The Wall Street Journal* makes an important point about Merrill Lynch's integrity:

> Poorly paid, shunned by upper-level managers and partners, compliance officers were kept from the center of the action. They were paid to maintain an appearance of self-policing in the securities industry—without actually instigating too many investigations.

Merrill Lynch, however, was more serious about compliance than most firms. Its general counsel, Stephen Hammerman, set the tone, insisting on thorough monitoring of customer and account-executive trading. Hammerman had built the largest compliance department on Wall Street, with a staff of 75.

And a final silver lining: The mortgage loss also provided important lessons that would be useful six months later in the market collapse.

By eight o'clock on the morning of Monday, October 19, 1987, John Leech knew it was going to be a rough day. Leech, who managed a group of thirteen Merrill Lynch over-the-counter traders, had seen nothing but disheartening signs for weeks. The previous Friday the market had closed down sharply, and everyone waited with trepidation for the markets to open on Monday. There were rumors of war in the Persian Gulf. Washington was full of talk about a tax on takeovers. The market had slumped 234 points the previous week, and brokers had been flooded with sell orders all weekend long. Some twelve hours earlier, the Tokyo exchange had opened for the week with a sharp drop. All night long the wave of despair rolled across the world's time zones and through the financial districts of Hong Kong, Frankfurt, Paris, and London on its way to Wall Street. Leech and his colleagues were broker-dealers whose job was to use ML capital to "make markets" in Apple Computer, Liz Claiborne, Yellow Transport, and fifty-two other OTC securities assigned to them; when the market opened at 9:30 A.M., the whole world was ready to dump stock in their laps. The ML traders did their best to keep trading in their assigned stocks as orderly as possible, and they didn't leave their office until nine-thirty that night after handling more than 6,000 trades. Many of their counterparts at other firms stayed on the sidelines, refusing to handle trades, causing prices on the OTC market to jump wildly. Investors complained about other firms, but Leech and his traders later got high marks up and down Wall Street for continuing to buy stocks.

Investors had been worried for months that a drop was coming, and now during one astonishing day they all seemed to be trying to get out at once. The Big Board's transactions tape could handle 900 trades per minute, but by early afternoon it was running nearly three hours late, and the NYSE itself came perilously close to shutting down. Panic-driven trading sent the Dow Jones Industrial Average plummeting 508 points—nearly 23 percent—a much larger drop than the 12.8 percent decrease on October 28, 1929, the infamous day of the Great Crash. The only certainty at the four P.M. closing bell was that Wall Street had stumbled into uncharted waters, and Schreyer and Tully moved quickly to project an image of calm control. In an unusual statement released first to ML employees, then to the firm's customers and the general public, they said: "We remain confident in the financial markets, and in the underlying value of financial assets in this climate. It is critical that reason and objectivity prevail. More than any other time, our customers will be relying on our financial strength, our proud tradition of trustworthiness and our leadership in providing the best professional guidance available anywhere." *The Wall Street Journal* picked up the statement and placed it high in its main story the next day on the worst single trading session in American financial history.

The following day, Schreyer put together a crisis management team to keep Merrill Lynch on course and active in all markets on behalf of its customers. Part of the plan was that at seven o'clock every morning the firm's top executives would meet with its key market and economic experts, trading managers, investment bankers, legal advisers, and communications personnel. "Today is going to be a day when we're going to be remembered by how we act," Schreyer told the assemblage. "I want you folks to get out there. I don't want you to be heroes, but I want you to be certain you answer the phones, treat our clients with respect, and give them good counsel and advice." To publicly reaffirm its own financial strength, Merrill Lynch authorized the repurchase of 5 million shares of its own stock. Then it announced it would buy A. B. Tompane, a troubled NYSE specialist unit and a venerable Wall Street institution that had survived the 1929 Crash. In doing so, ML became the first large securities firm to take over a Big Board specialist unit since rules on such acquisitions were eased.

There were Merrill Lynch ads running, as scheduled, between innings of the telecasts of the World Series games a few nights later, but they were very different from the originally planned images of a massive bull riding off into the sunset. Instead, there was the somber face of Bill Schreyer calling for an end to emotionalism. Harking back to the old ad campaigns of the 1970s, Schreyer said, "At Merrill Lynch, we're still bullish on America." There were also newspaper ads, which expanded on the same theme. This was Bill's finest hour and many credit this message for restoring calm to the markets. Although Larry Speakes did not last very long at Merrill Lynch as communications director (he resigned after fifteen months in 1988 after reports that he had fabricated quotes while serving as Ronald Reagan's former press secretary), Larry does deserve the credit for convincing Bill to make that TV ad. It was risky, but it worked, and I think as much as anything it solidified the legacy of Bill Schreyer, making it more apparent to all that he was the leader at Merrill Lynch.

Company executives faced the task of shoring up the morale not only of customers, but of the shell-shocked sales force as well. Many of ML's youthful brokers had known nothing but good times up until now, and in a single day, their world of eager clients and easy commissions had vanished. Schreyer and Tully turned to the ML Video Network. Just hours after the market closed on October 19, the network carried a twenty-six-minute telecast to all field personnel from the New York studio. It provided analysis, put the market drop into perspective, and gave brokers suggestions about what to say to customers. The network also put together the substitute commercials that aired during the World Series.

In stark contrast to the sentiment reflected in the "Bartles and James" comments earlier in the year, Bill and Dan were viewed as strong leaders and Merrill was seen as the stalwart firm on Wall Street. The *Pittsburgh Press* ran a cartoon depicting Ronald Reagan saying, "Get my financial advisers on the phone," and in the next frame, he said, "Hello, Merrill Lynch?" I purchased a copy of that memorable cartoon and have it hanging in my home today.

While some of Merrill's clients suffered vast losses, these were people who did not follow the asset allocation strategy that Launny had been preaching. The vast majority of the firm's financial consultants had their clients diversified so that most of them did not have a majority of their holdings in equities. Therefore, when the

Federal Reserve cut rates to stabilize the markets, bond prices went up, and many clients saw a far less severe decline in their monthly statements than they had feared. Launny's strategy was even more broadly embraced going forward.

The most important outcome of the firm's steady and decisive leadership during the crisis was that its loyal client base was retained. While many of the company's 6 million customers did pull money out of equities, for the most part they moved it to other forms of investments in their ML accounts and added steadily to them over the next year. In the wake of the crash, the firm pursued strategies designed to create broader and deeper relationships with clients—total financial relationships embracing both asset and liability management. It would be a further democratization of American finance, for the middle class would be offered services once available only to the very rich.

Critics who complained that Schreyer and Tully were sales-oriented executives who lacked the management skills needed to guide a Wall Street giant into the 1990s would be silenced over the next few years. One of the first important post-crash decisions made by the pair was not to buy E. F. Hutton, a troubled firm that put itself up for sale in 1988. Shearson Lehman Brothers had been courting Hutton; by acquiring the firm, Shearson would double its broker ranks and become more competitive with Merrill Lynch. Schreyer and Tully decided they would not make an offer—but left the clear impression that they would. As a result, Shearson came in with a hefty—and the only—bid for Hutton at $1 billion. It was a costly mistake that only made ML stronger.

The business climate became more difficult over the next few years, and it was clear that Merrill, like other firms, needed to take a hard look at its business. Dan Tully began his red-dot crusade in January 1990, patrolling the offices of the World Financial Center and slapping nickel-sized red-dot stickers on any object deemed unnecessary, excessive, duplicative, superfluous, obsolete, underused, unused, abandoned, or extravagant. Tully dotted furniture, computers, desk lamps, desks, bookcases, photocopiers. The stewards of these objects had twenty-four hours to prove they were needed, or they were gone. Nothing eluded Dan's single-minded campaign: He even found an extension telephone in Schreyer's thirty-second-floor office and slapped a red dot on that. After the first week, people began hiding from him. "They were afraid I'd put a red dot on their forehead," he joked. But Tully was serious. His two-week campaign made an infinitesimal dent in Merrill Lynch's expenses, which were running at about $11.5 billion a year, but he was trying to symbolize a new era for Merrill Lynch: Cost-cutting was going to receive more than the lip service it had for most of the nineteen years since the firm went public.

At the root of the parsimony was shareholder dismay over the company's performance. Ironically, Merrill Lynch—the giant of Wall Street whose experts could deftly analyze the capital structure of a corporation and dispense wisdom to the outside world on how to improve it—did a miserable job of managing itself. Between 1985 and 1989, while its competitors averaged a return on equity (ROE) of 15 percent, ML averaged under 11 percent, and in 1990 it plunged to 5.8 percent. "My kids could have done a better job running the company," Tully recalls. Merrill Lynch was America's largest brokerage, employed the most retail brokers, had the most comprehensive research team, and held more assets than any other firm on Wall Street. Everything was impressive about the company except its bottom line. The bounty of the go-go years and bull market of the 1980s never found its way to ML shareholders—at least from that portion of their portfolios. The firm took a pre-tax charge of $470 million for the fourth quarter of 1989, resulting in a loss for the year of $23 million. This was Merrill's first annual loss since 1941 and not something that either Schreyer or Tully wanted on their records. Bill later said, "You can get away with a write-off of this size once, but not twice." Some $125 million of the charge was related to the reduction of the work force, another $125 million went for costs involved in the disposal of assets, and $220 million was the result of excess office space in the World Financial Center.

ML had developed a reputation for free spending and weak controls, and much of it was deserved. Employees separated by one floor at the World Financial Center used United Parcel Service to send each other packages and ML trading floors were the largest on Wall Street, with desks piled high with expensive, unused computer equipment. (at one point, a newspaper cartoonist depicted a UPS plane flying from one floor to a lower one). When shareholders got wind of these loose controls, there was alarm and even talk of revolution. Eddie Lynch Jr. wrote a scathing letter to *The New York Times,* and Bill was furious over public criticism from "this pompous little ungrateful ass." It was years before they spoke again. Many people thought that Don Regan should be brought back, and there was talk inside and outside the company that Merrill would need to merge with someone else in order to survive. It was a challenging time, but the board supported Bill, who would later acknowledge that two former White Weld employees, Steve Hammerman and Tom Patrick, had probably saved him.

By 1990, Patrick had convinced Schreyer and Tully that ROE ought to be the yardstick for success and that an initial goal ought to be 15 percent. Reasoning that not all ML operations were a drag on the bottom line, Patrick took the forty-nine individual business units and placed them each in one of three categories: those that were achieving a 15 percent ROE (there were twenty-three), those that weren't (there were seventeen), and those that needed special consideration for one reason or another (there were nine). Under the performance measurement system, the executives running the seventeen underachievers were called into the boardroom and advised that they were about to be "BOPed"—that is, undergo a burden-of-proof scrutiny. They would have to justify the existence of their operations to the entire Executive Committee.

On the heels of the symbolic red-dot campaign came the next evolution of the firm's reorganization. While the two-sector approach (Capital Markets and Consumer Markets) had worked well to develop the global investment banking and institutional businesses, Bill and Dan believed the time had come for the next step. The firm was apportioned into six divisions—Private Client, Asset Management, Insurance, Investment Banking, Debt Markets, and Equity Markets—each headed by a manager with greater responsibilities for increasing revenues and reducing costs. The executives named to lead these areas were, respectively, Launny Steffens, Arthur Zeikel, Tom Patrick, Barry Friedberg, Roger Vasey, and Dave Komansky. Each was named an executive vice president of Merrill Lynch & Co. and became a member of the firm's Executive Management Committee, reporting directly to Dan. Additionally, Jerry Kenney was named EVP of Strategy. Many mistakenly thought that Jerry had been demoted, but they didn't realize what Dan, who was behind the appointment, had in mind: Jerry, a former analyst himself, had one of the best minds on Wall Street, and Dan felt that he would have even greater value to Merrill Lynch if he was focused on the future strategy of the firm.

While Bill was a strong ally of Tom Patrick's and felt that his "burden of proof" exercise when he was CFO may have helped save the Schreyer legacy, Dan was less enamored of him. He put him in charge of insurance, an area that Tom understood well, and replaced him as CFO with Herb Allison, the director of Human Resources, whom Dan had great confidence in. Herb was a person of the highest integrity. He also had a brilliant mind and was not nearly as political as many thought Patrick was. Behind the change was newly available management information showing just where ML was making money and where it wasn't. For many years the firm did not have a clear idea of how it was actually making money because so many of its transactions were interrelated. A consultant suggested an accounting system that would isolate each of the nearly fifty business lines and trace the profitability of each one.

From this evolved the performance measurement system that required each business unit that did not meet a 15 percent ROE to justify its continued existence. Some one hundred different employee-bonus plans were scrapped in favor of a system tied directly to return on equity. Until this time, only Schreyer and Tully had their compensation tied directly to the bottom line. Everyone else's was based on gross revenues. In 1990, the first year of the new system, the ROE was 5.8 percent and bonuses totaled only $19 million.

When the firm had decided to take a $470 million pre-tax write-off in 1989, Bill and Dan reduced the various cash bonus accruals by 15 percent and replaced them with a "synthetic equity" award called the ROE Incentive Compensation Plan. Employees were granted units, which would then be valued at a range of zero to 300 percent of the deferred amount, depending upon the firm's actual ROE in 1990 and 1991. The idea was to get everyone focused on the firm's overall return on equity, which, after all, was what shareholders wanted. There was anger throughout the organization about the use of units, which soon were dubbed "Herbies" since Herb Allison was credited with coming up with this unpopular idea. Employees felt that their bonus formulas had been unfairly adjusted, and they were angry. The branch managers who reported to me at the time felt that management had reneged on its word by changing the compensation plan arbitrarily at year's end. They were particularly bitter that a small area of the Capital Markets Division was impacting them.

At our December managers' meeting, my Mid-Atlantic regional managers presented me with a set of Daiwa golf clubs to acknowledge my recent promotion to the job of senior vice president of the Eastern Division. George Baskerville, who was our manager from Richmond, Virginia, made the presentation in his Southern accent. "Well, Win," he began, "we want to congratulate you and show you our appreciation for your leadership these past few years. We know you're an improving golfer and will probably have to play more in your new job, so this set of Daiwa clubs will hopefully help you remember us. There's only one thing. We've decided to hold back the eight iron and putter. If you perform better, we'll give them to you in three years." Everyone roared laughing. While they were irritated by the reduction in their cash bonus, they still had a sense of humor.

Almost everyone hated the Herbies, and few thought they would be worth anything. Traders were willing to sell them for cents on the dollars, but of course there was no market. At the annual Chowder and Marching Society luncheon, everyone was given a can of beans whose label, bearing the beaming face of Herb Allison, boasted that these "Fresh Herbies" were 85 percent pure. The label included a warning from the Surgeon General—"Contents of This Container May Be Hazardous to Your Compensation"—and instructions specifying that the can could be "opened when ML makes our ROE goal. Don't hold your breath." As always, this was good-natured but hard-hitting Chowder and Marching Society humor. And yet, despite all the grousing, in the end keying compensation to profitability proved to be a powerful incentive. When the ROE jumped to 21 percent in 1991, all of us received nearly three times the amount deferred in 1989, and the units came to be called "Sir Herberts."

By 1993, Schreyer and Tully had reined in ML's costs. Six business units had been red-dotted, a million square feet of office space had been relinquished, and there were 2,200 fewer employees. "If ever a chairman deserved well of his shareholders, Schreyer does," said *Forbes* magazine. "The great bull market in stocks and in underwriting was not, of course, of his making. What he did accomplish was to bring—and keep—Merrill's costs under control." The proof was on the bottom line. The $200 million loss in 1989 became a $200 million profit the following year, a $700 million profit in 1992, and in 1993 profits totaled nearly $900 million. ML was flexing its lean muscles to fight off stronger competition resulting from the merger of the brokerage operations of Shearson Lehman Brothers and Primerica Corp.'s Smith Barney. The price of ML shares skyrocketed in the early 1990s, and the return on equity consistently surpassed the stated goal of 15 percent. ML was the dominant force on Wall Street—the leader in almost every area of capital markets. Its brokers earned more commissions than any other, its investment bankers underwrote more corporate stock and bond issues, and its investment managers supervised more client assets than any financial institution except Fidelity, the giant mutual fund group.

Moreover, the firm had shed the stodgy image that had made it fair game for Wall Street mockery. Suddenly Merrill Lynch was chic, and its competitors were lackluster. Where it once had trouble recruiting top-tier executives, who preferred Morgan Stanley, Salomon, and Goldman, ML now was on the A list of top employers, with salaries and bonuses second to none. Kidder Peabody's No. 1 West Coast broker, who was producing $6 million a year in commissions and was sought by every major house on Wall Street, chose to go with Merrill Lynch.

The long metamorphosis that had expanded a purely retail operation into a combination brokerage and investment bank, begun in the 1960s and fostered by the 1978 purchase of White Weld, was finally beginning to pay off huge dividends. ML's considerable presence in both retail sales and investment banking enabled the firm to take risks not acceptable among its competitors. In addition, the two operations fed off each other in mutually profitable ways. The securities issued to finance institutional clients found a reliable outlet on the retail side. About 20 percent of the commission revenue of ML financial consultants came from underwritings managed by the Capital Markets Division. The fusion of the two financing worlds made ML what one analyst called "a unique beast" because other Wall Street behemoths specialized in only one or the other, but Merrill Lynch succeeded at both. By the mid-1990s, underwriting records were being set amid the longest bull market in Street history, and Merrill Lynch was, by far, Wall Street's No. 1 investment house.

Part of Merrill's rise was the result of its penetration into banking and other non-brokerage business, which it used as a link to its traditional brokerage operations. It offered mortgage and other secured loans and urged its clients who wanted loans for other purposes to borrow against their assets with the firm. It provided across-the-board banking services for individuals and companies. Just as small individual investors had been ignored by brokerages fifty years earlier, ML built a new revenue source by helping run the financial affairs of small businesses, offering them lines of credit, cash management, retirement planning, investment services, and business valuation advice. In its longtime goal to boost fee-based income to insulate itself against the fickleness of the stock market, Merrill Lynch not only provided financial services for the American middle class, it tried to anticipate them. Tully hoped that eventually fees would cover 100 percent of the firm's expenses. As ML drew more and more income from steady fees, it became far more stable than cyclical securities firms linked to market volatility—and its stock price soared.

The firm was cashing in on a revolution in the financial services industry that saw not just brokerages but thousands of entities, including investment firms, mutual fund companies, savings and loan associations, banks, and credit unions, competing to handle Americans' money. Not only had the stock market recovered from the disaster of October 1987, its popularity was growing rapidly. Between 1983 and 1995, the number of American households owning stocks, either directly or through mutual funds and pension plans, rose from 19 percent to 41 percent.

I n the year before his retirement, Bill spent much of his time traveling the globe to say good-bye to employees and clients, a farewell tour that became affectionately known as "the endless retirement." But it was important for Bill to leave his beloved firm in this fashion.

When Bill Schreyer turned over the role of CEO to Dan Tully in May 1993, he reflected on the enormous changes that had occurred at the company since he joined it in 1948. "And yet after all those years one thing had remained the same," he said. "Merrill Lynch was still a meritocracy, a place where talent and hard work were rewarded, and integrity and client service were the two most important principles; where every employee could be proud of our global reputation."

In other words, what really mattered was still in place, and the transition from Bill Schreyer to Dan Tully was seamless.

Bill was not the deepest thinker. He didn't have the intelligence of a Don Regan or the creativity of a Charlie Merrill. At times he could be a bit selfish. But he had two attributes that made him an extremely effective leader of Merrill Lynch: He recognized talent and surrounded himself with excellent people, and he was an unfailing optimist who woke up every day believing it was going to be a great day! Bill was always bullish, and it was infectious on the organization. His eight years had their ups and downs, but he left Merrill in better shape and well-positioned for the future.

Merrill Lynch & Co., Inc.

One Liberty Plaza
165 Broadway
New York, New York 10080
212 637 7455

 **Merrill Lynch**

August 20, 1986

Mr. and Mrs. Winthrop H. Smith, Jr.
11811 Piney Glen Lane
Potomac, MD 20854

Dear Win and Maggie:

The gala gathering at The New-York Historical Society to
mark our Centennial last fall remains a bright spot in our
memory and an inspiration to carry on the Legacy to which
your father contributed so greatly.

While it has taken time to sort through and assemble the
many fine pictures taken that evening, we hope you will
enjoy this souvenir album -- a souvenir not only of a grand
evening but of the legacy in which we all share.

Sincerely,

Bill

William A. Schreyer

J3's
Dan

Daniel P. Tully

Hellen Plummer, Dan Tully, Margaret and Ken Crosby

Charles Merrill and Merrill Magowan

Cinnie Magowan and Hal Berry

Dakin Ferris, Hellen Plummer, Joyce Ferris and Jim Merrill

Ken Crosby, Hellen Plummer, Jim Merrill, and Doris Magowan

Beth Smith, Beth Ross, George Beane, and Charles Ross

Arthur Urciuoli, Jane Shallcross, Mike and Margaret McCarthy

Bill Schreyer and Don Regan

Dan Tully, Bill Rogers, Bill Schreyer, and Jill Conway

Steve Hammerman

Alice Rooke with Ed Moriarty

Charles Merrill with Henry and Alice Hecht

General Wilson, Ned Ball, and Harry Anderson

Mary Lou and Roger Birk with Joyce Ferris

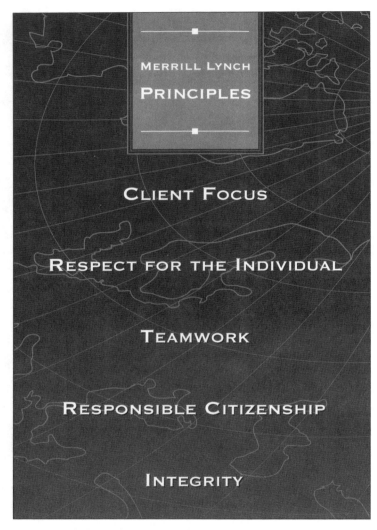

MERRILL LYNCH

PRINCIPLES

CLIENT FOCUS

RESPECT FOR THE INDIVIDUAL

TEAMWORK

RESPONSIBLE CITIZENSHIP

INTEGRITY

Many believe that Dan Tully's greatest achievement as CEO of Merrill Lynch was to capsulize the core values into five elements known as "The Principles." These words were etched outside company headquarters and displayed in offices worldwide in their local languages.

CHAPTER ELEVEN

Cementing
the Principles

(1993–1997)

D aniel Patrick Tully was the ninth leader of Merrill Lynch. Even though I admired all of his predecessors, Dan was the one I most respected, and the one who taught me the most about leadership. Dan was not as brilliant as Don Regan, as strategic as Charlie Merrill, as sophisticated as George Leness, or as worldly as Bill Schreyer. Dan was humble as well as genuine. He could be tough, but never rough. He was a leader with the highest of ethical standards. And he was also just a nice man whom people loved to work for. In style he was closest to my father, and like my father, Dan was loved and respected.

A graduate of St. John's University in New York, Dan was the son of Irish Catholics who lived in Queens. He studied accounting in college and landed a job in the operations area of Merrill Lynch in 1955. Dan often told the story of how when he told his mother he was going to work for Merrill Lynch, Pierce, Fenner & Beane, she said she was proud of him for joining a prestigious advertising firm. Almost immediately, Dan was told that he was being sent to Stamford, Connecticut, to work for Don Evers, the office manager there. Thinking he was headed for Stanford in California, he went home that evening to tell his wife, Gracie, the bad news. Dan had grown up in Queens and never strayed very far from his family, home, and church.

At first, Dan commuted by train to Stamford but eventually Evers told him that if he was going to be part of the team, he needed to be a member of the community (this was one of the firm's core principles), and so Dan moved to Connecticut and immediately became involved in the community, joining the Kiwanis and Rotary Club; later he became chairman of the local hospital board and oversaw a major capital campaign. A gregarious and affable Irishman who enjoyed a good beer and a round of golf, Dan met and got along with almost everyone. Despite his social skills, though, he was never great at remembering names, so he called everyone "pal." It didn't matter how well he knew you, you were often just "pal." Even Gracie, his wife, received that honor occasionally in public.

He was good with numbers, though, and it didn't take him long to understand that you could make a lot more money in sales than in operations, so, as he recalls, he "petitioned Mr. Evers" to let him go into the account executive training program, and Evers agreed. Upon graduation from the program, he returned to Stamford and became one of the office's top account executives. Before long Evers recognized Dan's management talents and made him the sales manager in addition to running his own book of business. Dan eventually became the unofficial office leader. As Evers neared retirement age, he spoke to Dan about succeeding him, but it was company policy that when you were promoted to management, you had to move to a new office. The thinking behind this rule was that one could more effectively lead account executives who had not once been one's peers.

But Dan is a persistent man and was a persuasive salesman, so he went down to visit Don Regan, who at the time supervised all the branch offices. He made his case to Don that he should be allowed to return to Stamford, and when the meeting ended, Don affectionately tapped him lightly on his chin with a fist and said, "Relax, kid." Dan was permitted to become the manager of the Stamford office.

For years, many of Dan's higher-ups tried to get him to take a "promotion" and move to headquarters in the heart of Wall Street, but he resisted, preferring instead to manage his successful office in Stamford and have enough free time to spend with Gracie and their young children. Finally, in the late 1970s, Dan relented and moved down to take over marketing, where he worked for Ross Kenzie, who was the executive vice president in charge of the retail side of Merrill Lynch. Dan said that what finally motivated him to move was that he wanted to make a difference—and be sure some "other stiffs didn't get the job."

In his memoir, *Still Bullish on America*, Bill Schreyer described Dan this way:

> He was a hands-on guy—exactly what you wanted in a chief operating officer—and sometimes he'd get his Irish up, and there would be a little bit of a confrontation with someone. But he tempered that beautifully as time went on—didn't lose his steadfastness or determination, but just mellowed a little bit. He was not a Ross Perot type—a dictator who ruled by fear.
>
> Dan had a great sense of humility, at least in terms of what the prospect of becoming CEO meant to him. He viewed each chairman and CEO as just part of a continuum of the history of an institution that was greater than any one individual. Even when he had record results, he was always careful to note that in ten, twenty, or one hundred years, each revenue and profit figure would have multiple zeroes behind it. In other words, don't get too full of yourself.

A few months before he stepped down as chairman in mid-1993, Schreyer turned to his successor at Merrill Lynch's Global Leadership Conference and said, "Danny Boy, we've got a great thing going. Let's not screw it up." Since he chose him for the No. 2 position in 1985, Schreyer had broken company tradition by giving Dan unprecedented powers, and this long association was an assurance that there would be no drastic changes. Nor were any needed.

In mid-1993, the *International Financing Review* observed:

> The transformation of Merrill from a lumbering also-ran to a streamlined international investment bank has essentially been achieved over the past 10 years. While Don Regan was probably Merrill's best known leader, it is the work of the less flamboyant Bill Schreyer and the new chief executive, Dan Tully, which has created the firm's present success. Under Regan, ML was a plodding, rambling organization involved in too many low-margin businesses.

This is probably a bit tough on Don, but the well-regarded *IFR* got it right about the Schreyer–Tully Merrill Lynch, and it was only going to get better over the next seven years.

That same week, the *Financial Times* said:

> During Mr. Tully and Mr. Schreyer's tenure, Merrill has grown from one of several dominant firms on Wall Street, to THE dominant force. Today, the firm is pre-eminent in almost every area of the US capital markets—its brokers earn more commissions than any other firm, its investment bankers underwrite the most corporate stock and bond issues and its investment managers handle more client assets than any financial institution except Fidelity, the mutual funds group.

By the time Dan took over in 1993, ML was a financial powerhouse and Wall Street's most profitable firm. Its underwriting skills teamed up with its distribution capabilities to produce pre-tax earnings of nearly $2 billion. Its twelve thousand brokers—the world's largest financial sales force—served more than 6 million clients. Suddenly Merrill Lynch was the first choice for the Street's talented elite. *The Wall Street Journal* offered this assessment:

> Merrill is the nation's biggest brokerage firm. It is the second-largest mutual-fund company, overseeing $115 billion in fund assets, and the largest vendor of money-market funds. It manages $71 billion in individual retirement accounts—more than the 102 largest banks combined. It is the top trader of exchange-listed stocks. In investment banking, it is the biggest underwriter; it helps bring to market nearly one-fifth of all new U.S. stock and bond issues, earning $878 million in underwriting fees so far this year. It has $13 billion of insurance assets, making it the nation's 24th-largest insurer, and services $5 billion of home-mortgage loans.

Clearly, the company was no longer focused solely on "bringing Wall Street to Main Street." But when CEM and my father had put that idea into practice, it was a sound business decision because there were middle-class Americans with money to invest. And it worked. The stock market had become a central feature of American life. What would Charlie and my father have thought about what the company had become? Even though they might not recognize the firm they had put together a half-century earlier, I think they would have approved. They would have liked the broadening of the company operations and the transformation of brokers into financial consultants. But most important, they would have been thrilled that the principles they'd operated under were still in sync with the mantra of one of their successors.

From his office overlooking New York Harbor (complete with kelly green carpeting in tribute to his Irish heritage), Dan Tully—the onetime ace stickballer from the sidewalks of Queens—dashed off memos with a green felt pen and directed the largest financial services corporation in the world. He told anyone who would listen that the greatest thing about his job was that, in terms of competition, he didn't have to contend with the likes of a Merrill Lynch. Dan was always careful to praise his predecessors rather than take sole credit for what the company achieved under his watch, and he always showed his respect by referring to "Mr. Merrill and Mr. Smith" rather than saying "Charlie and Win." Dan did many things very differently from Bill and prior CEOs, but he never publicly criticized them and always gave them the respect they deserved.

Dan put his own fingerprints on Merrill Lynch in his first Annual Report by emphasizing the company's "Principles for Performance":

> In 1993 Merrill Lynch was responsible to more countries, companies and individuals for more underwriting and financial advice in more markets and across more borders than any firm in history. We succeeded by letting our Principles light our way—the same unchanging Principles that have guided us for 100 years.
>
> **Client Focus** – Our clients come first. They are the driving force behind everything we do.
>
> **Respect for the Individual** – We believe in treating everyone with dignity, whether an employee, shareholder, client or member of the general public.

Teamwork – We strive for seamless integration of services because in our clients' eyes there is only one Merrill Lynch.

Responsible Citizenship – We seek to improve the quality of life in the communities where we live and work.

Integrity – No one's personal bottom line is more important than the reputation of our company.

Dan had many great achievements over his long career, but I and many others believe that his most important was taking the nine Merrill Lynch Principles (established by Charlie Merrill and my dad in 1940 and dubbed "the Ten Commandments") and distilling them into these five major elements: Client Focus, Respect for the Individual, Teamwork, Responsible Citizenship, and Integrity.

These words were etched in marble outside the headquarters at the World Financial Center. These words were displayed on executives' desks, outside elevators, and in hallways. These words appeared on plaques in company offices all over the world—Thailand, South Africa, Buenos Aires, London, Hong Kong—all in the local language. These words flashed by on computer screen savers. These words appeared on the ML Web site with this introduction:

Our corporate culture at Merrill Lynch is the sum total of what we believe and think, how we work together as colleagues and how we conduct ourselves as individuals. It is the way we treat our clients, our shareholders, our fellow employees, our neighbors and the public in general. It is *who we are*. And while our corporate culture is by nature indefinable, it begins and ends with certain Principles that underline our success as a business and as individuals. Our future growth and prosperity depends on our continued commitment to these Principles and our ability to instill them in others.

Dan always paid tribute to Charlie Merrill and my father, saying the original Principles had "helped guide me in my career." He said the Principles were "reworded, reformatted, and given a more physical profile" in order to "maintain and enhance" the corporate culture. He has always scoffed at the idea that the capsule Principles were his legacy, and insisted rather that he considered them to be part of an inviolate moral code that gave Merrill Lynch a distinct corporate culture. "Who can argue with them?" he asked. It's a rhetorical question.

There was nothing that Dan was more passionate about than these Principles. They were his compass, and he made them ours as well. There were many Executive Committee meetings when we debated a decision, and Dan would look up at the portraits of Merrill and my father that hung in our boardroom. Next to them were the Principles. "Okay, is this in our clients' interests?" he would ask. "Are we comfortable reading about this on the front page of *The Wall Street Journal* tomorrow?" Dan never allowed any decision to be made that he felt violated any of the five Principles.

I n addition to capsulizing the Principles, Dan also quickly put his executive team in place. He had an Executive Committee of sixteen: Herb Allison (EVP, Investment Banking), Paul Critchlow (SVP, Marketing and Communications), Barry Friedberg (EVP & Chairman, Investment Banking), Ed Goldberg (EVP, Operations, Systems and Technology), Steve Hammerman (Vice Chairman of the Board and General Counsel), John Heimann (Chairman, Global Financial Institutions), Jerry Kenney (EVP, Corporate Strategy, Credit and Research), Dave Komansky (EVP, Debt and Equity Markets), Dan Napoli (SVP, Risk Management), Tom Patrick (EVP and Chairman, Special Advisory Services), Win Smith (EVP and Chairman, Merrill Lynch International), Launny Steffens (EVP, Private Client Group), Roger Vasey (EVP, Senior Advisor), Pat Walsh (EVP, Human Resources), Joe Willett (SVP, Chief Financial Officer), and Arthur Zeikel (EVP, Asset Management Group). This was a first-class team whose members all respected one another.

But Dan also created two new organizational structures.

"As part of our ongoing evolution from a transaction-driven sales organization to one that is client-focused and market driven," he explained at the time, "we established the Office of the Chairman and the Office of the Chief Executive. In the Office of the CEO, Steve Hammerman and I are joined by Herb Allison, Dave Komansky, and

Launny Steffens." This made it clear that while there were sixteen Executive Committee members, Dan was relying on four in particular to be his "super committee." While the rest of us participated in most strategic discussions, it was really this group of five that made the final decisions. "In the Office of the Chairman," Dan said, "Mr. Hammerman and I are joined by Barry Friedberg, John Heimann and Tom Patrick. This office elevates client focus to the highest executive levels of the company, bringing to bear the full experience and resources of senior management on behalf of clients."

Dan had tremendous respect for Barry Friedberg but thought he was a much better investment banker than manager, so he'd replaced him as the leader of the Investment Banking Division with Herb Allison. In Dan's eyes he was in no way demoting Barry, but rather placing him in the right job where he could be most effective for Merrill Lynch. Putting Herb into his first important "line" job would allow Dan to see if Herb had the right stuff to become president. Since Launny had effectively taken himself out of contention, Dan was signaling early that Herb and Dave were the two contenders to become president and ultimately his successor. Dan also believed that John Heimann would play an important role in helping our investment bankers make inroads with governments and global financial institutions, and that being a member of the Office of the Chairman would signal the importance of his role: He had direct access to the CEO, after all.

Putting Tom Patrick into the Office of the Chairman was a bit more subtle. The truth is Dan didn't trust him and didn't want him in an executive role, but he also realized that Patrick had strong allies in Steve Hammerman and Bob Luciano, a board member, and was very close to Bill Schreyer, so rather than firing him or demoting him, he placed him in the Office of the Chairman and allowed him to work out of the investment banking office in Chicago. Even when he was CFO, Tom never moved his residence from Chicago and commuted back there every weekend. By this move, Tully had Patrick "out of sight and out of mind" and did not encourage him to come to New York for our weekly Executive Management Committee meetings.

Tully's team was in place.

I t was a great time to be on Wall Street. As Charles Geisst recalls in his 2004 book, *Wall Street: A History*:

> The strong market continued into the mid-1990s and became the largest bull market in Wall Street history. The merger trend continued on the back of low interest rates, a relatively cheap dollar and extraordinary demand for stocks, mostly by mutual funds. Merger activity increased to record amounts. Deals were being struck across the spectrum, from mining and manufacturing companies to transportation companies and utilities. Underwriting of new issues set records in both 1995 and 1996 as all sorts of new securities, from initial public offerings to exotic asset-backed bonds, increased in volume. Merrill Lynch was Wall Street's premier investment banking house, leading underwriting by a large margin over its nearest rivals, Lehman Brothers, Morgan Stanley and Goldman Sachs. Profitability for the Street hit record levels in almost every category.

In 1993, Merrill earned $1.4 billion and its stock hit a high of $51 per share in the fourth quarter. Total assets held in Merrill Lynch client accounts rose to $536 billion, and Launny Steffens set his sights on reaching $1 trillion by the end of the decade. Meanwhile, assets in Merrill Lynch Asset Management rose to $160 billion. *Investment Dealer's Digest* ranked the firm No. 1 in global debt and equity underwriting for the fifth consecutive year, and No. 1 in U.S. domestic debt and equity underwriting for the sixth consecutive year. Merrill was named "Equity House of the Year" by *International Financing Review* and took top honors in the *Institutional Investor* All-American Reseach rankings, for a total of fifty-six team positions. It was a great first year for Dan, and we felt enormous pride in being part of an organization that was rooted in great Principles and, in baseball parlance, was hitting the cover off of the ball. Morale was high and so, too, was our belief that we were part of something very special. We had a swagger that was plainly evident throughout every department of Merrill worldwide.

For most Wall Street firms, 1994 was not a good year, but ML did well. While earnings dipped to just over $1 billion from the prior years, we still made an 18.6 percent return on equity. Goldman Sachs was in turmoil, and for the first time in years, its managing directors were leaving to join other firms, including Merrill Lynch. We hired a number of superb professionals like Claudio Aguirre, who led Goldman's investment banking team in Spain. Claudio helped us win many important investment banking mandates, including the privatization of the Spanish telephone company. He later was promoted to work for me as the European director of our private wealth business.

Under Dan, Merrill Lynch continued to dominate retail brokerage (or Private Client, as we were now calling it), surged forward to commanding market shares in nearly all capital markets activities, and became a leader in offering strategic advice to businesses. The firm intensified its asset-gathering strategy and showed the rest of Wall Street how to minimize the impact of the historic volatility of the financial markets by increasing the share of its revenues coming from fees rather than from commissions, which were much more unpredictable. Its competitors in both the securities and banking industries could only look on in envy and admiration, and by this time Dan had earned the respect not only of his industry peers but of CEOs from many other industries as well.

Arthur Levitt, the chairman of the Securities Exchange Commission, appointed Dan to head a study of Wall Street compensation practices; he oversaw a committee whose members included business heavyweights like Warren Buffett and Jack Welch. Buffett had stepped in to salvage Salomon Brothers from a government trading scandal and Welch's General Electric had purchased Kidder, Peabody. When the study was completed, a press conference with Levitt and all members of the committee was held. Dan delivered the results and the floor was opened to questions from the press.

Dan chuckles when he recalls that all the questions were directed to Buffett, and the rest of the committee just sat by and listened. Afterward, Arthur Levitt took the committee members to lunch. "I'm paying," Levitt told them, "since I'm not allowed to be treated by anyone from the securities industry. In my opinion this is the best restaurant in Washington, and the steak tartar is to die for."

Dan recalled that when it came time for Buffett to order, he asked for two hamburgers and a Cherry Coke. Buffett and Tully were kindred spirits in many ways. Despite the attention on Buffett that day, Arthur Levitt was a huge fan of Dan Tully's and not only admired his leadership qualities, but also his integrity and the Principles that he continued to enunciate.

A fter years of trying to reach the top of the "glamorous" mergers and acquisitions field, ML's efforts paid off big-time on a single day, April 23, 1996, when it served as an adviser on two of the biggest deals in business history. The firm advised Bell Atlantic on its $23 billion merger with Nynex Corp., and Cisco Systems Inc. on its $4 billion acquisition of Stratacom Inc. For all of 1996, ML served as adviser on sixty-four deals, worth a total of $57 billion, placing it ahead of the those longtime M&A stalwarts, Goldman Sachs and Morgan Stanley. Merrill had structured another highly complex blue-chip deal a year earlier when it was used in Ingersoll Rand's hostile acquisition of the Clark Equipment Company. Of course, ML had first dipped its toes in the lucrative M&A market when it acquired White Weld back in 1978, and from there it was a long uphill march to the top. Initially it used a strategy of "moving up the yield curve."

After Roger Vasey was hired from AG Becker in 1979, he moved Merrill Lynch into the leadership position in commercial paper issuance, and he got the company into a dialogue with the treasurers of the largest corporations. Vasey then expanded Merrill's capabilities in all debt categories, and in a few years the firm was leading the league tables in almost all debt instruments for corporations and governments, with the notable exception of mortgages. Vasey built an aggressive team that sometimes sparred with the firm's investment bankers, who thought that all communication to a client should flow through them.

Barry Friedberg, another AG Becker alumnus, was named head of the Investment Banking Division in 1994. By this time Merrill had a leading research and institutional equity position, but it had not yet leveraged these capabilities into investment banking dominance. In changing Tom Chrystie's focus on selling the retail distribution strength of Merrill Lynch, Friedberg realized that the more effective message was selling the institutional placement excellence of the firm and thereby moving it from a co-manager spot into the book-running position, which meant we would control the allocation of the shares. Since CEOs of companies usually pay far more attention to equity issues than debt issues, being the lead manager of an equity issue allowed Merrill's investment bankers to deal directly with CEOs, who made the M&A decisions.

Meanwhile, under Launny Steffens and Arch Urciuoli, ML's Business Financial Services Division began an aggressive program of offering small businesses lines of credit, cash management, retirement planning, investment services, business valuation, and succession advice. As a result, small businesses that had met with resistance from the more traditional banks were getting the green light to grow with Merrill. For example, when a Brooklyn construction firm, Dak Electrical Contracting Corporation, found itself unable to expand its credit line from its longtime commercial bank, it turned to Merrill's BFS division. "The rates were terrific, the terms were fine, and there were no covenants we couldn't live with," Dak Chief Financial Officer Joseph Guddemi told *Crain's New York Business*. In 1996 the unit partnered with Mobil Oil Corp. to offer business planning, investment, and retirement services to Mobil's 7,700 service station franchisees. Merrill innovation once again was catching banks flat-footed and opening up opportunity for the firm's financial consultants to expand their services to small-business owners.

While Dan was CEO, the success of Merrill's strategy of bringing Wall Street to Main Street was confirmed when one of our clients, Anne Scheiber, died in 1993. She was a frugal Manhattan woman, and for twenty-two years ML financial consultant William Fay had her as a client. Scheiber had retired as an auditor for the Internal Revenue Service in 1944, and for the next half-century she, with the help of Merrill Lynch, grew a nest egg of $5,000 into $22 million. What got her national attention, though, was that she left almost every penny of it to Yeshiva University for scholarships for women to attend the Stern College for Women and the Albert Einstein College of Medicine. Soon after she died, Fay recalled that Scheiber had been difficult to deal with. "She was not particularly likable. She got in most people's hair. She was demanding. She came into the office two or three times a week—she never phoned—and she wouldn't hesitate to interrupt a conversation. But we developed a very good relationship over the years. She had a sense of humor, although she never showed it much. I could joke with her, but it took about ten years to get to that stage. She had a chip on her shoulder about never being promoted by the IRS because she was a woman. This eventually led to her interest to fund education for women."

D an Tully continued Bill Schreyer's focus on developing our international businesses, and as chairman of Merrill Lynch International, I was privileged to accompany him on many client calls throughout the world.

On March 7, 1994, the *China Daily* carried the headline LI IS BULLISH ON MERRILL LYNCH. Beneath it was a story describing a meeting between Chinese Premier Li Peng and Dan Tully at which ML was invited to open an office in Beijing and encouraged to continue providing financial assistance and advice to China, in particular with the financing of the Three Gorges Dam. The firm already had established a foothold in China in 1993 when it opened the office in Shanghai, and since then it had handled some two dozen major transactions for Chinese interests. Moreover, just a month before this newspaper article appeared, we had issued a $1 billion global bond for the People's Republic, and the very next day Alan Greenspan, the Federal Reserve chairman, raised interest rates, at which point we ended up buying back about half the issue to stabilize it. The Chinese Ministry of Finance thought we were heroes, so we looked forward to our meeting with Premier Li Peng.

The construction of the Three Gorges Dam was Li Peng's pet project, but because it was being opposed by most of the world's environmental organizations, it was a piece of business that we did *not* want to win, so we briefed Dan about the situation right before our meeting. "If he brings it up," we told him, "be diplomatic, but make sure you don't commit to anything." Sure enough, in the course of the conversation Li Peng asked, "Mr. Tully, have you ever been to the Three Gorges?" Pausing briefly to collect his thoughts as the rest of us watched apprehensively, Dan replied, "Well, no, but I would love to see them one day." Li Peng said he would arrange it. As we left the meeting Dan turned to us. "How did I do?"

"Dan," I said, "you blew it. You're going to the Three Gorges on your next trip."

"No problem, I'll probably enjoy that," he replied.

The next week when we were back in New York, I received a call from our investment banker in China, Zhang Liping. "Win, we have a problem," he said. "The Premier has arranged for you and Dan to visit the Three Gorges next week." I told him it was impossible to make the trip on such short notice.

Liping got emotional. "You don't understand. This is about face. The Premier has already made all the arrangements and you are his personal guests. If we turn him down, we will never do business there again."

I called Dan and asked if I could see him right away. When I arrived in his office, I said, "Dan, I have some good news. Do you remember when you told Li Peng that you'd love to see the Three Gorges? Well, he's already arranged for that to happen. Now the bad news. We're going back to China next week." I think most CEOs would have thrown me out of their office, but to Dan's credit he understood the importance of making the trip and also realized that he was the one who had committed to it, even if unintentionally.

"Okay," Dan said, "let's make an adventure out of this."

But it was the trip from hell. First, our corporate jet broke down in Sendai, Japan, so we had to take a train to Tokyo, which arrived very late at night, then catch a commercial flight to Beijing early the next morning, and finally board an antiquated China East charter jet with a fairly large delegation of Chinese bureaucrats who were our "hosts." From the airport we were packed into Toyota mini-vans and driven several hours over muddy dirt roads to the Yangtze River, where we boarded two large river boats. About an hour into the scheduled two-hour trip to the Three Gorges, one of the engines broke down and we were delayed an hour in the hot sun. When we got to the construction site, we noticed a large number of workers who were clearly prisoners doing manual labor. Under the constant glare of these unhappy workers, we were given a tour. Then we got back into the boats and were taken to a banquet with food we could not recognize. To be polite, we didn't ask what we were eating, but that night we made sure we drank enough red wine to kill any bacteria.

By the time we arrived back at the airport, it was totally dark. The gate was opened, and I noticed the light in the control tower go on. A lone person was up there looking up into the sky, and he gave a thumbs-up to our pilot. But then we just sat there, and through the plane window I saw Zhang Liping arguing loudly with a small group. Now even good-natured Dan was beginning to lose his patience as we approached midnight, so I went to the stairway and called Liping over.

"They've lost our flight plan," he explained. "No problem, though." Whenever Liping said "No problem," I knew there was a problem.

"Liping," I said, "get us the hell out of here right now." Five minutes later we were on our way back to Beijing for a short night's sleep before boarding our repaired corporate jet back to New York. Several months later an article appeared in *Vanity Fair* about the Three Gorges Dam, and there was a picture of us at the construction site. Fortunately, we were only referred to as a group of investment bankers ,so no environmental organizations picketed our building. The incident proved to me that Dan Tully was a man who kept his word and always put the interests of the firm ahead of his own. This was not a fun trip, but Dan understood the big picture of doing business in China. As it turned out, no investment bank would touch the dam project, and China financed it internally.

On another trip to China three years later, I saw wonderful examples of Dan's humility and self-deprecatory humor. Dan and I had an appointment with President Jiang Jemin that was meant to be a courtesy call that might last fifteen minutes. In preparation for the session, we reminded Dan of the importance of face to the Chinese, and we suggested that he pay a compliment to the Minister of Finance, Liu Jibin, who was our client and would be seated next to the President. After an exchange of greetings in front of television cameras, the President invited Dan to say something. "President Zhang," Dan began, mispronouncing the President's name. (Dan always had difficulty properly pronouncing foreign names and joked about his shortcoming.) "We are honored to be here today, and I must say that your Minister Loo [the correct pronunciation is something like "Lee-ooh," and of course "loo" is what the British sometimes call the toilet] is one of the most competent ministers we have worked with." Suddenly, Jiang scowled and had an earnest exchange in Mandarin with the translator. When Liu joined the discussion, we began to get nervous. Neither Dan nor I had a clue what was happening but it didn't look good. Finally, the President turned to Dan. "Mr. Tully," he said in perfect English, "you have confused my translator. The name is not Loo; it is Liu Jibin."

"Well, Mr. President," Dan answered without pause, "what do you expect from a guy from Queens?"

The President of China roared with laughter, and before the translator could speak, said, again in English, "Mr. Tully, let's make this a business meeting and forget the ceremony. My finance people tell me that assets minus liabilities equals shareholders' equity. Is that correct?"

What a perfect opening for a onetime accounting student like Dan, who replied that indeed that was so. For the next forty-five minutes, we conducted a meeting with the President of the People's Republic of China in English as he eagerly sought wisdom from "the world's largest and best financial firm" about finance and the capital markets. And this all happened because Dan could laugh at himself, make the President of China laugh, and set the kind of tone whereby the two of them related to each other as fellow human beings.

From the first time I visited China in the fall of 1992 until I retired in 2001, Merrill did well over thirty debt and equity transactions there, which culminated with us winning the mandate for a secondary equity offering of China Telecom in 2001, beating out Goldman, which had done its initial public offering. Dan clearly was a great help in making this happen.

But China wasn't the only place where we were making ourselves known. ML was strengthening its presence on every continent. Under Dan's leadership, *globalization* became the buzzword on Wall Street because of the growing demand for financial services around the world and because of the increased willingness of American investors to diversify internationally and of governments to shed companies that had been inefficiently run by bureaucracies for decades. ML played a major role in helping Latin America regain its footing in the global financial markets, bringing government and corporate issuers from

Argentina, Brazil, Mexico, Peru, Colombia, and Chile to the global scene. Merrill made inroads in the European market for acquisition advice, helping with the privatization of British Rail Telecom. Its Asian deals included the aforementioned Shanghai Petrochemical, as well as Indosat and Samsung Electronics, to name a few. By the middle of the 1990s, ML was atop the league tables, the widely watched rankings of debt underwriters which can be critical when firms are competing for investment banking business.

A nother one of Dan's great attributes was that he was a fierce competitor and believed that Merrill Lynch could and should win every mandate it sought. After becoming chairman of Merrill Lynch International in the spring of 1992, I traveled to Buenos Aires with Dan while he was still president. The trip was primarily to visit our remarkably successful Private Client office and our financial advisers there, but our newly formed investment banking team wanted Dan to visit government clients as well as some prospective corporate clients. Argentina had a new Minister of Finance, Domingo Cavallo, who was a free-market economist and had recently dollarized the Argentine currency and brought the country's hyper-inflation down dramatically. He had also convinced President Carlos Menem to privatize many of country's state-owned industries, notably Yacimentos Petrolieros Fiscales, or YPF, the large oil-and-gas company. Ever Since Goldman had led the privatization of Telemex, Mexico's telephone company, all the major investment banks were chasing privatization deals, and YPF was one of the largest prospects.

Merrill Lynch had a robust Private Client presence in Buenos Aires and was the only investment bank with a full-time presence in Argentina. Of course, we were managing the portfolios of wealthy Argentines who had moved their money out of the country decades before, so it was always a bit tricky to talk too much about what that business did for the Argentine economy. Nevertheless, we enjoyed a good reputation with this new government, and we had recently added a small investment banking office headed by Guillermo "Willie" Reca, a former J. P. Morgan banker. When Dan found out about the YPF opportunity, we spoke with Willie and said we should put all our efforts into winning this assignment, but Willie wasn't optimistic about our chances—he felt that Goldman, Credit Suisse, First Boston, Citibank, and J. P. Morgan had much stronger credentials. Merrill did not have the energy expertise in investment banking, and we had never led a major global privatization effort. After Goldman's success with Telemex, it was the clear favorite. When Willie suggested that we team up with J. P. Morgan and try to be a co-manager, Dan listened politely and then said, "Pal, I appreciate what you're saying, but we are Merrill Lynch, and we need to compete, and I believe that we can win."

And so we had a courtesy meeting with Cavallo and subsequently met with YPF's newly appointed CEO, Pepe Estensorro, a Bolivian who had a long, distinguished career in oil and had been the CEO of Hughes Tool back when Merrill Lynch took it public. We thought we had a great meeting, but a few days later we discovered we were not on the short list of investment banks invited to bid on the privatization. And yet we didn't let this discourage us, for we believed we had a secret weapon: Trey Fitzgibbons, who was now working with Merrill's private equity group, had been the lead banker on the Hughes Tool account, and had developed a very close friendship with Pepe. I called Trey to fill him in on the situation in Argentina, and after putting in a call to his old friend, Trey called me back. "Win, Pepe says he'll get you on the short list. The rest is up to you."

We were in the hunt. Shortly after we were put on the short list, Jack Hennessey, the CEO of CS First Boston, called Dan and suggested that Merrill and his firm team up and submit a joint bid. He argued that Goldman and Morgan Stanley were the front-runners but that if we would align forces, we would make for formidable competition. First Boston arguably had the best oil-and-gas investment banking team on Wall Street at the time, plus a track record in European privatizations. What we had was our commitment to Argentina, our research strength, and our dominant global "retail distribution"—all great assets to bring to the team. First Boston also had an equity interest in Banc General de Negocios, an Argentine bank whose owners were close to President Menem. The bank's adviser, Alberto Krieger, was a former Minister of Finance and a mentor of Cavallo's. Moreover, I had gotten to know Puchy Rolm, one of the local bank's owners, through a mutual friend, and while

Puchy's allegiance was naturally with First Boston, I was convinced that he and Krieger would put in a good word for us and thought that Merrill would make a great partner with First Boston. Of course, because of First Boston's oil-and-gas investment banking team, they expected to run the books should the deal go through. But Dan and I were of another mind.

Much to the chagrin of our competitors, especially Goldman Sachs, we won the mandate. Shortly afterward, David Mulford left the U.S. Treasury to join CS First Boston, and he became its point person on their YPF team. David, who had worked for Merrill Lynch after our acquisition of White Weld, had been recruited by Don Regan to join his team at Treasury, and later he had been instrumental in helping Cavallo restructure Argentina's debt, in the process becoming a well-known and popular person throughout Latin America. Since the government was a bit naïve in working with investment banks, they appointed two global leaders without designating who would run the books, and really believed we could work it out ourselves.

For months we jockeyed back and forth. Mulford and I liked each other personally, but we both refused to compromise on this matter. Mulford argued that his presence alone should win the day for First Boston and that, besides, Merrill lacked a track record in running a global privatization: We were a great retail firm and should be satisfied with being the non-book running manager, he thought. But Dan and I knew that this was a game changer for us if we could be the book runner. It would give us league table credit and put us in position to compete for a multitude of other privatizations. We would jump from being a never-ever to one who had managed a very challenging and large privatization. Both Mulford and I lobbied government officials to designate which firm should run the books, but their response was that "We hired the two of you for a reason and you work out the details." Finally, one day we had an update meeting with Cavallo. As we left his office and headed back for lunch, Puchy asked me to ride with him in his car. Getting into the backseat, he started in immediately: "Krieger says we've got to get this straightened out immediately. Daniel Mark [the Deputy Minister of Finance] is getting tired of us not working together, and he's beginning to wonder if they made the right choice. Goldman is still sniffing around and they're telling Marx that our two firms can't work together and this is going to jeopardize the deal."

"Puchy," I said, "let me be perfectly blunt with you. YPF is not going to be an easy deal to sell, and I doubt if we're going to get much institutional interest in it. Our only hope is that Merrill's retail system gets behind it, and I can assure you that if we don't manage the books, they won't. This is the way the system works. If we don't control the books, our advisers will spend months soliciting YPF and a non-Merrill book runner will allocate the shares away from them." I was counting on Puchy not really understanding our business that well, so I thought this bluff might work. I spent the rest of the ride with him asking me more about how deals are managed and what the difference was between a book-running manager and a non-book manager. I also reminded him that First Boston's highly regarded oil-and-gas investment banking team had recently jumped ship to join Merrill Lynch. When I got back to the United States, Mulford called me at home just as I was going out for a run on Saturday morning.

"Win, David Mulford here. I've been thinking about YPF, and I think we're at risk with Argentina. They're beginning to question whether our two firms can work together, and Goldman is feeding them a lot of bullshit about us. I have a creative idea that I want to run by you. This has never been done, but I propose that we become joint global book managers."

Pumping my fist in the air, I thought, *Yes! We won!* Then I said, "Well, David, I'm not sure. The devil is in the details. How would this actually work?"

David and I spoke for quite a while, discussing stuff that only investment bankers would care about, then he said, "Look, Win, you and I get along well and I know we both want this deal to be successful. I trust you, and I know that the two of us can make it work with our teams." I couldn't wait to get Dan on the phone at his Connecticut home. "Dan, we did it," I told him. He was delighted, but he said we couldn't let Jack Hennessey, First Boston's CEO, know how happy we were. When Hennessey called Dan the next day, Dan allowed that we were agreeing to this reluctantly, and only because I had pushed him to accept the deal. Dan loved to win, and he always believed that Merrill Lynch could do anything it set its mind to do.

YPF came to market in June of 1993. The 140-million-share of-fering was the largest original trade ever on the NYSE, and when the "green shoe" was exercised (i.e., we issued additional shares because the deal was hot), we raised $3 billion, the highest ever for a government privatization at that time. David and I did work well together and we were proud of our respective teams. Our bankers, equity traders, research analysts, retail and institutional salespeople, and our syndicate groups put their petty competitive selves on the shelf, and we worked as a team. In fact, YPF was named the Equity Deal of the Year by *International Financing Review*. At an Economics Club of New York dinner shortly after I retired, Jack Hennessey came up to me and said that the YPF deal was the best example of how investment banks should work together for the client's interest. Tully's competitive nature made this deal happen for Merrill Lynch, and this deal gave us the credibility to become, along with Goldman and Morgan Stanley, one of the dominant investment banking firms over the next decade.

Merrill Lynch could not have become a global power without its private clients' assets, which grew right along with the firm's determination to break free from its dependence on revenue from commissions in the cyclical, volatile business of selling stocks and bonds. Merrill's formidable retail base gave it a competitive advantage in the battle for underwriting mandates, and the firm successfully and uniquely created a novel and powerful combination of institutional and retail businesses that were two ventures under one umbrella. Because of the considerable culture differences between the two endeavors, other firms that had attempted this had failed at what ML was able to do. Bill Schreyer had understood the need to grant sufficient autonomy to the institutional business so that it did not get strangled under the yoke of a "retail approach," but he also recognized that Merrill had to be one integrated firm.

Dan Tully embraced this idea fervently and was keen on placing institutional people within the private wealth business and vice versa. He made Dave Komansky head of equity trading and then promoted him again to be head of debt and equity. He moved Joe Moglia from running Municipal Securities to a marketing executive position working for Launny Steffens in retail operations. Herb Allison served time in marketing in Private Client, running Human Resources, serving as CFO, and heading Investment Banking. Dan moved me, originally an investment banker, from Capital Markets to the position of regional director for the Mid-Atlantic Region in Private Client without my ever having been a financial consultant or having run an office.

All of these moves were intended to both develop his executives and help people in one sector of the firm understand the other sector. This was a unique approach on Wall Street and yielded many benefits. The decision to form dual, powerful franchises was made back in the 1960s, and ML stuck with it through some difficult times, particularly for the retail sector. But it paid off over the long haul because the two businesses fed off each other and enabled the firm to make capital outlays and take risks without jeopardizing overall results. By the year 2000, the firm would be involved in virtually every business on Wall Street—and doing very well in most of them.

It is important to remember that soon after he took over as chairman in 1971, Don Regan got down to the business of ending Merrill Lynch's servility to the whims of the bulls and bears. When fixed commissions were abolished in 1975, Merrill set about to offer a broader range of services to its clients and lock them into long-term relationships. In its 1982 vision statement, the firm resolved to be "all things to some people," and, as I recounted earlier, in 1985 the firm's brokers came to be called "financial consultants."

The linchpin of this effort was the Cash Management Account, which allowed financial consultants to gather assets and consolidate relationships at Merrill Lynch. And in the wake of the CMA's success, the firm began offering other similar accounts, such as the Working Capital Management Account, created in 1986 for small businesses—once again to a chorus of protest from the banking industry. ML also began managing 401(k) retirement plans. In 1998 the company established the Merrill Lynch Trust Co. and the Trust Management Account. This was an important part of Launny's strategy of being all things to some people and providing for more wealth planning, but it also was a way to ensure that family relationships stayed at Merrill Lynch through multiple generations. Banks for the most part charged high fees and delivered lousy investment performance, so Launny saw the trust company as a major opportunity to offer people an alternative to banks. By the end of the century, there was also the Capital Builder Account (CBA) for new and smaller emerging small investors, and the Key Client Account for wealthy investors, all derivatives of the original CMA concept. Other fee-based management services included Mutual Fund Advisor, which set up personalized fund portfolios, and ML Consults, which provides access to independent money managers.

During the 1990s, the firm's assets grew rapidly and there was an even sharper rise in dependable, fee-based revenues. The firm was no longer just a cyclical securities firm whose earnings dove any time the bulls ran for cover. It was a much more integrated global financial services company offering individuals, small businesses, and corporate clients an array of products such as loans, insurance, investment management, advice, access to capital, and, of course, stock brokerage. The better ML financial consultants were making far fewer cold calls and spending most of their time sitting down with existing clients to understand their needs, review long-term financial goals, and then allocate assets among a variety of investments. Step by step, these clients were brought closer to the firm—and made far less vulnerable to poaching by competitors.

"We had two general customer bases at the time: individuals and small companies, including partnerships," Launny summed up, speaking of the two-pronged structure that all the careful planning had brought about. "We decided their concerns, at different times in their life cycles, were savings, investment, taxes, insurance, and financing. Some people might be saving for a house; others for their children's college education. Younger people might want to invest; older people might prefer certificates of deposit. Everyone also has to consider insurance. Among businesses, we determined that their needs were cash management, investing, financing, and employee benefits. Next we decided we had to build genuine long-term relationships with our clients so we could solve whatever financial problems they had at particular times in their lives, not with just rote solutions but with things tailor-made. That's the heart of what we're doing, and that's what's behind founding a trust company. We wanted to put our sales force, our financial consultants, into a position where they could serve people's best interests."

Back in 1958, Merrill Lynch had been the first company on Wall Street and one of the first in any business to use computers. By installing the IBM 705, a first-generation mainframe, ML leaped into the Electronic Age ahead of the pack. "The Million Dollar Baby," as it was known, could process all the day's computations and records in a couple of hours, and with its arrival, Merrill Lynch became Wall Street's most efficient firm. Some twenty years later, the company again was at the electronic forefront when it unveiled the Cash Management Account, earning ML its first technology patent and articulating banking patent law for years to come.

On a chilly January day in 1991, nearly forty years after ML pioneered computer use on Wall Street with "the Million Dollar Baby," Dan asked Edward Goldberg to come to his office. Goldberg was a thirty-three-year ML veteran who had served well in administrative, sales, and marketing operations. "I have something in mind for you," Dan told him, "but I can't tell you what it is." Only a few weeks later, after the final decision had been made, did Goldberg find that he was to become executive vice president in charge of OS&T—Operations, Systems and Technology. Goldberg had virtually no on-the-job technology experience but he was a proven leader with a deep understanding of the private client business, and he leaped into his new duties with a massive re-engineering of ML's OS&T infrastructure, which moved the company toward a more centralized approach to technology.

"Goldberg believes firmly that technology can further enhance productivity by keeping brokers and investment bankers at their desks," said the magazine *Information Week*. "When brokers and bankers wander into other areas of the office, his thinking goes, they could miss an incoming phone call from a customer. But that's not all. Many brokers and bankers believe the only technology they need to do their job is the telephone. Goldberg's objective is to steer them well beyond that."

To stay atop Wall Street's elite, Dan had resolved to spend heavily on new technology. Under his and Goldberg's supervision, ML consolidated fourteen data-processing centers into two, taking advantage of more powerful computers and making the company's systems easier to use. Next it automated the processing of stock certificates and connected all 8,100 desktop computers in its institutional Capital Markets Group to one network.

But the keystone to this technological restructuring was a computer network connecting all brokers and providing market updates, client account information, financial-planning programs, and research reports.

With the inroads the firm was making with technology, along with its record profits and the high marks being won by its securities analysts, it seemed like Merrill Lynch could do no wrong under Dan Tully. But then on December 6, 1994, the government of Orange County, California, shocked Wall Street by filing for bankruptcy. It was the largest municipal bankruptcy in American history, and it shook the very foundations of municipal finance across the nation.

According to Orange County officials, its $7.4 million investment fund had lost about $1.6 billion in less than a year by borrowing heavily to buy securities whose value would increase if interest rates went down—but interest rates went up. It was an astonishing gamble, and Merrill was the county's underwriter and an adviser on many of these transactions. Orange County, which had been one of ML's biggest clients, sued the firm for $2 billion and alleged it had abetted an illegal investment strategy. Merrill denied the illegality charge and said the county's problem stemmed from inadequate accounting procedures and that the losses resulted from county officials' decision to declare bankruptcy at market bottom. Orange County's investment strategy had been designed by the county financial manager, Bob Citron, a sophisticated and arrogant man who, when his strategy failed, pleaded ignorance and pretended that Merrill had sold him on the strategy, one he did not understand.

While the county sharply curtailed education, health care, and other services, federal and state regulators investigated the bankruptcy, and the legal case got bogged down in the courts. Meanwhile, Merrill's reputation as a municipal bond underwriter and financial adviser was tarnished, and it began to lose much of the municipal bond business in California; this also began to affect Merrill's private client business in California. Finally, in June 1998, the firm—while still maintaining its innocence but fearing the negative impact of a highly publicized trial scheduled for September—agreed to pay a settlement of $437 million. "We are confident that we acted properly and professionally in our relationship with Orange County," the firm said in a statement announcing the settlement. "However, after weighing the substantial costs and distraction of continuing to litigate, we determined that it would be in the best interests of ML and all our constituents to definitively bring this matter to a close and end the uncertainty inherent in any judicial proceeding." Dan hated to settle when he firmly believed that Merrill Lynch had done nothing wrong, but Steve Hammerman, who had artfully negotiated the settlement, convinced Dan that this was in Merrill's best interests, and Dan agreed.

Dan's passion for supporting his ML teammates was never clearer than his confrontation one day with a very challenging client. One of our largest asset management accounts during the Tully years was with the Packer family from Australia. Kerry Packer was a very successful Australian businessman who had hired a ruthless American by the name of Al ("Chainsaw") Dunlap to manage his businesses. While the assets under management were large, the account was a most difficult one. Dunlap and Packer would constantly second-guess trades and even want to do their own. Once, on a visit to New York, Dunlap and Packer's son James made an appointment to "work things out with our asset management team." I was asked to host a luncheon for them after their meeting, and if all the problems appeared to have been resolved, I planned to take them, along with the account manager, to visit with Dan. The luncheon went very well, both Dunlap and young Packer were pleased, and so I brought them down to see Dan.

"How are you, pal?" Dan said to Dunlap. "I hear everything has been worked out. We're just delighted to be working with the Packer group and look forward to building a long-term relationship with you."

Dunlap barked back, "Tully, you have some of the dumbest people I have ever met. Your asset management people don't have a clue, and I'm not sure why we're even here." The Merrill Lynch relationship manager on the account had never met Dan, and now here was this important client telling Dan what an idiot he was. You could see him melting with embarrassment as he sunk low in his chair.

Dan shot back, "Hey, pal, you don't speak like that to me about a fellow Merrill Lyncher."

"Well, I will. I'm the client, and if you don't like it, any other Wall Street firm would love to have this account."

Dan stared at Dunlap for a moment, and his Irish face grew red. Then he rose from the conference table where we were sitting and picked up the phone. "Pal, tell me what number to call. I'll have the account transferred right now." There was a deep and profound silence that grew to the point that it was going to be hard to break. Finally, young James Packer took over in an attempt to defuse the situation. The entire tone of the conversation changed, and the meeting actually ended on a positive note. As Dan walked everyone to the elevator, he patted Al on the back. "Good luck, pal," he told him.

Dunlap, who had been silent for longer than he liked, shot back, "I don't need your luck." The elevator closed. However, before the elevator reached the first floor, talk of the meeting was already circulating around Merrill Lynch: Dan had stood up for his people in front of one of the corporate world's biggest bullies. No matter what it might cost in lost revenue, Dan was not going to let his people be demeaned. That's the type of leadership that makes one want to follow. Shortly afterward Dunlap was fired by Packer. He later became the CEO of Sunbeam and brought that company to its knees. In 2009, Conde Nast Portfolio.com named Dunlap the sixth-worst CEO of all time.

A s Dan Tully prepared to turn over the top job to Dave Komansky in 1997, *Forbes* magazine offered this assessment of the firm in its eighty-third year:

> Merrill Lynch is essentially two companies. One is an investment bank based in lower Manhattan, which serves the capital needs of corporations and governments. The other is a retail financial services firm based in Princeton, N.J., that operates out of 600 nationwide offices.
>
> It is a great accomplishment, in fact, that despite all the competition Merrill remains at the top of the brokerage heap. One hears a lot these days about Fidelity and Schwab, but Merrill overshadows both as a gatherer of public assets. Merrill boasts $830 billion in its client accounts, against Fidelity with $500 billion in managed assets and Charles Schwab with $253 billion. With 13,600 financial consultants

on its payroll—they are no longer called "brokers"—Merrill's sales force is far larger than runner-up Smith Barney, which has 10,400.

Merrill Lynch is also a leader in financing corporations. It is ranked number one or two in nearly every brokerage function, from global debt and equity underwriting to mergers and acquisitions and trading. On the rarefied big-money side of things, Merrill competes successfully with the likes of J. P. Morgan, Morgan Stanley, Goldman, Sachs and Salomon Brothers.

So, despite the competition, Merrill is scarcely losing the race at home. It earned $1.5 billion—$7.85 a share—on $24 billion in revenue last year. Its revenues have doubled in the past six years. Its return on equity has averaged 22% for the last five years, and in 1996 hit 26%.

Institutional Investor put it this way:

> Komansky inherits a firm that has never been stronger. It dominates retail brokerage in America. It has a commanding market share in virtually all capital markets areas. Increasingly, it is a power in strategic advice to companies (this year, for the 15th time in the feature's 25-year history, Merrill was again No. 1 in this magazine's All-America Research Team). With $1.17 billion earned through the third quarter, Merrill is well on its way to a record year—its fourth straight year of $1 billion-plus in profits. Thanks in part to an aggressive asset gathering strategy, Merrill has come closer than any other brokerage firm to smoothing out the endemic volatility of Wall Street earnings.

The 1996 Annual Report, which was published in early 1997, began with a message from the chairman. It was entitled "A Matter of Principles" and was vintage Tully:

> Merrill Lynch's history has been one of steady progress toward achieving the preeminence that our founders envisioned. Just in the four decades during which I have been

privileged to be associated with this great organization, our revenues have grown from $82 million to $25 billion, our profits from $4.6 million to $1.6 billion, the number of our employees from 5,000 to nearly 50,000 worldwide. However, the essential character of our company has not changed. Our Merrill Lynch Principles so evident since our inception—Client Focus, Respect for the Individual, Teamwork, Responsible Citizenship and Integrity—hang on our office walls today throughout the world.

Dan began and ended his chairmanship with a focus on the Principles.

A picture of a smiling Dan in shirtsleeves with his arm draped over a bronze casting of a bull and with the Principles hanging on the wall behind him was inserted in the middle of his message. He went on to talk about the people who inspired him and the satisfaction of helping people and making a better world. He wrote of being part of a great team and of how he viewed his role: "Equally rewarding has been the experience of being part of a continuum. Those who preceded me at Merrill Lynch were strong, visionary leaders who shaped and directed our company, and all my efforts as Chairman have been dedicated to passing that legacy to those who will follow." Dan ended his final chairman's letter this way: "Back in 1955, when most interoffice communications were conducted by old-fashioned wire, we used the old telegrapher's sign-off '73s' to convey thanks to a colleague for a job well done. As I end my career at Merrill Lynch, I would say to all of you who have helped sustain and build this great ongoing enterprise, 73s, Dan Tully."

Dan's final year was a remarkable one of achievement and it is worth noting just some of the main highlights that were listed in his final Annual Report:

> —No. 1 in announced U.S. M&A
> —No. 2 in global M&A
> —No. 1 in *Institutional Investor*'s All-America Research Team Survey
> —No. 1 in *Institutional Investor*'s All-America Fixed-Income Research Survey

—No. 1 in the U.S. in trading listed and NASDAQ equities

—No. 1 Municipal Institutional Trading House

—Business financial assets rose $38 billion

—IRA assets increased 16 percent to $105 billion, more than the top 163 banks combined

—Total 401(k) assets grew to $45 billion

–Trust assets totaled $3.6 billion

–Ranked Merrill Lynch as the No. 1 full-service brokerage firm in the U.S. by *Smart Money*

—*Euromoney* named ML International Equity Research House of the Year, Most Innovative Derivatives House, Best Brokerage Firm, and Best Lead Manager of Euro and Global Bonds

–Named the leading foreign securities firm in Japan in the Nikkei Survey

—Total Individual Client Assets held by Merrill Lynch were $839 billion [and would hit Dan and Launny's goal of $1 trillion in the summer of 1997]

Of course, it is also worth noting that the more success Merrill Lynch met with, the more its employees benefited. Back when he was director of Human Resources, Herb Allison had modified Merrill's compensation programs and made restricted stock and stock options a greater part of the year-end compensation for all ML professionals, who realized that they could achieve significant wealth if the company did well. All shareholders rode the same wave. When Dan became CEO, about 30 percent of all ML stock was owned by employees. Dan himself became a major shareholder by purchasing Merrill stock throughout his career and through his bonus allocations, and he never sold a share, always believing that the stock would go higher. There was no overt prohibition about senior executives selling ML shares, but everyone on the Executive Committee knew that Dan frowned on it. He felt that it sent a bad signal to other employees and the public. After Dan departed, most of us continued to hold our shares. The one exception was Stan O'Neal when he became an executive vice president. This angered Dan, but in retirement there was little he could do. This action demonstrated to many of us that O'Neal was far more concerned about his personal net worth than his long-term loyalty to Merrill Lynch. It was as though O'Neal were saying, *To hell with tradition, I will take what I'm entitled to.*

Dan turned over a remarkably healthy company, whose return on equity over the previous five years had averaged 23 percent. He left behind a company that managed risk well and had a capital structure that was able to provide liquidity under all market conditions. He left behind a performance-based compensation system that tied incentive compensation to earnings and ROE and aligned the interests of key managers and producers with those of shareholders by paying a significant portion of total compensation in restricted stock and options. He left behind a company whose stock price had increased 65 percent in 1996.

At his final annual meeting as chairman, Dan said: "The future of Merrill Lynch is now in the exceptionally capable hands of Dave Komansky, Herb Allison, our Board of Directors, and our Executive Management team. From my perspective, with the extraordinary leadership we have at all levels of this company, our prospects have never looked better." The rest of us were equally bullish on our future. As a tenor serenaded Dan with a rendition of "Oh, Danny Boy," we were clearly sad to see Dan retire, but we were looking forward to a bright future.

While Dan did retire in the spring of 1997, few knew that the Board of Directors had asked him to stay longer. They were not confident that his potential successors were ready. In fact, Dan was not really sure himself. He spoke to me and to Barry Friedberg and to several others about his reservations. While he had appointed Dave Komansky as president a couple of years earlier, he did so with some reservations. Dave was a good leader. He was popular with most people around the firm. He could be excellent with clients. However, in succession-planning discussions about prospective future leaders, Dave was seen as lacking intellectual curiosity and attention to detail. Dan worried about the Principles remaining a focus.

Dan's humble nature, however, compelled him to believe that Merrill Lynch CEOs traditionally retire at age sixty-five and he should respect that tradition. He later told me that he had really wanted Launny to be his successor, and it broke his heart when Launny told him he just wanted to be in charge of Private Wealth. "I don't like all that other stuff that you have to do," Launny had told Dan. Dan also told me after we'd both retired that he'd hoped that I would succeed Launny so that the Principles would endure.

In choosing Komansky, he knew he needed to appoint a president to make up for Komansky's shortcomings, and he really believed that a team of Komansky and Allison would work well. While Herb was not seen to be a great leader and often drove some subordinates to distraction by his micro-management style, still he was hardworking, diligent, and intelligent, a man of impeccable integrity who had broad experience in several areas of Merrill Lynch. In Dan's eyes, Dave would be the "outside" guy and Herb would be the "inside" one. Perhaps, he thought, they could form the same type of partnership that he had had with Bill Schreyer. Personally, I and some others thought this might work. Alas, it was not to be, and Dan's biggest mistake was not staying longer.

Bill Schreyer and Dan Tully each helped Merrill Lynch win two landmark equity deals.

AWARD OF THE YEAR

1993

presented to

YPF Sociedad Anonima

&

Merrill Lynch & Co. Inc [Joint]

in recognition of the most successful

Equity Deal

on the 11th day of January 1994

international **FINANCING** *review*   Editor

Bill Schreyer and I met with Premier Li Peng of China.

Photos and front page of China Daily after Dan Tully's visit in 1994.

Dan Tully and me at the Three Gorges project site.

Dan Tully and investment banker Charlie Li led the Merrill team in a rendition of "When Irish Eyes Are Smiling." China's Minister of Finance followed with a song of his own.

Makram Zaccour, John Dagher, Gary Neuser, and I at the site of Makram's family home that had been destroyed in Lebanon's civil war.

This cartoon depicted Merrill's move into post-Soviet Russia.

"Can you do the Merrill Lynch logo?"

This cartoon demonstrated ML's growing global importance throughout the 1990s.

Merrill's newest office for the long-term investor.

"THAT'S FOR THE LUCKY FEW WHO DID MANAGE TO TAKE IT WITH THEM."

Retired partners were invited every couple of years to a meeting with ML's executive management. This one took place in 1997. These meetings helped preserve the culture of the firm.

Komansky's first executive retreat with Executive Management Committee in 1998. Note: No O'Neal. Left to right: Jeff Peek, Carole Galley, Steve Zimmerman, me, Michael Marks, Barry Friedberg, Mary Taylor, Ed Goldberg, Launny Steffens, Dave Komansky, Curtis Brown, Herb Allison, Jerry Kenney, Dan Napoli, Tom Davis, John Heimann, Paul Critchlow, Steve Hammerman, Arthur Zeikel. In a few years, all but Kenney and Critchlow would be gone. Both Jerry and Paul would assume lesser roles during the O'Neal era.

Part Three

Compassion. Courage. Strength.

It has been said that we are all citizens of the global community. On September 11, 2001, that community was inexorably connected – by the bonds of shared grief, and the helping hands of human kindness.

In the aftermath of the tragedy, we mourned the loss of friends and colleagues, including three of our own – David Brady, Robert McIlvaine and Michael Packer – and joined together to demonstrate our resolve. Our reaction was swift and instinctive – from evacuating 9,000 employees in downtown Manhattan, to counseling calm and reason with clients... from rebuilding our trading floors virtually overnight, to helping rebuild lives in the places where we live and work.

The Merrill Lynch bull has always symbolized leadership, optimism and determination. In the face of enormously difficult circumstances, our employees showed their true mettle. We salute their compassion, courage and strength.

The 2001 Annual Report thanked all Merrill Lynch employees for their response to the September 11 terrorist attacks in New York. Just weeks later, newly appointed president Stan O'Neal began to unravel the successful culture at Merrill Lynch.

CHAPTER TWELVE

It Should Have
Been a Solid Legacy

(1997–2001)

I n 1968, David Herman Komansky, like Charlie Merrill some sixty years earlier, was a restless, free-spirited young man in Florida who had dropped out of college a few semesters short of a degree. When his father-in-law suggested that he ought to "work on Wall Street," he took the words literally and moved to New York. "It never occurred to me in a million years that I could work in this industry and live in Florida," he said. He applied to nearly two dozen firms, vowing that he would accept the first job offer he got, and soon he joined Merrill Lynch as a broker in the Forest Hills office in the borough of Queens. His base salary was $650 a month, and he and his wife, Phyllis, had to move in with her parents for the first several months. Within a few weeks he decided he wanted to move up to management: "I wanted to be one of the group that made things happen, as opposed to the group that things happened to." He proved himself as a producer, and in 1981, at the age of forty-two, he became the firm's youngest regional director up until then when he was given responsibility for Michigan, Indiana, and Ohio. Despite the fact that this area was hard-hit by a recession, it became Merrill's top-selling region. Komansky took over the New York Region in 1983.

Returning to New York was a homecoming for Komansky, who grew up in the Bronx with a Jewish father who was a post office foreman, an Irish mother who was a clerical worker, and a brother, Joseph. He went to public schools, where he liked history and geography, played baseball and football, swam competitively, and held odd jobs, including selling programs at Yankee Stadium so he could watch his beloved Bronx Bombers play for free. Both his father and brother suffered from allergies, so the family moved to Florida in 1956 to seek relief. There, Komansky attended University of Miami, where he occasionally studied but mostly partied. "I had a rough time dealing with the freedom of the new environment, and I enjoyed the good life," he recalled. He dropped out to join the Coast Guard, then became an electrician, then tried college again without success. He got married in 1964 and took a job with a printer.

From the time he joined Merrill Lynch in 1968, Komansky's career growth at the firm was balanced by a strong commitment to his wife and two daughters, and the two values clashed in 1985 when Bill Schreyer and Dan Tully asked him to become National Sales Manager, which was the No. 2 retail job. "It was the job I wanted more than any other," Komansky said, but he was reluctant to move his family from their home, set up just two years before, in Westport, Connecticut, to the division headquarters outside Princeton, New Jersey. When he was told he could not commute to Princeton, Komansky turned the job down. In many places on the Street, such refusals were career-ending. "That was, without question, professionally the most devastating moment of my career," he recalled. "I stress *professionally.* In those days saying no to an offer of promotion was not something that was politically correct. I was sure I had put a bullet in my career. But I was wrong. That's one of the reasons I feel about ML the way I do. We have a set of values here. We feel for each other. Many other firms would have been petulant about it, would say, 'Well, you know, that's it for him.' But that night when I got home, there was a huge basket of flowers that I could barely put my arms around from Dan and Bill with a note saying, 'Sorry you couldn't do it, but it is great that you are who you are.'"

That was a great example of what Mother Merrill really stood for.

As recounted earlier, Schreyer then put Komansky in charge of the firm's biggest problem child, Merrill Lynch Realty, which was headquartered in Stamford, relatively nearby to Westport, where Komansky was living. Ultimately, Komansky's recommendation was to sell, and it was accepted by the board. It was a tough, risky call, for had he been wrong, his career would probably be over for sure this time, but soon thereafter the real-estate market crashed, and Komansky's reputation blossomed. He was offered the National Sales Manager job again when it opened up in 1988, after Joe Grano was hired by Paine Webber (Grano had run into some personal financial problems with some of his private investments), and this time Komansky was told he could commute to Princeton from Connecticut.

I first met Dave when I was Human Resources Director and attending an annual Chairman's Club meeting in Palm Springs. My wife Maggie, and I had flown in commercially and taken a van from the airport to the Canyons Ranch resort with a group of our top financial consultants. As we were unloading our luggage, a white stretch limousine pulled up, and out lumbered Dave and his wife, Phyllis, leaving an empty bottle of champagne behind. Herb Ruben, the National Sales Manager at the time, had held a meeting of his regional directors in Los Angeles and sent all seven of them to Palm Springs in individual limousines complete with a bottle or two of champagne. Needless to say, the financial consultants who generated the firm's revenue were appalled that so much money was being spent frivolously, and Roger Birk, who was CEO at the time, was equally furious. While in this instance it was not Dave's idea to rent the limo, Dave never balked at enjoying the finer things in life. He lived well, dressed well, ate well, and enjoyed the finest wines. He also loved being in the company of people of wealth and cherished the trappings that he gained as he rode up the corporate ladder. While Dave was an athlete early in life, by the time I knew him he was overweight and not interested in any athletic activity. Dan Tully had told him he needed to stop smoking, lose weight, and learn to play golf if he wanted to become CEO. Dave pretended to do all three, but the truth is he hated golf, continued smoking, and remained the same weight.

Nevertheless, Dave had a unique leadership style that most people, especially men, related to and were motivated by. He made people feel good about themselves, and most people really enjoyed working for him. Dave was a genuinely caring person who always asked about one's family and was sincere in doing so. He could also be an excellent salesman, and I personally saw him in action around the world, where he was extremely effective in helping our investment bankers win large mandates. Dave learned to party early in life, and he was well known throughout his career for some of his amusements, a number of which were covered up by loyal employees. I have never doubted that Dave believed in the Principles of the firm, but he was never as passionate about them as Dan was, and he ultimately allowed them to be compromised by others.

Tully saw in Komansky a potential leader of the firm, and he recognized that he needed to broaden Dave's horizons beyond Private Client if he was to successfully lead a Merrill Lynch that was increasingly becoming a global institutional firm as well as a domestic private wealth company, In 1990, Komansky was named executive vice president of Equity Markets, and when Roger Vasey retired three years later, he became executive vice president of the Global Debt and Equity Markets Group. Many in the capital markets areas were skeptical that he would be successful, but Dave quickly gained the confidence of his troops and proved to be a capable leader in this new role. While he didn't know the businesses technically, he knew talent, built good teams, and had good instincts. When the firm named him president and Tully's heir apparent in early 1995, Komansky knew both sides of Merrill, retail and institutional, and his elevation was a clear message that ML was and planned to remain much more than a retail brokerage. When he became chief executive officer on December 28, 1996, Merrill Lynch was riding high as a many-faceted global powerhouse. "It's very scary," Komansky admitted upon taking over the helm. "How do we protect the organization from the arrogance of complacency? Everything that has happened up until this moment is history, so we have to create an environment where people are always reaching for greater levels of success."

Indeed, buoyed by a long bull market, Merrill Lynch was one of the largest financial services corporations in the world when Komansky took over. It dominated retail brokerage and was a formidable player in virtually all the capital markets areas. It was gaining strength as an adviser to businesses, and its research arm was considered No. 1. Moreover, it was approaching one trillion dollars in clients' money, and was involved in nearly every business on Wall Street—and was doing well in most of them as it became a global bank. Merrill alone had successfully integrated the traditional retail culture with an underwriting and trading mentality, and its envious competitors were scrambling to catch up, a process that some called "Merrillization." To take control of such a colossus was a daunting task.

As free enterprise spread around the globe, the need for financial services grew correspondingly, and ML moved to take advantage of the emerging international investor market. Governments were relaxing their longtime restrictions against foreign ownership of financial institutions and other industries, and once-conservative overseas investors were starting to take an interest in equities. Likewise, American retail and institutional investors were recognizing the need to diversify beyond the shores of the U.S. Merrill's interest in the deregulating international markets was heightened by the saturation of the U.S. market: In a word, America was "over-banked." Komansky, continuing the path begun by his predecessors, set his sights on establishing the firm as a universal bank that could handle business in any market in the world and in any currency. He wanted to convert Merrill Lynch's domestic brand identification to a global recognition—to make Merrill Lynch and its logo a recognizable worldwide presence like Coca-Cola, Levi Strauss, McDonald's, or Walt Disney. As *Institutional Investor* said: "The firm that took Wall Street to Main Street now wants to waltz down the streets of every major city in the world."

Komansky believed that ML did not have enough time to expand organically, and therefore, over the next five years, the firm would involve itself in more major acquisitions than it had in its entire history. Relying on the brilliance of Jerry Kenney's analysis and others' insights, including mine, Dave moved aggressively throughout the world. The explosion of activity had begun in 1995 with the purchase of Smith New Court, a British institutional brokerage firm, which gave Merrill an immediate 20 percent share of the equity market in the United Kingdom. At one of our Executive Committee strategy meetings held in London, Jerry outlined our strengths and weaknesses and the opportunities and threats that we faced. While we had become a leader in U.S. equities, we did not have a strong presence in non-dollar equities and had a particular gap in U.K. equities. Jerry felt we could not grow quickly enough and recommended that we approach Smith New Court before someone else did. The Executive Committee endorsed the idea, so Jerry and I paid a visit to Michael Marks and Paul Roy, the leaders of Smith New Court. We met in their London office and discussed the state of the world and the industry for a couple of hours, and it became apparent very quickly that we saw the future the same way, and that Merrill and Smith New Court would be a perfect fit because we had very little that overlapped. The acquisition was completed in a matter of months with Merrill paying $842 million for the firm. A key player in the final negotiations was Sir Evelyn de Rothschild, whose banking family owned 26 percent of Smith New Court. Tully and Komansky wanted Sir Evelyn's backing before making a final bid, and in return, Sir Evelyn wanted guaranteed access to Merrill's equities distribution network. Komansky sealed the deal in London's Dorchester Hotel at five A.M. after nightlong discussions with Sir Evelyn on an area of joint interest and expertise: wine. When Komansky returned to his hotel room, a case of 1982 Château Lafite Rothschild had been delivered. Many of us joked that the case of wine cost us at least $25 million in the purchase price.

The integration of the two firms is a textbook case for how mergers should happen. At one point in our merger discussions, Jerry and I asked Michael Marks if we should retain the Smith New Court name since it was a recognized brand in the U.K. and elsewhere. "Absolutely not," replied Marks. "We want to be part of one Merrill Lynch." Bob McCann, who headed Merrill's Global Equities Group, and Marks became co-heads of the new Global Equities Group. While they were different in many ways, it was a very effective partnership, and the impact of the acquisition was felt immediately.

With the Smith New Court acquisition, Merrill went from being a minor player to a major player in the European and Asian equity markets. Initial reaction on the Street was that ML had paid too high a price, but the skeptics were quickly silenced by a remarkably smooth transition, and within a few years the firm had established a substantial presence in Europe. The Smith New Court acquisition was the opening salvo for a series of big, strategic moves designed to dominate the booming global investment banking field and transform Merrill Lynch from a U.S.-centered firm to a worldwide equity giant.

Next up was Mercury Asset Management, which was widely regarded as the Rolls-Royce of Britain's fund managers. In December 1997, ML paid $5.3 billion for Mercury, making it the largest deal in Merrill's history. Komansky personally negotiated the purchase in the same suite at the Dorchester where he had completed the Smith New Court deal two years earlier, and he said he superstitiously ordered the same wine and food, including Peking duck, for the second deal as he had for the first. With the Mercury acquisition, the firm boldly made clear its belief that it could not only bring Wall Street to Main Street, but to *rues, strasses, carreras*, and *stradas* all over the world. This time, however, the cost of the wine might have been closer to $1 billion, and many saw the price we paid for MAM as a large premium that was based on expectations of aggressive growth.

The MAM acquisition was intended to counterbalance the company's dependence on retail accounts in the U.S., but this leap into institutional money management had its share of problems. Counter to how things had gone with the smooth integration of Smith New Court, Carol Galley and Steve Zimmerman of Mercury really wanted to remain independent of the Merrill brand, which they condescendingly viewed as representing "crude American retail brokers." The prospect of becoming a part of "the Thundering Herd" caused goose bumps to rise all over their bodies. In the end, the Mercury name was retained, and they avoided having to add the bull logo to their stationery and business cards. Beyond the symbolic, though, MAM executives dreaded having to participate in weekly Executive Management meetings and only reluctantly participated in anything at all involving Merrill Lynch. Dave had appointed Jeff Peek to succeed Arthur Zeikel as chairman of Merrill Lynch Asset Management, and while Peek did his best to try to integrate MAM into Merrill Lynch, he encountered tremendous resistance, and Dave was not willing to force the issue after paying such a high premium for Mercury's assets.

Smith New Court and Mercury were the bookends on an explosive period of global expansionism. Then, on November 24, 1997, the Japanese financial world was shaken to its roots when a tearful Shohei Nazawa, president of Yamaichi Securities, announced that after one hundred years of business, the nation's fourth-largest brokerage firm would shut down because of losses approaching

$2 billion from a racketeering scandal. Two weeks later, I received a call from Hisashi Moriya, the chairman of ML Japan, who said several Yamaichi executives had approached him with a novel idea: that Merrill Lynch assume certain of Yamaichi's assets, hire a number of its better retail brokers, and become the only non-Japanese investment firm in the nation.

While we had been in Japan since the 1960s, we'd always operated under a foreign license and were primarily an institutional and investment banking firm selling non-yen services to Japanese institutions. This move would allow us to compete in the Japanese market with big-name Japanese brokerages like Nomura, Nikko, and Daiwa. Japanese brokers were notorious for churning retail accounts and never placing their retail clients' interests first, but these Yamaichi executives were looking for something more. They had learned about Merrill's principles and its history in the U.S. "The time is right for Merrill to enter Japan and bring a new approach to the market as you did in the United States in 1940," one of them told me. After several weeks of due diligence and negotiations with them and discussions with Japanese regulators, Merrill announced that it would be hiring two thousand experienced Yamaichi employees in about thirty offices as the foundation to build a Japan-wide private wealth business. Suddenly Merrill Lynch had penetrated the tightly knit world of Japanese brokerage, and in combination with our established investment banking, institutional, and research capabilities in Tokyo, we were poised to become uniquely both a local as well as a global investment firm delivering services to Japanese individuals, institutions, and investment banking clients.

Because with Yamaichi we were effectively building rather than buying a business, we quickly set up Project Blossom, as we called it, under the leadership of Ron Strauss. In six months, and with the great teamwork of Merrill Lynchers from all over the world, from both Private Client and Capital Markets, we literally built a new firm, hiring and training two thousand former employees of Yamaichi's. This was a huge gamble approved by Komansky and the Merrill Lynch directors. The new company was budgeted to lose money for at least two years before sufficient assets were gathered, but after that, ML Japan would become a profitable venture and provide a good return on investment. We would have a unique franchise in the second-largest capital market in the world.

Next we acquired Midland Walwyn, a Canadian securities firm that was run by a former Merrill Lynch executive, and Smith Borkum Hare, a South African securities company. We bought a majority share of Phatra Securities, a Thai investment bank; a 40 percent interest in DSP, India's leading investment firm; FG Inversiones Bursatiles, a Spanish brokerage; Carnegie Italia, an Italian brokerage; and two Australian firms—McIntosh Securities and Centaurus Corporate Finance. In 1994, Merrill was a $3.7 billion enterprise with 73 percent of its business in the United States. By 1999 it was a $9.3 billion enterprise with half of it business outside the United States. By 2000, Merrill was serving half of the Fortune 200 clients, more than half of the FTSE (London Exchange) companies, and twenty-five of the biggest Japanese corporations. In addition, Merrill was the co-leader in a structured finance deal for the Kingdom of Denmark in which both retail and institutional investors were able to repay principal in one of four currencies. Finally, China awarded ML three lucrative bond deals.

As our international business grew, Dave was often there to facilitate things, helping our investment bankers win mandates, and meeting with tycoons like Li Kai Shiang in Hong Kong, members of various royal families like King Juan Carlos of Spain, and heads of state like President Suharto of Indonesia. Dave particularly liked visiting Hong Kong, Spain, Italy, the U.K., and China. At the same time, though, he refused to visit India despite our strong presence there and its growing importance, and only reluctantly went to Brazil once despite the growing opportunities there.

While Dave's daily agenda was limited to a few meetings, he could be an excellent salesman when he was on his game, and he developed a number of important relationships in those preferred countries. When he visited the king of Thailand, for example, he was told of a bold plan to deliver water from the moist northern highlands to the parched areas of the south. The king wanted access to Merrill Lynch OnLine to study the daily weather reports associated with the commodity markets, and so Dave immediately got him a password: Royal1. When the British government wanted to make a gesture in

1998 that would symbolize the importance of the City of London to the British economy, it was decided that Queen Elizabeth should call upon an investment bank. To the great chagrin of British banks, Merrill Lynch was singled out for the royal visit. Komansky presented the queen with a crystal Merrill bull and later met with her in Buckingham Palace. What a long road this kid from the Bronx had traveled! Later he met with the king of Spain and shared some of the king's finest wine while spilling a glass on his royal tan suit. Despite that faux pas, Merrill was awarded the mandate to privatize Spain's telephone company.

One controversial initiative during this period was our joint venture with HSBC, the huge banking and financial services firm, to create an online brokerage outside of the United States. Komansky had hired James Gorman, a McKinsey & Co. consultant who had worked closely with Launny Steffens, and made him executive vice president and head of marketing for Merrill Lynch & Co. Together Gorman and Komansky came up with this joint-venture idea. To Dave it was a way of getting closer to HSBC, which he considered Merrill's best "white knight" should anyone ever make a hostile offer for Merrill Lynch. Gorman was skeptical of my International Private Client Group strategy and believed a venture such as this made more sense. While I disagreed, I did join the board of the joint venture and encouraged Dave to appoint Ed Goldberg as its first CEO. I trusted Ed and also knew he was a Merrill Lyncher to the core and would make the right decisions for the firm. As this venture was dropped by Stan O'Neal in 2001 before it really got off the ground, we will never know how successful it might have been.

B ack in 1996, when Dave was preparing to become CEO in the days leading up to Dan's retirement, I remember one time when he and I flew back from a trip on our corporate jet. Dave said that when Herb Allison moved up to president after leading the Corporate and Institutional Client Group (CICG), he thought that there should be two leaders of CICG rather than just one. Goldman had operated successfully for years with co-leaders, and Dave believed that CICG was now too big and complex for one person to run it effectively. He told me that he thought I should be one of its leaders and we could merge my international role into it. He was considering either Jeff Peek or Tom Davis, two very talented investment bankers, for the other co-leader position.

A few weeks after Dan retired and Herb became president, I was once again on our jet, this time with Herb. As we took off for New York early one morning, Herb pulled a sheet of paper out of his briefcase while coffee was being served. "I bet you haven't had a performance appraisal in a long time," he began in a monotone voice. I had known Herb since my first few weeks in Investment Banking and had always liked and respected him. We had been peers for twenty-three years, and I was now reporting to him. After he finished highlighting all my faults, he said he wanted me to be one of the four Business Unit Executives working for him. "As you know," he said, "we have a huge opportunity to grow the Private Client business around the world. We should be in countries like Germany and France. I see our non-U.S. Private Client opportunity as big as any other one." Ironically, this case had been made by James Gorman while he was at McKinsey and advising us.

Given my conversation with Dave about co-leading CICG, I was flabbergasted. Herb went on to say my title would be president of the International Private Client Group (ICPG) and that the international private wealth area that currently reported to Launny Steffens would now report to me. He didn't see the need for me to have the title of chairman of Merrill Lynch International anymore and spend time helping to win investment banking mandates. As the plane touched down, I told Herb that I needed to sleep on this. Later that day, I visited with Dave and asked him what had changed from our earlier conversation.

"Well, Herb is the president now," he said, "and I need to let him decide on the organization he wants if I'm going to hold him accountable."

"Dave," I said, "I thought you were the CEO."

"I am, but I need to support Herb."

"Look, Dave, if you want me to do this job, I will out of respect for you, but it's just stupid, and not in Merrill's interests, for me to not continue holding the title of chairman of Merrill Lynch International and help us win international mandates. You more than anyone else understand this."

After a brief pause, Dave said, "Let me speak to Herb."

Leaving his office, I realized that things were going to be very different from the Tully years.

In the end, Herb reluctantly agreed to my continuing as MLI chairman, but he made it very clear that he wanted me spending as little time as possible on investment banking business, and said he was moving Archie Urciouli over from U.S. Private Client to work with me on developing the International Private Client strategy. "I want us in Germany and France as soon as possible," Herb added. Having worked both for and alongside of Arch, I was happy to have him on the team, and he took the lead in researching acquisition opportunities in the European markets. While I totally disagreed with Herb on the market opportunities there, and saw no way that we could successfully compete against the large local banks, we did, however, have opportunities to grow in markets where we already had an established institutional platform, as well as several where there wasn't strong competition. Though Herb had set his sights on Germany and France, Jerry Kenney and I felt that countries like Canada, Australia, the U.K., and Spain would cumulatively yield a much better return-on-investment for Merrill Lynch. We had the local currency capabilities, a strong CICG presence, excellent research coverage, and the strategic advantage of being able to offer both local and global services, something the local competition could not do.

We also recognized that our existing cross-border private wealth business had the potential to grow significantly. Owning a Swiss bank, having a Cayman Island trust, and in general offering a better array of products than most private banks gave us a leg up in competing for the offshore assets of the wealthiest people around the globe. (It is important to note that we did not allow U.S. citizens to open accounts in either our Swiss bank or our Cayman trust.)

We also had a very talented group of private wealth advisers in areas of the world such as Argentina, Lebanon, Hong Kong, Singapore, Spain, and the U.K. who were very productive in dealing with high-net-worth investors. Our No. 1 adviser, Francis Verstraeten in Buenos Aires, held nearly $1 billion in client assets and was a remarkably talented professional. For a couple of years he was actually the top producer at Merrill Lynch and the Argentina office was the firm's most profitable.

While Herb kept the pressure on me to focus on Western Europe, both Jerry Kenney and Dave understood and supported my priorities. By the end of 2000, IPCG had five thousand financial consultants and $150 billion in client assets, and our footprints in Japan, Canada, the U.K., and Australia were unique. We were able to be both local and global. Additionally, our offshore business and focus on the ultra-high-net-worth market was working and yielding excellent results. At the same time, I was able to continue supporting our investment banking business around the world and led a number of marketing initiatives that culminated, just before I left Merrill Lynch, in our winning the mandate for China Telecom's next global equity offer.

I n 1998 the firm's overseas expansion and technology development were put on hold by a summer market downturn and, in September, one of the worst financial failures in history: the collapse of Long-Term Capital Management, a hedge fund headquartered in Greenwich, Connecticut. The Russian debt crisis and the ensuing global credit squeeze had rocked Long-Term and brought it to the brink of bankruptcy. Markets around the world plunged, and the Federal Reserve Bank, fearing a domino effect that would topple other institutions, summoned fourteen major banks, including Merrill, to an emergency meeting to try to come up with ways to ease the crisis. The gravity of the situation was described by Roger Lowenstein in his award-winning book, *When Genius Failed*: "If Long-Term defaulted, all of the banks in the room would be left holding one side of a contract for which the other side no longer existed. In other words, they would be exposed to tremendous—and untenable—risks. Undoubtedly, there would be a frenzy as every bank rushed to escape its now one-sided obligations and tried to sell its collateral from Long-Term." Herb was Merrill's point person during the negotiations, and under his leadership, all but one of the fourteen banks displayed unusual harmony by forming a consortium to effect a $3.65 billion rescue of the hedge fund. Merrill contributed $300 million. In fact, many felt that it was Herb's leadership that enabled this important deal to get done. This type of project suited Herb's talents, and he really rose to the occasion.

While the immediate crisis ended, the overall market environment soured nonetheless and Merrill was forced into a cost-cutting campaign that included a 5 percent work-force reduction. Most of the cuts came in the units where the losses were mounting: bonds and emerging markets. As in past declines, the cuts were unpleasant but surgical—and they did not jeopardize future growth opportunities or compromise the Principles.

For a half-century, ever since Charlie Merrill decried Wall Street's "horse and buggy" technology, and ever since my father set up the first committee to study the feasibility of using computers in the brokerage business, Merrill Lynch had been a technological leader on Wall Street. More important, for most of those years technology had been viewed as an investment rather than an expense. But as the century and millennium drew to a close, the firm faced its biggest technological challenge ever. Between 1995 and 1998, American investors were bullish, just as ML advertising advised them to be, but in ever-increasing numbers they were using dozens of Web sites offering cheap trades and implying in their advertising that investors who used a full-service broker like Merrill Lynch were wasting their money.

The online brokers, such as Charles Schwab and E*Trade, catered to do-it-yourself investors and lured thousands of customers away from ML. By 1998 the firm was literally under siege, and on December 28 of that year Schwab's market capitalization overtook Merrill's, $25.5 billion to $25.4 billion. This was a shock to all of us. Many were pointing to firms like ours as dinosaurs. ML had already decided several months earlier to meet the online competition head-on and find a way to capture the benefits of the Internet as a trading tool, but the symbolic milestone reached by Schwab enraged Komansky. "That was about our manhood," he told *Business Week*.

There was criticism from within and outside the company that Merrill Lynch had waited too long to get with the times. One possible reason for the delay was the firm's own requirement that all employees keep their brokerage accounts with ML (the purpose being to discourage and monitor possible insider trading), making it so there was little firsthand awareness of the growing threat from the Internet. Another reason was that lower-cost trades would mean lower commissions, something likely to draw opposition from the firm's own brokers, who could have taken their talents—and their customers—elsewhere. But by the fall of 1998, Launny Steffens believed and Komansky concurred that the 17,000-member sales force was ready for online trading, and a task force was formed with the mandate to develop an Internet strategy by the year 2000—a deadline that would be met with only four hours to spare—that kept retail stockbroking as the company's No. 1 priority. To head the effort, ML hired John A. McKinley Jr., who had handled technology for General Electric under the legendary John F. Welch. McKinley replaced Ed Goldberg and was given a seat on the nineteen-member Executive Management Committee. Goldberg remained in charge of Operations for a few years before he moved over to run the Merrill–HSBC joint venture. "For financial services, the next eighteen to twenty-four months are a fundamental moment of truth," said *Business Week* magazine. "Firms that get it, that embrace technology and are willing to take bold steps and informed risks, they will win. If McKinley is any measure, technology isn't just out of the back room at Merrill, it's running down the hallways and ringing wake-up bells."

At meetings with Merrill customers in San Francisco and Texas, it was discovered that many of them used their existing Merrill accounts as vehicles to trade at discount firms, and the trend was growing. However, a majority of these clients said they would come back into the Merrill fold fully if the company offered an electronic trading service. Toward that end, Merrill acquired D. E. Shaw, a small investment company with a highly regarded online operation, and its forty software engineers promptly went to work designing a far larger, more complex system.

Beginning in April 1999, much of the work was conducted under tight security in a building on Manhattan's West Side. There was no sign or corporate logo to indicate the nature of what was going on there, and it was in every way a no-frills operation: Functional space was demarcated by masking tape, and decoration was provided by the children of employees, who made handprints in paint on the walls between flowcharts. When the firm announced in June 1999 that it would offer an Internet-based trading system, Merrill Lynch Direct, at $29.95 a trade, the impact was dramatic. Account transfers to rival firms slowed and then reversed. In little more than a year, ML Direct became a force in the Internet world, with special praise going to its research capabilities. "No big Wall Street firm had more to lose from the Internet," *The Economist* wrote about Merrill in June 2001, "and none has made better use of it."

But somewhat lost in all the attention given to Merrill's entry into the online investment world was the creation of a new retail product, Unlimited Advantage, which provided a full range of financial services, including online trading in conjunction with access to the firm's vast research and analysis apparatus, for a flat annual fee of 1 percent of assets. Under this system, Merrill clients would pay for advice rather than for trades, and the firm's financial consultants would be rewarded by how much they increased their clients' assets rather than by how many trades they executed. "Under the new structure," Komansky said, "the broker will be compensated the same for saying, 'No, don't do that,' as for executing a trade." Unlimited Advantage addressed the same problem that Charlie Merrill had attacked sixty years earlier: the commission system's inherent conflict between brokers and their clients. Launny received a lot of unfair criticism in the press and was misquoted as saying the Internet was "bad for your health." What he really was saying was that advice was still important and that those who day-traded were not likely to do well—indeed, that online trading was a threat to the financial well-being of the average investor. Launny recognized the growing importance and influence of the Internet, but he also knew that good financial advice would still be in demand and that clients would pay a fair price for it.

The success of Merrill's Internet strategy silenced many Wall Street critics who had ridiculed the firm for its go-slow approach, and by the year 2000, some $63 billion was invested in Unlimited Advantage accounts. "As Merrill Lynch's customers would obviously attest," said *Internet Week* magazine, "a critical new service done right, meeting the expectations that those customers develop over time, is often worth the wait."

At the same time, there were other major advances in technology throughout the firm. For one, to help its financial consultants set up, analyze, and update plans for their clients, ML spent $825 million on some 25,000 state-of-the-art IBM workstations. The system also allowed clients to communicate with their ML advisers, access their accounts, and review research reports. The firm's communications needs increased exponentially during the 1990s, and eventually it was decided to turn over the task of running the highly complex system to an outside firm, AT&T. On top of all this, during the final decade of the twentieth century, Merrill also spent sizable sums on technology to prevent rogue trading and to prepare for possible year-2000 problems with its computers.

D espite the highly competitive and complex financial services industry by the turn of the century, Merrill had come close to achieving brand identity. Though it fell short of the total power of Kleenex, Jeep, or Xerox, when people thought about securities, the name "Merrill Lynch" popped into their minds more than any other. A major factor was the advertising campaign that had begun with Charlie Merrill in the early 1940s, coalesced around Lou Engel's famous "What Everybody Ought to Know About This Stock and Bond Business" in 1949, and blossomed into the "Bullish on America" theme in 1971. The succeeding campaigns were "A Breed Apart" (1980), "Your World Should Know No Boundaries" (1986), "A Tradition of Trust" (1988), and "The Difference Is Merrill Lynch" (1993).

By 1998 online trading firms were engaged in heavy anti-broker advertising ("Boot Your Broker"), and to meet the challenge of online investing, ML's new agency, J. Walter Thompson, struck back at the discounters by touting its own Internet trading service; at the same time, it suggested that point-and-click trading was not for everyone and that the firm's 17,000 financial consultants stood ready to lend a hand. Most of the campaign was indirect, using the theme "Human Achievement" to make the point that it is people rather than machines that are responsible for the world's great accomplishments. ("We love technology. It's new and it's shiny and it inspires a certain awe. Technology is good at the heavy lifting. People are good at the heavy thinking. . . . Computers are plastic and metal and sand. People are brilliance and discernment and vision.") Then, to show that, nevertheless, Merrill was part of the high-tech world, it redesigned the bull to make it digital in form—a kind of cyber-bull. One ad showed scientists extracting DNA from the bronze bull statue, studying its genetic codes, and then transforming the inert beast into a living icon of the electronic age. The theme was "Be Bullish."

When the market turned bearish at the beginning of the new millennium, ML shifted advertising strategies again with the theme "Ask Merrill." The ads carried images of golf courses and yachts, signaling a new emphasis on wealthy investors.

I n 1999, some sixty-six years after it was enacted in response to the Great Depression, the Glass–Steagall Act was repealed by Congress. While the law had intended to address practices thought to have brought on the Crash of 1929, since then most economists had come to the conclusion that the practices in question had not contributed to the economic hard times. Proposals to repeal Glass–Steagall had come before Congress numerous times before without success, and the Chinese wall between banking and underwriting had remained in place.

Beginning in the 1970s, though, brokerages and banks began elbowing their way into each other's territories by exploiting loopholes in the law, and the lines between banking and securities began to blur. As mentioned earlier, Merrill Lynch's creation of the Cash Management Account in 1977 riled the banking industry in a big way. As bankers watched their depositors flee to greener pastures, they began actively lobbying for repeal or modification of Glass–Steagall and began pushing into the securities business. As the idea of the one-stop financial supermarket grew, Merrill Lynch was one of the first brokerages to seek change. But there were limitations on these expansions that resulted in added costs, and so the pressure for full repeal grew. Insurance companies joined the battle in 1996 when a U.S. Supreme Court ruling opened the door for banks to enter the insurance business. Financial globalization further fed the fires of change. Most foreign governments placed no restrictions on banking activities by financial service firms, and American firms needed that same flexibility if they were to compete globally.

In the closing days of its 1999 session, Congress again took up a proposal to repeal the law, for the thirteenth time in twenty-five years. This time it passed, and the defining financial law of the twentieth century was no more. The repeal placed the idea of a financial services supermarket squarely back on the front burner, and little time was lost in bringing investment and commercial banking fully under one roof. Citicorp combined with Travelers Group (which included Salomon Smith Barney) to become the largest financial services company in the world. Then Chase Manhattan Corp. joined forces with J.P. Morgan & Co. Of course, these new powerhouses posed a direct threat to Merrill, for they had the capitalization that enabled them to offer corporate clients lower prices and rates. There were similar challenges abroad from UBS Warburg, Deutsche Bank, Credit Suisse First Boston, and other European financial titans.

During this time there was intense speculation that ML would team up with a larger partner, or that it would be swallowed up by a larger firm, and in fact Dave did have some serious conversations with both Chase and UBS. When Walter V. Shipley was nearing retirement as Chase CEO, he was reluctant to name his president, Bill Harrison, as his successor and approached Dave about a merger, proposing that Dave would become president and COO and succeed him as chairman and CEO when he retired. When Dave spoke to me about it, I told him I favored the idea. Chase and Merrill had many complementary businesses and not very much overlap, and being larger would give us the capital base to compete against the other global banks, which were increasingly using their balance sheets to win deals. Importantly, a Merrill executive would lead the combined firm. Dave and Shipley came very close to a deal, but the negotiations fell apart when Shipley refused Dave's price of $130 per share and his insistence that the new entity be called Merrill Lynch Chase rather than Chase Merrill Lynch. Both Herb Allison and Stan O'Neal were opposed to the deal. Even more serious negotiations were carried on with UBS, and this deal also came very close to happening, but as Dave told me later, "I just could never get the courage to go home and tell Phyllis that I had sold Merrill Lynch."

History should have recorded the Komansky era as a great success—he built upon what Tully had done and put his own mark on the firm in many positive ways—but beneath the surface a growing problem was swirling. After Dave became CEO and Herb was named president, Dave delegated most of the operation to Herb and focused on business development and external relations, but the several executive vice presidents who reported to Herb were increasingly frustrated by his micro-management style. I'd known Herb for many years, thought of him as a friend and a colleague, and respected his mind and his integrity greatly, but I, too, found him difficult to work for. However, I underestimated how strongly some of the others felt and what they were up to.

In the summer of 1998, Herb returned from a week-long trip to Japan, where he had called on many of our top corporate clients and prospects, to a phone call from the boss. Dave invited him to his Connecticut home on a Saturday and fired him, telling him he wasn't permitted back in his office. Though Dave tried to persuade Herb to spin this as a resignation that was mutually agreed upon, Herb felt blindsided and refused. That Sunday, as I was hosting a dinner in New York for some of my International Private Client managers, my cell phone rang. "Win, this is Dave. I've let Herb go, effective immediately," he told me, "and I will be assuming the title of president as well as chairman for the foreseeable future." As much as Herb annoyed me at times, I was shocked by his sudden and unceremonious departure. He had been at Merrill for nearly thirty years and had succeeded in every role he had. He was hardworking, honest, smart, and loyal—and he had been an important part of our success. It was bad enough that he was fired without warning, but it was shocking that he was not permitted back in the office. The following day Herb was driven to New York by Ramon, his ML chauffeur, to go over the details of his termination arrangements with his personal lawyer. When he and his wife, Simin, left the meeting and went outside to get into his car to return home, Ramon was gone. Herb called Paul Critchlow, our EVP for marketing and communications, and anxiously implored, "Do you have any idea where my car and driver is?"

"I don't, Herb, but let me find out." Paul walked over to Steve Hammerman's office. "Steve, do you have any idea where Herb's driver is?"

Hammerman snapped, "I had it taken away. He doesn't deserve it."

Embarrassed, Paul phoned Herb to explain the situation to him, and this veteran of nearly three decades, who only a couple of days earlier had been the president of Merrill Lynch & Co., boarded a train back to his home in Connecticut. Years later, after Dave and I had both left Merrill Lynch, I asked him why he had not allowed Herb to return to his office. "You know," he said sheepishly, "I was surprised that Steve didn't want him back in the office." *God,* I thought, *who really was the CEO then?* If one were to point out the day that the culture began to change at Merrill, it was that Monday morning. The Principle of "Respect for the Individual" had been tossed out the window. If an honest, loyal, capable, hardworking man like Herb Allison could be treated with such disrespect, imagine what could happen to anyone else. It was a pattern that would repeat itself in the years ahead. Herb continued to have a distinguished career, serving as chairman and CEO of TIA-CREF until 2008. Then, in 2009, he took over the troubled Fannie Mae. Subsequently he was appointed Assistant Secretary of the Treasury and oversaw the Troubled Asset Relief Program ("TARP") until he retired in 2010. Herb passed away during the summer of 2013, and many of us, his former colleagues, attended his memorial service in New York City on September 9. He was eulogized, by family and friends alike, for his intellect, humanity, and impeccable integrity.

With Herb out of the way, Dave's weaker side was exposed, and a few ambitious people took advantage of it. While we will probably never know exactly what transpired, it is clear from conversations with many of my former colleagues and my own observations that Stan O'Neal and Tom Patrick, along with Arshad Zakaria, the senior VP for Risk Management, formed a cabal of sorts to first rid the firm of Allison and then to make a move on Komansky. Even though 1999 and 2000 showed record results, this group began to speak about Dave's unwillingness to control costs, his laziness, his lack of decisiveness, and his misguided acquisitions. They also turned their attention to U.S. Private Client and began to criticize Launny Steffens for building up such an expensive cost basis and for ignoring the trends in the growing use of the Internet. Patrick had a key ally on the board, Bob Luciano, and the support of Bill Schreyer, the former chairman.

Schreyer and Luciano began to push Dave to make a change in U.S. Private Client, and in 1998, Launny was replaced as its EVP by O'Neal, and Patrick was brought back from Chicago to replace Stan as CFO. Dan Tully was livid and called Dave to tell him that he had made a fatal mistake, but Dave ignored Dan and unknowingly created his own Brutus. Both Dan and I have always believed that Schreyer and Luciano effectively coerced Dave into appointing Patrick. I genuinely think that Bill had been convinced by the cabal that Dave was losing touch and needed a strong CFO like Patrick—after all, he had come to Bill's rescue after the market crash of 1987. As soon as O'Neal took over U.S. Private Client, he replaced Launny's executive team with his own, laid off some two thousand workers, and began the process of focusing on individuals with $1 million or more in assets. To Launny's credit, he never publicly criticized O'Neal, and he gave Dave his complete support even though O'Neal openly disparaged him and showed him no respect. O'Neal let anyone who would listen know what a mess he had inherited and he took credit for initiatives that were clearly Launny's. To those of us who knew the true story, it was shocking to see what was happening to our Merrill Lynch. The one place Launny put his foot down was at his retirement dinner in 2000: O'Neal was the only member of the Executive Committee he did not invite.

By the beginning of 2001, it was clear that the new year was going to bring a more challenging environment than the previous one, which had seen record profits, and we would have to pare down to maintain an adequate level of profitability. This played right into the hands of Patrick and O'Neal. Rumors began circulating and items appeared in the press saying that Komansky would soon announce his choice for president, and increasingly the focus was on Jeff Peek, the leader of our global asset management business and a well-liked and respected executive, and O'Neal. Some of these articles were critical of Komansky and his lack of decisiveness regarding his successor. I would learn much later from Komansky that the source for at least some of the leaks was Paul Critchlow, our director of communications, who was feeding the information to Charlie Gasparino, a reporter for *The Wall Street Journal*. Paul later confided to Greg Farrell, the author of *Crash of the Titans*, and to me that O'Neal had pressured him to choose sides in the succession race. "Life is a series of choices, Paul. It is time for you to make a choice," O'Neal threateningly said to him. Paul thought about the consequences of not siding with O'Neal and joined the effort, but later Paul told me how much he regretted this, as well as the stories he had leaked to the press that showed O'Neal in a favorable light and by contrast make Komansky look weak and indecisive.

Meanwhile, Patrick began giving the board selective data about various international acquisitions that cast them in an unfavorable light. At one point, after Jerry Kenney saw a presentation that was about to be sent to the board, he called Patrick and asked, "What the hell are you doing? That's misinformation, and if you don't retract it, I'm going to tell the board that you're purposefully giving them misinformation." The presentation was then corrected. Jerry called Steve Hammerman to tell him what was going on. "I will handle this," Steve told Jerry. "Don't mention this to anyone else." At the time, none of us realized the Machiavellian game that was being played, since this had never occurred in the history of Merrill Lynch. We were all too naïve. At some point it was suggested to O'Neal that he "get on the good side of Schreyer to play to Luciano" even though Bill had been retired for nearly seven years. But Bill was in his Princeton office most days, and O'Neal would visit him frequently to "ask his advice" and "seek his counsel." Launny had never felt the need to do this, and consequently Bill was less fond of him. There is nothing more flattering to former CEOs than to have their opinions sought, and so suddenly Schreyer became a "Stan Fan," and meanwhile, Patrick helped to convince Bill that Dave was not the right CEO, and that Stan would be much better for Merrill Lynch. As 2001 went on, the business climate became worse, and speculation about Dave's successor picked up.

Fast-forward to the July 2001 Board of Directors meeting: The lights dimmed and Tom Patrick began his PowerPoint presentation of MER's quarterly results. I half listened as he droned on, but when Patrick turned to highlighting each business unit's results, I was startled to see that those of my International Private Client Group were less than what we had reported. I had just reviewed them the evening before. Had there been some last-minute adjustment? When the board moved into executive session, I proceeded to the office of Dan Cochran, my financial officer, to ask, "Dan, did our results change from the ones I saw last night?'"

"No, they didn't."

"Then why the hell did Patrick show a different number to the board?"

"I have no idea," replied Dan incredulously. "Let me look into it."

Dan Cochran was one of the most hardworking and thorough executives I have ever known. He didn't make mistakes like that. Something was up.

I thought about Tom Patrick, someone I knew well from the early days after our acquisition of White Weld, his former firm. Tom had first held the CFO post under Bill Schreyer, who believed that Patrick had helped him survive in the turbulent times after the mortgage loss and the crash of 1987. Tom was a very smart and able financial mechanic and a creative investment banker who was always seeking to create high-margin products to sell to Merrill's corporate clients. He also had headed our insurance business and later equity trading. However, when Dan Tully became CEO, he "promoted" Patrick back to investment banking in Chicago. Dan didn't trust Patrick, who in turn was one of the few people who disliked Tully. Despite his dour expression, Tom had a witty and sarcastic sense of humor that had appealed to Bill Schreyer but not to Tully. Tom was also a pessimist by nature, so his presentations were often less than inspiring and dwelled on what was wrong and what could go wrong.

While I knew that Patrick was pushing to have Stan O'Neal named president and to succeed Komansky, I couldn't believe he would knowingly alter results. He, O'Neal, Arshad Zakaria, and Bob Luciano were frequent foursomes on the golf course. Many of us suspected that O'Neal, Patrick, and Zakaria had formed a secret pact and were lobbying the board through Bill Schreyer and Bob Luciano, who was the chairman of the Compensation and Benefits Committee.

Interestingly, Zakaria and Luciano's son, Richard, had worked for a unit together in Investment Banking from 1988 to 1991 when it was headed by E. S. P. Das, that created a series of complex tax partnerships and sold them to large companies. Tom Patrick, then a senior investment banker in our Chicago office, was somewhat of a mentor to them as well. Schering-Plough and Luciano, who was its chairman and CEO at the time, were one of the several beneficiaries of these tax advantage vehicles, which were later challenged by the IRS and discontinued by Merrill Lynch. In a *New York Times* article on August 3, 2003, it was disclosed that Luciano had retired from Schering-Plough with a retirement package of $51 million, which even by Wall Street standards was "seen as generous by corporate governance experts." At the time, Bill Schreyer was on Schering's board and was a close friend of Luciano's. Das and his group were very controversial and not at all liked or respected by most of the other investment bankers, who always felt that they played by a different set of rules and received preferential treatment by some predecessors of Barry Friedberg. At one point, when Barry Friedberg was in charge of Investment Banking, he had tried to fire Das for not telling him the truth about calling on a client without properly communicating first with the coverage officer (this was a violation of Merrill Lynch policy), and Das further compounded the problem by shading the truth after being confronted with the facts. Barry was summoned to a meeting with Tully (then president), Herb Allison (then head of Human Resources), and general counsel Steve Hammerman. Friedberg was later instructed to reduce Das's year-end bonus somewhat—but not fire him. I always thought this was highly unusual, since Hammerman was so adamant about integrity in every other situation. What role Schreyer and Luciano played in this decision is unknown. Later when Allison ran Investment Banking and Dan became CEO, the group was disbanded.

Meanwhile, that same morning of the board meeting, after I had asked Dan Cochran about the questionable numbers being presented, he phoned to tell me that the numbers for Jeff Peek's Asset Management business had also been understated while those for O'Neal's U.S. Private Client unit had been overstated. Jeff was beyond himself with anger when I called to ask him if that was true. Next I called Ahmass Fakahany, the ML controller, who worked directly for Patrick and was responsible for putting the board meeting information together. Ahmass had worked for me in Hong Kong and Tokyo, and I thought he was an able accountant, but in recent years he had gone to work for O'Neal and then Patrick, and I had begun to see him as a less objective numbers person and someone who had become much more political. He had also developed a swagger and arrogance that seemed to say, *I'm in the inner circle now.*

"Ahmass," I began, "what the hell is going on? The board was shown wrong numbers today."

"Yes, I know," he said without pause. "It was my mistake, and we will be sending them a corrected version of the board presentation later today." This was outrageous! It was like the front-page newspaper headline corrected two days later on page 92.

"Ahmass, you and I have known each other for a long time," I said then. "You're playing a game that will be your downfall. Integrity is everything. Don't do the bidding of others."

Fakahany's response? "Thank you."

I hung up and that was the last conversation I ever had with him. Little did I realize then that Fakahany was a founding member of the cabal and that he would ultimately become O'Neal's closest adviser and eventually responsible for risk management. Shockingly, in 2007 O'Neal named Fakahany co-president along with Greg Fleming. While many of us viewed Fleming as an able executive, we believed this appointment was premature given his level of experience at the time. On the other hand, we were stunned that someone like Fakahany was a possible heir apparent. The fact that he received a severance payment of $93 million still makes us nauseous. He is now in the restaurant business thanks to that severance. On the other hand, Fleming now runs the Private Wealth business at Morgan Stanley for James Gorman and is seen as a very able and ethical executive.

Maybe the incorrect numbers were an honest mistake, but Jeff and I doubted that. To us they were just another piece of evidence that the culture of Merrill Lynch was about to change. Past CEO successions at Merrill Lynch had been orderly and largely devoid of intrigue. Power passed smoothly from Charlie Merrill to my father, and then to Mike McCarthy, followed by George Leness, Jim Thompson, Don Regan, Roger Birk, Bill Schreyer, Dan Tully, and finally Dave Komansky. But this time it was different. Did the incorrect numbers ultimately make any difference? No! But in our opinion the fact that this happened was a sign of things to come. I later brought this to the attention of a longtime board member, Jill Conway, whom I had known since Don Regan first appointed her, but she obviously considered it an "innocent mistake," even though she said she would bring it to the attention of John Phelan, the chairman of the Audit Committee.

Right after the July board meeting, I got a phone call from Dave: "Win, I just want to let you know that in a few moments we will be issuing a press release announcing Stan as president and COO." Of course, this meant that O'Neal was the board's choice to succeed Komansky as CEO.

"I'm really sorry to hear that, Dave," I responded. "I think it's a big mistake for the firm. I would have preferred either Tom [Davis] or Jeff [Peek]."

"Give him a chance," Dave said in an imploring tone. "I'm going to be around for another two years. We'll continue to work on building our global business."

"Okay, Dave, I'll try to support your decision," I told him. Then I e-mailed my congratulations to O'Neal, and a few days later he appeared in my office unannounced and said he was really looking forward to working with me and having me on his team. That was nice, and I appreciated it.

Almost immediately, after O'Neal was appointed president, Dave moved into a passive chairman's role, deferring the executive power to O'Neal. I knew that Dave's back had been bothering him, and he seemed tired as the markets worsened and our quarterly earnings began a decline after our record year in 2000. Nevertheless, I was shocked to see him taking a backseat so quickly. A couple of weeks after Stan became president, we held our regular business unit quarterly reviews, but Dave was conspicuously absent. Ever since I had come on the scene in 1974, Don Regan, Roger Birk, Bill Schreyer, and Dan Tully had always made it clear that they were the boss until the day they retired, even after appointing their successors.

At my quarterly meeting, I was scheduled to update everyone on the restructuring initiatives we were making in Canada, Europe, and Japan in the International Private Client unit. We had had a great year at IPCG in 2000, but the technology bubble burst and 2001 was a much more challenging year for the private wealth business everywhere in the world. We had developed a plan (which Komansky had approved) to consolidate a number of our offices in Canada, Europe, and Japan, and things were proceeding according to that plan. This would have improved our profitability in these markets but still would have enabled us to keep a strategic presence that would position us well for when the financial picture improved. Our global platform was a unique competitive advantage. I was eager to share our progress with O'Neal. Patrick and James Gorman were also there. As we settled into our seats in the small conference room on the thirty-second floor, this time with

O'Neal at the head of the table, I asked him, "Would you like me to start with Canada?"

"Canada?" he said in a voice dripping with sarcasm. "They have more caribou than people, don't they? I don't need to spend any time on it."

It was a short and perfunctory meeting. It was obvious that the new president did not have any interest in leaning about the International Private Client business.

Later O'Neal held similarly perfunctory meetings with other leading executives. At a fifteen-minute session with Sue Dabarno, chairman of Merrill Lynch Canada, she reviewed the results of her unit. When we had purchased Midland Walwyn there in 1998, we viewed the acquisition as an integrated opportunity to build a leading private wealth, asset management, and investment banking and institutional firm in Canada, which would give us a strategic advantage over the existing Canadian banks and investment firms. We would be a leading domestic firm there with a global presence. Our acquisition analysis projected results out over five years. By 2000 we had forecast pre-tax earnings of $114 million; our actual results were $153 million. By 2001 we were expecting earnings of $136 million, and we were on target to do $143 million. Sue shared their numbers with O'Neal. "These numbers can't be right," he said to her.

Always blunt and to the point, Sue responded, "Well, Stan, they are. Numbers don't lie. We're exceeding the forecasts we made when Midland Walwyn was purchased. Given the environment, we're making some adjustments and consolidating a number of our retail branch offices, but this has been a great acquisition, and we're becoming the leading investment firm in Canada."

We in ICPG didn't see each business as a stand-alone—rather, they complemented and enhanced one another. So when we acquired Midland Walwyn, we modeled it this same way. A couple of months later as Sue was getting out of the elevator on a visit to our Calgary branch office, the manager greeted her with the news that ML's Canadian private wealth business had been sold to CIBC (Canadian Imperial Bank of Commerce). This came as a total shock to Sue. We later learned that before O'Neal had ever met with her, he had made up his mind to sell the Canadian business, no matter what the numbers were. At the time we held some $51 billion in client assets and were ranked as the No. 3 private wealth firm in Canada. Today former employees of ML Canada remember their years with Merrill fondly and lament the short-term decision that O'Neal made to sell the private wealth business. Of course, the other Canadian firms were delighted to see Merrill exit Canada. After leaving Merrill Lynch, I served on the Board of Directors at three firms in Canada where I encountered many of my former Canadian colleagues. To a person, they remembered their days at Merrill positively and confided to me that they were shocked and bitter about being sold to CIBC.

E. Stanley O'Neal's parents lived on a farm in the eastern Alabama town of Wedowee, but when his mother was ready to give birth to him, she was obliged to travel some twenty-five miles to Roanoke, Alabama, because the family's hometown hospital did not admit African-Americans. That was in 1951. Fifty years later, O'Neal would be the first African-American to become chief executive officer of a major Wall Street securities firm. In 1964, Earnest O'Neal moved his wife and four children to nearby Atlanta, where he worked on an assembly line at a General Motors plant and became a foreman.

O'Neal earned a bachelor of science degree by working at the General Motors plant in Doraville, Georgia, and attending the General Motors Institute (now Kettering University), a four-year college run by the company in Detroit. He would work six weeks in Georgia each semester and then go to school for six weeks in Michigan. After graduating in 1974, he worked as a supervisor in the same GM factory that employed his dad. Then he went to the Harvard Business School on a GM scholarship, graduated with an MBA in 1978, and went to work for GM's Treasury Office in New York.

He moved up rapidly at GM and by 1986 was working on mergers and acquisitions, a field that interested him to such an extent that he decided to become an investment banker, and following the lead of Courtney F. Jones, his mentor at GM, he joined Merrill Lynch. "I thought investment bankers were smart," he explained later, "but I didn't think they were five times smarter than me, which is about what they were making."

In 1991, O'Neal was named to lead the firm's high-yield bond group, which was already highly successful. Though he gained the attention of Herb Allison when Herb took over the Investment Banking Division, he was never considered a top banker by Barry Friedberg or many of his other peers. Nonetheless, Herb continued to promote O'Neal and, as recounted earlier, when Herb became president he made O'Neal chief financial officer. From this seat O'Neal steered the firm through the cash crisis that followed the collapse of Long-Term Capital and was actually a very effective CFO. Because of a funding program he established at that time, Merrill Lynch would be in a strong liquidity position when terrorists destroyed the World Trade Center three years later.

O n September 11, 2001, I had dinner in Tokyo and then returned to my room to place a prearranged call to a client of ours just before he began meeting with my colleagues at our head-quarters office in the World Financial Center. It was 8:50 A.M. in New York. I kept getting a busy signal on the client's cell phone, so after a few attempts, I phoned my executive secretary, Terry Cunningham, so she could patch me through to the conference room.

"I think a small plane has hit the World Trade Center," Terry said. "We can see smoke and some fire, but we really don't know much more." Merrill Lynch occupied two different buildings in the World Financial Center—the South Tower was directly across the street from the World Trade Center and the North Tower was one building removed, just behind the American Express Tower. I knew that many of our employees took the PATH train into the World Trade Center or walked right in front of that building every weekday morning to get to our headquarters. Terry mentioned that a notice had just come out over the loudspeaker that everyone should leave the building, and then she heard another explosion. We continued talking for a little bit, and then she said, "Security is here. I have to leave imme-diately." The phone went dead, and I wouldn't speak to Terry again for several days. Only later would I learn that she had walked down the thirty-four flights of stairs from the top floor of 250 Vesey Street, and was the last person out of our building that morning.

After my connection with Terry went dead, I turned on CNN. "Holy shit!" I exclaimed to no one as I saw the scenes of the two towers ablaze and I realized what was happening. As I would learn later, as soon as the evacuation was announced, members of the ML security force stationed themselves at street-level stairways and key intersections as they supervised the evacuation of some nine thousand employees from the North and South Towers. As the last evacuees left the buildings, security officials searched both towers from the roof down, looking for any stragglers. After Komansky, O'Neal, and other company leaders were escorted out of the North Tower and had started walking northward along the Hudson River promenade, they saw a billowing yellow cloud of smoke, dust, and powder as Two World Trade Center collapsed.

The coterie of Merrill Lynch leaders first headed for the firm's technology center at 570 Washington Street, but after only a few minutes there, they were forced to evacuate because of a gas leak. O'Neal ordered the party to separate, shouting, "We shouldn't be in one place—just in case." A few hours later they regrouped at Paul Critchlow's town house in the West Village, about a mile north of what would very soon be known as Ground Zero. That afternoon the command center was moved to a warehouse in Greenwich Village, and the effort to find temporary quarters began in earnest. As Dave moved into the background, O'Neal took charge, telling the senior managers that there would be daily meetings and that he wanted to be regularly updated on the firm's relocation efforts. As it turned out, three Merrill employees who were in the WTC at the time of the attack were killed, but some nine thousand others escaped from the North and South Towers of the World Financial Center without serious physical injury. Within five days nearly all of the displaced workers had been relocated.

Meanwhile, as the tragedy unfolded at the World Trade Center, many heroes emerged from the Merrill Lynch rank and file. Six nurses at the company's employee health-care clinic—Royanna Commisso, Karen Novello, Maureen Flanagan, Andrea Rizzo, Clorinda Hartman, and Janet Nagle—remained amid the horrors and established an outdoor triage center just outside the World Financial Center and across the street from the flaming towers. Fighting off their own fear and trauma, they set up chairs and cots, treated the victims for burns, shock, smoke inhalation, and lacerations, and then escorted them to ambulances. When the first tower collapsed, the ML nurses headed for safer areas and volunteered their skills at ad hoc treatment centers.

Stephen Newman, a director in the Structured Finance Section, arrived at the World Financial Center in a cab just minutes after the first plane slammed into the WTC. Almost immediately he came upon fifty-two-year-old Kenneth Summers, who was stumbling, dazed, bleeding, and badly burned by exploding jet fuel. Summers, who worked in One World Trade Center as a technical support analyst for a health insurer, appeared to be in shock. His hair was burned off his head, and his arms were charred. Newman escorted Summers to a ferry. En route they met firefighters who wrapped the victim's head in gauze and stemmed some of the bleeding. The two men got on the ferry and crossed the Hudson to New Jersey. Newman stayed with Summers for eleven hours until he was able to begin treatment in a hospital burn unit, and when the two former strangers parted company, the victim extended his bandaged hand in gratitude. Summers eventually recovered from his wounds.

Waleed Khoury, an ML assistant vice president, was inside One World Trade Center having breakfast with several colleagues when American Airlines Flight 11 crashed into the building. Khoury left the stricken North Tower and ran across the World Trade Center Plaza, where he came upon a woman who appeared to have been struck by falling debris and was bleeding badly from her abdominal area. Khoury grasped her legs while another man took her by the shoulders, and together they moved her to the safety of a nearby store. Khoury then returned to the horrific scene, where he and other Good Samaritans helped injured and dazed victims to safety, until they were forced to flee for their lives when the tower collapsed.

Many children drew pictures reflecting their image of the tragedy, including Amanda Wallbrink, whose parents, Jeff and Katy, both worked at Merrill Lynch. Amanda drew a haunting image of an angel hovering over the burning World Trade Center. Her mother had walked her to the first day of school just two blocks north of the towers that morning and had been standing outside the school when the first plane hit. From their apartment a block away, they watched both towers collapse and saw their own building enveloped in that awful cloud of smoke before they were forced to evacuate and march north along the West Side Highway.

In the days immediately following, Lisa Schwartz, an ML vice president, was desperate to do something to help. She offered to donate blood but was told no more was needed. She volunteered to make sandwiches for rescue workers but was told they didn't need any more help. Finally, she decided on a masquerade. She outfitted herself like a rescue worker—hard hat, work boots, utility belt, gloves, and mask—and on September 13 she was waved through several security checkpoints, and finally stood before the ash-covered, smoldering, five-story wreckage of the World Trade Center. Someone handed her a bucket; after several hours of work on what would become known as "the bucket brigade," she moved toward the desperate search for life in the rubble, passing equipment to firefighters and clearing space in the rubble for rescue workers to climb through.

Meanwhile, as all of this was going on in New York, I sat alone in my Tokyo hotel room. Even though cell phones were knocked out in New York, BlackBerries were still working for a while, and I immediately sent a message to Sue Dabarno, who was in New York for a conference and had been in our building. She e-mailed me back: "We're all okay and walking north, but I can't tell you how horrible it is. Bodies are falling on the pavement just across the street." As the hours went by, Seven World Trade collapsed, and then it was reported that a fire had broken out in the American Express garage which ML shared; I began to think that maybe our building would be next. What was this going to mean for Wall Street? For the economy? For Merrill Lynch? For all of us? However, the only enduring thought that night was for those families who had loved ones in those two towers and for the families of the first responders who had come to their rescue. God, what a horrible tragedy. I felt so remote and useless sitting in a hotel room in Tokyo.

The next morning I went into our Tokyo office and spent time on each floor, telling everyone that while this was certainly going to change many things, our firm would survive and pull though. Now was not the time to panic, but to remain calm, reassure our clients, and pray for those who had been lost. Like everyone, my colleagues were shocked, disgusted with those responsible, sad for those who had perished, and scared about the future. But their professionalism kept them doing their jobs and in particular speaking to our clients to reassure them. After a few hours, I knew that I needed to get back to New York, but of course there were no flights going into the United States—in fact, it might be a week or longer before I could even think of getting one. And so I booked a flight the next day to London. If I could get to London, I figured, perhaps I could get our corporate jet to pick me up there.

Boarding the JAL 747 on September 12, I met a few fellow Americans who were thinking the same way I was. One of them was Joe Carey, an investor along with Larry Silverstein in the World Trade Center. As we were landing in London, Joe said that he'd been in touch with Senator Charles E. Schumer of New York, and there was a good chance that his plane might be allowed to fly to London to pick him up. He offered to let me come along: "Call me when you get to your hotel, and I should know." When I got to my room I called him and learned that his plane had indeed been allowed to leave MacArthur Airport on Long Island, was overnighting in Newfoundland, and would fly into London to pick us up the next morning. And so on Friday, September 14, we touched down in Bangor, Maine, to clear customs and refuel. As I looked out the window, it was like the TV show *The Twilight Zone*. There were no planes and no people to be seen, and we just sat in the middle of the tarmac. Finally, a lone white SUV drove up, then unsmiling customs officials came on board and departed with our passports. After some time they returned, allowed us to refuel, and we took off for the final leg of our trip. As we flew into the New York metropolitan area early that afternoon, I had my first look at the site of the World Trade Center in the distance of downtown Manhattan, a vision that will always be etched in my memory. The towers were gone, but two plumes of smoke filled the air. Despite the devastation, it still felt good being home, but I knew that New York City would never be the same, nor would the firm my father had helped to build and where I had worked for over twenty-seven years.

Though Merrill Lynch would be forever changed by 9/11, the firm did recover, and part of what made the recovery easier was that three months earlier nearly every employee had taken part in an extensive two-day management exercise designed to enable a trillion-dollar international financial institution to survive and resume functioning after some cataclysmic event disrupted employees, facilities, and communications. The exercise had used the scenario of a hurricane striking Lower Manhattan. Emergency management officials from the city and from the states of both New York and New Jersey had taken part, and the duties of nearly every employee, from senior management to maintenance staff, were detailed. There were emergency command centers, telephone bridges, and wallet cards with critical telephone numbers. No one could have foreseen the full scope of the events of September 11, but this blueprint we'd established helped the firm recover with stunning speed.

The first urgent matter was letting employees, clients, and the public know that the company was open for business. The normal routes of communication—e-mail and telephone—were out of commission, but with great ingenuity and some improvisations, the company had by the evening of September 11 reestablished Internet-based contact with the nine thousand displaced workers and the additional three thousand employees who worked elsewhere in the New York area. Meanwhile, the company's public Web site—www.ml.com—became an emergency communications outlet rather than a marketing tool. At eight P.M. on the evening of the attacks, the company extended its "thoughts and prayers to the thousands of people affected" and assured clients that assets were "safe and secure, and we will continue to provide a full range of services." Media Relations officials set up a twenty-four-hour, toll-free hotline and had company executives speak to reporters from leading newspapers and magazines and appear on the top television and radio programs. As with the 1987 stock market crash, advertisements were published and commercials aired to calm investors. No avenue went unexplored, and a message to employees from Dave Komansky was sent to their homes via a telemarketing service.

Efforts to get the company back on its feet were helped enormously by the fact that right across the Hudson River, on Washington Boulevard in Jersey City, New Jersey, there was space waiting at the headquarters of Herzog Heine Geduld, a Nasdaq specialty trading company that ML had purchased just fifteen months earlier with a long-range plan for expanding its market-making capabilities. Most of the firm's institutional equities staff, some six hundred persons in all, set up a trading floor at Herzog. They arrived on Thursday, September 13, and by Friday were back in business. On the eve of the reopening of the Exchange on Monday, September 17, hundreds of new computers were in place at Herzog. Traders and salesmen were shoe-horned into trading rooms, sitting six inches apart, their words overlapping with their colleagues' shouts.

Just south of the Herzog operations, directly across the Hudson River from the WTC disaster site, the firm had additional office space that provided temporary quarters for, among others, the top executives. Others among the nine thousand displaced ML employees were scattered elsewhere in makeshift sites in New Jersey, New York, and Connecticut. Foreign exchange trading was moved to London.

In the days immediately following the attack, while there was little business to be conducted in the United States, activities picked up in the international markets. Komansky sent an internal memo to ML employees: "We have maintained normal operations in Asia and Europe and are implementing contingency plans to be prepared when the U.S. equity markets reopen. We are actively working with exchange and government officials to determine appropriate timing." As the anointed successor to Komansky as CEO, O'Neal took over operational command of the recovery and did a superb job. Komansky told the board that O'Neal's decisive leadership in the midst of this crisis proved he had made the right decision.

O'Neal believed that Merrill Lynch, as Wall Street's biggest player, must be there when trading resumed on the New York Stock Exchange. That would help show the world that the terrorists had failed in their attempt to cripple the American financial system. A massive technological recovery effort began almost immediately. Some 4,500 computer terminals were purchased and quickly programmed. Computer and communication links were built to replace and to back up the ones that were lost in the attack.

When trading did resume on Monday, Merrill Lynch was there. On that first day ML traders had to telephone orders to the floor because the faster electronic data feeds that were usually employed were not available. The firm accounted for only 3.2 percent of the NYSE volume that day—about 25 percent of its normal share—but on Tuesday this figure rose to 8.5 percent, and on Wednesday—eight days after the attack—the firm was back to its normal market share of about 12 percent. Merrill research analysts, many working out of their own homes, were sending reports as cut-and-paste e-mails, and occasionally asking clients to send them copies of reports they'd received that had been left behind at the World Financial Center. Robert McCann, the director of equity trading, told *Fortune* magazine: "If someone told me as I stood on the shore in Jersey City, watching the World Trade Center fall, that we'd have to start from scratch in so many places and that we'd be up and running the following Monday, I'd never have believed them. We were calling audibles from the line of scrimmage. It didn't always go smoothly, but it worked."

While the firm scrambled to return to normal business, it also faced the challenge of helping its employees and their families cope with losses far greater than those usually associated with Wall Street. The events of September 11 left thousands of ML workers bobbing a psychological wake. Many of the nine thousand Merrill Lynchers in Lower Manhattan on September 11 had literally fled for their lives, witnessed burning human beings leaping to their deaths from the World Trade Center, and known that friends and business associates would not survive when the towers collapsed. They were in emotional crisis, overwhelmed by depression, anxiety, fear, guilt, and anger.

The company set up a twenty-four-hour hotline offering professional counseling for distressed workers, and Komansky recorded a telephone message that was sent to all employees, advising them of the hotline number. Additional help and information was available at the Merrill Lynch Web site and at human resource locations throughout New York. Employees were urged to make their own decisions on when they were ready to return to work, and as the workers settled in to their temporary offices, counselors were there to help anyone who needed it. In addition, there were "Lunch and Learn" programs on how to deal with the added anxieties of new offices and commuting patterns, and a page called "Remembering, Helping, Healing" was opened on www.ml.com with stories of individual heroism by Merrill Lynch personnel. It also served as an outlet for workers and their families to express their feelings through essays, poetry, and art. All of these efforts did what they could to help ML employees, and in fact the firm's response to the human resources crisis won a "9/11 Recognition Award" from the New York State Psychological Association for "outstanding support and compassion extended to employees, their families and the community in response to the World Trade Center Disaster."

On the morning of September 15, 2001, Mike Shenot had stood in mute awe at the World Financial Center. As director of the company's Real Estate Planning and Transaction Group, it would be Shenot's job to oversee the reoccupation of the South Tower. What he saw before him was shattered glass, mangled marble, and foot-high dust. "We came back a few days after the attack to find the Winter Garden destroyed, a hole so big in the West Street entrance you could drive a bulldozer through it," Shenot said. "The workout center was ruined and there were mountains of glass and debris. It was just overwhelming." A cleaning crew of one thousand people was hired. For the next three months, they would work twenty-four hours a day, seven days a week to clean all forty-four floors and the roof of the South Tower—some 2.5 million square feet in all. I returned to my office in the North Tower a week after returning from Tokyo to collect some items my team needed. As I emerged from the car, the smell of death was palpable, and shortly afterward I could not believe the scene as I looked down from my office.

Members of Shenot's crew put on protective gear to remove asbestos that had been blown into the building when the Trade Center collapsed. They vacuumed air-conditioning vents, replaced 774 windows, and scrubbed mold and mildew. Some 2,200 pieces of marble (if laid end to end, they would have stretched four miles) were replaced in the facade. They removed massive steel beams that had been driven into the side of the building. Many items were beyond repair and had to be thrown out, including 1,800 computers, 3,000 chairs, and 1,400 desks and cubicle stations. "You had to put everything that happened on September 11 in the back of your mind and concentrate on the goal of getting the building back in working order," Shenot said. "For a few months, we lived, ate, and breathed South Tower."

The North Tower of the World Financial Center fared better because it had been partially shielded from the Trade Center collapse by the American Express Building. In addition, alert engineers had prevented huge dust problems by shutting off the building's ventilation system when the first plane struck. O'Neal gave returning to the North Tower headquarters the highest priority, and in late October members of the Executive Management Committee began moving back in, and they were followed by other employees in groups of eight hundred. Returning workers were given orientation programs that covered subjects ranging from where to find river ferries to the latest science on asbestos hazards. Counseling was offered by experts who had helped the surviving victims of the bombing of the Oklahoma City federal building.

Shenot and his corporate services team began moving back into the South Tower themselves on December 15, and on March 27, 2002, a forty-five-minute Merrill Lynch Homecoming ceremony was held to mark the return and to underscore the firm's determination to remain in Lower Manhattan. In a special video message, President Bush called the event "a tribute to the spirit and determination of every American," adding: "You showed the world that the acts of a few would not deter the hopes of many. In the face of enormously difficult circumstances, you showed us your true mettle."

The centerpiece of the World Financial Center, the ten-story glass-and-marble atrium known as the Winter Garden, was restored at a cost of $50 million and reopened in September 2002. On September 11, 2002, the company unveiled a memorial flag display overlooking Ground Zero and a plaque honoring the three ML employees who died in the attack. At a tree-planting ceremony, two of their colleagues read a poem they had written entitled "Branches of Hope":

> Here grows a tree
> For the hearts and hopes of the fallen.
> September 11, 2001 shall be forever woven
> With the branches of our nation.
> May their spirits serve to guide our actions,
> Hopes and dreams
> For a peaceful world.

*The only portraits that hung in the boardroom at
Merrill Lynch were those of Charlie Merrill and
Win Smith. After a meeting there one day, this photo
was taken of me beside my dad. After Bank of America
purchased Merrill Lynch, the retired chairmen's
portraits were deemed to be of "no value" and were
returned to their families.*

CHAPTER THIRTEEN

The Day
My Father Wept

(2001)

O ne day in August 2001, after he had effectively become CEO—that is, in every way except title—Stan O'Neal walked into my office, unannounced, and said: "Win, I'm going to be announcing some changes after Labor Day. I want you to be part of my new team, but I want you to play a different role that uses your client skills. We'll speak about it further in a couple of weeks." I was flattered but also concerned because I knew that he had no understanding of our non-U.S. business and had been very critical of many parts of it behind my back. Still, he said he wanted me on the team, and that was comforting for the moment, especially since I knew that several of my peers were not going to make that cut.

Several days later, Paul Critchlow, still our director of communications, popped his head in my office. "Did Stan come by to see you?" he asked. Paul had earlier sought my opinion of Stan's elevation, and I'd told him that I wasn't sure I would fit into his team. Paul and I had been friends and colleagues for several years. He was one of Bill Schreyer's closest aides and had also become a very useful member of Dan Tully's and Dave Komansky's teams as well. Paul had good media contacts and good judgments when it came to press relations. He was also a very able speechwriter and later would be one of the ghostwriters of Schreyer's book, *Still Bullish on America.* Only later did I learn, and did Paul confirm to me, that he had also become part of the O'Neal cabal due to his influence on Schreyer and Bill's influence with Bob Luciano.

"Yes, Paul," I answered. "We had a nice short conversation, and he said he wanted me on the team but didn't give me any details." Paul stepped over and hugged me. "You know, Win, I'm really just a sycophant, but I need the job." In hindsight, I think that was Paul's way of saying what he later explained to me: "I was a member of O'Neal's team, and I now really regret it. Had I known the real O'Neal, I would have done things differently, but I needed the job, and I knew that Komansky had to go. I lost all respect for him after he fired Herb Allison. I never imagined O'Neal would turn out to be the person he was and that he could bring down such a magnificent company." Like so many people, Paul was and is a very decent guy who really understood and loved the Merrill Lynch that we had known. But he needed a paycheck and there wasn't a better one available. Paul was not alone.

After that encounter with Paul, I remained focused on business and was inclined to give O'Neal the benefit of the doubt and wait to see what happened after Labor Day. As a gesture of support, I sent him a copy of the book *Co-Leaders: The Power of Great Partnerships*, which had a marvelous chapter about the special partnership between Charlie Merrill and my father. In just those twenty pages the authors captured the essence of Mother Merrill. Knowing that O'Neal did not really know our full history, I thought he would enjoy reading it. I inscribed it: "Stan, you are following a legacy of many great leaders, and I hope your leadership with take us to further heights." A couple of days later the book was returned with a note clipped to it: "Already read it."

Read? Maybe. Understood? No!

My meeting with O'Neal was delayed by the September 11 attacks, but near the end of the month, he called me over to his office and said that he wanted me to become vice chairman of Merrill Lynch & Co. and focus on our major government, corporate, and high-net-worth individual relationships around the world. I would also be a member of his new Executive Management Committee. He said that he planned to ask Kelly Martin, currently the director of Debt Markets, to take over the International Private Client Group, which had been part of my responsibilities. I tried to convince O'Neal that a change now in IPCG was not in the best interests of the firm because of the restructuring that was occurring in Japan, Canada, and Europe, and, aside from that, if there were to be a change, Kelly Martin would not be the right choice. I had great respect for Kelly, but I simply did not believe that he had the right personality for this job. (Little did I realize at the time what Stan's directions to Kelly would be.) I told him that Ron Strauss would be my recommendation to run IPCG if he was intent on making a change, but he said, "I have other plans for Ron." Then he asked: "Are you going to accept my offer?"

"I really appreciate the offer, Stan, and it sounds like a great opportunity," I said, "but I need to think it over for a few days and talk to my family." I was very concerned about taking a job with no line authority and no one reporting to me despite the lofty title.

"Okay," O'Neal said, his voice laced with irritation, "but I need an answer soon so I can move ahead with other changes."

Shortly after that Jeff Peek, my friend and fellow executive vice president who was head of our global asset management business, heard through the press that he had been fired. Tom Davis, who was executive vice president for the Capital Markets Group, was offered the lesser job of leading Research and Private Equity, and Arshad Zakaria was promoted to Davis's job. James Gorman, the former McKinsey consultant whom Komansky had brought into Merrill Lynch a few years before, was summoned to O'Neal's office. "I can't find anyone better, so I want you to run the U.S. Private Client Group," O'Neal told him. Gorman is a real gentleman and would never confirm this to me, but a number of others insist that this is how the conversation went. Some say that Gorman, who went on to become the CEO of Morgan Stanley, made the decision to leave Merrill Lynch that day. What an inspiring way to offer someone a promotion!

A couple of days later I received a late-afternoon call from Critchlow. "The press has the story about Kelly taking over IPCG," he told me. "It will read a lot better if they mention your new role as vice chairman, so it doesn't sound like you've been demoted." *What?* I asked myself. *Is this the Merrill Lynch that I knew and loved?*

"Goddamn it, Paul," I responded. "I told O'Neal I would give him an answer in a few days. I haven't decided. You can tell the press that I've been offered a significant senior position which I'm considering. I'm not going to be pressured into an answer." But someone had leaked this information to the press, and it was clearly a move to pressure me into accepting the job. Knowing that everyone who worked for me would see this story in the early hours of the next morning as the sun came up in Asia and then Europe, I had Terry Cunningham, my secretary, send an e-mail out to my nine thousand employees throughout the world saying that I would have a conference call with them the next morning.

I called Paul and told him what I was doing. "Can I help you with anything?" he offered.

"I've got it under control," I said, "but is there anything else I should know?"

Paul said there was: Michael Marks, the chairman of Merrill Lynch Europe, was going to become IPCG chairman along with Kelly Martin being named as president. I was somewhat comforted knowing that Marks would be involved with IPCG because I had great respect for him and knew he appreciated the value of the group. This appointment, however, was a surprise to Martin, and he almost declined the job. O'Neal had failed to let him know about Marks when he offered him, Martin, the job.

I telephoned Martin. "Kelly, I don't want our employees finding out about this through the press, so I'm having a conference call tomorrow morning. I'll make it positive and tell everyone I've been offered a very senior position which I'm considering, that I'm very supportive of Michael and you, and will do everything to make a smooth transition. After I speak, I'll turn it over to the two of you." I could tell that Kelly was not at all excited about taking this job and viewed it as a demotion, but Stan had held out the incentive of his taking over Gorman's job of running the U.S. Private Client Group after he "straightened out IPCG." What this allowed O'Neal to do was to put his own person in charge of Debt Markets, young Dow Kim. I next spoke to Marks, whose voice also betrayed his disappointment in what O'Neal was asking him to do, which was to unwind the regional chairman structure that we had put in place a decade earlier. I hardly slept that night. I could not believe what was happening not only to me but to so many others and how Komansky was allowing O'Neal to proceed the way he was. This was not the Merrill Lynch that we had worked for all these years.

The next morning many of my New York team members gathered in the conference room for my call, and the rest of the world phoned in. "This is not a call that I would have chosen to make," I began, "and I apologize that some of you have read about our change in the press. Change is tough and not always what we wish for, but change happens and life goes on. I have been proud to work with you and proud of our accomplishments in IPCG, and I remain confident about the future of IPCG. Michael and Kelly are great executives and good people. I will support them one hundred percent in the transition, and I am confident that they will do a good job in leading forward. I have been offered another senior position in the firm, and I'm giving it serious consideration." I went on to speak briefly about our Principles and the quality of the people in IPCG and then ended with this comment before turning it over to Michael and Kelly: "Someone once said you can never love a firm because it can't love you back. Well, that person never knew Merrill Lynch. Our firm is our people, and the love and respect you have shown me is why I love Merrill Lynch and each of you." Looking around the room, I saw tears in most people's eyes, and I fought back my own.

Almost immediately, the phone began ringing and e-mail poured in. An e-mail from Cecilia Fok, one of our leading private wealth advisers in Hong Kong, was representative of the messages I received over the next several weeks: "Your conference call and message were very moving, compelling me to respond with a few thoughts," she wrote. "The sentiment that stood out in both your conference call and message is the tight bond existing between the Company and its employees. In these final moments, you chose to stand for integrity and humanity—the heart behind Merrill Lynch. With such a heartened attitude, thinking of others besides yourself, you have already laid the foundations for success here and beyond. To me, you exemplified a hands-on leader who fought hard for your vision of the Company's future. I truly admire you for taking a stand for what you believed in. It is no wonder that many of my finest moments at this company were under your leadership." Messages like this made my twenty-seven years at Merrill worth every moment, and her words could have applied to so many others who were raised within the culture of Mother Merrill.

For their part, Michael and Kelly had spoken well and made good first impressions. Afterward I told them that no matter what I decided to do, I wanted to help them with the transition. I later spent several hours with Kelly and went over all the outstanding issues. That was the last time he and I ever spoke about the business, and as things turned out, he moved in a direction opposite from what I would have. Not that he had much choice. Kelly was charged with selling the private wealth business in Canada and essentially unwinding the private wealth businesses in Japan and Europe. I don't really fault him because these were the instructions he had from O'Neal and Patrick. He was just following orders. His reward for doing this, as I said, was supposed to be to succeed Gorman as head of U.S. Private Client, but that never happened, and Kelly left the firm shortly after he completed the dismantling of much of IPCG to become the CEO of the Irish drug company Elan.

Later on the day of my conference call, Bill Schreyer called and asked what my plans were, and I told him I was undecided. "Come on down to Princeton on Saturday, and we'll talk about your future," he said. "I'll get you the helicopter." I went down that Saturday to have lunch with Bill at our Plainsboro, New Jersey, office. Traditionally, all ML CEOs were given an office and a secretary when they retired, and Bill chose to have his there since he lived only a few miles away in Princeton. He began by asking about my wife at the time, Maggie. Bill and his wife, Joan, were very fond of Maggie and enjoyed her company tremendously. He once told me that Maggie was my greatest asset, and Joan and Maggie were great friends. We spoke about a number of different light topics and then went to lunch. The dining rooms at Plainsboro were named after the founding partners, and ironically, we ended up in the Smith Room. "Well, it's the weekend, so I think we should have a glass of wine," Bill said. We both ordered turkey sandwiches and a glass of Chardonnay.

The serious conversation began when Bill asked, "Are you going to accept Stan's offer? I think you should. You know that there's no better client guy in the firm than you, and Stan needs you on his team."

"Well, Bill," I responded, "I have some serious concerns."

"Like what?" he questioned.

"To begin with, I don't think he appreciates our culture and I don't like his tactics." I explained how Jeff Peek had been fired and how I had been treated a few days earlier. "And I'm very concerned about who he is surrounding himself with."

Bill looked at me, no longer smiling. "Like who?"

Knowing Bill's fondness for Tom Patrick, I hesitated but then responded, "Like Patrick. I don't trust him."

"Oh, come on, Win, you don't mean that."

"Yes, I do." And I told Bill about the board meeting in July, when Patrick had presented incorrect IPCG earnings numbers.

Bill changed the topic. "Win, you've been around long enough to know that things change. Take this job. In a couple of years, who knows, you might still be able to achieve your goal." Bill knew that I, like him years earlier, longed to be chairman and CEO of Merrill Lynch, and so, by saying what he did, he had set the hook.

"Okay, Bill, I really appreciate your advice, and I'm going to give it serious consideration."

For the rest of the weekend I weighed Bill's words carefully. He was someone who had always looked out for me. I knew of his affection for my father and for the history and culture of Merrill Lynch, and I genuinely believed that he wanted the best for Merrill Lynch and for me.

On Sunday night, Tom Davis and I spoke on the phone. "Win, I'm going to accept Stan's offer," he told me, referring to the Research and Private Equity job. "I'm really not excited about it, and I think I might be getting set up, but Dave [Komansky] is really pressuring me to stay. I'm going to give it a year. I hope you decide to stay, too. It would be better to have two of us to support each other."

By then I'd pretty much made up my mind, and I responded, "Tom, I'm seeing Stan tomorrow, and I think I'll also give it a year." After I got off the phone I told Maggie what I was likely to do, and she told me that she supported me whatever I decided.

I thought about how I'd been at Merrill Lynch for over twenty-seven years, and before that my father had spent forty-five years with the firm. I had had a great career, beginning on my twenty-fifth birthday as an associate in Investment Banking and subsequently being manager of the Financial Analysis and Budgets Department, manager of Compensation and Benefits, director of Human Resources, director of Strategic Planning and Marketing for the Capital Markets Group, director of Emerging Investor Services, director of the Mid-Atlantic Region, and director of the Eastern Sales Division for Private Client.

I had been the youngest division director and youngest executive vice president up to that point in the history of Merrill Lynch. For the last ten years I had been an executive vice president of Merrill Lynch & Co., a member of the Executive Management Committee, and chairman of Merrill Lynch International. Over that decade we had grown our global footprint to one that was arguably the envy of our competitors—even Goldman Sachs and Morgan Stanley grudgingly acknowledged that we were their toughest competition. I was proud of what our team had accomplished, and I was extremely fond of its members. I loved my job, and it would be very difficult to leave Merrill. My identity was so entwined with it.

As I drove into New York that autumn morning to meet with O'Neal, I thought about the conversations I had had with Schreyer, Komansky, and Tully over the past week. Bill and Dave wanted me to stay. Dan, on the other hand, was less supportive of my staying. Dan neither liked nor respected O'Neal. The day that O'Neal was appointed president in July he had phoned Dan and thanked him for his support, and Dan replied in his usual honest way: "I didn't support you, but I hope to hell you're going to uphold the Principles of our great firm." That was the last time Dan and O'Neal spoke. Despite Dan's reservations, I walked into O'Neal's office with the intent of staying, but I did want to ask him some questions that would help to clarify the new position. I had e-mailed him earlier with some questions, and he had printed it out and returned it with a bunch of scribbled comments in the margins: "Yes," "No," "Not now!" There were few complete answers, and I needed to know how he really viewed the position.

O'Neal and I got right down to business without chitchatting. As soon as I sat down, he said, "I hope that you're here to accept the job. I want you to be a core part of my team. We have a lot to do. After we get rid of Komansky, we have a lot of things to change about the way this place is being run."

Wow! I thought. *This new president who was appointed to the job only two months earlier by Dave Komansky is already talking about getting rid of his boss, who at least in title is still chairman of the board and chief executive officer of Merrill Lynch & Co.* I knew that Dave fully expected to be around for at least two more years. However, many of us doubted that O'Neal was really Dave's choice.

Even though to this day Dave denies it, we believed certain members of the Board of Directors had forced his hand. As I listened to O'Neal speak so confidently about his role and of Dave's irrelevancy, I realized that Dave was in some kind of denial about the truth.

After listening to Stan for a while, I asked him to clarify the job he had offered me and how I would fit into his management team. "I can see you becoming a member of the Board of Directors in the future, but now is not the right time," he offered, which still didn't answer my question. "You're one of the best client guys we have, and you can bring in a lot of business. I would also rely on you to give me good advice." Further definition of my role was not forthcoming from him. And so—in what turned out to be the defining moment of my life—I asked, "Stan, what do you think about our Principles, our values?"

Before accepting his offer, I wanted to know where he stood on this. But as soon as I asked the question, he launched into a diatribe about all that was wrong with "Mother Merrill" and how we had to raise our standards and get rid of all the incompetent people who had been kept around. "We've got to get rid of nepotism," he said, certainly an odd thing to say to me! O'Neal was usually composed and very measured, but that morning his disdain for Merrill's culture shone through. I can't remember everything he said because my blood was boiling as he disparaged our firm, its history, its culture, its values, and my fellow Merrill Lynch colleagues and friends. I remember thinking: *He's essentially saying that everything my father and I and most of my colleagues stood for was crap!* It was obvious that he knew and cared nothing about our history and our culture and was intent upon discarding it like trash. I looked Stan O'Neal in the eye and saw no soul. In the middle of his diatribe, I'd had enough and interrupted him.

"Stan," I said, "thanks for the offer, but I can't accept it. I'm going to retire. I'll help with a smooth transition, and I wish you the best." As he sat there in his shirtsleeves, staring at me in disbelief, I stood up, shook his hand, and walked out of his office. O'Neal never thought that Win Smith Jr. could ever leave the firm that bore his family's name and where my father and I had worked a cumulative seventy-two years. How wrong he was! How little did he understand the real Mother Merrill. In my opinion, O'Neal had no clue about leadership, principle, loyalty, and pride. He had no clue why a corporate culture as powerful as ours was one of the major reasons we had been so successful for so long. He had no clue what was important to my father and to me and to the so many thousands of loyal families that worked for Merrill Lynch. That morning I knew he was going to marginalize the firm and transform it in a way that I would not like and could not be part of, but I never suspected that he would ultimately destroy it.

I walked into Paul Critchlow's office next door and told him the news. "Paul, let's get a news release out immediately. Treat me honorably in the release. That will be in everyone's best interests." I phoned Maggie to tell her the news, and I will always appreciate her unconditional support of me in this decision and throughout my career. Over the years she had also become an important member of the Merrill Lynch family and, like so many Merrill Lynch spouses, understood the culture and embraced it. I returned to by office, where I spoke to Terry, my secretary, and a few of my closest colleagues. Then I telephoned my four children. The press release came out later that day under the names of Komansky and O'Neal, and after the initial announcement, it read:

> We are saddened by Win's decision to retire. He has made many important contributions to Merrill Lynch. As a leader, he has been especially instrumental in expanding our global franchise. He combines a deep sense of the history and tradition of Merrill Lynch with a keen understanding of the modern dynamics of our business, and is highly regarded and genuinely liked by all of us. No one has a deeper understanding of the needs of our clients and knowledge about the different cultures around the world. Our relationships with governments, corporations, institutions and individuals have been enhanced greatly because of his untiring work. While we regret Win's decision to leave the firm, we respect his reasons for doing so.

I really appreciated those words written by Paul.

A short while later, Komansky phoned me and asked me to stop by. "What the hell did you say to Stan? He said you made demands about compensation, your office, and the use of the corporate jet." Indeed, I had asked Stan what level of compensation he thought the job would be worth and if my office would be on the executive floor and if I would have some priority in continuing to use our jet to call on clients around the world. I believed the answers to these questions were relevant to how he viewed the position. But I hadn't made demands.

"That's not true, Dave. Would you like me to tell you what really happened? Dave, you've always treated me very fairly, and I have enjoyed working for you."

Dave interrupted. "Then why don't you stay at least another two years until I retire? We can have a lot of fun calling on clients."

Dave still refused to see what was happening. I was not going to indulge him in this. "Because, Dave, you won't be around for very much longer. You have no idea what you're up against." I told him about my conversation with Stan and how he'd effectively asked me to be part of his cabal that would rid the firm of Komansky.

"I've got it under control," Dave responded.

"No, you don't!" I told him, and though he attempted to change the subject, I said: "Dave, I love this firm, and I really do hope it all works out for the best. I want to leave honorably, and I want to help the transition in any way I can. I'd like to stay through year end. That will allow me to contact all the clients I have around the world and make them feel good about the change and to transition the business smoothly to Kelly. Just let me stay in my office and pay me fairly at year end. I trust you."

Dave agreed, and I went back to my office. As word of my resignation got out, I began to receive a stream of telephone calls and e-mails. One of the first was from Bill Schreyer.

"What happened?" he asked.

"Bill, I got to the altar, but when the veil was lifted, I just couldn't kiss the bride." He chuckled and wished me well.

A bit later, Terry said, "Mr. Regan is on the phone!" I picked it up.

"What the hell is going on up there?" Don asked in his usual demanding tone. "We need young guys like you. I sure as hell hope you're not going to disappear and become a hermit in Vermont." That was classic Don Regan. We spoke for a while, but having made my decision, I didn't want to say anything more than that I really didn't want to work for O'Neal and thought it best that I move on. I also received nice calls from both Roger Birk and Dan Tully. Little did I realize at the time what an impact my departure was going to have on so many. Over the next few weeks I received more than a thousand letters and e-mails and hundreds of phone calls from friends, colleagues, and clients around the world. One from Yaz Otsuka, the marketing and communications director for our private client business in Japan, had a special impact:

> Dear Win,
>
> It is with tears in my eyes that I have translated your message for JPC employees. It's quite an honor that I did this job for you and for people here. And I wish to extend my personal gratitude for what you gave me in the past few years. I would tell you that I've been feeling your presence at MLJS all the time. You have been a great part of my motivation to stay with this firm. Every time I saw you, you said to me, "Hi, Yaz." Your voice still echoes in my ears and heart. I have really been fortunate that I was able to see in person, a true leader in both physical and spiritual ways, since the very beginning of this great task "Project Blossom." It's my personal belief based upon experience not to love one's firm. However, I've felt and know that Merrill Lynch people and culture are the exception. I fully agree with your saying in the message, hoping that will remain unchanged. I will miss you profoundly.

Among all the phone calls, e-mails, and letters I received, not one was from a member of the Board of Directors, not even Jill Conway, whom I had known and worked closely with for twenty years. I later called her and met with her just prior to leaving in January and told her about my final meeting with O'Neal. It clearly fell on deaf ears. It was really quite incredible that during the transition from Komansky to O'Neal, no one on the board took the time to speak with senior executives, whom they had known well over the years. They were clueless about the negative impact this wholesale change would have on the culture of Merrill Lynch and what it would ultimately lead to.

A couple of weeks after my conversation with Komansky, Terry came into my office to sheepishly say that she had received a call from Terry Kassel, the new director of Human Resources. "We're being moved next week to an outplacement office," she told me. "That's where Jeff Peek is, so we'll have some nice neighbors."

"Bullshit," I blurted out. "Get Komansky on the phone for me."

I didn't hold back. "Dave, I've just been told that I'm being moved to an outplacement office next week. That's not what we agreed to. I thought I could trust your word." There was an embarrassed pause, then Dave said, "I don't know anything about this. I'll get back to you." A few hours later he called and said, "It's all set. You can stay until January, and everything we agreed to is the same." I knew Jeff Peek had retained a lawyer after he'd been terminated, so I called Jeff and asked him for the name. I no longer trusted this new Merrill Lynch. Regrettably, I felt I needed to draft a legal separation agreement, which I did and which Dave signed. How could it have come to this?

Shortly afterward, my New York team wanted to give me a retirement party, but they were told there was no money available, so John Rolander, a consultant we had used for years, said they could hold it at his apartment in Lower Manhattan. It was a fun and relaxed evening among colleagues and friends, and while it was tinged with sadness, it also reinforced why I had enjoyed working so much at Merrill. I would miss the company of these great people. Komansky later called and said he wanted to throw me a retirement party himself, but at that stage I thought it was an insincere and hypocritical offer. I declined.

In early January 2002, after bonuses were paid, I walked out the door of the Merrill Lynch office building in Midtown Manhattan and ended what had been a wonderful career for over twenty-seven years. I was not the only senior executive to leave. Eleven other members of our Executive Management Committee were either forced out or resigned in the eighteen months after O'Neal took over as president. Within a couple of years, the executive team and the Board of Directors looked very different from how they did in July 2001. O'Neal's team was in place and few on that team had the slightest idea about the real Merrill Lynch.

THE WALL STREET JOURNAL.

DOWJONES • • • • MONDAY, SEPTEMBER 15, 2008 • VOL. CCLII NO. 64 ★ ★ ★ ★ $2.00

Last week: DJIA 11421.99 ▲ 201.69 1.85 NASDAQ 2261.27 ▲ 0.25 NIKKEI 12214.76 unch. DJ STOXX 50 2858.68 ▲ 3.85 10-YR TREASURY ▼ 20/32, yield 3.7305 OIL $101.18 ▼ $5.05 EURO $1.4217 YEN 107.87

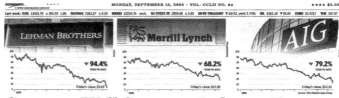

Crisis on Wall Street as Lehman Totters, Merrill Is Sold, AIG Seeks to Raise Cash

Fed Will Expand Its Lending Arsenal in a Bid to Calm Markets; Moves Cap a Momentous Weekend for American Finance

The American financial system was shaken to its core on Sunday. Lehman Brothers Holdings Inc. faced the prospect of liquidation, and Merrill Lynch & Co. agreed to be sold to Bank

By Carrick Mollenkamp, Susanne Craig, Serena Ng and Aaron Lucchetti

of America Corp.

The U.S. government, which bailed out Fannie Mae and Freddie Mac a week ago and orchestrated the sale of Bear Stearns Cos. to J.P. Morgan Chase & Co. in March, played much tougher with Lehman. It refused to provide a financial backstop to potential buyers.

Without such support, Barclays PLC and Bank of America, the two most interested buyers

mercial and investment banks announced Sunday night that they would post $70 billion of their own money to create a borrowing facility. The 10 institutions, which include Citigroup Inc., Credit Suisse Group, Deutsche Bank AG, could tap the pool to help them ride out the crisis. The banks also said they are mutually committed to trying to mitigate market volatility.

A sense of foreboding gripped Wall Street as top executives feared collateral damage from a Lehman liquidation. Attention was focused on Merrill Lynch, which boasts the largest force of retail brokers, and American International Group Inc., the insurance giant. Both firms have seen their stocks get hammered on worries that they

needed capital.

"Monday will be a day of reckoning for the financial markets," said Carlos Mendez, senior managing director of ICP Capital, a boutique investment firm in New York. On Sunday, he said, "it was like a fire alarm went off and people ran in all directions."

AIG executives spent the weekend trying to raise cash, either from asset sales or a capital infusion from private-equity firms, or both. AIG executives were meeting with regulators to see if they could transfer capital from some of its subsidiaries to the holding company.

As worries spread across Wall Street that Lehman wouldn't survive, brokerage firms, hedge funds and other

traders moved to disentangle themselves from trades with Lehman. When news of Lehman's peril date dimmed, a quiet Sunday on Wall Street turned into a mad rush. Executives and traders hurried to their offices or worked their phones to unwind outstanding contracts with Lehman and to gauge their overall exposure.

Merrill, whose brokerage force is known as the "thundering herd," quietly entered into discussions with Bank of America, which has retail bank branches stretching from coast to coast and has long coveted Merrill. Wall Street executives said the Federal Reserve was have been involved in orchestrating the sale, figuring that it was "better to save the rela-
Please turn to page A10

Ultimatum By Paulson Sparked Frantic End

One of the most tumultuous weekends in Wall Street's history began Friday, when federal officials decided to deliver a sobering message to the captains of finance: There would be no government bailout of Lehman Brothers Holdings Inc.

Officials wanted to prepare the market for the possibility that Lehman could simply fail. The best way to do that in an orderly way would be to get everyone together in a room.

Treasury Secretary Henry Paulson, Federal Reserve Chairman Ben Bernanke and his top New York lieutenant, Timothy Geithner, summoned some 30 Wall Street executives for a 6 p.m. Friday meeting at the Fed's offices in Lower Manhattan.

"There is no political will for a federal bailout," Mr. Geithner

By Deborah Solomon, Dennis K. Berman, Susanne Craig and Carrick Mollenkamp

told the assembled executives, according to a person familiar with the matter. "Come back in the morning and be prepared to do something."

Over the next 48 hours, these marching orders developed into a nerve-wracking test of the ability of the U.S. financial system to hold itself together amid the worst series of shocks it has faced in decades.

By taking the rescue option off the table, the U.S. government was declaring that there are limits to its role as backstop-in-chief. A week earlier it had seized mortgage giants Fannie Mae and Freddie Mac, and months prior had brokered the sale of Bear Stearns & Co. to J.P. Morgan Chase & Co. But now, Washington appears to want Wall Street to largely fix its own problems, and feels that finding institutions shouldn't expect the government to commit money to save them. "We've re-established 'moral hazard,'" said a person involved
Please turn to page A19

Please turn to page A10
Please turn to page A19

What's News—

Business & Finance

Lehman faces the possibility of liquidation, and Merrill Lynch agreed to be sold to Bank of America on Sunday, a day in which the U.S. financial system was shaken to its core. The Federal Reserve is expected to take new steps to stabilize the broader financial system. Meanwhile, AIG sought to raise cash and craft a survival plan amid investor pressure. **A1, A10, A16, C1, C3**

■ Regulators and investors prepare for Monday as Lehman's collapse, an AIG deal and talks between Bank of America and Merrill could rattle investors. **C1**

■ Oil futures pushed lower Sunday even after Hurricane Ike forced shutdowns of Gulf Coast refineries and platforms. Crude fell $2.05, or 2.1%, to $99.09 a barrel. **C1**

■ Exit packages for the deposed CEOs of Fannie Mae and Freddie Mac highlight a weak link in efforts to link executive pay with performance: severance deals. **B4**

■ Charles Prince, former Citigroup chairman and CEO, has a new job using his contacts to drum up business for a Washington consulting firm. **C5**

■ Electronic Arts dropped its bid for Take-Two, blaming its inability to get a deal by the holiday season was a factor. **B1**

■ China introduced a high-level commission to oversee enforcement of its new anti-trust legislation, which is facing a test from Coca-Cola. **Money & Investing**

■ Sirius XM's CEO detailed his plan for achieving the company's debt and proving satellite radio's potential. **B1**

■ GM on Tuesday aims to unveil the Chevrolet Volt, its battery-powered car set to hit the market by 2011. **B1**

■ The lengthening lead Japan's auto makers hold in securing batteries for the next generation of cars has become a rallying point for the U.S. auto industry. **B1**

World-Wide

■ The left is trail of damage from Texas to Louisiana. Destruction from the hurricane could squeeze energy supplies and strike a blow to the strong regional economy. More than 2.5 million homes and businesses lost power. Despite a broad evacuation effort, tens of thousands refused to leave their homes. Thirteen people were reported dead by Sunday. **A3**

Gulf Coast oil refineries appeared to have escaped major damage, but power problems prevented many from returning to service.

■ The NTSB was trying to determine the cause of a commuter-train crash in a Los Angeles suburb Friday. The train barreled into an oncoming freight train, and 25 people were killed. The wreck highlights the absence of key safety-equipment on the nation's rail network. **A6**

■ In New Delhi, bombings in popular shopping areas on Saturday killed 21. The five blasts followed three similar attacks that have hit other cities since May. **A10**

■ Obama raised a record $66 million from donors in August, but the money race between him and McCain is likely to be tighter than many originally thought. **A6**

■ Russian troops began pulling back from western Georgia checkpoints, part of an EU-brokered peace deal, but a new battle loomed over international access to Russia-backed separatist regions. **A16**

■ Bolivia's Morales agreed to talks over a clash with opposition-led provinces, after political violence killed as many as 30 last week. **A17**

■ Pakistani security forces killed 16 suspected militants in a tribal region bordering Afghanistan, the latest round of a military offensive with an end in sight, officials said.

Bank of America to Buy Merrill

Merrill Lynch CEO John Thain leaving the Federal Reserve Bank of New York Saturday, where U.S. officials and Wall Street executives met to discuss the turmoil facing U.S. financial institutions. More coverage on C1, C3 and C5.

By Matthew Karnitschnig, Carrick Mollenkamp and Dan Fitzpatrick

In a rushed bid to ride out the storm sweeping American finance, 94-year-old Merrill Lynch & Co. agreed late Sunday to sell itself to Bank of America Corp. for roughly $44 billion.

The deal, worked out in 48 hours of frenetic negotiating, could instantly reshape the U.S. banking landscape, making the nation's prime behemoth even bigger. Late Sunday night, the companies' boards had approved the deal, but lawyers were negotiating over fast-

vice and wealth management.

Driven by Chief Executive Kenneth Lewis, Bank of America has already made dozens of acquisitions large and small, including the purchase of ailing mortgage lender Countrywide Financial Corp. earlier this year. In adding Merrill Lynch, it would control the nation's largest force of stock brokers as well as a well-regarded investment bank.

The combination, if approved by shareholders, would create a bank of vast reach, involved in nearly every nook and cranny of the financial system, from credit cards and auto loans to bond and stock underwriting, merger ad-

Please turn to page A19

Please turn to page A19

Political Turmoil in Thailand Boosts Business for Astrologers

Mr. Luck Automates Fortunetelling; Some Rivals Want Industry Regulation

By James Hookway

BANGKOK—For a glimpse into the future of fortunetelling in Thailand, pay a visit to Luck Rakhanithes.

At Mr. Luck's plush, three-story bungalow of offices, a team of telephone operators guides anxious callers through the chaos of everyday life. Some know what their prospects are for securing a suitable love match or a well-paying job. Others are given auspicious dates for starting a new business.

At 36 years old, Mr. Luck is part of a new generation of business-savvy seers turning the ancient art of astrology into big business. He's a prime-time fixture on Thai television for sowing a red flag when he is 100% certain about his predictions ca

white flag goes up when he's less sure). He sells about 200,000 books a year, he says, thanks to a distribution deal with the local operator of the 7-Eleven convenience-store chain.

As Thailand comes to grips with two years of political unrest—including a coup, deadly riots and, last week, a television cooking show down for hosting a television cooking show—the country has tapped the prime minister to step down for hosting a television cooking show—the country has tapped Mr. Luck's confident forecasts.

"Every time there's a crisis in Thailand, it's a glorious time for astrologers," Mr. Luck says.

It's all too much for some in the old guard, whose predictions tend to be vaguer and more in keeping with the ancient traditions of seers here. These astrologers want about his predictions to
Please turn to page A17

Please turn to page A17

September 15, 2008, was one of Wall Street's darkest days. The Merrill Lynch so many of us knew and loved was brought down by the greed of a few top executives and lack of proper oversight by the Board of Directors.

CHAPTER FOURTEEN

The Death
of Mother Merrill

(2002–2007)

T hough my own time at Merrill Lynch had come to a close, I still cared deeply about the company, especially considering the direction it appeared to be taking, and I would continue to keep abreast of what was happening there.

What a decade it would be.

Of course, the decade began with adverse conditions on Wall Street growing out of the collapse of the Internet bubble, and even three months before 9/11 (an event that would only aggravate these conditions), Merrill Lynch's stock had dropped 30 percent from its record level at the start of the year. The company had thrived and grown as a result of the strong public support for equity investments, but suddenly the market seemed a more dangerous place than it had over the past few years.

Adding to the general downturn in sentiment were a couple of specific blows to the bottom line. While the company's 1997 purchase of Mercury Asset Management was a bold move into the field of global institutional fund management, it brought with it a problem unexpected at the time of the acquisition: The pension fund trustees for Unilever, an Anglo-Dutch conglomerate, sued Mercury for negligence and sought $190 million in damages for the alleged mismanagement of their $1.4 billion pension fund. The case was settled in December 2001, after a month-long trial in London, when ML agreed to pay Unilever an estimated $110 million. It was a large monetary settlement, but the damage to our reputation was even greater.

Another asset management acquisition, the Los Angeles firm of Hotchkiss and Wiley, which was purchased in 1996, also presented problems. The senior managers of the firm, feeling ignored by ML, left and took their best clients with them. Merrill eventually sold what was left of the firm at a loss.

As a result of these events as well as the downturn, revenues, funds under management, and pre-tax profit margins all declined significantly during 2001. The situation was stated clearly in that year's Annual Report:

> The events of September 11 exacerbated already weak economic conditions in the United States and the world's other major and developing economies. Equity indices posted their second consecutive year of declines, while new stock issuance and the value of global mergers both fell steeply. As 2001 progressed, we increasingly came to believe that while long-term growth drivers remain in place for our industry on a global basis, the rate of revenue growth in 1999 and 2000 was an aberration, rather than a sustainable trend—not only for Merrill Lynch, but for the entire industry. As the environment continued to weaken during 2001, we accelerated actions to improve profitability, and took decisive steps to reduce expenses and more sharply focus all our businesses to take maximum advantage of the best opportunities for growth.

The actions referred to here culminated in a fourth-quarter after-tax charge to earnings of $1.7 billion. Excluding this charge and expenses related to September 11, Merrill Lynch would have reported full-year net operating earnings of $2.4 billion—$2.50 per diluted share—net revenues of $21.9 billion, and a pre-tax margin of 16.9 percent. While the results were below those of the prior year, it was hardly a disastrous performance.

And yet at the same time, no one was happy about it. Among the "decisive steps" taken by O'Neal were cutting the firm's payroll by some 17,000 jobs, a reduction of almost 25 percent, from 72,000 to 55,000.

Nearly all Wall Street firms slashed jobs, but none as drastically as ML. In all, Merrill Lynch had made nineteen major acquisitions during the 1990s, but O'Neal believed that the firm had overextended itself, particularly in its global ventures. He trimmed back or eliminated major portions of our global private wealth businesses, drastically reduced the number of relationship managers in the Investment Banking Division, and made significant cuts throughout the U.S. private wealth business. Merrill Lynch had been through many cyclical downturns in the past, and while former leaders like Regan, Birk, Schreyer, and Tully had to cut costs, they never did it as harshly. In the past, Merrill usually gained market share in cyclical downturns. This time, however, the O'Neal team saw things differently. In their opinion, Merrill was "all screwed up" and it needed to be immediately changed fundamentally and then demonstrate short-term results.

By this time, Dave Komansky had been pushed almost entirely out of the picture by Stan O'Neal. Komansky was left out of nearly every critical decision. Dave's decline and O'Neal's emergence actually began immediately after the September 11 attacks when Dave stood by while O'Neal ordered people around. In June of 2002, O'Neal held a major management meeting while pointedly not inviting Komansky. It was clear that O'Neal was now running Merrill Lynch. At one point Don Regan phoned Komansky. "Dave, I understand that you're having some problems with your president," he said. Komansky was attempting to explain the situation when Regan barked, "Fire the bastard!"

"I don't think I can do that," Dave replied sheepishly. "I've already gotten rid of one president, and I don't think it will be good for the firm if I do it a second time."

"Hell, I fired at least two," replied Don. "Do it!"

When Don passed away in 2003, a memorial service was held at the Treasury Department. Among those asked to make official remarks were O'Neal, Vice President Dick Cheney, and Andrew Card, chief of staff to President Bush. O'Neal spoke about how he had grown close to Don and how Don had given him valuable counsel after he became CEO. It made me ill, because I knew the truth. I later asked Tom, Don's oldest son, how the family could have allowed O'Neal to represent Merrill Lynch at the service, rather than Birk, Tully, or Schreyer, who actually knew and worked with Don. "We had no choice" was his response.

During the time Dave was being pushed out, Tully also spoke to him about what was happening and asked for his permission to contact some of the directors. Dan told me that he believed that board members like John Phelan would be sympathetic to blocking O'Neal's accession to CEO, but he would only approach the board with Dave's permission. That was not to be. And thus, O'Neal officially took over as chairman in December 2002.

I t would not take long before the effects of his management were felt, and indeed the enormity of the downsizing he'd engineered as president had a profound impact on the culture of the firm and its future business model. By the end of 2003, not one member of Komansky's Executive Management Committee remained other than O'Neal himself. Jerry Kenney, the firm's leading strategist under Tully and Komansky, was still at the firm, but he no longer had any influence over corporate matters, and, moreover, had been moved from the executive floor to one of the investment banking floors. Even O'Neal's former allies in his quest for the presidency, Tom Patrick and Arshad Zakaria, had been fired. Of the twenty-three members of O'Neal's new executive team, only Bob Mulholland, who had been a financial adviser and office manager in the U.S. Private Client business, had a genuine appreciation for the real Mother Merrill. And he would not last long.

Soon after Patrick's and Zakaria's departure in August of 2003, O'Neal recruited Bob McCann back to Merrill. McCann had left Merrill for Axa Financial in 2002. To the surprise of executive vice presidents James Gorman and Bob Doll, McCann was brought in over them as vice chairman for wealth management, thus appearing to be the number-two executive now behind O'Neal. While McCann was a popular and able executive as co-leader of Merrill's global equity business in the late 1990s, most people thought it strange to bring him back in this position. His background was in equity trading, not private wealth or asset management. Before accepting this position, McCann had called Dan Tully for advice. Tully told him, "Bob, O'Neal is getting pressure to bring someone back who knows the old Mother Merrill. Negotiate hard and ask for the moon." Shortly after McCann's return, Gorman left to head private wealth at rival Morgan Stanley and ultimately succeeded John Mack as CEO. McCann did provide valuable leadership for the durable private wealth business, but it was soon apparent that he was not O'Neal's successor, and it became questionable how much real influence he had on the ultimate direction of the firm. Bob went on to lead private wealth management in the USA for UBS and one of his first recruits was Bob Mulholland.

Until this point in its history, Merrill Lynch had been like a family—a place where employees at all levels were appreciated and considered assets to be nurtured and preserved. For the past half-century, the company's unique culture had allowed it to grow and prosper and to survive in many challenging environments. As Launny Steffens said, "For over fifty years there was not an opportunity that Merrill Lynch didn't seize. We had different leaders with different styles and faced new and challenging environments, but I firmly believe it was our unique and strong culture that made the difference." It was a culture that generated tremendous pride and loyalty on the part of the entire Merrill team. But O'Neal never took the time to understand this culture. He dismissed longtime executives without batting an eye, and in their place he assembled a young management team with few durable ties to ML, little appreciation for the culture of the company, and very little experience in managing through difficult business cycles. Certainly his team consisted of smart and able people, but many lacked heart and were focused on maximizing short-term profitability and bonus pools, and all soon realized that you did not question O'Neal if you wanted to remain on the team. This was so different from how it was with leaders like Dan Tully, who had always encouraged open debate and sought counsel from many.

How much did Merrill change when O'Neal took over? Norman Brodsky, a highly successful entrepreneur, wrote a column called "Street Smarts" for *Inc.* magazine. One of his 2009 pieces was titled "Stan O'Neal Failed the First Rule of Leadership," and it read in part:

> I first became aware of Stan O'Neal through my daughter, Beth, who was working as an intern at Merrill Lynch the summer that he took over from his predecessor, David Komansky. She could hardly believe how quickly and how completely the culture changed. Overnight a chill settled on

the company. Komansky had made a point of eating lunch with his employees in the cafeteria from time to time. O'Neal never showed his face there. Beth and the other interns were given a strict set of rules governing how they should behave in the presence of the new CEO. If they saw him walking down the hall, they were to stay out of the way and not speak to him. If they were waiting for an elevator and the door opened and they saw him inside, they were not to get on. If they were already in the elevator and he got on, they were to step to the rear and keep their mouths shut. Given O'Neal's fear of interns, it's hardly surprising that he would fire Merrill Lynch's leading authority on asset- and mortgage-backed securities, Jeff Kronthal, when he dared warn about the risks the firm was running in that arena. Apparently, O'Neal never learned the most important rule of leadership as he made his way up the corporate ladder: A company is only as good as the people who work for it, and the CEO's main job is to create an environment in which they can thrive.

That was not how people like Charlie Merrill, my father, Bill Schreyer, and Dan Tully had run the company. For them, Merrill Lynch was a firm whose values mattered. The five Principles enunciated it well. We were a firm focused on the best interests of the client. We were a firm where teamwork was expected and rewarded. We were a firm that involved itself in the local communities. We were a firm that stood for integrity. We were a firm that valued its employees. This last trait is something that O'Neal never understood. While all the CEOs had high standards for performance and expected excellence, they also cared for their employees as individuals and often helped them personally. As Dan Tully so forcefully said, "You never throw a fellow employee down a flight of stairs. You always preserve one's dignity." Bill Schreyer may have had to fire or demote longtime colleagues and friends, but his generosity toward them was his way of trying to preserve their dignity. And, of course, I know from my own family history the importance of taking care of ML families.

After my father's death, his partners created the Winthrop H. Smith Memorial Foundation in his honor to help those employees who were facing financial hardships through no fault of their own, as well as to grant college scholarships to children of employees. The foundation was funded over the years by thousands of Merrill Lynchers who knew their generosity would aid their colleagues.

Where once the Annual Reports had cited the Principles, from 2003 on they spoke instead of "the New Merrill Lynch." One of the reports said it was a firm that had been remade to have focus, discipline, performance standards, and results, and was now "sized correctly." It was now a "performance-based culture." The image on the cover of the 2003 Annual Report was especially telling, as it showed two blurred people. While the intent was to demonstrate momentum, the surreal photo made them appear less than human.

Looking back, it is shocking to see how quickly Merrill Lynch had changed. Remember that back in 2001, O'Neal had taken over a vibrant company that still had reason to swagger. In the first quarter of 2001 our stock hit an all-time high of $80 (this was remarkable considering it had traded at a low of $0.75 on a post-split basis when I joined the firm in August of 1974). The prior year we had earned a record $3.8 billion—and we had all been very generously compensated for those results. We had a pre-tax margin of 21.3 percent and a return on equity of 24.2 percent. For the forty-eighth straight quarter, we had led the global underwriting leagues tables with a 13.3 percent market share and were ranked No. 3 in global mergers and acquisitions, with very little difference between us and No. 1. The only category of securities where we were not ranked highly was mortgages, and that was because we did not see it as a core business. Our global research was ranked No. 1 worldwide, and we were the dominant secondary equity-trading firm in the world. Over the past several years we'd gone head to head with Goldman Sachs and Morgan Stanley and won more than our fair share of the lucrative privatization mandates being awarded around the globe.

Our Private Client businesses held $1.5 trillion in client assets and our global asset management business held $557 billion in assets. We had 72,000 employees, 21,200 of whom were financial advisers. Our 975 Private Client offices were represented in forty-four countries.

Our global footprint was the envy of our competitors. By the end of 2003 the overall ML head count had been reduced by 33 percent to 48,100, and only 13,500 financial advisers remained. Adviser assets had fallen to $1.3 trillion.

Before O'Neal, we also had a very sound risk management system. The head of Risk Management was a member of the Executive Committee and reported directly to the chairman and CEO. In 1987, Bill Scheyer and Dan Tully, as CEO and COO respectively, were embarrassed by a trading loss that caused Merrill's first quarterly deficit since 1940. Recall that Dan Napoli, who was in charge of our Government Securities Division, was promoted to head Risk Management for the firm, and he instituted a system that worked very well and prevented many problems that other Wall Street firms faced in the ensuing years. Napoli was given full authority to not only monitor positions but to force them to be unwound if he deemed necessary, and since he had the full support of the CEO, he was not challenged.

Since that time, however, the risk management systems that had worked so well for the firm had weakened. Merrill was looking more and more like Goldman Sachs as its risk assets and leverage increased. In 2001 the firm's adjusted leverage stood at thirteen times shareholders' equity, but by 2007 it would grow to more than thirty-two times shareholders' equity. In the two years prior, nearly $340 billion of assets would be added to its balance sheet, many of which were the toxic assets that would lead to Merrill's demise.

L ess than two years into the new millennium, Wall Street was rocked by a series of scandals worse than any since the Great Depression. First, the Enron Corporation was accused of deceiving its shareholders and then collapsed. Its auditor, Arthur Andersen, was convicted of obstructing justice and was dissolved. Then Tyco International Limited, the Adelphia Communications Corporation, the Xerox Corporation, and WorldCom Inc. all were accused of misdeeds. Greedy executives, motivated by huge stock options intended to be incentives to boost performance, distorted profits while brokerage research analysts were shown to be intentionally steering investors toward stocks they knew were poor investments. Even Dick Grasso, the chairman of the New York Stock Exchange, was forced to resign amid controversy over his pay package.

The victims of all the wrongdoing were American investors, who saw their portfolios and nest eggs shrink drastically, and the legacy of this deception was the splintering of investors' faith in the American financial system. A 2003 Harris Poll showed that six out of ten Americans believed that "most people on Wall Street would be willing to break the law if they could make a lot of money and get away with it." Many of the respondents were small investors who were pursuing the opportunity to participate in the American free-enterprise system that was created for them a half-century earlier by Charlie Merrill and my father. No doubt the two of them were turning over in their graves.

On April 8, 2002, New York State Attorney General Eliot Spitzer accused ML analysts of giving the firm's investment banking customers overly optimistic stock recommendations. After a year-long investigation, Spitzer released a series of e-mails that he said showed sharply negative assessments of companies the analysts were urging the public to invest in. Other investment firms also came under scrutiny, and after a full-blown investigation of the securities industry, state and federal authorities reached a $1.4 billion settlement with some of the nation's largest investment firms. Without admitting any wrongdoing, Merrill agreed to pay $200 million of the settlement. The firm also agreed to sever analysts' compensation from its investment banking business, create a special committee to monitor stock ratings, and publicly disclose whether it would earn investment banking fees from recommended companies.

Merrill alone adopted tougher standards for its research analysts in early 2003, but as Wall Street's best-known brokerage, it came in for special criticism. Charles Schwab & Co. ran a series of television commercials that seemed to be a direct attack on ML. One spot showed a manager telling a group of brokers: "We've got a lot of stock to move today, people. Tell your customers this one's hot. Just don't mention the fundamentals—they stink. Now, let's put some lipstick on this pig." The CBS network refused to run the commercial on grounds that it unfairly impugned the ethics of all Wall Street firms and appeared to single out Merrill Lynch. However, it was widely played on other broadcast outlets.

Komansky, who was still nominally in charge at this time, made public apologies and appeared in newspaper ads detailing steps that had been taken to simplify ML's stock-rating system and to base analysts' pay on the accuracy of their ratings. "Lately, you've been hearing a lot about Merrill Lynch," said the ad copy. "Now you're going to hear from us. Leaders respond constructively to criticism; we've heard the criticism and are responding beyond what was asked." The ads heralded the adoption of a "new industry standard" for research integrity. In a major speech before an investors' conference, O'Neal acknowledged that "we've given ammunition to people who want to have a cynical view about us. That is inexcusable." But he added: "If we find people who do not operate with integrity, they will be gone."

To those of us with a long history at Merrill Lynch, the Spitzer investigation was painful—especially since it uncovered a few very troubling e-mails from an analyst named Henry Blodgett, who became the focus of the inquiry. Basically, Blodgett had written e-mails in which he expressed his opinion of stocks that were being represented in a different light to the public. Many of us felt that he was just a poor analyst and was not out to defraud anyone. I wrote an op-ed for the *Financial Times* that explained how research at Merrill Lynch had always been organized to protect the client's interest, and I received numerous messages of thanks from analysts who felt betrayed and misrepresented. Unfortunately, the public's perception was very different, and Merrill suffered a black eye.

Since its founding, Merrill Lynch had always believed that securities research had to be an independent division within the firm and protected from any undue influence, and management had always vigilantly protected the integrity of Merrill's independent research. This is why the Spitzer witch hunt was so appalling. I personally knew of numerous instances where CEOs whose investment banking business we either had or were soliciting called Schreyer, Tully, or Komansky to insist that we change a negative research opinion. We never did. Richard Margolis, a former member of our Asian institutional team who had joined us from Smith New Court, recently told me in an e-mail of his admiration for the ethics of the firm:

Although I only ever worked in the institutional business, you needed to be blind, deaf, and dumb not to realize that the retail business was the heart and soul of Merrill; the foundation which made everything else possible; and the source of the fine ethical standards which I remember being the hallmark of the firm when it acquired Smith New Court. I particularly remember an add-on equity financing for Samsung Electronics on which the firm lost money because Tom Kurlak went negative on the sector during the roadshow. But in aggregate, no money was lost, because institutional clients gave extra orders to reward the firm for having independent analysts. And there was, of course, a huge reputational dividend. None of this added anything to the bonus pool, but made loads of people feel good about working for Merrill.

Had Steve Hammerman, with his experienced legal mind, still been general counsel, I think the outcome of the whole Spitzer case might have been very different. Steve had the savvy and toughness to deal with unscrupulous politicians like Eliot Spitzer, but as it turned out, negotiations were in the hands of Merrill's new and young general counsel, Rosemary Berkery. She was capable but lacked Hammerman's experience and negotiating skills. After Spitzer threatened to use an arcane New York State law called the Martin Act to bring a felony charge against Merrill Lynch, knowing full well that no financial firm could realistically face a damaging felony charge, Merrill capitulated and set the stage for the broader settlement with Wall Street. This in turn set the stage for Spitzer to achieve his political goal of becoming governor of New York before having to resign in shame when he was caught hiring a prostitute in Washington, D.C.

And then, of course, there was Enron. After the company declared bankruptcy in December 2001, the SEC, Congress, and the Justice Department reacted to the justified outrage of Enron investors and other stakeholders, and initiated civil and criminal investigations in an attempt to identify all who had contributed to this debacle. The entire Arthur Andersen firm became a casualty, but then the Justice Department set its sights on Enron's investment bankers. Before its collapse, Enron had been a prized investment banking client, and Merrill's Houston oil-and-gas team, like all the major banks, had pursued them vigorously. However, we were not very successful until Enron presented a deal to the Houston team in December 1999.

At that time, Enron was building electric barges for the Nigerian government, and it told Merrill's bankers in Houston that they had a signed contract for the electricity that would be produced by these barges. The barges were not yet completely built, but Enron wanted to sell them prior to year's end, and so it asked Merrill's Houston team if Merrill would purchase the barges and then resell them once they were completed. Essentially, this would be a $7 million deal—not a large deal by Wall Street standards and, in fact, not something we would normally handle, but we figured we could use it to show our support for Enron in the hope of winning future profitable business. Even though it was small, the deal received tremendous attention and was taken through the entire commitment process, with about thirty Merrill Lynch lawyers, risk managers, finance staff members, and investment bankers reviewing the transaction. It was even discussed by the Executive Committee because Nigeria had a reputation for corruption. Ultimately, the ML commitment committee okayed the deal, subject to confirming that Andrew Fastow, Enron's CFO, was aware of the transaction, approved it, and would represent that Enron would complete the barges expeditiously. Dan Bayly, the head of Investment Banking, had not been involved up until now, but at this point he was asked by his boss, Tom Davis, the executive vice president of Capital Markets, to call Fastow and get these assurances.

Dan reached Fastow shortly before Christmas. Merrill's chief investment banking counsel, Kathy Zrike, was given the telephone number and may have actually been on the call with Fastow along with Bayly, but in later testimony she said she didn't remember. There were three people on the call from Enron and at least three from Merrill, and not one of these people, according to later testimony, thought the call was inappropriate in any way. Dan received the necessary assurances and the transaction went through.

Then in 2002, two years after the fall of Enron, the Justice Department discovered this deal and started to investigate Merrill's role with Enron. Dan was designated as the firm's representative in testimony before both Congress and the SEC. He agreed to this even though he was no longer the head of Investment Banking, had not been involved directly with the deal other than that one five-minute phone call, and was about to retire. "Why wouldn't I have?" Dan explained to me later. "This was a totally legitimate deal. Merrill did nothing wrong, and even though I was not engaged directly in the origination or the approval of the deal, I was happy to represent the firm."

That was vintage Dan, being loyal to the firm he'd joined in 1972 as one of the first MBAs hired by Tom Chrystie when Chrystie began expanding our investment banking practice. Eventually, Dan moved to our Chicago investment banking office and spent the bulk of his career there until he was promoted by Herb Allison to become the director of Merrill's global Investment Banking Division in 1998. I knew and worked with Dan from the time I joined ML in 1974, and I have never met a more honest, ethical, and loyal person. All over Wall Street, Dan was known as "Eagle Scout Bayly" because he would reject any deal that did not measure up to his strict standards.

Dan testified for hours without even thinking of invoking his Fifth Amendment rights and relied on the advice of Merrill Lynch's internal lawyers. Surprisingly to Dan, after being told by one of those lawyers that everyone at Merrill who was involved would testify, Tom Davis was called and he invoked his right not to testify under the Fifth Amendment.

In March 2003, after Merrill Lynch was threatened with a charge of fraud relating to the barge deal, O'Neal agreed to settle for $80 million and to cooperate in the investigation of Bayly and three other Merrill Lynch employees, Robert Furst, William Fuhs, and James Brown. At the time the deal had been made, O'Neal was the firm's CFO and would have known of it. In fact, in later discovery, Bayly's lawyers came across a handwritten note by Kathy Zrike that read, "Must inform Stan." Now that O'Neal was CEO, many of us wondered: Was it *his* role in the deal that caused him to settle for such a huge amount of money, and to agree to throw fellow Merrill Lynchers to the wolves of the Justice Department?

In hindsight Dan's willingness to testify was obviously a huge mistake. Between his testimony before Congress and the SEC, he generated 350 pages of testimony. When he agreed to testify, it was never pointed out to him by Merrill's attorneys that it would be easy for prosecutors to show inconsistencies if a defendant later testified in his own defense at a subsequent trial. After he testified before the SEC, Dan was not eager to represent Merrill before a Senate committee, but O'Neal threatened to fire him if he didn't. Other pressure was brought to bear as well. For example, Dan had been asked to write a chapter for a book on investment banking, and during a break in his SEC testimony, a Merrill attorney called him on his cell phone to say, "We're withholding permission for you to write this to see how your SEC testimony turns out." The message was clear!

On November 3, 2003, Dan, the three other Merrill employees, and four Enron employees were indicted by the Justice Department on conspiracy and fraud charges. The government also named everyone involved in the commitment process as unindicted coconspirators, essentially prohibiting them from testifying on behalf of their former colleagues. I was shocked. To me this was an attempt by some young politically ambitious lawyers in the Justice Department to make a name for themselves by going after a major firm. Along with many others, I reached out to Dan to see how I could help, and he asked me, along with Dan Tully and Susan Scherbel, a managing director in our Investment Banking Division, to be character witnesses at his trial. I didn't even need to think about it before saying yes.

When I first met with Dan's lawyers in New York and learned more about the case against him, it seemed incredible that any jury could convict him—even a jury in Houston, where there were many individuals who had been adversely and unfairly affected by the failure of Enron. The issue was whether Fastow had done a sham transaction by pretending to sell an asset to improve the balance sheet of the company prior to year's end, with a guarantee from Enron to repurchase the asset in the new year. If he had, that would have been fraud. Prior to trial the government lawyers told the judge (but never the jury) that if this was simply a purchase by LJM2, the ultimate buyer, they had no problem with it. It was the "guarantee" that was at the heart of the issue—that would have made the accounting wrong and thus a sham transaction. The December phone call that Dan made to Fastow was the primary evidence the Justice Department presented to support its indictment. But Fastow was never allowed to speak to Dan's lawyers or testify at the trial because earlier he'd entered a plea bargain that reduced his prison time for the actual fraud committed by him and others at Enron.

Nevertheless, the government was allowed to present hearsay evidence by others, who allegedly had heard from Fastow that he'd guaranteed to Bayly that Enron would repurchase the barges from Merrill. Thus it came down to Fastow's word against Bayly's, and that's why the issue of Dan's character was likely to be so important in the trial.

Unknown to Dan, the barges were indeed later sold to LJM2, a special-purpose vehicle, and some of the partners were employees of Merrill Lynch, a fact that the Justice Department used to great effect at the trial even after telling the judge it wasn't an issue. While this partnership was legally a third-party independent purchaser, there was the appearance of a conflict, and it was stupid on the part of someone at Merrill Lynch to allow employees to invest in it. The barges were later sold to the global power company AES Corporation, and to this day are still producing electricity in Nigeria.

I was scheduled to testify on behalf of Dan on a sweltering summer day. Dan Tully had done so the day before, and Susan Scherbel was on the stand ahead of me. As I sat waiting for my turn outside the courtroom, the door suddenly swung open and one of Dan's lawyers came over and said, "I'm really sorry to have dragged you down to Houston. Susan hit a home run, and we've decided to rest the case rather than put on another character witness. We think that might be overkill."

"That's great!" I said. All of us—Dan, his family, his lawyers, and ML colleagues—went out to lunch at a nearby restaurant, and I'll always remember what Dan's Houston attorney said: "Today was great, but we have a long way to go. The jury is through hearing about you, but now the other three Merrill Lynch people will be tried and then the Enron employees and then in a few weeks the jury will be asked to decide. Here's the summary that the prosecution is going to use: 'Ladies and gentlemen, over these past several weeks you have heard a lot of technical jargon and seen these slick lawyers from New York in action. What you now need to do is look into your hearts and do the right thing.' Translation: 'Forget the facts, and just put the bastards from New York in jail.'" (Incidentally, a very telling aspect of the trial was the positioning of Merrill's lawyers. Just as at weddings, one sits on the side of the aisle of the person who invited you. Merrill's lawyers sat on the government's side.)

In the end, the jury found all the defendants guilty. After the verdict was announced, the government lawyers were high-fiving one another and I can imagine them all thinking of which political office to run for. Before the sentencing, seventy of us had written letters to Judge Ewing Werlein about Dan's character and our belief in his innocence. The government was pushing for a sentence of fourteen years and wanted bail denied. Fortunately, Werlein took these letters into account. In fact, he said that in all his years on the bench he had never read anything like them. He even referred to Bayly as "Boy Scout–like" and called the barge scam a "rather small and benign fraud in the contemptible Enron fraud."

Werlein reluctantly sentenced Dan to thirty months in jail, and shockingly, Dan and the other three Merrill Lynchers were sent to hard-core prisons. Dan spent more than a year at a southern Virginia federal prison in a cell with five other inmates, all of whom had been incarcerated for violent or drug-related crimes. In November 2005, Dan was interviewed in prison by a *New York Times* reporter and told him: "It's a nightmare. Every day I wake up and say this is not possible. I loved the business. I loved helping clients, and I've always loved the firm."

It was a terrible miscarriage of justice, for in August 2006, after all of the defendants had served more than a year in prison, the Fifth Circuit Court of Appeals threw out most of their convictions. Though Dan's convictions were vacated on all counts, the ruling left the door open for the Justice Department to retry him, and a new group of young lawyers appeared ready to proceed. After several years of hell, the Damoclean sword was still hanging over Dan's head, but then an investigation by Dan and his lawyers found that the government had suppressed evidence, including the damning fact that Andrew Fastow had admitted to the Justice Department that he had never guaranteed that Enron would repurchase the barge. **This was the only thing that would have made the transaction illegal.** As Holman Jenkins later wrote in a *Wall Street Journal* editorial:

> The government's case on this vital point consisted of hearsay from Enron employees and emails between people who weren't party to the phone call. Kept from the defense, it later emerged, were FBI notes with Mr. Fastow in which

he explicitly denied making such a promise. As Mr. Fastow explained it, he only later fibbed to Enron colleagues about such a promise in order to "light a fire" under them to find a permanent owner of the barges.

But this evidence was never released in the trial. The discovery of this shocking abuse of prosecutorial power was enough to shake my faith in our justice system.

Today Dan Bayly is still a very good friend of mine and remains a remarkable human being. After a successful career of nearly thirty years, he had been about to retire when Komansky and O'Neal asked him to testify about the Enron deal, and he did it without hesitation because Mother Merrill, the firm that he trusted, had asked him to. He lost nearly a decade of his life fighting the charges by self-serving lawyers in the Justice Department, doing prison time, and then waiting another couple of years to see if he would be retried before the feds finally dropped the case with the proviso that Dan settle with the SEC without agreeing to their accusations and pay a modest fine. The use of the threat of a criminal case in order to force a defendant to settle a civil case is broadly considered an unethical and maybe even illegal tactic, but this is how the Justice Department wanted to save face after Fastow's exculpatory disclosure became known to Dan, who reluctantly agreed to the terms in order to move on with his life.

This injustice against him and the other three Merrill Lynch bankers is a book that needs to be written. While the obvious villains are the federal prosecutors who knowingly covered up evidence, I hold O'Neal and his legal team equally to blame. Dan Tully and other former principled leaders of Merrill Lynch would never have made Dan and the others sacrificial lambs. They would have fought the Justice Department because the firm had done nothing wrong, and any settlement they might have agreed to would have ensured the protection of all innocent Merrill employees. In fact, in retirement, Tully worked for years counseling Dan, speaking with and consoling his family, offering to raise money for his defense, and doing whatever he could to support the Bayly family during these horrible days. He even visited Dan in prison. This was what Mother Merrill was all about. She never abandoned one of her own. In contrast, O'Neal and others at Merrill Lynch knew that even if the transaction was fraudulent, which it was not, Dan was not the person to blame. However, they sat by and allowed a wonderful person and his family to go through years of personal agony, and Merrill's Board of Directors at the time concurred with this course of action. It was shameful.

Tom Davis, Dan's boss and a fellow executive vice president and member of the Executive Management Committee, went through his own personal hell for nearly a decade. At the same time the Justice Department began its investigation of the barge deal in 2002, the Securities and Exchange Commission opened its own inquiry. Tom was subpoenaed to testify about the deal, but because there was a parallel criminal investigation occurring, Tom's lawyers advised him to refuse to testify under his Fifth Amendment rights. Davis was immediately terminated by Merrill in a highly publicized fashion—despite the fact that he had offered to resign. His unvested restricted stock and options were forfeited but were eventually restored. In the spring of 2003 he was named in an SEC complaint along with Dan Bayly, Skyler Tilney, and Robert Furst and charged with aiding and abetting Enron's fraud. The complaint said very little about Davis or what he allegedly did. Later all parties named in this civil action agreed to a stay pending the resolution of the criminal case against Bayly and others.

A black cloud hung over Tom's head and effectively prevented him from getting another job in the industry. Then in early 2006, the judge "administratively closed" the case and granted all parties the right to reinstate it in the future at such time they deemed appropriate. Because he had not sought the dismissal, Tom was never sure why this happened, and while the closing of the case was welcome, the fact that it could be reinstated by the SEC at any time did not allay the cloud over Tom. Nothing more was heard from the SEC until December 2012 when Davis was notified that the case had been voluntarily dismissed as it related to him *with prejudice*. This meant the SEC could no longer bring back the case. Thus, after ten years of being under this blot of injustice, Tom could finally move on with his life. The stress on Tom and his family is just one more example of how Mother Merrill had left the scene and how a government agency abused its power—with terrible consequences for good, able, and loyal long-term executives like Tom Davis.

A s scandals like these, along with the burst of the technology bubble, pushed investors out of stocks in the early part of the decade, cash management became *sine qua non* for any financial services firm. ML was no exception. Company advertising dropped the "Be Bullish" slogan (though the bull itself reappeared after an absence of nearly a decade) and focused on the firm's newer products and services. "We want to reinforce that we are more than brokers and stock pickers," Paula Polito, head of marketing for Merrill's global brokerage operation, told *The New York Times*. To tie all its offerings together, the firm coined the phrase "Total Merrill" and the slogan "We see your financial life in total."

The year 2003 was only a week old when the company introduced Beyond Banking, a new cash management service that offered all the typical features of a checking and savings account, including ATM access, online bill payment, and a variety of short-term investment products, but in addition clients had access to innovative mortgage, credit, and lending products together with the advice and guidance of a Merrill Lynch financial adviser. Perhaps most significantly, Beyond Banking was a response to changing demographics in that some 78 million baby boomers were nearing retirement and moving from an emphasis on accumulation of wealth to preservation and liquidity. They were migrating from growth investments to a comprehensive, well-diversified strategy that was not tied disproportionately to the stock market and took into consideration the role of cash and liability management.

Beyond Banking was the final plank in Total Merrill, a comprehensive financial management platform. With Total Merrill, customers could organize all, or components, of their financial life—from everyday cash management to long-term investments and liabilities—at Merrill Lynch. While the new regime took credit for all of this, in reality most of the strategies and ideas had been developed by Launny Steffens and his team years earlier. In fairness, though, the new team executed them well. Despite what was happening to other parts of the organization and the overall culture, the private wealth business—the foundation of Merrill Lynch—continued to perform well, even if its many senior financial advisers bemoaned how the firm had changed.

In 2003 the company had a record profit of some $4 billion, and O'Neal celebrated by raising executive bonuses. For himself, he received a $28 million package—$14 million in cash, $11.2 million in stock, and options valued at $2.8 million. As the results improved, I thought that perhaps I had been mistaken and that O'Neal was getting the firm back on track after the recession following 9/11.

In the fall of 2003, Claudia Kahn, whom I had hired years earlier and who was now an assistant to O'Neal, invited me to lunch and spoke glowingly about O'Neal and the job he was doing. I bit my tongue and we had a nice reunion, recollecting many of the projects we'd worked on together over the years. A few days later she telephoned to ask if I would receive a call from her boss. "Of course, Claudia," I told her.

Shortly thereafter, O'Neal's secretary called. "Hi, Win, I understand that you would like a meeting with Mr. O'Neal."

"Well, actually," I answered, "I understand that Stan would like to see *me*. I'll be in town next week, if that works out." We made an appointment.

When I arrived, I was heartened by the greetings of several of our security personnel. "We hope you're coming back, Mr. Smith," one of them said. "We need you." As soon as I was ushered into O'Neal's office, I was struck by the décor. It was been totally redone and looked nothing like the other offices on the thirty-second floor of the World Financial Center—his private conference room had even been turned into a gym. (A few years later John Thain, who would replace O'Neal, was criticized for remodeling this same office, but there is no way that he would have fit into the décor O'Neal had chosen.) Several minutes after I arrived, O'Neal walked in. Once again, just as with our meeting two years earlier, there was no chitchat. He got straight to the point. "I'd like you to become an adviser to me on Asia," he said. He had difficulty clarifying what he was looking for, but I understood that it would be some sort of a consulting role. "You have a lot of knowledge about the area and a lot of contacts, so I think you'd help us greatly."

"Stan," I asked, "what is your vision for Asia?"

"That's why I want you to take this role: to help us figure that out," he responded. *Well, we did prior to 2001*, I thought, *but you changed all that.* He continued, "I'm on the board of General Motors, and they'll be selling more cars in China than in the U.S., so this has to be a big opportunity for us." Again, I thought, *No kidding! Why do you think I spent so much time helping to build our efforts, which you dismantled?* I thanked Stan for the offer and told him I'd consider it and get back to him. My decision was made before the elevator door opened, and I wrote him a polite letter the next day declining the position.

Before leaving the building after my meeting with O'Neal, I stopped by to see my good friend Jerry Kenney, the only member of the old executive team still at Merrill. As I mentioned earlier, he had been relegated to a small office on one of the investment banking floors and clearly had no influence anymore on strategic decisions. "You made the right decision leaving," Jerry said. "Carol [his wife] and Rose [his secretary] tell me I should get out, too, but I think I can still make a difference helping with financial institution relationships." He added with irony: "There aren't many people with some gray hair left." Jerry told me how the culture had changed and how the firm was now being run just by O'Neal and Ahmass Fakahany, the controller, who had become one of his major allies, and a few cronies. None of them had any interest in listening to anyone else. "Every time someone from the old guard left," Jerry said, "there were high-fives on the thirty-second floor." Over his three decades at Merrill, Jerry had done much to create our global success, but now he was being ignored and treated with great indignity. And yet he remained optimistic and thought that maybe he could outlast the new regime and make a difference in the meantime. He was wrong.

A few weeks later Landon Thomas of *The New York Times* wrote a critical article on O'Neal headlined "Dismantling a Wall Street Club," and he took a sentence from a speech I had given several months earlier at Duke University's Fuqua School of Business. It was a speech about Merrill's legacy and leadership, and in it I asked the question about whether the new leadership team could be as successful as prior ones:

> So the question is this: As a different firm, with a management team who may not understand and appreciate the culture and the principles in the same way as former teams, will Merrill Lynch continue to be an industry leader? As someone who is still a significant shareholder and who has many friends still there, I hope the answer is yes. Merrill is still a fabulous franchise and has many talented

people. However, in my opinion, the jury is out despite the strong financial results of last quarter, and we will not know the answer to this for several years. Merrill Lynch may be better for the shareholder in the near term, but will it be a better firm that endures for the long term? Cultures take a long time to create, but they can be cracked much faster.

The only part that made Thomas's article was "the jury is still out." Knowing the waves this would make, I sent Claudia Kahn a copy of the entire speech and asked her to show it to O'Neal, so he could read the quote in context. She called back and said O'Neal "has no interest in reading it." I heard from several others that he was extremely angry with me, so when the record quarterly earnings were announced, I sent him an e-mail: "Stan, congratulations on the great quarter. It is great to see these results. All the best, Win." I received a curt e-mail back the same day: "Not sure what to make of your e-mail given your percistent [*sic*] criticism." That was our last communication.

As the decade continued and economies and markets recovered, Merrill's financial results also continued to improve, and eventually its stock price neared $100 per share. Starting with net earnings of $2.5 billion in 2002, after the write-down of $1.7 billion in 2001, the firm reached an impressive and record level of $7.5 billion in 2006. O'Neal's star rose on Wall Street and the Board of Directors rewarded him with total compensation that reached $38 million annually. It was even rumored that O'Neal, who was a generous campaign bundler for President Bush's 2004 reelection campaign, was on the short list to replace John Snow as Treasury secretary. Word was he was actually working hard on this effort, and many believed it was his exit strategy from Merrill after he made his fortune.

Despite the record results, though, I and some others could see that not all was well within Merrill Lynch. Unfortunately, the ML directors, most analysts, and the media were clueless. They saw the short-term bottom-line results and dug no deeper. But a fissure was growing that would eventually rip the company apart. People whom I know and respected and who were still at Merrill would confide in me about a reign of terror, how employees were fearful of bringing bad news to O'Neal and disagreeing with him. As John Thain later observed, there was a "silo mentality" that prevented teamwork and understanding across business lines. Likewise, there was O'Neal's aloofness, his disdain of Mother Merrill and the Principles, and the perceived abuse by him of certain perks, such as the use of corporate jets and helicopter by certain members of the executive team. Many within the firm were whispering about O'Neal's passion for golf, which he often played alone, and his quest to belong to America's best golf clubs, such as Augusta National. According to members of the executive travel staff team, the corporate helicopter was on standby every Friday in case O'Neal wanted to play.

Later, after John Thain took over from O'Neal, we had lunch and John told me of many of the changes he would be making. "I'm getting rid of the helicopter, too. I looked at the flight log and since I don't play golf or have a house in Martha's Vineyard, I don't think we need it." Stories had circulated within the firm of how the helicopter had been used to transport a cooked turkey up to Martha's Vineyard for an O'Neal family holiday, and how it had been used to get the family dog to the island home. One year, O'Neal arranged some business meetings in South Africa around the Christmas holidays so that he could take his family there for vacation. John Thain also told me that he would be auctioning off the expensive wine cellar that Ahmass Fakahany particularly enjoyed partaking of while traveling on the corporate jet.

After the bear market of the early part of the decade came to an end, Merrill reversed its shrinkage mode with the addition of some twelve hundred employees, a move intended to increase business in hedge fund brokerage and electronic trading, and at the same time increased its acquisitions. In 2004, ML spent about $1 billion for the energy-trading business of Entergy-Koch, which came with 280 employees. Merrill had abandoned energy trading in 2001, and critics said it paid too much for Entergy-Koch. Net earnings rose to $4.4 million for the year and return on equity was 14.9 percent. However, these were not stellar results compared to other Wall Street powerhouses.

Then, in September 2005, ML purchased The Advest Group, Inc., a Hartford, Connecticut, company with some fifteen hundred employees engaged in three businesses: a private client group with 515 financial advisers in the Northeast, Midwest, and Florida; Boston Advisors, which managed $3 billion in balanced equity and fixed-income portfolios for individuals and institutional investors; and Capital Markets Group, with middle-markets and institutional-capital-markets divisions. This was a very curious acquisition. Advest advisers were very different from Merrill advisers. In hindsight, this did not turn out to be a very successful acquisition. However, Merrill's earnings rose to $5.1 million in 2005 and ROE improved to 16 percent.

But O'Neal's biggest acquisition moves were in the lucrative mortgage business. Between January 2005 and January 2007, he purchased a dozen mortgage-related companies or their assets. These included businesses in the United Kingdom, Germany, South Korea, and Italy. The largest of these was the $1.3 billion acquisition of First Franklin, which specialized in risky mortgages. Jeff Kronthal, a very capable executive who headed Merrill's mortgage business, opposed this acquisition and was fired by O'Neal, over the objection of his boss, Greg Fleming. O'Neal planned to issue in-house mortgages and package them into so-called CDOs—collateralized debt obligations. Clearly, the company was building a money machine—and moving into dangerous waters. The firing of Kronthal may have been the point at which Merrill's demise went from a possibility to a likelihood.

Another blockbuster deal was the merger of the company's $539 billion asset management business, Merrill Lynch Investment Management (MLIM), with BlackRock, Inc., to create a new independent company that became one of the world's largest asset management firms, with nearly $1 trillion in assets under management. Merrill Lynch's stake in BlackRock was 49.8 percent, but even before the deal was consummated in February 2006, Larry Fink, BlackRock's chief executive officer, began having misgivings about the mortgage market, and he expressed them to O'Neal. According to Charles Gasparino, in his 2009 book, *The Sellout*, the conversation went like this:

"Stan, we have these great risk models," Fink said. He was referring to BlackRock's mortgage bond analytics. These models had been carefully crafted since the time Fink had lost his shirt and nearly his career in the mortgage market, and they would now be available to Merrill after the deal went through. "O'Neal, uninterested, just changed the subject," Gasparino reported.

Low interest rates were propelling investors into riskier ventures in order to realize higher returns. Bundled mortgages like CDOs were pooled amid claims that the inherent risk was diluted by their broad diversity. By the time latecomer Merrill Lynch got into the act in 2005, the mania was in full bloom nationwide. Within a year, Merrill was the world's biggest CDO underwriter. Tom Guba, a good friend of mine, who was a partner in another Wall Street firm that specialized in mortgages, told me at the time that they were ceasing doing business with Merrill because of its exposure to CDOs and mortgages. "They now have the biggest exposure on the Street, and we're really concerned about them," he said. That comment in early 2007 really got my attention.

"But just as Merrill began moving deeper into mortgages, the housing market started to show its first signs of distress," notes Andrew Ross Sorkin in his book *Too Big to Fail.*

Nevertheless, O'Neal pushed on, reassuring investors that the new strategy would "not in any material way add to the risk profile of our firm."

Many disagreed. In *The Sellout*, Gasparino notes:

> Merrill Lynch had never been very good in the risk-taking department. The firm's business model had been built not on taking risk but on giving advice. Merrill had the nation's largest brokerage firm, its thousands of financial advisers peddling stocks to investors in cities across the country.
>
> The brokerage division was Merrill's heart and soul. Nearly every CEO at the firm had been a broker. It's the reason O'Neal had pushed to manage the brokerage department in 2000 on his way up the ranks. He'd viewed it as stepping-stone to the big time. And he was right. The problem is that while brokers are trained to sell stocks, they tend to make lousy risk managers.

Gasparino was clearly mistaken when he said Merrill was never good at risk-taking. Until recently, it had made some mistakes but we always learned from them and had developed a very good risk management controls. According to Gasparino:

O'Neal later said the realities of the business had left him no choice but to ramp up risk and leverage: fees were being squeezed due to greater competition, and investors were demanding that he crank out Goldman-type earnings. The data seemed to back him up. Over the previous ten years, underwriting fees had declined by 26 percent. Merrill had been hit particularly hard by the commoditization of the brokerage business [meaning people were choosing a broker on the basis of price alone], Fees declined by more than 80 percent because of increased competition and the advent of cheap online trading. Goldman had been the first to figure out that the only way to combat the decrease in fees was to fight it through risk-taking activities on the trading desk, and its earnings had soared, as had those of others that embraced the Goldman philosophy (a group that now included just about every firm on Wall Street). . . .

In O'Neal's mind, Merrill couldn't survive without taking more risk, even if taking risk put its very survival in jeopardy.

But while it is true that Merrill earnings lagged the Street, the actions O'Neal took in 2001 that cut back major portions of our business were the major reason why Merrill did not rebound as the markets recovered. O'Neal felt he had to take on new business quickly in order to ramp up earnings.

Early on, there were red flags. Indeed, ML's own chief economist, David A. Rosenberg, issued a paper entitled "Housing: If Not a Bubble Then an Oversized Sud" in August 2004, a detailed analysis of the precarious state of the American housing market and its threat to the entire economy. Then, in May 2005, François Trahan, the former chief equities investment strategist for Bear Stearns, warned about the threat of the declining housing market and raised the specter of a global credit crisis in a paper entitled "REIT All About It." But O'Neal did not heed these alerts, insisting, "We've got the right people in place, as well as good risk management and controls."

O'Neal's ally in these ventures was Ahmass Fakahany, who was given wide responsibility for ML's risk exposure. But Fakahany clearly failed in his oversight responsibility of watching the firm's growing leverage and the risk profile of the assets that were being added to the balance sheet.

One of the best overall accounts of the financial meltdown is *All the Devils Are Here: The Hidden History of the Financial Crisis*, by Bethany McLean and Joe Nocera. They tell the story of John Breit, who had been one of ML's best risk managers but saw his power stripped under O'Neal. Working on his own, Breit discovered that the company's losses were far greater than what was being projected. O'Neal got wind of this and summoned Breit to his office one day in 2007. According to McLean and Nocera, their encounter went like this:

> "I hear you have a model," O'Neal said.
>
> "Not a model," Breit replied. "Just a back-of-the-envelope calculation." The third quarter would end in a few weeks, and Merrill would have to report the write-downs in its earnings release. How bad did he think it would be? O'Neal asked. "Six billion," said Breit. But he added, "It could be a lot worse." Breit had focused only on a small portion of Merrill's exposure, he explained; he hadn't been able to examine the entire portfolio.
>
> Breit would never forget how O'Neal looked at that moment. He looked like he had just been kicked in the stomach and was about to throw up. Over and over again, he kept asking Breit how it could have happened. Hadn't Merrill Lynch bought credit default swaps to protect itself against defaults? Why hadn't the risk been reflected in the risk models? Why hadn't the risk managers caught the problem and stopped the trades? Why hadn't Breit done anything to stop it? Listening to him, Breit realized that O'Neal seemed to have no idea that Merrill's risk management function had been sidelined.
>
> The meeting finally came to an end; Breit shook O'Neal's hand and wished him luck. "I hope we talk again," he said.
>
> "I don't know," replied O'Neal. "I'm not sure how much longer I'll be around."

O'Neal went back to his desk to contemplate the disaster he now knew was unavoidable—not just for Merrill Lynch but for all of Wall Street. John Breit walked back to his office with the strange realization that he—a midlevel employee utterly out of the loop—had just informed one of the most powerful men on Wall Street that the party was over.

For several years, when journalists would call and ask my off-the-record opinion of how things were going at Merrill Lynch, I would try to explain to them what I thought was really happening in terms of changes to the culture of the firm. Few, however, were interested in looking beyond the reported record earnings, an indifference that frustrated me as well as many of my former colleagues like Dan Tully, Launny Steffens, Ed Goldberg, and Barry Friedberg, who also saw what was happening to Mother Merrill.

But suddenly in October 2007 I was being asked by numerous reporters about my views on the company, and the ML situation had deteriorated to the point that I was ready to be quoted on the record. I was in a hotel room at Parrot Cay in the Turks and Caicos Islands, where I was attending my daughter's wedding, and watching Maria Bartiromo on CNBC when I decided to e-mail my former assistant, Debbie Nikiper, who now worked for Maria, and ask if Bartiromo would be interested in speaking to me on the record. Debbie quickly e-mailed me back: "Are you serious?" I assured her I was, and a short while later Maria and I were talking on the telephone. She asked if she could arrange for a live interview on her show the following week after ML's earnings were released, and I gave her the go-ahead. The following week she had a production truck sent to Sugarbush, and she interviewed me on split screen, with her in New York and me sitting in front of a fireplace at Sugarbush.

"Win, welcome to *The Closing Bell*," Maria began. "I want to ask you a little about the culture of Merrill Lynch. Clearly, this has to be personal for you in many ways [with] your father, a founder of the company, and you having worked at the company for thirty years. How has the culture changed under Stan O'Neal?"

"Maria, it's heartbreaking in so many ways," I said. "The firm I knew, the firm I joined in 1974, was a terrific firm, and it still is by the way. But the culture then was really an embracing culture, one that had been built up over the years and dedicated itself to our five Principles. Importantly, the client's interests always came first. We had respect for one another. We really fostered teamwork. I had the opportunity to know every chairman of Merrill Lynch, and people like Dan Tully had an incredible ability to manage in good times and in a crisis, to pull people together, to lead us, to give us the momentum to carry forward despite the market environment and despite problems. And that was a culture that made Merrill Lynch a great firm that Stan inherited."

Maria continued: "You know, it's amazing how the tone has changed and how quickly the tone has changed against Stan O'Neal. Now, I know he came in and cut aggressively, but, Win, correct me if I'm wrong, but I feel that when he first came in and started, people celebrated. 'This is what we needed after 9/11. We need some harsh cuts.' What happened?"

"Well, look, Maria," I answered, "I think anyone there at the time knew that after 9/11 the world was different, things had to change. We had gotten a little bit fat. But it's not necessarily what you do, it's how you do it. I remember 1997 when we had to make some difficult decisions, but the way that a Bill Schreyer and a Dan Tully did it wasn't mean spirited. It was done, it was explained, and people rallied behind them, and we went on to new heights. So I think that's the difference."

"So in other words, Win, he didn't care about people's dignity the way he was cutting. You say it was done differently. How did Stan O'Neal do it?"

"I think it was done harshly, Maria. I think there were people who found out they were leaving the firm by leaks to the press. I think there wasn't an appreciation for people who had spent a lifetime at the firm, who had dedicated their lives, who had sacrificed their families to make Merrill the great place it was."

Within minutes of our interview ending, I began receiving calls and e-mails from numerous former colleagues thanking me for speaking so honestly and openly about the reign of terror that had led to this mess. Maria subsequently interviewed me for her *Business Week* column, and the less-than-flattering photo they chose to run with the piece was captioned "An Angry Win Smith." And I was angry—about the decline of Merrill Lynch and the impact it was going to have on so many families who had remained loyal to the firm. In fact, by the end of 2008, Merrill's stock price, which had been $80 a share in early 2001, had fallen to just over $3. Many had not sold their shares, believing that the firm would continue to prosper despite the despised CEO. "This, too, shall pass" was an expression I heard often. For my own part, it was after reading a *New York Times* article a few years earlier in which O'Neal was quoted that I made the decision to sell 100 percent of my stock. In the interview, O'Neal was asked—as he often was—about the definition of Mother Merrill. "I think this is a great firm, but greatness is not an entitlement," he said. "There are some things about our culture that I don't want to change, but I don't like maternalism or paternalism in a corporate setting, as the name Mother Merrill implies." That was the O'Neal I recognized the day I resigned, and it was when I read that quote that I knew for certain that Merrill would be marginalized. At the time, most of my family and friends thought I was reacting emotionally and impulsively in making the decision to sell my stock. But I didn't want to own the stock of a company run by O'Neal, so over the next few years I methodically sold all my shares. It turned out, however, that I had forgotten the five thousand shares I had in my IRA accounts, and I discovered them when MER was trading at the near-record high of $95, so I called Allan Linke, my nephew and one of my financial advisers, and told him to sell at the market. When Merrill Lynch collapsed, I did not own one share of my former firm.

Maria Bartiromo had wanted to conduct our interview after Merrill's third-quarter earnings were announced, no doubt because she suspected that they would be newsworthy, but they were more so than anyone might have guessed, for on October 24 O'Neal had reported a third-quarter loss that was six times greater than the firm had projected just three weeks previously. In the wake of this news, ML shares fell nearly 6 percent, but two days later they rebounded with an 8.5 percent jump, mainly on the widespread belief that O'Neal was about to be ousted. It was around this time that O'Neal was stunned to discover that his company had a $48 billion burden of collateralized debt and was facing the biggest losses in its nearly century of existence. In desperation, O'Neal approached Wachovia Bank to discuss a merger. This enraged the members of the ML board because they had not been advised of O'Neal's overtures. According to Andrew Ross Sorkin:

They were furious he had engaged in unauthorized merger talks. "But my job is to think about options," O'Neal protested. Two days later the board met without him and agreed to force him out. Few at Merrill Lynch were sympathetic. A former co-worker told the *New Yorker*: "I wouldn't hire Stan to wash windows. What he did to Merrill Lynch was absolutely criminal."

Within a week of the release of the abominable third-quarter numbers, the company announced it was ousting him and would write down $8.4 billion in losses. O'Neal left on November 1, taking with him about $161 million worth of stock options and retirement benefits.

My public criticism must have had some impact because a few weeks later I received a call from Alberto Cribiore, Merrill's lead independent director, whom I did not know. "Hello, this is Alberto Cribiore," he said in his thick Italian accent, and I had to listen carefully to understand his words. "I wanted to call to let you know that we have selected John Thain as the next CEO. We think he is the best-qualified person to deal with the issues at Merrill Lynch. I wanted to let you know before we announce it publicly, and I hope you will be supportive." I didn't know John well, but I had encountered him socially over the years, and I had had great respect for him at Goldman (where he was co-chief operating officer) and as the CEO of the NYSE. I thought his knowledge of mortgage-backed securities made him the right fit for that time. I also believed he was a man of high integrity. However, like others, I was saddened that for the first time in our ninety-four-year history, there was not an internal successor. But that was the given reality, and I supported the decision on the record in several newspaper and TV interviews over the ensuing weeks.

Tully also received a call prior to the Thain announcement. "I have some news to tell you," Cribiore began. He told Dan about the Thain appointment. Tully responded, "I have nothing against John Thain, and I hope he does a good job, and I wish you well. However, you should have called me before you made your decision. I could have given you some good advice about whom to select." It was actually shocking that a former chairman and especially such a respected leader as Dan Tully was not consulted after O'Neal departed.

After the announcement was made, I reached out to John to offer my congratulations and support, and he immediately responded and asked me to come down and have lunch with him after he officially joined Merrill Lynch. As I entered the building that day, security personnel welcomed me with a smile, then escorted me to the private elevator and took me to the thirty-second floor, where I was meeting John. As I walked through the Chairman's Gallery and viewed the portraits of Charlie Merrill, my father, and their successors, I knew they would have been stunned by the events of the past few years. Over lunch John told me about many of the issues he was facing and some of his dismaying discoveries about O'Neal and his management style. John was appalled by the silo mentality that he discovered, and was also surprised by the lack of experience of people trading billions of dollars of the firm's capital. As I mentioned, he was also very critical of the expensive wine cellar in the corporate dining room, and how the corporate jets and helicopter had been used. We spoke in great detail about the past culture of ML, and he clearly had great respect for it—and he asked for my thoughts about bringing it back.

A few weeks later I was invited to another lunch with Thain, this time along with Bill Schreyer, Dan Tully, Launny Steffens, Barry Friedberg, Dave Komansky, and Greg Fleming. (Dan was unable to attend but later did meet with Thain.) It was an interesting reunion. I had stayed in close touch with Dan, Launny, and Barry, and the four of us were in total agreement that O'Neal's tenure had been disastrous. Barry often joked that he was to blame for Merrill's failure since he had hired Stan three times. He had originally brought a young Stan O'Neal to Merrill from General Motors and placed him in the nascent high-yield group in investment banking. A few years later, O'Neal left to go to work for Bankers Trust and Barry convinced him to come back after just four days. Then, later when Stan was CFO and was about to accept an offer to go to work for Alberto Cribiore's private equity firm, Barry talked him out of it. "Just imagine," Barry would jest, "how things would be if I had been less convincing! I only wish I knew then what I know now."

When I walked into that second luncheon with Thain, the first person I saw was Bill Schreyer. He gave me his trademark smile, shook my hand, and referring to the Bartiromo interview, said, "You were at your best with Maria. Your father would have been proud." It was a great moment. Even though Bill had been my mentor for years, was a great friend of our family, and knew why I had left Merrill Lynch, he had done something a few years earlier that caused a rift in our relationship.

It happened right after I left Merrill officially in January of 2002, I was walking down Greenwich Avenue one day when I bumped into Hassan Tabbah, one of our Private Client office managers, who had worked for me in the past. I asked him how things were going, and he told me about a recent managers' meeting he had been at and what nice words Bill Schreyer had said about me and my father in a speech he gave on the history of the firm. I asked if he could get me a copy of the speech, and he e-mailed it to me a few days later. In it, after speaking about my father's role in building the firm, Bill said, "And I was sorry to see Win Jr. leave the firm, but I know he wanted a change of life and I supported that decision."

I was furious. He knew why I left, that it had everything to do with the abandonment of the ML culture, and by saying it was a "lifestyle choice," I felt he was trying to spin it in favor of O'Neal. In exchange for his support, O'Neal had rewarded Bill with a car and driver and use of the corporate jet and helicopter, something no other retired chairman had. In my anger at reading the speech, I wrote a long letter to Bill, which I asked Dan Tully to read before I mailed it. It was tough and may have gone too far because I ended it, "Bill, I hope that you will not be a pawn in another man's game." But I truly believed that Bill had been duped by O'Neal. I never heard back from him. I was taken off his and Joan's Christmas card list, and we didn't speak until the luncheon with John Thain. I have often regretted sending that letter because Bill had been so good to me over the years, but I felt compelled to let him know how offended I was by that comment. Fortunately, before Bill passed away, we were able to put this episode behind us.

I last visited Bill in the summer of 2010 and by then he was suffering a form of dementia. As we sat down for lunch in his office, he was drawn and clearly ill, but he still had his charm and wit and grace. "Have you seen Dan recently?" he asked me. "I saw him two weeks ago," I replied. I started to ask him a couple of questions for this book, but it was obvious that he was confused, so I started to reminisce, and he immediately came to life and spoke about some of the history we shared. "Have you seen Dan recently?" he asked again. "Yes, Bill, I saw him two weeks ago." Later, as I walked out, I thanked Ruth, his longtime executive assistant, for arranging the lunch, and George, his chauffeur, walked me to my car. "It's so sad, George, to see Bill like this," I said. "You and Ruth are terrific to take such good care of him." George had a tear in his eye as he said, "Thank you for coming down. I know it meant a lot to him." As I got into my car and buckled my seat belt, I, too, shed some tears. In many ways, Bill had been like a father to me. Back when I was a young investment banker, he reached out to me and clearly from that point forward helped me at every step of my career. Yes, I'd been sorely disappointed that Bill supported O'Neal, but I realized that he had been duped by a very clever and manipulative person and that he later regretted what he had done, even though he would never admit that publicly. At his memorial service in Princeton, I told Joan how sad I was by Bill's passing and how much I appreciated what he had done for Merrill Lynch and for me. "Bill was so fond of you," Joan said. That meant everything!

After our luncheon with John Thain, all of us left with mixed feelings. It was a shame that Merrill Lynch was now being run by a veteran of Goldman Sachs rather than a Merrill Lyncher, but we thought that given the circumstances that faced our firm, John Thain was the best person for the times. We were also pleased to see that he'd included Greg Fleming at the luncheon and not Ahmass Fakahany, the other "co-president." While Greg had only been at Merrill Lynch a decade or so, we viewed him as a highly ethical and competent young executive who knew and appreciated the real Mother Merrill. We did not think the same of Fakahany. In the void between the departure of O'Neal and the hiring of Thain, Greg provided strong leadership. At one point, I had dialed in to an all-employee conference call that was led by Greg, and afterward I called to let him know what an excellent job he had done to reassure the team that Merrill would survive.

While we were supportive of the board's decision to hire Thain, we were appalled that O'Neal was allowed to have a severance package of over $160 million. Rather than firing him for gross mismanagement, the directors had allowed him to "retire." Under our compensation plan he had sufficient age and tenure to be eligible for early retirement and have all of his restricted stock and options vested. This man who ruthlessly and consciously destroyed the culture of a great firm, who ridded the executive ranks of thousands of years of experience, and who now was accountable for an $8 billion quarterly loss was walking away with an egregious amount of money. Fakahany also walked away with a shocking sum of money and had the gall to sue for more but this was rejected in arbitration. It was wrong and shameful of the board to have allowed these payments to the people primarily responsible for Merrill's downfall. Not that O'Neal ever took responsibility for it, I should add, since in April 2010 he would resurface in an interview with *Fortune* magazine in which he claimed that he was surprised to learn the extent of Merrill's exposure to CDOs. That prompted this response from David A. Geracioti, the editor in chief of *RegisteredRep* magazine:

> O'Neal says that the CDO exposure "should have been more like $10 billion for us and probably was around $10 billion at the end of '06." (It wasn't $10 billion. In fact, that is such a laugher.) Basically, O'Neal argues that [there would have been no problem] if only a key board member had listened to him and allowed O'Neal to sell Merrill to BoA in 2007 at a price of as much as $100 a share.
>
> His assertion that he never meant for ML to get that deep into CDOs is directly contradicted by a guy I know who worked in the ML CDO department and was fired (along with his boss and a few others) about 15 months before Merrill's Sept. 2008 shotgun wedding to BoA. Their infraction? They weren't with the program; they told Stan O'Neal that ML needed to reduce its exposure to CDOs. For a while my friend was wondering if he had been correct. "I thought my career was over, that I had made a mistake," he told me some time ago. Turns out he was right; Stan was wrong.

But that didn't have an effect on his outrageous "golden parachute," as columnist James J. Cramer summed up perfectly in *New York* magazine:

> EUREKA! We have finally found the level of loss that sends the boss packing in corporate America: $8 billion. If a company's losses in a given quarter exceed that amount, as they just did at Merrill Lynch and Citigroup, the CEO is actually out of a job! Of course, even with that torrent of red ink, you can't get away from euphemisms. Merrill called its execution of CEO Stan O'Neal a retirement and carefully pointed out that the $161 million O'Neal got to take with him wasn't severance, but just what the firm was contractually obligated to pay him. There was no mention that perhaps, if you lose $8 billion, you can be fired for cause and be denied the contracted pay package. If $8 billion in losses isn't cause, what is? But it seems that no company will fire a CEO and then say "Sue us for the rest of your salary," no matter how deserving the firing might be, and this was the most compelling case for a firing that I've ever come across that didn't involve outright embezzlement.

It's a shame that the board didn't hear and heed the words of Don Regan: "Just fire him!"

*Leaders like Don Regan guided the company through
challenging times and made tough decisions without
forsaking the Principles or the culture of Mother Merrill.*

John Thain invited me to the podium at the final
Merrill Lynch shareholders meeting on December 5,
2008. Little did I know that day the impact my speech
would have on so many people throughout the world.

(Christopher Elston Photography)

CHAPTER FIFTEEN

Catching
Lightning in a Bottle

(2008)

O n December 1, 2007, John Thain took over a storied Wall
Street firm whose stock had fallen 30 percent in less than
a year. Andrew Ross Sorkin offered this thumbnail of the
new boss:

An ultra-straitlaced executive who was sometimes referred to as "I-Robot," Thain had appealed to Merrill's board
because of his newly minted reputation as a turnaround
artist. After rising rapidly through the ranks at Goldman,
he left to overhaul the New York Stock Exchange after the
extravagant compensation package for its CEO, Richard
Grasso, caused an outrage. . . . At the NYSE, Thain (who,
perhaps not surprisingly, took a post-Grasso $16 million
pay cut) unleashed a radical transformation, shaking the
world's largest stock exchange out of its clubby, anachronistic
ways. He cut perks—shutting the wood-paneled Luncheon
Club and firing the exchange's barber—and turned the exchange into a for-profit, publicly traded company. He took
on the powerful, entrenched constituency of floor traders
and specialists, who protested in vain as Thain dragged
them into the electronic trading age.

When he arrived at the World Financial Center, he
noticed that an entire bank of elevators was reserved just
for him—a policy established by O'Neal. If someone was on

>an elevator when [O'Neal] arrived they got off. Thain told
>them get back on, and everyone rode up together.

Within a few days of Thain taking over, ML announced plans to
raise some $6 billion in badly needed capital. Among the actions it
would take was selling its commercial finance business to General
Electric and selling off major shares of its stock to Temasek Holdings,
a Singapore investment group. Then, on January 17, 2008, the company reported a fourth-quarter loss of nearly $10 billion. In April
came more red ink, some $2 billion, for the first quarter of 2008,
and in July Thain announced $4.9 billion in second-quarter losses.
Between July 2007 and July 2008, the company lost $19.2 billion—or
$52 million a day! Merrill's 20 percent interest in Bloomberg was
sold as well to raise equity.

At the root of the company's downfall was the fact that billions of
dollars' worth of loans ML had purchased from sub-prime lenders
went bad. The firm that Charlie Merrill and my father had nurtured
so carefully ended up underwriting and packaging some of the most
worthless mortgages in America. Under O'Neal, Merrill Lynch had
gone from a solid broker, underwriter, and asset-gatherer to an
addict that squandered its assets on the toxic market for complex
debt instruments.

William Dallas, the founder of Ownit Mortgage Solutions, a
California-based lending business which Merrill bought in 2006,
offered this assessment to *The New York Times*: "The mortgage business at Merrill Lynch was an afterthought—they didn't really have
a strategy. They had found this huge profit potential, and everybody
wanted a piece of it. But they were pigs about it."

Thain desperately tried to purge the firm of its toxic assets, selling
some $31 billion in mortgage assets for pennies on the dollar. Because
he had brought the NYSE into the modern era, he gained a reputation
as "Mr. Fix-It." But our great company was beyond fixing.

At first Thain resisted entreaties to sell the company and laid out
an elaborate rescue plan, but the losses piled up, and at one point in
2008 he even lost his cool by throwing a chair against the wall at a
meeting where he had received more bad news. Already Bear Stearns
and Lehman Brothers had succumbed to the credit crisis, and the

betting was that Merrill Lynch would be next. Though Thain tried to get the company to remain independent, ultimately the combination of the mess O'Neal had left behind and the deteriorating macro-environment made him realize that Merrill Lynch could not survive the weekend of September 13–14.

That Sunday I received a call from Scott Swift, a successful ML financial adviser and father of the singer Taylor Swift, whom I had known for many years. "I hear Merrill is being sold," he said. "What do you know?" I was stunned. I knew things were tough, but I believed Merrill could survive. Later that night, I got a call from Thain's secretary asking if I would be available for a call from John sometime Monday morning. I was scheduled to speak to a group of Boston architects about our development at Sugarbush that morning, and just before I left my hotel I heard the news about the acquisition of Merrill Lynch by Bank of America. A bit later, Thain called and told me the reasons why he thought this was in the best interests of all Merrill Lynch stakeholders. Given the pressures of the previous week, it was incredibly thoughtful of John to take the time to call me.

"John," I said, "I really appreciate all you've done since coming to Merrill Lynch, and I think you had no choice except to do what you did. I just hope that you've negotiated a good role for yourself and will continue to lead Merrill Lynch under the new ownership." John said that he didn't have time to think about himself, but in due course would be speaking with Ken Lewis, the Bank of America CEO, about what, if any, role he was to play. (John Thain, in fact, would continue to lead ML for only a brief period until Ken Lewis unceremoniously flew up from Charlotte and fired him early in 2009. John later became CEO of CIT.)

And so, on September 14, 2008, ML was sold to Bank of America, creating the nation's largest financial services company. The sale price was $29 per share, or a total of some $50 billion, which at the time seemed like a remarkably good price for Merrill Lynch shareholders. With the consummation of the sale, Bank of America would become the nation's largest retail brokerage and a major player on Wall Street. It already was the nation's largest retail bank, the largest credit card issuer, and the largest mortgage lender.

It was the end of the line for the brokerage that brought Wall Street to Main Street.

The next day, Steve Fraser, the Wall Street historian and author of *Wall Street: America's Dream Palace*, said: "It is an enormous shock. Merrill was a kind of bedrock institution whose stability and longevity was taken for granted and was reassuring to people. Even in these very highly erratic and speculative marketplaces like we've been living through, you didn't think Merrill would be vulnerable."

A s we got closer to the final shareholders meeting in November, I was busy getting Sugarbush ready for the ski season, and I debated whether I should attend. Dan Tully told me he wasn't going, so after some thought I decided that I needed to be there and to say something on the record. I called John and told him that I planned to attend and would like to make some remarks and that they would be longer that the three minutes normally allotted to a questioner at such meetings. John said he looked forward to seeing me. He never asked anything about what I intended to say.

I drove down to New York City on the evening of December 4. The next morning I awoke early and walked from the Embassy Suites on Vesey Street to the New York Stock Exchange, where I was doing an early-morning interview with CNBC. Stepping onto the trading floor when no one else is there is surreal. This was also the first time I had been in that part of Wall Street since the terrorist attacks, and so I was struck by the security throughout the area.

It was a cool morning, so after my interview I walked briskly back to Vesey Street, entered the Merrill Lynch building, and made my way up to the second-floor conference room for the meeting. Coffee and muffins were available, and already a couple hundred people were chatting and milling about—as though at a wake. I saw Launny Steffens and Maddy Weinstein, a senior vice president and the company's senior woman executive. We chatted briefly about the passing of our firm. Bob Farrell, one of our great research icons, and I visited for a while and then George Shieren came over and spoke to me. George had been a very strong member of the legal team and also served as Dan Tully's assistant for two years. For Dan's retirement he was able to negotiate with Hermès to design a special tie that bore the Merrill Lynch logo. You have to look carefully to see the logo—most people won't notice anything other than a very attractive Hermès tie until it's pointed out to them. Later we all got the ties, and I had my tie on that day.

There were many former colleagues there that day, but what was most noticeable was who wasn't. Other than John Thain, no director had the courage or the respect for Merrill Lynch to come to that final meeting. Before the meeting began, I confirmed with John that I wanted to speak and also wanted to read a letter from Merrill Lynch Magowan, Charlie Merrill's grandson and a former employee of Merrill Lynch. Merrill and I had spoken days before the meeting and agreed that the offspring of Charlie Merrill and Win Smith really should be present at this meeting and speak frankly about what we felt was on the minds of most members of the Merrill Lynch family. Unfortunately, right before the meeting, Merrill came down with pneumonia and his doctor would not allow him to travel, so he asked me to read his letter.

Once everyone was starting to take seats, John Thain tapped me on the shoulder and said, "Sit in the first row. I'll call on you first before Evelyn begins her show." He was referring to Evelyn Davis, whom I had noticed sitting in the first row right in front of the podium. Evelyn was a woman of many professions, but most prominently an infamous gadfly who extorted many CEOs into buying her annual newsletter, *Highlights and Lowlights*, in exchange for her not disrupting meetings beyond a certain point.

John opened the meeting by thanking everyone for attending and then called for questions. He looked over to me, but before he could acknowledge me, Evelyn leapt to her feet and, as John had predicted, started her show. After many minutes, John said, "Evelyn, it's time to hear from some others. I'll call on you after others have a chance to speak. Win Smith, it's your turn."

I rose and started toward the microphone in the aisle, but John said, "Win, come up here and speak from the podium." I was really taken by surprise, and only when I looked around did I realize that the meeting was being filmed and the room was full. Normally, I don't read speeches, preferring to work from an outline, but today

I didn't want to miss a word. I had spent many hours writing this speech, and I had asked a few trusted friends, including Dan Tully, to read it and assure me that I hadn't gone too far. "It's perfect," Dan had said. "Go for it, good luck, and God bless."

To quell my nervousness, I looked down at Evelyn and said, "Good morning, Ms. Davis. Thank you for yielding to me. You look as beautiful as ever."

"It's MRS. Davis," she shot back, and I knew I had really irritated her. As it turned out, halfway through my speech she would try to interrupt me. ("John, he's gone over his time. Tell him to stop.") But I ignored her and kept reading after John said, "It's okay, Evelyn, you'll have your time."

Once I had the floor, I began by telling those assembled that Merrill had wanted to be there but, because he couldn't, I would be reading his letter. Then I proceeded to do so:

> Good morning. My name is Merrill Lynch Magowan. My grandfather was Charles E. Merrill, founder of Merrill Lynch. I am a member of the first fourth generation family to be employees of the company.
>
> In its 94 year history, Merrill Lynch has been led by 12 men. The first 10 were my grandfather, Win Smith, Mike McCarthy, George Leness, Jim Thomson, Don Regan, Roger Birk, Bill Schreyer, Dan Tully and Dave Komansky. I knew each of them, some quite well. I may be the only person in this room that can make such a claim. These men had many traits in common: They had a clear vision for the future of the company; they all had outstanding leadership abilities; they all developed management systems, whether seat of the pants as exemplified by my grandfather, or formal systems pioneered by Don Regan and improved by his successors. In the mid 1970s, the firm adopted the Louis Allen principles of management, focusing on planning, organizing, leading and controlling. The emphasis was on controlling, because if one could not control the brilliant plans conjured, the organization of those plans, the ability to motivate the people required to execute the plans, nothing would be gained.

In 2002, Stanley O'Neal became the CEO. He inherited a talented management team, but within months they had all left. In their stead he hired people from the outside who knew little of Merrill Lynch's culture, let alone the sophisticated and leveraged products they induced management to enter. At first, results were satisfactory, leading the Board of Directors to lavish extravagant compensation packages on senior management. [But as] a result of the increased leverage and the absence of adequate risk controls, assets were vastly overstated and led to a series of writedowns over the last 21 months that pushed the company to the edge of extinction, which cause this meeting today.

I feel the same as I would attending a funeral. It is appropriate that a member of the founding family be here; my grandfather was present for the birth, and I am here for the funeral. As at most funerals, there is a great deal of sadness. I am sad for the ending of a legacy, and I am particularly sad for the financial loss for our shareholders, who include our retirees and current employees who have seen their net worth greatly diminish. I am also bitter and angry that a management team could put Merrill Lynch in this position, and a Board of Directors who were clearly in over their heads and who served the shareholders who elected them poorly.

I paused and said that I was now speaking for myself. Here's what I said:

Thank you, John, for allowing me to say a few words on this most important morning. I will say more about you in a moment, but I just wanted to thank you up front for your leadership and all you have attempted to do this past year.

Fellow shareholders, I speak to you today as a twenty-eight-year employee, a shareholder, and the son of one of the founding fathers of Merrill Lynch.

On January 6, 1914, Charlie Merrill opened a one-man shop just a few blocks from where we are today. A year later he was joined by his friend Eddie Lynch, and the first

Merrill, Lynch & Co. was launched. One year later, my father joined the firm straight out of Amherst College. Thus began a wonderful partnership and friendship that lasted a lifetime.

Like Merrill Magowan, I have been privileged to know every CEO of Merrill Lynch from Charlie Merrill to John Thain. Most of them, including John, were principled leaders who never placed their interests ahead of those of the firm. Most of them valued and promoted the Principles that Charlie Merrill created, and most of them cared deeply for the welfare of their fellow colleagues.

Merrill Lynch grew and thrived through the tough as well as the good times. By 2001 we were one of the most successful and respected global financial firms in the world, with a stock price that hit $80 early that year. The ROI to both our employees and shareholders was superb. A hundred thousand dollars invested in the MER IPO was worth $2.3 million in early 2001.

But Merrill Lynch was more than a profitable company. It was a family. It was a culture. Merrill Lynch to so many of us was Mother Merrill, and it is so sad that the CEO who preceded John Thain and the Board of Directors had no understanding of what that meant. Arthur Levitt, the former chair of the SEC, once commented that of all the Wall Street firms, only Merrill Lynch had a soul. A soul! Can you imagine someone, much less the chair of the SEC, saying a company had a soul? Well, it did, because the tone, the culture, the ethics that we were all so proud of began that day, January 6, 1914.

It began with Charlie Merrill's first rule that the interests of the customer always came first. It began with his partners' understanding that they were a team and that no one's ego was more important than the team. It began with the knowledge that the primary assets of the firm went in and out of their door every day. They insisted on respect for everyone. It began with an understanding that Merrill was part of a broader community and that we had an obligation to support that community. It began with the simple belief that integrity was everything, and when a mistake was made, it was owned up to, corrected, and never covered up. These Principles of Charlie Merrill were passed to my father and then to Mike McCarthy and subsequent CEOs, and the culture endured because of the stories that were told to new Merrill Lynchers about our predecessors.

We knew the story of Charlie Merrill telling his clients to sell before the crash of 1929, of Don Regan testifying to Congress and saying "We goofed" and then making the clients whole for our mistake. We knew the story of Roger Birk realizing we erred in selling Baldwin United annuities to our clients and making them whole. We knew the story of Dan Tully facing down a CEO bully in his office when that person insulted one of Dan's teammates. Stories maintained the culture and created a bond between the founding partners and those who worked at Merrill eighty years later.

Merrill Lynch was a brand that we were so proud to wear on our hearts and even our ties. We had a swagger, and we were damn proud to be part of "the Thundering Herd." We loved being the underdog and doing things others thought we couldn't accomplish. We were optimists who always knew we would get better and better and be number one in whatever we chose to pursue.

People like Bill Schreyer reminded us that he had never met a rich pessimist.

We even took on Goldman Sachs in the eighties and nineties, and by the time I resigned in 2001, they were damned scared that we were competing with them successfully everywhere in the world. YPF, Shanghai Petrochemical, China Telecom, Indosat, CVRD, Telefónica de España were only some of the highly sought-after privatization mandates that we won around the world. Our Private Client assets totaled $1.5 trillion. We were proud of our founders, we were proud of our leaders, we were proud of our colleagues, we were proud of what Merrill Lynch was in 2001.

We were proud to be the leader in private wealth management. We were proud of our unique global footprint. We were proud of our leadership in both debt and equity underwriting as well as M&A. We were proud of our asset management business. But most of all, we were proud of our Principles, which we inherited from Charlie Merrill.

Many of us who have departed still get together. After one recent gathering a former senior executive of the Equity Division, Tom Joyce, and now a successful executive elsewhere, e-mailed this to the organizers: "I thought the setting was terrific, but it paled in comparison to the people gathered. What a wonderful collection of character and talent. Those years we had at Merrill were like catching lightning in a bottle." Like catching lightning in a bottle! That captures so much of what our culture created and what we felt and why Merrill was so successful! We were not about brick and mortar and cold numbers. We were about character, spirit, leadership, ethics, and pride.

As one former CEO said to us when times got tough, "Just remember, we are the only firm that doesn't have to compete against Merrill Lynch."

At this point I want to make it very clear that I support the merger with Bank of America, and I am thankful for John Thain's clear and decisive leadership at that moment of crisis this fall. I am encouraged by the respect that Ken Lewis says he has for our great franchise and for the many thousands of fine professionals who are still part of the Merrill Lynch team. I do hope Ken and his colleagues at Bank of America will allow the firm that they bought to thrive under its new ownership, and that they will appreciate the strong culture that made Merrill what it was by 2001, and will also appreciate the many fine people who hung in and are still with Merrill Lynch, including members of my own family.

All of us want this new organization to succeed and become preeminent. We all know that what has occurred is the given reality and it is time to move forward. However, before we do, some things need to be said for the record.

Today did not have to come. In the past it was Merrill Lynch that came to the rescue of Goodbody, White Weld, and Becker. It was Merrill Lynch that strong and successful firms like Fenner & Beane, C. J. Devine, Smith New Court, DSP in India, Midland Walwyn in Canada, and Mercury Asset Management wanted to join. Merrill always thrived in times of turmoil and grew market share. Today did not have to come.

Today is not the result of the sub-prime mess or synthetic CDOs. They are the symptoms. This is the story of failed leadership and the failure of a Board of Directors to understand what was happening to this great company, and its failure to take action soon enough.

I stand here today and say "shame" to both the current as well as the former directors who allowed this former CEO to wreak havoc on this great company.

Shame on them for allowing this former CEO to consciously and openly disparage Mother Merrill, throw our founding principles down a flight of stairs, and tear out the soul of the firm.

In the fall of 2001, I was asked to remain as vice chairman of Merrill Lynch. But in a private meeting it was obvious that this CEO-to-be had no respect for our history, for our culture, and for the Five Principles that had served us so well. I wanted to stay. My heart said stay. But I knew I could not. I would not have been able to look myself in the mirror each morning! That was a day I never thought could happen. Shame on members of the board for never asking any of us who loved this firm why we had to leave rather than remain part of something we could not in good conscience support. Some of us had the means to leave. Unfortunately, many others did not, and they will tell you how unpleasant it was. Just ask them.

Shame on these directors for allowing this former CEO to rid the firm of thousands of years of experience. Shame of them for allowing this former CEO to surround himself with many people who did not have the perspective of other market cycles and the experience of time. Shame for allowing this CEO to surround himself with many people who did not share the same values that made us great and appreciate our winning culture. Shame on them for allowing this CEO to cut costs and businesses so severely and bluntly for the sake of short-term earnings that he cut out future growth. Shame on them for allowing him to over-leverage the firm and fill the balance sheet with toxic waste to create short term earnings. Shame on them for allowing good people like Dan Bayly and a few others to be used as scapegoats to settle the U.S. government's Enron case against Merrill

Lynch and for allowing these wonderful human beings and loyal Merrill Lynchers to go to federal prison unjustly. Fortunately, the Court of Appeals overturned the sentence.

Shame on them for not knowing the Merrill Lynch helicopter and plane and other perquisites were being used irresponsibly.

Shame, shame, shame for allowing one man to consciously unwind a culture and rip out the soul of this great firm. Shame on them for allowing this former CEO to retire with a $160 million retirement package, and shame on them for not resigning themselves.

I am not alone in these sentiments. So many former and present Merrill Lynchers share this anger, this sadness, about what was allowed to occur. Just this week a former Merrill Lynch senior woman executive e-mailed me and said, "It is heartbreaking to see what greed and the absence of principles did to one of the finest companies in America."

What breaks my heart even more is to see the financial damage that has been inflicted on so many families that devoted their lives to the firm, and to all our stakeholders.

Where is the accountability? No wonder that the Main Street that learned to trust Merrill Lynch in the 1940s has lost faith in Wall Street in 2008. Merrill Lynch is not alone in this. But in the past Merrill Lynch rose above the crowd and distanced itself from the greed that brought others down. Our principled leaders steered us through many challenges, and we emerged stronger because of them.

But I must give the devil his due. I applaud the board for selecting John Thain. John inherited a mess, but he did so many of the right things. He reached out to the past; he reached out to the people of Merrill Lynch around the world and showed them his humanity as well as his intelligence. John had the intellect, the experience, the humility, the common sense, and the integrity to pull it off had not the markets melted down this past fall. Then he had the wisdom, as Kenny Rogers sang, to know when to fold them so that Merrill did not go the way of Lehman.

We thank you, John, not only for what you tried to do and what you did do, we thank you because we know you knew what Mother Merrill really stood for. As a competitor at Goldman Sachs, you respected our past and our present and you were serious about restoring our valued Principles once you became our leader.

I am personally pleased that you will be leading the new Merrill Lynch, which will operate under the Bank of America umbrella. So many of us are hopeful that the brand will survive, that the strengths in Global Private Wealth Management and Global Investment Banking in particular will be recognized and maintained. We hope that you and your colleagues will continue to tell the stories that will maintain the Principles and the culture that all began just down the block on January 6, 1914, and enabled Merrill Lynch to be the firm it was in 2001.

Merrill Lynch has always been Bullish on America. Now we hope that you, John, and Ken Lewis will make sure that Bank of America will not only be Bullish on Merrill Lynch but will carry forward the Merrill Lynch Principles along with those of Bank of America and continue a "Tradition of Trust" that will help to restore Main Street trust in Wall Street once again.

There are many parallels today with the world and the economy that existed in 1940 when Charlie Merrill and my dad and their talented teammates set upon the course of taking Wall Street to Main Street.

In 1999, Warren Bennis and Dan Heenan, two distinguished professors of business, wrote a book called *Co-Leaders*. One chapter was about the remarkable partnership and friendship that existed between Charlie Merrill and my father:

"When Charlie Merrill and Winthrop Smith entered Wall Street, Americans were wary stock buyers. At most only 15 percent of households were in the market. Today almost half of the adult population has money socked away in equities. The financial world has changed, in large part because of these farsighted co-leaders.

"Working together, Merrill and Smith made ordinary people Bullish on America. Thanks to them, people's capitalism is a reality. Besides democratizing investing, they helped provide the U.S. industry with much-needed capital for expansion. In tandem they were truly, in Merrill Lynch's famous catchphrase, 'a breed apart.'"

Now new co-leaders in the form of Ken Lewis and John Thain have that same golden opportunity—in fact the responsibility—to restore the trust and the confidence that Main Street must have in Wall Street at this time of turmoil. There is no reason why this new partnership of Bank of America and Merrill Lynch and its co-leaders of 2008 cannot achieve for America and the world what Charlie Merrill and my father did sixty-eight years ago.

While today did not have to come and should not have come, it did! So I wish all at Merrill Lynch and their colleagues at Bank of America the best of fortune in the years ahead. This new firm can and should be the leading global investment firm in the years ahead. It should be great and make all of you who will be part of it as proud as we were of the Merrill Lynch we knew and loved!

I will end by saying to my many Merrill Lynch friends, my extended Merrill Lynch family around the world: Thanks for the memories.

No one can ever take those away.

It was a hell of a run!

When I ended the room broke into applause and everyone rose to their feet. John, who had stood beside me the entire time, shook my hand. It was an incredibly emotional moment as I realized that I really had spoken for everyone in that room that day. My words were theirs and I was just the agent speaking on behalf of them. They were words they had wanted to say, and now they were said. What I didn't realize until days later was that rooms around the globe also had burst into applause, as the meeting and my speech had been broadcast live to Merrill Lynch offices throughout the world.

Over the next few months I received many calls, e-mails, and letters thanking me for speaking and bemoaning our great loss. The messages expressed sorrow at what O'Neal had done to the company, but also frustration and anger toward him and the Board of Directors.

One I received from Rob Mooney, who was head of business risk for Global Wealth Management, summarizes the sentiments of the many:

Win,

I just read your remarks from Friday and want to say Thank You! You said what so many of us who remained at ML (and thanks for recognizing us) could not over the years that Stan & Co ruined the firm and you captured well the character and values we grew up with. Thank you for caring enough to come back and commemorate a solemn event that many of us are struggling through. . . . In many ways, your words help bring closure and remind us how fortunate we were to have been a part of ML. Your words reminded me of all the things that made my first 20 years at ML the most formative of my life. I take heart knowing that the values I learned at ML will endure and that there will be opportunities to in some way continue the legacy.

Rob is like so many people at Merrill Lynch whom I was privileged to know and work with over the years. He was a smart and capable lawyer who spent his career at Merrill embracing our Principles and respecting our culture. To people like Rob, working at Merrill Lynch was more than a job. It was being part of a family where everyone strove not only to become the best, but to do it in a fashion that made us proud to say we belonged to Mother Merrill.

Epilogue

Mother Merrill was an incredible concept in corporate America and unique on Wall Street. It grew from a one-man shop in 1914 into arguably the leading and most admired investment banking and wealth management firm in the world.

Unfortunately, in 2008 I witnessed the demise of our great firm, the collapse of other Wall Street icons, and the ensuing distrust that Main Street America has for the financial sector. I am saddened and angry that an industry so crucial to a healthy global economy was hijacked by a group of selfish rogues who were only interested in self-enrichment and lacked the moral compass of men like Charlie Merrill, my father, Mike McCarthy, George Leness, Jim Thompson, Don Regan, Bill Schreyer, Dan Tully, and so many others who made Merrill Lynch great. I am enraged that certain directors allowed a person like Stan O'Neal to rip apart a powerful culture and destroy a successful company, destroy the net worth of thousands of employees, and be party to events that nearly brought down the capital markets and the economies of the world.

Where were these guardians of the shareholder? I am afraid that they were asleep. The signs were obvious.

To then have allowed O'Neal to leave with a "retirement" package worth $160 million was disgusting. The only thing worse is that no regulatory or legal actions have been taken against certain people who were accountable for the harm that thousands, if not millions, of people suffered and for the damage to the integrity of a critical industry.

Don Regan once said to Dan Tully, "After I leave, never let an accountant or a lawyer run Merrill Lynch." Don valued his financial and legal staff, but he knew that Merrill Lynch was a client business and that its leaders needed to be broad thinkers who understood client needs and the essence of what really made Merrill Lynch what it was. I think he would have also cautioned that character makes a difference and in choosing a future leader, one needs to look beyond just intelligence and technical skills and evaluate the full set of attributes found in great leaders. His choice of Roger Birk was evidence of that, as was Bill Schreyer's selection of Dan Tully.

Although Merrill Lynch was not perfect and made many mistakes over the years, it learned from these experiences and overcame its shortcomings primarily because its leaders believed in and maintained a set of guiding Principles that sustained the company through good times and bad. This culture was strong and made us proud to work there and to be a member of the Mother Merrill family.

Growing up, I never fully appreciated the role that my father played—along with his boss, mentor, partner, and friend, Charlie Merrill—in creating a brand-new concept in 1940 that brought Wall Street to Main Street and democratized the capital markets. This allowed millions of middle-class families to participate in the stock market in a fashion that had not been available previously. Subsequent leaders continued to innovate and evolve Merrill Lynch, but with one exception they were always careful to preserve the core Principles and the culture that Merrill, my father, and their partners had created.

As I was finishing this book, I received a call from David Decker, a financial adviser in Merrill Lynch's Boise, Idaho, office. He said: "I heard from Dan Tully that you were writing a book about the history of Merrill Lynch, and I wanted to share a story with you about something that made a tremendous impression on me years ago. In 1992, when I was manager of the Idaho Falls office, Tom Chrystie, then retired and living in Jackson Hole, Wyoming, hosted a dinner for Merrill's Executive Committee and invited me to join them. I was just a lowly office manager and had never really met the firm's executive team. They were an hour late arriving. I sat between Dan Tully and Launny Steffens. Dan apologized for being so late but explained to me that Bill Schreyer had started the day at a seven-thirty A.M. working breakfast and they had worked all day discussing the firm's strategic plan. Dan then related how Bill Schreyer had told his team that they had a sacred obligation at this meeting to come up with solutions that are good for the client, the shareholder, and the employees. As Dan said that, I noticed Launny Steffens and Steve Hammerman nodding their heads in affirmation, and I could see in their eyes how much they believed in that charge given to them by their chairman. This made a lasting impression, and I was particularly struck by the words 'sacred obligation.' In future years whenever a colleague criticized management, I would relate this story and let them know how proud I was to be working for a firm led by people like this. There are so many members of the Merrill Lynch family who felt the same way, and this is why we loved Mother Merrill."

F ate often takes us in a different direction than we expect. While I had fully intended to stay at Merrill Lynch until 2014 to witness its 100th birthday, things turned out differently. Today, for my second career, I am a ski bum running Sugarbush Resort in Warren, Vermont. It is satisfying, fun, and rewarding. In my own way, I have brought Wall Street to Main Street and feel proud to be building a business that provides guests with a great experience, employing hundreds of people, and having a positive impact on our local community. I will always be most proud that the Principles I learned from my mentors at Merrill Lynch are the same ones we strive to maintain here at Sugarbush: client focus, teamwork, respect for everyone, community involvement, and integrity. If practiced and embraced, these values are powerful and can become the foundation of success. But I often recall the wonderful twenty-eight years I spent at Merrill Lynch and think about the many colleagues whom I admired and liked and was privileged to know. I am still in contact with many (sometimes on the slopes), and when we get together our conversation immediately turns to fond memories of Mother Merrill.

I have two nephews, Allan and Scott Linke, and a son-in-law, Bob DiSabato, who are still with Merrill and enjoying successful careers there. I still have all my financial accounts with them. My youngest son, Cameron, joined Merrill's training program in Kansas City in

2011. After one year he realized that his passion was not in financial services, but the experience of working for Merrill Lynch was invaluable and the professionals he worked with there have left a lasting positive impression on him. When Lili and I visited Cameron, it was so refreshing to see the Principles hanging on the wall of the office and in plastic cubes on the desks of employees.

On his first day, Cameron e-mailed me a letter that was included in his welcome packet. It read:

> Welcome and congratulations. As a candidate in the Merrill Lynch financial advisor program, Practice Management Development (PMD), you have been accepted into an elite program alongside of some of the most qualified and talented financial advisor candidates in the industry.
>
> Since 1946, Merrill Lynch has been attracting, selecting, and developing some of the world's most talented financial advisors. Our award-winning professionals have been consistently recognized as being among the most elite financial advisors in the industry.
>
> Perhaps one of our founders said it best when he wrote to the 1946 Merrill Lynch Financial Advisor Training School Class:
>
> "On your shoulders rest the good name and reputation of the firm. Our cardinal policy, 'the interest of the Customer Must Come First,' should ever be kept in mind. You will find that reference to this policy will make many a problem easy to solve.
>
> "You are engaged in an honorable business which is an integral part of our entire economy. In the pursuit of your duties you will perform services to your fellow man no less important than those of the family doctor. As you go up the ladder your contacts will be more with the leaders of industry and thought in your community, and each of you will become numbered among those leaders.
>
> "We are well pleased with you. We look to you to provide the leadership that will make Merrill Lynch a better firm in the years to come. The road is long, the opportunities are bright."

That letter was written by Cameron's grandfather.

Merrill Lynch & Co. no longer exists as a legal entity. The remaining international private wealth business in Latin America, Europe and the Middle East has been sold to Bank Julius Baer & Co. Ltd., a Swiss private banking group. The investment banking and institutional businesses are now integrated within Bank of America and the jury is still out on whether they will regain the dominance that we once had. Fortunately, Merrill Lynch, Pierce, Fenner & Smith, Inc. is still one of BAC's major subsidiaries and remains focused on U.S. private wealth clients. It is doing well. Many former and capable colleagues, like James Gorman, Greg Fleming, Bob McCann, and Bob Mulholland, are now at rival firms and attempting to mold them into the "new" Merrill Lynch. Others, like Rob Mooney and Jose Malbran, have moved to newly created boutique brokerages. John Thain followed Jeff Peek as CEO of CIT Group. Merrill Lynch remains deep with talent, however, and I remain hopeful that the real MLFP&S will endure.

It is encouraging that John Thiel, a veteran of many years at Merrill Lynch, is now the leader of MLPF&S and has embraced its historical culture and our Principles. Moreover, he has reached out to me and other members of "the old guard" to help tell the history of our firm. As Merrill Lynch turns 100 on January 6, 2014, Thiel is planning to celebrate those first hundred years by honoring our cherished Principles, solidifying the culture, and preparing for the next generation. I am bullish on the prospects.

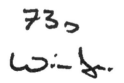

Founding
Partners and CEOs

(1914–2008)

Charles E. Merrill
Senior Partner 1914-1956
The first leader, Charlie was a
charismatic, creative visionary
who revolutionized both the
grocery and brokerage industries.

Edmund C. Lynch
Senior Partner 1914-1938
Charlie's first partner, Eddie was
the disciplined check-and-balance
of the relationship.

Winthrop H. Smith (Sr.)
Managing Partner 1940-1956
Directing Partner 1956–1958
CEO 1959–1961
A skilled leader and humble man,
Win's steady command brought
Wall Street to Main Street.

Michael W. McCarthy
CEO 1961–1966
A Safeway recruit, Mike reorga-
nized and modernized "backstage"
operations and began Merrill's
international expansion.

George J. Leness
CEO 1966–1969
A distinguished investment banker, George developed the foundation from which Merrill rose to prominence in future years.

James E. Thomson
CEO 1969–1970
A Canadian by birth, Jim was an important partner who oversaw the change to electronic data processing and brought discipline to the back office.

Donald T. Regan
CEO 1970-1980
Brilliant, feisty, visionary, and
courageous, Don took on the Street
establishment and was "Bullish
on America."

Roger E. Birk
CEO 1981–1984
Perhaps the most unappreciated
leader, Roger was an unselfish
man who acted with integrity
and kept Merrill Lynch
independent, setting the stage for
our success in the decades ahead.

William A. Schreyer
CEO 1985-1993
Never sweating the small stuff,
Bill's eternal optimism and focus
brought about the growth of
Merrill's investment banking,
institutional business, and
international markets.

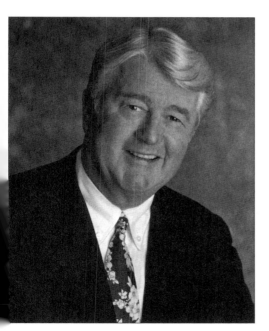

Daniel P. Tully
CEO 1993-1997
Dan's legacy is his devotion to
the Principles and the culture of
Merrill. A powerful leader who was
loved and respected just as my
father, Win Smith, had been.

David H. Komansky
CEO 1997-2003
A good man and able leader, Dave's successful career unfortunately was tarnished at the end.

E. Stanley O'Neal
CEO 2003–2007
A smart and competent man, but his disdain for the Mother Merrill culture embraced by all his predecessors brought down a great firm.

John A. Thain
CEO 2007-2008
He was dealt an impossible
hand but, in the end, John saved
Merrill Lynch from going the
way of Lehman Brothers.

Index